Power Tools for Literacy

Power Tools for Literacy

ACCELERATED PHONICS, SYLLABLES and MORPHEMES

Designed for Ages 9-21

Verena C. Rau

Boatman and Willener Press

Boatman & Willener Press
Post Office Box 2826
Castro Valley, CA 94546

www.powertoolsforliteracy.com

Copyright © 2007 by Verena C. Rau
All rights reserved. Persons who purchase this book may reproduce the lessons for their own use only.

"Boatman and Willener Press" is a registered trademark of Boatman and Willener Press.

Manufactured in the United States of America by Consolidated Printers Inc.

First Printing 2007

Senior Editor: Lenore A. Hirsch
Editors: Beverly E. Clayton and Laura M. Petersen
Cover Design: Adriane Bosworth

Library of Congress Cataloging-in-Publication Data

Rau, Verena Carol
Power Tools for Literacy: accelerated phonics and syllabication/ by Verena C. Rau
Includes bibliographical references and index.
ISBN-13: 978-0-9790925-0-3
ISBN-10: 0-9790925-0-7
LCCN: 2006910354

1. Reading—Phonetic method. 2. Word recognition. 3. English language—Orthography and spelling. I. Title.

Attention Corporations, Universities, Colleges, and Professional Organizations:
Quantity discounts are available on bulk purchases of this book for educational purposes. For information, please contact Boatman and Willener Press, P.O. Box 2826, Castro Valley, CA 94546.

This book is dedicated to my husband, Greg, to my students who helped shape this book, and to my fellow teachers who encouraged me along the way.

ACKNOWLEDGMENTS

I am profoundly grateful to my publishing professionals, friends, and colleagues for sharing their expertise and for their patience in critiquing numerous revisions:

Lenore Hirsch, Beverly Clayton, Laura Petersen, Adriane Bosworth, Sally Rayhill-Dellanini, Ed.D., Barbara Dahl, Kate Ingvoldstad, Linda Ridgeway, Susan Seipel, Martha Ritchie, Nancy Combs, Nancy Cushen White, Ed.D., Suzanne Gordon, Cecil Anison, Jeri Flinn, Philomena Buonsante, Deborah Hall, Simona Miller, and Horacio Miller.

Contents

Introduction 1

Overview and Procedures 3

CHAPTER 1
Closed Syllable 7

NOTE TO INSTRUCTOR 7
- 1 Introducing the Closed Syllable 11
- 2a Short a 12
- 2b Beginning Blends with Short a 13
- 2c-d Ending Blends with Short a 14
- 2e Sometimes a Says ô 16
- 2f (included on page 15)
- 3a Short i, First Rule of Syllabication 17
- 3b sh, ch, Second Rule of Syllabication 18
- 3c Consonant Teams ng and nk 19
- 3d Consonant Digraphs th, wh, and ng 20
- 3e-f Long i in Closed Syllables 22
- 4a Short e, Prefixes ex– and en– 24
- 4b Short Vowel Signals ff, ll, ss, zz 25
- 4c-d Short Vowel Signals ck and tch 26
- 4e Syllabication Practice 28
- 5a-b Short o 29
- 5c Review of Short o 32
- 6a Short u, Third Rule of Syllabication 33
- 6b-c Silent Initial Consonants, Medial y 35
- 7 Review of Closed Syllables 37
- 8 Review of Short Vowels 38
- 9 Suffixes –ful, –less, and –ness 39
- 10 Dictation Exercise 40
- 11 Plural –s and –es 41
- 12a-b Contractions 42

CHAPTER 2
Vowel-Consonant-e Syllable 45

NOTE TO INSTRUCTOR 45
- 1 Introducing the Vowel-Consonant-e Syllable 49
- 2a-b Long a, Fourth Rule of Syllabication 50
- 3a Long i 52
- 3b (included on page 51)
- 4 Long e 53
- 5a Consonants k and c 54
- 5b Hard and Soft c 55
- 5c-d Hard and Soft g 56
- 6 Long o, Fifth Rule of Syllabication 58
- 7a-b Long u 59
- 8a-b Ending v Sound 61
- 9 Review of Vowel-Consonant-e Syllables 62
- 10a Closed and Vowel-Consonant-e Syllables 63
- 10b Dictation Exercise 64
- 11a Sixth Rule of Syllabication 65
- 11b Dictation Exercise 66
- 12a Past Tense –ed 67
- 12b Pronunciation of –ed 68
- 12c-d Adding –ed to Verbs 69
- 13 Suffixes –en and –est 71
- 14a-b Adding –ing to Verbs 72
- 15 Prefixes a–, un–, dis–, non–, and mis– 74

CHAPTER 3
Open Syllable 75

NOTE TO INSTRUCTOR 75
- **1** Introducing the Open Syllable 79
- **2-3** Seventh Rule of Syllabication 80
- **4** Dictation Exercise 82
- **5a** Review: Seventh Rule of Syllabication 83
- **5b** Words with Three Kinds of Syllables 84
- **5c** (included on page 81)
- **6a** Open Syllable Prefixes 85
- **6b** Assimilated/Absorbed Prefixes 87
- **6c** Dictation Exercise 88
- **7a-b** Open and Closed Syllables 89
- **8** Applying Seven Syllabication Rules 91
- **9** Eighth Rule of Syllabication 92
- **10a-b** Three Sounds of y 93
- **10c** y in Accented Syllables 96
- **10d** (included on page 95)
- **10e** y in the Middle of Words 97
- **11** Suffixes –ate and –ite 98
- **12a** Word Endings –tion and –sion 99
- **12b** (included on page 90)

CHAPTER 4
R-Controlled Syllable 101

NOTE TO INSTRUCTOR 101
- **1** Introducing the R-Controlled Syllable 105
- **2a-c** R-Controlled Vowel ar 106
- **3a-c** R-Controlled Vowel or 109
- **4a-b** R-Controlled Vowel ir 112
- **5a** R-Controlled Vowel er 114
- **5b** (included on page 113)
- **5c** The Suffix –er 115
- **6a-b** R-Controlled Vowel ur 117
- **6c** Vowel-r-e 119
- **7a** Challenge Words 121
- **7b** Dictation Exercise 122
- **7c** (included on page 118)
- **8** Suffixes –ar and –or 123
- **9** Vowel-r-Vowel Rule 124
- **10** The Absorbed Prefix in– 125
- **11** The Word Ending –ture 126
- **12** The Suffix –al 127
- **13** Suffixes –ant, –ent, and –ment 128
- **14a** Word Endings –on and –an 129
- **14b** Connective i 130

CHAPTER 5
Vowel-Vowel Syllable 131

NOTE TO INSTRUCTOR 131
- **1** Introducing the Vowel-Vowel Syllable 135
- **2a-b** Vowel Teams ai and ay 136
- **3a** Vowel Team ea 139
- **3b-c** Another Sound for ea 140
- **4a** Vowel Team ee 142
- **4b-c** Vowel Team ey 144
- **4d** Plural After Vowel Teams ay and ey 146
- **5a** Vowel Team ie 147
- **5b** (included on page 145)
- **6a-b** Vowel Teams oa and oe 148
- **7a** Vowel Teams ue and ui 151
- **7b** (included on page 150)
- **8** Review of Vowel-Vowel Syllables 153
- **9** Syllable Review 154
- **10** Syllabication of Words with Five Syllables 155
- **11** Challenging Polysyllabic Words 156
- **12a** More Challenging Words 157
- **12b** Dictation Exercise 158
- **13** The Suffix –ize 159
- **14** Suffixes –ee and –ive 160

CHAPTER 6
Consonant-le Syllable 161

NOTE TO INSTRUCTOR 161
- **1** Introducing the Consonant-le Syllable 163
- **2** Ninth Rule of Syllabication 164
- **3** Spelling Rules for Consonant-le Syllables 165
- **4** Short Vowel Signal 166
- **5** Short Vowel Signal, spelling 167

6a Syllabication 168
6b Dictation Exercise 169
7 Challenge Words 170
8 (included on page 167)
9 Latin Roots and Consonant-*le* Syllables 171
10 The Suffixes *–able* and *–ible* 172

CHAPTER 7
Diphthong/Vowel Digraph Syllables 173

NOTE TO INSTRUCTOR 173
1a-b Diphthongs *oi* and *oy* 177
2a Diphthongs *ou* and *ow* 180
2b Other Sounds of *ou* 181
2c-d Four More *ou* Sounds 182
3a-b Diphthong *ow* (long *o*) 184
4a-b Vowel Digraphs *au* and *aw* 186
5 Review of *oi*, *oy*, *ou*, *ow*, *au* and *aw* 189
6a-b Vowel Digraph *oo* 190
7a-b Vowel Digraphs *oo*, *ew*, and *eu* 192
8 Diphthong and Vowel Digraph Review 1 194
9a Vowel Digraphs *ei* and *ie* 195
9b Review of Vowel Digraphs *ei* and *ie* 196
9c (included on page 193)
10 Review of Diphthongs and Vowel Digraphs 2 197
11 Journey to Glacier Bay 198

CHAPTER 8
Hard and Soft c and g 201

NOTE TO INSTRUCTOR 201
1 Hard and Soft *c* 203
2 Challenge Words with Hard and Soft *c* 205
3 The Syllables *–ace* and *–ice* 206
4 Spelling Patterns 207
5 Hard and Soft *g* 208
6 Prefixes and Suffixes with Soft *g* 210
7 Short Vowel Signal *dge* 211
8 Spelling Patterns 212
9 Three Sounds of *ch* 213
10 700 Years of Democracy 214

CHAPTER 9
Accented and Unaccented Syllables 217

NOTE TO INSTRUCTOR 217
1a Accented Syllables in Spoken Words 217
1b Identifying Accented Syllables 219
2 Accented and Unaccented Syllables 220
3a The *Schwa* Sound 221
3b The Dictionary's Phonetic Respelling 222
4 *Schwa* in Spelling Words 223
5a Accent Marks in Words with Prefixes 224
5b More Prefixes 225
6 Absorbed Prefixes 226
7 (included on page 223)
8 Accent Marks in Words with Suffixes 227
9 Accent Marks in Nouns and Verbs 228
10 Medial *Schwa* in Polysyllabic Words 229
11 A Tricky Spelling Rule 230
12 A Long Bike Ride 231

CHAPTER 10
Anglo-Saxon Suffixes 235

NOTE TO INSTRUCTOR 235
1a-b Suffix Pretest 240
2 Suffixes *–et* and *–let* 242
3 Review of Eight Suffixes 243
4a Adding Other Suffixes to *–y* 244
4b Plural After *–y* 245
5a Review of Suffixes *–or*, *–ar*, *–on*, *–an* 246
5b (included on page 241)
5c *i* before *–on*, *–an*, *–or*, *–ar* 247
6 Review of Accented Syllables 248
7a (see Note to Instructor, page 236)
7b Review *–ful*, *–less*, *–ness* 249

8a	(see Note to Instructor, page 237)	**9b**	The Word Ending –sion 285
8b	Suffixes –some, –hood, –ly, –ish 250	**10a**	(see Note to Instructor, page 266)
9a	(see Note to Instructor, page 238)	**10b**	The Word Ending –sion 286
9b	Suffixes –ship, –ward, –dom 251	**10c**	(included on page 282)
10a	Suffix Dictation 252	**10d**	ci, ti, and xi Before –ous 287
10b	(included on page 249)	**10e**	Accent Patterns for Five Suffixes 288
11a	Syllabication with Suffixes 253	**11**	Review of Latin Suffixes 289
11b-c	Dictation Exercise 254	**12**	Syllabication Challenge 1 290
12	Challenge Words 256	**13**	Words with Multiple Suffixes 291
13a	Dictionary Pronunciations 257	**14a**	Syllabication Challenge 2 292
13b	(included on page 255)	**14b**	Dictation Exercise 293
14	Review of Accented Syllables 258	**15a**	Dictionary Pronunciations 294
15	A Brief History of the English Language 259	**15b**	Prefixes, Base Words, and Suffixes 295
		16	Mount Everest 296

CHAPTER 11
Latin Suffixes, Part 1   261

CHAPTER 12
Latin Suffixes, Part 2   299

NOTE TO INSTRUCTOR 261		NOTE TO INSTRUCTOR 299	
1a	(see Note to Instructor, page 262)	**1a**	(see Note to Instructor, page 299)
1b	Suffixes –ment, –ist, and –ic 269	**1b**	The Suffix –al 304
1c-d	Accent Patterns for –ment, –ist, –ic 270	**1c-d**	Combinations ti, ci, tu, su, and du 305
2a	(see Note to Instructor, page 263)	**2a**	(see Note to Instructor, page 300)
2b	The Suffix –ous 272	**2b**	The Suffix –ive 307
2c	Vowels Before –ous 273	**3a**	(see Note to Instructor, page 300)
2d	i Before Word Endings 274	**3b**	The Suffix –ity 308
3a	(see Note to Instructor, page 263)	**3c**	(included on page 306)
3b	The Suffix –ine 275	**3d**	Multiple Suffixes 309
4a	(see Note to Instructor, page 264)	**3e**	(see Note to Instructor, page 301)
4b	The Suffix –fy 276	**3f**	Suffixes –ability and –ibility 310
4c	(included on page 271)	**4a**	(see Note to Instructor, page 301)
5a	(see Note to Instructor, page 264)	**4b**	The Suffix –ary 311
5b	The Suffix –ure 277	**5a**	(see Note to Instructor, page 301)
6a	(see Note to Instructor, page 264)	**5b-c**	The Suffix –ory 312
6b	The Suffix –age 278	**6a-b**	(see Note to Instructor, page 302)
6c	The Suffix –age in Sentences 279	**6c**	Suffixes –ent and –ence 314
6d	Accent Patterns for –ous, –fy, –ure, –age 280	**7a**	(see Note to Instructor, page 302)
7a	(see Note to Instructor, page 265)	**7b**	Suffixes –cy and –ency 315
7b-c	Suffixes –able and –ible 281	**7c**	ci, ti, and si Before –ent, –ence, –ency 316
7d	Review of –able and –ible 283	**7d**	(included on page 313)
8a	(see Note to Instructor, page 265)	**8a-b**	(see Note to Instructor, page 303)
8b	Suffixes –ion and –ian 284	**8c**	Suffixes –ant and –ance 317
9a	(see Note to Instructor, page 266)		

8d	Suffixes –ant, –ance, and –ancy	318
8e	Hard and Soft c and g Before Suffixes	319
9	Accent Rules for –al, –ive, –ent/ –ant, –ence/ –ance, –cy	320
10	Review of Latin Suffixes	321
11	Mixed Practice, Latin Suffixes	322
12a	Base words with Multiple Suffixes	323
12b	Dictation Exercise	324
13	Syllabication with Multiple Suffixes	325
14	Base words, Prefixes, and Suffixes	326
15	Climbing Mount Whitney	327

CHAPTER 13
Prefixes   329

NOTE TO INSTRUCTOR   329

1	Base Words, Prefixes, and Suffixes	332
2	Meaning of Prefixes	333
3a	Prefix Group Work	334
3b-c	First Set of Prefixes	335
3d	Vocabulary Test	337
4a	Prefix Group Work	338
4b-d	Second Set of Prefixes	339
4e	Vocabulary Test	342
5a	Prefix Group Work	343
5b-d	Third Set of Prefixes	344
5e	Vocabulary Test	347
6a	Prefix Group Work	348
6b-d	Fourth Set of Prefixes	349
6e	Vocabulary Test	352

CHAPTER 14
Latin and Greek Roots   353

NOTE TO INSTRUCTOR   353

1a-b	Latin Roots script, scribe	354, 358
2a-b	The Latin Root press	354, 359
3	The Latin Root port	360
4a-b	The Latin Root form	354, 361
5a-b	Latin Roots struct or stru	354, 362
6a-b	Latin Roots spect or spec	354, 363
7a-b	Latin Roots dict or dic	355, 364
8a-b	Latin Roots vis or vid	355, 365
9a-b	Latin Roots duct, duc, and duce	355, 366
10a-c	Latin Roots sist, stit, sta, tain	355, 367
11	Latin Roots ject or jec	368
12a-b	The Latin Root tract	356, 369
13a-b	Latin Roots vent or ven	356, 370
14a-b	The Latin Root rupt	356, 371
15a-b	Roots aud(io) and phon(o)	356, 372
16a-b	Roots nom, nym, and photo	356, 373
17	Greek Forms graph and gram	374
18a-b	Greek Forms chron and metr/meter	356, 375
19a-b	Latin Roots fact, fac, fect, and fic	357, 376

Answer Key   377

Appendix and Bibliography   420

Index   425

Introduction

Designed for ages 9-18, *Power Tools for Literacy* targets the problems of struggling readers, students with learning disabilities or dyslexia, and English learners. This program sustains motivation and brings about rapid improvement in reading, often resulting in higher test scores. Proven successful in grades 4-12, the book can be used in language-arts classes, reading intervention groups, special education programs, and private tutoring sessions. The lessons also have been used with adults who consequently made great strides. The look and feel of the lessons is appropriate for any age group; material that appears tailored to young children has been avoided.

A report by The National Institute of Child Health and Human Development (NICHHD, 1999) states, "For those children who are at risk for reading failure, highly direct and systematic instruction to develop phonemic awareness and phonics skills is required." In keeping with this principle, the 320 copy-ready lessons in this program develop a systematic understanding of the structure of English words. This technique develops the ability to "chunk" long words into predictable units, including syllables, base words, prefixes, and suffixes, thereby enabling students to read and spell difficult words they would otherwise skip. Instructors who have used the lessons report that even older students enjoy and are challenged by the program.

In the early chapters, every lesson starts with single-syllable words, then quickly progresses to longer words. Prefixes and suffixes are introduced from the beginning and throughout the program. The last four chapters concentrate on Latin and Greek prefixes, suffixes and roots. The meaning of these word parts is emphasized and practiced.

Power Tools for Literacy includes these topics:

- Short and long vowels with consonant blends and consonant digraphs
- Short vowel signals
- Configuration of seven kinds of syllables
- Rules for dividing polysyllabic words
- Accented and unaccented syllables
- Compound words
- Hard and soft **c** and **g**
- Reading, spelling, and defining 50 common suffixes
- Spelling rules for adding suffixes to base words
- Vocabulary enrichment by reading, spelling, and defining 50 common prefixes
- Assimilated prefixes
- Latin roots and Greek combining forms
- Weekly spelling lists

Power Tools for Literacy is teacher-friendly. Every chapter is prefaced by a **Note to Instructor**, which describes each lesson, provides background information, and gives directions for best practices.

Since recall improves when we engage more than one modality, *Power Tools for Literacy* is based on a multisensory approach involving the visual, auditory, kinesthetic (motion of writing), and oral (speaking) modalities. Multisensory principles activate every student's stronger learning style and strengthen the weaker modality.

In every chapter, each of the four modalities is engaged by specific exercises: discovering new syllable patterns, decoding lessons, dictation exercises, and weekly spelling lists. (Please see *Overview and Procedures* for more details.) Consistently, students have opportunities to discover phonemic concepts and to formulate the underlying rules for themselves. Whenever possible, it is important to associate meaning with the phonograms that are presented. Knowing the meaning of morphemes (meaningful units of words) develops instant recognition of elements that occur in thousands of words and greatly increases students' vocabulary.

The decoding and dictation pages will bring about improved spelling and decoding of phonemically regular words, and this in turn will generalize to thousands of other words with similar patterns. The weekly spelling lists parallel the presentation of phonemes and include phonemically irregular words and high frequency words.

Power Tools for Literacy is only one component of an effective reading program. It should be coupled with a literature-based curriculum, accompanied by intensive vocabulary development. The NICHHD states, "Reading fluency, automaticity, and reading comprehension strategies within a literature-rich environment must be included to obtain maximum gains."

Please modify and adapt this program to fit the needs of your students. Some middle and high school students may already have solid knowledge of short vowels, consonant blends, consonant digraphs, and long vowels. Therefore, it may be appropriate to omit some of the first lessons in the early chapters. The dictation and spelling lessons could serve as pretests to determine the pages that might be omitted and those that must be included. I hope your students will make great strides toward becoming proficient readers!

Verena Rau,
MS, Education of Learning Disabled Children
Resource Specialist

Overview and Procedures

Power Tools for Literacy provides decoding lessons, dictation exercises, and spelling activities for students who are placed in mainstreamed Language Arts classes, in reading intervention groups, in special education programs, or in private tutoring sessions. From our personal experience, we know that recall improves when we use more than one modality. For this reason, the lessons incorporate a multi-sensory approach. A multisensory method involves the visual, auditory, kinesthetic (motion of writing), and oral (speaking) modalities. In order to engage all four modalities, this technique alternates among the following four kinds of lessons:

Introduction of a New Concept or a New Syllable
Lesson 1 in each chapter is a visual exercise that introduces words with the same syllable or phoneme pattern. The teacher challenges students to find common aspects of the words and to formulate the underlying rules.

Decoding Exercises
The Decoding Exercises are copy-ready lessons comprised of a variety of activities that teach students to read polysyllabic words. Among the more prevalent activities are auditory discrimination exercises (in chapters 1,2,4 and 5), word sorts, matching prefixes or suffixes to base words, using words in sayings and expressions, solving puzzles, and separating words into syllables. When students are syllabifying words, they see the word (visual), divide the word (auditory and kinesthetic), and then pronounce it (oral). The challenging tasks are usually placed on the top half of the page, whereas the lower half of the page frequently consists of a fun activity.

The Code
The unique aspect of this program is the use of syllable codes. Each kind of syllable has a code abbreviation. Using codes in conjunction with a multisensory technique reinforces the structure of previously covered phonograms and morphemes (meaningful units of words) and addresses modality deficits.

Dictation Exercises
In the Dictation Exercises, the instructor writes the code of a polysyllabic word on the board or on the overhead and, then, dictates the word. Students hear the word (auditory), write it (kinesthetic), see it (visual), and then pronounce it (oral). Reversing the modality sequence improves the formation of sound/symbol association in both reading recognition and in spelling. After the instructor dictates ten to twenty words, the class reads the words aloud. It is often astonishing to see how quickly students respond to this method and learn to read and spell polysyllabic words.

Dictation Lists
The dictation lists are on the same page as the spelling lists, entitled **Reading and Spelling for Mastery**. The dictation lists are composed of phonemically regular, one-syllable words. The purpose of these lessons is to determine whether students have

internalized a given concept and whether they can reproduce that concept in writing. It is best to dictate these words soon after the corresponding lesson has been completed. If a student misses more than 20%, the preceding lesson needs to be reviewed.

Weekly Spelling Lists

The **Reading and Spelling for Mastery** lists, when combined with the **Proposed Spelling Activities** listed in the Appendix, provide a weekly spelling program that correlates with the presentation of phonemes. Therefore, it is imperative that the spelling program be used in conjunction with the decoding and dictation exercises. The purpose of these lists is to foster proficiency in reading and spelling three different kinds of words:
1. Practical words with the same phoneme pattern
2. Phonemically irregular words and exceptions called red words (printed in red)
3. High frequency words

    The teacher introduces the spelling list early in the week and requires students to complete two appropriate spelling activities each day for four consecutive days. Because students learn the high frequency words and numerous exceptions through the spelling program, **they must read the list prior to starting their daily practice**. Daily spelling practice is essential because the kinesthetic reinforcement helps to lock these words into long-term memory and simultaneously improves spelling as it strengthens reading. To reinforce retention even more, two additional activities are assigned as homework. The spelling test is given on the fifth day.

    If possible, the teacher has students read the words individually while the rest of the class works on other tasks. If individual reading is impractical, the class pronounces the words in unison.

    The words for the spelling program were selected from the following sources:
- Words with similar phonemic patterns were generated with the aid of the *Franklin Language Master*
- *The Gillingham Manual*
- *Words Their Way*
- *Dolch Words*
- *Solving Language Difficulties*
- *Top 100*

    Recommendation: Schedule these lessons at least three times per week for approximately thirty minutes per session. The spelling activities will take another ten minutes per day.

Decoding Binder
Students bring a binder and create six sections with the help of the teacher.
1. Phonograms   4. Rules
2. Red words   5. Prefixes
3. Homophones/Homographs   6. Suffixes

Phonograms: Students copy each new phonogram (a unit of sound represented in written form) in this section, and write four key words that illustrate it and a picture clue for all short vowel sounds.

Red Words: Immediately after the weekly spelling list has been discussed, students copy the red words (tricky or phonetically irregular words) in this section.

Homophones: Students copy homophones, also known as homonyms, along with a synonym or short definition, in this section. Homographs, marked **HG** (words with the same spelling but different pronunciations such as *bow*) are included in this category. Many of these words will also appear in the **Red Word** section.

Rules: After a rule has been explained, students copy it in this section, along with four examples that illustrate it.

Prefixes: Students copy prefixes in this section and include the pronunciation and definitions.

Suffixes: Students copy suffixes in this section and include the pronunciation, definitions, and parts of speech.

Review: The teacher finds a time slot every week to review the phonograms and rules and another time slot to read the red words, homophones, homographs, prefixes, and suffixes. If possible, a list of the prefixes and suffixes is displayed. The amount of review will depend on the age and strength of the group. The teacher reviews once a week for a minimum of five weeks. Many students will require more time before they achieve retention.

Recommendations:
1. Before you start using this program, learn how to administer an auditory discrimination test or have a speech and language pathologist give such a test. Children with auditory discrimination problems must first receive remediation in phonemic awareness. It is also highly desirable to administer diagnostic tests for word identification and reading comprehension.

2. As you start using this program, model and instill a curiosity about words and their etymology (history or derivation of words). Encourage students to use a good dictionary, a Language Master, or a computer and ask them questions about the origins of words.

The American Heritage Dictionary and Webster's New World Dictionary were used to check definitions and pronunciations.

CHAPTER 1
Closed Syllable

Note to Instructor

It is important that you read this **Note to Instructor** in its entirety as it explains the teaching techniques that apply to subsequent chapters.

Chapter 1 covers closed syllables, short vowels, consonant blends, consonant digraphs, and short vowel signals. Lesson 1 introduces closed syllables. Lesson 2 through Lesson 8 cover short vowels, one at a time, along with basic consonant concepts. Particular care must be given to ascertain students' mastery over the short vowel sounds because their differences are subtle and slight. Every lesson starts with single-syllable words and progresses to polysyllabic words.

The exercises in this chapter are especially important for learning-disabled students because their most common weakness in reading is blending phonograms (written representations of speech sounds) in the correct order. They also have great difficulties memorizing the short vowel sounds. The following lessons provide numerous exercises to remediate these weaknesses and spelling rules to solidify retention.

Some secondary students may already have solid knowledge of short vowels, consonant blends, and digraphs. Therefore, it may be appropriate to skip some of the early lessons, but do teach all of the lessons with syllabication rules (1, 3a, 3b, 6a, 7b). Without this knowledge, students will be lost in subsequent chapters. The dictation and spelling lists can serve as pretests to determine which pages to skip and which pages to include. The skills in this chapter provide a foundation not only for thousands of Anglo-Saxon words, but also for a great majority of Latin and Greek derivatives. Research by Stanback (1992) shows that 43% of all English words are closed syllables. Before you skip particular lessons, make sure students have complete mastery over the material.

Please help students create a **Decoding Binder** as outlined in *Overview and Procedures* and show everyone how to record each new phonogram, red word, homophone, homograph, prefix, suffix, and rule in the appropriate section. The phonograms that must be included are written in boldface. Ask students to write four words that illustrate every phonogram.

After students have completed a lesson, have them read all of the words and sentences again.

Lesson 1 introduces **closed** syllables. This type of syllable is called a closed syllable because the vowel is closed in by one or more consonants on the right side. The abbreviation for this syllable is **cl**. Copy page 11 as an overhead transparency. It may be necessary to use the transparency several times before students retain the characteristics of a closed syllable.

Ask students to answer the question, "What do these words have in common? at, stamps, crisp, in, end, kept, job, prompt, up, club." Record the correct responses on the overhead or on the board in any order, and direct your students to take notes. Correct responses are:

1. All are one-syllable words.
2. Every word has only one vowel.
3. Every vowel is followed by one or more consonants on the right side.
    (It doesn't matter whether there are consonants on the left side of the vowel.
    Many closed syllables start with vowels, *in, up, ant, end*)
4. All of the vowels are short.

Mark the vowels immediately after students discover that all the vowels are short. Mark a short vowel like this: stămp, hŏt. Explain that the marks above vowels are called **diacritical marks**. The name for a short vowel mark is **breve**, pronounced **brēv** or **brĕv** (derived from Latin **brevis**, which means *brief*). A long vowel mark is called a **macron**, pronounced **mācron** or **măcron** (derived from Greek **makros**, which means *long*).

Lesson 2a reviews the configuration of closed syllables and introduces the **short a** sound. This is an easy lesson. You might consider omitting it if you are teaching older students.

Lessons 2b and **2c** review the short **a** sound and introduce beginning and ending blends.

Lesson 2d is a **Reading and Spelling for Mastery** page, consisting of a dictation and a spelling list with words that contain short **a**, beginning blends, and ending blends. Please follow the format outlined in *Overview and Procedures* and select two appropriate spelling activities for daily practice from **Proposed Spelling Activities** in the Appendix, or use your own. Students must read the spelling words every day, before they begin the two activities. Ask students to write the red words in red pen or red pencil in the Decoding Binder, Red Words section.

Lesson 2e teaches an alternate sound of **a** embedded in closed syllables. Its phonemic symbol is ô. It usually occurs in words where **a** is followed by the letter **l**, *call, stall, talk, always, although*. Sometimes **a** also says ô when it is preceded by the letter **w**, *wasp, want, swat, swap, swamp*; however, when **wa** is followed by the letters **g, x,** or **ck**, (glottal stops) the **a** is short, *wag, wagon, wax, wacky, whack*. (Linguistics: The letters **g, x,** and **k** are called glottal stops, which are pronounced in the back of the throat.) It is difficult to talk about a phonetic rule when it applies usually, but not always. For this reason, give students credit if they notice that **a** = ô when **a** comes before **l** and after **w**. Note: Please help students with the sentences on the lower half of **Lesson 2e**.

Lesson 2f is a **Reading and Spelling for Mastery** list. It is on the same page as **Lesson 2d** and contains words with **a** = ô, as well as the exception **was** (wŭz). Some people pronounce **what** as **wŭt**. Therefore, **what** could be considered another exception. Please follow the format outlined in *Overview and Procedures* and **Lesson 2d**.

Lesson 3a introduces the **short i** sound and gives the **First Rule of Syllabication**: "Every syllable must have one vowel sound. A word has the same number of syllables as the number of sounded vowels." After completing the first exercise in this lesson, please introduce the above syllabication rule and teach the following mini-lesson on the board/overhead. Say the word *handbag* slowly and clearly. Ask students to write down the vowels they hear (ă,ă). Call on a volunteer to write the vowels on the board and mark them. Say the word again; and explain that *handbag* is a two-syllable word because we can hear two vowel sounds. Follow this procedure for these words: *backpack, swift, dismiss, landing, standstill, blast, Batman, catfish, hint, sandbag, tactic*. Students are now ready to do the last exercise on **3a**.

Lesson 3b teaches the consonant digraphs **sh** and **ch** and explains the **Second Rule of Syllabication**: "A word with two consonants between two vowels is divided between the consonants (*ad-mit, in-sist*)." Exception: do **not** divide between consonant digraphs. Since a consonant digraph stands for a single sound, treat it as a single letter. Students will learn to apply this rule in the last exercise. Please adhere to the following steps for writing words in syllables. Direct students to do these tasks:

- Highlight the vowels in each word and draw a red line between the medial consonants.
- Write the words in separate syllables, divided by dashes, and mark the vowels.
- Underline every word they are able to read. (If your teaching situation permits, help those who have not underlined all of the words.)
- When everyone is finished, ask students to raise their hands if they can read the first word.
- Once all the students raise their hands, direct the class to pronounce the word in unison when you say, "Now." (Insist that no one says the word before you say, "Now." Otherwise those who need remediation the most will be drowned out by those who need it the least.)
- Repeat the last two steps for each word. Pause between words to give everyone a chance to sound out the next one.
- If some students can't read the entire word, ask a volunteer to say the first syllable and another person to say the second syllable. Students then read the word in unison.

Lesson 3c The consonant team **ng** says the sound in **bring** or **sing**. When **ng** comes after **a**, the **a** is not exactly short. It makes a sound that is in between short **a** and long **a**, *hang, bang*. Let's call it the **ang** sound. The ending blend **nk** says **ng** + **k** *rank, tank*.

Lesson 3d introduces the consonant digraphs **th, wh**, and reviews **ng**. The second page provides a review of consonant digraphs.

Lesson 3e covers the exception of **long i** in closed syllables when followed by the consonants **nd, ld**, or **gh** (*mind, mild,* and *fight*).

Lesson 3f is a **Reading and Spelling for Mastery** page that consists of a dictation and a spelling list. Please follow the format outlined in *Overview and Procedures* and **Lesson 2**. Please select two appropriate spelling activities for daily practice. Explain the term homophone, also commonly called homonym: two or more words have the same pronunciation, but they differ in spelling and meaning. As you introduce the words on the spelling list, write the alternate spelling of each homophone on the board or overhead, and discuss the two different definitions. Follow this procedure whenever a lesson includes homophones.

Reminder: After students have completed a lesson, have them read all of the words once again.

Lesson 4a introduces the **short e** sound, as well as the prefixes **ex–** and **en–**. Ask students to enter the prefixes and definitions in the Prefixes section of their Decoding Binders: The prefix **ex–** means *out of, outside, away from*. The prefix **en–** means *into, onto,* or *within*. Prefixes change the meaning of a base word. The term *base word* is a word that has no prefixes or suffixes. Starting with this lesson, write all prefixes on a chart that is displayed in the classroom.

Lessons 4b and **4c** explain the short vowel signals **ll, ss, ff, ck, tch**, and sometimes **zz**. These short vowel signals usually apply to one-syllable words (*spill, press, stiff, check, patch, jazz*). If a one-syllable word has a prefix or a suffix, the short vowel signals continue to apply (*dispatch, packet, misspell*). Ask students to copy the short vowel signals and three examples for each in the Rules section of their Decoding Binders. Mnemonic device: Jeff will catch the ball and kick it to Russ.

Lesson 4b directs students to choose missing words in common expressions. Because many students may not be familiar with all of the phrases, group work might be appropriate. Please explain the meaning of each expression.

Lesson 4d is a **Reading and Spelling for Mastery** list with short **e** words and short vowel signals. Please follow the steps outlined in *Overview and Procedures* and select two appropriate spelling activities for daily practice. Students must read the words every day.

Lesson 4e is a review of the short vowels **a, i**, and **e**. The last exercise asks students to draw pictures of the symbols for the short vowels **a, i**, and **e** (*apple, igloo, elephant*).

Lessons 5a consists of two pages. The first page introduces the **short o** sound and contrasts it to **short e**. Consider allowing students to work with a partner on the activity with the common phrases/expressions. Provide assistance when necessary. The second page covers the exception of **long o** in closed syllables when followed by the consonants **l** or **st** (*roll, told,* and *most*). This rule has its own exceptions such as *cost* and *doll*.

Lesson 5b is a **Reading and Spelling for Mastery** page, which consists of a dictation and a spelling list. Please follow the previously discussed procedures.

Lesson 5c provides a review of words with short **o**.

Lessons 6a-6b introduce the **short u** sound, the silent consonant combinations **kn**, **wr**, and **gn**, as well as the **Third Rule of Syllabication**: "Words with three consonants between two vowels are often divided after the first consonant because the other two may form a blend (*hun-dred, pil-grim*). When the first syllable ends with a blend or a digraph, divide after the second consonant (*pump-kin, wind-mill*). This rule often applies to compound words or to words that start with prefixes.

Lesson 6c is a **Reading and Spelling for Mastery** page, which consists of a dictation and a spelling list. Please follow previously discussed procedures.

Lesson 7a (no worksheet) Say the word *inspect* slowly and clearly. Ask students to write down the vowels they hear (ĭ, ĕ). Call on a volunteer to write the vowels on the board and mark them. Say the word again; and explain that *inspect* is a two-syllable word because we can hear two vowel sounds. Follow this procedure for these words: *distract, prompt, enroll, invent, setback, inhabit, stock, cactus, contract, sprint, pickup, indent*.

Lesson 7b reviews the **First Rule of Syllabication** and elaborates on its four components. It teaches students how to determine the number of syllables in a word.

Lesson 8 directs students to write words in syllables and mark the vowels. Please follow the procedure outlined in 3b.

Lesson 9 introduces the suffixes **–ful** (*full of*), **–less** (*without*), and **–ness**, (*state or condition*), as well as the schwa sound. When a vowel other than short **u** says ŭ, it is called a schwa sound. Its symbol is ə. The **e** in **–less** and **–ness** says the schwa sound. Vowels in suffixes usually say the schwa sound because most suffixes are unaccented. Ask students to copy these suffixes in the Suffixes section of their Decoding Binders. Starting with this lesson and through subsequent chapters, write all suffixes on another chart that is displayed in the classroom.

Lesson 10 is the first dictation exercise. The purpose of the dictation exercises is to strengthen sound/symbol correspondence in spelling polysyllabic words. Initially, this activity may confuse students. They may need you to give detailed modeling and feedback on the board or on the overhead. This lesson requires students to remember the configuration of closed syllables and to produce two-syllable words according to the code. Please provide the code for each word orally and write it on the board or on the overhead. Then dictate the word. It is important that you pronounce each word slowly and clearly as one unit. Students must mark the vowels, but suffixes are not marked. Once students have completed the dictation exercise, ask them to underline every word they are able to read without help. Then ask your class to read the words individually if possible. If that is not practical, follow the procedure discussed in Lesson 3b.

Lesson 11 teaches the plural suffixes **–s** and **–es**. Use **–es** after nouns that end with **s, sh, ch, z,** or **x**. Use **–es** also after third person singular verbs that end with the above letters: *he catches, she dresses*.

Lesson 12a covers contractions.

Lesson 12b is a **Reading and Spelling for Mastery** list consisting of contractions. Please follow the previously discussed procedures. For one of the activities, give a practice test. Dictate the complete words, and have students write the contractions. When you give the test, dictate the words on the left only; students then write the correct contraction.

1 Closed Syllable

What is a syllable? A syllable is a word or part of a word that has one vowel sound. Often there are consonants before or after the vowel.

What do these words have in common?

at   stamps   crisp   in   end   kept   prompt   up   club

1. _____

2. _____

3. _____

4. _____

This kind of syllable is called *closed*. **The abbreviation is** *cl*. **Why do you think it has this name?**

_____

Fold back this bottom section, or place a sheet of paper over it. _ _ _ _ _ _ _ _ _ _ _ _ _ _ _ _ _ _

NOTE TO INSTRUCTOR: Please copy this page as an overhead transparency to introduce *closed* syllables. Record the following correct responses in any order.
1. All of these words have only one vowel.
2. The vowel is followed by one or more consonants on the right side.
3. The vowel is short. Mark the vowels immediately after students discover that all of the vowels are short.
4. All are one-syllable words. This type of syllable is called **closed** because the vowel is closed in by one or more consonants on the right side.

2a Short *a*

List three things that all **closed** syllables have in common.

1. _____
2. _____
3. _____

In the next few lessons, we will discuss the short vowel sounds. All the words you will study fit the pattern of **closed** syllables. Let's start with short **a**.

Draw an apple in the margin. Say the first sound in the word **apple**. You have just made a short **a** sound. We mark the short **a** sound like this: ă

Say the following words and listen to the short **a** sound

    1. add   2. at   3. as   4. ax   5. has   6. bag   7. tan

Say the word **at**. Write a new word with the letter **b** in front of **at** _____. Try the letter **c** in front of **at** _____. Write four words that start with the letters **h, m, p, s** and end with **at**. _____

Say the word **an**. Write a new word with the letter **c** in front of **an**: _____. Try the letter **m** in front of **an** _____. Write five words that start with the letters **b, f, r, p, t** and end with **an**. _____

Say the word **cap**. Write six words that rhyme with **cap**:

_____

Say the word **sad**. Write six words that rhyme with **sad**:

_____

Say the word **bag**. Write five words by changing the **b** to these letters: **n, r, s, t, w**

_____

2b Beginning Blends with Short *a*

Many words have two consonants before the vowel sound. When two different consonant sounds are right next to each other, they are called a **blend**. Blends that come before the vowel are called **beginning blends**.

Read the following words to yourself. Circle or highlight the words with beginning blends. Underline the words without blends:

1. hat	5. scam	9. mad	13. pan	17. had	21. clam
2. crab	6. tag	10. swam	14. clap	18. scan	22. cab
3. map	7. blab	11. grab	15. brag	19. glad	23. snag
4. plan	8. flag	12. sat	16. tap	20. drag	24. cram

Within each group, draw lines from the beginning blends on the left to the short **a** and consonant on the right to make new words. The word segments on the right may be used more than once. Write the new words on the lines.

gl   ab   ⇨   1. __glad__
sl   ap   ⇨   2. _____
sn   ad   ⇨   3. _____
tr   ⇨   4. _____
                     ⇨   5. _____

cl   an   ⇨   1. _____
sc   ab   ⇨   2. _____
bl   am   ⇨   3. _____
                     ⇨   4. _____
                     ⇨   5. _____
                     ⇨   6. _____

cr   an   ⇨   1. _____
br   ag   ⇨   2. _____
sp   ab   ⇨   3. _____
                     ⇨   4. _____
                     ⇨   5. _____

2c Ending Blends with Short *a*

Many words have two different consonants after the vowel sound. This is called an **ending blend**.

Say the word **and**. Listen to the ending blend. Write the consonants **l, h, b, br,** and **st** in front of **and**. Then read the new words.

1. ____and   2. ____and   3. ____and   4. ____and   5. ____and

Say the word **ant**. Listen to the ending blend. Write the consonants **r, gr, pl, sl,** and **sc** in front of **ant**. Read the new words.

1. ____ant   2. ____ant   3. ____ant   4. ____ant   5. ____ant

Say the word **ask**. Listen to the ending blend. Write the consonants **t, m, b, c,** and **fl** in front of **ask**. Then read the new words.

1. ____ask   2. ____ask   3. ____ask   4. ____ask   5. ____ask

Say the word **mast**. Listen to the ending blend. Change the first letter to the consonants **l, p, c, f,** and **bl**. Then read the new words.

1. ____ast   2. ____ast   3. ____ast   4. ____ast   5. ____ast

Say the word **camp**. Listen to the ending blend. Change the first letter to the consonants **r, l, d, cl,** and **st**. Then read the new words.

1. ____amp   2. ____amp   3. ____amp   4. ____amp   5. ____amp

Compound words connect two short words to form a new word, which combines both meanings. Draw lines from the words on the left to the ones on the right to make compound words. Write them on the lines. One word on the left will be used twice.

hand	nap	➪	1. __handbag__
back	man	➪	2. _____
crafts	bag	➪	3. _____
cat	stand	➪	4. _____
band	pack	➪	5. _____
		➪	6. _____

2d/f Reading and Spelling for Mastery

Words with short **a**, beginning blends, and ending blends:

a=ô, as in *tall, bald, talk, want*:

Dictation List

1. fad
2. mad
3. sat
4. cat
5. flat
6. drag
7. flag
8. snag
9. flap
10. clap
11. trap
12. grab
13. crab
14. slam
15. swam
16. task
17. flask
18. plant
19. draft
20. craft

2d Spelling List

1. am
2. bag
3. map
4. man
5. plan
6. ask
7. band
8. hand
9. stand
10. brand
11. has
12. had
13. have *(H)
14. half *
15. act
16. fact
17. lamp
18. stamp
19. fast
20. last

2f Spelling List

1. halt
2. salt
3. calm
4. walk*
5. talk*
6. stalk*
7. wad
8. want
9. all
10. call
11. wall
12. fall
13. wand
14. wasp
15. swan
16. swat
17. swap
18. swamp
19. what *
20. was * says **wuz**

*Red words, H=homophone

2e Sometimes *a* Says *ô*

Do you remember what the symbol is for the short **a** sound? Draw it in the margin.

All of the words you have studied so far are examples of **closed** syllables. In some **closed** syllables, the letter **a** has a different sound. Say the following words and listen to the vowel sound.

    1. all   2. ball   3. salt   4. swap   5. swat

We use the symbol **ô** to represent this sound. Read the following words and listen to the vowel sounds carefully. Write **ô** or **ă** next to each word.

1. draft ____	7. salt ____	13. wasp ____	19. swamp ____
2. call ____	8. stand ____	14. gasp ____	20. fall ____
3. hall ____	9. ball ____	15. bald ____	21. swat ____
4. grasp ____	10. mall ____	16. tall ____	22. bland ____
5. small ____	11. fact ____	17. halt ____	23. wall ____
6. ramp ____	12. stall ____	18. craft ____	24. scald ____

Study the pattern of the above words. Pay special attention to the letters that come before and after the **a** in each word. When does **a** say **ô**? What is the rule?

_____

_____

The letter **a** also says **ô** when **alk** comes after it, as in *talk*. Did you notice the letter **l** is silent?

Use the following words in the sentences below: balk, stalking, walk

    1. Don't _____ across the street without looking both ways.

    2. Some horses _____ when they try to jump over a hurdle.

    3. The cat was _____ a bird.

3a Short *i*, First Rule of Syllabication

Let's discuss the short vowel **i**. Say the word **igloo** and listen to its first sound. You probably know that an igloo is a small hut made of snow. Draw one in the margin. Say the following words and listen to the short **i** sound.

    1. in   2. hint   3. it   4. if   5. milk   6. fit   7. grin

Beginning blends have two consonants before the vowel; ending blends have two consonants after the vowel. Sometimes three consonants come before or after a vowel. This is called a **cluster**. We will now practice these skills with the short vowels **i** and **a**. Fill in the blanks with **i** or **a**, and mark them. Make sure the words make sense.

1. sk____p	6. cl____p	11. str____ct	16. br____sk
2. f____st	7. f____ct	12. m____sk	17. tw____st
3. f____st	8. sk____mp	13. str____p	18. s____lk
4. sw____ft	9. cr____sp	14. str____p	19. c____mp
5. cl____p	10. gl____nd	15. spr____nt	20. scr____pt

In the next few pages, you will learn some syllabication rules. They teach you how long words are put together. Your teacher will explain this rule and do a lesson with you.

First Rule of Syllabication	Every syllable must have one vowel sound. A word has the same number of syllables as the number of sounded vowels.

Compound words connect two short words to form a new word, which combines both meanings. Draw lines from the words on the left to the ones on the right to make compound words. Write the new words on the lines.

wind	nip	⇨	1. __windmill__
lip	stall	⇨	2. _____
cat	back	⇨	3. _____
pin	mill	⇨	4. _____
half	kin	⇨	5. _____
in	stick	⇨	6. _____
nap	ball	⇨	7. _____

3b *sh, ch*, Second Rule of Syllabication

Consonant digraphs consist of two consonants that make a single sound, such as **sh** in *shift* and **ch** in *chat*. Note: Do not divide long words between these consonants, unless the first syllable ends with the sound of **s**, and the second syllable starts with the sound of **h** (*mis-hap*).

Write **sh** or **ch** in the blanks below to make real words.

1. fi____
2. ____imp
3. sta____
4. ____ill
5. cra____
6. in____
7. ____ip
8. ____ip
9. sma____
10. ____ant
11. ____in
12. ____in
13. ____alk
14. spla____
15. ____ap
16. a____
17. pin____
18. da____
19. ____ift
20. bran____

Words with more than one syllable often have several consonants where the syllables connect. Here is an important rule for dividing words into syllables.

Second Rule of Syllabication	A word that has two consonants between two vowels is divided between the consonants (*ad-mit*).

Highlight the vowels in the words below. Draw a red line between the consonants in the middle. Then write the words in syllables, separated by dashes. Finally, mark the vowels. Do **not** divide between consonant digraphs; since they make one sound, treat them as one letter.

1. cat | fish   căt – fĭsh
2. attach
3. flashback
4. brandish
5. chipping
6. mishmash
7. picnic
8. chitchat
9. victim
10. dishpan

3c Consonant Teams *ng* and *nk*

The consonant team **ng** says the sound you hear in **bring** or **sing**. When **ng** comes after **a**, the **a** is not exactly short. It makes a sound that is in between the short and the long sound of **a**. Long **a** says its own name. Let's call it the **ang** sound. Listen to the **ang** sound in these words.

    1. bang   2. hang   3. fangs   4. rang

This in-between sound of **a** also occurs when **a** is followed by the ending blend **nk**. The ending blend **nk** first says **ng** and then adds **k**. Let's call it the **ank** sound. Listen closely to the **ank** sound in the following words.

    1. bank   2. rank   3. sank   4. drank

Complete the words by drawing lines to the correct consonant teams. The words must make sense.

	ng		ng		ng		ng
1. bla		2. fli		3. sla		4. cra	
	nk		nk		nk		nk

	ng		ng		ng		ng
5. swi		6. dri		7. fa		8. bli	
	nk		nk		nk		nk

Sometimes you can make two words by keeping all of the consonants the same and only changing the vowels. Try **a** or **i** in the blanks to make new words and write them on the lines. The words must make sense.

1. r___nk _____   5. s___ng _____

2. r___ng _____   6. bl___nk _____

3. s___nk _____   7. dr___nk _____

4. sl___ng _____   8. cl___ng _____

Write four rhyming words for **ink** _____

Write four rhyming words for **bang** _____

Write four rhyming words for **ring** _____

Write four rhyming words for **bank** _____

3d Consonant Digraphs *th* and *wh*

English has two more consonant digraphs (two consonants that make a single sound). They are **th** as in *thin* and **wh** as in *whip*. The digraph **wh** occurs in the beginning of a word or a syllable. **Th** can appear at the beginning, middle, or end of a word. Do not divide long words between these consonants, unless each makes its own sound.

In each group, draw lines from the word starters on the left to the consonant digraphs on the right to make real words. You may use the consonant digraphs on the right more than once. Write the new words on the lines. Please take note: These words do **not** start with **wh**: *with, wing, witch, will,* and *wish*. We will also review **ng**.

thi	th	⇨	1. __thing__
ba	ng	⇨	2. _____
cli	z	⇨	3. _____
whi		⇨	4. _____
		⇨	5. _____

sla	th	⇨	1. _____
fif	ll	⇨	2. _____
thri	ng	⇨	3. _____
whi	m	⇨	4. _____
		⇨	5. _____

spri	ft	⇨	1. _____
thra	p	⇨	2. _____
thri	ng	⇨	3. _____
whi	sh	⇨	4. _____
		⇨	5. _____

Try to solve this scrambled puzzle:

The digraph is at the end of the first syllable. Short **a** is in the second syllable. It is in the sink.

spinhad   _ _ _ _ _ _ _

3d continued

Write seven rhyming words for **ash**: _____
_____

Use a dictionary to copy three words that start with these digraphs: **wh, ch** and **th**.
_____

_____

Use the words in the box to solve the crossword puzzle; write in pencil.

> within   inkling   grandchild   bathmat   withstand
> signal   thrilling   sandwich   fabric   whiplash

Across
1. You have it for lunch.
2. Has two different vowels, the digraph **th** is in the middle.
3. Same vowels, means *inside*.
4. Same vowels, it rhymes with *twinkling*.
5. Starts and ends with consonant blends, digraph is in the middle.
6. No digraphs, first vowel is **i**

Down
1. Has two short **a**'s
2. Has two digraphs, you might get it in a crash.
3. Starts and ends with digraphs, same vowel in each syllable.
4. No digraphs, first vowel is **a**.

3e Long *i* in Closed Syllables

When the letters **gh** follow the vowel **i**, they are silent and make the **i** long. A long **i** says its own name, as in the word "I". We mark long **i** by writing a small dash above it (ī). The vowel **i** is also long when followed by the letters **ld** or **nd**.

Write the letter **i** next to each word and mark it long or short. You may need to try both sounds, and choose the one that makes a real word. There are two exceptions: wind (correct with long or short i) and gild.

1. mind ____	7. shrimp ____	13. kind ____	19. sigh ____
2. sick ____	8. light ____	14. wild ____	20. high ____
3. right ____	9. rind ____	15. hind ____	21. mild ____
4. thrill ____	10. blind ____	16. chip ____	22. flight ____
5. child ____	11. thing ____	17. bright ____	23. shrink ____
6. sight ____	12. grind ____	18. sling ____	24. find ____

Unscramble this word to solve the puzzle:

glafthilsh: _ _ _ _ _ _ _ _ _

1. It starts with the letter **f** and ends with the letter **t**.
2. The first syllable ends with a consonant digraph; the second syllable starts with the letter **l**.
3. You need it when it's dark.

Write seven rhyming words for **right:**

_____

_____

Write six rhyming words for **mind:**

_____

_____

Write two rhyming words for **wild:** _____

3f Reading and Spelling for Mastery

Words with short **i**, short **a**, and consonant digraphs:

Dictation

1. sing
2. string
3. spring
4. milk
5. silk
6. swift
7. shift
8. bank
9. drank
10. swing
11. sang
12. this
13. that
14. hang
15. ship
16. chips
17. split
18. blink
19. dish
20. fish

Words with short **i**, long **i**, and consonant digraphs:

Spelling List

1. did
2. give *
3. things
4. bring
5. with
6. wish
7. will
8. think
9. which* (H)
10. sign*
11. night (H)
12. might (H)
13. right (H)
14. flight
15. high (H)
16. mind
17. kind
18. find
19. child
20. children *

*Red words, H = homophones

4a Short e, Prefixes ex– and en–

Short **e** sounds just like the first letter in the word **elephant**. Say it several times and draw a small elephant at the bottom of this page. Read these words and listen to the short **e** sound.

    1. elf 2. end 3. egg 4. elm 5. else 6. red 7. pen 8. desk 9. left

Do you remember what the symbol is for short **i**? Draw it in the margin. Write ĭ or ĕ in the blanks to make real words. Let's talk about the sound of **qu**. It says **kw**.

1. m___lt
2. sl___p
3. k___pt
4. b___nch
5. fr___sh
6. th___ft
7. qu___t
8. qu___st
9. sh___ft
10. ch___st
11. tr___p
12. sh___lf
13. r___st
14. s___lf
15. st___ng
16. tr___nch
17. dw___ll
18. squ___d
19. fl___sh
20. qu___z

A prefix is a group of letters that comes before a word or a syllable and changes the meaning. Draw lines from the prefixes to the words or syllables to make new words. Write them on the lines. You will use each prefix more than once.

Prefixes   **Base words/Syllables**

              press ⇨ 1. _express_
ex–   it ⇨ 2. _____
              list ⇨ 3. _____
en–   act ⇨ 4. _____
              trench ⇨ 5. _____
                            6. _____

              chant ⇨ 1. _____
ex–   tract ⇨ 2. _____
              pand ⇨ 3. _____
en–   tinct ⇨ 4. _____
              trust   5. _____

What does the prefix **ex–** mean? _____

What does the prefix **en–** mean? _____

4b Short Vowel Signals *ff, ll, ss, zz*

English has several short vowel signals, which come right after the short vowel. They say, "The vowel in front of me is short!" Some of the most common short vowel signals are **ll** as in *fill*, **ss** as in *miss*, **ff**, as in *whiff*, and sometimes **zz** as in *jazz*. All of them have a single sound. These words do not follow the rule: **as, has, gas, was, is, if, his, us, bus, quiz, whiz,** and **yes**.

Draw lines from the word starters on the left to the short vowel signals on the right. Then write the new words on another sheet of paper. Read the new words.

1. sta	ss	5. spi	ss	9. swe	ss
2. cla	ll	6. dre	ll	10. pre	ll
3. ja	ff	7. fi	ff	11. fri	ff
4. be	zz	8. sni	zz	12. cli	zz

Use the words in the box to complete the expressions:

> class   shell   fall   fill   miss   wall   wills   cliff   call   dress

1. _____ the bill
2. hit the _____
3. _____ up
4. hit or _____
5. walk on egg_____

6. _____ it quits
7. _____ in love
8. a test of _____
9. a _____ act
10. a _____ hanger

Write six rhyming words for **bill**:

_____

Write five rhyming words for **call**: _____

Write four rhyming words for **mess**: _____

Write three rhyming words for **whiff**: _____

4c   Short Vowel Signals *ck* and *tch*

Two more short vowel signals are **ck** for the **k** sound and **tch** for the **ch** sound. Please note, the letter **t** in **tch** is silent. Remember, these signals are only used right after short vowels.

Draw lines from the consonants and vowel on the left to the correct short vowel signal on the right to make real words. Write them on the lines. Read all of the words.

ca		➪	1. __catch__
de	ck	➪	2. _____
cli		➪	3. _____
stre	tch	➪	4. _____
che		➪	5. _____

scra		➪	6. _____
fe	ck	➪	7. _____
bri		➪	8. _____
i	tch	➪	9. _____
sti		➪	10. _____
		➪	11. _____

Draw lines to the correct word endings. Make sure the words make sense and follow the rule! Use short vowel signals only when they come right after the vowel.

1. bra nch / tch
2. gli nch / tch
3. dre nch / tch
4. scra nch / tch

5. pe nk / ck
6. dri nk / ck
7. qui nk / ck
8. sna nk / ck

9. ske nch / tch
10. tra nk / ck
11. que nch / tch
12. tri nk / ck

4d Reading and Spelling for Mastery

Words with short **e**, short **a**, short **i**, and short vowel signals:

Dictation	Spelling List
1. tell	1. went
2. bell	2. them
3. sell H	3. that
4. mess	4. this
5. less	5. then
6. chess	6. class
7. then	7. guess *
8. tiff	8. well
9. sniff	9. still
10. fizz	10. quiz
11. jazz	11. back
12. neck	12. check
13. deck	13. wreck (H)
14. peck	14. quick
15. stick	15. stretch
16. black	16. scratch
17. fetch	17. says *
18. patch	18. said *
19. catch	19. when *
20. bench	20. watch *

* Red words, H = homophones

4e Syllabication Practice

Do you remember what a **closed syllable** is? Closed syllables have three things in common. What are they?

1. _____
2. _____
3. _____

In the last lesson, you learned the second rule of syllabication. Do you remember it? If not, here it is one more time.

| Second Rule of Syllabication | A word that has two consonants between two vowels is divided between the consonants (ad-mit). Do **not** divide between consonant digraphs. |

Highlight the vowels in the words below. Then draw a red line between the consonants in the middle. Next, write the words in syllables, separated by dashes. Finally, mark the vowels. When you're done, read the words at your teacher's direction.

1. expand   ĕx – pănd
2. invent   _____
3. affect   _____
4. helmet   _____
5. expect   _____
6. intend   _____
7. insect   _____
8. trespass   _____
9. fishnet   _____
10. inject   _____
11. embellish _____
12. establish _____

Draw the pictures of the prompts for short **a**, short **i**, and short **e** in the space below.

28

5a Short o

Let's discuss the short vowel **o**. Say the word **octopus** and listen to its first sound. You probably know that an octopus has many arms and lives in the sea. Draw one in the margin. Say the following words and listen to the short **o** sound.

1. on 2. off 3. opt 4. rock 5. stop 6. lock

We will now practice the short vowel **o** and contrast it to the short vowel **e**. Fill in the blanks with **o** or **e** and mark them. Make sure the words make sense. Read the words at your teacher's direction.

1. cl___th
2. str___ng
3. dw___ll
4. sp___ts
5. fr___g
6. h___nk
7. fl___ss
8. d___ll
9. c___st
10. b___nch
11. sh___ck
12. qu___st
13. cr___ss
14. cr___ss
15. bl___nd
16. bl___nd
17. st___ck
18. fr___st
19. cl___ck
20. st___mp
21. pr___mpt
22. f___lt
23. bl___ck
24. str___tch

Read the words in the box and use them to complete the phrases or expressions:

boss lock pop socks log strong shop dots clock hop doll lost

1. Stop the _____.
2. _____ till you drop.
3. Knocks your _____ off
4. _____ to it.
5. She is a _____.
6. _____ as an ox
7. Connect the _____.
8. _____ on.
9. You're the _____.
10. He _____ his senses.
11. _____ the question
12. They walk in _____ step.

Write five rhyming words for these examples:

1. log   _____
2. block   _____
3. stop   _____
4. not   _____

5a continued

Sometimes you can make several words by keeping all of the consonants the same and only changing the vowels. Let's see how many words you can make by changing the vowels. Use **a, i, e,** and **o**. The words must make sense.

1. b___nd (4) _____
2. ch___mp (3) _____
3. l___ft (3) _____
4. ch___p (3) _____
5. st___ck (3) _____
6. m___ss (4) _____
7. l___st (4) _____
8. bl___nd (4) _____
9. fl___p (3) _____
10. fl___ck (4) _____

Do you remember the picture prompt for the short **o** sound? Draw it in the margin.

Write all of the short vowel signals you have studied and add an example for each:

_____
_____

In some closed syllables the vowel **o** is not short. Sometimes **o** is long, even though it is the only vowel in the syllable. A long vowel says its own name. Therefore, long **o** sounds like the first sound in the word *old*. We mark a long vowel by writing a small line above it: **ō**.

Read these words and listen carefully to the vowel sounds. Write **ŏ** or **ō** next to each word.

1. most ___   5. roll ___   9. told ___   13. host ___
2. slosh ___   6. broth ___   10. poll ___   14. cold ___
3. post ___   7. prom ___   11. sold ___   15. fold ___
4. song ___   8. bold ___   12. cot ___   16. scold ___

Study words 1-16. When does **o** have a long vowel sound in closed syllables?

_____

5b Reading and Spelling for Mastery

Short **o** with blends, digraphs, short vowel signals, and some long **o** sounds:

Dictation List	Spelling List
1. dock	1. clock
2. lock	2. stock
3. rock	3. block
4. sock	4. socks
5. plot	5. cloth
6. frog	6. month *
7. smog	7. front *
8. drop	8. from *
9. stop	9. cross
10. long	10. long
11. fond	11. along
12. blond	12. strong
13. chomp	13. post
14. stomp	14. most
15. toss	15. almost
16. boss	16. roll * (H)
17. cost	17. comb*
18. lost	18. old
19. frost	19. told
20. broth	20. sold

*Red words, H = homophone

5c Review of Short o

Read the words in the box to solve the crossword puzzle. Underline the words you can read and ask for help with the rest. Your teacher will help you read the clues. Use a pencil!

> chopsticks   softball   bobsled   snapshot   liftoff   cobweb   hopscotch   watchdog
> crisscross   eggnog   slingshot   crosswalk   goblet   bottom   stopwatch   compacts

Across
1. It's like the letter *x*.
2. Small cars
3. You need it for crossing the street.
4. You eat with them.
5. It's a kind of picture
6. When a rocket rises
7. A nice glass
8. A game with teams
9. A kind of drink

Down
1. An animal
2. A children's game
3. It's used to time someone.
4. A spider makes it.
5. Hunters used it.
6. A winter sport
7. The opposite of *top*

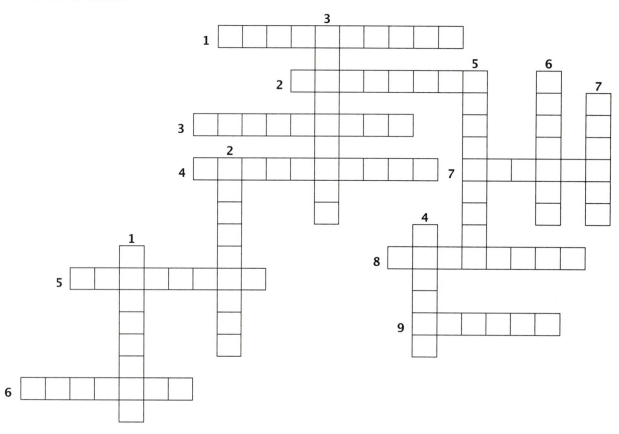

6a Short *u*, Third Rule of Syllabication

Let's discuss the short vowel **u**. Say the word **umbrella** and listen to its first sound. Draw an umbrella at the top of this page. Then read the following words and listen to the short **u** sound.

1. up   2. us   3. until   4. bug   5. luck   6. fun

We will now practice the short vowel **u** and contrast it to the short vowel **o**. Fill in the blanks with short **u** or short **o** and mark them. Make sure the words make sense.

1. dr___m	7. g___lp	13. c___st	19. cr___nch
2. br___sh	8. sk___nk	14. h___nk	20. h___lk
3. ch___p	9. st___mp	15. h___nk	21. cl___tch
4. cr___st	10. st___mp	16. gl___t	22. scr___b
5. s___lk	11. tr___t	17. str___ck	23. cr___ss
6. fl___sh	12. shr___g	18. pl___p	24. shr___b

Third Rule of Syllabication	Words with three consonants between two vowels are often divided after the first consonant because the other two may form a blend (*con-trast, sub-tract*). When the first syllable ends with a blend or digraph, divide after the second consonant (*trans-mit*).

Highlight the vowels in the words below. Draw a red line between the syllables. Then write the words in syllables, separated by dashes. Finally, mark the vowels.

1. hundred   _____
2. husband   _____
3. gumdrop   _____
4. unpack   _____
5. trumpet   _____
6. pumpkin   _____
7. subtract   _____
8. conduct   _____
9. unplug   _____

6a continued

What are beginning blends? _____

What are ending blends? _____

What are consonant clusters? _____

Say the word **pump**; listen to the ending blend. Change the first **p** to the following blends: **st, cl, sl, gr,** and **tr**. Read the new words.

    1. ___ump   2. ___ump   3. ___ump   4. ___ump   5. ___ump

Say the word **sunk**; listen to the ending blend. Change the letter **s** to the following blends or digraphs: **tr, ch, sk, pl,** and **s**. Read the new words.

    1. ___unk   2. ___unk   3. ___unk   4. ___unk   5. ___unk

Say the word **hunt**; listen to the ending blend. Change the letter **h** to the following blends or digraphs: **bl, gr, st, br,** and **sh**. Read the new words.

    1. ___unt   2. ___unt   3. ___unt   4. ___unt   5. ___unt

Say the word **lung**; listen to the ending digraph. Change the letter **l** to the following blends or clusters: **st, cl, sw, str,** and **spr**. Read the new words.

    1. ___ung   2. ___ung   3. ___ung   4. ___ung   5. ___ung

Solve these puzzles. Insert short vowels in the blanks to make real words and write them on the lines.

    1. Try **u** and **a**.   ___d___lt   ⇨   _____

    2. Try **u** and **i**.   ch___pm___nk   ⇨   _____

    3. Try **a** and **u**.   ___lb___m   ⇨   _____

    4. Try **i** and **o**.   ch___pst___cks   ⇨   _____

    5. Try **i** and **e**.   m___ssp___ll   ⇨   _____

    6. Try **i** and **u**.   r___bb___sh   ⇨   _____

    7. Try **a** and **e**.   ___x___ct   ⇨   _____

6b Silent Initial Consonants, Medial y

List the three things closed syllables have in common.

1. _____
2. _____
3. _____

The letters **k** and **g** are silent when paired with the letter **n** (kn, gn). When the letters **wr** are next to each other, the letter **w** is silent. Most words with the letters **kn, gn,** and **wr** came to English from Anglo-Saxon, the earliest form of English; however, we inherited some long words that start with **gn** from Greek.

Words that came to English from Greek use the letters **ph** for the sound of **f** and sometimes **y** for short **i**. Read the following words. Write the letter **G** next to the words we inherited from Greek, and the letter **A** next to the words we inherited from Anglo-Saxon.

1. knock _____	8. wrap _____	15. knapsack _____
2. knot _____	9. phonics _____	16. gnash _____
3. wrist _____	10. knight _____	17. Phillip _____
4. phlox _____	11. nymph _____	18. knack _____
5. gnat _____	12. lyrics _____	19. symptom _____
6. wrong _____	13. knob _____	20. graph _____
7. phantom _____	14. wrench _____	21. written _____

Go back over the last twenty-one words and cross out the silent consonants. Write the letter **f** when you hear its sound. Read the words at your teacher's direction.

Do you remember all of the symbols you have learned for the short vowel sounds? Draw them in the space below and write the short vowels above them. If you need more space, use another sheet of paper.

6c Reading and Spelling for Mastery

Short **u** with blends and digraphs:

Dictation

1. must
2. trust
3. stuck
4. buzz
5. fuzz
6. fuss
7. rush
8. brush
9. trunk
10. junk
11. dump
12. dusk
13. gulp
14. bulb
15. duct
16. hunt
17. grunt
18. fund
19. lungs
20. stung

Short **u** with short vowel signals and words with silent consonants:

Spelling List

1. us*
2. just
3. luck
4. truck
5. numb*
6. thumb*
7. does
8. stuff
9. clutch
10. much *
11. such *
12. full
13. pull
14. push
15. put
16. graph *
17. knock *
18. knob *
19. wrap * (H)
20. wrong *

*Red words, H = homophone

7 Review of Closed Syllables

Syllables are organized around sounded vowels. The number of sounded vowels determines how many syllables a word has. When we hear only one vowel sound in a word, it means the word has only one syllable. For example, the words **up, sat, hill, met** and **top** are all one-syllable words because they have only one vowel sound. An example of a two-syllable word is **admit**. Since we hear the short sounds of **a** and **i, admit** is a two-syllable word.

The first rule of syllabication is complicated because it has four parts. Memorize the following four parts of this rule:

1. Each syllable must have one vowel sound.
2. A syllable cannot have more than one vowel sound.
3. A one-syllable word is never divided.
4. A word has the same number of syllables as the number of sounded vowels.

Read the following words and answer the questions. Listen closely to the vowel sounds.

	How many vowels can you hear?	How many syllables?
1. think		
2. drumstick		
3. attic		
4. camp		
5. absent		
6. swim		
7. Thanksgiving		
8. Atlantic		
9. dentist		
10. tent		
11. inventing		
12. ticket		
13. sprint		
14. establishment		

8 Review of Short Vowels

Do you remember three rules for dividing long words into syllables? Highlight the vowels in the words below. Then write the words in syllables, separated by dashes. Finally, mark the vowels. Read the words at your teacher's direction.

1. nonstop _____
2. subject _____
3. impress _____
4. inspect _____
5. checkup _____
6. suppress _____
7. publish _____
8. dispatch _____
9. chestnuts _____
10. mollusk _____

Draw lines from the syllables on the left to the syllables on the right to make new words. Write them on the lines below. Read the words at your teacher's direction.

ad	el	⇨	1. _____
zig	mit	⇨	2. _____
trav	sect	⇨	3. _____
in	zag	⇨	4. _____

con	pect	⇨	1. _____
rel	trast	⇨	2. _____
sus	off	⇨	3. _____
bas	ish	⇨	4. _____
kick	ket	⇨	5. _____

9 Suffixes –*ful*, –*less*, and –*ness*

A **suffix** is a group of letters that is added to the end of a word. A suffix changes the meaning of the word. How does the meaning of the word *rest* change when you add the suffix –**less** *(restless)* or the suffix –**ful** *(restful)*? How does the meaning of the base word *sick* change when you add the suffix –**ness**? When you have finished this page, answer these questions at the bottom.

Read the following words and listen carefully to the sound **e** makes: softn<u>e</u>ss, sadn<u>e</u>ss, fitn<u>e</u>ss, windl<u>e</u>ss, mindl<u>e</u>ss, strapl<u>e</u>ss. What sound does the **e** say? _____

Good job if you noticed that the **e** in –**ness** and –**less** sounds like a short **u**. When a vowel other than **u** says short **u**, we call it a schwa sound. Its symbol is ə. Many long words have schwa sounds. Look up the word **American**. How many schwa sounds does it have? ____

Draw lines from the base words on the left to the suffixes on the right to make new words. Write them on the lines below.

Base word	Suffix		
thank		⇨	1. _____
spot		⇨	2. _____
kind	–**ful**	⇨	3. _____
watch		⇨	4. _____
thick	–**less**	⇨	5. _____
self		⇨	6. _____
help	–**ness**	⇨	7. _____
mind		⇨	8. _____
		⇨	9. _____
		⇨	10. _____
		⇨	11. _____

Sometimes it is possible to add the suffix –**ness** after another suffix and make still more words, as in *thanklessness*. Create as many of these words as possible and write them on the lines.

thanklessness, _____

_____

What does the suffix –**ful** mean? _____

What does the suffix –**less** mean? _____

How does the suffix –**ness** change a base word? _____

10 Dictation Exercise (Teacher Page)

Provide the code orally and write it on the board or on the overhead. Then dictate the word slowly and clearly, as one unit. Students write each word in syllables, separate the syllables with a dash, and mark the vowels. The code for a prefix is **pref** and for a suffix **s**. Prefixes and suffixes are NOT marked.

1. closed-closed or (cl-cl)   ŭp-sĕt
2. closed-closed or (cl-cl)   pŭb-lĭsh
3. closed-closed or (cl-cl)   măs-cŏt
4. closed-closed or (cl-cl)   căm-pŭs
5. prefix-closed or (pref-cl)   en-ăct
6. prefix-closed or (pref-cl)   ex-prĕss *
7. closed-closed or (cl-cl)   slĭng-shŏt
8. closed-suffix or (cl-s)   thănk-ful
9. closed-suffix or (cl-s)   dămp-ness
10. closed-closed or (cl-cl)   păd-lŏck
11. closed-suffix or (cl-s)   stĭll-ness
12. prefix-closed or (pref-cl)   en-gŭlf
13. prefix-closed or (pref-cl)   ex-trăct
14. closed-closed or (cl-cl)   mŭs-tăng
15. closed-suffix or (cl-s)   tăct-less

* Please remind students to use the short vowel signals **ss** and **ll**.

Ask students to read the words. Please follow the same procedure as was recommended in **Note to Instructor**.

11 Plural –s and –es

The suffixes –s and –es change a noun from singular (one) to plural (more than one), *one flower, two flowers*. Add **–es** also to verbs (action words) when they are used after **he**, **she**, **it**, or one person's name: *I blush, you blush, he/she* blush**es**, *Matt* pitch**es** *the ball*. This is called third person singular. Most of the time, we simply use –s to show plural or third person singular, but in nouns or verbs that end with the letters **s**, **sh**, **ch**, **z** or **x**, you must add **–es**.

Write the plural form for each singular noun.

1. one box, two _____
2. one dog, six _____
3. a brush, lots of _____
4. a stamp, seven _____
5. one dress, two _____
6. you catch, he/she _____
7. a tax, lots of _____
8. one glass, ten _____
9. I stretch, he/she _____
10. one dish, too many _____

Rewrite the phrases by changing the underlined noun to mean *more than one*, or the plural. The verb *was* is used with one thing or noun. Use *were* for more than one thing or noun.

1. The <u>bench</u> was wet.   The benches were wet.
2. He lost his <u>ticket</u>. _____
3. My <u>wish</u> was granted. _____
4. The <u>fox</u> runs up the hill. _____
5. The <u>sandwich</u> is in the bag. _____

Rewrite the phrases by changing the pronoun **I** to **he** or **she**.

1. I watch a tennis match on t.v. _____
2. I bring six pens to class. _____
3. I munch on a snack. _____
4. I cash a check at the bank. _____
5. I ask for help. _____

12a Contractions

The word *contract* can mean to make smaller or shorter. When we speak quickly, we often combine two words into one. The combined words are called *contractions*. In a contraction, one or more letters are missing. An apostrophe (') shows where the missing letters used to be.

Below, you will see the complete words and their contractions. Study the contractions carefully and write the missing letters on the lines.

1. cannot = can't _____
2. do + not = don't _____
3. did + not = didn't _____
4. does + not = doesn't _____
5. is + not = isn't _____
6. was + not = wasn't _____
7. are + not = aren't _____
8. has + not = hasn't _____
9. have + not = haven't _____
10. will + not = won't _____

11. I + am = I'm _____
12. you + are = you're _____
13. we + are = we're _____
14. he + is = he's _____
15. he + has = he's _____
16. I have = I've _____
17. it + is = it's _____
18. what + is = what's _____
19. I + will = I'll _____
20. we + will = we'll _____

Now fold this paper in half to hide numbers 1-20. Write the contractions for these words.

1. can + not = _____
2. do + not = _____
3. did + not = _____
4. does + not = _____
5. is + not = _____
6. was + not = _____
7. are + not = _____
8. has + not = _____
9. have + not = _____
10. will + not = _____

11. I + am = _____
12. you + are = _____
13. we + are = _____
14. he + is = _____
15. he + has = _____
16. I + have = _____
17. it + is = _____
18. what + is = _____
19. I + will = _____
20. we + will = _____

12b Reading and Spelling for Mastery

Short vowels with blends, clusters and short-vowel signals:

Contractions:

Dictation

1. shrug
2. split
3. spring
4. struck
5. scrub
6. strong
7. stretch
8. thrill
9. scratches
10. script
11. crunch
12. trenches
13. shrimp
14. shrink
15. clock
16. strict
17. brisk
18. crosses
19. bulk
20. squint

12b Spelling

1. cannot = can't
2. do not = don't
3. does not = doesn't*
4. did not = didn't
5. has not = hasn't
6. have not = haven't
7. is not = isn't
8. are not = aren't
9. was not = wasn't
10. will not = won't*
11. I am = I'm
12. you are = you're* (H)
13. he has = he's   (H)
14. he is = he's   (H)
15. we are = we're
16. I have = I've
17. it is = it's   (H)
18. what is = what's
19. I will = I'll
20. we will = we'll

*Red words, H=homophone

CHAPTER 2
Vowel-Consonant-e Syllable

Note to Instructor

Some secondary students may already have solid knowledge of long vowels and consonant-e syllables. Therefore, it may be appropriate to skip some of the early lessons, but do teach all of the lessons with syllabication rules (1, 2, 6, 9, 12a, 12b, 13, 14a, 15). Without this knowledge, students will be lost in subsequent chapters. The dictation and spelling lists can serve as pretests to determine which pages to skip and which pages to include.

Lesson 1 introduces **vowel-consonant-e** syllables. The abbreviation for a vowel-consonant-e syllable is **vce**. Copy this page as an overhead transparency. It may be necessary to use this transparency several times before students retain the characteristics of vowel-consonant-e syllables.

Ask students to answer the question, "What do these words have in common? ate, scrape, hike, smile, eve, these, drove, broke, cute, use." Record the correct responses on the overhead or on the board in any order. Direct your students to take notes in the Rules section of their Decoding Binders. Correct responses are:

1. All are one-syllable words. (Every syllable has only one vowel sound; silent vowels don't count.)
2. Each word has two vowels. The second vowel is always an **e**.
3. A consonant is between the vowels.
4. The first vowel is long; the **e** is silent.

Mark the vowels immediately after students discover that the first vowel is long and the **e** is silent. Mark the vowel-consonant-e syllable as follows: rōpe̸. The long vowel mark is called a **macron**.

Reminders:
1. **Have students reread all the words in every lesson once they have completed the exercises.**
2. Ask students to copy each new phonogram, red word, homophone, homograph, prefix, suffix, and rule in the appropriate sections of their Decoding Binders. Include homographs, marked **HG**, in the Homophone Section. When entering a phonogram, prefix, or suffix, students must list four key words that illustrate it. Students must also add four words for every rule and definitions for the homophones and homographs.
3. Review all sections of the binder once a week for a minimum of five weeks. Younger children or the severely learning disabled may need more time for review.
4. Use the **Proposed Spelling Activities**, located in the Appendix, for all **Reading and Spelling for Mastery** lists, or use your own. Students must read the list every day before they start the two practice activities.

Overview: Lessons 2-6 introduce long vowels, one at a time, embedded in vowel-consonant-e syllables. Students tend to master the long vowel sounds with relative ease. Every lesson starts with single-syllable words and progresses to polysyllabic words. Consonant digraphs, blends, clusters, and short vowel signals are also reinforced.

Lesson 2a covers the long **a** sound and requires students to remember the configuration and the abbreviation for closed and vowel-consonant-e syllables. It also introduces the **Fourth Rule of Syllabication**: Divide a vowel-consonant-e syllable after the silent e *(juke-box)*.

Lesson 2b is a **Reading and Spelling for Mastery** page (**Lesson 3b** is also listed on this page). It consists of words with long **a** and silent **e**. Please select two appropriate spelling activities for daily practice from **Proposed Spelling Activities** in the Appendix, or use your own. Students must read the spelling words every day before they begin the two activities. Ask students to write the red words in red pen or red pencil in the Decoding Binder, Red Words section.

Lesson 3a introduces the long **i** sound and reviews closed syllables that have a long **i** sound. The code is introduced for the first time. A word that consists of two vowel-consonant-e syllables, such as *snakebite* has a code of **vce-vce**. A word that consists of a closed and a vowel-consonant-e syllable, such as *sunshine* has a code of **cl-vce**. The second activity requires students to create compound words and write them in pencil under the correct code. Provide help as needed.

Lesson 3b (on the same page as **Lesson 2b**) is a **Reading and Spelling for Mastery** page. The Spelling List contains the homograph **live**. Explain that a homograph is a word that is spelled like another word but has a different meaning and sometimes a different pronunciation. Homographs with two different pronunciations are indicated with **(HG)**. Ask students to include homographs in the Homophone section of their **Decoding Binders**, but clearly mark them as homographs. Then follow the direction from **2b**.

Lesson 4 covers the long **e** sound. The second exercise requires students to write words in syllables and denote the code for each word. For example, the word **athlete** is divided like this: ath-lete, with a code of cl-vce; the word **makeup** is divided like this: make-up with a code of vce-cl. Ask students to mark **ex–** as a prefix (abbreviated **pref**) and **–less**, as well as **–ness** as a suffix (abbreviated **s**). Prefixes and suffixes are not marked. Treat the prefixes that have not yet been introduced as closed syllables.

Lesson 5a presents words with the letters **k** and **c** and asks students to figure out the following rule: Use **k** in front of the letters **e** and **i**, otherwise use **c**. The letter **k** is also used in one-syllable, Anglo-Saxon words as part of an ending blend or after long vowels or diphthongs *(tank, bulk, shake, hawk)*. Latin and French do not use the letter **k**.

Lessons 5b and **5c** give the reason for the previous rule and introduce **hard** and **soft c** and **g**. The letter c says the **s** sound when **e, i**, and **y** follow it *(cell, city, ice, civic, cyst)*. This is called **soft c**. When any other letter follows **c**, it makes the **k** sound you hear in *cat*. This is called **hard c**. The suffixes –ance and –ence are also introduced. Both say ǝns and mean *state* or *condition*.
When **e, i**, or **y** follow **g**, it is soft and says **j**, *gem, gist, gym*; otherwise it is hard and says **g** as in *go* and *game*. At this point, students are just exposed to these two concepts. Chapter 8 covers **hard** and **soft c** and **g** more thoroughly. The exceptions to soft **g** are words that derived from Anglo-Saxon: *gift, give, girl, gig, giggle, get, gimmick*. Here is a mnemonic that might help: Race a circus bicycle in a huge, giant gym. The last exercise introduces the short vowel signal **dge**, *bridge, hedge, dodge*.

Lesson 5d is a **Reading and Spelling for Mastery** page, which consists of a dictation list and a spelling list with hard and soft **c** and **g** words, as well as **dge**.

Lesson 6 introduces the long **o** sound and the Fifth Rule of Syllabication: A compound word is divided between the words that create it (cup-cake, pot-hole).

Lesson 7a discusses the two sounds of long **u**. The letter before the **u** determines whether **u** says its name or is pronounced o͞o. When **u** follows the consonants **r** and **l**, it says o͞o *(lure, rule)*. This is also usually true for the consonants **d, j, t,** and sometimes **n,** *(duke, June, tune, nude)*. (When the tongue forms the consonant preceding o͞o, it is on the palate, right behind the upper incisors.) When **u** follows any other consonant, it says its own name *(cute, fuse)*. Here is a mnemonic device that may help students remember this sound pattern: "Dudes just love to rule."

Lesson 7b is a **Reading and Spelling for Mastery** page comprised of words with long **o**, long **u**, and red words. Please follow the usual procedures and select two activities for daily practice.

Lesson 8a introduces this rule: "When **v** is at the end of a word, it must be followed by silent **e**."

Lesson 8b: There is no worksheet; please teach this lesson on the board/overhead. At the end of words, the letter **s** is doubled after a short vowel *(miss, gloss)*; however, after a short vowel and a consonant, **s** is usually followed by a silent **e**. Write these words on the board/overhead: sense, base, chose, tense, false, rise, else, glimpse, rinse, pose, lapse. Tell students to draw two columns on a sheet of paper with these two headings: 1. long vowel 2. short vowel. Direct everyone to write the words under the correct category. Ask students, "How can we know whether the first vowel is long or short?" (The words with short vowels have two consonants between the first vowel and the **e**. The extra consonant protects the short vowel from the vce rule.)

Lesson 9 teaches the rules for recognizing the number of syllables in words with closed and vowel-consonant-e patterns.

Lesson 10a requires students to syllabify words with closed and vowel-consonant-e syllables. After students complete the worksheet, direct them to check every word they are able to read without help. (Follow the procedure discussed in Chapter 1, Lesson 3b.)

Lesson 10b is a dictation exercise that requires students to remember the configuration of closed and vowel-consonant-e syllables and to produce two-syllable words according to the code. You provide the code for each word orally and write it on the board or on the overhead. (The code for each word is supplied for you.) Then dictate the word. It is important that you pronounce each word slowly and clearly, as a unit. Once students have completed the dictation exercise, ask them to underline every word they are able to read without help. Follow the procedure in Chapter 1, **3b**.

Lesson 11a introduces the Sixth Rule of Syllabication: A word that has four consonants between two vowels is often divided after the second consonant. However, this doesn't always work. Look for beginning or ending consonant blends, digraphs, or clusters. Then decide where to divide. The second activity requires students to create compound words and write them under the correct code.

Lesson 11b is a dictation exercise. It may be necessary to model the more difficult items on the board or on the overhead before independent work begins.

Lesson 12a introduces the subject of past tense and the suffix **–ed** with its three sounds. Explain the following rule: when **–ed** makes the sound of **d** or **t**, it does not form a separate syllable because there is no additional vowel sound *(planned, stopped)*. When **–ed** is added to verbs that end with the letters **d** or **t**, there is another sounded vowel, and therefore, another syllable *(landed, rated)*; **–ed** says əd, which gives you the opportunity to reinforce the concept of the schwa sound.

Lesson 12b covers the rules for adding **–ed** to verbs with closed and vce syllables.
- In verbs with a **vce** pattern, drop the silent **e** before adding **–ed** *(hoped, liked)*.
- In verbs with one consonant after a short vowel, double the consonant before adding

- **–ed** to protect the short vowel from the vce rule *(stopped, hummed)*.
- Make no changes when the verb has two consonants because the short vowel is already protected by two consonants (same or different) after the vowel *(planted)*.

Lesson 12c reinforces the rules for adding **–ed** to verbs and introduces irregular past tense verbs. Please ask students to record these rules in the Rules Section of their Decoding Binders.

Lesson 12d is a **Reading and Spelling for Mastery** page with **–ed** words.

Lesson 13 introduces the suffixes **–en** and **–est**.

Lesson 14a introduces the suffix **–ing** and the rules for adding it to base words. Please ask students to record these rules in the Rules section of their Decoding Binders.

Lesson 14b is a **Reading and Spelling for Mastery** page with **–ing** words.

Lesson 15 introduces the prefixes **a–, un–, dis–, non–,** and **mis–**. The prefix **a–** means *on, in,* or *without*. **Un–** and **non–** mean *not;* **dis–** means *not, opposite of, without;* **mis–** means *bad* or *wrong*. Explain that using a prefix is a shortcut in expressing an idea. Please help students read the sentences in the second activity.

1 Vowel-Consonant-e Syllable

What do these words have in common?

ate   scrape   hike   smile   eve   these   drove   broke   cute   use

1. _____

2. _____

3. _____

4. _____

This type of syllable is called *vowel-consonant-e*. The abbreviation is *vce*. What does the abbreviation *vce* mean?

_____

Fold back this bottom section, or place a sheet of paper over it._ _ _ _ _ _ _ _ _ _ _ _ _ _ _ _ _ _ _ _

NOTE TO INSTRUCTOR: Please copy this page as an overhead transparency to introduce vowel-consonant-e syllables. Record the following correct responses in any order.
1. All are one-syllable words. (Every syllable has only one vowel sound; silent vowels don't count.)
2. Each word has two vowels. The second vowel is always an **e**.
3. A consonant is between the vowels.
4. The first vowel is long; the **e** is silent.

Mark the vowels immediately after students discover that the first vowel in each word is long and the **e** is silent (āte̷).

The abbreviation **vce** stands for vowel-consonant-e.

2a Long *a*, Fourth Rule of Syllabication

The long **a** sound is easy to learn because it says its own name. Do you remember the pattern of vowel-consonant-e syllables? The first vowel is long, followed by a consonant and a **silent e**. The **silent e** has the power to make the first vowel long. Mark it like this: lāte.

Say the following words and listen to the long **a** sound in each of them.

    1. made   2. cake   3. ate   4. grape

Read the words below and mark the vowels. Write the name of the syllable next to each one. Use the abbreviation **cl** for closed syllables and the abbreviation **vce** for vowel-consonant-e syllables. Then read the words.

1. made ____
2. mad ____
3. back ____
4. bake ____
5. stamp ____
6. shape ____
7. plate ____
8. ants ____
9. blade ____
10. flask ____
11. skate ____
12. snake ____
13. snack ____
14. blaze ____
15. plant ____
16. quake ____
17. brave ____
18. scrape ____
19. scrap ____
20. strand ____

Fourth Rule of Syllabication	Divide a vowel-consonant-e syllable after the silent **e**.

Highlight the vowels in the following words and draw a red line between the syllables. Then draw a line from the first syllable of each word to the correct syllable abbreviation on the left. Next, draw a line from the second syllable of each word to the correct syllable abbreviation on the right. Finally, read the words.

cl	inflate	**cl**
	takeoff	
	stalemate	
	handmade	
pref	engrave	**s**
	blameless	
	shameful	
	exhale	
vce	makeshift	**vce**

On another sheet of paper, write five rhyming words for **save**, **late**, and **cake**.

2b/3b Reading and Spelling for Mastery

Vowel-consonant-e words
and irregular spelling patterns:

2b Spelling List

1. have*
2. gave
3. save
4. made (H)
5. plane (H)
6. name
7. came
8. same
9. take
10. make
11. shake
12. safe
13. sale (H)
14. late
15. date
16. rate
17. gate
18. state
19. plate
20. trade

Vowel-consonant-e words:

3b Spelling List

1. time
2. like
3. five
4. drive
5. ride
6. side
7. wide
8. nine
9. ninth
10. file
11. life
12. fine
13. tire
14. fire
15. mile
16. smile
17. white*
18. while*
19. live (HG)
20. give*

*Red words, H = homophones, HG= homograph: Words that are spelled alike, but have a different meaning and sometimes a different pronunciation.

3a Long *i*

The long i sound is easy to learn because it also says its own name. Read these words and listen to the long i sound in each of them.

1. hide   2. pipe   3. like   4. dime

Read the following words and mark the vowels. Write the name of the syllable next to each one. Use the abbreviation **cl** for closed syllables and the abbreviation **vce** for vowel-consonant-e syllables. Then read the words.

1. crime _____   4. flip _____   7. split _____   10. spine _____
2. shine _____   5. bribe _____   8. stripe _____   11. spin _____
3. shin _____   6. spite _____   9. chime _____   12. glide _____

Use the chart to create compound words. Combine a first-syllable word with a second-syllable word. Write the new words on notebook paper first. Then write them under the correct code in pencil. Do the easy ones first.

First-Syllable Words				Second-Syllable Words			
snake	sun	like	side	cone	wise	walk	size
cap	life	pin	line	tap	shine	time	man
pine	wire			bite	stripe		

vce-vce   cl-vce   vce-cl

1. __snakebite__   1. _____   1. _____
2. _____   2. _____   2. _____
3. _____   3. _____   3. _____
4. _____

Review: Some closed syllables have a long **i** sound. The letters **gh** are silent when they follow the letter **i**; they make the **i** long. The vowel **i** is often long when followed by the letters **ld** or **nd**. Write **i** next to each word and mark it long or short.

1. mind ____   4. shrimp ____   7. plight ____   10. find ____
2. slight ____ 5. bright ____   8. grind ____   11. kind ____
3. trip ____   6. child ____   9. thrill ____   12. mild ____

4 Long e

You've probably already guessed that the long **e** sound says its own name. Say the following **vowel-consonant-e** words and listen to the long **e** sound in each of them.

1. eve   2. these   3. Pete   4. theme   5. sphere

Review the first three rules of syllabication listed in your binder. Afterwards, highlight the vowels in the words below and draw a red line between the syllables. Next, write the words in syllables, separated with a dash. Finally, mark the vowels and denote the code. The code for a prefix is **pref** and for a suffix **s**. Prefixes and suffixes are not marked.

1. eve|ning   ēvé–nĭng   vce – cl
2. athlete
3. herein
4. adhere
5. extreme
6. makeup
7. concrete
8. nameless
9. expect
10. discrete
11. stampede
12. cashmere
13. lateness
14. atmosphere

List the four things all **vowel-consonant-e** syllables have in common.

1.
2.
3.
4.

5a Consonants *k* and *c*

The **k** sound is spelled in two different ways. Sometimes we use **k**, but more often we use **c**. Highlight the following words you can read and try to figure out the rule.

1. crime	5. fact	9. bike	13. Ken	17. scratch
2. kept	6. like	10. club	14. cave	18. kennel
3. act	7. quake	11. crave	15. clutch	19. sketch
4. kill	8. cape	12. kind	16. stake	20. ketchup

When do we use **k**? _____

The consonant **k** is also used in ending blends *(blank, silk)*. Use **c** before all other letters. The words *skate, skunk* and *skull* are exceptions.

Use the rule to fill in the blanks with the letters **c** or **k**. Read the words at your teacher's direction.

1. ___lap	5. ___iss	9. ___ids	13. sa___e	17. ___rib
2. ___ake	6. ___lock	10. ___ram	14. ___op	18. sna___e
3. ___ick	7. ___ite	11. ___ut	15. s___ill	19. ___lose
4. ___it	8. ___loth	12. ___ing	16. ta___e	20. s___id

Review: The consonants **ck** make the **k** sound. When do we use **ck**?

_____

Let's practice the **k** sound after long and short vowels. Draw lines from the word starters on the left to the correct word endings on the right. Write the new words on another sheet of paper and read them.

1. bra		1. li	
2. sti	ke	2. de	ke
3. ca		3. qua	
4. ne		4. bi	
5. qui	ck	5. sna	ck
6. stri		6. sta	

54

5b Hard and Soft c

When do we use the letter **k**? Write down the rule. _____

Read the following words. What does the letter **c** say in these words? _____

    1. cent   2. place   3. nice   4. cinch   5. face   6. cyst   7. twice   8. cite

Study words 1-9. When does the letter **c** say **s**? _____

Highlight the following words you can read and write them under the correct heading.

act	civil	cell	expect	space	fence
citrus	crate	cost	since	cake	cross

Hard c (c = k)   **Soft c (c = s)**

_____   _____
_____   _____
_____   _____
_____   _____
_____   _____
_____   _____

These two common suffixes have a soft **c** sound: **–ance** and **–ence**. They are both noun endings and say **əns**, *balance, existence*. They mean *state* or *condition*. What is the name of this symbol **ə** and what does it say? _____

Highlight the following words you can read. Many of them are challenging. Write the number of syllables each word has on the lines.

1. entrance ____   7. graceful ____   13. trace ____
2. price ____   8. evidence ____   14. attendance ____
3. sentence ____   9. distance ____   15. presence ____
4. dance ____   10. slice ____   16. trace ____
5. instance ____   11. spacecraft ____   17. residence ____
6. dice ____   12. absence ____   18. central ____

5c Hard and Soft g

The rule you learned in the last lesson also applies to the letter **g**. The letter **g** makes the **j** sound when the letters **e, i,** and **y** follow it (*stage, gist, gym*). This is called **soft g**. When any other letter follows **g**, it makes the **g** sound you hear in *gave* and *got*. This is called **hard g**.

Highlight the words you can read. On the lines, write the sound that **g** says: **g** as in *go* and **j** as in *gym*. This rule has many exceptions. Some of them are *girl, get, gift* and *give*.

1. grass _____
2. gymnast _____
3. gem _____
4. twig _____
5. range _____
6. game _____
7. gel _____
8. age _____
9. grove _____
10. sponge _____
11. fringe _____
12. glide _____
13. page _____
14. globe _____
15. genes _____

Do you remember short-vowel signals from the last chapter? Here is another short-vowel signal, **dge**. It says **j**. The letter **d** is silent and protects the short vowel from the power of the silent **e**. Use **dge** right after a short vowel: *judge, edge*. After a long vowel use **ge**: *cage, sage*. After a consonant use **ge**: *hinge, bulge*.

In the words below, mark the first vowel. If the first vowel is short, followed by the **j** sound, use **dge**. If the first vowel is long or there is a consonant after the short vowel, use **ge**. Next, draw an arrow to the correct ending.

1. ri dge / ge
2. ple dge / ge
3. pa dge / ge
4. bin dge / ge

5. hu dge / ge
6. bri dge / ge
7. hin dge / ge
8. a dge / ge

9. sle dge / ge
10. gru dge / ge
11. sta dge / ge
12. plun dge / ge

Write the correct spelling next to the phonetically spelled words:

1. băj _____   2. rāj _____   3. ĕj _____

5d Reading and Spelling for Mastery

Vowel-consonant-e words:

Dictation

1. shame
2. rake
3. chime
4. shine
5. stake (H)
6. crime
7. shave
8. drape
9. bride
10. gripe
11. frame
12. swipe
13. crate
14. prime
15. blaze
16. scale
17. twine
18. pride
19. prize
20. strike

Vowel-consonant-e words:

Spelling List

1. face
2. pace
3. place
4. race
5. space
6. trace
7. ice
8. rice
9. nice
10. twice
11. price
12. slice
13. spice
14. age
15. page
16. stage
17. wages
18. pledge
19. judge
20. bridge

*Red words, H = homophone

6 Long *o*, Fifth Rule of Syllabication

You probably already know that the long **o** sound says its own name. Read the following vowel-consonant-e words and listen to the long **o** sound in each of them.

1. ode   2. rode   3. note   4. phone   5. hose   6. scone

Read the phonetically spelled words below. Then write the correct spelling of the words on the lines. Use the rules for vce and closed syllables and remember your short vowel signals!

1. chōs _____   7. thrōn _____   13. flŏk _____
2. brōk _____   8. crŏs _____   14. clōs _____
3. glōb _____   9. chōk _____   15. glŏs _____
4. flŏs _____   10. blŏk _____   16. shōn _____
5. stŏk _____   11. stōn _____   17. bŏs _____
6. stōk _____   12. strŏb _____   18. frōz _____

| **Fifth Rule of Syllabication** | Divide a compound word between the words that create it. |

Draw lines from the syllables on the left to the syllables on the right to make new words. Write the words next to the numbers. (Use **dis**, **hole**, **pose**, and **close** more than once.)

pot ⇨ ⇨ ⇨   1. _____
sup ⇨ ⇨ ⇨   2. _____
en   ness ⇨   3. _____
rose   hole ⇨   4. _____
like   pose ⇨   5. _____
op   close ⇨ 6. _____
pin   bud ⇨   7. _____
dis ⇨ ⇨ ⇨   8. _____
                   9. _____

On another sheet of paper, write four rhyming words for **stone**, **broke**, and **chose**.

7a Long *u*

Read these vowel-consonant-e words and listen to the long **u** sound in each of them.

    1. use   2. cute   3. fume   4. pure   5. cube   6. fuse

Long **u** makes a different sound when it follows the letters **d, j, l, r, t** and sometimes **n**. Read the following words and listen to the **u** sound in each of them. The dictionary uses the phonetic spelling o͞o for this sound. Notice, how your tongue is on your palate, right behind your upper front teeth when you make these consonant sounds.

    1. dune   2. June   3. lure   4. nuke   5. rule   6. tune

Read the words below carefully and listen to the two different sounds of **u**. Next to each word write ū or o͞o. This mnemonic device might help you remember the consonants that cause the **u** to say o͞o. "Dudes just love to rule!"

1. fluke ____	6. cube ____	11. tube ____	16. prune ____
2. cure ____	7. duke ____	12. mute ____	17. crude ____
3. mule ____	8. pure ____	13. spruce ____	18. plume ____
4. lure ____	9. brute ____	14. fuse ____	19. dude ____
5. muse ____	10. truce ____	15. rule ____	20. ruse ____

Highlight the vowels in the following words, and draw a red line between the syllables. Then draw a line from the first syllable in each word to the correct syllable abbreviation on the left. Next, draw a line from the second syllable to the correct syllable abbreviation on the right. Finally, read the words at your teacher's direction.

	confuse	
cl	rudeness	cl
	endure	
	purebred	
pref	pollute	s
	jukebox	
	excuse	
vce	useful	vce
	include	

7b Reading and Spelling for Mastery

Vowel-consonant-e words:

Vowel-consonant-e words and irregular spelling patterns:

Dictation

1. rode (H)
2. note
3. vote
4. nose (H)
5. tone
6. hope
7. joke
8. broke
9. spoke
10. froze
11. drove
12. quote
13. chose
14. tune
15. rule
16. flute
17. cute
18. pure
19. cure
20. cube

Spelling

1. phone
2. home
3. roll* (H)
4. hole (H)
5. whole* (H)
6. wrote* (H)
7. close (H)
8. clothes* (H)
9. those
10. some*
11. come*
12. done*
13. none*
14. gone*
15. move*
16. prove*
17. sure*
18. use (HG)
19. June
20. huge*

*Red words, H = homophones, HG = homograph

8a Ending *v* Sound

Our language has this strange rule: No word shall end with the letter **v**. It must be followed by silent **e**. This causes some confusion because it is hard to know whether the **e** is part of a vowel-consonant-e syllable, or whether it is there because a word can't end with the letter **v**. Therefore, we often don't know whether the preceding vowel is long or short.

There are three common words that we must memorize: **have**, **give**, and **live**. These words have short vowels, even though they end with silent **e**. The word **live** is a homograph. It says **lĭve** and **līve**. Notice the two different meanings. Memorize these words.

The letter **o** is affected in strange ways by the **ve** ending. It often says the short **u** sound. When it sounds like short **u**, it is called **Scribe o**. In the Middle Ages when scribes would copy whole books by hand, the letters **u, v, w, m,** and **n** all looked very similar. To make the book easier to read, the scribes simply changed **uve** to **ove**.

Read the following words, and write them under the correct category.

1. stove	5. strove	9. love	13. grove	17. move
2. shove	6. glove	10. clove	14. novel	18. drove
3. cove	7. wove	11. prove	15. cover	19. hovel
4. above	8. grovel	12. rove	16. shovel	

o says ō   **o says ŭ**   **o says o͞o**

o says ŏ

Copy **have, give,** and **live** (**live** with a long and a short **i** and its two meanings) in the Phonograms section of your Decoding Binder. Write a sentence for each word.

9 Review of the Vowel-Consonant-e Syllable

Syllables are organized around sounded vowels. The number of sounded vowels determines how many syllables a word has. When we hear only one vowel sound in a word, it means the word has only one syllable. For example, the words *take, drove,* and *shine* are all one-syllable words because they only have one vowel <u>sound</u>. The **e** is silent, and silent vowels don't count. An example of a two-syllable word is *homemade*. Since we only hear the long sounds of **o** and **a**, *homemade* is a two-syllable word.

Do you remember the four parts of the First Syllabication Rule?

1. Each syllable must have one vowel sound.
2. A syllable cannot have more than one vowel sound; silent vowels don't count.
3. A one-syllable word is never divided.
4. A word has the same number of syllables as the number of sounded vowels.

Read the following words and answer the questions. Listen closely to the vowel sounds.

	How many vowels can you see?	How many vowels can you hear?	How many syllables are in the word?
1. hopeful			
2. spoke			
3. sideswipe			
4. crisp			
5. reptile			
6. atmosphere			
7. basement			
8. incomplete			
9. watch			
10. imbalance			
11. likewise			
12. closeness			

10a Closed and Vowel-Consonant-e Syllables

Highlight the vowels in the words below. Then write the words in syllables, separated by dashes. Next, mark the vowels and denote the code. Finally, read the list.

1. expire _____
2. stagehand _____
3. district _____
4. advise _____
5. fireplace _____
6. entwine _____
7. stalemate _____
8. compensate _____

Use the words in the box for the crossword puzzle. Remember to use a pencil!

> trumpet, complete, combine, address, limestone, instruct, explode, confiscate

Across
1. cl-cl, starts with a vowel, to teach
2. cl-cl, makes music
3. vce-vce
4. cl-cl, where you live
5. pref-vce, starts with a vowel

Down
1. has three syllables, to take something away
2. cl-vce, second syllable has a long **e** sound
3. cl-vce, starts with a consonant, to put together

63

10b Dictation Exercise (Teacher Page)

Provide the code orally and write it on the board or on the overhead. Then dictate each word. Have students write the word in syllables, separate the syllables with a dash, and mark the vowels. The code for a prefix is **pref**. Prefixes that have been taught previously are not marked (en–, ex–). Treat suffixes that have not been taught as of now as closed syllables. The code for a suffix is **s**. Suffixes are not marked.

1. closed – vowel-consonant-e or (cl-vce)   mĭs-tāke
2. closed – closed or (cl-cl)   cŏn-quĕst
3. closed – closed or (cl-cl)   shăm-rŏck
4. vowel-consonant-e – suffix or (vce-s)   blāmé-less
5. closed – closed or (cl-cl)   plăs-tĭc
6. closed – vowel-consonant-e or (cl-vce)   mĭs-plāce
7. vowel-consonant-e – suffix or (vce-s)   grāté-ful
8. closed – closed or (cl-cl)   pĭl-grĭm
9. vowel-consonant-e – vowel-consonant-e or (vce-vce)   fīré-sīdé
10. closed – closed or (cl-cl)   ĭm-prĕss *
11. closed – vowel-consonant-e or (cl-vce)   ăd-mīré
12. closed – vowel-consonant-e or (cl-vce)   trăns-pōsé
13. prefix – closed or (pref-cl)   ex-trăct
14. prefix – vowel-consonant-e or (pref-vce)   en-clōsé
15. vowel-consonant-e – vowel-consonant-e or (vce-vce)   dātē-līné

Ask students to read the words.
Please follow the procedure recommended in Chapter 1, Note to Instructor, 3b.

*You will see the direction **"Give doubling hint,"** on many pages with dictation exercises: It pertains to the following rule:

The last consonant is doubled in most one-syllable words ending with the letters **f, s, l**, and sometimes **z**. This rule also applies to many multisyllabic words with a prefix and a base word that ends with this pattern *(dismiss, express, instill, etc.)*. This is a review of short vowel signals. Mnemonic device: the **sluff** rule.

11a Sixth Rule of Syllabication

Sixth Rule of Syllabication: A word that has four consonants between two vowels is often divided after the second consonant. This doesn't always work. Look for beginning or ending consonant blends, digraphs, or clusters. Then decide where to divide.

Highlight the vowels in the words below. Then write the words in syllables, separated by dashes. Next, mark the vowels, and denote the code. Finally, read the list.

1. sandblast _____
2. transgress _____
3. landslide _____
4. crosscheck _____
5. grandchild _____
6. inscribe _____
7. stovepipe _____
8. illustrate _____
9. satellite _____
10. sidetrack _____
11. transplant _____

Read the following words. Write **cl** next to each word that is a closed syllable and **vce** next to each word that is a vowel-consonant-e syllable.

1. hand _____   4. home _____   7. bush _____   10. shake _____
2. whole _____ 5. grave _____ 8. fire _____   11. sick _____
3. brush _____ 6. rose _____   9. stone _____ 12. sale _____

Use words from numbers 1-6 above and add words from numbers 7-12 to make compound words. Write them on a separate sheet of paper first. Then write them in pencil under the correct heading.

cl-vce   **vce-vce**   **vce-cl**

_____   _____   _____

_____   _____   _____

11b Dictation Exercise (Teacher Page)

Provide the code orally and write it on the board or on the overhead. Then dictate each word. Have students write each word in syllables, separate the syllables with dashes, and mark the vowels. The code for a prefix is **pref**. Prefixes that have been taught previously are not marked (en–, ex–). The code for a suffix is **s**. Suffixes are not marked. The reason prefixes and suffixes are not marked is that the vowel often says the schwa sound. Words # 2, 5, 11, and 12 start with prefixes that haven't been covered yet; just treat them as closed syllables.

1. closed – vowel-consonant-e or (cl-vce)   ĭg-nīte
2. closed – closed or (cl-cl)   cŏn-trăst
3. vowel-consonant-e – suffix or (vce-s)   shāme-less
4. closed – closed or (cl-cl)   văn-ĭsh
5. closed – vowel-consonant-e or (cl-vce)   ĭn-trūde
6. prefix – vowel-consonant-e or (pref-vce)   ex-cūse
7. closed – closed or (cl-cl)   bănk-rŭpt
8. closed – vowel-consonant-e or (cl-vce)   vŏl-ūme
9. closed – closed – vowel-consonant-e or (cl-cl-vce)   rĕc-ŏg-nīze
10. closed – closed – vowel-consonant-e or (cl-cl-vce)   ĕs-tĭm-āte
11. closed – closed or (cl-cl)   dĭs-rŭpt
12. closed – closed – closed or (cl-cl-cl)   dĭs-ĭn-fĕct
13. vowel-consonant-e – vowel-consonant-e or (vce-vce)   sīde-līne
14. closed – closed – vowel-consonant-e or (cl-cl-vce)   dĕm-ŏn-strāte
15. vowel-consonant-e – suffix (vce-s)   clōse-ness

Ask students to read the words.
Please follow the procedure recommended in Chapter 1, Note to Instructor, 3b.

12a Past Tense –ed

Many words that end in closed or in vowel-consonant-e syllables are verbs (action words). Verbs frequently have suffixes. A suffix is a group of letters that is added to the end of a base word. A suffix changes the base word's meaning. Here's an example that uses the verb **talk** by itself and with the suffix **–ed**.

> Jason and Jeff **talk** on the phone almost every day. On Tuesday, they **talked** for more than an hour.

Fill in the blanks with the verbs **hike** and **hiked**.

> Julia and her family like to _____ on weekends.
>
> Last Saturday they _____ six miles.

How did adding **–ed** to the verbs **talk** and **hike** change the meaning of the verbs?

_____

The suffix **–ed** has three different sounds. Sometimes it makes the **d** sound you hear in the words **planned** and **filled**. Sometimes it makes the **t** sound you hear in the word **scraped** and **thanked**. When **–ed** says **d** or **t**, it is a part of the previous syllable.

The third sound **–ed** makes is **əd**, as in the word **melted**. The **rotated e** is called a **schwa sound**. It says the same thing as short **u**. When **–ed** says **əd**, the suffix becomes a separate syllable.

Read each word below and listen closely to the sound **–ed** makes. Then write **t**, **d**, or **əd** next to the word.

1. planted ____	8. landed ____	15. rusted ____
2. tuned ____	9. honked ____	16. piled ____
3. inspected ____	10. smiled ____	17. shrugged ____
4. talked ____	11. scraped ____	18. trusted ____
5. stomped ____	12. melted ____	19. snaked ____
6. ruled ____	13. sloped ____	20. hinted ____
7. phoned ____	14. hummed ____	21. stopped ____

This mnemonic device might help you remember the three sounds of **–ed**.
I jumped, I yelled, and then I landed.

12b Pronunciation of –ed

What three sounds does the suffix –ed make? _____

Read these words and write them under the correct heading. Here is a sentence that might help you remember the three sounds: I jumped, I yelled, and then I landed.

rested trapped shined prodded planned packed chatted stuffed jogged
waxed ended poked buzzed trotted slipped pulled funded inflamed

-ed = d	-ed = t	-ed = əd

What letters come before –ed when it says əd? _____

English has important spelling rules for adding the suffix –ed to verbs. Mark the first vowel in each verb below. Then study the verbs carefully, and answer questions 1-3.

1. grip – gripped
2. shrug – shrugged
3. like – liked
4. plan – planned
5. spot – spotted
6. scrape – scraped
7. stop – stopped
8. hum – hummed
9. hop – hopped
10. hope – hoped
11. grade – graded
12. slam – slammed
13. smile – smiled
14. thank – thanked
15. drift – drifted
16. ask – asked
17. melt – melted
18. camp – camped
19. chime – chimed
20. trim – trimmed

1. What is the rule for a adding –ed to verbs that have a short vowel followed by only one consonant? _____

2. What is the rule for adding –ed to verbs that have a long vowel followed by one consonant and a silent e? _____

3. What is the rule for adding –ed to verbs that have a short vowel followed by two consonants? _____

12c Adding –ed to Verbs

What are the rules for adding **–ed** to closed and vowel-consonant-e syllables?

1. _____
2. _____
3. _____

Write the past tense for the following verbs. (Many present tense verbs are also nouns).

1. hike _____	9. joke _____
2. step _____	10. drift _____
3. test _____	11. base _____
4. tug _____	12. wilt _____
5. drum _____	13. grin _____
6. hire _____	14. blink _____
7. sulk _____	15. scrub _____
8. strap _____	16. prune _____

You've learned the spelling rules for adding the suffix **–ed** to base words. Now we need to talk about exceptions.

Usually, **vce** syllables have only one consonant before the silent **e**; however, the letters **st** are an exception. Even though there are two consonants before the silent **e** in words like **taste**, **waste**, **baste**, **paste**, and **haste**, we put these words in the vce category. To make these verbs past tense, drop the silent **e** and add **ed**.

Most verbs form the past tense by adding **–ed**; however, there are a number of verbs that form their past tense differently. Draw a line to the correct past tense for each of these verbs.

1. rise — rised / rose
2. cut — cutted / cut
3. sink — sank / sinked
4. drink — drank / drinked
5. bite — bit / bited
6. drive — drove / drived
7. hide — hided / hid
8. ride — rided / rode
9. make — made / maked

69

12d Reading and Spelling for Mastery

Adding the suffix **–ed** to verbs with closed and vowel-consonant-e patterns:

Dictation

1. clapped
2. slipped
3. drummed
4. piled
5. trimmed
6. timed
7. flipped
8. stacked
9. smiled
10. lucked
11. shrugged
12. faded
13. quoted
14. flopped
15. fumed
16. strapped
17. taped
18. scrubbed
19. planted
20. shifted

Spelling

1. stopped
2. planned
3. voted
4. dragged
5. stepped
6. graded
7. skipped
8. tricked
9. laughed*
10. hopped
11. hoped
12. dropped
13. used
14. liked
15. grabbed
16. hated
17. closed
18. moved*
19. melted
20. asked

*Red words

13 Suffixes –en and –est

The suffix **–en** says ən. How does the suffix **–en** change the meaning of the underlined base words in numbers 1-3? Fill in the blanks with these words: flatten, lighten, widen.

1. Your backpack is <u>light</u> compared to mine. Would you mind taking my jacket to _____ my backpack?

2. The sidewalk in front of school is not <u>wide</u> enough for all the kids. The principal asked the district office to _____ it.

3. It is best to recycle <u>flat</u> cans. Please _____ your cans before you toss them in the bin.

In sentences 1-4, the suffix **–en** changes an adjective to a verb (action word). Now it means to make light, to make wide or whatever the quality described by the adjective.

The suffix **–en** is also added to verbs to show that something happened in the past. This is called **past participle**. We use **has**, **have**, and **had** along with a verb + the suffix –en (has tak<u>en</u>, have chos<u>en</u>).

Fill in the blanks with these words: hidden, stolen, written, driven

1. My dad has _____ me to school for the last month.

2. The pen-pals have _____ to each other for a long time.

3. The policeman said, "The robbers have _____ the laptop, but they didn't find the five dollar bills which were _____ in the bottom of the desk.

The suffix **–est** says əst and changes the meaning of an adjective. Read these examples: *a long race, the longest race, a bright light, the brightest light, a brave firefighter, the bravest firefighter.* How does the suffix **–est** change the meaning of the adjectives?

_____

The rules for adding **–en** and **–est** are the same as for adding **–ed**.

Add –est	Add –est	Add –en
1. safe _____	6. red _____	11. sad _____
2. cold _____	7. late _____	12. damp _____
3. slim _____	8. grim _____	13. rot _____
4. fine _____	9. hot _____	14. spoke _____
5. big _____	10. wide _____	15. got _____

14a Adding –ing to Verbs

We often use verbs that are followed by the suffix **–ing**. It is usually used after the verb **to be** or its conjugated forms (**am, is, are, was, were, been,** and **be**) and is called the present participle.

Mark the first vowel in each of the words below. Study the spelling patterns of the words carefully, and notice the changes when the suffix **–ing** is added.

1. drive – driving
2. swim – swimming
3. shift – shifting
4. blame – blaming
5. act – acting
6. slip – slipping
7. shop – shopping
8. strike – striking
9. squint – squinting
10. tug – tugging
11. gripe – griping
12. bump – bumping
13. get – getting
14. help – helping
15. hope – hoping
16. shine – shining
17. scrub – scrubbing
18. blink – blinking

What are the rules? _____

_____

Write the above **–ing** words in the correct column below.

Last consonant in the base word is doubled	The **e** in the base word is dropped	No changes are needed

Thumbs up, if you discovered that the rules for adding the suffix **–ing** are the same as for adding the suffix **–ed**! The suffix **–ing** has the same power as the **e** in a vce syllable. It makes the vowel before it long.
- In a base word with a vce pattern, drop the **e** before adding **–ing**.
- In a base word with a closed pattern that ends with only one consonant, double the consonant before adding **–ing**.
- Make no changes when the base word has two consonants at the end.

14b Reading and Spelling for Mastery

Adding the suffixes –**ing**, –**en**, and –**est** to base words with closed and vowel-consonant-e patterns:

Dictation

1. chipping
2. trapping
3. joking
4. shrugging
5. fretting
6. slipping
7. chasing
8. stepping
9. plotting
10. shaving
11. grading
12. planting
13. fuming
14. choking
15. bragging
16. dating
17. clogging
18. lifting
19. piling
20. shifting

Spelling

1. stopping
2. liking
3. checking
4. wrapping* (H)
5. chopping
6. writing* (H)
7. quoting
8. planning
9. strapping
10. using
11. saving
12. asking
13. making
14. hoping
15. moving*
16. coming*
17. biggest
18. widen
19. happen
20. happening

*red words, H = homophones

15 Prefixes a–, un–, dis–, non–, and mis–

A prefix is a group of letters that comes before a base word and changes its meaning. The prefix **a–** means *on, in,* or *without*. Listen to the sound of the prefix **a–** in these words.

    1. aside   2. along   3. awake   4. awhile   5. amiss   6. adrift

The prefix **a–** does not have a long or a short **a** sound. What sound does **a–** say? _____

Here are some other common prefixes, which are closed syllables: **un–** as in *unfit*, **dis–** as in *dismiss*, **non–** as in *nonsmoking* and **mis–** as in *misplace*.

Draw lines from the prefixes to the base words to make real words.

1. un   spell   5. un   tract

2. mis   fat   6. mis   stop

3. dis   grateful   7. dis   take

4. non   connect   8. non   kind

The prefixes **un–**, **dis–**, and **non–** have the same meaning. What do they mean? _____

What does the prefix **mis–** mean? _____

Using prefixes is a shortcut to expressing ideas. For example, isn't it faster to say *I distrust her* than *I do not trust her*? Insert the prefixes **un–**, **dis–**, **non–**, and **mis–** to shorten the definitions of the following underlined phrases.

1. If you <u>do not like</u> it, you _____ it.
2. I was <u>not happy</u> with my grade in math; I was _____ with my grade.
3. Manuel put his book <u>in the wrong place</u>; he _____ his book.
4. My father did <u>not</u> want our phone number <u>listed</u> in the phone book; he wanted an _____ number.
5. What my little brother said <u>made no sense</u>; what he said was _____.
6. The teacher said, "Kids who <u>behave badly</u> while I'm gone will face consequences; so, do not _____".
7. My mother says it is <u>not safe</u> to walk home after dark; she says it is _____.
8. To bake chicken, I like to use a pan <u>that doesn't stick</u>. I will use a _____ pan.

CHAPTER 3

Open Syllable

Note to Instructor

This chapter contains challenging information that is vital in subsequent chapters. Therefore, older students should complete all pages.

Students will be studying prefixes in this chapter, because many prefixes are open syllables. It is important at this point to introduce some basic linguistic terms that will explain how words are put together. Let's start with the term **morpheme**. A morpheme is the smallest unit of meaning. For example, the word **unlikely** consists of a base word, **like**, which is modified by the prefix **un–** and the suffix **–ly**. Therefore, the word **unlikely** has three morphemes, or three units of meaning. Most Anglo-Saxon base words are **free morphemes**. A free morpheme can occur alone and make sense by itself. It can also attach affixes (prefixes and suffixes), as in these examples *sight, foresight, hindsight, unsightly, print, reprint, reprinting*. Most Latin base words, called **roots**, are **bound morphemes**, which means they don't occur by themselves; prefixes and or suffixes will precede or follow them. For example, the Latin root **sist**, which means *to stand*, occurs with many different prefixes or suffixes: *insist, insistent, consistency, desist, assistance, persist, irresistible*; however, **sist** does not appear by itself. To become good readers, students need to be aware of morphemes as well as of phonograms. Knowing the meaning of prefixes, base words, and suffixes strengthens instant recognition of elements that occur in thousands of words and greatly increases students' vocabulary. Teach these terms before you begin Lesson 6a and 6b: **morpheme, free morpheme, bound morpheme,** and **root**. Explain that every prefix and suffix represents one morpheme.

Lesson 1 introduces the **open syllable.** This kind of syllable is called **open** because the vowel is the last letter in the syllable, and it is NOT closed in or followed by consonants. The abbreviation for an open syllable is **op**. Copy this page as an overhead transparency. It may be necessary to use the transparency several times before students retain the characteristics of an open syllable.

Ask students to answer the question, "What do these words have in common? he, I, so, a, she, we, hi, go, and be." Record the correct responses on the overhead or on the board in any order. Direct your students to take notes in the Rules section of their Decoding Binders. Correct responses are:

1. All of these words have only one vowel.
2. Every vowel is at the end of a syllable. Or, every word ends with a vowel.
3. The vowels are long.
4. All are one-syllable words.

Mark the vowels immediately after students discover that all the vowels are long. Mark the open syllable as follows: shē.

Reminders:
1. **Have students reread all the words in every lesson once they have completed the exercises.**

75

2. Ask students to copy each new phonogram, red word, homophone, homograph, prefix, suffix, and rule in the appropriate sections of their Decoding Binders. Include homographs, marked **HG**, in the Homophone Section. When entering a phonogram, prefix, or suffix, students must list four key words that illustrate it. Students must also add four words for every rule and definitions for the homophones and homographs.
3. Review all sections of the binder **once a week** for a minimum of five weeks. Younger children or the severely learning disabled may need more time for review.
4. Use the **Proposed Spelling Activities**, located in the Appendix, for all **Reading and Spelling for Mastery** lists. Students must read the list every day before they start the two practice activities.

Lesson 2 Before you start this lesson, ask students to write down all of the things each of the following syllables has in common: 1. closed 2. vowel-consonant-e 3. open. Discuss the answers and have everyone correct the wrong answers. The first activity in Lesson 2 requires students to name the syllables on a list of words and mark the vowels. The second paragraph introduces the Seventh Rule of Syllabication: "A word that has one consonant between two vowels is often divided after the first vowel (ro-tate)." This creates an open pattern in the first syllable, resulting in a long vowel. This rule doesn't work all of the time. Sometimes the first syllable is closed, resulting in a short vowel. This means the word must be divided after the consonant (lev-el). Tell students that they may have to pronounce the word with both a long and a short vowel, and then pick the one that makes a real word.

Lesson 3 is a **Reading and Spelling for Mastery** page, which also includes **Spelling List 5c**. The spelling lists consist of high frequency words with open, closed, and vce patterns.

Lesson 4 is a Dictation Exercise, which requires students to apply the Seventh Rule of Syllabication. It is particularly challenging to apply this rule to the dictation exercises. Students will need quite a bit of coaching to understand whether the medial consonant stays with the first syllable or must be moved to the second syllable. Here is an example. The first dictation word on this page is *humane*, *hū-māne*. Supply the code, **op-vce**, orally and write it on the board or on the overhead. Then say, "Humane." If some students write *hum-ane*, ask them to mark the vowels and pronounce the word with a short **u**. Demonstrate on the board or on the overhead that the **m** must be moved into the second syllable to make the first syllable open. Then mark the **u** long, repeat the correct pronunciation of the word. This lesson includes some open-syllable prefixes, which students will learn later in this chapter. For now, the code for these prefixes is *open* or *op*.

Lesson 5a provides more practice on the Seventh Rule of Syllabication. Ask your students to highlight the vowels and draw a red line before or after each medial consonant. When a student divides a word incorrectly, ask her to pronounce the word based on the way she divided it. Once she mispronounces the word, this difficult rule will start to make sense. Here is a suggestion. Ask everyone to syllabicate (divide the word into syllables) the first word only. Then call on a volunteer to write it on the board. Ask students to give reasons why they think the word is divided correctly or incorrectly. Use these steps for every word.

Lesson 5b is a crossword puzzle that applies the previously covered rules.

Lesson 5c (on the same page as **Lesson 3**) is a **Reading and Spelling for Mastery** list with difficult words. For younger children substitute these words for the most difficult ones: we, me, he, she, be, so, go, do.

Lesson 6a (two pages) introduces prefixes that have open-syllable configurations and establishes that meaning is associated with prefixes. Introduce the terms **morpheme**, **free morpheme**, **bound morpheme** (the second paragraph under Notes to Instructor contains definitions). Explain that every prefix and suffix represents one morpheme. If you are teaching fourth graders or severely learning disabled students, introduce these terms gradually or wait until Chapter 10. Once students make the connection between the definition of prefixes and their pronunciations, instant recognition should ensue. After students have completed all of the exercises in this lesson, direct them to record the following prefixes and their definitions in the Prefixes section of their Decoding Binders; the previous terms should be included in the Rules section. Because this lesson may be too difficult for younger children, you may need to modify it. Continue to write all prefixes on a chart that is displayed in the classroom.

re–	*again, anew*	**pro–**	*ahead, for,* or *supporting of*
pre–	*before*	**e–**	*out of, outside of, away from*
de–	*the opposite of, away from* or *down*	**ex–**	*out of, outside of, away from*

The assimilated prefix **e–** is introduced, which is a variant of **ex–**. An assimilated prefix changes its last letter to sound better with the first letter of a Latin root: **ex–** + rase = erase, **ex–** + ject = eject. The proper term for this is the Greek word **euphony** (the prefix **eu** means good and **phon** means sound). For the sake of our middle school students, this program will use the term *absorbed prefix* instead of *assimilated prefix*.

Lesson 6b introduces the absorbed prefixes **co–**, **col–**, and **com–**. They are variants of **con–**. An absorbed prefix often changes its last letter to match the first letter of the root, **con–** + lapse = collapse, **con–** + mute = commute. When **con–** precedes a root that starts with **b**, **p**, and **m**, it changes to **com–** (**con–** + bat = combat, **con–** + pile = compile, **con–** + mute = commute). The prefix **co–** is used before vowels or the letter **h**. (The absorbed prefix **cor–** will be covered in Chapter 4.) The accent in most two and three syllable words is on the first syllable; however, in words with prefixes, the accent is on the base word. Please see Chapter 9 for more details.

Many of the words in **Lessons 6** through **Lesson 10** consist of three- and sometimes four-syllable words. Younger children or the severely learning disabled will need lots of support to succeed.

Lesson 6c is a Dictation Exercise, which requires students to apply seven syllabication rules.

Lesson 7a provides more practice with words that have one consonant between two vowels.

Lesson 7b is a **Reading and Spelling for Mastery** page, which also includes **Lesson 12b**. **Lesson 7b** is comprised of words with open-syllable prefixes and –a endings, *(extra, comma, soda)*.

Lesson 8 requires students to apply all seven syllabication rules.

Lesson 9 discusses the Eighth Rule of Syllabication: "Divide a word after a prefix or before a suffix and keep the base word intact, if possible." This rule takes precedence over the Second and Third Rules of Syllabication. The Second Rule states: "A word that has two consonants between two vowels is divided between the consonants (hel-met)." The Third Rule states: "A word that has three consonants between two vowels is often divided after the first consonant (pil-grim, hun-dred.)" The following words illustrate how the Eighth Rule of Syllabication takes precedence over the second and third rules: re-strict-ing, de-frost-ed, re-print-ed. In Anglo-Saxon words, the prefixes and suffixes are usually separate syllables (fast-est, un-fund-ed). In the following words it is <u>not</u> possible to keep the base word intact because the **e** in the vce syllables needs to be dropped: wid-en, fad-ed, rip-en, vot-ing. When a word has a doubled consonant before a suffix that starts with a vowel, divide the word between those consonants to keep the base word intact (flat-ten, run-ning). These complicated rules have purposefully been kept off the worksheet. Teach them gradually, especially to younger children.

For your information: The rules for Latin derivatives are different. In Latin derivatives, the last letter of the root often joins a suffix that begins with a vowel (ac-tive, vi-sor, in-ter-nal). Unless students bring up this point, it might be wise to skip this topic for now. It will be covered extensively in subsequent chapters.

Lesson 10a (two pages) Before you begin this lesson, give this short review quiz. Dictate these words to see if students remember the rule that deals with adding suffixes that begin with vowels: 1. widen 2. hidden 3. hottest 4. latest 5. raked 6. jumped 7. scrubbed 8. chopping 9. smiling

Do not grade this quiz, but review as necessary because students will need to know this rule for adding the suffix –**y** to base words.

This lesson deals with three sounds of **y**.
1. As a consonant in words such as *yes* or *yet*
2. As a vowel, **y** says **long i** at the end of a one-syllable word, *dry, by, cry, my*. This reflects a rule that no word in English shall end with the letter **i** (exceptions: *pi, ski, taxi, khaki, rabbi, chili, safari, salami* and other words derived from foreign languages).
3. Y says **long e** at the end of a two-syllable word, *funny, silly, dressy*. In this position, **y** is usually a suffix. It means *having to do with, like something*, or *characterized by*.
    This mnemonic device might help students remember the two ending sounds: m**y** hobb**y**.

This lesson also introduces the suffix –**ly**, which usually changes an adjective to an adverb (softly) and a noun or verb to an adjective (lovely). It is easy to add a suffix that begins with a consonant. Just add the suffix unless the base word ends with **y**, which requires changing the **y** to **i** before adding the suffix, handy + –ly = handily, happy + –ly = happily; however, do not change **y** to **i** before the suffix –**ing**. Use these words to teach this rule on the board/overhead: *cry, crying, fly, flying, spy, spying, buy, buying, fry, frying, empty, emptying, baby, babying, copy, copying, vary, varying*).

Lesson 10b is a **Reading and Spelling for Mastery** page, which also includes **Lesson 10d**. These two lists consist of words with **y** in all positions.

Lesson 10c covers the letter **y** in accented syllables. Then **y** usually has the **long i** sound, *supply, comply* and *apply*. This lesson also introduces the suffix –**fy**, which is usually preceded by **i**, –**ify**, pronounced –əfī. This suffix has a secondary accent; however, do not teach this fact to your class unless you have a strong group of students.

Lesson 10d (on the same page as **Lesson 10b**) is a **Reading and Spelling for Mastery** list with **y** at the end of two and three syllable words (**y** = ē as in an**y**bod**y** and **y** = ī as in suppl**y**).

Lesson 10e covers the two sounds of **y** in the middle of a word where **y** functions like the vowel **i**: long **i** in open or vowel-consonant-e syllables (*hydrant, style*) and short **i** in closed syllables (*myth*).

Lesson 11 introduces the word endings **ate** and **ite**. At the end of verbs, **ate** is pronounced with **long a**, (*simulate, dedicate, evaluate*). When **ate** occurs at the end of a verb, it has a secondary accent. (Share this rule with strong students only.) When **ate** is part of a noun or an adjective it says ət (*climate, private*). As a verb ending, **ite** says –ītε; at the end of a noun or an adjective it says ĭt or ət.

Lesson 12a (two pages) introduces the suffix –**ion**. In its most common form, –**ion** is preceded by the letters **t** or **s** as in –**tion**, –**sion**, and –**s-sion**, which are covered more thoroughly in chapter 11. The word endings –**tion**, and –**s-sion** say *shən*. The ending –**sion** says *zhən* when a vowel or the letter **r** precede it (confusion, emersion). It says **shən** when a consonant precedes it (mansion, expulsion). These word endings are usually nouns and mean *state or condition*. The letter **t** in –**tion** comes from the Latin root (*act, action, instruct, instruction, promote, promotion*). The **at** in **ation** frequently comes from the word ending **ate** (*create, creation, locate, location, vacate, vacation, relate, relation, dedicate, dedication*). When the root ends in **te**, the **e** is dropped. The syllable right before these suffixes is accented.
For strong students: Use the following words to show how the accent shifts from the Latin root to the syllable directly before the suffix in words that end with the above suffixes: ac-cuse' ac-cu-sa'tion, mi'grate mi-gra'tion, con-trib'ute con-trib-u'tion, ac-com'mo-date ac-com-mo-da'tion. If you feel that your students are ready to learn the rules for accented and unaccented syllables, select relevant lessons from Chapter 9.

Lesson 12b (on the same page as 7b) is a **Reading and Spelling for Mastery list** with –**tion**, –**sion**, and **s–sion** words. Give this list to strong students or older students.

1 Open Syllable

What do these words have in common?

he   I   so   a   she   we   hi   go   be

1. _____

2. _____

3. _____

4. _____

This type of syllable is called *open*. The abbreviation is *op*. Why do you think it has this name?

_____

Fold back this bottom section, or place a sheet of paper over it. _ _ _ _ _ _ _ _ _ _ _ _ _ _ _ _ _

NOTE TO INSTRUCTOR: Please copy this page as an overhead transparency to introduce **open syllables**. Record the following correct responses in any order.
1. All of these words have only one vowel.
2. The vowel is at the end of every word/syllable, or this syllable ends with a vowel.
3. The vowels are long. (Mark the vowels immediately after students discover that all of the vowels are long.)
4. All are one-syllable words.

This type of syllable is called an **open syllable** because it ends with a vowel and the vowel is NOT closed in by consonants on the right side.

79

2 Seventh Rule of Syllabication

Read the words below. Next to each word, write the abbreviation **cl** for closed syllables, **vce** for vowel-consonant-e syllables, or **op** for open syllables. Then mark the vowels.

1. branch _____
2. go _____
3. throne _____
4. script _____
5. these _____
6. cute _____

7. we _____
8. quake _____
9. end _____
10. me _____
11. frost _____
12. be _____

13. crime _____
14. chunk _____
15. pro _____
16. scrape _____
17. hi _____
18. blend _____

Seventh Rule of Syllabication	A word with one consonant between two vowels is often divided after the first vowel (lā-bel). This means the first syllable is open and the vowel is long. Sometimes, however, the word is divided after the consonant (lĕv-el). This means the first syllable is closed and the vowel is short.

- In words that have one consonant between two vowels, try to say the word with a long vowel. If the word makes sense, divide it after the first vowel. This creates an open pattern in the first syllable and makes the first vowel long (hū-man).
- If the word doesn't make sense when you pronounce it, try to say the word with a short vowel. Then divide it after the consonant. This creates a closed pattern in the first syllable and makes the first vowel short (rĕl-ish). Write the code after the divided words.

1. pilot _____
2. hero _____
3. medic _____
4. rotate _____
5. rapid _____
6. canine _____
7. mimic _____
8. lilac _____
9. volume _____
10. memorandum (cl-op-cl-cl)_____

3/5c Reading and Spelling for Mastery

Words with open, closed, and vowel-consonant-e syllables:

3 Spelling List
1. who*
2. who is = who's (H)
3. whose* (H)
4. be (H)
5. being
6. begin
7. belong
8. behind
9. beside
10. behave
11. become*
12. believe*
13. hello
14. final
15. equal
16. quiet*
17. also
18. open
19. even
20. evening

5c Spelling List
1. basic
2. unit
3. music
4. human
5. zero
6. minus
7. silent
8. depend
9. defend
10. decide*
11. refund
12. rebate
13. provide
14. produce* (HG)
15. product
16. protect
17. elect
18. radio*
19. idea
20. area

*Red words, (H)=Homophones, HG=homograph

These lists may be too difficult for younger students; please modify as necessary.

4 Dictation Exercise (Teacher Page)

Provide the code orally and write it on the board or on the overhead. Then dictate each word. Have students write the word in syllables, separate the syllables with dashes, and mark the vowels. This lesson includes some open-syllable prefixes, which students will learn later in this chapter. For now, the code for these prefixes is *open* or *op*.

Please teach students the following concept: Sometimes a vowel can be a syllable all by itself (e-rupt). When this happens, the vowel is an open syllable.

Code abbreviations: cl = closed
vce = vowel-consonant-e
op = open
s = suffix

1. (op-vce)   hū-māne
2. (cl-op)   měm-ō
3. (op-vce)   crē-āte
4. (cl-cl)   tĭm-ĭd
5. (op-cl)   ū-nĭt
6. (op-vce)   ū-nīte
7. (op-cl)   ē-vĭct
8. (op-cl)   bō-nŭs
9. (cl-op-op)   vĭd-ē-ō
10. (cl-cl)   văl-ĭd
11. (op-vce)   dī-lāte
12. (op-cl-s)   ē-věnt-ful
13. (cl-op)   băn-jō
14. (op-cl-s)   bē-hōld-en
15. (op-cl-cl) dē-mŏl-ĭsh

Ask students to read the words. Please follow the procedure recommended in the **Note to Instructor**, Chapter 1, 3b.

5a Review: Seventh Rule of Syllabication

Let's discuss the tricky aspects of the Seventh Rule of Syllabication.

- Sometimes a vowel can be a syllable all by itself (e-rupt). When this happens, the vowel is an open syllable.
- In words that have one consonant between two vowels, try dividing the word after the first vowel. This creates an open pattern in the first syllable and makes the first vowel long (hū-man).
- If the word doesn't make sense when you pronounce it, divide the word after the consonant. This creates a closed pattern in the first syllable and makes the first vowel short (rĕl-ish).

Highlight the vowels in each word below. Then decide whether the consonant between the two vowels goes with the first or the second syllable. Next, draw a red line between the syllables and write the code after each word.

1. polite _____
2. Venus _____
3. travel _____
4. lemon _____
5. elect _____
6. spinach _____
7. melon _____
8. omit _____
9. photo _____
10. donate _____
11. tulip _____
12. vanish _____
13. finish _____
14. profile _____
15. comic _____
16. minus _____

Now try dividing these three syllable words.

1. volcano _____
2. synonym _____
3. antonym _____
4. pantomime _____
5. tomato _____
6. monument _____
7. equipment _____
8. dislocate _____

Some words that have a consonant between two vowels can be pronounced two ways. That means you can divide the word two ways. If you divide it before the consonant, the first vowel is long. If you divide it after the consonant, the first vowel is short. Divide each of these words two ways, and pay attention to the different definitions.

1. refuse _____
   refuse _____
2. present _____
   present _____

5b Words with Three Kinds of Syllables

Read the words in the box and use them to solve the crossword puzzle.

revive	bright	placemat	prohibit	document	potato	giant
album	violin	revolve	develop	microscope	defense	react
		evacuate	isolate	frequent		

Across:
1. A fight against an attack
2. To exit an unsafe building
3. To respond to someone's action
4. Full of light
5. It enlarges very small items.
6. To build up, to create
7. To bring back to life
8. An instrument
9. You put a plate on it.

Down:
1. Often
2. A book for photographs
3. Very large
4. To separate
5. Something to eat
6. Legal paper
7. To go around
8. To forbid

84

6a Open Syllable Prefixes

A **morpheme** is a unit of meaning. A **prefix** is a morpheme that is added to the beginning of a base word. A prefix changes the base word's meaning. Many prefixes are open syllables. How does the prefix **re–** change the meaning of the base words?

    1. rewrite   2. redo   3. restate   4. remake   5. rehire   6. resell

What does the prefix **re–** mean? _____

Most prefixes and suffixes are syllables by themselves. Therefore, when you try to sound out a word, cut off its prefixes and suffixes and look for the base word.

Sometimes prefixes occur in front of base words that start with a vowel. In such cases, the two vowels belong to two separate syllables (re-en-list, re-act).

The words below begin with the prefix **pre–**. Divide each word by writing its syllables under the correct headings. Do you remember the rule that says, "Drop the **e** in a vowel-consonant-e syllable before adding –ing or –ed"? If the base word has a vowel-consonant-e pattern, you will have to put the missing **e** back on.

	Prefix	Base word	Suffix
1. prefix	_____	_____	
2. prewriting	_____	_____	_____
3. preshrunk	_____	_____	
4. pretended	_____	_____	_____
5. pretest	_____	_____	

What does the prefix **pre–** mean? _____

Let's divide some words that begin with the prefix **de–**. Write each syllable under the correct heading.

	Prefix	Base word	Suffix
1. defrost	_____	_____	
2. degrading	_____	_____	_____
3. deducted	_____	_____	_____
4. dethrone	_____	_____	
5. depressing	_____	_____	_____

What does the prefix **de–** mean? _____

6a continued

Let's divide words with the prefix **pro–**. Write each syllable under the correct heading.

	Prefix	Base word	Suffix
1. profile	_____	_____	
2. proposing	_____	_____	_____
3. protested	_____	_____	_____
4. program	_____	_____	
5. prolonging	_____	_____	_____

What does the prefix **pro–** mean? This one is difficult! _____

The prefix **e–** is an **absorbed prefix**. It is another form of the prefix **ex–**. One of the reasons for absorbed prefixes is to make the last letter of the prefix and the first letter of the base word sound better when they are put together **ex–** + vent = event. The prefix **e–** is an open syllable, which means it says ē. The prefix **e–** has the same meaning as the prefix **ex–**.

Most of the following base words are Latin. Latin roots are **bound morphemes**, which means they don't make sense as separate words. They need prefixes or suffixes to become real words. When we talk about a Latin base word, we call it a Latin **root**.

Draw lines from the prefixes **ex–** and **e–** to the Latin roots.

ex–	ject	**ex–**	cuse
	pel		rupt
e–	plode	**e–**	pire
	rase		valuate

ex–	lastic	**ex–**	lect
	press		pand
e–	lapse	**e–**	pect
	treme		vent

What do the prefixes **ex–** and **e–** mean? _____

What is a morpheme? _____

What is a free morpheme? _____

What is a bound morpheme? _____

What is the name of a Latin base word? _____

6b Absorbed Prefixes

Let's divide some words with the prefix **co–**. Write each syllable under the correct heading. Some of these base words have more than one syllable.

	Prefix	Base word	Suffix
1. cohosting	_____	_____	_____
2. coed	_____	_____	
3. coexisting	_____	_____	_____

What does the prefix **co–** mean? _____

The prefix **co–** is an **absorbed prefix**. It is another form of **con–**. An absorbed prefix changes its last letter to match the first letter of the Latin root, **con–** + late = collate. Another reason for absorbed prefixes is to make the last letter of the prefix and the first letter of the root sound better when they are put together **con–** + bat = combat.

Create real words by changing the last letter of the prefix **con–** to fit the first letter of the Latin root. Most Latin roots are **bound morphemes** and do <u>not</u> make sense by themselves. You will use **con–**, **col–**, and **com–**. Some prefixes don't need to be changed.

1. con + pose   _____   7. con + pact   _____
2. con + lect   _____   8. con + mit   _____
3. con + mute   _____   9. con + lide   _____
4. con + tribute   _____   10. con + tract   _____
5. con + bine   _____   11. con + pass   _____
6. con + lapse   _____   12. con + plete   _____

We use **col–** in front of what letter? _____ We use **com–** in front of what letters? _____

Study the three words at the top of the page that start with the absorbed prefix **co–**.

We use **co–** in front of what types of letters? _____ and **h**.

What do the prefixes **con–**, **col–**, and **com–** mean? _____

Even though the prefixes **con–**, **col–**, and **com–** are closed syllables, they do not always have a short **o** sound. What sound does **o** say in words 1-6 above? You are right if you heard a schwa sound (ə) in some of them. Usually the vowel sound in **con–**, **col–**, and **com–** says ə. Sometimes these prefixes do have a short **o** sound as in *contact* and *comment*.

Read the words below and write ŏ or ə above the **o** in the prefixes.

1. combine   2. contact   3. confuse   4. comprehend   5. collapse   6. concentrate

6c Dictation Exercise (Teacher Page)

Provide the code orally and write it on the board or on the overhead. Then dictate each word. Have students write the word in syllables, separate the syllables with dashes, and mark the vowels.

Code abbreviations: cl = closed
vce = vowel-consonant-e
op = open
pref = prefix
s = suffix

1. (pref-vce) re-sāle
2. (pref-vce) con-spīre
3. (pref-vce) pro-mōte
4. (op-op) hē-rō
5. (pref-cl-s) en-chănt-ed
6. (pref-vce) de-vōte
7. (pref-cl) com-păct
8. (pref-vce) ex-pīre
9. (pref-pref-cl-s) dis-en-chănt-ed
10. (pref-cl-op-vce) e-văc-ū-āte
11. (pref-cl-cl) de-pŏs-ĭt
12. (op-op) vē-tō
13. (op-op-vce) vī-ō-lāte
14. (pref-cl-vce) dis-trĭb-ūte
15. (pref-vce) e-vāde

Ask students to read the words. Please follow the procedure recommended in the **Note to Instructor**, Chapter 1, 3b.

7a Open and Closed Syllables

Let's review the trickiest part of syllable division: A word that has one consonant between two vowels is often divided after the first vowel (ba-con). This creates an open syllable, which makes the vowel long. Sometimes the first syllable is closed. This means the word must be divided after the consonant and, therefore, the vowel is short (cab-in).

Study the following words carefully. The Syllabication Choices give you two possible ways to divide each word. Mark the first vowel in each numbered word. Then circle the correct syllabication and write the code in the box. (Remember, a long vowel in the first syllable means that the syllable is open.) Use **op** for an open syllable and **cl** for a closed syllable.

Word	Syllabication Choices	Code
1. total	to-tal or tot-al	
2. figure	fi-gure or fig-ure	
3. tribute	tri-bute or trib-ute	
4. local	lo-cal or loc-al	
5. female	fe-male or fem-ale	
6. topic	to-pic or top-ic	
7. rival	ri-val or riv-al	
8. human	hu-man or hum-an	
9. item	i-tem or it-em	
10. panic	pa-nic or pan-ic	
11. donate	do-nate or don-ate	
12. edit	e-dit or ed-it	

Divide each word into syllables, mark the vowels, and write the code on the line.

1. legalize _____
2. tabulate _____
3. idolize _____
4. illustrate _____
5. reinvent _____

7b/12b Reading and Spelling for Mastery

Words with prefixes and ending **a**:

7b Spelling

1. request
2. require
3. revise
4. refuse (HG)
5. react
6. regret
7. define
8. decline
9. develop
10. deposit
11. donate
12. prepare
13. pretend
14. prevent
15. present (HG)
16. locate
17. program
18. extra
19. comma
20. pasta

Words with the suffixes **–tion**, **–sion** and **s–sion**:

12b Spelling

1. action
2. reaction
3. fraction
4. fiction
5. section
6. mention
7. option
8. question
9. nation
10. motion
11. vacation
12. station
13. solution
14. election
15. location
16. division
17. decision
18. occasion
19. admission
20. discussion

*Red words, **HG**=homographs

8 Applying Seven Syllabication Rules

Review the syllabication rules in your binder. Then highlight the vowels in the words below. Draw a red line between the syllables. Next, write the words in syllables, separated by dashes. Finally, mark the vowels and write down the code.

1. in | vite   in - vīte   cl - vce
2. silent
3. crisis
4. wiretap
5. resentful
6. stimulate
7. humid
8. inspected
9. evaluate
10. allocate
11. reliance   pref-op-s
12. accumulate

Highlight the vowels in the words below, and draw a red line between the syllables. Draw a line from the first syllable in each word to the correct syllable abbreviation on the left. Then draw a line from the second syllable to the correct syllable abbreviation on the right.

op	provide	vce
	mandate	
	tirade	
	remind	
pref	complex	
	demand	
	erase	
	vacate	
cl	duet	cl

9 Eighth Rule of Syllabication

Eighth Rule of Syllabication	Divide a word after a prefix or before a suffix and keep the base word intact, if possible (*re-print-ed, de-press-ing, un-fund-ed*).

The Eighth Rule of Syllabication overpowers the Second and Third Rules of Syllabication. The Eighth Rule of Syllabication tells you to separate the prefixes and suffixes from the base word so you can sound it out.

In words such as **wid-en** and **vot-ed**, it is not possible to keep the base words intact because the **e** needed to be dropped.

When a word has a doubled consonant before a suffix that starts with a vowel, divide the word between the consonants to keep the base word intact (prod-ded, run-ning).

Draw a red line between each prefix, base word, and suffix. Then underline the base word.

1. de | fend | ed
2. untwisting
3. preshrunk
4. prolonging
5. prescribe
6. refreshing
7. defrosted
8. restricted
9. disgraceful
10. describing
11. misquoted
12. reminded
13. knotted
14. scrubbing
15. dropping
16. strutted

Do you remember the rules for determining how many syllables are in a word? Read the following words and answer the questions.

	How many vowels can you see?	How many vowels can you hear?	How many syllables are in the word?
1. reunite			
2. limelight			
3. distribute			
4. eliminate			
5. preprogrammed			
6. deposit			
7. involvement			
8. grapevine			

10a Three Sounds of *y*

The letter **y** may be a consonant or a vowel. It is a consonant when it occurs at the beginning of a word or a syllable. Read these words and listen to the sound **y** makes.

    1. yet   2. yes   3. you   4. yank   5. beyond   6. yell

The letter **y** is a vowel when it occurs in the middle or at the end of a word. Most often, the letter **y** occurs at the end of words. In this position, it has two sounds. Sometimes it says long **i**, but frequently it sounds like long **e**.

Read the following words and listen to the two different sounds of **y**. Then write ī or ē on the lines. If you are not sure which one is correct, try both. Then choose the one that makes a real word.

1. spy ____	6. funny ____	11. sly ____	16. bossy ____
2. messy ____	7. cry ____	12. pony ____	17. flashy ____
3. fly ____	8. lazy ____	13. entry ____	18. pry ____
4. rosy ____	9. ruby ____	14. happy ____	19. flimsy ____
5. puppy ____	10. dry ____	15. salty ____	20. cranky ____

Study the patterns of the two different sounds of **y**. What is the rule?

_____

Sometimes **y** is a suffix. It is a suffix when you can see a base word before it <u>messy</u>, <u>funny</u>, <u>salty</u>. It is usually an adjective ending that means *like* or *resembling*.

Do you remember the rule for adding the suffixes **–ed** or **–ing** to verbs? The suffix **–y** follows the same rule. When you add the suffix **–y** to a word with a short vowel, you must have two consonants before the **–y** (*dusty, plenty, flimsy*). If the word has only one consonant, you must double the consonant before adding **–y** (*puppy, muddy, witty*). When the first vowel is long, as in a vowel-consonant-e syllable, drop the **e** before you add **–y** (*shine = shiny, shake = shaky*).

Rewrite the following words by adding the suffix **y**. Mark the first vowel in each word.

1. shake	_____	6. pop	_____
2. draft	_____	7. haze	_____
3. lace	_____	8. crisp	_____
4. skin	_____	9. bag	_____
5. fog	_____	10. spice	_____

10a continued

Mark the first vowel and draw an arrow to the correct ending. Then read the words.

1. slop   py / y
2. dust   ty / y
3. mud   dy / y
4. dad   dy / y
5. wind   dy / y
6. nos   sy / y
7. laz   zy / y
8. fun   ny / y

Rewrite the following words by adding the suffix **y**. Mark the first vowel in each word.

1. wave _____
2. chop _____
3. silk _____
4. shade _____
5. crab _____
6. smoke _____
7. nut _____
8. grub _____

How does the suffix –y change the meaning of a base word?

_____

Here are a few words that do not follow the rules: *body, study, city, copy, busy, pity, lily.* Also, with the exception of the word *savvy*, do not double the consonant in words that end with **v** or **x**: *levy, bevy, waxy, boxy.*

Another common suffix is **–ly**, pronounced **lē**. It usually changes a noun or a verb to an adverb (describes a verb) or an adjective (describes a noun) and means *like* or *resembling.*

Highlight the words you can read. Try to figure out the rule for adding –ly to base words.

1. last – lastly
2. love – lovely
3. happy – happily
4. time – timely
5. hasty – hastily
6. light – lightly
7. cost – costly
8. right – rightly
9. lazy – lazily
10. rapid – rapidly
11. busy – busily
12. brave – bravely

What is the rule? _____

Add –ly to these base words and write the new words on the lines:

1. like _____
2. bright _____
3. angry _____
4. nice _____
5. body _____
6. high _____
7. clumsy _____
8. late _____
9. safe _____
10. open _____
11. cagy _____
12. huge _____
13. most _____
14. lazy _____
15. fine _____
16. kind _____
17. calm _____
18. lucky _____

10b/10d Reading and Spelling for Mastery

Words with y as a consonant and as a vowel:

10b Spelling

1. yet
2. yell
3. yellow*
4. yank
5. you* (H)
6. your* (H)
7. yourself
8. you + will = you'll* (H)
9. you + are = you're* (H)
10. my
11. myself
12. sky
13. cry
14. try
15. trying
16. flying
17. shy
18. by (H)
19. buy* (H)
20. why*

10d Spelling

1. any
2. body
3. anybody
4. anyone
5. anything
6. every
7. everybody
8. everything
9. tiny
10. baby
11. study*
12. copy*
13. empty
14. very
15. funny
16. lovely
17. twenty-two
18. deny
19. supply
20. reply

*Red words, H = homophones

10c *y* in Accented Syllables

In some two-syllable words, the **y** ending has a long **i** sound. This only happens when the second syllable is **accented**. **Accented** syllables are pronounced more forcefully than unaccented ones. Each word must have at least one accented syllable. The dictionary shows accented syllables with an apostrophe *(ad-mit', do'-nate)*. When the first syllable is **accented**, the **y** is usually a suffix and has a long **e** sound *(ang'ry, dust'y)*. When the second syllable is accented, the **y** has a long **i** sound *(re-ly', ap-ply')*.

Read each of the following words. Highlight the accented syllable and write the sound of **y** on the line.

1. sup-ply	____	5. com-ply	____	9. fluff-y	____
2. re-ply	____	6. bulk-y	____	10. im-ply	____
3. trend-y	____	7. de-fy	____	11. snap-py	____
4. de-ny	____	8. Ju-ly	____	12. oc-cu-py	____

English has a suffix that has a long **i** sound. It is **–fy** and says **fī**, *satisfy*. Usually it has the letter i before it **–ify**, *mod<u>i</u>fy, simpl<u>i</u>fy, magn<u>i</u>fy*. What does the underlined **i** say? _____

You are correct if you noticed that the **i** says the schwa sound (ə). The suffixes **–fy** or **–ify** change a noun or an adjective to a verb and mean **to make**.

Change the following nouns or adjectives to verbs by adding **–ify**. Next, write the new words on the lines. Drop the silent **e** before you add the suffix.

1. just	_____	6. humid	_____
2. test	_____	7. solid	_____
3. false	_____	8. note	_____
4. class	_____	9. pure	_____
5. intense	_____	10. null	_____

Sometimes more than one letter needs to be dropped before you add the suffixes **–fy** or **–ify**. In some words the vowel sound also changes. Read these words and write the missing letters on the lines.

1. clear	clarify	_____	5. quality	qualify	_____
2. electric	electrify	_____	6. quantity	quantify	_____
3. syllable	syllabify	_____	7. unit	unify	_____
4. signal	signify (sign)	_____	8. identity	identify	_____

10e *y* in the Middle of Words

Let's go back to words that have the letter **y** embedded in the middle. Reminder: In the middle of words, treat **y** just like **i**. The letter **y** has a short **i** sound when it is in a closed syllable *(myth)*. The letter **y** has a long **i** sound when it is at the end of an open, accented syllable *(nylon)*, or when it follows the vowel-consonant-e pattern *(type)*.

Highlight the words you can read. Then draw a line to the sound that the **y** makes.

1. myth
2. crystal   ĭ
3. style   ī
4. hymn

5. hybrid
6. synonym   ĭ
7. rhyme   ī
8. analysis

9. system
10. hydrant   ĭ
11. pyramid   ī
12. tyrant

13. lyrics
14. nylon   ĭ
15. syllable   ī
16. rhythm

Highlight the following words you can read. Listen to the sound of **y** and write the words under the correct heading.

1. oxygen
2. byte
3. homonym
4. cycle
5. bicycle
6. cyst
7. type
8. unicycle
9. lynx
10. physical
11. hydrate
12. onyx
13. gym
14. antonym
15. cyclone
16. sympathize

y says short i	y says short i	y says long i	y says long i

11 Suffixes –ate and –ite

The word ending **ate** usually follows the vowel-consonant-e rule and is pronounced just like the small word **ate** in *locate*. Sometimes, however, it says ət as in *private* or *delicate*. Words with the sound of āte are usually verbs.

Read the following words and listen closely to the sounds of **ate**. Write āte or ət next to each word.

1. dic-tate _____
2. pri-vate _____
3. col-late _____
4. cli-mate _____
5. e-quate _____
6. pal-ate _____
7. reg-u-late _____
8. ac-cu-rate _____
9. tab-u-late _____

Although the suffix **ite** usually follows the vowel-consonant-e rule and is pronounced īte, sometimes it also says ĭt or ət.

Read these words and listen to the vowel sound of **ite**. Write īte or ĭt or ət on the lines.

1. u-nite _____
2. po-lite _____
3. in-vite _____
4. gran-ite _____
5. fi-nite _____
6. de-spite _____
7. sat-el-lite _____
8. op-po-site _____
9. hyp-o-crite _____

Use words from the above lists to solve the crossword puzzle.

Across:
1. object that orbits earth
2. top of your mouth
3. to keep track of points
4. typical weather in an area

Down
1. no mistakes
2. to make equal
3. ask someone to your home
4. saying please or thank you

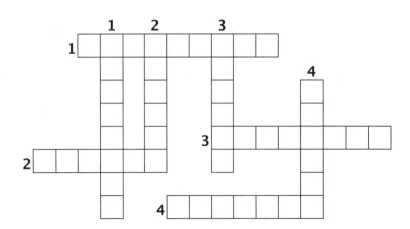

98

12a Word Endings –*tion* and –*sion*

The Latin suffix **–ion** often has the letter **t** before it, **t + –ion = –tion**, which says **shən**. It means state or condition. Most words that end with **–tion** are nouns. Write **–tion = shən** five times on the back of this sheet. Many words with open and closed syllables are followed by **–tion**. The **t** in **–tion** comes from the Latin root (*instruct, instruction, act, action*).

Write the following words in syllables, separated by dashes. Then mark the vowels and denote the code. The code for a suffix is **s**. Suffixes are not marked.

1. nation   nā – tion   op-s
2. motion
3. emotion
4. promotion
5. election
6. devotion
7. accusation
8. fraction
9. invention
10. prescription

A Latin noun that ends with **–tion** often has a related verb (action word). Highlight the words you can read. Then draw a line to match each noun with its related verb:

1. reflection	erupt	5. locate	calculation
2. collection	reflect	6. calculate	location
3. eruption	select	7. hesitate	vacation
4. selection	collect	8. vacate	hesitation

Study words 5-8 above. What happens to the word ending **ate** when the verb becomes a noun (*locate, location*)? _____ What letter needs to be dropped? _____

Write nouns for these verbs:

1. inspect _____
2. motivate _____
3. instruct _____
4. create _____
5. migrate _____

Write verbs for these nouns:

6. disruption _____
7. hesitation _____
8. attraction _____
9. prediction _____
10. donation _____

12a continued

Sometimes **–sion** sounds like **–tion** as in *expansion* and *tension*. More often, however, **–sion** sounds like **zhən** as in *confusion* or *decision*. Words with these endings are nouns and mean *state or condition*.

Highlight the words you can read and write them under the correct headings.

| explosion | invasion | occasion | pension | division |
| tension | expulsion | extension | illusion | mansion |

–sion says zhən   **–sion says shən**

_____   _____
_____   _____
_____   _____
_____   _____
_____   _____

Study the above pattern. When does the suffix **–sion** say **zhən**? _____

When does the suffix **–sion** says **shən**? _____

Write the verbs for these nouns:

1. division _____   3. decision _____   5. erosion _____
2. invasion _____   4. extension _____   6. explosion _____

What is the pattern? _____

Many words have another **s** before **–sion**: *mission, session, passion*. What does **s-sion** say? Highlight the following words you can read. Then draw a line from the noun to the verb:

1. expression   possess   5. omission   compress
2. possession   oppress   6. submission   omit
3. transmission   express   7. compression   depress
4. oppression   transmit   8. depression   submit

Highlight the following words you can read; then write the matching verbs on the lines:

   1. discussion _____   2. impression _____
   2. confession _____   3. admission _____

When is **s–sion** used? What is the pattern? _____

CHAPTER 4
R-Controlled Syllable

Note To Instructor

Some secondary students may already have solid knowledge of r-controlled vowels. Therefore, it may be appropriate to skip some of the early lessons. The dictation and spelling lists can serve as pretests to determine which pages to skip and which pages to include.

Lesson 1 introduces the **r-controlled** syllable. This syllable is called r-controlled because the **r** changes or controls the vowel sound. The abbreviation for an r-controlled syllable is **rc**. Copy this page as an overhead transparency. It may be necessary to use the transparency several times before students retain the characteristics of an r-controlled syllable.

Ask students to answer the question, "What do these words have in common? art, March, or, sport, shirt, birth, her, clerk, fur and turn." Record the correct responses on the overhead or on the board in any order. Direct your students to take notes in the Rules section of their Decoding Binders. Correct responses are:
1. All of these words have only one vowel.
2. The vowels are followed by the letter **r**. You will probably need to repeat this rule often. (Example: The word *form* is r-controlled, but *from* is closed.)
3. The letter **r** controls the vowel and changes it to say **ar** as in *art* and **or** as in *sport*. The other three vowels have the same sound: **ur** as in *turn*, **ir** as in *birth*, and **er** as in *her*.
4. All of these examples are one-syllable words.

Mark the vowels immediately after students discover that the **r** changes or controls the sound of the vowels. Circle the vowel and the **r** as follows: sp(ar)k

Certain phonemes present particular problems. The r-controlled vowels are a case in point. They are very difficult to learn because there are at least five different ways to spell the **ur** sound: **er** as in *verb*, **ir** as in *girl*, **ur** as in *burn*, as well as the suffixes **–or** as in *major* and **–ar** as in *grammar*. Students need a great deal of practice to master these difficult phonemes. There are eight **Reading and Spelling for Mastery** lists in this unit. Since you might not want to spend eight weeks on this chapter, you might need to tailor these spelling lessons to your students' needs. To reduce the number of spelling words, consider using these lists as pretests, so your more capable students are not practicing words they already know. By pre-testing, you can create individualized lists. You could even pair up students and let them test each other. Other possibilities are to divide the class into groups, or **to postpone using the more difficult lists until later in the chapter**. Even though each student may not cover every spelling lesson, everyone should practice pronouncing all of the lists.

Reminders:
1. **Have students reread all the words in every lesson once they have completed the exercises.**
2. Ask students to copy each new phonogram, red word, homophone, homograph, prefix, suffix, and rule in the appropriate sections of their Decoding Binders. Include homographs, marked **HG**, in the Homophone Section. When entering a phonogram, prefix, or suffix, students must list four key words that illustrate it. Students must also add four words for every rule and definitions for the homophones and homographs.
3. Review all sections of the binder **once a week** for a minimum of five weeks. Younger children or the severely learning disabled may need more time for review.
4. Use the **Proposed Spelling Activities**, located in the Appendix, for all **Reading and Spelling for Mastery** lists. Students must read the list daily before they start the two practice activities.

Lesson 2a (two pages) introduces the r-controlled vowel **ar** and contrasts it to short **a** and long **a**, embedded in closed and vowel-consonant-e syllables. The second page discusses the influence **silent e** has on the pronunciation of **ar** (*care, dare,* and *stare*). The American Heritage Dictionary indicates this sound with the symbol â. The second activity uses homophone pairs with **are** and the irregular spelling pattern of **air**. Please provide dictionaries, computers, or Franklin Spellers and ask students to look up the words they don't know. This lesson will also help them with the next two spelling lists.

Lesson 2b/2c is a **Reading and Spelling for Mastery** page comprised of a dictation and two spelling lists with **ar** words. The spelling lists contain more difficult **ar** words, high frequency words, and irregular r-controlled vowel patterns. (To reduce the number of spelling words, please see suggestions on the previous page.) Students must read the spelling lists daily before they begin their spelling practice. Modify the third activity in the Proposed Spelling Activities as follows: Make three columns on a sheet of paper. Write **Long V.S. (Vowel Sound)** at the top of the first column, **Short V.S. (Vowel Sound)** at the top of the second column, and **R-Controlled V.S. (Vowel Sound)** at the top of the third column. The spelling words with r-controlled vowels in the first syllable should be written under the heading **R-Controlled Vowel Sound**.

Lesson 3a (two pages) introduces the r-controlled vowel **or** and contrasts it to short **o** and long **o**, embedded in closed and vowel-consonant-e syllables. The second exercise features a true story about the explorer Robert Peary. (The vowel in Peary makes the short **e** sound.) Students are asked to underline or highlight all words with the phonemes **ar** and **or**. Because some of the words are difficult, provide lots of support for your younger children or those with severe learning disabilities. The second page introduces irregular spelling patterns for the **or** sound (**oor** *door*, **our** *four*, and **oar** *soar*) and asks students to use homophone pairs in sentences. Offer dictionaries, etc. for this exercise. Most of these words will be reviewed in Chapters 5 and 7.

Lessons 3b and **3c** are on the same page, which consists of two **Reading and Spelling for Mastery** lists with **or** words. A dictation list is also included. To reduce the number of words, consider pretesting. The second spelling list includes the irregular spelling patterns **oor,=or** *(door)*, **our=or** *(court)*, and **oar**. Since these words are difficult for younger students, please modify as necessary.

Lesson 4a discusses the r-controlled vowel **ir** and requires students to differentiate among r-controlled, closed, and vowel-consonant-e syllables. The exercise at the bottom of the page is designed to help students distinguish between r-controlled syllables and closed syllables that contain the letter **r**. This might be confusing to those with dyslexic tendencies. You might consider writing each word pair on the board or on the overhead and discussing the correct answers.

Lesson 4b is a **Reading and Spelling for Mastery** list with **ir** words. It also contains **Lesson 5b**.

Lesson 5a introduces the r-controlled vowel **er**.

Lesson 5b is a **Reading and Spelling for Mastery** list with **er** words (on the same page as **Lesson 4b**). Please note how the vowel sound changes from **er** to short **e** when the letter **r** is doubled, *berry*.

Lesson 5c: Before you begin this lesson, give students a short quiz. Dictate the following words to ascertain whether students remember the rule for adding suffixes that start with vowels: Cramming, hiked, reddest, melted, ripen, clogged, and planting. Review as necessary.
Lesson 5c is two pages and introduces **–er** as a suffix, which serves two functions:
1. **–er** is added to adjectives to compare two things *(bigger, higher)*
2. **–er** changes a verb to a noun. The noun describes a person or thing in the process of performing a certain activity *(shopper, camper)*.

This lesson also reiterates the spelling rule for adding suffixes that start with vowels. Two sets of riddles provide more practice for these concepts.

Lesson 5d (no worksheet) provides practice for the second part of the Eighth Rule of Syllabication: "Divide a word after a prefix or before a suffix and keep the base word intact, if possible." Write these words on the board or the overhead, but **do not write them in syllables**: *swim-mer, plan-ner, rob-ber, chat-ter, dip-per, shut-ter, slip-per, trap-per, drum-mer, dress-er, blend-er, small-er, blink-er, blind-er, check-er, catch-er, shop-per, charm-er, drop-per, flip-per, quick-er, part-ner, print-er, ranch-er*. Ask students to copy the words, underline the base word, and syllabicate the words. Here is an added complication for words with two consonants before **–er**: apply the rule to divide before **–er** only in base words that have a clear meaning (camp-er, fast-er, dress-er), as opposed to words that don't have a clear meaning (De-cem-ber, plas-ter). If this seems too confusing, skip this last part.

Lesson 6a discusses the r-controlled vowel **ur**. As in previous lessons, the first exercise requires students to differentiate among closed, vowel-consonant-e, and r-controlled syllables. The second and third activities direct students to apply these skills to polysyllabic words.

Lesson 6b is a **Reading and Spelling for Mastery** list with **ur** words. This page includes **Lesson 7c**.

Lesson 6c (two pages) introduces silent **e** after **r**. It also discusses how the suffix **–y** affects the vowel sound in r-controlled syllables. Finally, this lesson introduces the irregular spelling of **ear** as in *pearl* and *search*. Because the second page is difficult; consider teaching it as a whole-class lesson.

Lessons 7a consists of a crossword puzzle with challenging words.

Lesson 7b is a dictation exercise with all r-controlled vowels, integrated with previously taught syllables.

Lesson 7c is a **Reading and Spelling for Mastery** list (on the same page as **Lesson 6b**). This spelling list includes **ear** *(search)* and is another exception to the rule that states **r-controlled** syllables have only one vowel. This lesson also contains words with **wor** *(word, worth)*.

Lesson 8 presents the Latin/Greek suffixes **–ar** and **–or**, which say ər, just like **–er** does. (Many Latin roots also use **–er**, *computer, designer, consumer*, but Anglo-Saxon words generally do not use –**ar** and **–or**.)

Lesson 9 explains this very complex rule: "When an r-controlled phoneme is followed by a vowel, it is **not** pronounced with the r-controlled sound. Instead, it is long (more frequently) or short (less frequently) as in *impurity, spirit, scary*." This worksheet is probably not appropriate for younger students or for those students who struggled with the concepts in this chapter.

If you are working with 4th graders or severely learning-disabled students, provide lots of support for the next five lessons. You might consider teaching these lessons as whole-class activities. The accent rules for all suffixes in this chapter are the same: The first syllable is accented, unless the word starts with a prefix, in which case the base word is accented. All of these suffixes are unaccented. See Chapter 9 for more details.

Lesson 10 introduces the assimilated or absorbed prefixes **in–**, **im–**, **il–**, and **ir–**. They mean **not** or **in**, **into**, and **within**. Use **im–** before base words that start with **m**, **b**, and **p** *immediate, imbalance, impossible*; use **il–** before **l**, *illegal, illiterate* and **ir–** before **r** *irresponsible, irrational*.

Lesson 11 is a mini-lesson on dictionary skills and presents the suffix **–ture**.

Lesson 12 introduces the suffix **–al**, which says əl. The second activity uses multiple suffixes.

Lesson 13 introduces the suffixes **–ant**, **–ent**, **–ment**. This lesson also reviews the schwa sound.

Lesson 14a and **14b** cover the word endings **–on** and **–an**, which say ən and the connective **i**. **Lesson 14b** may be too difficult for younger students. Have students write **ion**, **ian**, **ial**, **ient,** and **iate** in their Decoding Binders, Suffixes section along with three examples from the worksheet.

1 R-Controlled Syllable

What do these words have in common?

art   March   or   sport   shirt   birth   her   clerk   fur   turn

1. _____

2. _____

3. _____

4. _____

We call this type of syllable *r-controlled*. **The abbreviation is** *rc*.
Why do you think it has this name?

_____

Fold back this bottom section, or place a sheet of paper over it._ _ _ _ _ _ _ _ _ _ _ _ _ _ _ _ _ _ _

NOTE TO INSTRUCTOR: Please copy this page as an overhead transparency to introduce **r-controlled** syllables. Record the following correct responses in any order.
1. All of the words have only one vowel.
2. The vowels are followed by the letter **r**.
3. The letter **r** controls the vowel and changes it to say **ar** as in *art* and **or** as in *sport*. The other three vowels have the same sound: **ur** as in *turn*, **ir** as in *birth*, and **er** as in *her*.
4. All are one-syllable words.

Mark the vowels by circling the vowel and the **r**, a͡rt.
This syllable is called **r-controlled** because the **r** changes the vowel sounds.

2a R-Controlled Vowel *ar*

The r-controlled vowel **ar** is not long or short. The letter **r** controls the **a** and changes it to say **ar** as in **art, arm, arch,** and **park**. A syllable that contains the **ar** combination is called an **r-controlled syllable**.

The letter **r** is part of an r-controlled vowel. The abbreviation is **rc**. We mark it by circling the vowel and the **r**: (ar)m.

Read the following words. Next to each word, write the abbreviation **rc** for r-controlled syllables, **cl** for closed syllables, or **vce** for vowel-consonant-e syllables. Then mark the vowels and read the words again.

1. charm ____	7. phrase ____	13. harm ____	19. brand ____
2. stand ____	8. scarf ____	14. crash ____	20. starch ____
3. card ____	9. blast ____	15. Mars ____	21. farm ____
4. blaze ____	10. chart ____	16. smart ____	22. shave ____
5. barn ____	11. sharp ____	17. brave ____	23. start ____
6. March ____	12. grace ____	18. dark ____	24. black ____

Draw lines from the syllables on the left to the syllables on the right to make new words. Next, write them on the lines.

mar	arm	⇨	1. _____
harm	ket	⇨	2. _____
dis	pet	⇨	3. _____
de	ful	⇨	4. _____
part	ling	⇨	5. _____
car	ness	⇨	6. _____
har	ly	⇨	7. _____
dar	part	⇨	8. _____

On another sheet of paper, write four rhyming words for **car** and four for **dark**.

2a continued

The letters **ar** have a different sound when they are followed by a silent **e**. Listen to the vowel sound in the words **care**, **share**, and **scare**. If you listen closely, you will notice that **ar + e** together say the word **air**. Another pattern makes the same sound. Listen to the vowel sound in the words **hair, fair,** and **pair**. The dictionary uses the symbol **âr** (a with a roof over its head) for the sound you hear in **care** or **air**.

Read the following words and listen to the vowel sounds. Write **ar** or **âr** next to each word.

1. spark ____
2. spare ____
3. lair ____
4. dart ____
5. pair ____
6. car ____
7. care ____
8. chair ____
9. star ____
10. stare ____
11. stairs ____
12. mark ____
13. flare ____
14. fair ____
15. tarp ____
16. square ____
17. scar ____
18. scare ____
19. far ____
20. fare ____

Use the homophones in the box to complete the sentences below. You may consult a dictionary if you need help.

| fair | stare | pair | flair |
| fare | stair | pare | flare |

1. Make sure you have exact change for the bus _____.
2. The Student Body President won the election _____ and square.
3. The driver prevented an accident by setting out a _____ after his car stalled.
4. Sabrina has a _____ for acting.
5. It is very rude to _____ at people.
6. You will get in shape if you take the _____ case instead of the elevator.
7. Use the sharp knife to _____ the apple.
8. I need a new _____ of shoes for the dance.

The letters **ar** have one more sound. Listen to the vowel sound in the words **war, warm, warn,** and **quarrel**. The rule is, "When the letters **ar** follow **w** or **qu**, they sound like the word **or**."

Read the following words. On another sheet of paper, write a sentence with each word.

1. warp
2. warming
3. warning
4. ward
5. warden
6. warrant
7. quart
8. quarter
9. quarrel
10. quarry

2b/2c Reading and Spelling for Mastery

Ar as in art:

Words with **ar**, **arr**, and **war**:

Words with **are** and **air**:

Dictation

2b Spelling

2c Spelling

1. car
2. far
3. jar
4. star
5. art
6. cart
7. part
8. tart
9. smart
10. barn
11. hard
12. card
13. park
14. dark
15. mark
16. spark
17. barb
18. arm
19. farm
20. charm

1. are*
2. start
3. sharp
4. harm
5. alarm
6. starve
7. March
8. yard
9. guard*
10. garden
11. market
12. army
13. apart
14. separate* (HG)
15. quart*
16. war*
17. warn*(H)
18. warm*
19. marry*(H)
20. carry*

1. care
2. dare
3. rare
4. share
5. ware (H)
6. wear (H)*
7. scare
8. scary
9. glare
10. stare (H)
11. stairs (H)
12. square*
13. air (H)
14. hair (H)
15. pair (H)
16. pare (H)
17. fair (H)
18. fare (H)
19. upstairs
20. airplane

*Red words, H=homophones, HG = homograph: two pronunciations, two meanings

3a R-Controlled Syllable *or*

The r-controlled vowel **or** is not long or short. The letter **r** controls the **o** and changes it to say **or** as in **for, fork,** and **born**. A syllable that contains the **or** combination is called an **r-controlled syllable**. When the **or** sound comes at the end of a one-syllable word, it is followed by silent **e**, except for the words **or, nor,** and **for**. Words such as **bore, tore,** and **more** are still considered r-controlled syllables; however, the **e** is silent, so cross it out.

The letter **r** is part of an r-controlled vowel. The abbreviation is **rc**. We mark it by circling the vowel and the **r**   sp(or)t.

Read the following words and highlight the vowels. Write the vowel sound next to each word and mark it.

1. sport ____	7. broke ____	13. core ____	19. close ____
2. moth ____	8. shore ____	14. grove ____	20. scorn ____
3. north ____	9. torch ____	15. storm ____	21. cord ____
4. spoke ____	10. prod ____	16. honk ____	22. port ____
5. slot ____	11. chore ____	17. cork ____	23. rock ____
6. short ____	12. stork ____	18. throb ____	24. norm ____

On another sheet of paper write five rhyming words for **port** and five for **torn**.

Read the following story first. Go back over it and underline or highlight all of the words with **ar** and **or**.

An American Explorer

Robert E. Peary (short e) loved to travel to cold places in the far North. While exploring Greenland in the 1890s, he hiked 600 miles over snow and ice to map the area. Afterwards, he informed the world that Greenland was not part of a continent. Instead, it was a large island.

Peary had an even bigger goal for himself. He wanted to be the first human to reach the North Pole! Before he started, he organized an exploring party of six hardy men. Their ship departed from the port of New York in July 1908. While stopping at a port in Canada, Peary hired 17 Eskimos to support this enormous effort.

In March 1909, he set sail for the frozen North. His ship carried 23 men, 133 dogs, and 17 dog sleds. Because the days were short, they traveled mostly in darkness. They endured bitter cold and harsh storms. Peary's remarkable party made history on April 6, 1909. On that date, they recorded planting the American flag on the North Pole.

(Paraphrased from <u>100 Years of Adventure and Discovery</u>, National Geographic Society, 1987)

3a continued

The **or** sound is complicated because it has several other spellings. Listen to the **or** sound in the words **floor**, **four**, and **soar**. Even though there is another vowel between the letter **o** and the letter **r**, it still says **or**. Many words with the extra vowel are homophones.

Use the following words in the sentences below. You may consult a dictionary.

bore	horde	horse	bored	course	sore	morning
boar	hoard	hoarse	board	coarse	soar	mourning

1. Norm's older brother is taking a college _____.
2. Start with _____ sandpaper when you refinish the walnut chair.
3. After the football game, the fans were _____ from yelling for their team.
4. The jockey rode the _____ around the track.
5. The hunter shot a wild _____.
6. Carl is a _____ because he talks too much about himself.
7. Make sure you copy the homework from the _____ before the bell rings.
8. The crowd was restless and _____ because the singer was late.
9. In times of war, many people _____ food.
10. After the football team won, a _____ of people ran onto the field.
11. An eagle can _____ through the air.
12. After hiking for nine miles with a full backpack, my back was _____.
13. Oh, what a beautiful _____, oh, what a beautiful day!
14. The family was in _____ after Grandma's death.

The **or** spelling also has a different sound. Listen to the vowel sound in the words **world**, **work**, and **worse**. Here is the rule: "When **or** follows the letter **w**, it says **ûr**."

Read the following words. Write **or** or **ûr** on the lines. Underline the two words that do not follow the rule **wor** says **wûr**.

1. fort ____   4. world ____   7. dorm ____   10. worst ____
2. worm ____   5. worry ____   8. worth ____   11. wore ____
3. sport ____   6. north ____   9. sword ____   12. worship ____

3b/3c Reading and Spelling for Mastery

Words with **or** as in corn:	Words with **ore** as in score:	Words with **our** as in four, **oor** as in door **oar** as in oar
Dictation	3b Spelling	3c Spelling
1. or (H)	1. order	1. door*
2. for (H)	2. forth (H)	2. floor*
3. fort	3. north	3. poor (H)*
4. forty	4. before	4. pour (H)*
5. born (H)	5. bored (H)	5. four (H)*
6. corn	6. sore (H)	6. fourth (H)
7. torn	7. shore	7. mourn (H)*
8. horns	8. wore (H)	8. mourning (H)
9. sworn	9. more	9. court*
10. worn (H)	10. score	10. course (H)*
11. scorn	11. store	11. coarse (H)*
12. thorn	12. story	12. oar (H)
13. cord	13. corner	13. roar
14. sort	14. record (HG)	14. hoard (H)*
15. sport	15. history *	15. board (H)*
16. short	16. morning (H)	16. boarding
17. pork	17. correct	17. aboard
18. fork	18. report	18. skateboard
19. form	19. support *	19. soar (H)*
20. storm	20. according *	20. soaring

When the **or** sound comes at the end of a one-syllable word, it is followed by **silent e**, except for the words **or, nor,** and **for**.
*Red words, H = homophone, HG = homograph

4a R-Controlled Vowel *ir*

The r-controlled vowel **ir** is not long or short. The letter **r** controls the **i** and changes it to say **ir** as in **bird**, **girl**, and **sir**. A syllable that contains the **ir** combination is called an **r-controlled syllable**.

The letter **r** is part of an r-controlled vowel. The abbreviation is **rc**. We mark it by circling the vowel and the **r**: g(ir)l.

Read the following words. Next to each word, write the abbreviation **rc** for r-controlled syllables, **cl** for closed syllables, or **vce** for vowel-consonant-e syllables. Then mark the vowels and read the words again.

1. first ____
2. thrill ____
3. swirl ____
4. crime ____
5. chirp ____
6. third ____
7. flirt ____
8. brink ____
9. shirt ____
10. thrift ____
11. pride ____
12. dirt ____
13. shrink ____
14. twirl ____
15. smirk ____
16. thirst ____
17. irk ____
18. strike ____
19. brick ____
20. quirk ____

Highlight the vowels in the words below and draw a red line between the syllables. Then draw a line from the first syllable of each word to the correct syllable code on the left. Next, draw a line from the second syllable of each word to the correct syllable code on the right.

cl	firsthand	**cl**
	confirm	
	whirlwind	
	skirmish	
rc	rebirth	**rc**
	blackbird	
	birthstone	
	affirm	
pref	stirrups	**vce**

Decide if each word below is a closed syllable or an r-controlled syllable. Then write **cl** or **rc** next to the word.

1. girl ____
2. grill ____
3. grid ____
4. gird ____
5. frock ____
6. fork ____
7. form ____
8. from ____
9. crock ____
10. cork ____
11. arm ____
12. ram ____
13. tarp ____
14. trap ____
15. barn ____
16. bran ____

4b/5b Reading and Spelling for Mastery

Words with **ir** as in bird :

Words with **er** as in her :

4b Spelling

1. first
2. third
3. thirty
4. thirteen
5. thirst
6. thirsty
7. birth (H)
8. girl
9. skirt
10. shirt
11. sir
12. stir
13. dirt
14. dirty
15. bird
16. firm
17. confirm
18. flirt
19. squirt
20. shirk

5b Spelling

1. her
2. after
3. were*
4. other
5. another
6. mother
7. brother
8. father
9. sister
10. number
11. together
12. over
13. river
14. perhaps
15. understand
16. different*
17. desert (H, HG)*
18. dessert (H)*
19. person*
20. merry (H)*

When the letter **r** is doubled, the **e** is short as in *berry* and *merry*.

*Red words, H = homophones, HG = homograph

5a R-Controlled Vowel *er*

The r-controlled vowel **er** is not long or short. The letter **r** controls the **e** and changes it to say **er** as in **her**, **fern**, and **clerk**. You may have noticed that **er** sounds just like **ir**. A syllable with the **er** combination is called an **r-controlled syllable**.

The letter **r** is part of an r-controlled vowel. The abbreviation is **rc**. We mark it by circling the vowel and the **r**, f(er)n.

Read the following words and highlight the vowels. Write the first vowel sound next to each word and mark it.

1. stern ____	5. clerk ____	9. spend ____	13. herd ____
2. term ____	6. rent ____	10. serve ____	14. shred ____
3. eve ____	7. nerve ____	11. theme ____	15. perch ____
4. germ ____	8. Steve ____	12. fern ____	16. verb ____

Highlight the vowels in the following words. Write the words in syllables and mark the vowels. Then denote the code. Next, read the words at your teacher's direction.

1. corner _____
2. order _____
3. perform _____
4. expert _____
5. former _____
6. server _____
7. observer _____

Use the clues to help you unscramble these words.

1. rettuprin   i __ __ __ r r __ __ __

   a) cl-rc-cl   **b)** The third and last letters are **t**'s.   **c)** It is a rude thing to do.

2. betilare   __ __ __ __ __ __ __ __

   a) cl-rc-vce   **b)** The vowel in the rc syllable is **er**.   **c)** The consonant in the **vce** syllable is **t**.
   d) It means *to set free*.

3. dreefla   __ __ __ __ __ a __

   a) cl-rc-cl   **b)** The word starts with the letter **f**.   **c)** It is a kind of government.

5c The Suffix –er

When the r-controlled vowel **er** occurs at the end of a word, it is usually a suffix. A suffix changes the base word's meaning. The suffix –**er** often changes a verb to a noun and can mean *a person or thing performing an activity* as in the words *shopper, camper,* and *singer*. It is also added to adjectives to compare two things as in the phrases *the faster car* and *the older person*. Sometimes, **er** does not have a clear meaning as in the words *otter, corner,* or *offer*.

Read the following words. If the suffix –**er** compares two things, write **c** next to the word. If the suffix changes a verb to a noun and means a person or a thing, write **n** next to the word.

1. camper ____
2. sticker ____
3. longer ____
4. drummer ____
5. buzzer ____
6. darker ____
7. quitter ____
8. taller ____
9. quicker ____
10. golfer ____
11. shopper ____
12. stronger ____

Choose two rhyming words from the box to finish each sentence.

| clipper   bender   better   twitter   letter   glimmer   flutter   shimmer   skipper   fender |

1. On sunny days, waves _____ and _____.
2. Most birds do this _____ and _____.
3. A minor car accident is a _____ _____.
4. The captain of a sailing ship is the _____ of a _____.
5. The editor of the newspaper picked the _____ _____.

English has an important spelling rule for adding suffixes that start with vowels to base words. (You studied this rule in Chapter 2.) Write the rule on another sheet of paper.

Read each word and mark the vowels. Next, add –**er** and write the new words on the line.

1. time _____
2. wrap _____
3. print _____
4. scrape _____
5. chat _____
6. broke _____
7. camp _____
8. drop _____
9. joke _____
10. shut _____
11. line _____
12. flip _____

5c continued

Give yourself a pat on the back if you noticed that the rule for adding the suffix –er to base words is the same as the rule for adding the suffixes –ed or –y. When a word has a short vowel in the first syllable and ends with only one consonant, you must double the consonant before adding –er *(chatter)*. This protects the short vowel from the power of the **e** in the suffix –er. When the first vowel is long as in vce syllables, drop the **e** before adding –er *(baker)*. Words like *camper* or *printer* do not require any changes because they already have two consonants.

Mark the first vowel in the following words. Then draw an arrow from each word starter to the ending with the correct spelling:

1. pep — per / er
2. vot — ter / er
3. saf — fer / er
4. fin — ner / er
5. slip — per / er
6. log — ger / er
7. drum — mer / er
8. clos — ser / er
9. ship — per / er
10. stop — per / er
11. scan — ner / er
12. min — ner / er

Choose two words from the box to answer each riddle.

| winner | litter | mutter | pitcher | copper | chatter | patter |
| silver | pitter | brother | runner | catcher | critter | sister |

1. An animal's young: _____'s _____
2. The sound of rain: _____ _____
3. Two people in a family: _____ and _____
4. Players on a baseball team: _____ and _____
5. Ways of talking: _____ and _____
6. Two types of metal: _____ and _____
7. The fastest _____ will be the _____.

6a R-Controlled Vowel *ur*

The r-controlled vowel **ur** is not long or short. The letter **r** controls the **u** and changes it to say **ur** as in **fur**, **burn**, and **curl**. Did you notice that **ur** sounds exactly like **ir** and **er**? A syllable that contains the **ur** combination is called an **r-controlled syllable**.

The letter **r** is part of an r-controlled vowel. The abbreviation is **rc**. We mark it by circling the vowel and the **r**: b(ur)n.

Read the following words and highlight the vowels. Write the vowel sound next to each word and mark it.

1. curb ____	6. hurt ____	11. blur ____	16. hurl ____
2. surf ____	7. struck ____	12. trump ____	17. shrug ____
3. fume ____	8. turf ____	13. blurt ____	18. curl ____
4. brunt ____	9. rude ____	14. church ____	19. strum ____
5. flute ____	10. turn ____	15. cute ____	20. slurp ____

Highlight the vowels in the words below. Use a red pencil to divide them into syllables. Then read the words and write them under the correct code.

1. occur	4. sunburst	7. incur	10. sunburn
2. surfer	5. surprise	8. perturb	11. racehorse
3. current	6. burner	9. survive	12. turnstile

rc-rc	cl-rc	rc-vce
rc-cl	**vce-rc**	

6b/7c Reading and Spelling for Mastery

Words with **ur** as in **burn**:

Words with **ear** as in **learn** and **wor** as in **work**:

6b Spelling

1. fur (H)
2. blur
3. burn
4. burner
5. turn (H)
6. return
7. hurt
8. curl
9. curb
10. curve
11. nurse
12. purse
13. church
14. further*
15. hurry*
16. hurried
17. hurrying
18. surface*
19. current
20. sure *

7c Spelling

1. earn (H)
2. learn
3. heard (H)
4. pearl (H)
5. earth
6. early
7. rehearse*
8. search
9. searching
10. research
11. word
12. world (H)
13. work
14. worker
15. worry*
16. worried
17. worrying
18. worst
19. worse
20. worth

*Red words, H = homophones

6c Vowel-r-e

Review the Rules of Syllabication in your binder. Then highlight the vowels in the words below. Write the words in syllables, separated by dashes. Finally, mark the vowels and write the code next to each word.

1. distortion _____
2. turpentine _____
3. cornerstone _____
4. coordinate _____
5. refrigerate _____
6. excursion _____
7. reimburse _____
8. injury _____
9. scornfully _____
10. furthermore _____

Silent e is usually more powerful than the letter **r** in an r-controlled syllable. Say the following words and listen to the vowel sounds.

    1. cure   2. pure   3. fire

Did you notice that the first vowel is long? This means that the silent **e** affects the first vowel sound and makes it long. Mark the vowels in these words.

1. cure	6. spur	11. dirt	16. stir
2. lurch	7. fir	12. hire	17. sir
3. pure	8. fire	13. her	18. wire
4. purr	9. mire	14. here	19. sphere
5. lure	10. mirth	15. spire	20. stern

Here is a very common word you should memorize: **sure**. There is one letter you hear in the word **sure** that is missing. What letter is it? _____

Silent e is only able to wield its long vowel power when it comes after **ir**, **er**, and **ur**. It does not affect **or**. When **or** occurs at the end of words, it usually has a **silent e** after it.

Do you remember how **silent e** changes the **ar** sound? _____

6d continued

Write these word starters in front of **ire**: **ent**, **adm**, **emp**, and **requ**. Then read the words.

    1. _____ire   2. _____ire   3. _____ire   4. _____ire

Write **end**, **sec**, **obsc**, **and fig** in front of **ure**. Then read the words.

    1. _____ure   2. _____ure   3. _____ure   4. _____ure

Write **expl**, **rest**, **enc**, and **ign** in front of **ore**. Then read the words.

    1. _____ore   2. _____ore   3. _____ore   4. _____ore

Write **soft**, **hard**, and **silver** in front of **ware**. Then read the words.

    1. _____ware   2. _____ware   3. _____ware

Do you remember what the suffix **–y** says in polysyllabic words? It usually says the long **e** sound, as in **silky** or **plenty**. The suffix **–y** has the same power as a **silent e**. In words with one **r**, the **–y** makes the first vowel long. When the **r** is doubled, the first vowel is usually short *(berry)*, except for **ur**, which is not changed by double **r**.

Read each word. Write the first vowel sound on the line and mark it. What is the symbol for **ar** when it is followed by silent **e**, or in this case **–y**? _____

    1. fury ____   4. berry ____   7. vary ____   10. scary ____
    2. furry ____   5. hurry ____   8. merry ____   11. scurry ____
    3. wiry ____   6. cherry ____   9. ferry ____   12. sorry ____

Read these words.

    1. marry   2. tarry   3. carry   4. Harry   5. harried

What does the vowel **a** say when it is followed by double **r**? _____

Here is a strange exception. The word **bury** means *to dig a hole and put something in it*.

What sound does **ur** say in **bury**? _____

The words *pearl, learn, yearn,* and *heard* say the **û**r sound, which you learned earlier (*worry, world.*) This is somewhat confusing because **ear** can also say **ē**r (*near, spear, hear*).

Read the following words, listen to the vowel sound, and write **û**r or **ē**r on the lines.

    1. earth _____   3. dear _____   5. earn _____   7. search _____
    2. fear _____   4. early _____   6. rear _____   8. rehearse _____

7a Challenge Words

Read the words in the box below and use them to solve the crossword puzzle.

> supervise   wilderness   surrender   hibernate   porcupine   start
> exploring   cooperation importer   argument   northern   perspire
> enterprise generation   prehistoric harmonize   cucumber   advertise

Across
1. One who sells items from other countries
2. An animal
3. Singers do this in a group.
4. To give up
5. Opposite of end
6. Discovering
7. An area without human activity
8. People of the same age
9. A time before any records were kept

Down
1. Ability to work well with others
2. A vegetable, used in salads
3. Your body does this when you run
4. A business organization
5. A verbal fight
6. To tell the advantage of a product
7. A bear does this.
8. What a boss does
9. rc-rc

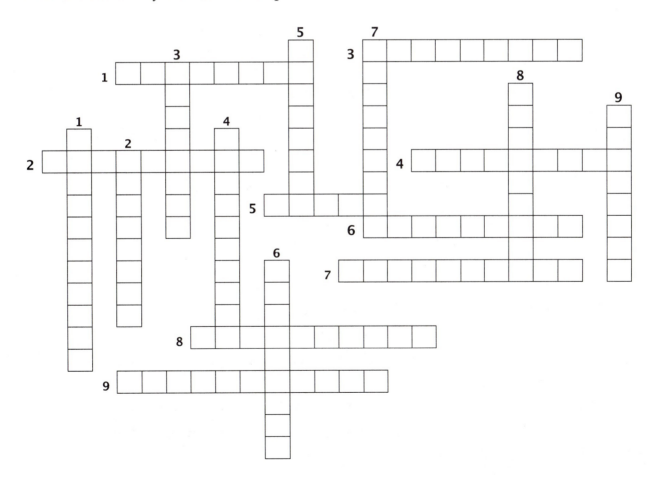

121

7b Dictation Exercise (Teacher Page)

Provide the code orally and write it on the board or on the overhead. Then dictate each word. Have students write the word in syllables, separate the syllables with dashes, and mark the vowels.

Before you start this lesson, please review prefixes. Prefixes and suffixes are not marked, but do not take off points for students who mark prefixes. Four words (# 1, 5, 12, and 13) start with prefixes that have not yet been introduced. For now, treat them as *r-controlled* syllables.

*For this exercise, accept **er**, **ir**, and **ur** for the ər sound; however, please point out the correct spelling.

For fourth graders or students with severe learning disabilities, shorten the list and select the easier words only.

Also, remind students that –er often occurs at the end of words as a suffix.

Code abbreviations: cl = closed   rc = r-controlled
                          vce = vowel-consonant-e pref = prefix
                          op = open   s = suffix

Students will circle the vowel + r. On this page, the r-controlled vowels are shown in red.

1. (rc-vce)   sur-vīve*
2. (pref-rc-s)   non-start-er
3. (pref-rc)   ex-pert*
4. (cl-rc-vce)   ŏp-er-āte *
5. (rc-vce)   sur-prīse*
6. (pref-rc)   de-serve
7. (cl-rc-s)   wŏn-der-ful*
8. (cl-rc-rc)   thŭn-der-storm*
9. (cl-cl-s)   pŭb-lĭsh-er
10. (pref-rc)   dis-arm
11. (pref-rc-s)   un-chart-ed
12. (rc-vce)   per-fūme*
13. (rc-rc-s)   per-form-er*
14. (cl-rc-rc-cl) kĭn-der-gar-tĕn*
15. (pref-rc-s)   pro-por-tion

Ask students to read the words. Please follow the procedure recommended in the **Note to Instructor**, Chapter 1, 3b.

8 Suffixes –ar and –or

Do you remember the suffix **–er**? It is used to compare two things *(faster, bigger)*. Or, it may mean a person or thing that does a certain activity *(runner, swimmer)*. Words with the suffix **–er** are derived from Anglo-Saxon or old English. Many other words end with the sound of **–er (ər)**, but they are spelled with **–or** and **–ar**. Words that end with the suffixes **–or** and **–ar** are usually derived from Latin or Greek.

Read the following words and write **A** for Anglo Saxon or **L+G** for Latin and Greek. Remember, when they are suffixes, **–er**, **–or**, and **–ar**, all say **ər**.

1. spinner _____
2. major _____
3. grammar _____
4. flavor _____
5. miner _____
6. minor _____
7. doctor _____
8. cluster _____
9. calendar _____
10. banner _____
11. lunar _____
12. error _____
13. visitor _____
14. beginner _____
15. popular _____
16. farmer _____
17. singular _____
18. conductor _____

In previous lessons you learned the rules for adding the suffix **–ed**, to base words. This rule also applies to other suffixes that start with vowels. Go back and mark the vowels directly before the suffixes in the words above. Then write the rule.

_____

_____

This rule usually applies to the suffixes **–or** and **–ar** too. Which word in the first activity does not follow the rule? _____

Think about this rule as you combine each word and suffix below.

1. advise + –or _____
2. jog + –er _____
3. equate + –or _____
4. swim + –er _____
5. act + –or _____
6. locate + –or _____
7. fact + –or _____
8. scan + –er _____
9. tract + –or _____
10. create + –or _____
11. educate + –or _____
12. elevate + –or _____

What does **–or** mean in numbers 7, 13, and 18 (top) and 1, 5, 6, 10, 11, and 12 (bottom)?

_____

Words with the suffix **–ar** are often adjectives: singular, popular, lunar, spectacular.

9 Vowel-r-Vowel Rule

Here is one more important rule for syllables with an **r**. Do you remember what an **accented** syllable is? It is the part of the word that we say with more force. When there is a vowel <u>after</u> the **r** as in **spir<u>a</u>l**, **spir<u>i</u>t** or **mur<u>a</u>l**, the vowel before the **r** will **not** be r-controlled. It will be either long or short. We call this the **vowel-r-vowel rule**. This is only true when the syllable with the **r** is **accented** (pronounced more forcefully).

The only exception is for the letter **a**. The letter **a** in this kind of syllable will always say **âr**, as in **p<u>a</u>ragraph**.

Highlight the vowels that come before and after the letter **r**. Now, try reading these challenging words. Highlight the ones you can read.

1. parents
2. inherit
3. caramel
4. Carolyn
5. spirit
6. spiral
7. plural
8. caravan
9. enduring
10. admiring
11. experiment
12. alluring
13. American
14. cherub
15. clarinet
16. sheriff
17. mural
18. scary
19. there
20. impure
21. peril
22. rural
23. tariff
24. floral

We mark an **accented** syllable by placing an apostrophe right after it: ex per'i ment, spi'ral, sher'iff. Write the accent mark in the following words. Then decide whether the vowel-r-vowel rule applies and highlight or underline the words that follow this rule.

1. be ware
2. there fore
3. nu mer al
4. per ish
5. con spire
6. car a way
7. in quire
8. var y
9. fed er al
10. pre pared
11. gen er al
12. re quire ment
13. sev er al
14. ver y
15. min er al
16. com pared
17. re tired
18. mar-a-thon

This was very hard! If you finished, you should be very proud of yourself.

124

10 The Absorbed Prefix *in–*

The prefix **in–** is an absorbed prefix. This means its last letter sometimes changes to the beginning letter of the base word (in + regular = irregular). In some words, the last letter of the prefix changes to a letter that sounds better with the first letter of the base word (in + possible = impossible). This is called **euphony**. The prefix **eu** is Greek and means good; the base word **phon** means sound. In many words **in–** doesn't change.

Use **in–, im–, il–, in–,** and **ir–** to make real words.

1. _____perfect
2. _____secure
3. _____resistible
4. _____literate
5. _____balance
6. _____digestion
7. _____polite
8. _____legal
9. _____regular
10. _____valid
11. _____proper
12. _____logical
13. _____reverence
14. _____mature
15. _____direct

1. We use **im–** in front of what letters? _____
2. We use **il–** in front of what letter? _____
3. We use **ir–** in front of what letter? _____
4. We us **in–** in front of all the other letters.

What do the prefixes **in–, il–, im–,** and **ir–** mean?_____

These same prefixes can have another meaning. Try to figure out what they mean in the words below. Highlight the words you can read.

1. insight
2. inscribe
3. injection
4. invite
5. inhabit
6. inhale
7. incorporate
8. insert
9. immerse
10. import
11. impression
12. imprinted
13. illuminate
14. illustration
15. irrigation
16. irritate

What else do the prefixes **in–, im–, il–,** and **ir–** mean in words 1-16? _____

Do you remember the absorbed prefixes of **con–**? They are _____ and mean _____. The prefix **con–** has one more variant. It is **cor–**. It also means *together or with*. Highlight the following words you can read:

1. correct   2. correction   3. corporation   4. corrugated   5. corrode   6. corrupt

125

11 The Word Ending –*ture*

The dictionary provides us with lots of useful information.
- The entry word is written in syllables.
- A phonetic spelling follows every entry word. This tells us how to pronounce words.
- The part of speech is listed for every entry word.
- All definitions are listed.
- A good dictionary tells us the history of the word, or from what language the word derived (came from).

1. Look up the word **adventure** and copy the phonetic spelling: _____

2. What part of speech is the word **adventure**? _____

3. Copy the first two definitions: _____

_____

4. What languages did **adventure** come from? _____

5. What is the phonetic spelling for the word ending –**ture**? _____

6. What are the two words at the top of every page in the dictionary called and why are they there? _____

Match the phonetically spelled words from the dictionary with the entry words.

1. lĭt′ ər ə chər′   signature
2. dĭ par′ chər   nature
3. jĕs′ chər   texture
4. fyo͞o′ chər   literature
5. kŭl′ chər   recapture
6. sĭg′ nə chər   departure
7. fur′ nĭ chər   culture
8. nā′ chər   gesture
9. rē kăp′ chər   structure
10. tĕks′ chər   future
11. frăk′ chər   furniture
12. strŭk′ chər   fracture

Write the word ending that says **chər** three times: _____

12 The Suffix –al

The suffix **–al** means *relating to, characterized by*. Most words that end with **–al** are adjectives *(informal, federal, normal)*. A few words, however, are nouns *(principal)*. Listen to the vowel sound of the suffix in the following words:

1. formal   2. terminal   3. hospital   What does **–al** say? _____

Add **–al** to these base words and write the new words on the lines. Remember to drop the silent **e** before you add **–al**.

1. person _____   8. herb (silent h) _____
2. arrive _____   9. remove _____
3. propose _____   10. globe _____
4. rent _____   11. front _____
5. sign _____   12. approve _____
6. tribe _____   13. culture _____
7. nature _____   14. rehearse _____

Highlight the above words you can read. Underline the words with two suffixes.

Now that you're becoming a pro with suffixes, you are ready to deal with words that have two suffixes. When **–ture** and **–al** join, the silent **e** must be dropped.

Draw lines from the word starters to the correct suffixes to create real words. Write the new words on the lines.

nă

emo   –tional

struc

op   –tural

fic

1. _____
2. _____
3. _____
4. _____
5. _____
6. _____

Highlight the following words you can read. Write the base words on the lines. The base word may be quite different.

1. marginal _____   4. referral _____
2. digital _____   5. central _____
3. refusal _____   6. numeral _____

13 Suffixes –ant, –ent, and –ment

What is the name of the symbol ə ? _____ What does is say? _____

The vowel in many suffixes or word endings says ə. Read the following words and listen to the vowel sounds in the suffixes:

   1. contin<u>e</u>nt   2. inst<u>a</u>nt   3. curr<u>e</u>nt   4. inf<u>a</u>nt

Because the vowel sounds in –ant and –ent say ə, these two suffixes sound the same. Both say ənt. Many words with these two suffixes are adjectives (describing words). They mean *of* or *relating to*. Sometimes –ant can be a noun ending, which means *a person or thing performing an action*.

Highlight the following words you can read and draw an arrow to **adjective** or **person**.

1. constant
2. occupant   person
3. current   adjective
4. servant

5. merchant
6. recent   person
7. frequent   adjective
8. contestant

Do you remember the suffixes –ance and –ence? What do they say? _____

Many adjectives that end with –ant and –ent can be turned into nouns. To turn such an adjective into a noun, drop the suffix –ant or –ent, and add –ance or –ence. Words with the suffix –ant go to –ance and words with the suffix –ent go to –ence.

Change the following adjectives to nouns and highlight the ones you can read.

1. distant _____
2. attendant _____
3. important _____
4. fragrant _____

5. present _____
6. resident _____
7. confident _____
8. innocent _____

The suffix –ment says mənt. Words that end with mənt are usually nouns and mean *act of* or *state of*.

Highlight the following words you can read and write the phonetic spelling of the suffix on the lines: **mənt** or **ənt**.

1. movement _____
2. vacant _____
3. enrollment _____

4. resentment _____
5. hesitant _____
6. enforcement _____

7. ignorant _____
8. excellent _____
9. replacement _____

14a Word Endings –on and –an

What does the suffix –en, say? _____ You are correct if you remembered that is says ən. The word endings **on** and **an** say exactly the same thing. Most words that end with **on** and **an** came to English from Latin or Greek.

Word endings are usually unaccented, and the vowel in unaccented syllables says the schwa sound. Therefore, **on** and **an** say ən. In a few words, however, the accent is on the ending. Then –**on** and –**an** sound just like the little words **on** and **an**.

Highlight the words you can read and write the sound of the suffix on the lines: ən, on, an.

1. cotton _____
2. slogan _____
3. gallon _____
4. crayon _____
5. dungeon _____
6. organ _____
7. hexagon _____
8. canyon _____
9. nylon _____
10. common _____
11. horizon _____
12. caravan _____
13. human _____
14. pentagon _____
15. pecan _____
16. veteran _____
17. prison _____
18. suburban _____
19. skeleton _____
20. marathon _____
21. comparison _____

Choose two words above that mean *jail* _____
Choose two words that are *types of fabric* _____
Choose two words that are *shapes* _____

Highlight the following words you can read and listen to the suffixes. Then write each word in the box under the correct heading:

1. current
2. cannon
3. agent
4. argument
5. instant
6. attachment
7. person
8. resident
9. orphan
10. investment
11. exuberant
12. retirement
13. pelican
14. compartment
15. cotton

-ənt	-ən	-mənt

14b Connective *i*

Sometimes the letter **i** is right before a suffix that begins with a vowel. Listen to the sound of **i** in these words: super*i*or, Cana*di*an, immed*i*ate, memor*i*al. What does the **i** say? _____
You are correct if you heard a long **e** sound. Memorize this rule: when **i** occurs before a suffix that starts with a vowel, it usually says **ē**.

Highlight the words you can read. Write **ē** above every **i** that says long **e**. Then draw lines to the sound of the word endings.

1. warrior
2. interior
3. champion   **ēr**
4. librarian
5. exterior   **ēən**
6. scorpion
7. comedian

8. nutrient
9. jovial
10. radiant   **ēənt**
11. obedient
12. memorial   **ēəl**
13. ingredient
14. material

What do **–ion** and **–ian** mean in the words 3, 4, and 7 ? _____

Do you remember the two ways the word ending **ate** is pronounced? _____
You are correct if you wrote **āte** (*deviate*) and **ət** (*immediate, appropriate*).

The letter **i** can occur before many other suffixes that start with vowels.
Highlight the following words you can read and write them under the correct heading.

| tutorial | radiate | variant | trivial | alleviate | expedient |
| gradient | burial | infuriate | recipient | mediate | imperial |

ēāt	ēənt	ēəl

Exceptions: Verbs that end with **y** saying **ī**, keep the long **i** sound: comply, compliant, rely, reliant, defy, defiant, deny, denial, supply, supplier.

CHAPTER 5
Vowel-Vowel Syllable

Note to Instructor

Some secondary students may already have solid knowledge of vowel-vowel syllables. Therefore, it may be appropriate to skip some of the early lessons. The dictation and spelling lists can serve as pretests to determine which pages to skip and which pages to include.

Lesson 1 introduces the vowel-vowel syllable. This kind of syllable contains two vowels that are next to each other. The abbreviation for a vowel-vowel syllable is **vv**. Copy this page as an overhead transparency. It may be necessary to use the transparency several times before students retain the characteristics of a vowel-vowel syllable.

Ask students to answer the question, "What do these words have in common? aim, stay, eat, steam, sweep, tree, pie, tie, roast, throat, due, and fruit." Record the correct responses on the overhead or on the board in any order. Direct your students to take notes in the Rules section of their Decoding Binders. Correct responses are:

1. All of these words have two vowels next to each other.
2. The first vowel in each word is long.
3. The second vowel in each word is silent.
4. All are one-syllable words.

Remind students that every syllable has only one vowel sound; silent vowels don't count. Another important point is to keep the two vowels in the same syllable. Do not divide between them.

Mark the vowels immediately after students discover that the first vowel is long and the second vowel is silent: thrōat.

Many phonics manuals classify all vowel pairs as digraphs or diphthongs. This manual uses the term vowel-vowel syllable because it covers a large number of words that follow the simple phonics rule: "The first vowel is long, the second one is silent." (The two vowels themselves will be referred to as a vowel team.) Diphthongs and vowel digraphs also consist of vowel pairs (house, down, clause, straw, joy, moist, brief, cool, and new), but their vowel combinations do not have a clear sound/symbol relationship. Chapter 7 covers diphthongs and vowel digraphs.

Reminders:
1. **Have students reread all the words in every lesson once they have completed the exercises.**
2. Ask students to copy each new phonogram, red word, homophone, homograph, prefix, suffix, and rule in the appropriate sections of their Decoding Binders. Include homographs, marked

HG, in the Homophone Section. When entering a phonogram, prefix, or suffix, students must list four key words that illustrate it. Students must also add four words for every rule and a brief definition for the homophones or homographs.
3. Review all sections of the binder **once a week** for a minimum of five weeks. Younger children or the severely learning disabled may need more time for review.
4. Use the **Proposed Spelling Activities**, located in the Appendix, for all **Reading and Spelling for Mastery** lists, or use your own. Students must read the list every day before they start the two practice activities.

Lesson 2a (two pages) introduces the vowel teams **ai** and **ay**. If you are teaching younger students, reinforce the rule: "When two vowels go walking, the first one does the talking." Students are asked to figure out that **ai** is used at the beginning or in the middle of words, whereas **ay** occurs at the end of words or syllables.

Lesson 2b is a **Reading and Spelling for Mastery** page. It consists of three spelling lists with **ai** and **ay** words. To reduce the number of spelling words, consider using these lists as pretests, so your more capable students are not practicing words they already know. By pre-testing, you can create individualized lists. You could even pair up students and let them test each other. Another alternative is to group students according to their ability levels and to use the harder list for the stronger students. **You could also postpone some of the lists until later in this chapter.** Use these two suggestions for all spelling lists in this chapter. Please select two appropriate activities from **Proposed Spelling Activities**, located in the Appendix and require students to read the list before they start their daily spelling practice.

Lesson 3a introduces the vowel team **ea**. The first exercise directs students to insert **ea** or **ai** in words with missing vowels. The last activity asks students to highlight vowel teams in a brief story.

Lesson 3b discusses the short **e** sound of the **ea** spelling in words like *head, thread,* and *breath*. This lesson also includes the long **a** sound of the **ea** spelling in *they, great, break, steak*.

Lesson 3c is a **Reading and Spelling for Mastery** page. It consists of three spelling lists with **ea** words. Follow the usual procedures. (Consider pre-testing for the same reasons cited in Lesson 2b.)

Lesson 4a (two pages) introduces the vowel team **ee**. The first exercise asks students to insert **ee, ai**, or **ay** in words with missing vowels. The second activity requires students to combine two base words to create compound words. Tell everyone to write the compound words on a sheet of binder paper before writing them under the appropriate code. The second page requires students to add letters before word endings and to syllabify words. Some polysyllabic words have an open syllable or a prefix followed by another syllable that starts with a vowel (re-en-list, me-an-der). Alert your class to the possibility of false vowel-vowel patterns. Ask students to record this information in the Rules section of their Decoding Binders.

Lesson 4b discusses the phonogram **ey**.

Lesson 4c is a **Reading and Spelling for Mastery** page (Lesson 5b is also listed on this page). This lesson consists of two spelling lists with **ee** and **ey** words. Directions are listed in **Lesson 2b**.

Lesson 4d explains the rules for adding plural or third person singular to words that end in **y**. When **y** follows a vowel team (also diphthongs and vowel digraphs), just add **s**, *days, keys*. When **y** follows a consonant, change the **y** to **i** and add **es**, *puppies, ponies, copies, he/she studies*.

Lesson 5a discusses the rule: "No word shall end with the letter **i**." The exceptions to this rule are the following words: *ski, pi, taxi, kiwi, alibi, khaki, quasi, rabbi, salami, bikini, safari* and the plural of Greek words such as *cacti*, as well as and other words derived from foreign languages. When a word ends with **i**, we must add a silent **e**. This lesson also explains the two sounds of **ie**. In a one-syllable word, **ie** says **long i**, *tie, die*. At the end of a polysyllabic word, –**ie** is a suffix that says **long e**, *cookie, brownie*.

Lesson 5b (on the same page as 4c) is a **Reading and Spelling for Mastery** list with **ie** words. It reiterates the previously covered spelling rules for adding plurals, past tense endings, and present participles to base words that end with **ie** or **y**. Directions are listed in **Lesson 2b**.

Lesson 6a (two pages) introduces the vowel teams **oa** and **oe**. The first two exercises require students to discriminate among vowel-vowel, vowel-consonant-e, and r-controlled syllables. In the third activity, students insert different vowel pairs in words that have the same consonants. The final exercise reviews the vowel team **oar** in words such as *roar*, *board*, *coarse*, and *hoarse*.

Lesson 6b is a **Reading and Spelling for Mastery** page (Lesson 7b is also listed on this page). It consists of words with the vowel teams **oa** and **oe**. Follow the directions outlined in **2b**.

Lesson 7a (two pages) introduces the vowel teams **ue** and **ui**. This lesson reiterates that long **u** has two different sounds: **u** as in *argue* and *rescue* and $\overline{oo}$, as in *glue* and *fruit*. The letter before the **u** determines whether **u** says its name or is pronounced $\overline{oo}$. When **u** follows the consonants **r** and **l**, it says $\overline{oo}$, (*true, clue*). This is also usually true for the consonants **d**, **j**, **t**, and **s**, (*due, juice, Tuesday, sue*). When **u** follows any other consonant, it says its own name. The word *value* is an exception. In the first exercise, students categorize words under the headings **ue** and $\overline{oo}$. This lesson also covers the silent **ue** ending in French derivatives (*vague, league*). The last exercise uses common expressions with missing vowel-vowel words. Consider allowing students to work in groups because these phrases may not be familiar to everyone. Provide help for younger students.

Lesson 7b (on the same page as Lesson 6b) is a **Reading and Spelling for Mastery** list with **ue** and **ui** words. Follow the directions outlined in **Lesson 2b**.

Lesson 8 asks students to highlight or underline the vowel-vowel patterns in a condensed version of the Cinderella story. Please point out that not all vowel combinations fit the rule: "First vowel long, second vowel silent." This is an opportunity to teach the difference between diphthongs and true vowel-vowel patterns. (Note: Consider omitting this lesson if you feel the subject matter is inappropriate for older students.)

Lesson 9 reinforces the First Rule of Syllabication: "A word has the same number of syllables as the number of sounded vowels." Students determine how many vowels they see, how many vowels they hear, and how many syllables are in words with vowel teams.

Lessons 10, 11, and **12a** provide decoding practice with more challenging words. The polysyllabic words on these pages review all vowel teams introduced in this chapter. Alert your class to the possibility of false vowel-vowel patterns, which have been included.

Lesson 12b is a dictation exercise; do not disseminate these pages to students. Since it is difficult to deduce the silent vowels on the dictation pages, encourage students to think of the base word first. If they know the spelling of the base word, they may choose the correct silent vowel. Otherwise, encourage them to ask for the silent vowel and supply it without hesitation.

Lesson 13 introduces the suffix –**ize** and reviews the suffix –**al**. This lesson also explains the spelling rules associated with adding –**ize** and –**al** to base words. These exercises may be difficult for younger students. You might consider allowing students to work in groups.

Lesson 14 introduces the suffixes –**ee** and –**ive** and reiterates the spelling rules for adding suffixes that start with vowels. This lesson may be difficult for younger students. You may consider allowing students to work in groups. The suffix –**ive** will be covered thoroughly in Chapter 12.

Lesson 15 is designed for stronger or older students. There is no worksheet; please cover this concept on the board/overhead. Ask students to write the suffix **–tion** on a piece of binder paper. If they don't remember, review the spelling and pronunciation. Write the words **realize, capitalize, itemize, utilize, modernize, colonize, stabilize,** and **victimize** in a column on the board. Ask students to copy these words and underline the ones they can read. Then say, "Watch what happens to the suffix **–ize** when we add **–tion** to it." Then write **realization** next to **realize** and ask students what the changes are in the spelling and pronunciation of **–ize**. Next, ask students to add **–tion** to the rest of the words and practice pronouncing them. Review the concept of **accented syllables**. Ask where the accent falls in words that end with **–ize**. (The first syllable is accented.) Then ask where the accent falls in the words that end with **–tion**. (The syllable directly before **–tion** is accented.)

If you are teaching older students or a strong group, you might consider using some of the lessons from Chapters 13 to continue the process of acquiring prefixes. This instruction could be taught as a supplementary vocabulary unit; however, continue teaching the syllable patterns in Chapters 6 and 7.

1 Vowel-Vowel Syllable

What do these words have in common?

| aim | eat | sweep | pie | roast | due |
| stay | steam | tree | tie | throat | fruit |

1. _____

2. _____

3. _____

4. _____

This kind of syllable is called *vowel-vowel*. **The abbreviation is** *vv*. **Why do you think it has this name?**

_____

Fold back this bottom section, or place a sheet of paper over it._ _ _ _ _ _ _ _ _ _ _ _ _ _ _ _ _ _ _

NOTE TO INSTRUCTOR: Please copy this page as an overhead transparency to introduce **vowel-vowel** syllables. Record correct responses in any order.
1. All of the words have two vowels next to each other.
2. The first vowel is long.
3. The second vowel is silent. Mark the vowels right after students discover the sounding rule.
4. They are all one-syllable words. Remind students that every syllable has only **one vowel sound**. Another important concept is that the two vowels must be kept in the same syllable. Do not divide between them.

This type of syllable is called **vowel-vowel** because two vowels are next to each other. The **vowel-vowel** syllable is not to be confused with diphthongs. Diphthongs also have two vowels next to each other, but they follow an arbitrary sounding rule that must be memorized.

2a Vowel Teams *ai* and *ay*

In a vowel-vowel syllable, the first vowel is _____, and the second one is _____. Read the following words slowly and listen to the vowel sound in each of them.

    1. aim   2. aid   3. paid   4. day   5. stay

What do the vowel teams **ai** and **ay** say? _____

You are right, if you noticed that together they say a long **a** sound. Therefore, the first vowel is long and the second one is silent. Mark the letter **a** long and cross out the silent **i** or **y**, āi̸m, dāy̸.

Read the following words. Highlight the vowels and mark them. Next to each word, write the abbreviation **vv** for **vowel-vowel** syllables, **vce** for **vowel-consonant-e** syllables, or **rc** for **r-controlled** syllables.

1. train _____	7. scrape _____	13. frail _____	19. trait _____
2. quail _____	8. chart _____	14. stay _____	20. faint _____
3. plane _____	9. pray _____	15. drain _____	21. march _____
4. sway _____	10. paint _____	16. shape _____	22. claim _____
5. arch _____	11. spray _____	17. strait _____	23. straight _____
6. tray _____	12. sharp _____	18. strain _____	24. stray _____

Underline words 1-24 with **vowel teams**. Study the pattern. When do you use **ai**? When do you use **ay**?

_____

Write the following letters in front of **ail**: **s, p, b, m, n, f, t, r**. Read the new words.

1. _____   3. _____   5. _____   7. _____

2. _____   4. _____   6. _____   8. _____

Write these letters in front of **ain**: **m, p, r, v, g, br, ch, st**. Read the new words.

1. _____   3. _____   5. _____   7. _____

2. _____   4. _____   6. _____   8. _____

Read all of the words!

2a continued

Highlight the vowels in the following words. Write the words in syllables, separated by dashes. Next, denote the code.

1. acclaim _____
2. entertainer _____
3. railway _____
4. fingernail _____
5. display _____
6. ponytail _____
7. underpay _____
8. terrain _____
9. portray _____
10. remainder _____

There are two common words that do not follow the rule you have just learned. They are **said** and **says**. On the back of this sheet of paper, write each word in a sentence. Then memorize these words.

Draw lines from the syllables on the left to the syllables on the right to make new words. Write them on the lines. You will use one syllable on the left and three syllables on the right twice. Read the words.

shirt		⇨	1. _____
brides	tail	⇨	2. _____
Thurs	nail	⇨	3. _____
pay	tray	⇨	4. _____
de	way	⇨	5. _____
high	maid	⇨	6. _____
hang	tain	⇨	7. _____
be	day	⇨	8. _____
mer		⇨	9. _____
		⇨	10. _____

On the back of this sheet of paper, write five rhyming words for **way** and five for **nail**.

2b Reading and Spelling for Mastery

Words with the vowel teams **ai** and **ay**:

Dictation List	Spelling List 1	Spelling List 2
1. pain (H)	1. pail (H)	1. pay
2. gain	2. mail (H)	2. lay (H)
3. grain	3. rain (H)	3. bay
4. chain	4. main (H)	4. may / May
5. stain	5. plain (H)	5. say
6. brain	6. paid	6. says*
7. sprain	7. wait (H)	7. way (H)
8. strain	8. claim	8. away
9. train	9. raise	9. always
10. contain	10. praise	10. today
11. container	11. paint	11. holidays
12. rail	12. painter	12. gray, grey
13. jail	13. daily	13. stay
14. sail (H)	14. waist (H)	14. pray (H)
15. tail (H)	15. straight* (H)	15. displays
16. retail	16. said*	16. spray
17. nail	17. again*	17. stray
18. fail	18. against*	18. essay
19. frail	19. captain*	19. delay
20. trail	20. bargain*	20. betray

*Red words, H = Homophones, HG = homograph

3a Vowel Team *ea*

Do you remember the rule for the vowel sound in vowel-vowel syllables? Read the following words, and listen closely to the vowel sound in each of them.

    1. eat   2. tea   3. seat   4. deal

What does the vowel team **ea** say? _____ As you have learned in the previous lesson, the first vowel is _____ and the second one is _____. Mark the vowels in the words above.

Fill in the blanks with **ea** or **ai** to make real words. Read the words at your teacher's direction.

1. n____t
2. b____m
3. p____n
4. dr____m
5. sp____k
6. str____k
7. ch____p
8. squ____k
9. st____n
10. tw____k
11. tr____l
12. ch____t
13. str____m
14. p____nt
15. scr____m
16. cl____n
17. fr____l
18. sm____r
19. spr____n
20. squ____l

Read the paragraph below. Underline or highlight the twenty-three words that contain the vowel team **ea**. Then write the words on the lines and read the paragraph one more time.

Eastern California has many hot springs. Hot Creek is one that is easy to reach because it is near a resort called Mammoth Lakes. Several small hot springs are right in the middle of a clear, clean stream. The heat from the springs releases steam that hovers above the water. In any season of the year, people love wading and swimming in Hot Creek. Some eager beavers leap right into the stream; while others appear to retreat in fear. Some folks think hot springs have the power to heal disease. Spending a day at Hot Creek is a great treat!

_____

_____

_____

Find the **ea** word that doesn't follow the rule: _____

3b Another Sound for *ea*

The vowel team **ea** is complicated because it doesn't always say long **e**. Read the following words and listen to the vowel sound in each of them.

    1. head   2. ready   3. bread   4. steady

What does the vowel team **ea** say in the above words? _____ The vowel team **ea** also represents one other sound. Say the following words and listen to their vowel sound.

    1. they   2. great   3. break   4. steak

What does the vowel sound say in these words? _____ Memorize these four words! Try this mnemonic device: "During lunch break, they ate a great steak."

Read these words carefully. Then write them under the correct vowel sound. If you are not sure, try both sounds and choose the one that makes a real word.

1. preacher
2. sweat
3. instead
4. uneasy
5. hear
6. threat
7. plea
8. increase
9. dread
10. meant
11. sneaky
12. threads
13. breath
14. breathe
15. queasy
16. spread

ea=ĕ	ea = ē

Memorize the four common words in which **ea** says the long **a** sound: they, break, great, steak. Then use them in these sentences.

1. My favorite meal is barbecued _____ with mashed potatoes, gravy, and beans.
2. The _____ Wall of China was built as a defense against western invaders.
3. Please wash the glasses carefully; _____ _____ easily.

3c Reading and Spelling for Mastery

Words with the vowel team **ea**:

Dictation	Spelling List 1	Spelling List 2
ea = long e	ea = long e	ea = short e
1. fear	1. leave	1. head
2. clear	2. read (HG)	2. ahead
3. seat	3. lead* (HG)	3. bread (H)
4. beat (H)	4. each	4. spread
5. heat	5. reach	5. dead
6. meat (H)	6. teach	6. death
7. deal	7. hear* (H)	7. breath
8. heal (H)	8. tear* (H, HG)	8. sweater
9. steal (H)	9. near	9. ready
10. sea (H)	10. reason	10. already
11. plea	11. least	11. bear (H)
12. peach	12. easy	12. wear (H)
13. beach (H)	13. mean	13. heavy
14. clean	14. breathe*	14. instead
15. team (H)	15. please	15. weather (H)
16. steam	16. beneath	16. meant
17. stream	17. they*	17. measure*
18. east	18. great* (H)	18. treasure*
19. feast	19. break* (H)	19. pleasure*
20. leash	20. steak* (H)	20. heart*

*Red words, H = homophones, HG= homographs

4a Vowel Team ee

Do you remember the rule for the vowel sound in **vowel-vowel** syllables? Read the following words and listen closely to the vowel sounds in each of them.

    1. bee   2. see   3. need   4. beef   5. meet   6. week

What does the vowel team **ee** say? _____ As you have learned in previous lessons, the first vowel is _____ and the second one is _____. Mark the vowels in this word: keep

Fill in the blanks with **ee**, **ai**, or **ay** to make real words. Afterwards, read all of the words.

1. d____d	6. ch____n	11. sn____ze	16. sw____p
2. sw____	7. sl____p	12. sn____l	17. j____p
3. d____p	8. ch____ks	13. fr____ze	18. cl____m
4. r____f	9. str____	14. g____se	19. sw____t
5. cr____k	10. qu____n	15. tr____l	20. sh____t

Create compound words by combining words from numbers 1-12 with words from numbers 13-24. Write them on another sheet of paper first. Then write them in pencil under the correct code. Finally, read the words.

1. bee	7. up	13. back	19. way
2. six	8. knee	14. hole	20. deed
3. week	9. screen	15. hive	21. play
4. feed	10. tree	16. cap	22. cake
5. in	11. free	17. teen	23. keep
6. cheese	12. peep	18. top	24. day

cl-vv	vv-vce	vv-cl	vv-vv

On another sheet of paper, write four rhyming words for **bee** and four for **deep**.

4a continued

Write these letters in front of **ee** and read the words: **f, fl, fr, tr, thr, gl, spr, kn**.

1. _____   3. _____   5. _____   7. _____
2. _____   4. _____   6. _____   8. _____

Write these letters in front of **eed** and read the words: **f, s, w, d, gr, bl, fr, cr**.

1. _____   3. _____   5. _____   7. _____
2. _____   4. _____   6. _____   8. _____

Write these letters in front of **een** and read the words: **s, t, k, gr, sh, scr, spl, qu**.

1. _____   3. _____   5. _____   7. _____
2. _____   4. _____   6. _____   8. _____

Do you remember the prefixes **re–** and **pre–**? Sometimes they occur in front of base words that start with the letter **e**. When this happens, the two **e's** do not form a **vowel-vowel** syllable. Instead, they belong to two separate syllables: re-en-list (pref-pref-cl).

Highlight the vowels in the following words. Write them in syllables, separated by dashes. Then write the code. In a true vowel-vowel syllable, keep the two vowels in the same syllable. In words that we inherited from Latin, the consonant before a suffix that begins with a vowel often joins the suffix (ed-u-cate, cl-op-c+s).

1. reenter _____
2. proceed _____
3. reevaluate _____
4. preempt _____
5. canteen _____
6. reeducate _____
7. tweezers _____
8. preexist _____
9. reelect _____
10. reenact _____

4b Vowel Team ey

The vowel team **ey** follows the same rules as other **vowel-vowel** syllables. The letter **e** is _____ and the **y** is _____. We will discuss some exceptions later.

Use the words in the box to complete the sentences below.

> valley   turkey   volley   chimney   jersey   kidneys
> honey   monkey   alley   jockey   money   donkeys

1. The disk _____ played one of Carlos' favorite songs.
2. Sarah wore her red _____ to the tryouts for the _____ball team.
3. The river winds through the lush, green _____.
4. Tom's mother gave him some _____, but told him not to buy any candy.
5. Most people like sugar in their tea; the beekeeper prefers _____.
6. In many countries, farmers still use _____ to transport their grain to market.
7. Dad always parks his car in the _____ behind our house.
8. Little kids like to climb on the _____ bars.
9. Your _____ remove waste and toxins from the body.
10. My favorite part of the Thanksgiving feast is the _____!
11. Our _____ was damaged during the last earthquake.

In a few words, **ey** says another sound. Read these words. What does the vowel team **ey** say? _____

    1. they   2. prey   3. obey   4. survey   5. purvey   6. convey

Memorize these words. On another sheet of paper, write a sentence with words 1-6. The word **prey** is a homophone. What does it mean? Write you answer on the bottom.

4c/5b Reading and Spelling for Mastery

Words with the vowel team **ee**:

Words with the vowel team **ie**:

Dictation

1. free
2. three
3. sheet
4. sweet
5. deep
6. sleep
7. steep
8. sweep
9. teen
10. green
11. greed
12. steer
13. cheer
14. heel (H)
15. feed
16. deed
17. indeed
18. seed
19. speed
20. speech

4c Spelling List

1. steel (H)
2. meet (H)
3. seem (H)
4. speech
5. people*
6. greetings
7. been* (H)
8. seen (H)
9. feel
10. feelings
11. between
12. wheel*
13. knee*
14. freeze
15. cheese
16. money*
17. valley
18. they*
19. obey*
20. survey*

5b Spelling List

1. lie (H)
2. lied
3. lying
4. tie
5. tying
6. die (H)
7. dying
8. cry
9. cried
10. crying
11. try
12. tries
13. tried
14. trying
15. fly
16. flies
17. pie (H)
18. friend*
19. movie
20. goalie

*Red words, H = Homophones

4d Plural After Vowel Teams *ay* and *ey*

When **y** is part of a vowel team, it is the silent vowel *(play, hockey)*. Do you remember what **y** says at the end of a two or a three-syllable word?

    1. fluffy   2. plenty   3. happy   4. sloppy   5. dressy   6. muddy

What does **y** say? _____

To form the plural (more than one) in nouns that end with the letter **y**, change the **y** to **i** and then add **–es**. Use this rule only when a consonant comes before the **y** *buddy, buddies*. When a vowel precedes **y**, make no changes, simply add **–s** *tray, trays*.

Draw lines from the singular nouns to their correct plural. Read all of the words and write them on the lines.

story   1. _____

key   2. _____

puppy   **–ies**   3. _____

play   4. _____

cherry   5. _____

daisy   **–s**   6. _____

chimney   7. _____

pony   8. _____

This rule also applies to third person singular as in these examples.

1. Tony play<u>s</u> soccer.   2. He appl<u>ies</u> himself.   3. Paula obey<u>s</u> her mom.

Add the plural to these nouns: Change the verb to third person singular:

1. One lady, two _____   1. I pay, he _____

2. A turkey, three _____   2. You study, she _____

3. An essay, two _____   3. We delay, he _____

4. One party, many _____   4. They stray, it _____

5. A penny, ten _____   5. I apply, she _____

6. One valley, five _____   6. They say, he _____

7. A hobby, two _____   7. We reply, she _____

8. One tardy, four _____   8. I try, he _____

5a Vowel Team *ie*

English has some strange rules. Here is one of them: "No word shall end with the letter **i**." When a word ends with the letter **i**, we must add a silent **e** to it or use **y** instead. Some foreign words such as *ski* or *pi* do not follow this rule. The vowel team **ie** has two sounds. Sometimes it says long **i**, but more frequently it says long **e**.

Read the following words, and listen closely to the sound of **ie**. Write **i** or **e** on the lines and mark them. If you are not sure, try both and choose the one that makes a real word:

1. collie _____
2. lie _____
3. birdie _____
4. pie _____
5. goalie _____
6. beanie _____
7. tie _____
8. oldie _____
9. caddie _____
10. prairie _____
11. die _____
12. zombie _____
13. movie _____
14. vie _____
15. eerie _____
16. sweetie _____

Study the pattern of the two different sounds of **ie**. What is the rule?

_____

_____

You are correct if you noticed that the vowel team **ie** says long **i** at the end of a one-syllable word; however, the letters **ie** say the long **e** sound at the end of a word that has two or more syllables. In this position, the vowel team **ie** is often a suffix.

Four of the one-syllable words above are verbs (action words). Select the verbs and write them on the line.

_____   _____   _____   _____

Do you remember the rules for adding –**ed** or –**ing** to verbs? When the verb ends with the letter **e**, you must drop the **e** before adding a suffix that starts with a vowel.

Here is another strange rule: "No word may have two **i**'s next to each other." Therefore, in verbs such as tie + ing, you must change the letters **ie** to **y** as in **tying**.

Rewrite the verbs you listed above by adding –**ed** and –**ing**.

_____   _____   _____   _____

_____   _____   _____   _____

6a   Vowel Teams *oa* and *oe*

Do you remember the rule for the vowel sound in **vowel-vowel** syllables? Read the following words and listen closely to the vowel sounds.

　　1. oak　　2. boat　　3. coat　　4. soap　　5. toe　　6. foe

What do the vowel teams **oa** and **oe** say? _____ The first vowel is _____ and the second one is _____. The vowel team **oe** occurs at the end of words and is less common.

Read the following words, highlight the vowels, and mark them. Next to each word, write the abbreviation **cl** for **closed** syllables, **vce** for **vowel-consonant-e** syllables, **rc** for **r-controlled** syllables, and **vv** for **vowel-vowel** syllables.

1. coal	____	7. goat	____	13. sport	____	19. road	____
2. rode	____	8. foe	____	14. groan	____	20. cork	____
3. gloat	____	9. throat	____	15. stock	____	21. doe	____
4. roam	____	10. floss	____	16. spoke	____	22. poach	____
5. Joe	____	11. stork	____	17. broach	____	23. roast	____
6. gloss	____	12. float	____	18. broke	____	24. coach	____

Highlight the vowels in the following words and draw a red line between the syllables. Then draw a line from the first syllable to the correct abbreviation on the left. Next, draw a line from the second syllable to the correct abbreviation on the right.

vv	coaster	vv
	oatmeal	
	tiptoe	
	scapegoat	
	encroach	
vce	toaster	vce
	seacoast	
	coalmine	
	lifeboat	
	approach	
cl or pref	roadside	rc or s

On the back of this sheet of paper, write four rhyming words for **boat** and three for **coast**.

6a continued

You can make several words by keeping all of the consonants the same and only changing the vowel pairs. Use the vowel teams **oa**, **ea**, **ee**, and **ai** to fill in the blanks in the following words. Make sure the words make sense. There are several homophones. You may use a dictionary.

1. s____k   s____k
2. b____st   b____st
3. p____ch   p____ch
4. fl____t   fl____t
5. s____l   s____l
6. f____l   f____l   f____l
7. m____t   m____t   m____t
8. m____n   m____n   m____n
9. gr____n   gr____n   gr____n
10. cr____k   cr____k   cr____k
11. b____t   b____t   b____t   b____t
12. r____d   r____d   r____d   r____d

Review: In some words, the vowels **oa** are followed by the letter **r**. You studied the phoneme **oar** in the last chapter. Read the words in the box and use them to complete the sentences.

board   soar   coarse   boars   roar   hoarse   hoard   oars

What does **oar** say? _____

1. Do not throw the _____ over_____, otherwise you might not make it back to shore!

2. If you keep screaming, you will become _____.

3. Eagles _____, lions _____, and wild _____ grunt.

4. In my woodworking class, I learned to use _____ sandpaper as the first step in refinishing my grandmother's dresser.

5. Please don't _____ the cookies; we have plenty for everyone!

6b/7b Reading and Spelling for Mastery

Words with the vowel teams **oa** and **oe**:

6b Spelling List

1. road (H)
2. load (H)
3. coat
4. boat
5. float
6. throat
7. coal
8. goal
9. loan (H)
10. groan (H)
11. roast
12. toast
13. coast
14. boast
15. soap
16. coach
17. approach
18. toe (H)
19. foe
20. shoe* (H)

Words with the vowel teams **ue** and **ui**:

7b Spelling List

1. due (H)
2. hue
3. blue (H)
4. flue (H)
5. clue
6. glue
7. true
8. cue (H)
9. queue* (H)
10. argue
11. issue*
12. tissue*
13. value
14. avenue
15. fruit
16. juice*
17. suit
18. suite* (H)
19. suitcase
20. pursuit

*Red words, H = Homophones

7a Vowel Teams *ue* and *ui*

Do you remember the rule for the vowel sound in vowel-vowel syllables? Read the following words and listen closely to the vowel sound in each of them.

    1. cue   2. hue   3. argue.   What does the vowel team **ue** say? _____

You are right, if you noticed that together **ue** says the long **u** sound.

Write the rule for marking vowels in vowel-vowel syllables. Then mark the vowels in numbers 1-3 above. _____

When you studied long **u** in **vowel-consonant-e** syllables, you learned that it has two different sounds. It often says its own name as in *use, cute,* and *fume*. Long **u** also makes the sound you hear in *plume* and *rule*. The dictionary uses the phonetic spelling of o͞o for this sound. The vowel team **ue** also says these <u>two</u> sounds; but **ui** only says o͞o *(suit)*.

Read the following words and highlight the vowels. Listen to the two different sounds of **u**. Write the words under the correct category.

1. due
2. rescue
3. sue
4. avenue
5. suit
6. imbue
7. glue
8. argue
9. barbecue
10. bruise
11. venue
12. fruit
13. queue
14. cruise
15. true
16. miscue
17. revenue
18. clue
19. pursuit
20. continue

ū	o͞o

Study the above lists. What sound does the vowel team **ui** say? _____ The vowel team **ue** says o͞o after what consonants? _____

7a continued

When the letters **u** and **e** or **u** and **i** are next to each other, they sometimes do not form a vowel team. When this happens, it is because they belong to two different syllables. Highlight the vowels in the words below and draw a line between the syllables. Listen to the two distinct vowel sounds. Beware of false vowel pairs!

1. fluid 2. cruel 3. ruin 4. fluent 5. influenza

In words that we inherited from French or Latin, the letters **ue** often occur after the letter **g**. In such words, **ue** is silent. The vowel before **g** may be long, short, or r-controlled. Read the following words and underline the ones you know.

1. vague   4. league   7. plague   10. vogue
2. rogue   5. monologue   8. prologue   11. colleague
3. catalogue   6. tongue   9. dialogue   12. morgue

One more refresher of a former rule: Drop the letter **e** before adding a suffix that starts with a vowel. On the back of this sheet of paper, write the following three words by adding the suffixes **–ed**, **–er**, and **–ing**:

1. rescue   2. subdue   3. pursue

Practice using all of the vowel teams you have studied so far: Use the words in the box to complete the common phrases below. Do the ones you know first.

break	heat	keynote	sea	cream	moaned
coat	free	esteem	toe	dream	dreams
blues	coast	pursuit	clean	teeter	groaned

1. the _____ is clear
2. in hot _____
3. sweet _____
4. _____ of arms
5. _____ totter
6. from _____ to shining _____
7. made a _____ break
8. _____ wave
9. _____ speech
10. give me a _____
11. sing the _____
12. Everyone _____
13. a _____ come true
14. _____ speaker
15. good self _____
16. the _____ of the crop
17. toe to _____
    and _____ about the homework.

8 Review of all Vowel-Vowel Syllables

Read the story first. Go back over it and underline or highlight all of the words with true vowel teams (first vowel long, second one silent). There are 53; if you can get 48, you're doing well! The phoneme **air** is not a vowel team.

Cinderella

At the stroke of midnight, Cinderella remembered to keep her promise to her fairy godmother. There was no time to explain! She ran away from the prince and down the steep steps. The prince's feelings were hurt by her speedy retreat. They had danced with each other all night, and she was his dream come true! As Cinderella raced down the staircase, she lost one of her glass slippers. The prince grabbed the slipper and vowed to return it to the sweet maiden.

That night, sleep defied the prince; he could hardly wait to seek out Cinderella. In the wee hours of the morning, he began to visit each house in town. He coaxed all the young girls he met to try on the glass slipper. To his dismay, it fit no one. At last, he came to Cinderella's home. Her stepsisters were eager to meet the prince and complied with his request. They screamed with pain as they tried to force their big feet into the tiny slipper.

In the meantime, Cinderella was sweeping the porch and cleaning the floor with a pail of soapy water. The prince approached her, but the mean stepsisters said with disdain, "Pay her no heed; we treat her just like a maid." The angry prince prevailed. He beseeched Cinderella to try on the glass slipper. It fit her to a tee! The beaming prince got down on his knees and pleaded with her to become his wife. Tears filled Cinderella's eyes and rolled down her rosy cheeks. She replied sweetly, "I will be your faithful wife and someday your queen." They lived happily ever after.

9 Syllable Review

Syllables are organized around sounded vowels. The number of sounded vowels determines how many syllables a word has. When you hear only one vowel sound in a word, it means the word has only one syllable. For example, the words *at, grease, throat, cheese, and spoke* are all one-syllable words because they have only one vowel sound. Silent vowels don't count. An example of a two-syllable word is *roadside*. Since we hear the long sounds of **o**, and **i**, *roadside* is a two-syllable word.

Do you remember the four parts of the First Rule of Syllabication? Write them here.

1. _____
2. _____
3. _____
4. _____

Read the following words and answer the questions. Listen closely to the vowel sounds.

	How many vowels can you see?	How many vowels can you hear?	How many syllables are in the word?
1. raise			
2. sweepstakes			
3. increase			
4. soapsuds			
5. trailblazer			
6. squeeze			
7. spray			
8. railroad			
9. disagreement			
10. appraise			
11. keepsake			
12. cheeseburger			
13. misconstrue			
14. undefeated			

10 Syllabication of Words with Five Syllables

Review the Rules of Syllabication in your Decoding Binder. Then highlight the vowels in the words below. Write the words in syllables, separated with dashes. Finally, mark the vowels and denote the code. Watch out for false vowel pairs! Read the words!

1. goalkeeper _____
2. reelection _____
3. freeloader _____
4. coastline _____
5. incongruent _____
6. maintenance _____
7. unprotected _____
8. encroachment _____
9. streamline _____
10. unexplained _____

Make a sentence out of these words: great, patterns, makes, word, mastering, reader
Watch for the syllable clues: (s=suffix)

_____   _____   _____
   cl-rc-s   rc   cl-rc

_____ you a _____   _____.
   vce-s   vv   vv-rc

Make another sentence out of these words:

praised Bay Raiders defeat Buccaneers team his Oakland after coach
The plural **s** is a suffix.

The _____ of the _____   _____
        vv   vv-cl   vv-s-s

_____   _____   _____   _____
   vv-s   cl   vv   cl-rc

the _____ of the Tampa _____   _____.
      pref-vv   vv   cl-op-vv-s

155

11 Challenging Polysyllabic Words

Read the words in the box and use them to solve the crossword puzzle:

blueberry	leadership	skirmish	committee	
scribbler	arboretum	constrain	squeegee	toasty
arcade	squeamish	career	strengthen	

Read the clues carefully:

Across:
1. Pleasantly warm
2. Afraid of germs and blood
3. A short fight or battle
4. A small kind of berry
5. To make strong
6. An area that displays different types of trees
7. A person's chosen work

Down:
1. A person who writes or draws carelessly
2. An amusement center with shops and video games
3. To hold back, to restrict
4. A group of people who meet to solve problems
5. A person's ability to get other people to follow him or her
6. Used for washing windows

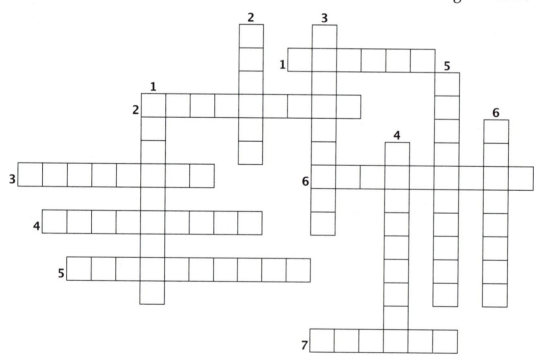

Read all the words one more time!

12a More Challenging Words

Highlight the vowels in the words below. Write the words in syllables, separated by dashes. Next, mark the vowels and denote the codes. (Beware of false vowel teams.)

1. creation _____
2. seamstress _____
3. betrayal _____
4. avenue _____
5. acquaintance _____
6. volunteer _____
7. endeavor _____
8. feature _____
9. pioneer _____
10. disappearance _____
11. misdemeanor _____
12. discontinue _____

Draw lines between the first set of syllables and the second set to make new words. Write them on the lines below.

		⇨ 1. _____
		⇨ 2. _____
main	load	⇨ 3. _____
de		⇨ 4. _____
up	tain	⇨ 5. _____
over		⇨ 6. _____
con	crease	⇨ 7. _____
un		⇨ 8. _____
enter	stream	⇨ 9. _____
		⇨ 10. _____

12b Dictation Exercise (Teacher Page)

Provide the code orally and write it on the board or on the overhead. Then dictate each word. Students write the word in syllables, separate the syllables with dashes, and mark the vowels.

Usually the vowel combinations in vowel-vowel syllables are **ai, ay, ea, ee, ey, ie, oa, oe, ue,** and **ui**. Encourage students to think of the base word first. If they don't know it, and if they ask for the silent vowel, supply it without hesitation.

For the purposes of this exercise, tell students to use **ey** when they hear long **e** at the end of a word. This exercise will not use **ie**. Since **ea** and **ee** sound the same, accept either one, but point out the correct spelling.

Remind students that **–er** often occurs at the end of words as a suffix. Students mark r-controlled vowels by circling the vowel + the **r**. On this answer key, they are shown in red.

Code abbreviations: cl=closed   vv=vowel-vowel
                      vce=vowel-consonant-e   pref=prefix
                      op=open   s=suffix
                      rc=r-controlled

1. (pref-vv)   ex-plāin
2. (pref-vv)   re-pēat
3. (cl-vv)   hŏck-ēy
4. (op-vv)   bē-mōan
5. (vv-vce)   swēep-stāke
6. (cl-vv)   rĕs-cūe
7. (cl-rc-vv)   ŭn-der-nēath
8. (vv-vv-rc) or (vv-vv-s)   chēer-lēad-er
9. (vv-vce)   wāist-līne
10. (cl-vv)   kĭd-nēy
11. (vv-vv)   rāin-gēar
12. (pref-vv)   re-prōach
13. (vv-vv)   frēe-wāy
14. (pref-vv-s)   re-tāin-er
15. (pref-cl-vv)   con-tĭn-ūe

Ask students to read the words. Please follow the procedure recommended in **Note to Instructor** in Chapter 1, Lesson 3b.

13 The Suffix –ize

A common suffix that you may already know is **–ize**. It follows the vowel-consonant-e rule and says īzé. It means to become or to resemble.

Read these words and write the base word on the lines:

1. itemize _____
2. customize _____
3. tenderize _____
4. modernize _____
5. winterize _____
6. motorize _____
7. symbolize _____
8. realize _____
9. finalize _____
10. organize _____
11. civilize _____
12. humanize _____

When a base word ends with **y**, drop the **y** before adding **–ize**. Add **–ize** to these words.

1. memory _____
2. harmony _____
3. agony _____
4. sympathy _____
5. summary _____
6. fantasy _____
7. economy _____
8. colony _____

Do you remember the rules for hard and soft **c** and **g**? The letter **c** says **s**, and the letter **g** says **j** when followed by **e, i,** and **y**. Underline the words below that you can read.

1. energy   2. energize   3. apology   4. apologize

Read these words. What happens when you add **–ize** to words that end with hard **c**? Underline the words you can read.

1. critic   2. criticize   3. public   4. publicize   5. italic   6. italicize

Another common suffix that you studied in Chapter 4 is **–al**, pronounced əl. It means *relating to*. This suffix often appears before **–ize**. Add **–al** and **–ize** to these base words.

1. form + al + ize = _____
2. verb + al + ize = _____
3. norm + al + ize = _____
4. person + al + ize = _____

Add **–ize** to these words.

5. capital + ize = _____
6. central + ize = _____
7. legal + ize = _____
8. local + ize = _____

14 Suffixes –ee and –ive

The suffix **–ee** follows the vowel-vowel rule and says the long **e** sound. Read words 1-12 and try to figure out what the suffix **–ee** means. Write the base word on the lines.

Some of these base words end in silent **e**. The **e** was dropped to add the suffix **–ee**. You will have to add an **e** to the base words that are **vce** syllables; * means tricky.

1. absentee _____
2. honoree _____
3. escapee _____
4. enlistee _____
5. detainee _____
6. refugee _____
7. evacuee* _____
8. nominee* _____
9. trustee _____
10. trainee _____
11. retiree _____
12. referee _____

What does the suffix **ee** mean? _____

A very common suffix is **–ive**. It is pronounced ĭv. It is derived from Latin and means *doing a certain action* or *like a certain action (act, active, attract, attractive)*. Sometimes **–ive** is not a suffix. Instead, it is part of a word with a vowel-consonant-e pattern. These words tend to be shorter.

Read each of these words. Listen to the sound of **–ive** and write ĭv or īve on the lines:

1. secretive _____
2. elective _____
3. arrive _____
4. assertive _____
5. alive _____
6. strive _____
7. detective _____
8. inventive _____
9. cursive _____
10. defective _____
11. survive _____
12. executive _____

The last letter of the base word may change when **–ive** is added. Read these words and write the base words on the lines. Remember to add silent **e** to base words that are **vce** syllables.

1. inclusive _____
2. explosive _____
3. exclusive _____
4. offensive _____
5. decisive _____
6. divisive _____
7. defensive _____
8. evasive _____
9. expensive _____
10. intensive _____
11. intrusive _____
12. corrosive _____

What is the last sound of the base word? _____

Read all of the words one more time!

CHAPTER 6
Consonant-le Syllable

Note to Instructor

Lesson 1 introduces the consonant-le syllable. This syllable is comprised of a consonant and the letters **le**. The abbreviation for a consonant-le syllable is **cle**. Copy this page as an overhead transparency. It may be necessary to use the transparency several times before students retain the characteristics of a consonant-le syllable.

Ask students to answer the question, "What do these words have in common? trample, riddle, settle, nozzle, struggle, able, idle, eagle, noble, and bugle." Record the correct responses on the overhead or on the board in any order. Direct your students to take notes in the Rules section of their Decoding Binders. Correct responses are:

1. All of these words end with the letters **le**.
2. The letter **e** in the consonant-le syllable is silent.
3. There is at least one consonant before the **le** ending.
4. The consonant-le syllable usually occurs at the end of words.

Explain that the consonant-le syllable is divided right before the consonant that precedes **le**. If this is confusing to students, tell them to count back three letters from the end of the word and divide there.

Reminders:
1. **Have students reread all the words in every lesson once they have completed the exercises.**
2. Ask students to copy each new phonogram, red word, homophone, homograph, prefix, suffix, and rule in the appropriate sections of their Decoding Binders. Include homographs, marked **HG**, in the Homophone Section. When entering a phonogram, prefix, or suffix, students must list four key words that illustrate it. Students must also add four words for every rule and definitions for the homophones and homographs.
3. Review all sections of the binder **once a week** for a minimum of five weeks. Younger children or the severely learning disabled may need more time for review.
4. Use the **Proposed Spelling Activities**, located in the Appendix, for all **Reading and Spelling for Mastery** lists. Students must read the list daily before they start the two practice activities.

Lesson 2 reviews the Ninth Rule of Syllabication introduced in Lesson 1, "Divide words with the consonant-le syllable before the consonant that precedes **le** (pud-dle, puz-zle, sim-ple)." The next exercise requires students to add word starters to consonant-le syllables. There is a short story on the lower half of this worksheet. Ask everyone to highlight or underline the twenty-one words that end with consonant-le syllables.

Lesson 3 provides decoding practice for words with consonant-le syllables and teaches the following rules:

1. When the first vowel is short, the word must have two consonants between the first vowel and the **le** ending (can-dle). This pattern creates a closed syllable in the beginning of the word. In words that have only one consonant sound between the short vowel and the **le** ending, double the consonant (bub-ble). Mark the first vowel short and cross out the silent e: căn-dle̸, bŭb-ble̸.

2. When the first vowel is long, the word has only one consonant between the first vowel and **le** (fa-ble). This pattern creates an open syllable in the beginning of the word. Mark the first vowel long and cross out the silent e: fā-ble̸.

Lesson 4 alerts students to the special rules associated with words that end in **ckle**. Please remind students that **ck** is a short vowel signal; it shows that the vowel before it is short. In words that have a **k** sound right after the short vowel, the letter **k** is not doubled. Teach students to use **ck** instead (pickle, tackle). Additionally, the rule for dividing words with the **ckle** ending is different than the rule for other consonant-le syllables. The letters **ck** stay together as part of the first syllable (pick-le, tack-le). Therefore, the code is **cl-le**.

Lesson 5 consists of a **Dictation** list and two **Reading and Spelling for Mastery** lists (Lesson 8 is also included.) Please select two appropriate activities from **Proposed Spelling Activities**, in the Appendix. Require students to read the list every day before they start their spelling practice.

Lesson 6a introduces words that have two different consonants between the short vowel and the consonant-le syllable *(sim-ple, han-dle)*. In such words, the medial consonants are not doubled. The second exercise asks students to select words to answer riddles.

Lesson 6b is a dictation exercise. This page is for teacher use only. It requires students to remember the rules that deal with consonant-le syllables. After you have dictated the list and corrected it, write these words on the board: bundle, bungle, trample, struggle, trickle, startle, chuckle, swindle, and rekindle. Ask students what changes are needed to add past tense **–ed** to these words (drop the **e**). Next, have students rewrite the words by adding **–ed**.

Lesson 7 provides two activities for integrated practice with more challenging words. Please remind students to use a pencil to complete the crossword puzzle.

Lesson 8 (on the same page as **Lesson 5**) is a **Reading and Spelling for Mastery** list. Review the *drop-e* rule for # 1, 7, and 9. Please select two appropriate activities from **Proposed Spelling Activities** in the Appendix and require students to read the list before they start their daily spelling practice.

Lesson 9 deals with Latin derivatives that end with the letters **cle**. Because these are difficult words, students should consult a dictionary and use the pronunciation guide.

Lesson 10 covers the two common suffixes **–ible** and **–able**. Spelling rules that explain when to use each of these suffixes are included in chapter 12.

1 Consonant-le Syllable

What do these words have in common?

| trample | riddle | settle | nozzle | struggle |
| able | idle | eagle | noble | bugle |

1. _____
2. _____
3. _____
4. _____

This type of syllable is called *consonant-le*. The abbreviation is *cle*. What do the letters *cle* stand for?

Fold back this bottom section, or place a sheet of paper over it. _ _ _ _ _ _ _ _ _ _ _ _ _ _ _ _ _

NOTE TO INSTRUCTOR: Please copy this page as an overhead transparency to introduce **consonant-le** syllables. Record the following correct responses on the overhead in any order.
   1. All of the words end with the letters **le**.
   2. There is at least one consonant before the **le** ending.
   3. The consonant-le syllable usually occurs at the end of polysyllabic words.
   4. The letter **e** in the consonant-le syllable is silent. Therefore, cross it out.

This kind of syllable is called **consonant-le** because it consists of a consonant and the letters **le**.

2 Ninth Rule of Syllabication

The **consonant-le** syllable usually occurs at the end of a word *(puddle, marble, simple,* and *settle).*

Ninth Rule of Syllabication	Divide words with the consonant-le syllable before the consonant that precedes **le** (pud-dle, puz-zle, sim-ple).

An easier way to think of this is to count back three letters from the end of the word and divide there. The letter **e** is silent.

Write these word starters in front of the **dle** ending: **sad, cud, bun, grid**. Read the new words.

1. _____dle   2. _____dle   3. _____dle   4. _____dle

Write **tat, ket, tur,** and **star** in front of the **tle** ending. Read the new words.

5. _____tle   6. _____tle   7. _____tle   8. _____tle

Write **rip, sam, dim, tem** in front of the **ple** ending. Read the new words.

9. _____ple   10. _____ple   11. _____ple   12. _____ple

Read the story first. Then go back over it and highlight all of the words that end with consonant-le syllables. Many words that end with this syllable are followed by suffixes *(tickled, bubbles).*

Drama in the Backyard

This morning, I saw two baby robins huddled behind the maple tree. After leaving their nest a couple of days ago, they were learning to pick for seeds in the grass. Just like all little robins, their breasts were speckled and flying was still a big struggle. The adult robins tirelessly searched for worms and other nibbles, which the babies gobbled up eagerly. When the parents approached the chicks, they jostled and squabbled to be the first in the feeding line. Suddenly Snuggles, the cat from next door, appeared and startled the little robins! They trembled because they were afraid. Their parents were there in an instant, ready to do battle. Screeching loudly, both were flying and diving towards the cat. Clearly rattled, he retreated, backing into a puddle of water. Snuggles had no desire to tangle with the fearless birds and decided to forego this scuffle for another time. For now, the enemy was scuttled and all was well with the Robin Family. I chuckled as the wet cat slinked away.

3 Spelling Rules for Consonant-le Syllables

The consonant-le syllable usually occurs at the end of a word. When the preceding vowel is short, the word must have two consonants before **le** (tumble). In words that have only one consonant sound between the short vowel and the **le** ending, you must double the consonant (sizzle). Therefore, the first syllable is **closed** (sĭz-zle). When the preceding vowel is long, the word has one consonant before **le** (fable). Therefore, the first syllable is **open** (fā-ble). Divide words right before the consonant-le syllable (mid-dle, han-dle, a-ble).

Write the following words in syllables, separated by dashes. Mark the vowels and cross out the silent **e**. Then denote the code. The code for a consonant-le syllable is **cle**. Read the words at your teacher's direction.

1. shuttle _____
2. cuddle _____
3. stable _____
4. apple _____
5. bugle _____
6. hobble _____
7. rifle _____
8. topple _____
9. middle _____
10. cradle _____

Draw a line from each word starter to the correct word ending:

1. se — tle / ttle
2. ri — dle / ddle
3. gi — gle / ggle
4. pu — zle / zzle
5. bri — dle / ddle
6. ma — ple / pple
7. ca — tle / ttle
8. smu — gle / ggle
9. pe — ble / bble
10. bu — ble / bble
11. ti — tle / ttle
12. bo — tle / ttle

4 Short-Vowel Signal

Do you remember the short vowel signal **ck**? It shows that the vowel directly before it is short. This same rule also applies to consonant-le words. When you hear the **k** sound in the first syllable and **k** comes right after a short vowel, do NOT double it, write **ck** instead (*pickle, tackle*).

Write **ck** or **k** in the blanks to make real words. Remember to use **ck** only when the **k** sound comes right after the short vowel.

1. pi____le
2. cra____le
3. twin____le
4. tri____le
5. ti____le
6. chu____le
7. bu____le
8. sprin____le
9. spar____le
10. knu____les
11. wrin____le
12. spe____le

The dictionary does not follow the same rules for dividing words with the **ckle** ending as with other consonant-le syllables. It keeps the letters **ck** together and puts both letters in the first syllable (pick-le, tack-le). The code for the last syllable is **le**. The code for *pickle* and *tackle* is **cl-le**.

Highlight the vowels and use a red pencil to divide the words. Then write them according to the rule you just learned. Denote the code. If the first syllable ends with **ck**, the code for the second syllable is **le**.

1. hackle   _____
2. freckle _____
3. tackle   _____
4. buckle   _____
5. shackle _____

Draw lines from the syllables on the left to the syllables on the right to create new words and write them on the lines. Then read all of the words on this page.

knuckle	suckle	1. _____
un	shuffle	2. _____
honey	buckle	3. _____
dis	bones	4. _____
re	mantle	5. _____

5/8 Reading and Spelling for Mastery

Words that end with the **cle** syllable:
Note: Use **el** after the letter **v**.

Dictation List	5 Spelling List	8 Spelling List
1. saddle	1. middle	1. handled
2. bottle	2. meddle (H)	2. candle
3. maple	3. settle	3. simple
4. brittle	4. little	4. sample
5. cradle	5. battle	5. example
6. scribble	6. cattle	6. uncle*
7. buckle	7. shuttle	7. sprinkled
8. tackle	8. apple	8. ankle
9. chuckle	9. smuggle	9. sparkled
10. bugle	10. struggle	10. castle*
11. riddle	11. double*	11. whistle*
12. staple	12. trouble*	12. single
13. grapple	13. couple*	13. angle
14. noble	14. triple*	14. pickle
15. ladle	15. able	15. cycle*
16. giggle	16. cable	16. people*
17. stifle	17. table	17. idle
18. kettle	18. stable	18. level*
19. fable	19. title	19. travel*
20. puzzle	20. rifle	20. label*

*Red word, H=homophones

6a Syllabication

Write the words in syllables, separated by dashes. Mark the first vowel in each word and cross out the silent **e**. Then denote the code. Do not double the consonant in words that have two different consonant sounds. When **st** is part of the consonant-le syllable, the letter **t** is silent as in the words *castle* and *whistle*. Syllable division: *cas-tle, whis-tle*.

1. gurgle _____
2. nestle _____
3. rekindle _____
4. unable _____
5. crumble _____
6. thistle _____
7. ladle _____
8. jungle _____
9. wrestle _____
10. example _____

Find two words that answer each riddle. Most of them rhyme (5, 6, 7, and 9 do not).

> tackle   trouble   snuggle   sparkle   stumble   giggle   candle   huddle   grumble
> jingle   cuddle   fumble   handle   mumble   single   double   twinkle   chuckle

1. Your mom is angry, you are in _____ _____
2. A clumsy person might _____ and _____
3. To hold a light _____ a _____
4. One song is a _____ _____
5. Football players do this _____ and _____
6. Ways of laughing _____ and _____
7. What stars do _____ and _____
8. Ways of talking _____ and _____
9. A baby likes to _____ and _____

6b Dictation Exercise (Teacher Page)

Provide the code orally and write it on the board or on the overhead. Then dictate each word. Ask students to write the word in syllables, separate the syllables with dashes, and mark the vowels.

Remind students of these rules:
- Double the consonant in words that have one consonant sound between a short vowel and the **cle** syllable.
- Do not double the consonant in words that have two consonant sounds between the vowel and the **cle** syllable.
- Do not double the consonant in words that have a long vowel in the first syllable.

Code abbreviations: cl=closed
op=open
cle=consonant-le

After you have completed this exercise, please do the follow-up lesson listed in **Note to Instructor 6b**.

1. (cl-cle)   fĭz-zle
2. (cl-cle)   scrăm-ble
3. (cl-cle)   bŭn-gle
4. (rc-cle)   tur-tle   (Accept er and ir, but point out the correct spelling.)
5. (cl-cle)   grăp-ple
6. (op-cle)   ī-dle
7. (cl-cle)   strŭg-gle
8. (cl-cle)   quĭb-ble
9. (op-cle)   sī-dle
10. (rc-cle) star-tle
11. (cl-cle) thrŏt-tle
12. (cl-cle) swĭn-dle
13. (op-cle) gā-ble
14. (pref-cl-cle) re-kĭn-dle
15. (pref-cl-cle) ex-ăm-ple

Ask students to read the words. Please follow the procedures recommended in the **Note to Instructor** Chapter 1, 3b.

7 Challenge Words

Write the words in syllables, separated by dashes. Mark the vowels and denote the code. Read the words at your teacher's direction.

1. stranglehold _____
2. bumblebee _____
3. settlement _____
4. entangle _____
5. mishandle _____
6. tablecloth _____
7. embezzle _____
8. candleholder _____
9. middleman _____
10. encircle _____

Word Bank
steeple   pickles
atmosphere   rustle
cockroach   reporter
correspond   drizzle
comprehend
wrestler

Across
1. cl-cle, a soft sound
2. pref-pref-cl, understand
3. pref-pref-cl, write
4. cl-vv
5. cl-cle-s, tries to pin you down

Down
1. cl-cle, a sour food
2. pref-rc-rc,
3. cl-cl-vce,
4. vv-cle, on a roof
5. cl-cle, rain

9 Latin Roots and Consonant-le Syllables

Let's practice some consonant-le words that came to us from Latin. Usually the vowel before the **cle** syllable is unaccented, which means that it is pronounced like a schwa sound (ə) or short **u**. These words do not follow the rules you learned earlier.

With the help of a dictionary, use the following words in the sentences below:

> article   vehicle   obstacle   cubicles   particles   barnacles
> clavicle   miracle   spectacle   cuticles   tentacles   pinnacle

1. It was a _____ that he survived the shipwreck.
2. _____ is another name for collar bone.
3. Have you read the _____ about the world's fastest runner in Sports Illustrated?
4. The first team to complete the _____ course will win the race.
5. Smog is the result of tiny, polluting _____ in the air.
6. Since my car has 140,000 miles on it, I've decided I need a new _____.
7. It is very time-consuming to remove _____ from the hulls of ships.
8. Most large offices are divided into _____.
9. The _____ are pushed back when you have a manicure.
10. An octopus has eight _____.
11. During halftime at the Super Bowl, the cheerleaders put on a fabulous _____.
12. We climbed to the topmost _____ of the mountain.

Find three words from the box that have a long vowel in the first syllable and copy them:
_____

Find five words from the box that have a short vowel in the first syllable and copy them:
_____

Go back over the last six words. Highlight the accented syllables. What do the vowels in the unaccented syllables say? _____

10 The Suffixes –able and –ible

The suffixes **–able** and **–ible** both say **əble.** You probably remember that the symbol ə is called a schwa sound and says short **u**. These two suffixes usually turn verbs and sometimes nouns into adjectives. Adjectives are words that describe nouns.

Turn the following verbs/nouns into adjectives by adding –able and –ible. Remember to drop the silent **e** before you add a suffix that starts with a vowel. Sometimes you must drop two letters to make a real word. Write the new words on the lines.

1. pay + able = _____
2. wash + able = _____
3. distract + ible = _____
4. tax + able = _____
5. sense + ible = _____
6. size + able = _____
7. use + able = _____
8. convert + ible = _____
9. adore + able = _____
10. advise + able = _____
11. terror + ible = _____
12. horror + ible = _____

Look up the words **sizable** and **usable** in the dictionary. Copy the other acceptable way to spell these words: _____

In everyday conversation, the suffix **–able** is used more often than the suffix **–ible**. Draw lines from the prefixes to the base words. Next, draw another line from the new two-syllable words to the suffix **–able** to create adjectives. Then write them on the lines. Use **re** twice.

dis	fund		1. _____
re	vent		2. _____
de	mark	–able	3. _____
pre	fort		4. _____
com	pose		5. _____
	pend		6. _____

CHAPTER 7
Diphthong/Vowel Digraph Syllables

Note to Instructor:

This chapter introduces **diphthong/vowel digraph** syllables. Linguistically speaking, a **diphthong** is defined as "a complex speech sound or glide that begins with one vowel and gradually changes to another vowel within the same syllable" (from the *American Heritage Dictionary*). The vowel pairs **oi**, **oy**, **ou**, and **ow** are diphthongs. **Vowel digraphs** are vowel combinations that make a single sound. The most common vowel digraphs are **au**, **aw**, **oo**, **ew**, **ie** (as in *brief*), and **ei**. Diphthongs and vowel-digraphs can't be sounded out and must be memorized. Therefore, they are not marked. The abbreviation for both is **d.** Teach students to keep the two vowels in the same syllable; do not syllabicate between them.

Diphthongs and vowel digraphs may easily be confused with vowel-vowel syllables because all of them are vowel pairs. Vowel-vowel syllables differ from diphthong and digraph syllables in that they follow a predictable sounding rule, whereas diphthongs and digraphs use vowel combinations that do not form clear sound/symbol relationships. Some examples are *brief*, *aunt*, or *new*. This program finds the distinction useful. (Many phonics books classify *vowel-vowel* syllables as digraphs.) Most words with diphthongs and digraphs are derived from French, Anglo Saxon, Middle English, German, and Greek. Therefore, we're coping with phonemic rules from five different languages! Because they are the most difficult phonemes and graphemes to master, they are presented individually.

A great deal of practice is needed to master diphthongs and digraphs. There are seven **Reading and Spelling for Mastery** lists in this unit. Since you might not want to spend seven weeks on this chapter, you might need to tailor these spelling lessons to your students' needs. To reduce the number of spelling words, consider using these lists as pretests, so your more capable students are not practicing words they already know. By pre-testing, you can create individualized lists. You could even pair up students and let them test each other. Other possibilities are to divide the class into groups, or to postpone using the more difficult lists until later in the chapter. Even though each student may not cover every spelling lesson, everyone should practice pronouncing all of the lists because students learn the phonemically irregular words (sight words) from the spelling units.

Reminders:
1. **Have students reread all the words in every lesson once they have completed the exercises.**
2. Ask students to copy each new phonogram, red word, homophone, homograph, prefix, suffix, and rule in the appropriate sections of their Decoding Binders. Include homographs, marked **HG**, in the Homophone Section. When entering a phonogram, prefix, or suffix, students must

list four key words that illustrate it. Students must also add four words for every rule and definitions for the homophones and homographs.
3. Review all sections of the binder **once a week** for a minimum of five weeks. Younger children or the severely learning disabled may need more time for review.
4. Use the **Proposed Spelling Activities**, located in the Appendix, for all **Reading and Spelling for Mastery** lists. Students must read the list daily before they start the two practice activities.

Lesson 1a (two pages) introduces the diphthongs **oi** and **oy**. After reading a list of words with **oi** and **oy**, students are asked to deduce the following rule: use **oi** in the beginning or middle of words (*oil, point*); use **oy** at the end of a word or at the end of a syllable: (*boy, loy-al*). On the next page, students read a list of words and use them in sentences.

Lesson 1b is a **Reading and Spelling for Mastery** page with the diphthongs **oi** and **oy**. Please select appropriate spelling activities and require students to read the list before they start the daily spelling practice. To foster retention, select one word from each list and ask students to draw an illustration of it. This will become the picture prompt for that diphthong or digraph. Follow this procedure for all of the lists. For the third spelling activity, please add the category **diphthongs/digraphs** or **d**. All words with diphthongs or vowel digraphs in the first syllable should be written under this new category.

Lesson 2a covers the difficult diphthongs **ou** and **ow** (*out, found, mouth, owl, now, brown*). The letter **w** is considered a vowel in diphthongs and vowel digraphs. Sometimes **ow** also has a long **o** sound, which will be discussed later. English has two fairly strong rules that help us decide whether **ou** or **ow** is the correct spelling in a word.
Rule 1: **ou** is used in the beginning or middle of words, whereas **ow** is used at the end of a word or a syllable (*our, proud, how, powder*).
Rule 2: **ow** is used in the middle of words when followed by a single **l** or **n**, or **er** and **el** (*owl, frown, power, towel*). The words *crowd* and *foul* are exceptions. *Foul*, as in foul ball and *fowl*, as in poultry are homophones.

Lesson 2b discusses three alternate sounds of the diphthong **ou**. This is clearly the most difficult and confusing vowel combination in our language! As previously mentioned, the most common sound of **ou** is the one you hear in *out, found*, and *proud*. When **ou** is followed by the silent letters **gh** (*ought, thought*), it says **ô**. To make matters more confusing, **ou** may also sound like a **short u** (*double, couple*). In this lesson, students are asked to read a list of words and write them under the appropriate sound category. Please provide lots of help, because this is a very tricky exercise. Since most of these categories (aside from **ou** as in out) have less than ten common words, it's best to memorize them by phoneme patterns. The reason this grapheme is so difficult is that French and Anglo-Saxon derivatives represent different sounds with the **ou** spelling.

Lesson 2c introduces four more **ou** sounds. Sometimes **ou** is pronounced like the vowel sound you hear in *group*. The dictionary represents this phoneme as $\overline{oo}$. When **ou** is followed by the letter **r**, it may sound like the r-controlled syllables **ur** (*journal*) and **or** (*court*). In a few words, **ou** says **long o** (*dough, shoulder*).

Lesson 2d consists of two **Reading and Spelling for Mastery** lists and categorizes words according to the various **ou** sounds. Follow the same procedure outlined in **Lesson 1b**.

Lesson 3a covers words with **ow** pronounced as long **o** (*throw, yellow*). It also covers this spelling rule: double the medial consonant in words that have a short vowel, followed by one consonant sound and the diphthong **ow**. This rule does not apply to the letter **d** in the medial position (*widow*).

Lesson 3b consists of two **Reading and Spelling for Mastery** lists with **ou** words. Follow the procedure outlined in **Lesson 1b**.

Lesson 4a introduces the vowel digraphs **au** and **aw**. A **vowel digraph** is a vowel pair that makes a single sound. Unlike vowel-vowel syllables, digraphs don't follow a clear sounding rule and, therefore, must be memorized. The abbreviation for the vowel digraph syllable is **d**. The vowel digraphs **au** and **aw** both say ô *(cause, draw)*. This sound has already been introduced in the previous lesson *(ought)*. Most words with the digraph **au** are French derivatives. In this lesson, students read and study the vowel patterns in a list of words with **au** and **aw** and deduce two spelling rules that are almost identical to the rules for **ou** and **ow**.

Rule 1: **au** is used in the beginning or the middle of words, whereas **aw** is used at the end of a word or a syllable *(haunt, saw, drawer)*. There are a few exceptions: awe, awesome, awful.

Rule 2: **aw** occurs in the middle of words when it is followed by a single **n, l,** or **k** *(crawl, fawn, gawk)*. This rule also applies when suffixes are added to these words *(crawler, gawking)*.

Lesson 4b is a **Reading and Spelling for Mastery** list with **au** and **aw** words. Follow the procedure outlined in **Lesson 1b**.

Lesson 5 is a review of the diphthongs **oi, oy, ou, ow** and the digraphs **au** and **aw**.

Lesson 6a teaches the two sounds of the digraph **oo**. The more common sound is the one you hear in *moon*, o͞o. The second sound is the one you hear in *took*, o͝o. Mnemonic device: Look at the moon.

Lesson 6b is a **Reading and Spelling for Mastery** list with the digraph **oo**. Follow the procedure outlined in **Lesson 1b**.

Lesson 7a covers four more difficult spelling patterns for the o͞o sound. The first is **ew** as in *new, crew* and *flew* (**ew** says **long u** in *few* and *pew*). Students are presented with a list of words and asked to deduce this sounding rule: Use **ew** when the o͞o sound is at the end of a word. Use **oo** in the beginning or middle of words. As always, there are just a few exceptions. The most common ones are *zoo, too, shoo, coo, woo, bamboo, igloo, shampoo,* and *kangaroo*. The second spelling pattern is less common: **eu** says long **u** *(Europe, eulogy, eulogize, euphony)*. The prefix **eu** is Greek and means **good**. The **eu** spelling also occurs in the middle of a few French derivatives and says o͞o or long **u**. The last exercise reviews the vowel-vowel syllables **ue** and **ui**. They also say o͞o, *true, blue, fruit* and *pursuit*.

Lesson 7b is a **Reading and Spelling for Mastery** list with the vowel digraphs **ew** as in *new*, **oo** as in *zoo*, **ui** as in *suit*, and **ue** as in *blue*. (**Lesson 9c** is also listed on this page.) Please follow the procedures outlined in **Lesson 1b**.

Lesson 8 is a diphthong and vowel digraph review.

Lesson 9a and **Lesson 9b** deal with the thorny digraphs **ei** and **ie**. The digraph **ei** has two pronunciations. They are **long e** *(seize, receive)* and **long a** *(rein, weight)*. The digraph **ie** usually says **long e**. This rule may be helpful: i before e, except after c, or when it sounds like ā in neighbor or weigh. It has several exceptions *(either, neither, weird, seize* and *leisure)*. This is already a very confusing lesson. Use your discretion as to whether students can deal with these added complexities:

Ei and **ie** represent several other sounds as in these seven words:

1. **eigh** says **long i** *(height, sleight)*
2. **ei** says **short i** *(forfeit, counterfeit)*
3. **ei** says the **schwa sound** *(foreign, sovereign)*
4. **ie** says **short e** *(friend)*

Lesson 9c (on the same page as **Lesson 7b**) is a **Reading and Spelling for Mastery** page with **ei** and **ie** words. Please follow the procedure outlined in **Lesson 1b.**

Lesson 10 provides a review of all diphthongs and vowel digraphs.

Lesson 11 is a true story. Before students read the story, write these words on the board and ask everyone to read them: enormous, dangerous, hazardous, and gorgeous. Point out that **ous** is a suffix and ask your class what it says. It is pronounced ŭs or əs. Have students record this suffix in their Decoding Binders.

1a Diphthongs *oi* and *oy*

The <u>American Heritage Dictionary</u> defines **diphthongs** as glides that begin with one vowel sound and gradually change to another vowel sound within the same syllable. The abbreviation for diphthongs is **d**. The first two diphthongs you will study are **oi** and **oy** (*oil* and *boy*). You will notice that they have the same sound.

English has an easy rule to help us decide whether **oi** or **oy** is the correct spelling in a word. Let's see if you can discover this rule. Read the following words. Highlight the words with **oi**; underline the ones with **oy**.

1. oil	4. voice	7. joist	10. ointment	13. joy
2. convoy	5. cowboy	8. ploy	11. corduroy	14. rejoin
3. poise	6. point	9. soy	12. moist	15. foil

What is the rule? _____

_____

Write **oi** and **oy** in the blanks to make real words:

1. c___l
2. c___
3. sp___l
4. t___
5. c___n
6. v___d
7. overj___
8. h___st

Use the clues to help you unscramble these words.

pomely   _ _ _ _ _ _
1. It starts with a vowel.
2. It ends with a diphthong.
3. The second letter is **m**.

nisoop   _ _ _ _ _ _
1. The diphthong is in the first syllable.
2. It starts with the letter **p** and ends with **n**.
3. It could make you sick.

pantompinet   _ _ _ _ _ _ t _ _ _ _
1. It starts with the letter **a** and ends with with the letter **t**.
2. The letter **p** is doubled.
3. The base word has a diphthong and means *sharp end* or *dot*.

1a continued

Read the words in the box and use them to complete the sentences below:

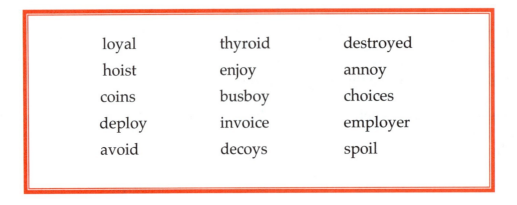

1. The _____ cleared the dirty dishes from our table.
2. You can _____ the heavy traffic if you stay away from Main Street.
3. The _____ is a gland that regulates the growth of one's body.
4. The army will _____ troops overseas.
5. In January, we received an _____ for the toys we ordered.
6. Tom uses wooden _____ when he goes duck hunting.
7. Have fun and _____ your vacation.
8. The _____ gave all of the _____ workers a big bonus.
9. The _____ you make as a teenager will affect the rest of your life.
10. Please put the milk in the refrigerator, otherwise it will _____.
11. Alex has an interesting collection of rare and valuable _____.
12. His bad habits _____ me.
13. The mechanic raised the car with a _____.
14. The earthquake _____ several small villages.

Read all of the words one more time!

1b Reading and Spelling for Mastery

Words with the diphthongs **oi** and **oy**:

Dictation

1. coil
2. foil
3. boy
4. hoist
5. joist
6. ploy
7. avoid
8. broil
9. convoy
10. toy
11. toys
12. toil
13. boys
14. coy
15. soy
16. void
17. decoy
18. broiler
19. envoy
20. deploy

Spelling

1. oil
2. coin
3. boil
4. spoil
5. moist
6. join
7. point
8. appointment*
9. poison
10. noise
11. voice
12. choice
13. joy
14. enjoying
15. employ
16. annoy
17. annoying
18. destroy
19. loyal*
20. voyage*

*Red words, Use **oi** in the beginning or in the middle of a word; use **oy** at the end of a base word or a syllable.

179

2a Diphthongs *ou* and *ow*

The diphthongs **ou** and **ow** usually have the same sound and say **ou** as in *out* and **ow** as in *now*. The letter **w** is considered a vowel in diphthongs. English has two fairly strong rules that help us decide whether **ou** or **ow** is the correct spelling in a word.

Read the following words and highlight the diphthongs. Then study the different spelling patterns and try to figure out the first rule that tells us when to use **ou** and when to use **ow**.

1. ground	7. mouth	13. endow	19. vow
2. eyebrow	8. bounce	14. spouse	20. sound
3. thousand	9. Moscow	15. cow	21. pronounce
4. ounce	10. allow	16. pound	22. foundation
5. how	11. account	17. chow	23. powwow
6. plow	12. rebound	18. announce	24. shout

When do we use **ou**? _____

When do we use **ow**? _____

The second rule covers specific exceptions to the first rule. Sometimes **ow** occurs in the middle of words. Read words 1-24 and highlight the diphthongs. Study the different spelling pattern to discover the rule that tells us when to use **ow** in the middle of words.

1. clown	7. growl	13. shower	19. trowel
2. flower	8. towel	14. owl	20. fowl
3. howl	9. drown	15. cower	21. down
4. power	10. scowl	16. town	22. dowel
5. vowel	11. renown	17. prowl	23. gown
6. tower	12. crown	18. frown	24. brown

When do we use **ow** in the middle of words? _____
_____

2b Other Sounds of *ou*

The diphthong **ou** is clearly the most difficult vowel combination because it represents seven different sounds. Here are three of the seven phonograms.
1. Review: the most common sound is the one you hear in the words *out* and *found*.
2. The second sound occurs in words like *ought* and *bought*. The dictionary symbol for this diphthong is ô. Usually the silent letters **gh** follow the ô sound *(thought)*; however, the letters **gh** are not always silent. Sometimes they say **f** as in *cough*.
3. The diphthong **ou** can also say short **u** as in *double, enough, tough,* and *rough*.

Highlight the following words you can read and underline the diphthongs. Then write the words under the matching phonograms:

1. young
2. amount
3. bought
4. couch
5. thoughtful
6. rough
7. counter
8. enough
9. wrought
10. grouchy
11. touch
12. mountain
13. cousin
14. sought
15. sprout
16. country
17. brought
18. scout
19. trouble
20. fought
21. cough
22. announce
23. tough
24. trough (trôf)

ou as in out	ou=ô (ought)	ŭ

List five words from the above list that do **not** follow this sounding rule: **gh** is silent.

_____   _____   _____   _____   _____

181

2c Four More *ou* Sounds

Sometimes **ou** says the sound you hear in *cool*. The dictionary symbol for this phoneme is ōō. When the letter **r** follows **ou**, it may sound like the r-controlled vowels **ur** *(journal)* and **or** *(course)*.

Highlight the following words you can read and underline the diphthongs. Then write each word under the correct heading below.

1. fourth
2. group
3. journey
4. youth
5. nourish
6. through
7. course
8. courtesy
9. pour
10. souvenir
11. source
12. journal
13. concourse
14. soup
15. courage
16. cougar
17. adjourn
18. court
19. coupon
20. resource

ou = ōō	ou = ur	ou = or

We must cover one more pattern that occurs in only a few words:

though, although, dough, thoroughly, shoulder, boulder, poultry

What does **ou** say in these words? _____

Use the above words to fill in the blanks in these sentences.

1. Even _____ Jenny studied for hours, she didn't ace the math test.
2. You must knead the _____ before you bake it.
3. He hurt his _____ when he was rock climbing on the large _____.
4. Please wash your hands _____ after you handle raw _____.
5. _____ we worked very hard, we didn't get a raise.

2d Reading and Spelling for Mastery

The diphthong **ou** as in *out, group,* and *through*:

Spelling

1. our   (H)
2. hour (H)
3. ounce*
4. noun
5. house
6. loud
7. out
8. about
9. without
10. thousand
11. round
12. around
13. found
14. pound
15. count
16. account*
17. amount
18. group
19. youth
20. through* (H)

Irregular **ou** as in *ought, could, rough* and *though*:

Spelling

1. ought
2. bought
3. fought
4. brought
5. thought
6. cough*
7. could*
8. couldn't*
9. would* (H)
10. should*
11. touch
12. tough*
13. rough*
14. enough*
15. double
16. trouble
17. young
18. country*
19. though*
20. although*

*Red words, **H**=homophones

3a Diphthong *ow* (ō)

The diphthong **ow** represents the sound you hear in *cow*. It also makes a second sound. Say the following words slowly and carefully.

    1. snow   2. grow   3. flow   4. tow   5. yellow   6. pillow

What does **ow** say in these words? _____

You're correct if you noticed that **ow** can say long **o** when it is at the end of a word (*owe* and *own* are exceptions). There are more words with **ow** as **ō** than the sound you hear in *cow*.

Pronounce the following words. Draw a line to the sound that is made by **ow**. Use **ō** for the sound you hear in *snow* and **ow** for the sound you hear in *cow*.

show		stow		flow	
now		fellow		brow	
grow	**ow=ō**	plow	**ow=ō**	sparrow	**ow=ō**
know	**ow=owl**	swallow	**ow=owl**	mellow	**ow=owl**
vow		crow		throw	
shallow		allow		anyhow	

In most two-syllable words that end with **ow**, the consonant before **ow** is doubled. Use this rule only when a word has one consonant sound between the short vowel in the first syllable and the **ow** ending. There is one exception to this rule. Do not double the consonant **d**.

Use the letters in the parentheses to complete each of these words.

    1. ye____ow (l)   6. so____ow (r)   11. mea____ow (d)
    2. ma____ow (r)   7. wi____ow (d)   12. tomo____ow (r)
    3. bo____ow (r)   8. a____ow (r)   13. be____ow (l)
    4. sha____ow (d)   9. wa____ow (l)   14. bu____ow (r)
    5. ho____ow (l)   10. na____ow (r)   15. fo____ow (l)

Did you notice that number 13 is correct with one or two l's? Read these two words and write a sentence with each: **below**, **bellow**. _____

_____

3b Reading and Spelling for Mastery

Diphthong **ow** as in *down* and *snow*:

Spelling

1. cow
2. plow
3. flower (H)
4. tower
5. powder
6. vowel
7. towel
8. down
9. town
10. crown
11. brown
12. frown
13. crowd
14. row (H)
15. low
16. flow
17. mow
18. tow (H)
19. window
20. swallow

Spelling

1. how
2. now
3. allow
4. power
5. shower
6. drown
7. show
8. shown
9. blow
10. snow
11. throw
12. thrown (H)
13. grow
14. know* (H)
15. known*
16. borrow
17. follow
18. narrow
19. tomorrow*
20. below

*Red words, H=homophones

4a Vowel Digraphs *au* and *aw*

Vowel digraphs are vowel pairs that make a single sound. They don't follow a clear sounding rule as do vowel-vowel syllables, so you must memorize them. The abbreviation for the vowel digraph syllable is **d**.

The vowel digraphs **au** and **aw** represent the sound you hear in *cause, haunt, draw* and *shawl*. The dictionary uses the symbol ô for this phoneme. You have already been introduced to this sound in the previous lesson (ought). Most words with the digraph **au** are French derivatives.

We have two rules that help us decide whether **au** or **aw** is the correct spelling in a word. Read words 1-20 and highlight the vowel digraphs. Try to figure out the first rule.

1. draw
2. haunt
3. thaw
4. saw
5. sauce
6. auburn
7. flaw
8. fault
9. straw
10. applaud
11. fraud
12. coleslaw
13. laundry
14. claw
15. author
16. paw
17. flaunt
18. gnaw
19. autograph
20. automatic

When do you use **au**? _____

When do you use **aw**? _____

Sometimes the digraph **aw** also occurs in the middle of words. Read the following words and highlight the vowels. Then study their spelling pattern to discover the second rule:

1. shawl
2. lawn
3. awl
4. spawn
5. brawl
6. gawk
7. prawn
8. scrawl
9. squawk
10. drawl
11. fawn
12. crawl
13. pawn
14. trawl
15. hawk
16. bawl

When do you use **aw** in the middle of words? _____

The words *haul* and *maul* are exceptions.

Write **au** or **aw** to complete the words.

1. h____nt
2. g____k
3. cr____l
4. g____dy
5. y____n
6. l____nch
7. spr____l
8. p____se
9. ____nt
10. d____n
11. g____nt
12. p____nch

4a continued

The following words have the silent letters **gh** after the **au** sound: caught, taught, naughty, daughter, haughty, and slaughter. Create a silly sentence (called a mnemonic) to help you memorize these words. Write it on the back of this sheet of paper.

Use the words in the box to complete the crossword puzzle.

taunt	automatic	autobiography	autumn	autograph
audit	audible	faucet	vault	authority
saucer	sausage	automobile	Australia	auditorium

Across:
1. Something to eat
2. The author's own story
3. A country
4. To insult, to tease, to provoke
5. Works by itself
6. The government's review of taxes
7. A small plate
8. A safe place for storing valuables

Down
1. Someone who knows a lot
2. A spigot
3. A place to hear music or speeches
4. A car
5. Loud enough to be heard
6. A famous person's signature
7. A season

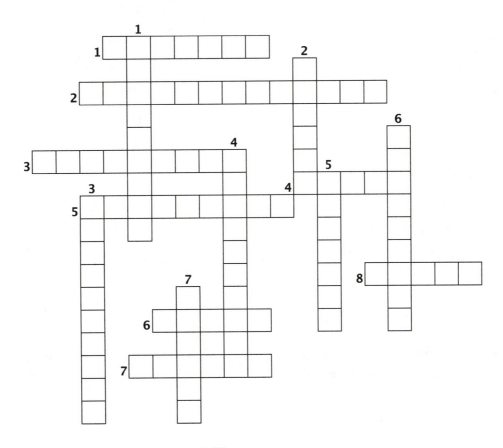

187

4b Reading and Spelling for Mastery

Vowel Digraphs **au** and **aw**:

Dictation	Spelling
1. jaw	1. law
2. thaw	2. lawyer *
3. claw	3. draw
4. flaw	4. drawn
5. straw	5. drawer
6. gawk	6. paws (H)
7. hawk	7. crawl
8. squawk	8. lawn
9. yawn	9. awesome*
10. fawn	10. awful*
11. dawn	11. cause
12. pawn	12. because
13. prawns	13. haul (H)
14. spawn	14. fault
15. shawl	15. August
16. sprawl	16. caught *
17. fraud	17. taught* (H)
18. haunt	18. daughter*
19. flaunt	19. caution*
20. vault	20. author

*Red words, H=homophones

Use **au** at the beginning or in the middle of words. Use **aw** at the end of a word or a syllable. In one-syllable words use **aw** before **n**, **l**, or **k** when they are the last letter in the word.

5 Review of *oi, oy, ou, ow, au* and *aw*

Let's review the diphthongs **oi**, **oy**, **ou**, and **ow** and the digraphs **au** and **aw**. Use the words in the box to complete the expressions or phrases. Write in pencil and do the ones you know first. Remember to capitalize the first word in a sentence. Use one word twice.

tomorrow	straws	spoiled	enough	show
showers	applause	tough	royal	coin
join	flawless	fought	point	owl
fault	thrown	flowers	auto	enjoy
	through	announcements		

1. The movie attendant told me to _____ the _____.
2. Jose has always been a night _____.
3. When things get _____, the _____ get going.
4. Let's give a round of _____.
5. _____ the crowd.
6. It wasn't my _____.
7. They _____ like cats and dogs.
8. _____ is another day.
9. England's Prince William and Prince Harry are part of a _____ family.
10. Those kids are _____ rotten.
11. They were friends _____ thick and thin.
12. The principal makes _____ over the intercom.
13. Don't take too much. There is not _____ to go around.
14. Let's decide by tossing a _____.
15. You're missing the _____.
16. The runner was _____ out at first base.
17. April _____ bring May _____.
18. It was a _____ performance.
19. She was grasping at _____.
20. They were on _____ pilot.

6a Vowel Digraph *oo*

The digraph **oo** has two different sounds. The more common sound is the one you hear in *moon*. The dictionary uses the symbol o͞o to represent this phoneme. The second sound says **oo** as in *look*. The dictionary uses the symbol o͝o for this phoneme. Here is a mnemonic device that may help you remember these two sounds: Look at the moon.

Pronounce the following words and write the correct dictionary symbol next to each one. Remember, o͞o as in *room* and o͝o as in *look*.

1. choose _____
2. book _____
3. redwood _____
4. raccoon _____
5. outlook _____
6. bassoon _____
7. paratroopers _____
8. brook _____
9. rookie _____
10. shampoo _____
11. caboose _____
12. shook _____
13. rainproof _____
14. poodle _____
15. hood _____
16. teaspoon _____
17. cookbook _____
18. pontoon _____
19. understood _____
20. mushroom _____
21. noodles _____

The **oo** spelling frequently occurs in compound words. Draw lines from the words on the left to the ones on the right to make compound words and write them on the lines.

honey	groom	1. _____
bare	noon	2. _____
after	pool	3. _____
proof	foot	4. _____
bride	moon	5. _____
whirl	read	6. _____
sea	book	7. _____
table	wood	8. _____
year	stick	9. _____
Holly	food	10. _____
room	spoon	11. _____
broom	mate	12. _____

6b Reading and Spelling for Mastery

Vowel digraph **oo** as in *look* and **oo** as in *moon*:

Dictation	Spelling
1. hook	1. book
2. nook	2. took
3. foot	3. look
4. brook	4. cook
5. crook	5. shook
6. hoof	6. wood (H)
7. wool	7. stood
8. good	8. blood*
9. hood	9. flood*
10. room	10. school*
11. moon	11. food
12. spoon	12. afternoon
13. booth	13. soon
14. tooth	14. tools
15. pool	15. troops
16. cool	16. choose (H)
17. boots	17. proof
18. mood	18. shoot
19. root H	19. smooth
20. cartoon	20. loose*

*Red words, H=homophones

7a Vowel Digraphs *oo*, *ew*, and *eu*

The digraph **ew** is another way to spell the **ōō** or **ū** sounds. Read the following words and highlight the vowel digraphs. Then study the pattern to discover when we use **ew** and when we use **oo**.

1. chew	5. grew	9. new	13. flew	17. blew
2. dew	6. moon	10. food	14. crew	18. stew
3. cool	7. threw	11. drew	15. ooze	19. oodles
4. few	8. cartoon	12. pool	16. pew	20. strew

The rule is: _____

_____

Good for you, if you noticed that **ew** is used when the **ōō** sound is at the end of a word; whereas **oo** is used in the beginning or middle of words. As always, there are just a few exceptions. The common ones are *zoo, too, shoo, woo, bamboo, igloo, shampoo,* and *kangaroo*.

English has an interesting prefix that came to us from Greek. It is **eu** and means *good* (*eulogy, Europe*) and is pronounced with a long **u**. Look up these four words in the dictionary, and write their definitions on another sheet of paper:

1. eulogy   2. euphemism   3. euphoria   4. euphony

The **eu** spelling also occurs in the middle of a few French derivatives and says **ōō** or long **u**. Read these words and write the sound of **eu** on the lines (**ōō** or **ū**):

1. feud ____   2. feudal ____   3. neutral ____   4. neutron ____   5. neurology ____

Review

When the **ōō** sound occurs at the end of words, it can also be spelled **ue.** You might remember **ue** from Chapter 5, which dealt with vowel-vowel syllables.

Read these words and highlight the vowels. Listen to the vowel sounds and write **ōō** or **ū** on the lines.

1. due ____	5. true ____	9. rescue ____	13. issue ____
2. cue ____	6. queue ____	10. pursue ____	14. tissue ____
3. blue ____	7. value ____	11. barbecue ____	15. revenue ____
4. clue ____	8. avenue ____	12. statue ____	16. sue ____

When the **ōō** sound is in the middle of words, it can also be spelled **ui**; however, this only occurs in these common words: *juice, cruise, bruise, fruit, suit, recruit, pursuit, sluice*.

7b/9c Reading and Spelling for Mastery

Vowel digraphs **ew**, **oo**, **ui**, and **ue**:

Vowel digraphs **ie**, **ei**:

Dictation

1. dew (H)
2. blew (H)
3. crew
4. stew
5. chew
6. chewing
7. spew
8. brew
9. renew
10. slew H
11. zoo
12. shoo (H)
13. igloo
14. bamboo
15. cruise
16. bruise
17. due (H)
18. true
19. blue H
20. clue

7b Spelling

1. few
2. new (H)
3. knew (H)
4. flew (H)
5. threw (H)
6. drew
7. grew
8. view
9. review
10. sew (long o)(H)*
11. too (H)
12. two (H)*
13. who*
14. suit
15. fruit
16. juice
17. value
18. rescue
19. avenue
20. issue*

9c Spelling List

1. field
2. piece* (H)
3. niece*
4. pier (H)
5. grief
6. belief
7. believe
8. achieve
9. friend*
10. eight* (H)
11. eighty
12. weigh*(H)
13. weight (H)
14. neighbor*
15. height*
16. either
17. neither
18. receive*
19. receipt
20. weird

*Red words, H=homophones

8 Diphthong and Vowel Digraph Review 1

Write the words in syllables, separated by dashes. Next, mark the vowels and denote the code. Diphthongs are not marked. Finally, read the words at your teacher's direction.

1. raccoon   răc-coon   cl-d
2. journalist
3. compound
4. turquoise
5. lawnmower
6. aloofness
7. moisturizer
8. astronaut
9. dewdrops
10. pronounce

Use the words in the box to fill in the blanks in the story. Study the code underneath the lines. One word will be used twice.

filled	greed	first	goose	astounded
laid	each	now	farmer	overjoyed

The suffix **ed** shows past tense. The code for a suffix is **s**.

A _____ had a _____ that _____ a golden egg
       rc-rc   d   vv

_____ and every day. At _____ he was _____
    vv   rc   cl-d-s

and _____. Then the farmer's heart became _____
     op-rc-d-s   cl-s

with _____. He said to himself, "I want it all _____!"
     vv   d

So he killed the _____. No more golden eggs!
             d

9a Vowel Digraphs *ei* and *ie*

The vowel digraph **ie** usually says long **e** *(field, yield, chief)*. Have you ever heard the spelling rule, "**I** before **e**, except after **c** or when it sounds like **ā** in neighbor and weigh?" This rule tells us to use **ei** right after the letter **c** *(receive, deceive)*. The **ei** spelling says long **e**, when it occurs after the letter **c**. There are five exceptions to this rule: *either, neither, weird, leisure,* and *seize*. In these five words, **ei** says long **e**, even though it does not follow **c**.

When the digraph **ei** does not follow the letter **c**, it often says long **a** *(neighbor, weigh)*.

Read the words in the box and write them under the correct heading below. Try long **e** or long **a** in words with the **ei** spelling. Then pick the one that makes a real word.

believe	rein	weird	eighty	seize	shriek	freight
veil	conceited	weight	priest	reign	deceive	shield
receive	thief	perceive	deceit	feint	niece	pier

       ei = long a   **ei = long e**   **ie = long e**

_____   _____   _____
_____   _____   _____
_____   _____   _____
_____   _____   _____
_____   _____   _____
_____   _____   _____

Write the five words that are exceptions to the rule, "**I** before **e**, except after **c**."
_____

On another sheet of paper, write a silly sentence with these exceptions and memorize it.

Here are some words with **ei** and **ie** that say a different sound.

What does **eigh** say in the words *height* and *sleight*? _____

What does **ei** say in the words *forfeit* and *counterfeit*? _____

Three more words you should memorize are *friend*, *foreign*, and *sovereign*. What do the letters **ie** and **ei** say in these words? _____

9b Review of Vowel Digraphs *ei* and *ie*

Use the words in the box to complete the crossword puzzle.

believe	relieve	eighth	thieves	brief	
cashier	deceive	eighteen	grieve	neighbor	perceive
sleigh	conceited	ceiling	achieve	receipt	

Across
1. Between 10-20
2. The digraph says long **a**, she lives close to you.
3. The digraph says long **e**, you pay him.
4. **I** before **e**, except after **c**, to mislead
5. The digraph says long **e**, to lessen, to take someone's place
6. The digraph says long **a**, used in winter.
7. The digraph says long **e**, it's above you.
8. The digraph says long **e**, very short.

Down
1. The digraph is in the second syllable, stuck up.
2. The digraph says long **e**, to reach a goal.
3. **I** before **e**, except after **c**, to see
4. The digraph says long **e**, people who are not nice.
5. The digraph says long **a**, between 1-10.
6. The digraph says long **e**, proof of payment.
7. The digraph is in the second syllable, to trust.
8. To be sad over a loss

10 Review of Diphthongs and Vowel Digraphs 2

1. Diphthongs are glides that begin with one vowel sound and change to another vowel sound within the same syllable. The most common diphthongs are: oi, oy, ou, and ow.
2. Vowel digraphs are vowel combinations that say a single sound. The common vowel digraphs are: au, aw, oo, ew, eu, ie, and ei.
3. Diphthongs/digraphs can't be sounded out and must be memorized.
4. The abbreviation for a syllable with a diphthong or a vowel digraph is **d**. Do **not** mark this syllable.

Write the words in syllables, separated by dashes. Then mark the vowels in the syllables that do not have diphthongs or digraphs. Next, denote the code.

1. harpoon _____
2. authorize _____
3. powerhouse _____
4. disappoint _____
5. insurmountable _____
6. unemployment _____
7. disbelief _____
8. authentic _____
9. retriever _____
10. boomerang _____
11. announcement _____

Use a red pencil to divide the words into syllables. Draw a line from the first syllable in each word to the correct syllable abbreviation on the left. Then draw a line from the second syllable to the correct syllable abbreviation on the right.

pref	exhaust	s
	boycott	
	withdrew	
d	discount	d
	decoy	
	scooter	
cl	drawback	cl

197

11 Journey to Glacier Bay

Several years ago, my husband and I, along with four friends, planned a kayaking (kī-ăck-ing) trip to beautiful Glacier (Glāsher) Bay in Alaska. We had several group meetings to chart our course and organize the food. Because Glacier Bay is a huge national park, there are no restaurants or hotels, only the great outdoors. Therefore, we thought carefully about all of the camping gear, cooking equipment, and food we needed.

After meeting up in Juneau, we transferred to two floatplanes that flew us to our starting point. The views of surrounding mountains and sea channels were stunning and made up for the rough and very noisy flight. Touching down on water brought about a smooth landing.

The following day we rented our kayaks, transferred our food into bear-proof, metal boxes, and crammed all of our camping gear into the bows and sterns of our little boats. As we pushed away from the pier, we were finally ready to embark on our paddling cruise.

Once we were launched, it suddenly dawned on me that our three tiny boats were in water that was barely above freezing and was often bordered by sheer cliffs. What if one of our kayaks capsized? I swallowed hard and tried not to allow fear of the unknown to cloud our new adventure! My husband perceived my feelings of distress and boosted my courage.

We encountered a few, brief rain showers that first morning, but the afternoon brought clear skies and bright sunshine. We had lunch on a small island where we discovered lovely flowers and munched on wild strawberries. After paddling for another three hours, we steered through a narrow channel into Mouse Cove, an inlet off Glacier Bay. Luckily, we found a mile-long beach providing us with a perfect camping spot. As we assembled the stoves to boil water for soup and freeze-dried stew, we heard heavy, deep breathing and saw waterspouts rising from the bay. To our delight, we spotted two massive humpback whales cavorting. They entertained us until midnight, when the light finally faded and the moon started to rise. Right after we crawled into our tents, we heard the hooting of an owl and the loud howl of a wolf nearby.

The next few days brought us alongside the enormous tidewater glaciers of Reed and Lamplugh. From our tiny boats, we were staring up at cragged walls of ice, more than one-hundred fifty feet in height and many miles in length. Waterfalls of recently thawed ice cascaded down the frozen cliffs. What an awesome sight! We were careful not to get too close, because huge pieces of ice often break off and cause dangerous tidal waves.

As our course took us to the most northerly glacier, we began to encounter an astounding number of icebergs. They are stunning to look at, but also hazardous. Remembering the fate of the Titanic, we tried to exercise caution and avoided them as best we could. Gorgeous (gor-jus) Mount Fairweather, a snow-capped peak over 15,000 feet high, was towering above us.

After crossing Glacier Bay, we headed south. Finally, we allowed ourselves a rest day. My husband wanted to fish from shore, two friends wanted to kayak, and two other friends and I decided to climb a mountain. We set off around 9:30 in the morning and announced that we thought we'd be back by 3:00.

In this remote countryside there are no trails; we had to bushwhack through the dense underbrush in the forest. After we gained about seven hundred feet of altitude, I was a bit ahead of Chris and Kelly. Suddenly, about two hundred feet away, I saw three giant grizzly bears! They stood up on their hind legs! I let out a blood-curdling scream, and they quickly took off into the woods. My friends caught up with me and asked me what was wrong. I could hardly talk; my voice trembled when I explained the frightful sighting. They exclaimed, "Too bad we didn't see them."

When the mountain became steeper, we had to do some rock climbing. After reaching a small ledge, we turned around to look at the view. It was then that we realized the bears were following us! We tried to make ourselves look big and screamed at them. The grizzlies were unimpressed. We kept climbing, and they kept up their pursuit. At this point we were terrified! Our only advantage was that we were above them. I told my friends, "I'm going to throw rocks down the mountain!" Chris replied that this might make the bears mad. We were clearly in big trouble because the grizzlies were quickly gaining on us. I picked up a huge rock and threw it down the mountain, and then another and another. Bouncing wildly, the rocks headed towards the grizzlies! The falling rocks spooked the bears, and they quickly disappeared into the underbrush.

After breathing a sigh of relief, we continued climbing the peak. Once we reached the summit, we took out our binoculars and soon realized the bears were foraging in the very area of our descending route. We stayed on top of the mountain for five hours, waiting for them to move somewhere else. Around eight o'clock in the evening, we decided to go down as far as we could without alerting the bears. Finally, the three grizzlies wandered over to a nearby snowfield, curled up, and went to sleep. Here was our chance! We down-climbed silently, taking care not to loosen any rocks that might make noise!

As the ridge became less steep, we ran through the underbrush getting scratched up by branches and twigs. We didn't even notice because we were so scared the grizzlies could have awakened from their nap and might be hunting for us. After an hour, we finally reached level ground and saw our tents nearby. It was 9:30 when we walked into camp. My husband and our friends had been extremely worried. One of them said, "What were you fools doing on top of that peak for five hours?" They tracked our movements with binoculars and couldn't make heads or tails out of our actions. After a full debriefing, everyone was relieved and happy that we came back alive!

The next day, we paddled back to the ranger station, turned in our kayaks and bear boxes and headed home. Luckily our trip had a happy ending. That was enough adventure to last us a good long time!

Comprehension Questions

1. Why did the campers have to think carefully about the items they brought along?
_____

2. Why were the kayakers cautious about not getting too close to the tidewater glaciers?
_____

3. What spooked the bears?
_____

4. What did the bears do that gave the hikers a chance to escape?
_____

5. Why were the other friends and the author's husband worried?
_____

6. How did the hikers feel once they returned to camp?
_____

CHAPTER 8
Hard and Soft *c* and *g*

Note to Instructor

Chapter 8 covers **hard c**, **soft c**, **hard g**, and **soft g**. Soft c says the **s** sound you hear in *city, center,* and *space*. When the letters **e**, **i**, or **y** come directly after **c**, c says **s** (**soft c**). Otherwise, **c** usually says the **k** sound you hear in *care, close,* and *curl* (**hard c**). This rule applies to words that were incorporated into English from French and Latin. In words that came to English from Anglo-Saxon or German the letter **k** is used in front of **e** or **i** (*keep, kid, kiss,* and *kettle*).

Soft **g** says the **j** sound you hear in *age, gentle,* and *gym*. When the letters **e**, **i**, or **y** come directly after **g**, g says **j** (**soft g**). Otherwise, **g** says the sound you hear in *go, grill,* and *foggy* (**hard g**). This rule has many exceptions because it only applies to words that are derived from French and Latin. These rules do not apply to words that came to English from German or Anglo-Saxon. Examples of exceptions are *give, girl, gear,* and *get*.

Reminders:
1. **Have students reread all the words in every lesson once they have completed the exercises.**
2. Ask students to copy each new phonogram, red word, homophone, homograph, prefix, suffix, and rule in the appropriate sections of their Decoding Binders. Include homographs, marked **HG**, in the Homophone Section. When entering a phonogram, prefix, or suffix, students must list four key words that illustrate it. Students must also add four words for every rule and definitions for the homophones and homographs.
3. Review all sections of the binder **once a week** for a minimum of five weeks. Younger children or the severely learning disabled may need more time for review.
4. Use the **Proposed Spelling Activities**, located in the Appendix, for all **Reading and Spelling for Mastery** lists. Students must read the list daily before they start the two practice activities.

Lesson 1 (two pages) lists words with **hard c** and **soft c** and asks students to figure out the rule for the two ways to pronounce **c**. The second page covers the suffixes **–ance**, **–ence**, and **–cy**. After students have completed this lesson, please call on volunteers to share their perception of the rule.

Lesson 2 presents words with both sounds of **c**, as well as words with **sc** (*science, scene, scent*).

Lesson 3 introduces the phonograms **ace** and **ice**. The phonogram **ace** has two pronunciations. When **ace** is part of a base word, it is accented and follows the *vowel-consonant-e* rule: **long a** as in *misplace, disgrace*. (Accented syllables are pronounced with more force than unaccented syllables.) When **–ace** is unaccented, it is usually a suffix that says əs or ĭs as in *furnace* or *surface*.
The phonogram **ice** also has two pronunciations. When **ice** is part of a base word, it is accented and follows the *vowel-consonant-e* rule: **long i** as in *advice* or *overpriced*. (It is also accented in few longer words that don't have a clear base word as in *suffice*.) In most polysyllabic words, **ice** is an

unaccented suffix that says ĭs or əs as in *justice, notice*. Please simplify these explanations for younger students or those with severe learning disabilities.

Lesson 4 is a **Reading and Spelling for Mastery** page. Use List 1 for younger students or those with severe learning disabilities. Point out that most words with the sound of āse are spelled **ace**, *face, ace, place, pace, space, trace, grace*. The words *base, case, vase,* and *chase* are the only four common words that end with **ase**. (Steer, Peck & Kahn, 1971). Consider giving pretests for individualized lists. All students should read both lists. Please select two appropriate spelling activities from **Proposed Spelling Activities** in the appendix and require students to read the list before they start their daily spelling practice.

Lesson 5 (two pages) lists words with **hard g** and **soft g** and asks students to figure out the rule for the two ways of pronouncing **g**: The second exercise requires students to write words under the categories **hard g, soft g**, and **hard and soft g** (both sounds within the same word). The last exercise is a crossword puzzle. Please remind students to use a pencil for the crossword puzzle.

Lesson 6 introduces the prefixes **geo–** and **gen–** and the suffixes **–age** and **–ology**. Students are instructed to highlight the words they can read. Please help students with the words they can't read. Have students write these prefixes and suffixes in the relevant sections of their Decoding Binders.

Lesson 7 introduces the short vowel signal **dge**. Ask students to write this phonogram in the rules section of their Decoding Binders.

Lesson 8 is a **Reading and Spelling for Mastery** page. Please explain the following rule: When the vowel sounds **e** or **i** follow **hard g** in Latin or French words, the letter **u** is inserted as in *guest, guide, guilt* and *guitar*. Use List 1 for younger students or those with severe learning disabilities. Consider giving pretests for individualized lists. All students should read both lists. Follow the usual directions.

Lesson 9 discusses the three sounds of the digraph **ch** (*chapel, chronicle* and *parachute*).

Lesson 10 reviews **hard** and **soft c** and **g** in the context of a challenging article about the history of democracy. Students will need lots of guidance and support. Please give every student a copy of the following words. Ask students to write **k** over every hard **c** and **s** over every soft **c**, as well as **g** over every hard **g** and **j** over every soft **g**. Go over all of the words and the definitions. If your situation permits, ask students to read the list individually. After the article, there are five comprehension questions.

1. democracy   2. democratic   3. Greece   4. country   5. region
6. central   7. conquered   8. occupied   9. Hapsburg   10. directly
11. citizens   12. decades   13. governor   14. enraged   15. secret
16. organize   17. villages   18. delegates   19. discuss   20. pledged
21. allegiance   22. excellent   23. crudely   24. occupiers   25. combat
26. experience   27. recognized   28. huge   29. tactics   30. disadvantage
31. regiment   32. general   33. galloped   34. perceived   35. danger
36. successful   37. decided   38. elect   39. convene   40. civic
41. decisions   42. government   43. century   44. distinction

1 Hard and Soft c

The letter c has two different sounds. It usually says the **k** sound you hear in the word *call*. This is called the **hard c** sound. Sometimes the letter c says the **s** sound you hear in the word *mice*. This is called the **soft c** sound. Let's see if you can figure out the rule for the two ways to pronounce **c**.

Read the following words and study the patterns. Then highlight the words with **soft c** (**c** says **s**), and underline the words with **hard c** (**c** says **k**).

1. cost
2. city
3. close
4. center
5. spicy
6. crying
7. decide
8. coffee
9. closet
10. price
11. space
12. doctor
13. mascot
14. discuss
15. fancy
16. lacy
17. twice
18. reflect
19. citizen
20. crime

When does **c** say **s**? What is the rule? _____

_____

In front of **e** or **i**, use the letter **k** to make the hard **c** sound, *keep, kid, kiss,* and *kettle*.

Read each word in the box and listen to the sound that the letter **c** makes. Write **s** next to the word if it makes a **soft c** sound. Write **k** next to each word that makes a **hard c** sound.

Next, write the words under the correct heading.

| grocery | crunchy | subject | perceive | decision |
| clutter | cinema | mercy | crumble | direct |

      hard c (c = k)   **soft c (c = s)**

_____   _____

_____   _____

_____   _____

_____   _____

_____   _____

Lesson 1 continued

Read each word and listen to the sound that the letter **c** makes. Write **s** next to each word that makes the **soft c** sound. Write **k** next to each word that makes the **hard c** sound.

1. central _____
2. secret _____
3. contest _____
4. celery _____
5. impact _____
6. cement _____
7. trace _____
8. slice _____
9. elect _____
10. decade _____
11. dance _____
12. acrobat _____
13. advice _____
14. commit _____
15. chance _____
16. force _____
17. tactics _____
18. juice _____
19. cellar _____
20. proceed _____

Two common suffixes that have a **soft c** sound are **–ance** and **–ence**. Both say **əns**. The schwa sound (ə) says **short u**. Another suffix with a **soft c** sound is **–cy**, which says **sē**.

Draw a line from the word starters to the appropriate suffix and read the words.

attend
bal   ance
vacan
entr
fluen   cy
poli

priva
abs   ence
resid
truan
secre   cy
differ

Most dictionaries have a pronunciation guide right after the entry word. It is usually inside parentheses. Read each phonetically spelled word on the left and draw a line to its correctly spelled counterpart on the right.

1. krok′ ə dīl   curfew
2. ĭk spĭr′ ē əns   allowance
3. ŏk′ yə pī   evidence
4. ĕv′ĭ dəns   crocodile
5. ə lou′ əns   democratic
6. kur′ fyōō   license
7. ĭn′ ə səns   occupy
8. lī′ səns   experience
9. dĕm ə krăt′ ĭk   cucumber
10. kyōō′ kŭm bər   innocence

2 Challenge Words with Hard and Soft c

Sometimes hard and soft **c**'s are in the same word. Find all of the **c**'s in the words below. Highlight the ones that make a **soft c** sound. Underline the ones that make a **hard c** sound.

1. circulate
2. confidence
3. concept
4. occurrence
5. civic
6. concert
7. commerce
8. democracy
9. recycle
10. excellence
11. concern
12. conference
13. clearance
14. circle
15. circus
16. bicycle

A number of words have two **c**'s next to each other, followed by the letters **e** and **i**. Read the words in the box and listen closely to the two different sounds of **c**. Highlight the words you can read.

| accept   success   accent   successful   vaccine   accident |

What does the first **c** say? _____   What does the second **c** say? _____

Some words have the letters **sc** in front of **e**, **i**, or **y**. Read the words in the box with the help of a dictionary. Highlight the ones you can read. What sound does **sc** make? _____

| science   scientific   resuscitate   scent   scene   scenery   reminisce   fascinating |

Select words from both boxes to complete the following sentences.

1. Please _____ my apologies.
2. Finding a _____ for smallpox was a great _____ achievement.
3. After the _____, the doctor attempted to _____ Mrs. Smith; fortunately, he was _____.
4. The experiment we did in _____ class was _____.
5. The lovely _____ of the mountains and the lake caused me to _____ about swimming there as a child.

3 The Syllables –ace and –ice

The syllable **ace** has two pronunciations. When **ace** is part of a base word, it is accented and follows the vowel-consonant-e rule *(place, grace)*. (Accented syllables are pronounced with more force than unaccented syllables.) When **–ace** is a suffix, it is unaccented and says əs as in *furnace* or *surface*.

Read the following words. Write **ace** next to each word when **ace** follows the vowel-consonant-e rule. Write **əs** next to each word when **–ace** is unaccented. If you are not sure, try both and use the one that makes sense.

1. misplace _____
2. furnace _____
3. embrace _____
4. palace _____
5. necklace _____
6. disgrace _____
7. terrace _____
8. retrace _____
9. boldface _____
10. preface _____
11. surface _____
12. replace _____

The syllable **ice**, also has two pronunciations. When **ice** is part of a base word, it is accented and follows the *vowel-consonant-e* rule *(advice, overpriced)*. (It is also accented in a few longer words that don't have a clear base word.) In most polysyllabic words, **–ice** is an unaccented suffix that says **əs**. The word *police* does not fit the rule. It says pə-lēs'.

Read these words and draw a line from each word to the correct pronunciation of **–ice**.

1. notice
2. price   īce
3. office
4. advice
5. practice   īs or əs
6. service
7. sacrifice
8. justice   īce
9. solstice
10. prejudice
11. entice   īs or əs
12. apprentice

Use rhyming word pairs from this list to answer each riddle:

slice, notice, place, justice, nice, prejudice, spice, service, price, race

1. After Maria ran the _____, she took first _____ and won a trophy.
2. Sugar and _____ and everything _____
3. The judge said, "There is no room for _____ in the Halls of _____.
4. At Round Table my friend asked, "What's the _____ of a _____ of pizza?"
5. A tip lets the server know you took _____ of his or her _____.

4 Reading and Spelling for Mastery

Words with hard and soft c:

Spelling List 1
1. face
2. race
3. place
4. space
5. ice
6. nice
7. price
8. twice
9. force
10. since
11. once *
12. chance
13. dance
14. cent (H)
15. center
16. city
17. citizen *
18. except
19. accept *
20. success *

Spelling List 2
1. exercise *
2. decide *
3. decision *
4. receive *
5. receipt *
6. certain *
7. science *
8. piece (H) *
9. peace (H) *
10. produce (HG)
11. service
12. notice
13. office
14. practice
15. justice
16. advice
17. circle *
18. recycle *
19. bicycle *
20. ocean *

*Red words, H=homophones, HG=homograph

C says s when the letters e, i, or y come right after it. Otherwise the letter c says the k sound. Some of the words on this list also follow the spelling rule: "i before e, except after c."

5 Hard and Soft g

The letter **g** has two different sounds. **Hard g** says the sound you hear in *grab* and *frog*. When **g** is soft, it says the **j** sound you hear in *gem* and *large*. Read each of the following words. Underline the letter **g** when it says **g** as in *go* (hard g). Highlight each **g** when it says **j** as in *gym* (soft g).

1. golden
2. huge
3. gallon
4. ginger
5. gym
6. angle
7. angel
8. gloomy
9. danger
10. gallon
11. gasoline
12. giant
13. gentle
14. glow
15. grape
16. age
17. golf
18. government
19. change
20. margin

Now read the words again and study the patterns. Can you figure out the rule for the two ways of pronouncing **g**? Here's a hint: The letter right after **g** determines how it will be pronounced.

What is the rule? _____

_____

Write each of the following words under the correct heading below.

1. guess
2. ranger
3. glitter
4. agent
5. sponge
6. garden
7. baggage
8. recognize
9. geography
10. magic
11. gigantic
12. organize
13. engage
14. engine
15. wagon
16. luggage
17. language
18. energy

Hard g as in go	Soft g as in gym	Both hard and soft g

Lesson 5 continued

Read the words in the box and use them to complete the crossword puzzle. Write in pencil.

| grudge | governor | tragedy | refrigerator | gorgeous | digest | gargle |
| garbage | ginger | guitar | gymnastics | enlarge | engagement | |

Across:
1. Soft **g**, a sport
2. Soft **g**, starts and ends with the same letter, five syllables
3. First **g** hard, second **g** soft, beautiful
4. Soft **g**, to make bigger
5. Soft **g**, the stomach does it
6. Hard **g**, the head of state government

Down:
1. Hard and soft **g**, starts with a vowel
2. Both **g**'s are soft, a spice
3. Hard and soft **g**, goes in a can
4. Ends with a consonant-le syllable
5. Soft **g**, a sad event
6. Hard and soft **g**, no forgiveness
7. Hard **g**, an instrument

209

6 Prefixes and Suffixes with Soft g

Do you remember what prefixes and suffixes are? A **prefix** is a morpheme that comes before a base word. A **suffix** is a morpheme that goes after a base word. Prefixes and suffixes change the meaning of a base word. The prefix **geo–** is derived from Greek. Use your dictionary to find eight words with this prefix. Write them on the lines below. Study the definitions and use the dictionary's pronunciation guide to help you read the words.

1. _____   5. _____

2. _____   6. _____

3. _____   7. _____

4. _____   8. _____

What does the prefix **geo–** mean? _____

The prefix **gen–** is derived from Latin. It means *producer* or *one that is produced*. Circle the prefixes in the following words and try to figure out what the words mean; look up any you don't know. Highlight all of the words you are able to read. (Hint: the prefix **gen–** is not the first syllable in words 13-16.

1. general   5. generalize   9. genetic   13. agent
2. generate   6. generator   10. genocide   14. agency
3. gender   7. generally   11. gentle   15. agenda
4. generic   8. generous   12. gentleman   16. urgent

There are two common suffixes that contain the **soft g** sound. They are **–age** as in *manage* and **–ology** as in *biology*. The suffix **–age** means *condition, collection, an action*. The suffix **–ology** means *a branch of learning*.

Draw lines from each base word to its correct suffix.

man   ap
radi   ology   vill   ology
post   dam
anthrop   ge
advant   age   ec   age
band   pack

7 Short Vowel Signal for Soft *g*

Do you remember the short vowel signals? The rule states that you must double the letters **l**, **s**, **f**, and sometimes **z**, after a short vowel in one-syllable words. Two other short vowel signals are **ck** and **tch**. Here is one more rule: "Use **dge** right after short vowels." The silent **d** in **dge** protects the short vowel from the power of the silent **e**. The short vowel signal **dge** says **j**.

The following words are spelled phonetically. Write the correct spelling of each word. Remember to use **dge** right after a short vowel. Use **ge** after long vowels or consonants.

1. brĭj _____
2. ĕj _____
3. cāj _____
4. charj _____
5. hūj _____
6. plĕj _____
7. plŭnj _____
8. smŭj _____
9. pāj _____
10. lŏj _____
11. grūj _____
12. larj _____
13. stāj _____
14. rĭj _____
15. crĭnj _____
16. jŭj _____
17. rāj _____
18. hĕj _____
19. merj _____
20. trŭj _____
21. forj _____

Draw an arrow from each word starter to the correct ending. Remember, **dge** is only used right after short vowels.

1. nu — dge / ge
2. hin — dge / ge
3. we — dge / ge
4. sa — dge / ge
5. bul — dge / ge
6. bu — dge / ge
7. wa — dge / ge
8. ver — dge / ge
9. lun — dge / ge
10. do — dge / ge
11. gor — dge / ge
12. sle — dge / ge

8 Reading and Spelling for Mastery

Words with hard and soft **g**:

Spelling List 1
1. age
2. stage
3. huge
4. change
5. strange
6. large
7. gym
8. gentle
9. giant
10. danger
11. edge
12. pledge
13. lodge
14. bridge
15. grudge
16. judge
17. judgment *
18. guess *
19. guide *
20. guest *

*Red words

Spelling List 2
1. college *
2. magic
3. merge
4. urge
5. register
6. emergency *
7. arrange
8. general
9. energy
10. agent
11. engine
12. original *
13. region
14. religion *
15. baggage
16. village
17. language *
18. garbage *
19. biology *
20. geography *

G says **j** when the letters **e**, **i**, and **y** come right after it. Otherwise **g** is hard as in *go*. Use **dge** after a short vowel in one-syllable words. In the second list, words 15, 17, 18, and 20 have both sounds of **g**.

9 The Three Sounds of ch

Usually the digraph **ch** is pronounced like the first sound in the words *chart* and *chance*. In words we inherited from Greek, **ch** says the **k** sound you hear in *chord* and *character*.

Read the following words. Write **k** next to each word in which **ch** says **k**. Write **ch** next to each word that says the sound you hear in *chart* and *chance*. You may have to try both sounds, before deciding which one makes sense:

1. chime _____
2. character _____
3. chimney _____
4. chaos _____
5. chemistry _____
6. charge _____
7. chose _____
8. chorus _____
9. technology _____
10. chisel _____
11. branches _____
12. scholar _____
13. echo _____
14. schedule _____
15. children _____
16. anchor _____
17. headache _____
18. churches _____
19. chips _____
20. stomach _____
21. chronicle _____

In words that came to English from French, the digraph **ch** is often pronounced as **sh**. Use the dictionary to help you pronounce the words in the box. Then select words to complete the following sentences.

> chef   charades   parachutes   chandelier   chartreuse   chalets   chauffeur

1. The President's _____ drove him to the airport.
2. A light green color is called _____.
3. For dessert, the _____ made chocolate cake with fresh raspberries.
4. We played _____ at the birthday party.
5. After the skydivers jumped out of the airplane, they opened their _____.
6. In the Swiss mountains, most people live in _____.
7. The castle had a huge _____ in the dining room.

10   700 Years of Democracy

From our history classes, we have learned that the world's oldest democracy thrived in Greece over 2,000 years ago. Another country with a long democratic history is Switzerland. It became a nation in 1291 and has lasted over 700 years. The events that led to her beginning were similar to the events that triggered the American Revolution.

A region with lovely peaks and lakes, now known as Central Switzerland, was conquered and occupied by the Hapsburgers, a kingdom directly to the East. Their king oppressed Swiss citizens and taxed them heavily for decades. In the year 1291, after the Hapsburg governor tried to impose even more taxes, the people became enraged and began to organize a secret meeting.

All of the villages sent delegates to a central meeting place to discuss a response to the new taxes and the harassment. These representatives pledged allegiance to each other and vowed to wage war to gain their freedom. Even though Hapsburg had an excellent army and the Swiss had only crudely formed spears, they were determined to try to force the occupiers out. Since the Swiss had little combat experience, they recognized the risks and knew the chances of being crushed.

Overcoming their huge disadvantage by using clever tactics, the Swiss attacked a Hapsburg regiment of knights in shining armor. General Leopold and his men galloped single file along the shore of a lake. The Swiss waited for them on the steep slopes above the lake, ready with an arsenal of huge rocks and boulders. The knights perceived the danger too late. As the rocks and boulders were unleashed, some knights were crushed to death while others drowned. After many bloody battles, the Swiss people were successful in defeating their enemy and gaining their freedom.

Once they rid themselves of foreign forces, the Swiss, like the early Americans, rejected being ruled by a king. They decided to elect their leaders and convene regular town-hall meetings to discuss civic matters. Important decisions were debated by the people and required a vote by a show of hands. This type of government is called a direct democracy. During the last century, the Swiss laws have been changed to allow voting booths and secret ballots. Switzerland has the distinction of being the world's longest lasting democracy.

Some 500 years later, the colonists in America engaged in a similar struggle. To finance his many ventures, King George of England oppressed the people and demanded ever-increasing taxes. Finally, in 1776 delegates from all parts of the colonies met in secret and drafted the Declaration of Independence. After a hard-fought war, the colonists won their freedom and decided for a government founded on democratic principles. Even though Switzerland and the United States are separated by thousands of miles, they became independent countries in very similar ways.

1. What year did Switzerland become a nation?

   _____

2. Why did the Swiss people become enraged?

   _____

   _____

3. What did the representatives at the secret meeting decide to do?

   _____

   _____

4. What kind of government did the Swiss people choose after they forced the Hapsburgers out of Switzerland?

   _____

   _____

5. In what ways is the history of Switzerland similar to the history of the United States?

   _____

   _____

CHAPTER 9
Accented and Unaccented Syllables

Note to Instructor
The concept of **accented** and **unaccented** syllables is difficult for students to comprehend. Every polysyllabic word has one syllable that is pronounced more forcefully than the others. This is called the primary accent. Two- and three-syllable words have one accented syllable. Words with four or more syllables also have secondary accent. This chapter only deals with primary accents. Secondary accents will be discussed in Chapters 11 and 12.

Lesson 1a (no worksheet) Please demonstrate accented syllables by slowly pronouncing the word **entertainment**. Ask students to repeat the word and pick out the part of the word that is pronounced more forcefully than the other two (en ter tain'ment). The third syllable is accented, which is shown with an apostrophe directly to the right of the accented syllable. Follow the same procedure for these words: pen'cil, nu'mer al, an nounce'ments, his'to ry, mag'net, ap point'ment, de part'ment, prin'ci pal, e lect'ive, hu'mor ous.

Lesson 1b presents a list of syllabified words. Disseminate the worksheet and use the following procedure for each word: Ask students to read the word silently and raise their hands when they can read it. Direct the class to pronounce the word in unison. Ask students to highlight the syllable that is accented or stressed. Elicit responses and discuss each word. A bit of exaggeration is probably necessary to get the point across. Many students will need lots of practice to master this concept.

If students have difficulty understanding this concept, you might provide additional practice by selecting fifteen to twenty polysyllabic words from one of the textbooks. Write each word in syllables on the board or on the overhead and direct your class to write down the accented or stressed syllable. Discuss each word.

Reminders:
1. **Have students reread all the words in every lesson once they have completed the exercises.**
2. Ask students to copy each new phonogram, red word, homophone, homograph, prefix, suffix, and rule in the appropriate sections of their Decoding Binders. Include homographs, marked **HG**, in the Homophone Section. When entering a phonogram, prefix, or suffix, students must list four key words that illustrate it. Students must also add four words for every rule and definitions for the homophones and homographs.
3. Review all sections of the binder **once a week** for a minimum of five weeks. Younger children or the severely learning disabled may need more time for review.
4. Use the **Proposed Spelling Activities**, located in the Appendix, for all **Reading and Spelling for Mastery** lists. Students must read the list daily before they start the two practice activities.

Lesson 2 provides students with independent practice in placing accent marks on forty polysyllabic words. Direct your class to highlight the accented syllable in words 1-20. After everyone has completed the first section, discuss each word separately and follow the directions from **Lesson 1b**. Ascertain the level of understanding. If everyone seems to catch on, proceed to the next section, which is somewhat more difficult. If students are struggling with this idea, provide more practice with two-syllable words. After the entire page has been completed, direct students to go back and place accent marks (an apostrophe) right after the highlighted syllables.

Lesson 3a introduces the schwa sound, represented by this symbol ə. Many vowels in unaccented syllables say the schwa sound as in these examples: a cross, chick en, per son. The second exercise asks students to read a list of words. For every word, they must decide which syllable is accented, and mark it with an apostrophe. The final step is to read the words again and to mark the vowels. Tell your class to write the schwa symbol (ə) above the vowels that sound like a short **u**.

Lesson 3b teaches students how to read words using the pronunciation guide from the American Heritage Dictionary.

Lesson 4 is a **Reading and Spelling for Mastery** list with words that contain the schwa sound. (**Lesson 7** is also listed on this page.) Reduce the number of spelling words for younger children. Follow the usual directions.

Lesson 5a reviews prefixes that were introduced in chapter 3 and covers two rules that govern accent placement. 1. In most two and three-syllable words, the accent falls on the first syllable. If the word starts with a prefix, the accent falls on the base word, often the second syllable. Although prefixes are not usually accented, there are some nouns with accented prefixes (see **Lesson 9**).

Lesson 5b reviews the prefixes **un–**, **dis–**, and **non–**.

Lesson 6 reviews the absorbed prefix **in–** with its variants **im–**, **il–**, and **ir–**, which mean **not** (*inaction, impossible, illegal, irrational*). **In–** and its variants can also means *inside, within, into*. Technically speaking, the proper term for these prefixes is **assimilated** prefixes. Since many of you are working with middle school students, we'll call them **absorbed** prefixes.

Lesson 7 (on the same page as **Lesson 4**) is a **Reading and Spelling for Mastery** list, consisting of words with the schwa sound and prefixes. Reduce the number of spelling words for younger children.

Lesson 8 deals with words comprised of base words and suffixes. In this configuration, the accent falls on the base word. Another important rule is included in this lesson: the accent falls on the second syllable or the base word, when the configuration is prefix, base word, suffix. Please ask students to write these four rules in their Decoding Binders:
1. The accent is on the first syllable in most two and three-syllable words.
2. In words that have a prefix and a base word, the accent is on the base word.
3. In words that have a base word and a suffix, the accent is on the base word. Most suffixes are not accented.
4. In words that consist of a prefix, a base word, and a suffix, the accent falls on the base word.

Lesson 9 covers a conflicting pronunciation rule: English has some words that are pronounced in two different ways depending on whether the word is used as a noun or a verb (*conduct, object, suspect*). In nouns, the accent is on the first syllable, or the prefix. When these words function as verbs, the accent is on the second syllable or the base word.

Lesson 10 explains another challenging issue. Many long words have a vowel in the middle of the word that looks like it belongs to an open syllable, but it actually says the schwa sound, *ref e ree, par a graph,* and *or na ment*.

Lesson 11 explains a very complicated spelling rule. We have Webster himself to thank for this one! Exercise caution in teaching this rule to your class. If your students function below the middle fifth grade level, it might be a good idea to skip this page. The rule states: Do NOT double the last consonant after a short vowel or schwa in words that end with an **unaccented** syllable as in *traveled, happening, developer*. In words that end with **accented** syllables, follow the rules covered in chapter 2, as in *committed, occurring, planner*.

Lesson 12 is a true story of an adventure by one of the author's friends.

1b Identifying Accented Syllables

In polysyllabic words, we say one syllable more forcefully than the other ones. The syllable that is pronounced with more force is called the **accented syllable**. Read the words and highlight the accented syllable in each.

1. de part
2. bas ket
3. re quire ment
4. sup ply
5. spark plug
6. ad mire
7. free way
8. big gest
9. pen cil
10. Eng lish
11. de pos it
12. Sep tem ber
13. un der stand
14. ar tist
15. teach er
16. af ter
17. pre dict
18. fast
19. ra di o
20. to ma to
21. re cov er

2 Accented and Unaccented Syllables

In words that have more than one syllable, we say one more clearly and forcefully than the others. The syllable that is stressed (pronounced forcefully) is called the **accented syllable**. The syllables that are not stressed are called the **unaccented syllable(s).** The dictionary uses an apostrophe to show accented syllables *(dis'-trict)*. Pronounce each of the following words. Decide which syllable is accented and highlight it. Then mark the accented or highlighted syllable with an apostrophe *(con-fess')*.

1. dol lar
2. in flate
3. bi cy cle
4. a gree
5. la bel
6. skate board
7. mu sic
8. mis take
9. ac count
10. free dom
11. mem ber
12. ex plode
13. al bum
14. per fume
15. li on
16. al low
17. trum pet
18. sup pose
19. sud den
20. ad vice

Highlight the accented syllables and place the accent mark in these three-syllable words.

1. com put er
2. grand moth er
3. im po lite
4. tel e phone
5. rep re sent
6. e lec tric
7. buf fa lo
8. um brel la
9. vid e o
10. lib er ty

Look up the first word below in your dictionary. Notice that the dictionary gives the accent mark in the phonetic respelling. Use your dictionary to place accent marks in numbers 1, 3, 4, and 9. Do the rest by yourself.

1. en ter tain ment
2. in ter rupt
3. ed u ca tion
4. e lec tron ics
5. dis trib ute
6. bar be cue
7. val en tine
8. his to ry
9. re fer ral
10. a part ment

Read all of the words one more time!

3a The Schwa Sound

The vowel sound in an accented syllable is usually long, short, r-controlled or a diphthong. In unaccented syllables the vowel often says something different. Read the following words and listen to the underlined vowel sounds.

1. a cross'
2. tun' nel
3. chick' en
4. les' son
5. con nect'
6. im por' tant
7. Can' a da
8. or' na ment

What sound do the underlined vowels say? _____

Read each of the following words. Decide which syllable is accented, and mark it with an apostrophe. Then go back over all the words. Listen to the vowel sounds and mark them. Write the schwa symbol (ə) above the vowels that sound like **short u**.

1. chan nel
2. at tend
3. moun tain
4. chil dren
5. ad mire
6. vow el
7. a round
8. pen cil
9. strength en
10. com mand er
11. ab sent
12. sev enth
13. com plete
14. per son al
15. thou sand
16. el e phant
17. sea son al
18. un der stood
19. fish er man
20. A mer i can

Does the **schwa** sound occur in accented or in unaccented syllables?

_____

3b The Dictionary's Phonetic Respelling

The dictionary shows a phonetic version of each word right after the entry word, so we can figure out how unfamiliar words are pronounced. Memorize these four rules:

1. An apostrophe on the right side of a syllable shows that it is accented.
2. We say accented syllables more forcefully than unaccented ones.
3. Vowels in unaccented syllables often say the **schwa** sound.
4. The symbol for the **schwa** sound is ə; it says **short u**.

Match the phonetically spelled words on the left with their correctly spelled counterparts on the right.

1. kəm plē′ shən	seventeen
2. pou′ ər fəl	attend
3. chăl′ ənj	powerful
4. pī′ lət	recommend
5. ə tĕnd′	pollution
6. sĕv′ ən tēn	backward
7. ăk′ sə dənt	pilot
8. rĕk′ ə mĕnd	construction
9. ə pēr′ əns	avoid
10. ŏb′ stə kəl	challenge
11. ə void′	completion
12. pə lōō′ shən	shovel
13. kən strŭk′ shən	appearance
14. băck′ wərd	obstacle
15. shŏv′ əl	accident

Read each of the following words. Place an apostrophe after the accented syllable, and write ə whenever you hear the **schwa** sound. Listen closely to the ending letter **a**. What does it say?

1. so da	5. com ma	9. pan da	13. stan za
2. tu na	6. del ta	10. scu ba	14. piz za
3. ex tra	7. i de a	11. ar o ma	15. dra ma
4. par ka	8. so fa	12. ar e a	16. cam er a

4/7 Reading and Spelling for Mastery

Words with the schwa sound:

4 Spelling List

1. area
2. extra
3. sofa
4. idea
5. camera
6. sugar*
7. answer*
8. woman*
9. women*
10. common
11. often
12. minute *(HG)
13. second
14. difficult
15. breakfast*
16. captain
17. certain
18. mountain
19. fountain
20. American

*Red words, HG=homograph

Words with the schwa sound and prefixes:

7 Spelling List

1. unsure*
2. unfriendly*
3. unfinished
4. appoint
5. disappoint
6. disagree
7. disappear
8. disguise
9. nonsense
10. afford
11. address
12. arrange
13. attract
14. install
15. illegal
16. irresponsible*
17. prevent
18. describe
19. promise
20. remove

5a Accent Marks in Words with Prefixes

Let's review some prefixes you studied in **Chapter 3**. After each set of words, write the prefix and its meaning.

	Prefix	Meaning
1. rewrite, rebuild, reread	_____	_____
2. preshrunk, preheat, precook	_____	_____
3. depart, descend, derail	_____	_____
4. provide, protect, promote	_____	_____
5. coordinate, cooperate, coincide	_____	_____

The prefix **a–** means **on**, **in**, or **without**. Listen to the sound of the prefix **a–** in the following words.

    1. around   2. ajar   3. afloat   4. arise

What does **a–** say? _____

Where does the accent fall in the above words? _____

Read each of the following words. Place an accent mark next to the syllable that you pronounce more forcefully.

1. car pet	4. pup pet	7. mo ment	10. west ern
2. mar gin	5. cam er a	8. val en tine	11. jour nal ist
3. far mer	6. cal en dar	9. nar row	12. por cu pine

What is the accent rule for words with two and three syllables?

_____

Read each of the following words. Circle the prefix and place an accent mark next to the syllable that you pronounce more forcefully.

1. a bove	4. pro long	7. pro duce	10. de glaze
2. pre vent	5. con trol	8. re ply	11. re act
3. de tect	6. a miss	9. pre dict	12. pro ceed

What is the accent rule for two-syllable words that start with a prefix?

_____

5b More Prefixes

Some other common prefixes are **dis–**, **un–**, and **non–**. Add these prefixes in front of the following base words to make new words. Make sure they make sense!

1. sense   _____
2. honest   _____
3. armed (2)   _____   _____
4. fat   _____
5. cover (2)   _____   _____
6. expected   _____
7. stop   _____
8. locate   _____
9. certain   _____

What do the prefixes **dis–**, **un–**, and **non–** mean?   _____

Synonyms are words that have the same meaning. Read each word in the left column. Then draw a line to its synonym in the right column.

1. distracted   unlucky
2. undefeated   disorder
3. unfortunate   unavailable
4. disconnect   disgusting
5. disagreeable   unbeaten
6. unreachable   unfocused
7. disarray   unfriendly
8. uncertain   unplug
9. disagreement   unsure
10. distasteful   dispute

Where does the accent fall on words that have two or three syllables and no prefixes?

_____

Where does the accent fall on words that have a prefix and a base word?

_____

225

6 Absorbed Prefixes

Another common prefix is **in–**. What do you think **in–** means in the following words? _____

    1. indoors   2. insight   3. inside   4. inflate   5. invite   6. install

Sometimes a prefix like **in–** will change its last letter to match the first letter of the base word. Other times, the last letter changes to an entirely different letter that is easier to say with the first letter of the base word. Such prefixes are called **absorbed prefixes**. Let's see if you can make real words by combining the prefix **in–** with the base words below. (Not all base words will change.)

1. in + legal   _____   5. in + responsible   _____
2. in + perfect   _____   6. in + moral   _____
3. in + correct   _____   7. in + human   _____
4. in + regular   _____   8. in + logical   _____

What else does the prefix **in–** and its absorbed forms mean? (**il–**, **im–**, and **ir–**) _____

Another absorbed prefix is **con–**. Try to make real words with **con–** and these Latin roots.

1. con + mute   _____   5. con + lect   _____
2. con + rect   _____   6. con + pare   _____
3. con + nect   _____   7. con + mit   _____
4. con + mittee   _____   8. co + pilot   _____

What do the prefixes **con–**, **com–**, **col–**, and **cor–** mean? _____
What does the **o** in words 1-7 say? _____
Do you remember the prefix **co–**? It is another absorbed prefix of **con–**.

One more absorbed prefix is **ad–**. Try to make real words with **ad–** and these base words.

1. ad + range   _____   5. ad + point   _____
2. ad + ford   _____   6. ad + locate   _____
3. ad + tract   _____   7. ad + dress   _____
4. ad + count   _____   8. ad + sume   _____

What does the prefix **ad–** and its absorbed forms mean? (**ac–**, **af–**, **al–**, **ap–**, **ar–**, **as–** and **at–**)

_____

8 Accent Marks in Words with Suffixes

Let's review the following suffixes you studied in **Chapter 2** and **Chapter 4**: –ful, –less, –ness, –ed, –est, –en, –ing, –er, –ly, –ment, –ive, and –y. Mark the accented syllable in the following words.

1. hand ful
2. teach er
3. part ly
4. crowd ed
5. camp er
6. kind ness
7. frost y
8. roast ing
9. po ny
10. tall est
11. sense less
12. soft en

In words 1-12, is the accent on the base word or on the suffix?
_____

Mark the accented syllable in the following three-syllable words. All of the words start with a prefix and end with a suffix.

1. in tense ly
2. un fair ness
3. pre tend ed
4. de fend ing
5. at trac tive
6. com plain er
7. re gard less
8. pre pay ment
9. com plete ly
10. un luck y
11. pre serv er
12. non smok ing
13. pre vent ed
14. im port ed
15. un worth y

What is the rule for placing accent marks in words with a prefix, a base word, and a suffix?
_____

Use these words in the blanks to complete the sayings: different, minding, helping, away, pulling, kitchen, bushy, thinking, shoulder, meeting

1. I was _____ out loud!
2. Are you all squared _____?
3. If you can't stand the heat, get out of the _____.
4. He was just _____ my leg.
5. She gave me the cold _____.
6. Different strokes for _____ folks.
7. Give a _____ hand.
8. Fancy _____ you here!
9. She was bright-eyed and _____-tailed.
10. You should be _____ your own business!

9 Accent Marks in Nouns and Verbs

English has words that are pronounced in two different ways, depending on whether the word is a noun or a verb. A **verb** is an action word; a **noun** is a person, place, thing, or idea.

The words below are homographs and can be pronounced in two different ways. The accent is on the fist syllable in nouns and on the second syllable in verbs. Pronounce each of the words two ways by stressing the accented syllable. Write the word in each sentence, and decide if it is used as a noun or a verb. Then place the accent mark to match the meaning.

con duct'   **con' duct**

1. Her _____ during the assembly was not acceptable.
2. Metals _____ heat more quickly than things made from plastic.

per mit'   **per' mit**

3. Manuel is studying for his driver's _____.
4. My parents will not _____ me to stay out late on a school night.

in' sult   **in sult'**

5. Please don't _____ my intelligence.
6. That was an _____, and you should apologize.

sus' pect   **sus pect'**

7. I _____ the flight will be delayed due to the stormy weather.
8. The policeman arrested the _____.

pres' ent   **pre sent'**

9. I just love the birthday _____ you gave me.
10. Are you prepared to _____ your speech?

ob' ject   **ob ject'**

11. The defense attorney will _____ to the prosecutor's questions.
12. There's an _____ in the exhibit that is made of pure gold.

Where does the accent fall in verbs? _____

Where does the accent fall in nouns? _____

10 Medial Schwa in Polysyllabic Words

Review: Try to remember the four accent rules and write them on the lines.

1. _____
2. _____
3. _____
4. _____

Here is a very tricky concept. Many long words have a vowel that connects the first and second part of a word. Sometimes there is a consonant before the vowel. These vowels or consonant/vowels look like they belong to an open syllable; however, they are frequently not long. Figure out what the red vowel (also underlined) says in each word below and write its true sound right above it.

1. hes **i** tate
2. cent **i** me ter
3. par **a** dise
4. e rad **i** cate
5. par **a** graph
6. fan t**a** sy
7. ge og r**a** phy
8. ref **e** ree
9. im pl**e** ment
10. ad **e** quate
11. his t**o** ry
12. mar m**a** lade
13. ju v**e** nile
14. ther m**o** stat
15. des t**i** ny
16. lig **a** ment
17. mag n**i** fy
18. prin c**i** pal
19. sac r**i** fice
20. mo t**i** vate
21. e quiv **a** lent
22. cin **e** ma
23. nom **i** nate
24. hip po pot **a** mus

You are correct if you noticed that the red vowels in the words above say the **schwa** sound. The vowels in the middle of long words often say the schwa sound.

Use a dictionary to find six words with one or more schwa sounds.

1. _____ 4. _____
2. _____ 5. _____
3. _____ 6. _____

11 A Tricky Spelling Rule

Let's review the rules for adding the suffixes **–ed, –ing,** and **–er** to one-syllable base words with long or short vowels.
- Words that have a short vowel must have two consonants before a suffix that starts with a vowel.
- When a word ends with only one consonant, that consonant must be doubled.
- When the first vowel is long as in **vowel-consonant-e** syllables, drop the **e** before adding **–ed, –ing,** or **–er**.
- Words such as *camped* or *melted* do not require any changes because they already have two consonants.

Keeping the above rules in mind, add the designated suffix to each of the following words.

1. vote + er _____
2. stomp + ing _____
3. hop + ed _____
4. hope + ed _____
5. plan + ing _____
6. drum + er _____
7. step + ed _____
8. strap + ing _____

Now that you have become familiar with accented and unaccented syllables, here is one more rule that deals with adding suffixes to base words. This rule applies to suffixes that start with vowels (–er, –ed, –ing, –al, –ant, –ent, etc.) and are added to polysyllabic base words that end with unaccented syllables. The rule states: "When a word ends in an **unaccented** syllable, do **not** double the last consonant after a short vowel or schwa (*credited, developer*)." In words that end with **accented** syllables follow the previously mastered rules (*referring, omitted*).

Highlight the accented syllables in the following verbs. Then add the designated suffix to each word and write the new word on the line.

1. prof it + ed _____
2. e quip + ed _____
3. re bel + ing _____
4. em bed + ed _____
5. de vel op + er _____
6. vis it + ed _____
7. per mit + ing _____
8. be gin + er _____
9. ad mit ed _____
10. hap pen + ed _____
11. gal lop + ing _____
12. com mit + ed _____
13. car pet + ed _____
14. lim it + ing _____
15. oc cur + ed _____
16. com pel + ing _____
17. pro pel + er _____
18. cred it + ing _____
19. pre fer + ed _____
20. riv et + ing _____

12 A Long Bike Ride

Have you ever gone on a really long bike ride? Can you remember how tired you were afterwards? My friend Janis Turner, along with her biking buddies Celeste and Rose, challenged each other to a very long ride. They wanted to pedal from the Pacific Ocean across the whole United States to the Atlantic Ocean! Can you figure out how many miles that is? Luckily, Walt, a friend of Celeste's, offered to accompany them by van to haul their camping gear and food and to drive ahead looking for motels or campgrounds. The four undertook this journey as a fundraiser for Hope Hospice, an organization that supports people with terminal illnesses. When the local radio station, KKIQ, got wind of their plans, they interviewed the foursome and asked them to call in every Friday to inform the listeners of their progress. The announcer never missed a chance before or after the phone calls to mention what a deserving, worthy organization Hope Hospice is. Many listeners, friends of the riders, and their coworkers pledged a penny or a nickel per mile.

After negotiating a two-month leave from work, the foursome started their adventure at Baker Beach in San Francisco, California on July 31, 2005. A crowd of friends and Hospice supporters gathered to watch them dip their rear wheels in the ocean before they rode through the streets of San Francisco, across the Golden Gate Bridge, and eastward over the hills, all in one day.

After a day of fast riding through the flat Central Valley, their pace slowed as they muscled their way up the Sierra Nevada Range. They conquered their highest point in Eastern California, Carson Pass, at an altitude of 8,573 ft (2,613 m). Congratulating each other with hugs and high fives, they were rewarded with easy coasting, down the mountainside into the Nevada high desert.

Because the day-time temperatures in Nevada reach 115 degrees Fahrenheit (45 degrees Celcius), the trio started breaking camp at 5:00 am and began riding at the crack of dawn. They would ride for six or seven hours until the heat became unbearable and then try to find a park with some shade. When Walt found a campground or motel with a swimming pool, they felt particularly lucky. Route 50 is a very lonely road with only a few small towns along the way, which often have no accommodations. If no campgrounds or motels were available, they would go to the police station and ask where they could camp. The sheriff usually allowed them to pitch their tents in the city park and often offered them showers at the fire station.

From the Nevada desert, they entered Utah, which was equally hot, but much more mountainous. On a particularly grueling day, the trio ascended three steep passes with temperatures reaching 110 degrees! Since there was no water anywhere, Walt met them on the crest of every pass to supply them with as much cool water as they wanted. His kindness was the proof of true friendship! In spite of the heat and the elevation gain, they rode 85 miles that day! Their route led them through beautiful Capitol Reef National Park with its magical reddish rock formations, sandstone bridges carved by millennia of erosion, and its phantom castles and fortresses. Two days later, during a lunch break, they went swimming in Lake Powell. Soon afterwards, they reached their 1,000 mile mark (1,610km)!

For the next few days, Janis, Rose and Celeste burned thousands of calories as they rode up, up, up the Rocky Mountains to the top of Monarch Pass, at 11,312 ft (3,448 meters), which is on the Continental Divide. Looking westward, all of the rivers flow into the Pacific Ocean, and looking eastward, all of the rivers flow into the Atlantic Ocean, or the Gulf of Mexico. Having expended such great effort, they now delighted in miles and miles of downhill coasting!

Soon they were in Kansas where they made great time. Because it's flat, they averaged 95 miles a day and reached their 2,000 mile mark (3,220km) in Heston, Kansas! On a particularly windy day, Janis fell off her bike and was scraped up badly. Within minutes, a pickup truck screeched to a stop. The friendly couple insisted on loading her bike in their truck and taking Janis to their home to bandage her wounds. After offering her a tall glass of lemonade, they drove her back to the spot where her concerned buddies were waiting.

Upon entering Missouri, they realized they were facing a very different experience. It was tough going because it was constant up and down, up and down for hundreds of miles. Crossing the Mississippi River at St Genevieve, they rode through Southern Illinois and into Kentucky. Kentucky was beautiful with its green hills but also challenging because of the renewed, rolling terrain. In the eastern part of the state, they rode through the Cumberland Gap into Tennessee.

Crossing the Appalachian Mountains was one last challenge before them. They conquered two more passes each time gaining more than four thousand feet, before they faced the final stretch through Virginia. In Charlotteville, they met a wonderful lady named June, the Cookie Lady, who invited them to spend the night, free of charge. She had fixed up her second home for bike riders and offered them the use of the kitchen, which was stocked with free food and lots of cookies.

They were now getting close to the end. A couple of days later, exhilarated and very tired, the threesome celebrated their incredible feat by dipping their front tires into the Atlantic Ocean at Virginia, Beach. They hugged Walt and thanked him for his unwavering support. It would not have been possible to ride across the United States in sixty days without his help.

After flying home, they were greeted at the airport by dozens of friends and several representatives of Hope Hospice who congratulated them on their remarkable achievement and thanked them for raising over $ 10,000!

Janis, Celeste, and Rose rode 3,815 miles (6,150 km) in exactly sixty days! Never once did they succumb to the temptation to ride with Walt. They averaged 65 miles a day, through blistering heat and many storms with a total elevation gain of approximately 100,000 ft (30,480 m). What an astonishing accomplishment!

Comprehension Questions:

1. How did Walt help the three bike riders? _____
   _____

2. Their journey was a fundraiser for what organization? _____
   _____

3. Who helped spread the word of the riders' adventure and consequently helped them raise more money?_____

4. Why was riding through Nevada and Utah so difficult? _____
   _____

5. What is "The Continental Divide"? _____

6. Why was riding through Missouri and Kentucky very difficult? _____
   _____

7. How many miles did the three women ride and how much money did they raise?
   _____

CHAPTER 10
Anglo-Saxon Suffixes

Note to Instructor

This section will teach students how to read and spell additional Anglo-Saxon suffixes and will review the ones that were introduced in earlier chapters. A few Latin suffixes will also be reviewed. Please explain that a suffix is a morpheme that follows a base word and changes its meaning. Most Anglo-Saxon base words are **free morphemes**, which means they make sense when they occur by themselves. It is very important that students learn to read and spell these word endings to the automatic level, because they occur in thousands of words. The suffixes in this chapter are fairly easy to learn because their sound/symbol correspondence is strong (greatest, widen, helpful, careless, lovely).

Students will review the following suffixes in Lessons 1-6: –**er**, –**y**, –**est**, –**en**, –**ed**, –**ing**, –**ar**, –**or**, –**an**, and –**on**. The suffixes –**et** and –**let** are introduced, as well as the rules for adding a second suffix to words that end with –**y**. The suffixes –**ed**, –**en**, –**est**, and –**ing** were covered in Chapter 2 and –**er**, –**ar**, –**or**, –**on**, and –**an** were covered in Chapter 4. The tricky factors are the rules for adding these suffixes to base words. Although these rules were previously covered in Chapter 2 and Chapter 4, they are reviewed because they are complicated and difficult to remember.

Lessons 7-15 cover these suffixes: –**some**, –**ish**, –**hood**, –**ship**, –**ward**, and –**dom** with a review of –**ful**, –**less**, –**ness**, and –**ly**, which were covered in Chapters 1 and 3.

Many teachers have made color-coded flashcards for each set of suffixes (a different color for each set). The most effective method is to have students make their own sets. The suffix is written on one side; the definition, pronunciation, and three examples are written on the reverse side.

Reminders:
1. Have students reread all the words in every lesson once they have completed the exercises.
2. Ask students to copy each new phonogram, red word, homophone, suffix, and rule in the appropriate sections of their Decoding Binders. When entering a phonogram or suffix, students must list four key words that illustrate it. Students must also add four words for every rule.
3. Review all sections of the binder once a week for a minimum of five weeks. Younger children or those with severe learning disabilities may need more time for review.
4. Use the **Proposed Spelling Activities**, located in the Appendix, for all **Reading and Spelling for Mastery** lists. Students must read the list daily before they start the two practice activities.

Lesson 1a is a quiz that reviews how to add Anglo-Saxon suffixes to one-syllable words when the suffix starts with a vowel. When the first vowel is short, the word must have two consonants before the suffix. If there is only one consonant, it must be double *(stopped)*. In a vowel-consonant-e word, drop the **e** and add the suffix *(widen)*. Just add the suffix to base words that end with two consonants or that contain diphthongs, r-controlled vowels, or vowel teams *(cutest, spoiled, dreamer)*.

Lesson 1b is a **Reading and Spelling for Mastery** page, consisting of base words with these suffixes: **–er**, **–en**, **–ed**, **–ing**, **–est**, and **–y**. Assign two appropriate activities from **Proposed Spelling Activities** for daily spelling practice. Students must read the spelling words every day.

Lesson 2 introduces the suffix **–et** and **–let**, pronounced ət, and lət. Sometimes these suffixes mean a small amount of a particular item, such as *book* and *booklet*, *lock* and *locket*. The second half of the page provides more practice with these suffixes in the context of common expressions. Please ask students to use a pencil! This activity might be appropriate for group work.

Lesson 3 is a review of the previous suffixes in the form of a crossword puzzle. Remind students to use pencils.

Lesson 4a explains how to add a second suffix to **–y**. The suffix **–y** usually says long **e** at the end of polysyllabic words. Sometimes it is followed by other suffixes such as **–s**, **–er**, or **–est**. In an earlier lesson, students learned that the suffix **–y** changes to **i** before adding a second suffix as in *lazy, lazier*. It's very important to remember that the letter **i** continues to say the same sound as the **y** it replaces *(puppy, puppies, try, tries)*. Do **not** change **–y** to **i** if a vowel precedes the **–y** or when adding **–ing** or **–ish** *(plays, played, player, playful, flies, flying, babies, babying)*. The words **said** and **paid** are exceptions.

Lesson 4b is a spelling quiz that shows whether students can apply the rules stated in **Lesson 4a**.

Lesson 5a reviews the Latin/Greek suffixes and word endings **–or**, **–ar**, **–on**, and **–an**. They were previously covered in chapter 4.

Lesson 5b (on the same page as **Lesson 1b**) is a **Reading and Spelling for Mastery** list, which consists of words that end with **–or**, **–ar**, **–on**, **–an**, **–et**, and **–let**. Follow the directions listed in **Lesson 1b**.

Lesson 5c discusses the Latin sound of the letter **i**, pronounced like our long **e** sound. When **i** precedes **–on** and **–an**, the combinations **–ion** and **–ian** are suffixes that say ēən; **–ion** means *action or process*, whereas **–ian** means *resembling* or *a person who belongs to*. The combinations **–ior** and **–iar** say ēər. There are very few words with the **–iar** ending. These combinations will be covered more extensively in Chapter 11.
The dictionary shows the following phonetic spelling: After the letters **n** and **l**, **–ion** and **–ian** sound like yən and **–ior** and **–iar** sound like yər. For most students it is too confusing to introduce this variation at this point; however, if you have a strong group, use the following words to teach these phonograms: *onion, stallion, union, civilian, million, opinion, billion, senior, junior*. Since the two sounds ēən and yən, as well as ēər and yər are very similar, students will arrive at the correct pronunciation with either explanation.

Lesson 6 reinforces accent placement, which was previously covered in Chapter 9.

Lesson 7a (No worksheet) Dictate the following words to review the suffixes **–ful**, **–less**, **–ness**, and **–ly**: *cheerful, fearless, sickness, partly, pointless, slowly, careful, sweetness*. Ask students to write the meaning of the suffixes next to the first four words. (These suffixes were covered in Chapters 1 and 3.) Review as necessary. Most students will probably remember that **–ful** means *full, with much* and **–less** means *without*. The suffix **–ness** means *state of being, condition of*. Most common grammatical change: **–ness** changes an adjective to a noun. Please teach students the following rule: When a base word ends with the letter **n** and the suffix **–ness** is added, both **n**'s are kept *(evenness, keenness, leanness, openness)*. The suffix **–ly** means *like, in the manner of*. Most common grammatical changes:

–ly tells how and changes a noun to an adjective *(lovely)* and an adjective to an adverb *(softly)*. Explain these two rules: 1. When **–ly** is added to a *consonant-le* syllable, the letters **le** are dropped *(simple, simply, humble, humbly)*. 2. When adding the suffix **–ly** to a word that ends with the letter **l**, keep both **l's** *(cruelly, gravelly)*. This rule also applies to words that end with the suffixes **–al** and **–ful** *(equally, carefully)*.

Lesson 7b (On the same page as Lesson 10b) is a **Reading and Spelling for Mastery** list consisting of words with these suffixes: **–ful**, **–less**, and **–ness**. Please select two appropriate activities from **Proposed Spelling Activities**, located in the Appendix. Students must read the words before they start their daily spelling practice.

Lesson 8a (No worksheet) introduces the suffixes **–some**, **–ish**, and **–hood**.

A) 1. Write the suffix **–some** on the board/overhead (or show the card). 2. Tell students that they will be studying words with the suffix **–some** and write three words that end with **–some** next to the suffix. Ask for volunteers to read the words. 3. After everyone understands the concept, elicit a minimum of ten words from your class and write them on the board/overhead. In case not enough words are volunteered, a list is supplied for your convenience: *(lonesome, threesome, worrisome, meddlesome, awesome, troublesome, handsome, tiresome, foursome, wholesome, cumbersome, burdensome, gruesome)*. 4. Ask how **–some** is pronounced and what it means: (səm), *having the quality of*. 5. Students write the suffix, pronunciation, definition, and four examples in their binders. Most common grammatical changes: **–some** converts a noun, a verb, or an adjective to another adjective or a noun. This grammatical explanation is probably too complex for most students.

Suggestion: Divide the class into small groups that are balanced in abilities. After you have presented the first suffix with examples, set a timer for two or three minutes (longer for younger students) and have the groups compete against each other. Allow students to use textbooks or dictionaries. The group that generates the most words (they must be valid) wins the first round. If this format works well, do this for the next five suffixes.

B) 1. Write **–ish** on the board or overhead. 2. Add three words. 3. Elicit words from students and write their words on the board/overhead *(selfish, Scottish, stylish, sheepish, snobbish, feverish, clannish, foolish, Swedish, reddish, skittish, sluggish, childish)*. 4. Ask how **–ish** is pronounced and what it means, (ĭsh), *having the quality of*. 5. Students write the suffix, pronunciation, definition, and four examples in their binders. Most common grammatical change: **–ish** converts a noun to an adjective or an adjective to another adjective. When **–ish** is part of a verb, it is not a true suffix *(publish, admonish, languish, refurbish, finish, banish)*. Since **–ish** begins with a vowel, review the following two rules:

a) Using the words *snobbish, clannish, reddish, skittish* and *sluggish*, ask your class why the middle consonant is doubled. Then review the rule for adding suffixes that start with vowels **(Lesson 1a)**. In a word that ends in a vowel-consonant-e syllable, a consonant-le syllable, or a vowel-vowel syllable, drop the **e** before adding the suffix *(prudish, ticklish, bluish)*. Just add the suffix to base words ending with two consonants.
b) The following rule applies to the suffix **–ish** (also **–ing**). When a word ends with **y**, do not change the **y** to **i** before adding **–ish** or **–ing** *(babyish, grayish, boyish, trying, playing)*. Ask students if they remember this rule from **Lesson 4a** and **4b**. The rule states that no word shall have two **i's** next to each other.

C) 1. Write **–hood** on the board or overhead. 2. Add three words. 3. Elicit words from students and write their words on the board/overhead *(neighborhood, childhood, motherhood, fatherhood, livelihood, statehood, likelihood, falsehood, sisterhood, brotherhood, parenthood, womanhood, manhood)*. 4. Ask how **–hood** is pronounced and what it means: (hŏŏd), *state of, having the quality of*. 5. Students write the suffix, pronunciation, definition, and four examples in their binders. Most common grammatical change: **–hood** changes an adjective or a noun to another noun, often with a collective connotation.

Lesson 8b requires students to add suffixes to base words. Explain that suffixes that begin with consonants can be added without any changes. The only change that needs to be made is for base words that end with the letter **y**. In words that end with a consonant + **y**, change the **y** to **i** before adding the suffix *(plentiful)*. There are six exceptions: shy *(shyly, shyness)* dry *(dryly, dryness)* sly *(slyly, slyness)* spry *(spryly, spryness)*, wry *(wryly, wryness)* and sky *(skyward)*. Teach these exceptions only to strong students. If a vowel precedes **y**, <u>no</u> changes are needed *(playful)*. The words *paid* and *said* are exceptions. Words 23-30 require students to add **–ish** to base words.

Lesson 9a: (No worksheet) Introduce the suffixes **–ship**, **–ward**, and **–dom**.

A) 1. Write **–ship** on the board or overhead. 2. Add three words. 3. Elicit words from students and write their words on the board/overhead *(hardship, fellowship, leadership, penmanship, membership, ownership, township, clerkship, courtship, companionship, relationship, readership, partnership)*. 4. Ask how **–ship** is pronounced and what it means: (**shəp**), *rank, having the quality of*. 5. Students write the suffix, pronunciation, definition, and four examples in their binders. Most common grammatical change: **–ship** converts an adjective or a noun to another noun, often with a collective connotation.

B) 1. Write **–ward** on board/overhead. 2. Add three words. 3. Elicit words from students and write their words on the board/overhead *(outward, homeward, awkward, inward, afterward, northward, southward, upward, forward, seaward, backward, westward, eastward)*. 4. Ask how **–ward** is pronounced and what it means: (**wərd**), *in the direction of*. 5. Students write the suffix, pronunciation, definition, and four examples in their binders. Most common grammatical change: **–ward** changes a noun to an adjective or an adverb. This suffix is not very common.

C) 1. Write **–dom** on the board or overhead. 2. Add three words. 3. Elicit words from students and write their words on the board/overhead *(freedom, serfdom, boredom, kingdom, wisdom, seldom, chiefdom, martyrdom, dukedom, stardom, fiefdom)*. 4. Ask how **–dom** is pronounced and what it means: (**dəm**), *condition, state of, rank, position*. 5. Students write the suffix, pronunciation, definition, and four examples in their binders. Most common grammatical change: **–dom** converts an adjective or a noun to another noun, often with a collective connotation. This suffix is not very common.

Lesson 9b requires students to add suffixes to base words. Review the **y** rule from **Lesson 4a** and the rule for adding suffixes that begin with vowels from **Lesson 1a**.

Lesson 10a consists of a reading and a dictation exercise. Write all of the suffixes on the board or on the overhead (or display the cards) and ask students to read them individually, if possible. If that is not practical, ask your class to read them in unison. Next, dictate the words from Lists A and B. Students should copy the suffixes only. After completing List B, erase the suffixes from the board or remove the cards. Ask students to turn over their sheets of paper and dictate the words from List C and D. Students write the suffixes from memory. When they forget, write it on the board (or show the particular card) and ask them to copy it.

Lesson 10b (on the same page as **Lesson 7b**) is a **Reading and Spelling for Mastery** list with the suffixes **–ly**, **–some**, and **–ness**. Follow the directions listed in **Lesson 1b**.

Lesson 10c (No worksheet) First, dictate the words from Lists E and F (see **Lesson 10a**) and have your class write the suffixes from memory. Afterwards write all of the suffixes on the board (or use the cards) and ask students to read the suffixes one more time.

Lesson 11a reviews the seven different syllables in conjunction with suffixes. Prefixes and suffixes are not marked. The code (s-s) is used in words that have two suffixes as in *helpfulness* (cl-s-s). The second exercise is a condensed version of the fairy-tale *Snow White* with suffixes that are missing. If you are teaching grades 8-12, you might consider skipping this paragraph. After students have completed filling in the blanks, ask your class to read the story aloud. Familiarity of the story helps students to know where the suffixes should go.

Lesson 11b is a dictation exercise. Please reiterate the following rule: When syllabicating a word with a double consonant and a suffix that begins with a vowel, the second consonant usually joins the suffix to keep the base word intact *(slug-gish, big-gest, slip-per)*. This rule does not apply to base words that end in a double consonant, because the base word must be kept intact *(bull-ish, stress-ing, tall-er)*.

Lessons 11c (on the same page as **Lesson 13b**) is a **Reading and Spelling for Mastery** list with these suffixes: **–ish**, **–hood**, and **–ship**. Follow the directions listed in **Lesson 1b**.

Lesson 12 is a crossword puzzle. Please ask students to use a pencil.

Lesson 13a requires students to match phonetically spelled words with their correct counterparts.

Lesson 13b (on the same page as **Lesson 11c**) is a **Reading and Spelling for Mastery** page with these suffixes: **–ship**, **–dom**, and **–ward**. Follow the directions listed in **Lesson 1b**.

Lesson 14 reviews syllabication of words with base words, prefixes, and suffixes, as well as accent placement. Please prompt students to remember the following rules and record their responses on the board or overhead. In most two and three-syllable words, the accent falls on the first syllable; but if the word starts with a prefix, the accent falls on the base word, often the second syllable.

Lesson 15 is a story entitled *A Brief History of the English Language*. It explains why English is so difficult to read and spell. It is particularly important for students to have this information before they begin Chapter 11, which deals with challenging Latin suffixes.

Before your class reads the article, please write these difficult words on the board or copy them as a transparency for the overhead. Ask students to practice reading the list silently. Next, have students read them in unison. The story will explain why some of these words are hard to read.

1. languages
2. symbol
3. surrounded
4. brutally
5. centuries
6. confusion
7. negative
8. German
9. realize
10. treacherous
11. original
12. intermarried
13. monarch
14. conclusion
15. Italian
16. complicated
17. conquered
18. Anglo-Saxon
19. intention
20. positive
21. especially
22. correspondence
23. difficult
24. collapsed
25. similarities
26. fiercely
27. Westminster Abbey

1a Suffix Pretest

This is a quiz to see how well you remember the rules for adding suffixes to base words.

Add –er

1. flip _____
2. shop _____
3. time _____
4. blend _____

Add –y

1. crab _____
2. haze _____
3. trend _____
4. rose _____

Add –en

1. damp _____
2. ripe _____
3. flat _____
4. spoke _____

Add –est

1. hot _____
2. fine _____
3. slim _____
4. strong _____

Add –ed

1. chat _____
2. step _____
3. lift _____
4. scrape _____

Add –ing

1. hope _____
2. jump _____
3. scrub _____
4. quote _____

Let's see if you can do the reverse. Write the base word next to each two-syllable word.

1. slipper _____
2. cutest _____
3. shaken _____
4. choppy _____
5. swimmer _____
6. pricing _____
7. rotten _____
8. sliced _____

9. foggy _____
10. strutted _____
11. reddest _____
12. shined _____
13. chatter _____
14. wavy _____
15. bumpy _____
16. shaking _____

1b/5b Reading and Spelling for Mastery

Words with the suffixes –er, –en, –ed, –ing, –est, and –y:

Words with the endings –or, –ar, –on, –an, –et, and –let:

1b Spelling

1. suffer
2. remember
3. teacher
4. driver
5. discover
6. happen
7. happened
8. happening
9. written*
10. forgotten
11. fasten*
12. lengthen
13. strengthen
14. straightened*
15. greatest *
16. thinnest
17. strongest
18. hungry
19. empty
20. plenty

*Red words

5b Spelling

1. motor
2. visitor
3. regular
4. particular
5. grammar
6. familiar
7. gallon
8. common
9. cotton
10. season
11. reason
12. weapon*
13. onion
14. human
15. woman
16. packet
17. pocket
18. jacket
19. ticket
20. bracelet*

2 Suffixes –et and –let

The suffix **–et** says ət. Sometimes it has the same meaning as the suffix **–let**, which says lət. Highlight the base words in numbers 1-12.

1. droplet
2. ringlet
3. helmet
4. packet
5. snippet
6. cabinet
7. booklet
8. leaflet
9. locket
10. starlet
11. coverlet
12. wavelet

How do these suffixes change the meaning of the base words? _____

You are correct if you noticed that **–et** and **–let** mean a small amount of a particular item, such as **book** and **booklet**. Often, however, they do not have a clear meaning.

Use the words in the box to complete the phrases and expressions. Do the ones you know first.

| budget | basket | hatchet | rocket | carpet | ticket |
| pockets | bonnet | Musketeers | racket | blanket | market |

1. This is not _____ science.
2. He is on trial because he lined his own _____.
3. This is my _____ out of here.
4. In a job interview, you must learn to _____ yourself.
5. Cut out that _____; I'm trying to concentrate.
6. Grandma gave me a goody _____ for my birthday.
7. They were just like the Three _____.
8. It's time to forgive and bury the _____.
9. Don't be a wet _____; let's go to the party.
10. She put a bee in my _____.
11. Because of the lawsuit, our company is facing a huge _____ crunch.
12. My boss called me on the _____ for giving the customer incorrect information.

3 Review of Eight Suffixes

Read the words in the box and use them to solve the crossword puzzle. Write in pencil.

recovery   shiny   leakiest   entered   emboldened   oxygen   droplet   early
toughen   locket banners   happening straightened steepest quietest kitten

Across
1. Cleaned up, tidied
2. Occurring
3. A component of air
4. Nose of Rudolf
5. Could be the condition of a very old faucet
6. Came inside
7. A tiny drop
8. Improved health

Down
1. Not at all loud
2. A tiny silver or gold case that holds pictures
3. To make less fragile
4. An adjective for a slope
5. Pieces of cloth or paper with a message or logo
6. A young animal
7. Before the appointed time
8. Eager to try, not afraid, encouraged

243

4a Adding Other Suffixes to –y

Do you remember the sound of the suffix –y? It frequently says long **e**. Sometimes it is followed by other suffixes such as –s, –er, and –est. In an earlier lesson, you learned that the suffix –y changes to **i** before you add a second suffix *(lazy, lazier)*. This only applies when a consonant comes before **y**. If a vowel precedes **y**, do not change it *(player)*. It's very important to remember that the letter **i** says the same sound as the **y** it replaces *(puppy, puppies, try, tries.*

Add these suffixes to the following words: **–er, –est**

1. happy
2. curly
3. angry
4. juicy
5. gray
6. pretty
7. funny
8. bulky
9. lucky
10. sloppy

In numbers 1-12, remove the suffixes –**er** and –**est**, and write the base words on the lines.

1. laziest
2. carrier
3. shakiest
4. baggier
5. sunnier
6. spiciest
7. crazier
8. foggiest
9. tiniest
10. rainiest
11. smokiest
12. muddiest

Some two-syllable words that end in **y** have a long **i** sound. This only happens when the second syllable is accented. Read these words: **reply, supply, comply, deny, rely, imply**.

Add the suffixes –**s**, –**ed**, and –**ing** to **reply, deny, supply** *(relies, relied, relying)*.

1. reply:
2. deny:
3. supply:

4b Plural After –y (Teacher Page)

Tell students that you will give them a quiz on a spelling pattern they learned in Chapter 5. Dictate the following words and review as necessary.

This lesson covers the following three rules:
1. To form the plural or third person singular in words that end with **y**, change the **y** to **i** and add **–es**. Use this rule only when a consonant comes before **y**. When a vowel comes before **y**, simply add **–s**.
2. Past tense: When a verb ends with the letter **y**, change the **y** to **i** and add **–ed**. In verbs that have a vowel before **y**, simply add **–ed**. Common exceptions: said, paid, laid.
3. Present participle: When adding **–ing** to a verb that ends with **y**, do **not** change the **y** to **i**, just add **–ing**. The rule states that we cannot have two **i's** next to each other.

Dictation

1. berry – berries (H)
2. story - stories
3. penny - pennies
4. lady - ladies
5. twenty - twenties
6. baby - babies
7. key - keys
8. turkey - turkeys
9. day - days
10. play, plays, playing
11. buy* (H), buys, buying
12. delay, delays, delaying
13. carry, carried, carrying
14. try, tried, trying
15. dry, dried, drying
16. fly, flies, flying
17. deny, denied, denying
18. reply, replied, replying
19. say, said, saying*
20. pay, paid, paying*

Red words, H=homophone

5a Review of Suffixes –or, –ar, –on, –an

Words with the suffixes –**er** are derived from Anglo-Saxon or old English. Many other words end with the same sound (ər) but are spelled with –**or** and –**ar**. These two suffixes often change a noun to a verb and mean *one who does or performs a certain action*. Words that end with the suffixes –**or** and –**ar** are usually derived from Latin or Greek.

The suffixes –**or** and –**ar** say ər. The Anglo-Saxon suffix –**en** says ən. The word endings –**on** and –**an** are usually attached to Latin or Greek derivatives and say ən. Most suffixes are unaccented. The vowel in unaccented syllables usually says the schwa sound (ə).

Read words 1-15 and listen to the sound of the suffixes. Then write ər or ən on the lines.

1. cotton _____
2. escalator _____
3. jugular _____
4. horizon _____
5. monitor _____
6. humor _____
7. governor _____
8. urban _____
9. similar _____
10. veteran _____
11. human _____
12. scissors _____
13. ancestor _____
14. reason _____
15. projector _____

Synonyms are words that have similar meanings. Choose words from the following list to find synonyms for numbers 1-8.

> calendar   professor   canyon   narrator   prison   ventilator   advisor   sugar

1. counselor _____
2. dungeon _____
3. planner _____
4. lecturer _____
5. storyteller _____
6. sweetener _____
7. respirator _____
8. gorge _____

Antonyms are words that mean the opposite. Choose words from the following list to find antonyms for numbers 1-8.

> honor   uncommon   supervisor   veteran   circular   major   urban   liberator

1. minor _____
2. worker _____
3. dishonor _____
4. rural _____
5. conqueror _____
6. angular _____
7. rookie _____
8. common _____

5c *i* before *–on, –an, –or, –ar*

When the letter **i** is in front of the word endings **–on** and **–an**, two suffixes are created: **–ion** and **–ian**; **–ion** means *an action or process* and **–ian** means *a person belonging to* or *resembling*. Latin or French do not have long or short vowels. The Latin or French sound for our letter **i** says our long **e** sound; the suffixes **–ion** and **–ian** say **ēən**. When the letter **i** is in front of **–or** and **–ar**, the two combinations (**ior** and **iar**) say **ēər**.

Read these word starters and draw lines to the correct sound of the word endings.

1. warrior
2. librarian
3. historian   **ēən**
4. interior   **ēər**
5. comedian
6. scorpion

7. custodian
8. guardian
9. exterior   **ēən**
10. champion   **ēər**
11. superior
12. Canadian

Highlight the following words you can read and write the <u>sound</u> of the **i** above it.

1. ruffian   2. barbarian   3. mammalian   4. Australian

Highlight the words you can read. Listen to the sound of the word endings and write them under the correct heading below.

regular   familiar   popular   grammar   peculiar   instructor   Indian
criterion   Italian   inferior   amphibian   conductor   median   ulterior

You are correct if you heard a long **e** sound. Memorize this rule: when **i** occurs before a suffix that starts with a vowel, it usually says **ē**.

ar/or = ər	–iar/–ior = ēər	–ion/–ian = ēən

6 Review of Accented Syllables

Do you remember the accent rules for two and three-syllable words?

Read these words. Highlight the accented syllables, and mark them with an apostrophe.

1. car pet
2. al ler gy
3. gold en
4. fol low er
5. bas ket ball
6. loos en
7. tall est
8. stock bro ker
9. free hand
10. clean est
11. brace let
12. brav er y
13. gadg et
14. flow ers
15. nois y
16. i vor y

Where does the accent fall in two and three-syllable words?

_____

Read these words. Highlight the accented syllables and mark them with an apostrophe. Here are the prefixes you learned in previous chapters: re–, pre–, de–, pro–, co–, con–, com–, col–, cor–, in–, il–, im–, ir–, dis–, un–, non–, mis–, and ad–.

1. de scend
2. un sure
3. pro claim
4. dis arm
5. pre serve
6. re port
7. con tempt
8. de rail
9. in tact
10. pre scribe
11. im pose
12. re act

Where does the accent fall in words that start with a prefix?

_____

Read these words. Highlight the accented syllables and mark them with an apostrophe.

1. re cord er
2. im plant ed
3. un pack ing
4. pre vent ed
5. un luck y
6. mis tak en
7. in hu man
8. un like ly
9. con duc tor
10. ac count ing
11. un eas y
12. de light ed

Where does the accent fall in words with a prefix, a base word, and a suffix?

_____

248

7b/10b Reading and Spelling for Mastery

Base words with the following suffixes: –ful, –less, –ness, –ly, and –some.

7b Spelling
1. careful
2. useful
3. carefully
4. legally
5. wasteful
6. wonderful
7. peaceful*
8. thoughtful *
9. beautiful *
10. doubtful*
11. senseless
12. painless
13. worthless
14. needless
15. endless
16. harmless
17. happiness *
18. carelessness
19. thankfulness
20. fearlessness

10b Spelling
1. lovely
2. mainly
3. slowly
4. really
5. lonely
6. friendly *
7. finally
8. perfectly
9. handsome
10. tiresome
11. lonesome
12. gruesome
13. troublesome *
14. bothersome
15. goodness
16. illness
17. kindness
18. forgiveness
19. worthiness
20. loneliness

*Red words

8b Suffixes –some, –hood, –ly, –ish

It's easy to add suffixes that start with a consonant to base words, because usually no changes are needed. Just add the suffix and keep silent **e's**. There are two exceptions:
1. When a base word ends with a consonant + **y**, change the **y** to **i** before adding a suffix (*lazy, laziness*), but when the base word ends with a vowel + **y**, do not change the **y** (*play, playful*).
2. When you add **–ly** to base words that end with a consonant-le syllable, drop the letters **le** before you add **–ly** (*bubble, bubbly*).
Do you remember the rules for adding **–ish** to base words?

Rewrite the words by adding **–some** and read them:

1. trouble _____   4. three _____
2. whole _____   5. worry _____
3. bother _____   6. meddle _____

Rewrite the words by adding **–hood** and read them.

7. likely _____   10. parent _____
8. woman _____   11. lively _____
9. brother _____   12. knight _____

Rewrite the words by adding **–ly** and read them: Keep both **l's** when **–ly** follows **–al** and **–ful**.

13. forceful _____   18. personal _____
14. angry _____   19. lucky _____
15. probable _____   20. possible _____
16. happy _____   21. incredible _____
17. careful _____   22. legal _____

Rewrite the words by adding **–ish** and read them. Do **not** change **y** to **i** before **–ish**.

23. snob _____   27. slug _____
24. baby _____   28. style _____
25. gray _____   29. tickle _____
26. Scot _____   30. boy _____

9b Suffixes –ship, –ward, –dom

It's easy to add suffixes that start with a consonant, because usually no changes are necessary. Just add the suffix and keep silent **e**'s. There are two things to remember: 1. When a base word ends with a consonant + **y**, you must change the **y** to **i** before adding a suffix *(lively, livelihood)*. 2. When the base word ends with a vowel + **y**, keep the **y** *(key, keyless)*.

Rewrite the words by adding **–ship** and read them:

1. partner _____
2. friend _____
3. censor _____
4. hard _____
5. penman _____
6. guardian _____

Rewrite the words by adding **–ward** and read them.

7. side _____
8. down _____
9. after _____
10. up _____
11. home _____
12. out _____

Rewrite the words by adding **–dom** and read them.

13. free _____
14. bore _____
15. wise _____
16. star _____
17. king _____
18. chief _____

Write the base words on the lines for the following words.

19. sluggish _____
20. clannish _____
21. silliness _____
22. liveliness _____
23. playfully _____
24. greedily _____
25. plentiful _____
26. penniless _____
27. sisterhood _____
28. equally _____

10a Suffix Dictation (Teacher Page)

A) 1. neighborhood
    2. childish
    3. timeless
    4. chiefdom
    5. backward
    6. careful
    7. troublesome
    8. neatly
    9. citizenship
    10. happiness

B) 1. softly
    2. quarrelsome
    3. kindness
    4. helpful
    5. sideward
    6. painless
    7. kingdom
    8. foolish
    9. hardship
    10. nationhood

C) 1. courtship
    2. greenish
    3. plainly
    4. inward
    5. childhood
    6. illness
    7. playful
    8. twosome
    9. nameless
    10. fiefdom

D) 1. upward
    2. irksome
    3. knighthood
    4. lately
    5. rubbish
    6. fearful
    7. friendship
    8. awareness
    9. wisdom
    10. priceless

E) 1. downward
    2. madness
    3. needless
    4. conveniently
    5. girlhood
    6. boredom
    7. dictatorship
    8. hateful
    9. reddish
    10. meddlesome

F) 1. stylish
    2. wishful
    3. judgeship
    4. burdensome
    5. desperately
    6. careless
    7. goodness
    8. onward
    9. boyhood
    10. seldom

11a Syllabication with Suffixes

Write the words in syllables, separate them with dashes, and mark the vowels. Prefixes and suffixes are not marked. Next, denote the code. Finally, place an apostrophe right after the accented syllable. Read the words at your teacher's direction.

1. nationhood _____
2. membership _____
3. Scottish _____
4. awkwardly _____
5. meaninglessness _____
6. respectfully _____
7. boredom _____
8. unwholesome _____
9. thankfulness _____
10. relationship _____
11. adventuresome _____
12. gratefully _____

Read the story and fill in the blanks with the correct suffixes so that it makes sense.

You will use these suffixes: –ly, –ful, –ness, –hood, –wards, –some, –less.

After Snow White ate the poisonous apple, she fainted. When the usual_____ cheer_____ dwarfs saw the love_____ maiden, they felt sad_____. They felt hope_____ because they thought that she was dead. The dread_____ news traveled quick_____. The whole neighbor_____ cried. After_____ they laid her in a coffin and carried her to the graveyard. Fortunate_____ a hand_____ prince came by. He loved her instant_____. His kiss awakened Snow White, and they lived happi_____ ever after.

Read the story again to check whether it makes sense.

11b Dictation Exercise (Teacher Page)

Provide the code orally and write it on the board or on the overhead. Then dictate each word. Ask students to write the word in syllables, separate the syllables with dashes, and mark the vowels.

Students must circle the vowel + r to mark r-controlled vowels. On this page, they are printed in red.

Code abbreviations:
  cl=closed   vv=vowel-vowel
  vce=vowel-consonant-e   cle=consonant-le
  op=open   d=diphthong/vowel digraph
  rc=r-controlled   s = suffix
     pref = prefix

1. (rc-s)   scorn-ful
2. (cl-rc-s)   sĭs-ter-hood*
3. (cl-rc-s)   clĕv-er-ness*
4. (cl-cle-s)   mĕd-dle-some
5. (vce-s)   brāve-ly
6. (vv-rc-s)   rēad-er-ship*
7. (pref-rc-s)   re-gard-less
8. (rc-s)   serf-dom*
9. (vv-m+s)   squēa-mish
10. (d-s)   out-ward

1. (cl-g+s)   slŭg-gish
2. (pref-vce-s)   en-tīre-ly
3. (cl-s)   rĕst-less-ness
4. (rc-s)   north-ward
5. (rc-rc-s)   part-ner-ship*
6. (cl-s)   kĭng-dom
7. (d-s)   boy-hood
8. (vv-s-s-s)   mēan-ing-ful-ly
9. (vce-s-s)   shāme-less-ness
10. (vv-s)   thrēe-some

* Accept **er**, **ir**, and **ur** in these *r-controlled* syllables, but point out the correct spelling of these words.

Ask students to pronounce the words.

11c/13b Reading and Spelling for Mastery

These lessons will cover base words with the following suffixes: –ish, –hood, –ship, –dom, and –ward. For the first spelling activity, ask students to write the words in syllables and mark the accented syllable with an apostrophe.

11c Spelling

1. selfish
2. childish
3. English
4. reddish
5. furnish
6. foolish
7. rubbish
8. publish
9. finish *
10. parenthood
11. fatherhood
12. sisterhood
13. livelihood*
14. brotherhood
15. nationhood*
16. neighborhood*
17. childhood
18. hardship
19. worship*
20. friendship*

*Red words

13b Spelling

1. fellowship
2. township
3. ownership
4. membership
5. leadership
6. relationship *
7. citizenship*
8. freedom
9. kingdom
10. random
11. seldom
12. wisdom
13. boredom
14. backward
15. forward
16. frontward
17. afterwards
18. downward
19. northward
20. southward

12 Challenge Words

Use the words in the box for the crossword puzzle. Write in pencil.

masterful	indirectly	tenderness	falsehood	distrustful	frequently
noiselessly	accomplish	forgiveness	gracefully	quarrelsome	workmanship
		boyhood			

Across

1. The act of letting grudges go
2. A statement that is not true. The suffix has a double vowel.
3. cl-rc-s, outstanding, highly skilled
4. op-cl-s, often
5. cl-cl-cl, to meet a goal
6. The time of a man's childhood
7. cl-cl-s, not trusting

Down

1. d-s-s, without sound
2. vce-s-s, how a dancer moves
3. cl-rc-s, gentleness, sweetness
4. rc-cl-s, hard to get along with
5. Antonym of straightforwardly
6. rc-cl-s, the quality of a person's work

13a Dictionary Pronunciations

The dictionary shows a phonetic version of each word right after the entry word, so we can figure out how an unfamiliar word is pronounced.

Reminder:
1. When an apostrophe comes right after a syllable, it means that it is **accented**.
2. Accented syllables are pronounced more forcefully than unaccented ones.
3. Vowels in unaccented syllables often say the schwa sound.
4. The symbol for the schwa sound is ə and is pronounced as a short **u**.
5. Most four-syllable words also have a secondary accent.

Match the phonetically spelled words on the left with their correctly spelled counterparts on the right.

1. byoo' tə fəl   governorship
2. kə rĕkt' nəs   outwardly
3. wurth' ləs   unexpectedly
4. out lăn' dĭsh   guardianship
5. gə' vər nər shĭp'   correctness
6. sək sĕs' fəl   outlandish
7. out' wərd lē   beautiful
8. gar' dē ən shĭp'   worthless
9. ŭn ĕk spĕk' təd lē   successful

1. jĭb' ər ĭsh   ghostly
2. gōst' lē   tasteless
3. ôk' wərd nəs   randomly
4. nīt' hŏod   cowardliness
5. tāst' ləs   purposeful
6. krăfts' mən shĭp   awkwardness
7. kou' ərd lē nəss'   gibberish
8. pər' pəs fəl   knighthood
9. răn' dəm lē   craftsmanship

14 Review of Accented Syllables

An Anglo-Saxon base word makes sense by itself. It may stand alone, or it may have prefixes and suffixes attached in the beginning or at the end.

1. Write the base word, prefix, and suffix(es) next to the numbered words.
2. Mark the accented syllable by placing an apostrophe right after it. Try to remember the rules you learned in chapter 9.

Hint: The spelling and pronunciation of the base word may change when it stands alone.

	base word	prefix	suffix	suffix
1. yellowish	_____		_____	
2. leadership	_____		_____	_____
3. disorderly	_____	_____	_____	
4. unselfishness	_____	_____	_____	_____
5. downward	_____		_____	
6. motherhood	_____		_____	
7. foolishness	_____		_____	_____
8. delightful	_____	_____	_____	
9. chiefdom	_____		_____	
10. unwholesome	_____	_____	_____	
11. wilderness	_____		_____	_____
12. imperfectly	_____	_____	_____	
13. ownership	_____		_____	_____
14. carelessness	_____		_____	_____
15. disgracefully	_____	_____	_____	_____
16. wisdom	_____		_____	
17. childhood	_____		_____	
18. insightful	_____	_____	_____	

15 A Brief History of the English Language

First of all, you are right if you think English spelling is really hard! Other languages like German, Italian, and Spanish are easy to spell because their words are usually written the way they sound. The proper term for this is **sound/symbol correspondence**. It means that one letter stands for one sound. We all realize that many English words are not spelled the way they sound. Let's explore why this is so.

Why is English so difficult to read and spell? The answer to this question has a lot to do with the history of England. Even though England is an island, surrounded by treacherous waters, it was invaded over and over. The Romans conquered England roughly 2,000 years ago and ruled it for 500 years. To this day, there are Roman ruins that prove the vastness of their empire.

After the collapse of the Roman Empire in the 5th century, bloodthirsty Germanic tribes called Angles, Saxons, and Jutes sailed across the English Channel. They brutally plundered and burned the houses, villages, and towns of the original people. Thousands were killed. After forcing the native people to flee into Scotland, Wales, and Ireland, the Anglo-Saxons started settlements in England and have lived there to this day.

These Germanic tribes spoke Anglo-Saxon, a language somewhat similar to German. Over time, Anglo-Saxon evolved into Old English. Many of our common words still have clear similarities to German words. Some examples are: water = Wasser, garden = Garten, man = Mann, father = Vater, mother = Mutter, brother = Bruder, sight = Sicht, right = recht, etc. To this day, many of our common words have their origin in Anglo-Saxon or early German.

In the late eighth century, Viking pirates and warriors sailed to England and began raiding the coastline. Although the Anglo-Saxons defended their country bravely for two centuries, the Vikings defeated them in 1013. As the saying goes, "What goes around, comes around." The Vikings settled in England and intermarried with the Anglo-Saxons. Over time, traces of Danish, the language of the Vikings, were mixed in with Anglo-Saxon or Old English. Such words as *skin, neighbor, skirt, husband,* and *sky* are examples of words we inherited from Danish. England was ruled by many different kings during the next fifty years. Then a Viking named Harold came to the throne 1066.

In the same year, King William of northern France set sail across the English Channel with the intention of conquering England. The generals of the French and the English armies readied their troops for battle. King William and King Harold confronted each other at the Battle of Hastings on October 14th. King Harold and his five-thousand-man army fought fiercely to defend their country. Toward evening, King Harold was wounded by an arrow and fell from his horse. In the confusion of battle, he was trampled to death. Without their leader, The English were defeated! King William I, also known as William the Conqueror, was crowned at Westminster Abbey on Christmas Day in 1066.

Coming from northern France, the new monarch, his army, and his many servants only spoke French. Everyone who needed to deal with the king had to learn French. Eventually, the rich and powerful began to speak French, whereas the peasants continued to speak Anglo-Saxon or Old English. After many centuries, these two languages became all mixed up. To this day, more than half of the words we use came to us from French. The result of the melding of Anglo-Saxon and French had a huge impact on the English language. On the positive side, English has a very rich vocabulary. On the negative side, it has made reading and spelling very challenging because the spelling rules of French and Old English are very different. French inherited most of its words from Latin and Greek. For this reason, we inherited spelling patterns from Latin and Greek along with French. This means that we must learn some spelling patterns from these **five** languages: Anglo-Saxon, Danish, French, Latin, and Greek. That's a tall order!

Keep this story in mind as you study suffixes in **Chapters 11** and **12**. French, Latin, and Greek suffixes are especially challenging to learn because many of them are **not** spelled the way they sound.

1. What does the term **sound/symbol correspondence** mean? _____

2. Who conquered England in the 5th century A.D.? _____

3. Where did the Angles and Saxons come from and what language did they speak?

4. Who conquered England in the year 1013 and what language did they speak?

5. Who conquered England in the year 1066?

6. What language did the new king and his followers speak?

7. What two languages became all mixed up in England?

8. Whether we realize it or not, we have to learn spelling rules from how many different languages? List the languages:

CHAPTER 11
Latin Suffixes, Part 1

Note to Instructor

As you begin teaching Latin suffixes, it is important to realize how challenging this section is for students with learning disabilities or poor visual memories. Essentially, they have to learn some aspects of the orthography of several foreign languages, namely Latin, Greek, and French. Whereas these suffixes have good sound/symbol correspondence in the original language, in English the sound/symbol correspondence is complicated. For example, the words *nature, conscientious,* and *negotiation* illustrate the difficulty students are up against. Therefore, it is very important to take time and teach each suffix as a unit of meaning, sound, and sight with lots of review along the way. A great deal of repetition and practice is needed before these suffixes are committed to long-term memory. Many teachers have made color-coded flashcards for each set of suffixes (a different color for each set). The most effective method requires students to make their own cards. The suffix is written on one side of the card; the definition, pronunciation, and four examples are written on the reverse side.

Anglo-Saxon base words are free morphemes, which means they make sense when they appear by themselves. Most Latin roots are bound morphemes, which means they are not real words by themselves. They need prefixes or suffixes to become usable words. This section deals with the first set of Latin suffixes: **–ment, –ist, –ic, –ous, –ine, –fy, –ture, –sure, –ure, –age, –able, –ible, –tion, –sion,** and **–s-sion**. With the exception of **–fy**, the suffixes in this chapter are unaccented.

Most middle school and high school students are capable of doing all of the ensuing lessons with minor modifications for those with severe learning disabilities; however, when signs of frustration begin to appear, review the concept and do the worksheet as a whole-class lesson. Most fourth and fifth graders will probably not reach this chapter. In the event that they progress this far, consider doing the worksheets as whole-class lessons and cross off words that seem too difficult.

Reminders:
1. **Have students reread all the words in every lesson once they have completed the exercises.**
2. Ask students to copy each new phonogram, red word, homophone, homograph, prefix, suffix, and rule in the appropriate sections of their Decoding Binders. Include homographs, marked **HG**, in the Homophone Section. When entering a phonogram, prefix, or suffix, students must list four key words that illustrate it. Students must also add four words for every rule and definitions for homophones and homographs.
3. Review all sections of the binder **once a week** for a minimum of five weeks. Younger children or those with severe learning disabilities may need more time for review.
4. Use the **Proposed Spelling Activities**, located in the Appendix, for all **Reading and Spelling for Mastery** lists. Students must read the list daily before they start the two practice activities.

Lesson 1a: Because this lesson is teacher-directed, there is no worksheet. First, we will discuss the suffixes **–ment**, **–ist**, and **–ic**, which have strong sound/symbol correspondence.

A) Write the suffix **–ment** on the board/overhead (or display the card). Next to the suffix, write three words that end with **–ment**. Call on volunteers to read the words. After students understand the concept, elicit ten or more words from your class and write them on the board/overhead. In case not enough words are volunteered, a list is supplied for your convenience: *(agreement, fragment, monument, enjoyment, document, amusement, movement, ointment, shipment, basement, argument, deployment, appointment)*. Ask everyone to deduce the phonetic spelling **(mənt)** and the definition: *action or process*. Many words that end with **–ment** are formed from verbs and name ideas. Students write the suffix, pronunciation, definition, and four examples in the Suffixes section of their binders.

Suggestion: Divide the class into small groups that are balanced in abilities. After you have presented the first suffix with examples, set a timer for two or three minutes (longer for younger students) and have the groups compete against each other. The group that generates the most words wins the first round. To find words, allow students to use textbooks, dictionaries, and Franklin spellers, if available. Ask a volunteer from every group to write the words on the board/overhead and have students read the cumulative list in unison. If this format works well, do this for every suffix and keep track of points. Consider giving the winners a small reward. If the same group of students always wins or loses, change the makeup of the groups.

B) Write the suffix **–ist** on the board/overhead (or display the card) and add three words that end with **–ist** *(dentist, tourist, florist, lobbyist, motorist, finalist, artist, novelist, optimist, humorist, receptionist, soloist, therapist)*. Elicit ten words from your class and write them on the board/overhead. Ask everyone to deduce the phonetic spelling **(ĭst)** and the definition: *a noun that names a person*, or *a specialist*. Most words that end with **ist** are nouns. Students write the suffix, pronunciation, definition, and four examples in their binders. There are some verbs that end with **–ist** *(assist, resist, subsist)*, but in this case **–ist** is not a suffix but derives from the Latin verb *sistere* which means to stand.

C) Follow the same procedure for **–ic** *(comic, topic, athletic, clinic, traffic, metric, cosmetic, historic, allergic, Pacific, graphic, electric, tragic)*. Ask everyone to deduce the phonetic spelling **(ĭc)** and the definition: *relating to, characterized by*. Most words that end with **–ic** are adjectives; however, some are nouns, especially when **–ic** is followed by the letter **s** *(politics, Olympics, ethics, physics)*. Students write the suffix, pronunciation, definition, and four examples in their binders. Because Latin doesn't have long or short vowels, it is sometimes difficult to tell whether the vowel preceding the suffix is long or short: *mimic, tunic, panic, epidemic*; however, in many words the root will provide the clue: *cube, cubic, base, basic*.

Lesson 1b: Before you hand out the worksheet, teach this short review to determine if students have retained the spelling of the suffixes **–ment**, **–ist**, and **–ic**. Dictate the words *appointment, enjoyment, tourist, artist, panic,* and *organic*. Ask students to write the suffixes only. Check for spelling errors and review if necessary. Then write **–ment**, **–ist**, and **–ic** on the board/overhead and have students read them to you, individually if possible. Students are now ready for **Lesson 1b**, which provides more practice with these three suffixes.

Lesson 1c requires students to add **–ment**, **–ist**, and **–ic** to base words. The second exercise deals with accent placement. The rules are as follows: the accent usually falls on the first syllable in words with the suffixes **–ment** and **–ist**. If there is a prefix, the accent moves to the root. If students are confused by 7-10 in the first set, ask if these last four words have a different pattern. In words that end with the suffix **–ic**, the accent falls on the syllable directly before **–ic**.

Lesson 1d (on the same page as **Lesson 4c**) is a **Reading and Spelling for Mastery** list with these suffixes: **–ment**, **–ist**, and **–ic**. Please find **Proposed Spelling Activities** in the Appendix. Students are required to read the list before they start the daily practice.

Lesson 2a: (No worksheet) Write the suffix **–ous** on the board/overhead, and add three words that end with **–ous** (*famous, joyous, dangerous, hazardous, horrendous, thunderous, disastrous, enormous, poisonous, numerous, nervous, marvelous, fabulous*). Elicit ten words from your class and write them on the overhead/board. Ask everyone to deduce the phonetic spelling (əs) and the definition: *full of, like, possessing*. Students write the suffix, pronunciation, definition, and four examples in their binders. Most words that end with **–ous** are adjectives. The accent is usually on the first syllable. If there is a prefix, the accent is on the root. The noun suffix **–ess**, which means *female*, sounds the same as **–ous**. Have students record **–ess** and four of these examples and the definition in their binders: *seamstress, governess, hostess, actress, goddess, heiress, princess, lioness*. Since **–ess** is not very common, there is no worksheet for it.

Lesson 2b requires students to complete sentences with synonyms that end in **–ous**.

Lesson 2c discusses the connective **u**, which often precedes the suffix **–ous**; it is usually long (*strenuous*). It may be followed by the letter **l** (*fabulous*). Sometimes **u** combines with the last letter of the root, **tu** and says **choo**, *contemptuous* (*contempt*), *tumultuous* (*tumult*); **du** says **joo**, *deciduous, assiduous, arduous,* or **jə**, *incredulous,* and **xi** says **sh**, *anxious, obnoxious*. Ask students to record **tuous = chooəs**, **duous = jooəs**, and **xious = shəs** in the Suffixes section of their Decoding Binders, along with examples for each. When **e** precedes **–ous**, it is usually long. It can also be silent when it is there to keep **g** soft (*outrageous*).

Lesson 2d reviews a phonics lesson from Chapter 10: Latin, French, and Spanish do not have long or short vowels. In these languages the letter **i** always says our **long e** sound, and words with **i** before suffixes are usually Latin and French derivatives. This rule often applies to the connective **i**, when it precedes a suffix that starts with vowels, (*tedious, superior, immediate*). There is a second reason **i** says the long **e** sound: when a base word ends in **y** saying long **e**, this long **e** sound continues when the **y** changes to **i** (*envy, envious, vary, various, glory, glorious, fury, furious, library, librarian*). The vowel right after **i** usually says the schwa (ə) sound (*appropriate, superior, guardian*). The accent falls on the syllable directly before the connective **i**. Ask students to record **–ious (ēəs)** in the Suffixes section of their Decoding Binders, along with four examples.

Lesson 3a: (No worksheet) Write the suffix **–ine** on the board/overhead and add three words. Because this suffix is difficult, do not try to elicit words from your class. Often **–ine** says ən¢, which is unaccented (*determine, examine, doctrine, medicine, margarine, feminine, masculine, discipline, imagine*). It also frequently says ēn¢, with the Latin sound for **i**, and the accent on the suffix (*machine, routine, sardines, vaccine, chlorine, histamine, marine*). Sometimes **–ine** has a vowel-consonant-e pattern and says īn¢, (*feline, porcupine, valentine, turpentine, combine, confine, decline*). Write these headings on the board: 1. ən¢ 2. ēn¢ 3. īn¢. Select words at random from the three sound categories and write them on the board/overhead, one at a time. Then ask students to write these words under the correct heading. It means *having the nature of, like*. Nouns, adjectives, and verbs can end with **–ine**. Ask students to record all three suffixes in their Decoding Binders, along with the pronunciation of all three, examples for each, and the definition:

Lesson 3b provides more practice with words that have the pronunciations ən¢ and ēn¢. Since students have practiced pronouncing vowel-consonant-e syllables in earlier chapter, words with this pattern are not covered in detail on the worksheet.

Lesson 4a: (No worksheet) Review the previous five suffixes and check for retention. Review as necessary. If retention has been achieved, write the suffix **–fy** on the board/overhead. Since **–fy** is almost always preceded by the letter **i**, also write **–ify** and add three words that end with **–fy** and **–ify** (*unify, verify, amplify, gratify, satisfy, fortify, horrify, disqualify, certify, testify, identify, modify, clarify*). Elicit ten words from your class and write them on the board/overhead. Ask everyone to deduce the phonetic spelling (**fī**), (**əfī**) and the definition: *to become, to make*. Most words that end with **–fy** or **–ify** are verbs. The accent is usually on the first syllable, unless there is a prefix. The letter **i** in **–ify** is unaccented, and says the schwa sound. The suffix **–fy** has a secondary accent, which is pronounced less forcefully than the primary accent. Do not dwell on secondary accents unless you teach a strong group of students. Students write the suffix, pronunciation, definition, and four examples in their binders.

Lesson 4b teaches students how to add or eliminate the suffix **–fy**. It also deals with adding the suffixes **–ing** and **–ed** to words that end with **–fy** (*classifying, unified*).

Lesson 4c (on the same page as **Lesson 1d**) is a **Reading and Spelling for Mastery** list with these suffixes: **–ic**, **–ous**, and **–fy**. Follow the previously discussed directions.

Lesson 5a: (No worksheet) Write the previous six suffixes on the board or overhead and check whether mastery has been attained. Provide additional practice if necessary. Then write the word ending **–ture** on the board/overhead, and add three words that end with **–ture** (*picture, nature, culture, capture, feature, future, mixture, vulture, fracture, creature, moisture, signature, adventure*). The actual suffix is **–ure**. In its most common use, it is preceded by the letter **t**, resulting in the unvoiced pronunciation **chər**. It means *act, process, condition*. Students must write the suffix, pronunciation, definition, and four examples in their binders.

Please alert students to the difference between **cher** as in *pitcher, teacher, preacher, butcher*, and **–ture** as in *culture, nature, rupture*. The former are usually Anglo-Saxon, and the base word ends with the **ch** sound, *pitch, teach, preach*. Frequently, the suffix **–er** in these words means **one who performs an action**, *teacher, preacher*.

To keep students from feeling overwhelmed by this difficult lesson, you may want to tackle the next two word endings in another session. The related endings **–sure** and **–zure** (**–zure** is not common) say **zhər**, which is voiced. Elicit words from you class and write them on the board/overhead (*pleasure, measure, treasure, closure, leisure, exposure, enclosure, displeasure, foreclosure, seizure, azure*). Also less common, **–sure** may say **shər**, which is unvoiced (*pressure, fissure, censure*). Ask students to make three columns on a sheet of paper with these headings 1. **chər** 2. **zhər** 3. **shər**. Select words at random from the three lists and write one at a time on the board/overhead. Students write the word under the correct heading.

The true suffix **–ure** says **yər** and can occur by itself, *failure, figure, tenure*. Afterwards, ask students to deduce the definition: *act, process, condition*. Students write the last two endings, the pronunciation for each, the definition, and four examples for each suffix in their binders.

Words that end with **–ure** are usually nouns. The accent is on the first syllable, unless there is a prefix, which moves it onto the root. Some verbs or adjectives are accented on the second syllable: **endure, secure, insure, assure, procure, obscure, mature**, and **brochure**. In these words **ure** is not a suffix. These words are introduced in **Lesson 6d**.

Lesson 5b requires students to write the sound of the above endings next to words. The second activity directs students to match dictionary pronunciations with their correctly spelled counterparts. It also covers accent placement, as well as the pronunciations **oor** and **ūr** as in *endure* and *secure*, which have the accent on the second syllable.

Lesson 6a: (No worksheet) Write the previous nine suffixes/endings on the board/overhead and ask students to pronounce them individually, if possible. Provide additional practice if necessary.

Then write the suffix **–age** on the board/overhead, and supply three words that end with **–age** (*postage, beverage, average, package, pilgrimage, voltage, language, blockage, stoppage, passage, garbage, encourage, baggage*). Elicit words from your class and write them on the board/overhead. Ask everyone to deduce the phonetic spelling (**ĭj**) and the definition: *condition, state*. Most words that end with **–age** are nouns, although some are verbs. Students must write the suffix, pronunciation, definition, and four examples in their binders.

The ending sound **ĭj** also occurs in these Anglo-Saxon words: *knowledge, cartridge, partridge,* and *porridge*. These Latin derivatives also end with the **ĭj** sound: *college, privilege, sacrilege,* and *vestige*.

Lesson 6b lists words that end with **–age** and reviews this previously taught spelling rule, "When a word has one consonant sound between a short vowel and **–age**, the consonant is usually doubled, if the syllable before the suffix is accented, *village, cabbage, luggage*." Three common exceptions are *damage, manage, savage*.

Lesson 6c requires students to use words with the suffix **–age** in sentences.

Lesson 6d presents words with the suffixes **–ous, –age, –fy** and the endings **–ure, –ture, –sure**, and asks students to deduce accent rules. The rules are as follows: the accent usually falls on the first syllable. If there is a prefix, the accent moves to the root. In verbs and some adjectives, the accent is on the second syllable. This lesson also broaches the concept of secondary accents, which occur in words with the suffix **–fy**. The primary accent is on the first syllable, the secondary accent is on the suffix **–fy**. If there is a prefix, the primary accent is on the base word or the Latin root.

Lesson 7a: (No worksheet) Write the previous ten suffixes on the board/overhead and check for retention. Provide additional practice if necessary. Then write the suffixes **–able** and **–ible** on the board/overhead, and supply three words that end with **–able** and **–ible** (*reasonable, sensible, workable, suitable, permissible, favorable, possible, moveable, adorable, visible, usable, audible, terrible*). Elicit ten words from your class and write them on the board/overhead. Ask everyone to deduce the phonetic spelling (both say əbl) and the definition: *able, capable*. Words with these suffixes are adjectives. Students must write the suffixes, pronunciation, definitions, and four examples in their binders.

Lesson 7b lists prefixes, base words, and the suffixes **–able** and **–ible** and asks students to compose words that consist of these three components.

Lesson 7c (on the same page as **Lesson 10c**) is a **Reading and Spelling for Mastery** list with these suffixes **–ture, –sure, –ure, –able, –ible** and **–age**. Follow the previously discussed procedures.

Because both of the suffixes **–able** and **–ible** say əbl, it is difficult to know which one to choose. Here are several rules that may help in selecting the correct suffix for əbl. A strong group of students might benefit from learning these rules, whereas weaker students will probably just become confused. 1. Use **–ible** after a base word that ends with soft **c** and **g** (*reproducible, invincible, eligible, incorrigible*). 2. Some base words retain **e** after **soft c**, therefore go to **–able** (*noticeable, changeable, manageable*). 3. To keep hard **c** and **g**, use **–able** (*applicable, despicable, navigable*). 4. If a related word ends with **–ation**, go with **–able** (*applicable, observable, admirable*). Related words with the suffixes **–sion, s–sion,** and **–ive** go to **–ible** (*comprehensible, repressible, permissible*).

Lesson 7d is a review of the suffixes **–able** and **–ible**.

Lesson 8a: (No worksheet) Write the previous twelve suffixes on the board/overhead, and check for retention. Provide additional practice if necessary. You will now teach a very important pattern that applies to thousands of words. Write these combinations on the board/overhead: **ti, si, ci,** and **xi**. They appear right before a suffix or become part of a suffix. Write the following words on the board/overhead: *fiction, action, extension, mission, musician, magician, anxious, obnoxious, appreciate, negotiate*. Ask your class to deduce what **ti, si, ci,** and **xi** say (all say **sh**). Then write the word ending **–tion** on the board/overhead, and supply three words that end with **–tion** (*nation, equation, position, fraction, completion, tradition, quotation, education, donation, selection, reception, definition, situation*). The actual suffix is **–ion**; The letter **t** in the word ending **–tion** comes from the root (*act, action, instruct, instruction, promote, promotion*). The **at** in **ation** frequently comes from the word ending **ate** (*create, creation, locate, location, vacate, vacation, relate, relation, indicate, indication, dedicate, dedication*). When the root ends in **te**, the **e** is dropped. Elicit ten words from your class and write them on the board/overhead. Ask everyone to deduce the phonetic spelling (**shən**) and the definition: *action, process, condition*. Most words with the ending **–tion** are nouns and are formed from related verbs. Even though the dictionary breaks **–tion, –sion,** and **–cian** into two parts, this program treats them as a single unit.

Write the ending **–cian** on the board/overhead, and supply three words that end with **–cian** (*magician, musician, politician, beautician, physician, electrician, pediatrician, obstetrician, dietician*). This suffix is not as common. Ask everyone to deduce the phonetic spelling (**shən**) and the definition: *a person who performs a certain function or action*. The ending **–tion** is Latin, whereas **–cian** is Greek. Students must write both suffixes, pronunciation, definitions, and four examples for each in their binders.

Lesson 8b: The first exercise asks students to syllabify twelve words and answer five questions about the vowels preceding **–tion** and **–cian**. Remind your class that prefixes and suffixes are not marked. The vowels **a, o,** and **u** are long when they precede **–tion**, whereas **i** is always short and **e** can be long or short.

Lesson 9a: (No worksheet) Write the previous fourteen suffixes on the board/overhead and check for retention. Then write the combinations **ti, si, ci,** and **xi** on the board/overhead. Ask everyone to write down the phonetic spelling for each. Then write the suffix **–sion** on the board/overhead, and tell your class that this suffix has two different sounds. Supply three words that end with **–sion** (*version, conclusion, explosion, confusion, collision, invasion, occasion, abrasion, mansion, tension, pension, extension, expansion*). Elicit words from your class and write them on the board or overhead. Ask if the suffix **–sion** always says the same sound. Hopefully students can hear the difference between the voiced and the unvoiced pronunciation of **–sion** (*decision* is voiced, *extension* is unvoiced). Then write two columns on the board with these two headings 1. **zhən** 2. **shən**. Ask students to copy the headings and write all of the words under the appropriate column. Point out that **–sion = zhən** is much more common than **–sion = shən**, which occurs after a consonant, frequently the letters **n** or **l**. (Students will discover in the next lesson that **–sion** says **zhən** after vowels or the letter **r**, *confusion, explosion, decision, version*. Check the work and repeat this procedure with different words for students who can't discriminate between the sounds. Ask everyone to deduce the meaning of **–sion**: *action, process, condition*. Students must write the suffix, pronunciation, definition, and four examples in their binders. Most words with the **–sion** ending are nouns.

Lesson 9b: The first exercise requires students to discriminate between **–tion** saying **shən** and **–sion** saying **zhən**. The second activity asks students to find base words from nouns with **–sion**. The last questions prompts students to discover the following pattern: base words (usually verbs) that end with **d** or **de** will go to **–sion**, *suspend, suspension, extend, extension, expand, expansion, conclude, conclusion, divide, division*.

Lesson 10a: (No worksheet) 1. Write the previous fifteen suffixes or endings on the board/overhead and check for retention. 2. Write **ti, si, ci,** and **xi** on the board/overhead. Ask everyone to write down the phonetic spelling. 3. Write the ending **s–sion** on the board/overhead, and supply three words that end with **s–sion** (*session, mission, permission, expression, discussion, confession, profession, impression, admission, depression, commission, recession, transmission*). Elicit ten words from your class and write them on the board/overhead. Ask everyone to deduce the phonetic spelling and the definition: (**shən**, exactly the same as for *–tion*), *action, process, condition*. Ask students to write the suffix, pronunciation, definition, and four examples in their binders.

As an aside, tell your class that *–xion* is very rare. The only two common words are *complexion* and *crucifixion*. Both of their roots end with the letter **x** (complex, crucifix).

Lesson 10b displays four patterns of verbs that go to **s–sion** *(permit-permission, express-expression, recede-recess-recession,* and *succeed-success-succession)*. Students will study the patterns and apply them to new words. One way to remember the application of **s–sion**, is roots that end with **mit**, double **s**, **cede**, and **ceed** will go to **s–sion**. Her is another way to remember when to use **s–sion**: words that end with **–mission**, **–pression**, **–cession**, or **–cussion**, use **s–sion**.

Lesson 10c (on the same page as **Lesson 7c**) is a **Reading and Spelling for Mastery** list with these endings: **–tion**, **–sion**, and **s–sion**. Follow the previously discussed procedures.

Lesson 10d displays words with **ti**, **ci**, and **xi** followed by the suffix **–ous**. Students will use the words to complete sentences. Ask students to record **–cious**, **–tious**, and **–xious** (all say **shəs**) in the Suffixes section of their Decoding Binders, along with the following examples for each: *precious, delicious, gracious, spacious, nutritious, ambitious, cautious, fictitious, anxious, obnoxious*. The syllable directly before **ti**, **ci**, and **xi** is accented.

Lesson 10e discusses accent placement for the suffixes **–able/–ible**, **–tion**, **–sion**, and **s–sion**. In words that end with **–able/–ible**, the accent falls on the first syllable. If there is a prefix, the accent is on the root. In words that end with **–tion**, **–sion**, **s–sion**, **–cian**, and **–xion**, (also **–ic**), the syllable directly before the suffix is accented, no matter how many syllables are in the word.

Lesson 11 is a reading and dictation review of the suffixes covered in this chapter.

Lesson 12 is a syllabication exercise, which includes the previously covered suffixes. Prefixes and suffixes are **not** marked. If students do mark prefixes, do not count it as a mistake. Some words will have an open syllable with a short **i** or short **e** (coded **ŏp**), before **ti**, **si**, and **ci** (e-lec-tri-cian, par-ti-tion). When dividing syllables, the last letter of the root often joins the suffix. This happens especially in words with two consonants between the last vowel and a suffix that begins with a vowel, reflecting the Second Rule of Syllabication (rŭs-tic, cl-t+s, e-nor-mous, pref-rc-m+s). Demonstrate that words with **s-sion** are divided between the first and second **s**: dis-cus-sion, per-mis-sion, pro-gres-sion.

Lesson 13 covers words with multiple suffixes and introduces the suffix **–fication**, which derives from Latin verb **fiacre**, which means **to make** or **to produce**. Because this is a challenging page, please provide lots of support for younger children or those with severe learning disabilities.

Lesson 14a is a syllabication exercise with all of the suffixes in this chapter.

Lesson 14b is a dictation exercise. Some of the words are difficult, therefore, grade leniently.

Lesson 15a lists dictionary pronunciations, which must be matched with the correct spelling.

Lesson 15b requires students to categorize words according to their components.

Lesson 16 is a story about the author's experiences on a trip to Nepal.

1b Suffixes –*ment*, –*ist*, and –*ic*

Match the word starters on the left with the appropriate suffix to make real words. Write them on the lines.

gar		1. _____
organ		2. _____
pave	–ic	3. _____
scient		4. _____
plast	–ment	5. _____
announce		6. _____
stat	–ist	7. _____
invest		8. _____
solo		9. _____
econom		10. _____
		11. _____
		12. _____

Highlight the following words you can read and use them to complete the sentences:

> erratic   cyclists   enforcement   violinist   Department   measurements   aerobic

1. The English _____ planned a field trip to watch the Shakespeare play, Romeo and Juliet.
2. Getting _____ exercise is one of the best methods of preventing heart disease.
3. After an excellent performance, the _____ received a standing ovation.
4. A career in law _____ is very challenging and often dangerous.
5. The world's most famous _____ compete in the Tour de France.
6. Watch out for the _____ driver in the left lane, he might cause an accident.
7. Before you install new carpeting, make sure you have precise _____.

1c Accent Patterns for –ment, –ist, –ic

Add the suffixes –ic, –ist, and –ment to the following word starters. When you add –ic and –ist to a base word that ends with **y** or silent **e**, drop the **y** or **e** and add the suffix (history + –ic = historic).

Write new words by adding the specified suffix. Then read the new words.

add –ic

1. scene _____
2. academy _____
3. hero _____
4. base _____
5. economy _____

add –ment

1. adjust _____
2. govern _____
3. enjoy _____
4. replace _____
5. appoint _____

add –ist

1. style _____
2. flute _____

add –ist

3. botany _____
4. therapy _____

Let's examine what happens to accent patterns in words with the suffixes –ment, –ist, and –ic.

Read the following words and highlight the accented syllable.

1. pun ish ment	3. ar gu ment	5. or na ment	7. de rail ment	9. in vest ment
2. gov ern ment	4. state ment	6. pay ment	8. com mit ment	10. de vel op ment

What is the rule? _____

1. den tist	3. tour ist	5. ter ror ist	7. sci en tist	9. re serv ist
2. hy gien ist	4. fi nal ist	6. op ti mist	8. or gan ist	10. de feat ist

What is the rule? _____

1. re pub lic	3. a tom ic	5. dra mat ic	7. bar bar ic	9. O lym pics
2. e las tic	4. fab ric	6. vol can ic	8. me chan ic	10. pan ic

What is the rule? _____

1d/4c Reading and Spelling for Mastery

Words with the suffixes
–ment, **–ist**, and **–ic**:

1d Spelling

1. movement
2. statement
3. government
4. develop
5. development
6. experiment
7. treatment
8. appointment
9. agreement
10. payment
11. equipment
12. employment
13. artist
14. dentist
15. scientist*
16. florist
17. basic
18. traffic
19. public
20. electric

*Red words

Words with the suffixes
–ic, **–ous**, and **–fy**:

4c Spelling

1. historic
2. plastic
3. terrific
4. electric
5. electronic
6. comic
7. famous
8. enormous
9. tremendous
10. generous *
11. jealous*
12. poisonous
13. anxious*
14. satisfy
15. satisfied
16. identify
17. clarify
18. simplify
19. qualify
20. qualified

2b The Suffix *–ous*

Write the phonetic spelling for the suffix *–ous* _____. Just a quick reminder, it means *full of, characterized by, possessing*. Most words with this suffix are adjectives.

Highlight the following words you can read. Choose two synonyms (words with similar meanings) to fill in the blanks. Use a pencil and do the easier ones first.

vigorous	hazardous	humorous	boisterous	tremendous
jealous	strenuous	glamorous	dangerous	traitorous
venomous	gorgeous	anxious	treasonous	rambunctious
hilarious	nervous	fabulous	envious	poisonous

1. Aerobic exercise is _____ and _____.
2. Many students are _____ and _____ before a test.
3. A funny movie is _____ and _____.
4. Swimming in a fast-moving river is _____ and _____.
5. Someone who betrays his country is _____ and _____.
6. A person who wants what others have is _____ and _____.
7. A fashion model is _____ and _____.
8. Kids who get carried away are _____ and _____.
9. Snakebites can be _____ and _____.
10. Something great and wonderful is _____ and _____.

Go back over the words and highlight the two words with soft **g**.

2c Vowels Before –ous

Read the following words, highlight the vowel right before the suffix –ous, and mark it.

1. hideous
2. erroneous
3. conspicuous
4. courteous
5. tenuous
6. innocuous
7. bounteous
8. vacuous
9. continuous
10. strenuous
11. spontaneous
12. ambiguous
13. extraneous
14. incongruous
15. homogeneous
16. simultaneous

What kind of vowel sounds can you hear before –ous? _____

When the **e** is there to make the letter **g** soft, it is not pronounced. Read these words:

1. courageous   2. gorgeous   3. outrageous

All of the following words have the combinations **tu**, **du**, or **xi** directly before the suffix –ous, which says əs. Together the letters **tu** say **choo**, the letters **du** say **joo**, or **jə**, and the letters **xi** say **sh**. Keeping these sounds in mind, try to pronounce words 1-12; they are challenging. Draw a line from each word to its ending sound.

1. contemptuous
2. virtuous
3. deciduous
4. tumultuous   **choo-əs**
5. assiduous
6. anxious   **jə-ləs**
7. incredulous
8. tortuous   **joo-əs**
9. sumptuous
10. obnoxious   **shəs**
11. arduous
12. presumptuous

Go back over all of the words and study the accent pattern. Where does the accent fall in words that have **e, u, tu, du,** and **xi** before –ous? _____

2d *i* Before Word Endings

Suffixes often have the letter **i** right before them. Say these words and listen closely to the sound of **i**: *serious, mediate, previous*. What does **i** say? You are correct if you heard a long **e** sound. We inherited the previous words from Latin and French. In Latin, French, and Spanish the letter **i** always says our **long e** sound. There is another reason for this long **e** sound: a base word that ends with **y** keeps the **e** sound when **y** changes to **i**, *envy, envious, vary, various, glory, glorious*. Try to memorize this rule: **i** usually says **long e** before suffixes that start with vowels. The vowel right after **i** says the schwa sound (ə).

Highlight the words you can read and write them under the correct heading in the boxes.

retaliate	librarian	interior	suburbia	comedian	abbreviate
stadium	bacteria	humiliate	superior	insomnia	gymnasium
various	curious	premium	median	exterior	mysterious
inferior	criteria	guardian	aquarium	victorious	appreciate

ē-əm	ē-əs	ē-ən

ē-ər	ē-ə	ē-ate

Go back over all of the words you wrote in the boxes and highlight the accented syllables. Study the accent patterns. What is the rule? Write it on the back of this sheet of paper.

3b The Suffix –ine

The word ending **ine** sometimes says **ən** (*examine, determine, imagine*). In many other words **ine** says **ēn** (the Latin sound of **i** is long **e**) *chlorine, mezzanine*. In a few words **ine** says **īne**. Many of them are compound words (*deadline*). Some words have a **vce** pattern with a prefix (*define, combine, decline*). Read these words (**ine** says **īne**):

1. feline 2. canine 3. bovine 4. divine 5. iodine 6. incline 7. turpentine 8. valentine.

Use two words from the lists below to fill in the blanks. Try **ən** or **ēn** for the **ine** endings.

List A: masculine, vaccine, nectarine, limousine, feminine, medicine, gasoline, tangerine

1. A _____ requires _____ to run.
2. Two kinds of fruit: _____ and _____
3. A _____ is a kind of _____ that keeps you from getting sick.
4. Adjectives for female and male traits: _____ and _____

List B: engine, sardines, routine, margarine, magazine, trampoline, machine, caffeine

5. They are both foods: _____ and _____
6. An _____ is a _____ that makes a car run.
7. I read in a _____ that drinking too much _____ is harmful.
8. The acrobats did an amazing _____ on a _____.

Use these words for the crossword puzzle:

submarine, adrenaline, examine, discipline, pristine, famine, imagine, determined, destined

Across: 1. Intent on doing a task
2. A ship that moves below the surface
3. To enforce rules for behavior
4. A hormone that helps you escape fast.
5. Wild, untouched, beautiful
6. Bound to happen, no matter what you do.

Down: 1. To look at carefully
2. To picture something in your mind
3. A time of starvation

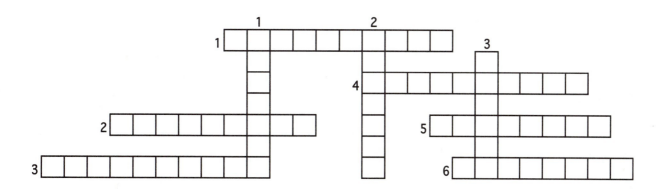

275

4b The Suffix –fy

Adding the suffix –**fy** to base words changes an adjective or noun to a verb and means *to make* or *to become*. Remember that –**fy** is usually preceded by the letter **i** which says the schwa sound (ə). Just a quick reminder: when a word ends with silent **e**, you must drop it before adding a suffix that starts with a vowel.

Add –**ify** to these base words and write them on the lines. Read the new words. Sometimes the accent changes, creating a change in the pronunciation.

1. just _____
2. fort _____
3. mode _____
4. type _____
5. diverse _____

6. pure _____
7. note _____
8. test _____
9. humid _____
10. intense _____

Read the words and write each base word on the lines. Some of the base words are quite a bit different. You may use a dictionary.

1. classify _____
2. horrify _____
3. beautify _____
4. solidify _____
5. personify _____

6. falsify _____
7. simplify _____
8. signify _____
9. syllabify _____
10. exemplify _____

Add the past tense –**ed** and the present participle –**ing** to these words. Remember to use the rules for adding suffixes to words that end with **y**.

	Add –ed	Add –ing
1. unify	_____	_____
2. satisfy	_____	_____
3. certify	_____	_____
4. terrify	_____	_____
5. specify	_____	_____
6. gratify	_____	_____

5b The Suffix –ure

The suffix **–ure** means *act, process, condition*. It often has the letter **t** directly before it (*nature, future, culture*) and says **chər**. Sometimes it is preceded by the letter **s** (*treasure, enclosure*) and says **zhər**; however, it may also appear by itself (*figure, tenure*).

Highlight the words you can read. Listen closely to these endings: **ture**, which says **chər** and **sure**, which says **zhər** or **shər**. When **sure** says **zhər**, it is voiced (*measure*). When **sure** says **shər**, it is unvoiced (*pressure*). Can you hear the difference?

Write **chər**, **zhər**, and **shər** next to the following words. Highlight the ones you can read.

1. capture _____
2. nature _____
3. fissure _____
4. pleasure _____
5. texture _____
6. leisure _____
7. picture _____
8. treasure _____
9. nurture _____
10. mixture _____
11. censure _____
12. measure _____
13. future _____
14. venture _____
15. exposure _____

The suffix **–ure** can occur by itself, but sometimes it is preceded by the letter **d**. When it is by itself it says **yər** (*figure*), but when it is preceded by **du**, it says **jər** (*procedure*). When the letter **z** precedes **ure**, it says **zher** (*seizure*).

Highlight the words you can read and listen to the ending sound: Write **yer**, **jər**, or **zhur** on the lines.

1. figure ____ 2. azure ____ 3. failure ____ 4. tenure ____ 5. procedure ____

Match the phonetic version from the dictionary with its correct spelling.

1. jĕs′ chər   departure
2. dĭs clō′ zhər   sculpture
3. lĭt′ ər ə chər   failure
4. prə sē′ jər   disclosure
5. scŭlp′ chər   leisure
6. fāl′ yər   gesture
7. dē par′ chər   legislature
8. lē′ zhər   measure
9. mĕ′ zhər   procedure
10. lĕj′ əs lā chər   literature

The Latin root **jur** says **jər** and occurs in verbs and nouns: injure, perjure, jury.

6b The Suffix –age

Read these words and listen closely to the suffix **–age**: damage, outage, savage, voyage. What does **–age** say? _____ It means *condition, state, an action*.

The following spelling rule usually applies to words that end with the suffix **–age**: When a word has one consonant between a short vowel and **–age**, the consonant is usually doubled if the final syllable in the base word is accented. Do **not** double the consonant after r-controlled vowels or diphthongs and digraphs. Do you remember this rule from previous chapters? There are some exceptions to this rule.

Highlight the following words you can read. Then write them under the correct category. Write the exceptions on the line between the boxes.

storage	sausages	cabbage	average	message	percentage
damage	luggage	villages	advantage	salvaged	savage
cottage	coverage	footage	manage	rummage	discouraged

Exceptions to the doubling rule: _____

Double consonant after short vowel	2 different cons. after short vowel	R-Controlled v. before –age	Diphthong+cons. before –age

The ending sound **ĭj** also occurs in these Anglo-Saxon words, but it is spelled with the short-vowel signal **dge**: knowledge, cartridge, partridge, and porridge.

These Latin derivatives also end with the **ĭj** sound, but they are spelled with **ege**: college, privilege, sacrilege, and vestige.

6c The Suffix –age in Sentences

Use these words to complete the sentences. Write in pencil, and do the easy ones first:

shortage	sausages	cabbage	storage	message	percentage
damage	luggage	villages	rummage	salvaged	discouraged
	coverage	drainage	seepage	advantage	

1. Because of the severe _____ to our truck, it could not be _____. Fortunately, we had good insurance _____.
2. Last night we had potatoes, _____, and _____ for dinner.
3. After my flight home, I received a _____ that my lost _____ was found.
4. A high _____ of high school dropouts becomes _____ with low salaries and lack of benefits.
5. A college degree will always give you an _____ in the job market.
6. After the earthquake, there was a _____ of food in the small _____ around the epicenter.
7. Please don't _____ around in the _____ area.
8. To get rid of water _____ in the basement, you must improve the _____ around the building.

In words we inherited from French, the suffix –age says äzh. Highlight the words you can read and use some of them to complete the sentences:

1. ga rage   3. mas sage   5. cor sage   7. sab o tage
2. fu se lage   4. en tou rage   6. es pi o nage   8. cam ou flage

1. The President has a huge _____ when he travels to foreign countries.
2. Too much stuff is stored in our _____.
3. The armed forces need _____ clothing when they fight a war.
4. My sister's boyfriend gave her a beautiful _____ for the prom.

6d Accent Patterns for –ous, –fy, –ure, –age

Highlight the accented syllables in these words:

1. fa mous
2. se ri ous
3. nerv ous
4. slan der ous
5. cour te ous
6. en vi ous
7. fu ri ous
8. poi son ous
9. con tin u ous

Highlight the accented syllables in these words:

1. nur ture
2. cul ture
3. sig na ture
4. per jure
5. trea sure
6. ag ri cul ture
7. de par ture
8. dis clo sure
9. re cap ture

Highlight the accented syllables in these words:

1. hos tage
2. bro ker age
3. lan guage
4. foot age
5. pil grim age
6. rough age
7. bag-gage
8. her i tage
9. hem or rhage

The same accent rule applies to all of the above words. What is the rule?

_____

_____

Some words with the **ure** ending have the accent on a different syllable. Read these words and highlight the accented syllable.

1. pro cure
2. ob scure
3. se cure
4. in sure
5. en dure
6. bro chure (bro shoor)
7. ma ture

Where does the accent fall in the last seven words? _____

Words that end with the suffix –**fy** have a secondary accent on –**fy**. A secondary accent is not pronounced as forcefully as the primary accent, but it is stressed more than unaccented syllables. Highlight the syllables with primary accents and mark the secondary accent with an apostrophe.

1. clar i fy
2. sat is fy
3. mag ni fy
4. u ni fy
5. tes ti fy
6. am pli fy
7. in ten si fy
8. ex em pli fy

Where does the primary accent fall in words with the suffix –**fy** or –**ify**?

_____

7b Suffixes –able and –ible

Do you remember what the suffixes **–able** and **–ible** say? Read these words and listen closely: *possible, payable, visible, taxable*. The suffixes **–able** and **–ible** say əbl and mean *able* or *capable*.

Create new words by combining a prefix, a base word, and **–able** or **–ible**. The words must make sense.

	pose		1. _____
	break		2. _____
un	excuse		3. _____
dis	deny		4. _____
im	use	–able	5. _____
in	move		6. _____
	agree		7. _____
	rely		8. _____

	response		1. _____
in	digest		2. _____
ir	resist	–ible	3. _____
	flex		4. _____

Read these words and write the base words on the lines. Sometimes there is a change in spelling. The ones with an * are challenging.

1. indigestible _____
2. unaffordable _____
3. unforgivable _____
4. indispensable _____
5. uncontrollable _____
6. irredeemable _____
7. irreversible _____
8. nondeductible _____
9. indestructible* _____
10. impermissible* _____
11. nonflammable* _____
12. indivisible* _____

7c/10c Reading and Spelling for Mastery

Spelling rule for words with the suffix –age: when a word has one consonant between a short vowel and –age, the consonant is usually doubled. The three common exceptions are *manage, damage* and *savage*. Spelling rules for –able/–ible are cited in the Note to Instructor.

7c Spelling

1. nature
2. capture
3. picture
4. furniture
5. temperature *
6. pressure*
7. measure *
8. figure
9. valuable
10. breakable *
11. probably
12. possible
13. terrible
14. responsible
15. message
16. village
17. package
18. luggage
19. average *
20. language *

*Red words

10c Spelling

1. action
2. station
3. question
4. attention
5. solution
6. position
7. population
8. directions
9. addition
10. information
11. situation*
12. education *
13. fashion*
14. permission
15. admission
16. decision *
17. invasion
18. conclusion
19. vision
20. television

7d Review of –able and –ible

Highlight the following words you can read and use them to solve the crossword puzzle:

reversible   avoidable   eligible   sensible   impossible
portable   achievable   noticeable   enjoyable   convertible   edible
terrible   incapable   adorable   treatable   available

Across:
1. Preventable, able to avoid
2. Easy to see or hear
3. Made to use in two ways
4. Unable to do a task
5. Designed to be carried around
6. Awful, horrible
7. Very cute and sweet
8. Qualified to do something

Down:
1. Ready for use, obtainable
2. Unworkable, without solution
3. Pleasurable
4. Reachable, a goal that can be reached
5. A fun kind of car
6. Showing good judgment, practical
7. Curable
8. Suitable or fit for eating

283

8b Suffixes –ion and –ian

What do **ti** or **ci** say? _____ They often appear before the suffixes **–ion** and **–ian**: together **ti + ion = tion**, and **ci + ian = cian**.

Syllabify the following words, mark the vowels, and denote the code. Then underline the words you can read. Prefixes and suffixes are not marked. You will notice that some words have an open syllable with a short vowel. In such situations, use this code ŏp.

1. locomotion _____
2. formation _____
3. musician _____
4. discretion _____
5. conversation _____
6. revolution _____
7. politician _____
8. electrician _____
9. completion _____
10. institution _____

1. Go back over words 1-12 and highlight the vowels before **–tion** or **–cian**. What vowels are long right before **–tion**? _____
2. What vowel comes before **–cian** _____? Is it long or short? _____
3. What does the ending **–cian** mean? _____
4. What vowel is short right before **–tion**? _____
5. What vowel can be long or short right before **–tion**? _____

Read these words and write down the verb for each. It might be quite different.

1. injection _____   6. correction _____
2. education _____   7. admiration _____
3. invitation _____   8. irritation _____
4. definition _____   9. reflection _____
5. expiration _____ 10. graduation _____

Study words # 1, 6, and 9. Where does the **t** in **–tion** come from? _____

Study words # 2, 8, and 10. Where does that **at** in **ation** come from? _____

9b The Word Ending –sion

What are the two ways the word ending –sion is pronounced? _____ , _____

Read each word starter and draw a line to its correct ending. Drop the silent **e** of the base word. Then write the new words on the lines. Sometimes one or two letters must be dropped before adding the ending. When you add a –**sion** or –**tion**, the last vowel sound in the base word may change.

1. react
2. divide
3. operate
4. decide   –tion
5. televise
6. infect
7. vacate   –sion
8. persuade
9. graduate
10. direct

1. _____
2. _____
3. _____
4. _____
5. _____
6. _____
7. _____
8. _____
9. _____
10. _____

What word endings go to –**tion**? _____

What kind of a letter comes right before –**sion** when it says **zhən**? _____

The word ending –**sion** also says **zhən** after the letter **r**, as in *excursion, submersion, diversion*.

The word ending –**sion** doesn't always say **zhən**. Often it says exactly the same thing as –**tion**.

Read these words and write down the base words. Some letters may need to change.

1. suspension _____
2. extension _____
3. expansion _____
4. apprehension _____
5. comprehension _____
6. expulsion _____
7. compulsion _____
8. repulsion _____

What consonants does the suffix –**sion** follow? _____

There are many more words with the –**sion** = **zhun** ending than –**sion** = **shən** ending.

10b Word Ending *sion*

How do you pronounce the ending **–sion**? _____

What other endings say the same thing? _____

Let's examine how we can decide when to use **s–sion**. Read these words, study the patterns, and fill in the blanks.

1. admit (verb) = admission (noun)
2. permit (verb) = permission (noun)
3. commit (verb) = commission (noun)
4. possess (verb) = possession (noun)
5. oppress (verb) = oppression (noun)
6. impress (verb) = impression (noun)
7. transmit (verb) = _____ (noun)
8. submit (verb) = _____ (noun)
9. omit (verb) = _____ (noun)
10. express (verb) = _____ (noun)
11. discuss (verb) = _____ (noun)
12. depress (verb) = _____ (noun)
13. confess (verb) = _____ (noun)

Read these words, study the pattern and fill in the blanks.

1. recede (verb) = recession (noun), related to *recess*
2. succeed (verb) = succession (noun), also *success*
3. proceed (verb) = _____ (noun)
4. concede (verb) = _____ (noun)
5. secede (verb) = _____ (noun)
6. intercede (verb) = _____ (noun)

Study all of the verbs on this page. What word endings in verbs go to **s–sion** in nouns?

_____

Study the last six examples. What does the addition of the ending **s–sion** do to the last vowel of the base word? _____

10d *ci*, *ti* and *xi* Before *–ous*

Write down the phonetic spelling of the suffix **–ous**: _____ In the last lesson, you learned how to pronounce **ti, si, ci,** and **xi**. What do they say? _____

Sometimes **ci, ti,** and **xi** come right before the suffix **–ous**: ci + –ous = –cious, ti + –ous = –tious, and xi + –ous = –xious. Together, they say **shəs**. The consonant before the connective *i* comes from the Latin root *(space, spacious)*.

Highlight the following words you can read and use them to complete the sentences.

suspicious	gracious	cautious	delicious	ferocious	superstitious
nutritious	obnoxious	infectious	predacious	fictitious	rambunctious

1. The _____ hostess served a wonderful meal that was both _____ and _____.
2. When kids get rowdy, they can be _____ and _____.
3. Hungry lions and tigers are _____ and _____.
4. Nurses and doctors must be _____ when they treat people with _____ diseases.
5. The detective became _____ after she discovered the suspect was using a _____ name.
6. A _____ person believes that Friday the 13th brings bad luck.

Sometimes it's hard to know whether to use **ci** or **ti** before **–ous** because they both say **sh**. Two rules will help you spell these difficult words. First of all **–cious** is much more common than **–tious**. When in doubt, think of the related noun. If that noun ends with **–tion**, the adjective will end with **–tious**, *fiction, fictitious*. Otherwise, use **–cious**.

Use these rules to change the phonetic spelling to the correct spelling in words 1-6.

1. spa shəs _____
2. pre shəs _____
3. cau shəs _____
4. am bi shəs _____
5. rep e ti shəs _____
6. de li shəs _____

Study all of the words on this page. Where does the accent fall in words with **ci** and **ti**?

_____

10e Accent Patterns for Five Suffixes

Read these words and highlight the accented syllables. Write the words under the appropriate category. Do the easy ones first.

1. vo ca tion
2. el i gible
3. char i table
4. ag gres sion
5. sea son able
6. grad u a tion
7. man age able
8. pos ses sion
9. leg is la tion
10. meas ur able
11. an i ma tion
12. vul ner a ble
13. prof it able
14. dam age able
15. dec or a tion
16. con fig u ra tion
17. per ish able
18. ap pli cable
19. con ver sa tion
20. ex plo sion

The syllable directly before the suffix is accented	The first syllable is accented. If there is a prefix, the root is accented

You have now studied sixteen suffixes/word endings. Only five of these follow the rule, "The syllable right before the suffix is accented". What are the five suffixes?

_____

All of the other suffixes follow the accent rule you already learned in the previous two chapters. Write the rule again.

_____

11 Review of Latin Suffixes

First session: Write all of the suffixes on the board/overhead (or show the cards) and ask students to read them individually, if possible. If that is not practical, ask your class to read them in unison. Dictate the words from the first column. Students should copy the suffixes only. Erase the suffixes, ask students to turn over their papers, and dictate words from the second and third lists. Students write the suffixes from memory. Check for accuracy.

Second session, dictate the words from the fourth and fifth lists. After you have checked the work, write the suffixes on the board/overhead and ask students to read them individually if possible. If more practice is required, use the sixth list.

Accept either suffix for –**able**/–**ible**. Since –**tion** and –**cian** sound the same, prompt students by saying, "Which one means *a person who does a certain job*?"
To avoid confusion, the suffix **s-sion** is not included.

A)
1. devotion
2. reasonable
3. picture
4. qualify
5. apartment
6. television
7. courageous
8. marriage
9. archeologist
10. electric
11. physician
12. pleasure
13. examine

B)
1. cabbage
2. outrageous
3. nullify
4. occasion
5. typist
6. magician
7. treasure
8. changeable
9. frantic
10. submarine
11. capture
12. addition
13. placement

C)
1. fanatic
2. tourist
3. exposure
4. mountainous
5. pediatrician
6. terrify
7. breakable
8. voyage
9. jasmine
10. collision
11. monument
12. transportation
13. furniture

D)
1. persist
2. subtraction
3. technician
4. routine
5. monstrous
6. enjoyable
7. future
8. decision
9. horrify
10. amusement
11. measure
12. rustic
13. baggage

E)
1. lecture
2. feasible
3. conspicuous
4. pacify
5. artist
6. mortgage
7. traffic
8. exposure
9. inspection
10. precision
11. requirement
12. musician
13. imagine

F)
1. profitable
2. subtraction
3. nature
4. composure
5. amazement
6. electrician
7. chlorine
8. terrific
9. organist
10. clarify
11. mileage
12. division
13. vigorous

12 Syllabication Challenge 1

Rewrite the words in syllables, separate them with dashes, and mark the vowels. Then denote the code. Prefixes and suffixes are **not** marked. Some words will have an open syllable with a short vowel, coded ŏp.

In divided syllables the last letter of a Latin root often joins the suffix. This happens especially in words with two consonants between the last vowel and a suffix that begins with a vowel. For example, the word *rustic* is divided like this: rus-tic. The code is cl-t+s. This is a review of The Second Rule of Syllabication.

1. fantastic _____
2. entertainment _____
3. generous _____
4. excursion _____
5. concentration _____
6. indispensable _____
7. determine _____
8. voyage _____
9. orthodontist _____
10. departure _____
11. disclosure _____
12. automatic _____
13. profession _____
14. musician _____

Go back over the last fourteen words and highlight the accented syllables.

Choose suffixes from the list below to make complete words. Do the easy ones first. Use **–fy** and **–ible** twice.

–ous, –ment, –sion, s–sion, –ist, –ic, –age, –ify, –ture, –sure, –ible, –ine, and –cious.

1. terrif_____
2. conclu_____
3. tremend_____
4. revers_____
5. refresh_____
6. stor_____
7. incred_____
8. qual_____
9. mea_____
10. anthropolog_____
11. deli_____
12. ident_____
13. struc_____
14. permi_____
15. imag_____

13 Words with Multiple Suffixes

Do you remember the suffix –**ize**? It says **īz**. Add the following suffixes to the base words. Then add more suffixes to create new words. You must remember the rules for adding suffixes that start with vowels. When you add –**ous**, change the **y** to **i**.

1. equal + ize = _____ + er = _____
2. organ + ize = _____ + er = _____
3. energy + ize = _____ + er = _____
4. vapor + ize = _____ + er = _____
5. moist + ure = _____ + ize + er = _____
6. press + ure = _____ + ize + ing = _____

To change a verb that ends with –**ify** to a noun, drop –**fy**, (but not the **i**) and add –**fication** (fĭ cā′shən). This word ending derives from the Latin verb **ficare**, which means *to make*.

1. class + ify = _____ + fication = _____
2. note + ify = _____ + fication = _____
3. false + ify = _____ + fication = _____
4. just + ify = _____ + fication = _____
5. pure + ify = _____ + fication = _____
6. fort + ify = _____ + fication = _____

Add suffixes to these base words: an asterisk (*) means tricky!

1. pack + age = _____ + ing = _____
2. envy + ous = _____ + ly = _____
3. please + ure = _____ + able = _____
4. profit + able = _____ + ly = _____
5. remark + able = _____ + ly = _____
6. advance* + age = _____ + ous = _____

Read the words again and highlight the accented syllables. What are the accent rules?

_____

_____

14a Syllabication Challenge 2

Write the words in syllables, separate them with dashes, and mark the vowels. Then denote the code. Prefixes and suffixes are **not** marked. In divided syllables the last letter of the Latin root often joins the suffix. This happens especially in words with two consonants between the last vowel and a suffix that begins with a vowel. This is a review of the Second Rule of Syllabication.

1. engagement _____
2. organic _____
3. technician _____
4. simultaneously _____
5. nonrenewable _____
6. embezzlement _____
7. impressionable _____
8. consciously con-scious-ly   pref-sci+s-s _____
9. repercussion _____
10. scientist _____

The following words have a schwa sound. Highlight the words you can read:

1. gasoline   3. modify   5. magnify   7. verify
2. medicine   4. modification   6. magnification   8. verification

To complete the puzzle, find the base words in these polysyllabic words. Use a pencil.

Across:
1. extremist
2. unfavorably
3. arrangements
4. dissatisfaction

Down:
1. undeniable
2. therapist
3. reservist
4. transformation

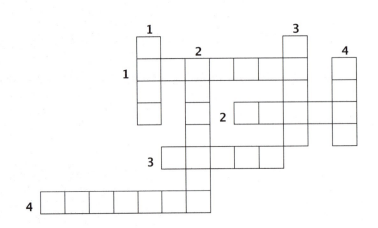

14b Dictation Exercise (Teacher Page)

Provide the code orally and write it on the board/overhead. Then dictate each word. Ask students to write the word in syllables, separate the syllables with dashes, and mark the vowels. Prefixes, suffixes, and schwa in open syllables are not marked.

Code abbreviations:
- cl=closed
- vce=vowel-consonant-e
- op=open
- rc=r-controlled
- vv=vowel-vowel
- cle=consonant-le
- d=diphthong/vowel digraph
- s=suffix
- pref=prefix

The suffixes **–able/ –ible** are both pronounced əbl. Therefore, accept either one. Remind students to circle r-controlled vowels, shown in red on this worksheet.

1. (pref-vv-s)   mis-trēat-ment
2. (cl-tr+s)   dŏc-trine
3. (rc-s)   short-age
4. (pref-op-s)   in-trū-sion
5. (pref-vv-s)   un-trēat-able
6. (op-rc-s)   nū-mer-ous
7. (cl-op-s)   jŭs-ti-fy   Ask, What letter precedes –**fy**?
8. (pref-cl-s)   in-strŭc-tion
9. (cl-cl-t+s)   Ăt-lăn-tic
10. (op-s-s-s)   fū-tur-ist-ic

1. (pref-pref-op-s)   un-re-lī-able
2. (rc-cl-t+s)   sar-căs-tic
3. (pref-cl-s)   pre-scrĭp-tion
4. (d-s)   mois-ture
5. (pref-cl-op-s)   in-těn-si-fy   Ask, What letter precedes –**fy**?
6. (pref-op-s)   in-vā-sion
7. (pref-cl-s-s)   un-măn-age-able
8. (d-s-s)   joy-ous-ly
9. (pref-rc-s)   con-form-ist
10. (cl-s-s)   măn-age-ment

Accept **er**, **ir**, and **ur** in these **rc** syllables, but point out that **er** is the correct spelling.

Asks students to pronounce the words.

15a Dictionary Pronunciations

Reminders:
1. When an apostrophe comes right after a syllable, it means that it is **accented**.
2. We say accented syllables more forcefully than unaccented ones.
3. Vowels in unaccented syllables often say the schwa sound.
4. The symbol for a schwa sound is ə; it has the same sound as a **short u**.
5. Some words with four or more syllables have a secondary accent.

Match the dictionary pronunciations on the right with the words on the left.

1. or′ thə dŏn′ tĭst   qualification
2. kəm′fər tə bəl   gigantic
3. mĕd′ ə sən   fictitious
4. jī găn′ tĭc   organization
5. grăj ōō ā′ shən   comfortable
6. fĭc tĭ′ shəs   temperature
7. kwŏl′ ə fĭ kā′ shən   medicine
8. jĕn′ ər əs lē   orthodontist
9. or′ gə nĭ zā′ shən   generously
10. tĕm′ prə chər   graduation

1. ĕn kur′ ĭj mənt   appreciation
2. rē bĕl′ yəs nəss   signature
3. grăt′ ə fī   rebelliousness
4. ŭn-sī ən tĭf′ ĭk   communication
5. sĕm′ ē prĕsh′əs   unselfconsciously
6. ə prē′ shē ā′ shən   gratify
7. ŭn ăk sĕp′ tə bəl   encouragement
8. sĭg′ nə chər   unscientific
9. ŭn′ sĕlf kŏn′ shəs lē   semiprecious
10. kə myōō′ nĭ kā′ shən   unacceptable

15b Prefixes, Base Words, and Suffixes

When used in English, Latin roots are bound morphemes. This means they are not real words by themselves; they need prefixes or suffixes to make sense. Some of the words below have several suffixes. 1. Write the base word, prefix, and suffix(es) next to the numbered words.
1. When **ci**, **ti** or **i** precede **–ous**, write them with the suffix.
2. Mark the accented syllable by placing an apostrophe right after it.
3. The spelling and pronunciation of the base word may change when it stands alone.

	base word	prefix	suffix	suffix
1. deductible				
2. unemployment				
3. nectarine				
4. expressionless				
5. noninfectious				
6. indefensible				
7. allergic				
8. objectionable				
9. laboriously				
10. perfectionist				
11. ungraciously				
12. disclosure				
13. artistic				
14. postage				
15. nonpoisonous				
16. disagreement				
17. unspeakably				
18. contemptuously				

16 Mount Everest

Several years ago, my husband, our friend Mary, and I decided to make a long-held dream come true. We planned a trip to Nepal to see the beautiful Himalayas and Mount Everest with our own eyes. I want to emphasize the word **see**, **not climb!** Do you know why Mt. Everest is one of the world's most famous mountains? You are right if you knew that it is the highest mountain on earth.

After careful research and many planning sessions, we made the decision to go over winter vacation, because we wanted to avoid the monsoon rains during the summer months. With the realization that we were going to face extremely cold temperatures, we were advised to bring two down sleeping bags per person. We wondered whether the guide, the cook, and their assistants would have warm clothes to brave the elements. Therefore, our trip preparation included visits to the Salvation Army store where we bought warm jackets, and to a department store where we purchased woolen hats and socks. We managed to stuff all of the extra clothing into our luggage.

After an interminable flight via Korea, Hong Kong, and Thailand, we arrived in Katmandu, the capital of Nepal. Nepal is a small country, northeast of India. Much of its territory is inaccessible because of the extremely rugged and mountainous terrain. Upon our arrival in Katmandu, we were suddenly immersed into a fascinating mixture of Buddhist and Hindu cultures. Just like typical tourists, we visited temples, palaces, museums, and, of course, treated ourselves to delectable meals at exotic restaurants.

A couple of days later, we met up with our guide and his staff to fly to Lukla (Lookla), a small village at 9,200 feet (2,827 meters) in the foothills of the Himalayas. The most memorable aspect of Lukla was its amazing silence. After the plane's departure, we realized we heard no passing cars, busses, motorcycles, or any other traffic noise! That's because there were no roads! The only means of transportation was your own two feet and a sizeable system of footpaths and trails. So began our trek. A trek is a series of long hikes over the course of many days.

That first day, we were huffing and puffing up steep trails for eight hours until we reached the capital of the Khumbu. The Khumbu is the highest state in Nepal, inhabited by the Sherpa people. We had gained 2,000 feet and were now at 11,300 feet (3,446 meters). Fortunately, our guide, Nuru, had made reservations at a guesthouse, where we had dinner and were going to spend the night.

Suddenly, I began to feel dizzy and nauseous. I had a pounding headache and my heart was racing wildly! We became seriously worried about my condition, because we could identify the symptoms of altitude sickness. The only treatment was to descend; but we were in no mood to lose our hard-fought gain. I took some aspirin, and we decided to spend the night and evaluate the situation in the morning. Awakened by the excited voices of children outside, we opened the windows to be greeted with a fresh blanket of snow. Kids were having a snowball fight! Luckily, I felt much better.

We continued our trek, through a gorgeous valley ringed by jagged, glacier-covered peaks. Every three or four miles there were beautifully carved prayer wheels right along the path. Each passing person gave them a twirl, which, according to Buddhist belief, sent prayers to heaven. Farther along, we came upon a large boulder that was engraved with prayers. Our guide explained that Sherpas must walk completely around the boulder in a clockwise direction to honor Buddha.

Towards evening, we reached Tengboche (Teng-bo-she) Monastery, inhabited by Buddhist monks. It was perched on a ledge, above a rushing gorge, surrounded by 20,000 foot peaks. In this spectacular setting, we caught our first glimpse of Mount Everest. The monks were welcoming and very hospitable. As there was no room in the guesthouse, we were invited to spend the night in a small room inside the monastery. It was bitterly cold; we were very happy to snuggle in our double down bags. At two o'clock in the morning, we were awakened by the mysterious sound of a gong that called the monks to prayer service. We heard musical instruments and chanting for at least two hours. The only thing the monks were wearing was a thin robe! We shuddered and shivered on their behalf.

The next morning, Nuru got everyone up and going bright and early. After a couple of miles, we had to walk across a rickety, hanging bridge suspended above a raging river. None of us wanted to be first, but with Nuru's encouragement, we all made it! He was a perfect guide who spoke good English and taught us about Nepalese culture, religion, and geography. A native Sherpa, he and the other support staff were always joking, laughing, or singing, as they guided us along the trail.

For the next five days we wandered upwards, getting closer and closer to Mount Everest. As we passed through small villages and settlements, we were often greeted by Nuru's friends and relatives, who invited us into their homes for tea, or to spend the night. Every evening there was a party!

On our eighth day, we reached a guesthouse close to the Everest Base Camp with a fantastic view of the big hulk! We were now at 17,000 feet (5,184 meters) and felt somewhat weak and wobbly from the altitude. At dinner, we met a large group of climbing Sherpas who were going to guide a Korean climbing expedition to the summit of Mount Everest. What captivating stories they told! We were totally in awe of their courage and mountaineering skills.

The next day, we slowly climbed a high hill, which afforded the best views of Mount Everest and the surrounding peaks. We stopped often, gasping for air, but eventually we did reach the top at 18,450 feet (5,623 meters). Mount Everest towered above us, more than 10,000 feet higher. What a thrill to gaze across the valley at this spectacular, breathtaking panorama of the tallest mountains in the world. We stayed for hours reveling in the momentous, awesome beauty!

As the peaks turned pink in the waning light, we reluctantly returned to the guesthouse. Over the next several days, we walked back towards Lukla. Again we were fortunate, a friend of Nuru's invited us to spend Christmas with his family. Now it was our turn to teach them about our culture.

Soon we reached Lukla, and the time came to leave our newfound friends. It was hard to say good-bye to our providers, teachers, guides, and entertainers, all wrapped in one. We tried to hold back tears as we boarded the plane to Katmandu. We already missed their fun-loving company! Two days later, as we flew back home, we felt enriched and dazzled by this once-in-a-lifetime experience.

1. Why did the trekkers decide to visit Nepal over winter vacation? _____

_____

2. Why was it quiet in Lukla? _____

3. What are the symptoms of altitude sickness? _____

4. What did the trekkers learn from Nuru, the guide? _____

_____

5. Who invited the trekkers for tea or to spend the night? _____

_____

6. What was the highest altitude the trekkers reached? _____

_____

7. On what occasion did the trekkers share their culture with the Nepalese? _____

_____

8. How did the trekkers feel about their trip? _____

_____

CHAPTER 12
Latin Suffixes, Part 2

Note to Instructor

This section deals with the second set of Latin suffixes. As was stated previously, Latin suffixes are very challenging to master because the sound/symbol correspondence is often weak and the accent rules are complicated. Therefore, it is very important to take time and teach each suffix as a unit of meaning, sound, and sight with lots of review along the way. A great deal of practice is needed before these suffixes are committed to long-term memory. Many teachers have made color-coded flashcards for each set of suffixes (a different color for each set). The most effective method requires students to make their own cards. The suffix is written on one side of the card; the definition, pronunciation, and four examples are written on the reverse side. Please modify these lessons for younger students or for those with severe learning disabilites. Cross out the most difficult words or consider using the difficult pages as whole-class activities.

Anglo-Saxon base words are free morphemes, whereas Latin roots are bound morphemes. Therefore, most Latin roots are not real words by themselves and don't make sense unless they are attached to prefixes or suffixes. This section covers the following Latin suffixes: **–al**, **–ive**, **–ity**, **–ability**, **–ibility**, **–ary**, **–ory**, **–ent**, **–ence**, **–cy**, **–ency**, **–ant**, **–ance**, and **–ancy**. The suffixes in this chapter are unaccented, except for these five suffixes: **–ary**, **–ory**, which have a secondary accent, as well as **–ability** and **–ibility**, which have the accent on the syllable before **–ity** (**–a bil′ity** and **–i bil′ity**). The word ending **–ate** is also reviewed; it has a secondary accent when it's part of a verb.

Reminders:
1. **Have students reread all the words in every lesson once they have completed the exercises.**
2. Ask students to copy each new phonogram, red word, homophone, homograph, prefix, suffix, and rule in the appropriate sections of their Decoding Binders. Include homographs, marked **HG**, in the Homophone Section. When entering a phonogram, prefix, or suffix, students must list four key words that illustrate it. Students must also add four words for every rule and definitions for the homophones and homographs.
3. Review all sections of the binder **once a week** for a minimum of five weeks. Younger children or those with severe learning disabilities may need more time for review.
4. Use the **Proposed Spelling Activities**, located in the Appendix, for all **Reading and Spelling for Mastery** lists. Students must read the list daily before they start the two practice activities.

Lesson 1a: (No worksheet) Write the suffix **–al** on the board/overhead (or show the card). Next to the suffix, write three words that end with **–al** (*equal, normal, legal, total, rival, floral, central, removal, musical, journal, global, terminal, carnival*). After students understand the concept, elicit ten words from your class and write them on the board/overhead. Ask everyone to deduce the phonetic spelling and the definition: (əl), *of, relating to*. Most words that end with the suffix **–al** are adjectives, although some are nouns. Students write the suffix, pronunciation, definition, and four examples in the Suffixes section of their binders.

Suggestion: Divide the class into small groups that are balanced in abilities. After you have presented the first suffix with examples, set a timer for two or three minutes (longer for younger students) and have the groups compete against each other. The group that generates the most words wins the first round. Allow students to use textbooks and dictionaries to find words. Ask a volunteer from every group to write the words on the board/overhead and have students read the cumulative list in unison. If this format works well, do this for every suffix and keep track of points. Consider giving the winners a small reward. If the same group of students always wins or loses, consider changing the makeup of the groups.

Lesson 1b requires students to add –al to base words and to apply the drop **e** rule and the **y** rule (change **y** to **i** before adding a suffix, unless the **y** is preceded by a vowel).

Lesson 1c deals with the combinations **ti, si, ci, xi, tu, su,** and **du** when they occur before **–al.** They were already discussed in chapter 11. Here is the accent rule that students will discover: the syllable directly before these combinations is accented *(com mer'cial, u'su al, es sen'tial)*. Ask students to record these phonic elements in the Suffixes section of their Decoding Binders, along with four examples: **cial, (shəl)** *commercial, artificial, special, social;* **tial, (shəl)** *initial, potential, partial, essential;* **tual, (chooəl)** *mutual, actual, ritual, eventual;* **sual, (shooəl)** *usual, casual, visual, sensual;* **dual (jooəl)** is less common *individual, gradual;* **du, (joo or jə)** *educate, graduate, procedure, schedule*.

Lesson 1d (on the same page as **Lesson 3c**) is a **Reading and Spelling for Mastery** list, consisting of words with the suffix **–al**. Because this list is difficult, please modify it for younger students or the severely learning disabled. Please see **Proposed Spelling Activities**, located in the Appendix. Students are required to read the list before they start the daily practice. Challenge your class to find the following pattern: In words that end with **–al**, the accent is on the first syllable, unless there is a prefix, which shifts the accent onto the base word.

Lesson 2a: (No worksheet) Write the suffix **–ive** on the board/overhead and add three words that end with **–ive** *(motive, cursive, massive, relative, adhesive, native, elective, fugitive, attentive, defective, effective, narrative, offensive)*. Elicit ten words from your class and write them on the board/overhead. Ask everyone to deduce the phonetic spelling and definition. It says **ĭv**, even though it has a **silent e** at the end. It means *performing* or *like a certain action*. Have students write the suffix, pronunciation, definition, and four examples in their binders. Most words that end with the suffix **–ive** are adjectives, although some are nouns. Words with the suffix **–ive** are accented on the first syllable, unless there is a prefix, which shifts the accent onto the base word.

Lesson 2b provides practice with adding and eliminating the suffix **–ive**. Please check whether students remember the **drop e** rule for adding suffixes that start with vowels. The second exercise encourages students to figure out this pattern: when a base word ends with the letter **d**, it will usually change to **s** before **–ive** *(expand, expansive; respond responsive; explode, explosive)*. In the last exercise, accept either **–able** or **–ible**.

Lesson 3a: (No worksheet) Write the suffix **–ity** on the board/overhead and add three words that end with **–ity** *(gravity, sanity, quality, reality, capacity, charity, purity, clarity, security, quantity, necessity, cavity, humanity)*. Elicit ten words from your class and write them on the board/overhead. Ask everyone to deduce the phonetic spelling and definition: **(ĭtē)**, *state, quality*. Ask students to write the suffix, pronunciation, definition, and four examples in their binders. Most words that end with the suffix **–ity** are nouns. The syllable directly before **–ity** is accented.

Lesson 3b requires choosing words that end with **–ity** to complete sayings or expressions. Please provide support with the more difficult ones and ask students to use a pencil.

Lesson 3c (on the same page as **Lesson 1c**) is a **Reading and Spelling for Mastery** list, consisting of words with the suffixes **–ive** and **–ity**. Since this list is difficult, please modify it for younger students or those with severe learning disabilities. Follow the usual procedures. For the first activity, ask students to write the words in syllables and mark the accented syllables with an apostrophe. Alert students to this spelling rule: when **–ity** follows **–ive**, the silent **e** must be dropped.

Lesson 3d presents students with words that have multiple suffixes. When separating words into their components, the letter **e** must be added to **iv** for words such as activity *(act = base word, -ive = suffix, -ity = suffix)*. For a strong group, determine if students can deduce the plural form of **–ity** (**–ities**), but point it out to a weaker group. The word components for # 10 are *exclude ive, ity*. This page is difficult, consider presenting it as a whole-class activity.

Lesson 3e (No worksheet) Review the suffixes **–al**, **–ive**, and **–ity**. Provide more practice if necessary. Then write the suffixes **–ability** and **–ibility** on the board and add three words that end with **–ability** and **–ibility** (*liability, probability, reliability, suitability, availability, flammability, irritability, insurability, desirability, possibility, capability, responsibility, visibility, legibility, feasibility, flexibility, plausibility, eligibility*). Elicit as many words as possible from your class and write them on the board/overhead. Ask everyone to deduce the phonetic spelling and definition: both say ə bĭl′ə tē, and mean *ability or inclination for*. Students must write the suffixes, pronunciation, definitions, and three examples for each in their binders.

Lesson 3f requires students to add the suffixes **–ability** and **–ibility** to Latin roots and points out that these two suffixes form nouns from adjectives that end with the suffixes **–able** and **–ible**. Words that end with **–able** go to **–ability** and words that end with **–ible** go to **–ibility**. Words with **–able/–ible** are accented on the first syllable or the base word. Words that end with **–ability** and **–ibility** are accented on **bil**, which is the syllable before **ity**. The last exercise asks students to find base words from short lists of related words.

Lesson 4a: (No worksheet) Write the suffix **–ary** on the board/overhead and add three words that end with **–ary** (*library, February, contrary, itinerary, customary, summary, imaginary, vinegary, vocabulary, voluntary, exemplary, secretary, glossary, secondary, ordinary*). Elicit ten words from your class and write them on the board or the overhead. Ask everyone to deduce the phonetic spelling. Students may notice that **–ary** has two different pronunciations. The more prevalent one is **ĕrē** (or **airy**, if you prefer); however, sometimes it says **ərē**. To explain the difference, we must raise the difficult issue of secondary accents, which are stressed, but not as forcefully as primary accents. The **ĕrē** pronunciation has a secondary accent on the suffix, whereas **ərē** is unaccented. Once students notice the difference, have them copy the generated words under two headings: 1. **ĕrē** 2. **ərē**. Most words that end with the suffix **–ary** are nouns or adjectives. As an adjective it means *relating to, characterized by*. As a noun, it can mean *a place or thing used for or connected with*. Have students write the suffix, two pronunciations, three examples for each, and the definition in their binders.

Lesson 4b deals with the two pronunciations of **–ary** and secondary accents. Even though the suffix **–ary** is technically a two-syllable suffix, for the purpose of these exercises, we will treat it as a single unit.

Lesson 5a: (No worksheet) Write the suffix **–ory** on the board/overhead and add three words that end with **–ory** (*dormitory, victory, ivory, memory, obligatory, migratory, history, factory, observatory, directory, auditory, territory, mandatory*). Elicit ten words from your class and write them on the board/overhead. Ask everyone to deduce the phonetic spelling and definition. As with the previous suffix, there are two pronunciations: **orē** when it has a secondary accent and **ərē** when it is unaccented. Once students notice the difference, have them copy the list under these two headings: 1. **orē** 2. **ərē**. It means *relating to, characterized by*. Have students write the suffix, two pronunciations, three examples for each, and the definition in their binders. Most words that end with the suffix **–ory** are nouns or adjectives.

Lesson 5b deals with the two pronunciations of **–ory** and secondary accents. Even though the suffix **–ory** is technically a two-syllable suffix, for the purpose of these exercises, we will treat it as a single unit. When the suffix says **orē**, it has a secondary accent. When it says **ərē**, it is unaccented.

Lesson 5c (on the same page as **Lesson 7d**) is a **Reading and Spelling for Mastery** list, consisting of words with the suffixes **–ary** and **–ory**. Please follow the usual procedures. Students are required to read the list before they start the daily practice.

Lesson 6a: (No worksheet) Review the suffixes **–ability/–ibility**, **–ary**, and **–ory**. Provide more practice if necessary. Then write the suffix **–ent** on the board/overhead and add three words that end with **–ent** (*student, resident, decent, present, ancient, silent, recent, solvent, excellent, accident, continent, independent, persistent*). Elicit ten words from your class and write them on the board/overhead. Ask everyone to deduce the phonetic spelling (**ənt**) and the definition: *promoting or causing a specified action*. Students must write the suffix, pronunciation, definition, and four examples in their binders. The suffix **–ent** is unaccented. Words with this suffix are nouns or adjectives and are accented on the first syllable, unless there is a prefix, which shifts the accent onto the base word. When **ent** occurs in verbs, it is not a suffix but part of the root (*pre<u>vent</u>, re<u>sent</u>, in<u>vent</u>*).

Lesson 6b: (No worksheet) Write the suffix **–ence** on the board/overhead and add three words that end with **–ence** (*patience, science, residence, evidence, audience, sentence, absence, silence, innocence, reference, independence, confidence, consequence*). Elicit ten words from your class and write them on the board/overhead. Ask everyone to deduce the phonetic spelling (**əns**) and the definition: *state or condition*. Students must write the suffix, pronunciation, definition, and four examples in their binders. Most words that end with the suffix **–ence** are nouns and are accented on the first syllable, unless there is a prefix, which shifts the accent onto the root.

Lesson 6c asks students to add the suffixes **–ent** and **–ence** to base words. The second exercise deals with synonyms and antonyms.

Lesson 7a: (No worksheet) Write the suffix **–cy** on the board/overhead and supply three words that end with **–cy** (*policy, emergency, agency, presidency, secrecy, privacy, residency, pharmacy, conspiracy, frequency, democracy, candidacy*). Elicit ten words from your class and write them on the board/overhead. Many of these words are difficult, so please take some time to explain their meaning. Ask everyone to deduce the phonetic spelling (**sē**) and definition: *state, condition, quality*. Students must write the suffix, pronunciation, definition, and four examples in their binders. Most words that end with the suffix **–cy** are nouns and are accented on the first syllable, unless there is a prefix, which shifts the accent onto the base word. Please point out the rule for soft **c**.

Lesson 7b asks students to think of the adjective form for nouns that end with **–cy**. (Review the suffix **–ate** with its two pronunciations: **āte** as in *calculate, tabulate, evaluate, hydrate, regulate* and **əte** or **ĭt** as in *accurate, climate, private, pirate, palate*). The rule addresses the fact that the suffix **ate + cy = –acy** and **ent + cy = –ency**. Students must write the two suffixes, pronunciations, definitions, and four examples in their binders. By thinking of related words, students should be able to deduce the spelling of the schwa sound before the suffix **–cy**. Even though the suffixes **–acy** and **–ency** are two-syllable suffixes, for the purpose of these exercises, we will treat them as a single unit.

Lesson 7c reviews the suffixes **–ent**, **–ence**, and **–ency**, as well as the combinations **ti**, **ci**, and **si** before suffixes. Ask students to record these combinations and the added suffixes, along with the following examples: **cient**, *efficient, sufficient, proficient, ancient;* **tient**, *patient, quotient;* **cience**, *conscience;* **tience**, *patience,* **ciency**, *proficiency, efficiency, sufficiency, deficiency*. The **i** before **ti, ci,** and **si** is always short.

Lesson 7d (on the same page as is **Lesson 5c**) is a Reading **and Spelling for Mastery** list, consisting of words with the suffixes **–ent, –ence, –ency,** and **–cy**. Follow the usual procedures.

Lesson 8a: (No worksheet) Review the suffixes **–ent**, **–ence**, **–cy**, **–ency**, and **–ate**. Provide more practice if necessary. Then write the suffix **–ant** on the board/overhead and add three words that end with **–ant** *(pleasant, hydrant, important, remnant, peasant, tenant, buoyant, distant, instant, warrant, inhabitant, merchant, consonant)*. Elicit ten words from your class and write them on the board/overhead. Ask everyone to deduce the phonetic spelling **(ənt)** and definition. Words with the suffix **–ant** are adjectives when they mean *causing a certain action;* however, when they mean *one who performs a certain action,* they are nouns. Students must write the suffix, pronunciation, definition, and four examples in their binders. Ask students what other suffix is pronounced exactly the same way.

Lesson 8b: (No worksheet) Write the suffix **–ance** on the board/overhead and add three words that end with **–ance** *(balance, clearance, appliance, attendance, entrance, fragrance, ignorance, tolerance, elegance, importance, reluctance, alliance, guidance)*. Elicit ten words from your class and write them on the board/overhead. Ask everyone to deduce the pronunciation **(əns)** and definition: *state, action,* or *condition*. Students must write the suffix, pronunciation, definition, and four examples in their binders. Most words with the suffix **–ance** are nouns and are accented on the first syllable, unless there is a prefix, which shifts the accent onto the base word. The suffix **–ance** is unaccented. Ask your students what other suffix is pronounced exactly the same way.

Lesson 8c provides syllabication practice with words that contain **–ant** and **–ance** and reviews the connective **i** before suffixes that start with vowels.

Lesson 8d explains the relationship among **–ant/ –ance/ –ancy** and the consistency in the spelling patterns. For the purpose of this exercise, we will treat the two-syllable suffix **–ancy** as a single unit.

Lesson 8e reviews hard and soft **c** and **g** before the suffixes **–ent/ –ence/ –ency** and **–ant/ –ance/ –ancy**. Soft **c** and **g** must be followed by **–ent/ –ency/ –ency**; whereas hard c and g must be followed by **–ant/ –ance/ –ancy**.

Lesson 9 reviews accent rules for the following suffixes: **–al, –ive, –ent/–ant, –ence/–ance,** and **–cy**.

Lesson 10 provides a review of all of the suffixes covered in this chapter.

Lesson 11 is a syllabication exercise, which includes the previously covered suffixes. Four-syllable words are usually accented on the second and fourth syllables.

Lesson 12a lists related words with a common base word and asks students to select the base word.

Lesson 12b is a dictation exercise with multiple suffixes.

Lesson 13 is a syllabication exercise with multiple suffixes. The last exercise is difficult; therefore, ask students to write the words they know and provide help with the rest.

Lesson 14 requires students to categorize words according to their components.

Lesson 15 is a story about the mountaineering experience of one of the author's friends.

1b The Suffix –al

The suffix **–al** says ǝl and means *of, relating to*. Most words that end with **–al** are adjectives (*informal, seasonal, national*), but there are also some nouns with **–al** (*principal, appraisal, disposal*).

Add **–al** to these base words and write the new words on the lines. You must remember some tricky spelling rules from previous chapters.

1. person _____
2. origin _____
3. propose _____
4. arrive _____
5. season _____
6. sign _____
7. nature _____
8. deny _____
9. margin _____
10. colony _____
11. globe _____
12. memory _____
13. approve _____
14. culture _____
15. rehearse _____
16. option _____

Read the words and highlight the ones with major changes in pronunciation. There are five.

Now that you're becoming a pro with Latin suffixes, you are ready to deal with words that have multiple suffixes.

Draw lines from the word starters to the correct suffixes and write the new words on the lines.

cler

emo

myth   –tional

struc

na   –ical

rad

fic   –tural

agricul

class

1. _____
2. _____
3. _____
4. _____
5. _____
6. _____
7. _____
8. _____
9. _____
10. _____

1c Combinations *ti, ci, tu, su,* and *du*

What do the combinations **ci** and **ti** say when they come directly before a suffix? _____ The combinations **ci** and **ti** when added to the suffix –al say **shəl**. In trying to decide whether to spell a word with –**cial** or –**tial**, think of how a related word ends. Usually words that end with **ce** go to –**cial**, *face, facial; office, official* and words that end with **t** go to –**tial**, *potent, potential; resident, residential*. The exceptions are *beneficial, spatial, substantial, sequential,* and *essential*.

Highlight the following words you can read and use them to complete the expressions.

| financial   special   impartial   official   social   initials   crucial   facial   potential |

1. Write your _____ here.
2. A judge must be _____.
3. She expects _____ treatment.
4. He is here on _____ business.
5. A bank is a _____ institution.
6. He/she has the _____ to be a great student.
7. _____ expression
8. _____ butterfly
9. Your appearance in court is _____.

Let's talk about the combinations **tu, su,** and **du,** as in *mutual, usual,* and *gradual*; **tu** says **choo**, **su** says **shoo**, and **du** says **joo**. They appear right before suffixes.

Write words 1-9 in phonetic spelling.

1. mutual   ____mūchooəl_____
2. visual   _____
3. individual _____
4. spiritually _____
5. unusual   _____
6. actually _____
7. gradually _____
8. factual   _____
9. habitual _____

What sound does the letter **i** say when it precedes **tu, su,** and **du**? _____ Read all of the words again and highlight the accented syllables. What is the accent rule?

_____

1d/3c Reading and Spelling for Mastery

For the first spelling activity, write the words in syllables and mark the accented syllables with an apostrophe. What are the accent rules?

Words with the suffix –al:

1d Spelling
1. several
2. usual*
3. usually*
4. capital (H)
5. signal
6. personal
7. natural
8. equal
9. central
10. general
11. national
12. annual
13. material*
14. actual*
15. gradual*
16. individual*
17. crucial*
18. social*
19. special*
20. especially*

Words with the suffixes –ive and –ity:

3c Spelling
1. active
2. activity
3. creative
4. creativity*
5. expensive
6. native
7. negative
8. positive
9. relative
10. elective
11. massive
12. security
13. authority
14. nationality
15. majority
16. equality
17. abilities
18. possible
19. possibility
20. responsibility*

*Red words, (H)=Homophone

2b The Suffix –ive

Do you remember how to pronounce the suffix –ive? It says ĭv, even though it has a silent **e** at the end. It means *performing* or *like a certain action*. Most words with the suffix –ive are adjectives, although some are nouns.

Underline the following words you can read. Next, add the suffix –ive and write the new words on the lines.

1. act _____
2. effect _____
3. secret _____
4. expense _____
5. object _____
6. attract _____
7. create _____
8. assert _____

Underline the following words you can read and write the verb (action word) on the lines. They may be quite different. Some end with a **vce** pattern. Do the ones you know first.

1. explosive _____
2. inclusive _____
3. defensive _____
4. corrosive _____
5. divisive _____
6. decisive _____
7. offensive _____
8. conclusive _____

What letters have changed? _____

Several different suffixes can be added to certain base words. The meaning, spelling, and pronunciation might be slightly different.

Read each word, remove the suffix –ive, and write down the verb. Then add the suffix –tion or –sion. Next, go back to the verb and add the suffix –able or –ible. Write the new words on the lines.

	Base Word	Add –tion/–sion	Add –able/–ible
1. detective	_____	_____	_____
2. digestive	_____	_____	_____
3. collective	_____	_____	_____
4. divisive	_____	_____	_____
5. expand	_____	_____	_____
6. preventive	_____	_____	_____

Circle the base word below that can attach all of these suffixes: –able, –ive, –tion, or –sion, and –age.   1. deduct   2. act   3. pass

3b The Suffix –ity

What does the suffix –ity say? _____ You are correct if you remembered that –ity says ītē and means *state, quality*. Most words that end with –ity are nouns.

Highlight the following words you can read and use them to complete the expressions or sentences. Do the ones you know first and use a pencil.

> formality   eternity   publicity   majority   opportunity
> immunity   security   identity   familiarity curiosity
> popularity equity   density   maternity   quantity
>   necessity

1. We want quality not _____.
2. Home _____ loan
3. In a democracy, the _____ rules.
4. We all must guard against _____ theft.
5. The _____ system is on 24/7.
6. This is just another _____ stunt.
7. _____ knocks.
8. This is no _____ contest.
9. _____ breeds contempt.
10. Let's do away with _____, and dig right in.
11. _____ is the mother of invention.
12. She is out on _____ leave.
13. For all _____
14. _____ from prosecution
15. _____ killed the cat.
16. Most cities have high _____ housing.

The suffix –ity is unaccented. Read the above words one more time and highlight the accented syllables. What are the accent rules?

_____

308

3d Multiple Suffixes

Now that you have advanced to the fourth set of suffixes, you will come across many words that have two suffixes. Often there is a slight change in spelling.

Read these words and use your creativity to divide them. Write the base word and each suffix (in its original form) under the correct heading. The tricky ones have an asterisk (*).

	Base Word	Suffix	Suffix
1. formality			
2. activities			
3. normality			
4. commonality			
5. impulsivity			
6. originality			
7. personality			
8. creativity			
9. musicality			
10. exclusivity*			
11. objectivity			
12. nationalities*			

Where does the accent fall in the words on the left? _____

Write the plural for **–ity** _____

Draw lines from the word starters to the correct suffixes to make real words.

crit		fest	
ment	ality	vert	ality
capt	ical	gener	ical
med	ivity	class	ivity
sensit		pass	

309

3f Suffixes –ability and –ibility

Two very long suffixes are **–ability** and **–ibility** (*durability, responsibility*). Both are pronounced with a schwa sound in the beginning and say **ə bĭl′ə tē**. These two suffixes are the noun forms of adjectives that end with **–able** or **–ible** and mean *ability* or *inclination*.

As you have probably already guessed, words with the suffix **–able** go to **–ability** and words with the suffix **–ible** go to **–ibility**.

Change the following adjectives to nouns and write the new words on the lines. (Drop the suffixes **–able** or **–ible** and add **–ability** or **–ibility**.)

1. capable _____
2. feasible _____
3. plausible _____
4. available _____
5. eligible _____

6. legible _____
7. livable _____
8. portable _____
9. reliable _____
10. vulnerable _____

The suffixes **–ability** and **–ibility** cause a change in spelling, accent, and pronunciation. Read words 1-6 and highlight the accented syllables.

1. flexible, flexibility
2. visible, visibility
3. probable, probability
4. possible, possibility
5. accountable, accountability
6. readable, readability

What is the change in the accent pattern when you go from words with the suffixes **–able/–ible** to words with the suffixes **–ability/–ibility**?

_____

Sometimes a base word can add several different prefixes or suffixes. The meaning will then change slightly, but it is usually still related. Highlight the words you can read and write down the base word they share. There may be a slight change in spelling.

1. society, socially, unsociable, sociability _____
2. employment, unemployed, employability, employable _____
3. sensation, sensible, sensibility, senseless _____
4. variation, variable, invariably, variability, varying _____
5. admission, inadmissible, admissibility, admitted _____
6. deduction, deductible, deductibility, nondeductible _____
7. application, applicable, applicability, reapplying _____
8. irritation, irritability, irritable, irritating _____

4b The Suffix –ary

The suffix **-ary** usually says **ĕrē** and means *relating to*. Sometimes, however, it says **ərē**. Read words 1-10 and draw lines to the phonetic spelling of the two suffixes.

1. January		6. secondary	
2. sanctuary	ĕrē	7. boundary	ĕrē
3. salary		8. elementary	
4. dictionary	ərē	9. stationary	ərē
5. glossary		10. anniversary	

The pronunciation of the suffix **-ary** depends on accent placement. Sometimes **-ary** has a secondary accent, which is pronounced with less force than a primary accent.

Read words 1-12 and write **ĕrē** or **ərē** next to each. Then highlight the accented syllables.

1. or din ary _____
2. pri mary _____
3. sug ary _____
4. mil i tary _____
5. nec es sary _____
6. mo men tary _____
7. bur glary _____
8. tem po rary _____
9. in fir mary _____
10. doc u men tary _____
11. vol un tary _____
12. budg et ary _____

Does **-ary** have a secondary accent when it says **ĕrē** or **ərē**? _____

Use the words from the lists above to solve the crossword puzzle. Write in pencil.

Across:
1. The base word is a food
2. The base word means *important papers*
3. The base word rhymes with *round*.
4. The base word means *a fraction of a minute*

Down:
1. The base word means *a place where a bus or a train stops*
2. The base word means *a plan for spending money*
3. The base word means *short amount of time*

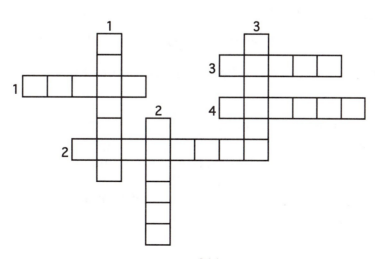

311

5b The Suffix –ory

The suffix **–ory** usually says **orē** and means *relating to*. Sometimes, however, it says **ərē**. Most words with the **–ory** ending are nouns or adjectives.

Read the following words and listen carefully to the sound of the suffix. Write **orē** or **ərē** on the lines.

1. memory _____
2. observatory _____
3. history _____
4. theory _____
5. territory _____
6. dormitory _____
7. compulsory _____
8. auditory _____
9. category _____
10. victory _____
11. factory _____
12. laboratory _____
13. inventory _____
14. accessory _____
15. explanatory _____
16. directory _____

Does the suffix **–ory** have a secondary accent when it says **orē** or **ərē**? _____

Write the plural for # 1, 4, 5, 9, and 11 on the back of this sheet.

Many words of Latin origin have open syllables that do not say a long vowel sound. Instead, the vowel says the schwa sound (ə).

Highlight the following words you can read and write the schwa symbol (ə) over the vowel wherever you hear it. Then write the base words for # 1, 2, 3, 7, 8 and 9. These base words are quite different, use your imagination and consult a dictionary if necessary.

1. man da tory _____
2. cir cu la tory _____
3. ac cu sa tory _____
4. pred a tory _____
5. au di tory _____
6. de rog a tory _____
7. ex plor a tory _____
8. mi gra tory _____
9. ex plan a tory _____

Did you notice that the last letter of the syllabicated word joins the suffix?

Read the clues carefully to unscramble the word.

trecodyri

_ _ _ _ _ _ _ _ _

1. It starts with d, ends with **ərē**.
2. The first syllable is **r-controlled**.
3. It contains information.

312

5c/7d Reading and Spelling for Mastery

Words with –ary and –ory:

Words with –ent, –ence, –ant, –ance and –cy. Please remind students that –ant/–ance and –ent/–ence are used consistently with the same base words.

5c Spelling

1. January
2. February*
3. dictionary
4. secretary
5. ordinary
6. military
7. temporary
8. primary
9. secondary
10. summary
11. salary
12. necessary*
13. history
14. victory
15. memory
16. theories
17. factory
18. category
19. territory
20. inventory

*Red words, HG = homograph

7d Spelling

1. present (HG)
2. independent
3. sentence
4. resident
5. president
6. accident*
7. different
8. difference
9. absent
10. absence
11. experience*
12. distant
13. distance
14. important
15. importance
16. policy
17. secrecy
18. emergency*
19. emergencies*
20. privacy*

6c Suffixes –*ent* and –*ence*

The suffix **–ent** says **ənt** and means *promoting or causing an action*. The suffix **–ence** says **əns** and means *state or condition*. A base word can often add **–ent** to create an adjective or **–ence** to create a noun.

Add **–ent** and **–ence** to the base words and write the new words in the correct column. Remember the doubling rule for # 3 and 7. Use your imagination to deal with # 8 and 10. The last one is tricky!

	Add –*ent*	Add –*ence*
1. persist		
2. depend		
3. excel		
4. differ		
5. insist		
6. exist		
7. recur		
8. reside		
9. indulge		
10. diverge		

Read each word below and draw a line to the matching synonym (similar definition).

1. occurrence	competent	5. transparent	indulgent
2. evident	incident	6. equivalent	hostility
3. proficient	frequent	7. belligerence	translucent
4. recurrent	apparent	8. lenient	identical

Read the words and fill in the blanks with antonyms (opposite definition):

appearance   absence   descent   independence

1. ascent _____   3. disappearance _____
2. dependence _____   4. presence _____

7b Suffixes –cy and –ency

The suffix **–cy** says **sē** and means *state, condition, quality*. Most words with the suffix **–cy** are nouns. This suffix is not accented.

Read the following words and write the adjective forms on the lines.

1. privacy   __private__
2. intricacy   _____
3. accuracy   _____
4. adequacy   _____
5. literacy   _____
6. delicacy   _____

The adjectives above have what word ending? _____ What letters are dropped when **–cy** is added to **–ate**? _____

Use your newly acquired skills to add the suffix **–cy** to these adjectives or nouns.

1. intimate + cy ⇨ _____
2. pirate + cy ⇨ _____
3. advocate + cy ⇨ _____
4. obstinate + cy ⇨ _____
5. candidate + cy ⇨ _____
6. democrat + cy ⇨ _____

The suffix **–cy** often follows a base word with **–ent** and **–ence**, as in these examples: resident, residence, residency. The suffix **–ency** is a variant of **–ence** and says **ənsē**.

Rewrite the following words by dropping the suffix **–ent**, then adding **–ence** or **–ency**.

1. agent   _____
2. turbulent   _____
3. decent   _____
4. insistent   _____
5. confident   _____
6. independent   _____
7. nonviolent   _____
8. current   _____

Use your skills to make new words. Some letters may need to be dropped. #4 and #5 are tricky!

1. emerge + ent ⇨ _____ + cy ⇨ _____
2. absorb + ent ⇨ _____ + cy ⇨ _____
3. urge + ent ⇨ _____ + cy ⇨ _____
4.* reside + ent ⇨ _____ + cy ⇨ _____
5.* preside + ent ⇨ _____ + cy ⇨ _____
6. solve + ent ⇨ _____ + cy ⇨ _____

7c *ci, ti,* and *si* Before *–ent, –ence, –ency*

What do the combinations **ci**, **ti**, and **si** say when they appear right before a suffix? _____

You are correct if you remembered that they say **sh**. Actually, **ci** is usually the one that is used in front of **–ent** or **–ence**. Together they are spelled **–cient** or **–cience** and say **shənt** or **shəns**, as in *sufficient* or *conscience*. The only two common words with **ti** are *patient* and *quotient*. The word *transient* is the only common word with the **–sient** ending.

Read the words on the right and write **sh** above **ci** or **ti**. Next, draw a line between the phonetic pronunciation of each word on the left and the correct spelling on the right.

1. ĭm pā′ shəns	deficient
2. prə fĭsh′ ən sē	conscience
3. ĕ fĭsh′ ən sē	efficient
4. dē fĭsh′ ənt	impatience
5. kwō′ shənt	sufficiency
6. ān′ shənt	proficiency
7. ŏm nĭsh′ ənt	sufficient
8. kŏn′ shəns	efficiency
9. sŭf fĭsh′ ən sē	conscientious
10. ə fĭsh′ ənt	ancient
11. sŭf fĭsh′ ənt	quotient
12. kŏn′ shē ĕn′ shəs	omniscient

Highlight the vowel **i** when it occurs directly before **ti** and **ci**. What does the **i** say? _____

1. Where does the accent fall in words with **ti** and **ci**, ?
   _____

2. Write the two different ways of spelling **shənt**: _____

3. Write the two different ways of spelling **shəns**: _____

4. How do you spell **shənsē**: _____

8c Suffixes –*ant* and –*ance*

The suffix **–ant** says ənt and is usually an adjective when it means *causing a certain action*. When it means *one who performs a certain action*, it is a noun. The suffix **–ance** says əns and means *state, action,* or *condition*. What other suffixes are pronounced exactly the same way? Write them in the margin.

In Latin words there are many open syllables with short vowels or the schwa sound. Also, the last letter of a Latin root frequently joins the suffix. A word like *applicant* is syllabicated like this: ap-pli-cant, with a code of cl-ŏp-c+s.

Write the following words in syllables, separated by dashes. Then mark the vowels and denote the code.

1. occupant _____
2. ambulance _____
3. defendant _____
4. exorbitant _____
5. tolerance _____
6. inhabitant _____
7. endurance _____
8. importance _____
9. descendant _____
10. appearance _____

In previous lessons you learned that Latin does not have long or short vowels. What does the letter **i** say in Latin? _____ You are correct if you remembered that the letter **i** says our **long e** sound. This sound occurs frequently before Latin suffixes that start with a vowel.

Read these words and write ē over the letter **i** whenever it says **long e**:

1. radiant   4. valiant   7. ingredient   10. experience
2. variant   5. nutrient   8. oriental   11. obedient
3. variance   6. recipient   9. lenient   12. obedience

There are some base words that do not follow this rule. If the base word ends with a **long i** sound, its sound continues when the suffix is added, as in *comply, compliant, compliance*. Highlight the following words you can read:

1. rely 2. reliant 3. reliance 4. apply 5. appliance 6. defy 7. defiant 8. defiance.

317

8d Suffixes –ant, –ance, and –ancy

In lesson 7c, you learned that the suffix –ent is often followed by –cy, as in *resident, residency*. What letter is dropped when the suffix –cy follows –ent? _____ The same is true for –ant, as in *vacant, vacancy*. However, some words add –tion or –ation instead of –cy.

Create as many words as possible with the following base words and the four suffixes above them. You must remember some spelling rules. Sometimes the base word changes significantly. Write the words on another sheet of paper.

	–ant	–ance	–ancy	–ation
	1. attend	2. defy	3. inform	4. expect

	–ant	–ance	–ancy	–ation
	5. resist	6. rely	7. hydrate	8. occupy

	–ant	–ance	–ancy	–ation
	9. vacate	10. consult	11. hesitate	12. apply (tricky!)

Because the suffixes –ant/–ent, –ance/–ence, –ancy/–ency sound the same, it's difficult to know whether to use the letter **e** or **a**. Here are some important spelling rules. You already realize that some base words can add several of these suffixes. The letters **a** or **e** will be consistent for all suffixes. Here are two examples: radi<u>a</u>te, radi<u>a</u>nt, radi<u>a</u>nce, radi<u>a</u>tion, or compet<u>e</u>nt, compet<u>e</u>nce, compet<u>e</u>ncy.

Choose –ant/–ance/–ancy to keep an ending **c** or **g** hard: vacant vacancy, elegant
Choose –ent/–ence/–ency to keep an ending **c** or **g** soft: decent, decency, indulgent

Read the words, cross out the incorrect letter, and write the correct letter above it. The first word in each series is spelled correctly.

1. relevant, relevence, relevancy
2. excellent, excellence, excellancy
3. competent, competance, competency

4. adolescent, adolescance
5. negligent, negligance
6. significant, significence

8e Hard and Soft *c* and *g* Before Suffixes

What letters make the letter **c** say **s** and the letter **g** say **j**? Write them in the margin.

Read the words and write the letter **s** over soft **c** and the letter **j** over soft **g**. Write the letter **k** over hard **c**, and circle the letter **g** for hard **g**.

1. florescent
2. vacancy
3. applicant
4. negligent
5. detergent
6. accent
7. urgency
8. innocence
9. significance
10. acceptance
11. adolescent
12. extravagant
13. recent
14. magnificence
15. reminiscent
16. acceptance

What is the rule for **hard** and **soft** **c** and **g** before the suffixes –ant/–ance/–ancy or –ent/–ence/–ency? _____

Solve the crossword puzzle by choosing words from the above list.

Across:
1. op-rc-soft **g** + s
2. a person who applies for a job
3. freedom from guilt
4. not long ago
5. a teenager

Down:
1. one hard **g** two soft **c's**
2. one hard and one soft **c**, unoccupied space
3. hard **g**, hard and soft **c's**, importance
4. one soft **g**, one soft **c**, attention is needed now
5. pronounced with more force

9 Accent Rules for *al, ive, ent/ant, ence/ance, cy*

You have already learned the accent rules for the other suffixes in this chapter. We will now cover the more complex rules that deal with the above suffixes. All are unaccented.

Read these words and highlight the accented syllables.

A) 1. stu dent   2. dom i nant   3. ev i dence   4. am bul ance   5. fre quen cy

What is the rule? _____

Just when you thought this was easy, a thorny issue arises. Read these words and highlight the accented syllables.

B) 1. de ter gent   2. in tol er ant   3. de fi ance   4. in sis tence   5. con sis ten cy

What is the rule? _____

Read these words and highlight the accented syllables.

C) 1. gen er al   2. dig i tal   3. cap i tal   4. hos pi tal   5. per son al

What is the rule? _____

Read these words and highlight the accented syllables.

D) 1. non ver bal   2. re ver sal   3. dis loy al   4. re fer ral   5. ap prov al

What is the rule? _____

Read these words and highlight the accented syllables.

E) 1. se cre tive   2. rel a tive   3. neg a tive   4. pos i tive   5. dec o ra tive

What is the rule? _____

Read these words and use apostrophes to show accent.

F) 1. pro tec tive   2. dis rup tive   3. con clu sive   4. im press ive   5. pre dic tive

What is the rule? _____

10 Review of Latin Suffixes (Teacher Page)

First session: Write all of the suffixes on the board/overhead (or show the cards) and ask students to read them individually, if possible: **–ability/–ibility, –al, –ive, –ity, –ary, –ory, –ent, –ence, –cy, –ency, –ant, –ance, –ancy**. If that is not practical, ask your class to read them in unison. Dictate the words from the first column. Students should copy the suffixes only. Erase the suffixes and ask students to turn their sheet of paper over. Dictate the words from the second and third lists. Students write the suffixes from memory. Check for accuracy.

Second session: Dictate the words from the fourth and fifth lists; students only write the suffixes. After you have checked the work, write the suffixes on the board/overhead and ask students to read them individually, if possible. If more practice is required, use the sixth list.

For **ənt**, accept **–ent** or **–ant**. For **ənce**, accept **–ence** or **–ance**. For **əncy**, accept **–ency** or **–ancy**; for **əbility**, accept **–ability** or **–ibility**, but please point out the correct spelling. Suggestion: Ask students to write both possible suffixes and circle the one they think is correct.

1. consistency
2. observatory
3. general
4. legacy
5. active
6. diversity
7. excellence
8. divisibility
9. coronary
10. inhabitant

1. majority
2. coastal
3. stability
4. impulsive
5. distance
6. accuracy
7. vacancy
8. mandatory
9. turbulent
10. preliminary

1. laboratory
2. relative
3. secondary
4. unusual
5. plausibility
6. difference
7. brilliant
8. contingency
9. humanity
10. secrecy

1. commentary
2. category
3. seasonal
4. aggressive
5. decent
6. insurance
7. charity
8. confederacy
9. urgency
10. probability

1. intelligence
2. delicacy
3. visibility
4. customary
5. quality
6. inventory
7. visual
8. passive
9. merchant
10. efficiency

1. gravity
2. bankruptcy
3. positive
4. tolerance
5. dormancy
6. opponent
7. reliability
8. territory
9. classical
10. imaginary

11 Mixed Practice, Latin Suffixes

Write the words in syllables, separate them with dashes, and mark the vowels. Next, denote the code. Prefixes and suffixes are **not** marked. The last letter of a Latin root often joins the suffix, as in the word **internal** (in-ter-nal, pref-rc-n+s), which reflects the Second Rule of Syllabication: a word with two consonants between two vowels is divided between the consonants. Reminder: an open syllable can have a short vowel, ŏp.

1. discrepancy _____
2. correspondence _____
3. advisory _____
4. subversive _____
5. financial _____
6. discretionary _____
7. feasibility _____
8. belligerent _____

Use these words for the crossword puzzle and write in pencil.

temporary, formality, reference, universal, secretive, dependent, ignorance, voluntary

Across:
1. cl-rc-s, not much knowledge
2. cl-rc-s, not permanent
3. op-cl-rc-s+s, everywhere
4. op-cl-d+s, a small word within means a writing utensil
5. cl-cl-t+s, the suffix says ĕrē

Down:
1. tending to keep information private
2. rc-s-s, proper etiquette or procedure
3. cl-rc-s, the suffix says əns, has useful information

322

12a Base words with Multiple Suffixes

Read each set of words and find the hidden base word. It may be quite different. Consult a good dictionary when you're stumped. Highlight all of the words you can read.

1. significance, insignificant, signature, signal, design _____
2. preferential, preferentially, preference, preferred _____
3. horizontal, horizontally, horizons _____
4. visual, visually, visible, invisible, visibility, envisioned _____
5. reception, receipt, receiver, receptive, receptively, receiving _____
6. deceptive, deception, deceiving, deceit, deceitful _____
7. recognition, recognizable, recognizance, unrecognizable _____
8. national, nationality, internationally, nationhood, nationalistic _____
9. circulatory, circulation, circuit, circling, circumnavigation _____
10. pleasantly, pleasure, unpleasant, pleasurable, pleasing _____
11. clarity, clarify, clarification, declaration, clearly _____
12. sufficient, sufficiency, insufficient, sufficiently, sufficing _____
13. productivity, unproductive, production, producing _____
14. repetition, repetitive, unrepeatable, repetitious _____
15. comprehensive, comprehension, incomprehensibility _____

Unscramble the words below. Read the clues carefully; they give you all the needed hints.

larasy

_ _ _ _ _ _

1. cl-s; The suffix says ərē.
2. The a's stay in the same place.
3. Adults need it to pay the bills.

desrepint

_ _ _ s _ _ _ _ _

1. cl-cl-s
2. The suffix says ənt.
3. The first syllable starts with **p**, the second syllable starts with **i**.
4. We have had many, but we can only have one at a time.

Do you remember the suffix **–ology** from Chapter 8? It says **ŏ′lə jē** and means *a branch of learning*. Highlight the following words you can read:

1. biology   3. ecology   5. psychology   7. zoology   9. morphology
2. phonology   4. astrology   6. archeology   8. geology   10. anthropology

12b Dictation Exercise (Teacher Page)

Provide the code orally and write it on the board/overhead. Then dictate each word. Ask students to write the word in syllables, separate the syllables with dashes, and mark the vowels. Prefixes and suffixes are not marked. For the purpose of this exercise, we will treat the following two- and four-syllable suffixes as a single unit: **–ory, –ary, –ity, –ancy, –ency, –ability** and **–ibility**.

Code abbreviations: cl=closed   s = suffix
                          vce=vowel-consonant-e   pref=prefix
                          op=open
                          rc=r-controlled

The suffixes **–ent** and **–ant** are both pronounced ənt. The suffixes **–ence** and **–ance** are both pronounced əns. The suffixes **–ability** and **–ibility** are both pronounced ə bĭl'ĭ tē. The suffixes **–ancy**, and **–ency** are both pronounced ənsy. Therefore, accept either of the two spellings, but point out the correct one.

Students must circle the vowel + **r**, in r-controlled syllables. They are highlighted in red on this answer key.

1. (pref-op-s)   com-plī-ance (ence)
2. (pref-cl-t+s)   in-věn-tory
3. (pref-pref-cl-s+s) com-prē-hěn-sive
4. (cl-cl-t+s)   vŏl-ŭn-tary
5. (op-c+s)   vā-cancy
6. (rc-op-l+s)   tur-bū-lent*
7. (pref-rc-m+s)   in-for-mal
8. (cl-s)   crĕd-ibility
9. (op-cl-s)   hū-mĭl-ity
10. (cl-op-s-s)   ŏc-cā-sion-al

> Remind students to think of the base word first.

1. (rc-rc-s)   per-form-ance (ence)*
2. (pref-op-n+s)   ex-pō-nent
3. (cl-rc-s)   fĕd-er-al*
4. (pref-cl-s+s)   ex-pĕn-sive
5. (cl-s-s)   dĭc-tion-ary
6. (cl-t+s)   rĕc-tory
7. (cl-t+s-s)   căp-tiv-ity
8. (rc-m+s)   dor-mancy
9. (rc-m+s-s)   nor-mal-cy
10. (op-s)   lī-ability

*Accept **er, ir,** and **ur** in these **rc** syllables, but point out that **er** is the correct spelling. Ask students to pronounce the words.

13 Syllabication with Multiple Suffixes

Rewrite the words in syllables, separate them with dashes, and mark the vowels. Write the code next to each word. Write **ti** and **ci** with the suffix. Pay attention to what happens to the suffix **–ic** when it is followed by the suffix **–ity**.

1. superficial _____
2. simplistic _____
3. simplicity _____
4. confidential _____
5. eventually _____
6. authentic _____
7. authenticity _____
8. sanctuary _____
9. casually _____
10. substantially _____

Add the suffixes to the base words. You will need to drop or add some letters. This might change the pronunciation. The tricky ones are: 5, 7, 12, 16, 17, and 20.

1. cave + –ity ⇨ _____
2. secure + –ity ⇨ _____
3. sane + –ity ⇨ _____
4. grave + –ity ⇨ _____
5. clear + –ity ⇨ _____
6. define + –tion ⇨ _____
7. office + –cial ⇨ _____
8. public + –ity ⇨ _____
9. toxic + –ity ⇨ _____
10. vary + –ability ⇨ _____
11. resident + –cy ⇨ _____
12. destroy + –ive ⇨ _____
13. describe + –tion ⇨ _____
14. admit + s-sion ⇨ _____
15. category + –ize ⇨ _____
16. type + –ical ⇨ _____
17. extend + –ive ⇨ _____
18. electric + –ity ⇨ _____
19. vacant + –cy ⇨ _____
20. explode + –ive ⇨ _____

14 Base words, Prefixes, and Suffixes

Each base word on this worksheet makes sense by itself. It will have prefixes and/or suffixes attached to it. A prefix is a morpheme that comes before a base word and changes its meaning. You will learn more about prefixes in the next section. 1. Write the base word, prefix, and suffix(es) next to the numbered words. 2. Mark the accent by placing an apostrophe right after it. The spelling and pronunciation of the base word may change when it stands alone.

	base word	prefix	suffix	suffix
1. impulsivity	_____	_____	_____	_____
2. deodorant	_____	_____	_____	
3. unresponsiveness	_____	_____	_____	_____
4. disappearance	_____	_____	_____	
5. unreliability	_____	_____	_____	_____
6. conservancy	_____	_____	_____	
7. inaccuracy	_____	_____	_____	
8. nonobservant	_____	_____	_____	
9. inexpensively	_____	_____	_____	_____
10. unsuitability	_____	_____	_____	_____
11. nonproductive	_____	_____	_____	
12. independently	_____	_____	_____	_____
13. unavailability	_____	_____	_____	_____
14. personality	_____		_____	_____
15. acceptance	_____		_____	

The following words have a medial schwa sound. Highlight the words you can read:

1. cardinal   4. intelligent   7. confidence   10. original   13. secretary

2. adequate   5. contradictory   8. primitive   11. auditory   14. solitary

3. heredity   6. negativity   9. mandatory   12. relative   15. separate

15 Climbing Mount Whitney

Several years ago my friends Cecil-Anne, John, and Herb decided to climb Mount Whitney, the highest peak in the continental United States. They could have hiked up the trail, but they decided they wanted a bit more excitement and opted for a challenging rock-climbing route. This meant they would have to carry ropes and a lot more heavy equipment, in addition to their backpacks stuffed with camping gear. The first day, they hiked for several hours through meadows with lovely wildflowers and eventually camped next to a granite-lined lake.

After getting an early start the following morning, they bushwhacked their way to the bottom of the cliffs. They roped up, with one person anchored to the rock while belaying the others. Since only one person could climb at a time, this was a very time-consuming endeavor. At first everything went smoothly, as there were plenty of handholds and footholds. After lunch, the cliffs became increasingly steep, and the group was feeling the effects of being at high altitude. Herb, the least experienced climber, inadvertently dropped his pack, which tumbled hundreds of feet down the mountain. This was dangerous because all of his survival gear was gone in one fell swoop!

Although the group was getting tired, they tried to keep a fast pace because Herb needed to get down before nightfall. When Cecil-Anne was on a particularly vertical section, one of her footholds suddenly broke off, leaving her swinging in a pendulum motion. She tried to brace herself as best she could against the oncoming rock wall, but in a split second, she was smashed against the cliff. After the rope stopped swinging, Cecil-Anne let out a scream. Her ankle was in excruciating pain! She waited for a few minutes hoping the pain would subside, but it got worse. What was she to do? She had to keep climbing as best she could, in spite of the unbearable pain. After she reached the other climbers, they were horrified by the bad news. They bandaged her foot, gave her aspirin, and weighed their options. Since they had already climbed two-thirds of the way, rapelling down was much too time-consuming and would require more endurance than they could muster. More importantly, they would not get down in daylight. The trio came to the grim conclusion that they must continue towards the summit.

Slowly, carefully, trying not to put all of her weight on her throbbing foot, Cecil-Anne concentrated on climbing the cliffs. With the help of her friends, she eventually made it to the top! After John handed her all of his warm clothes, he and Herb hurried down the trail to contact emergency services for a helicopter rescue.

Several other climbers had reached the summit by then, and for a while, Cecil-Anne had lots of company. One by one, they descended, and brave Cecil-Anne gave them assurance that she would be ok. Now all by herself, she began to shiver as the last rays of sunshine faded from the peak. Still no helicopter! At 14,496 feet there is a sudden temperature drop after sunset. Trying to fend off hypothermia, she put on her down jacket and wrapped John's around her legs. As it grew dark, she began to recognize the danger she was in. Not only was she in severe pain, but she might freeze to death! She exercised her upper body and arms to try to keep warm. It was very dark and lonely on the summit of Mount Whitney.

Hours later, after midnight, Cecil-Anne thought she saw the appearance of a faint light off in the distance. Was she hallucinating? No, she saw it again, coming closer. She called out for help and heard a muffled response. After a few minutes, the mysterious person approached her. He explained that he was a ranger who had been alerted by John and Herb and had hiked up the mountain for many hours to help the stranded climber. From his huge backpack, he pulled out a sleeping bag, brought especially for Cecil-Anne. After firing up his stove, he made her hot soup and tea. Soon she was toasty warm. The good Samaritan had just arrived in time! The ranger stayed with her all night, and by early morning, the helicopter appeared and whisked her away to the hospital. Her ankle was broken, so the emergency physician had to put her leg in a cast.

After hobbling around on crutches for a few weeks, Cecil-Anne made a full recovery! By the following summer, she was right back to climbing her beloved mountains!

Comprehension Questions

1. Why did the group need to get down before nightfall?

_____

2. Why did Cecil-Anne fall? _____

3. Why did Cecil-Anne stay on top of Mt. Whitney? _____

_____

4. How did she try to stay warm? _____

5. Who was the mysterious person who appeared in the middle of the night?

_____

6. How did he help her? _____

7. How was Cecil-Anne rescued? _____

_____

CHAPTER 13
Prefixes

Note to Instructor

The purpose of Chapter 13 is to improve students' vocabulary by teaching the most common prefixes. The concepts of base words and suffixes are also reviewed and integrated within the prefix exercises. See Appendix for a list of the included prefixes, as well as their definitions.

Reminders:
1. **Have students reread all the words in every lesson once they have completed the exercises.**
2. Ask students to write each new prefix in the Prefixes section of their Decoding Binders. After the entry, include the phonetic spelling, definition, and four examples of words with the particular prefix. Students must also add three or more key words for every rule.
3. Review all sections of the binder **once a week** for a minimum of five weeks. Younger children or the severely learning disabled may need more time for review.

Lesson 1 requires students to circle prefixes and suffixes and copy the base words.

Lesson 2 reviews prefixes that students studied in chapters 1-4 and chapter 9. Use this worksheet as a pretest to ascertain what students remember. Because the prefixes **re–**, **un–**, **non–**, and **dis–** have been used frequently in previous lessons, they are not included in Chapter 13. If review is needed, go back to Chapter 9, Lessons 5a and 5b.

Lesson 3a introduces the first set of prefixes: **pre–**, **de–**, **mis–**, **ex–**, **e–**, **ef**, **– pro–**, **trans–**, **super–**, **anti–**, **counter–**, and **mid–**. The prefix **ex–** is an absorbed prefix. Its variants are **e–** and **ef–**. Use **ef–** before Latin roots that start with **f**; use **e–** before roots that start with **d, l, m, n,** or **v**.

Ask your class to think of words that start with the prefix **pre–**. Write the words on the board or the overhead. After students have offered different examples (at least seven), ask everyone to deduce the meaning of the prefix. Disseminate the worksheet. Students copy the five best examples (words that clearly show the meaning of the prefix) and the definition on the worksheet; this will be their study guide for the first prefix test. (Definitions are listed at the top of **Lesson 3b**.) The dictionary is the arbiter as to whether a word is acceptable.

Suggestion for an alternative presentation: Divide your class into small groups and set up a competition. Introduce one prefix at a time. Each group should elect a recorder and brainstorm for words with the particular prefix. The recorder writes the words on notebook paper, not the worksheet. Impose a time limit and keep track of points. Perhaps the winning team might earn some small tangible rewards after all of the nine prefixes have been covered. If your students work in groups, do not allow them to use dictionaries. Otherwise this competition might not be challenging enough. Next, hand out the worksheet and ask students to copy the five best examples. Follow this procedure for the rest of the prefixes.

For your convenience, possible words choices are listed below:

1. precook, preheat, preschool, prefix, preset, preface, predominant
2. destroy, deduct, descend, decline, depart, dehydrate, descendant,
3. misprint, misread, mistake, misbehave, misfortune, misguided, misperceive
4. export, exterior, external, exhaust, expand, eject, erase, evaporate, emerge, evaluate evade, effect, effective, effort, efficient
5. prolong, proceed, produce, propose, progress, proclaim, proactive
6. transport, transact, transmit, transition, transparent, transit, transcript
7. supervise, supermarket, superpower, supernatural, superhuman, superhighway, superior
8. antisocial, antibody, antibiotic, antiseptic, anticrime, antifreeze, antiperspirant
9. counterattack, counterculture, counterclockwise, counterinsurgency, counterproposal, counterclaim, counterargument
10. midweek, midsummer, midwinter, midstream, midtown, midway, midnight

Lesson 3b and **Lesson 3c** provide exercises with the first set of prefixes.

Lesson 3d is the first prefix test. Consider giving students several days to study, and tell them when the test will be given. The test requires students to remember two words that clearly illustrate the meaning of each prefix, as well as the definition.

Follow the same procedure for the next four sets of prefixes.

Lesson 4a introduces the second set of prefixes: **sub–**, **post–**, **mal–**, **semi–**, **multi–**, **uni–**, **mono–**, **bi–**, **tri–**, **quadr–**, **quar–**, **cent–**, and **centi–**. Ask students to explain why using prefixes is a shortcut to communicating ideas. The prefix **sub–** is an assimilated prefix. This means that the last letter of the prefix, in this case **b**, changes to the first letter of the root: **sub–** + ceed = succeed, **sub–** + fix = suffix, **sub–** + gest = suggest, **sub–**, + pose = suppose, **sub–** + reptitious = surreptitious. Even though the term *assimilated prefix* is technically the correct term, for the sake of our middle school students, we will use the term *absorbed prefix*. Next, follow the same procedure outlined in **Lesson 3a**.

1. substitute, submit, sublet, subdue, submerge, subtraction, subtitle, success, successor, succumb, suffice, sufficient, suffuse, suggest, suggestion, support, supply, supplement
2. postpone, posttest, postscript, posterity, postdate, postoperative, posttraumatic
3. malnourished, malfunction, malignant, malicious, maladjusted, maladapted, malign
4. semicircle, semiweekly, semimonthly, semiprecious, semisweet, semitropical, semiprivate
5. multiplication, multicolored, multipurpose, multimedia, multicultural, multilateral, multitude
6. uniform, university, unique, union, universal, united, community
7. monorail, monotone, monogram, monolith, monopoly, monologue, monotony
8. bicycle, bifocals, binoculars, bicoastal, bipartisan, bisect, billion
9. triangle, triathlon, triplets, triplex, tripod, triplicate, trifocals
10. quarter, quart, quartet, quarterback, quadrangle, quadruple, quadriplegic
11. centimeter, centennial, centipede, century, centiliter, centigrade, percent

Lesson 4b and **Lesson 4c** provide exercises with the second set of prefixes.

Lesson 4d covers the absorbed variants of **sub–**.

Lesson 4e is the second prefix test.

Lesson 5a introduces the third set of prefixes: **fore–**, **tele–**, **inter–**, **a–**, **bio–**, **per–**, **auto–**, **in–**, **il–**, **im–**, **ir–**, **con–**, **col–**, **com–**, **cor–**, **co–**. The prefixes **in–** and **con–** are absorbed prefixes, which were introduced in Chapters 3 and 4. This means that the last letter of the prefix, in this case **n**, changes to the first letter of the base word: **in–** + mature = immature, **con–** + mission = commission, **in–** + legal = illegal, **con–** + league = colleague, **in–** + regular = irregular, **con–** + respond = correspond. The prefix **con–** changes to **co–** before vowels and **h**: **con–** + incidence = coincidence, **con–** + host = cohost, also copilot. Use **im–** and **com–** before the letters **b**, **p**, and **m**: *imbalance, impact, immature,*

combine, compile, commiserate. If the root starts with other letters, use **in–** and **con–**, *invitation, insulate, incapable, conspire, contact, condition*. Next, follow the same procedure outlined in **Lesson 3a**.
1. foreground, forestall, forehead, forearm, foremost, foretell, foreword
2. telescope, television, telephone, telegram, telephoto, telegraph, telemarketing
3. interstate, interlock, interview, intermission, intersection, interrupt, interact
4. around, alone, ajar, alive, align, along, amass
5. biology, biography, biodegradable, antibiotic, biopsy, bionic, biohazard
6. perform, perfume, perspire, percent, permission, perception, perjury
7. autograph, autobiography, automatic, automobile, automotive, autocratic, automation
8. **in– (not)** inaccurate, indirect, inactive, inappropriate, insensitive, indifferent, inefficient
    in– (inside, within) inbound, include, indent, income, infect, input, inject
    im– (not) impossible, improper, impractical, immature, immortal, impartial, immovable
    im– (inside, within) import, impress, immigrate, imprison, implant
    ir– (not) irrational, irregular, irresponsible, irresponsive, irresistible, irreplaceable
    ir– (inside, within) irrigate, irrigation, irradiate
    il– (not) illegible, illegal, illegality, illiterate, illogical, illusion, illicit
    il– (inside, within) illumine, illuminate, illustrate, illustration
9. conspire, contest, context, conduct, confront, constrain, concourse,
    compound, commission, composition, combat, compress, compartment, compile
    correlate, correspond, corrode, correct, corroborate, corrugate, corrupt
    collect, collate, colleague, collateral, collapse, collide, college
    cooperate, copilot, coordinate, coherent, coauthor, coincide, coerce,

Lesson 5b-d provide exercises with the third set of prefixes.

Lesson 5e is the third prefix test.

Lessons 6a introduces the fourth set of prefixes: **ab–, intro–, ad–, ac–, ap–, en–, em–, ob–, op–, syn–, sym–**. The prefix **ad–** is an absorbed prefix. This means that the last letter of the prefix, in this case **d**, changes to the first letter of the base word: **ad–** + count = account, **ad–** + point = appoint. The prefix **ad–** has more assimilated variants than any other prefix. Students will only be tested on **ad–, ac–**, and **ap–**, but the following variants are introduced in **Lesson 6d**: **af–**, affirm, **ag–**, aggressive, **al–**, allocate, **ar–**, arrest, **as–**, assign, **at–**, attire. The prefix **ab–** is **not** a variant of **ad–**. The prefix **en–** is also an absorbed prefix. Its common variant is **em–**, which is used before **b** and **p**, *emboldened, empower*. Another absorbed prefix is **ob–**. Its variants are **oc–, of–, op–** *occupy, occasion, office, offend, oppose, opposite*. Next, follow the same procedure outlined in **Lesson 3a**.
1. absent, absorb, absentee, abduct, absolute, absolve, abbreviate
2. adventure, admission, advice, adjust, administer, advantage, advise
3. account, accurate, accord, accomplish, access, accident, accept,
4. appoint, appear, applaud, appropriate, appendix, appreciate, apparel,
5. enjoyment, envelope, envision, endure, enlighten, enforce, enlarge
6. embattled, empower, embroider, employ, embrace, embark, emphasis
7. observe, obstacle, obnoxious, object, obligation, obstruction, obsess
8. oppose, oppress, opponent, opportunity, opportunist, opposite, oppressive
9. synonym, synthesize, synchronize, syndrome, synthetic, synopsis, syntax
10. symphony, symptom, symmetry, sympathy, symbol, sympathetic, symbolic

Lesson 6b and Lesson 6c provide exercises with the fourth set of prefixes.

Lesson 6d covers the other absorbed variants of **ad–**.

Lesson 6e is the fourth prefix test.

1 Base Words, Prefixes, and Suffixes

Base word: A base word (also called a stem) is a word that makes sense by itself. This is not always clear when the base word derives from a foreign language. In the word *preheating* the meaning of the base word is easy to understand. In the word *confiscate*, the Latin root is *fiscus*, which means *public treasury* in Latin. For those of us who have never studied Latin, it is sometimes difficult to know the meaning of such roots. Most Anglo-Saxon base words are **free morphemes**. A free morpheme can occur alone and make sense by itself. It can also attach prefixes and suffixes, as in these examples *sight, foresight, hindsight*. Most Latin roots are **bound morphemes**, which means the root doesn't occur by itself; prefixes and or suffixes will precede or follow it. For example, the Latin root **sist** does not appear by itself, *insist, insistent, consistency, desist, assistance, persist, irresistible*.

Prefix: A prefix is a morpheme that comes before a base word and changes its meaning. A prefix may have one or more syllables (re–, super–).

Suffix: A suffix is a morpheme that follows a base word and changes its meaning.

Circle the prefixes and suffixes in the following words. Write the base words on the lines. Sometimes the spelling and accent of the base word will change when suffixes are added. Highlight the words you can read.

1. prehistoric _____
2. unusable _____
3. mistaken _____
4. disagreement _____
5. unnoticeable _____
6. indifferent _____
7. replaceable _____
8. reaction _____
9. impulsive _____
10. misgivings _____
11. contributor _____
12. department _____
13. irresponsible _____
14. nonexistent _____

2 Meaning of Prefixes

Prefix: A prefix is a morpheme that comes before a base word and changes its meaning. It is a shortcut to conveying ideas. Saying *rewrite it* is faster than saying *write it again*.

You have studied the following prefixes in earlier chapters. Circle each prefix and write the base word on the first line. Next, write the meaning of each prefix on the second line.

	Base word	Meaning of Prefix
1. nonfat	_____	_____
2. unsafe	_____	_____
3. disprove	_____	_____
4. resupply	_____	_____
5. disorder	_____	_____
6. unhealthy	_____	_____
7. displease	_____	_____
8. replacement	_____	_____
9. nondairy	_____	_____
10. unfocused	_____	_____
11. nonfiction	_____	_____
12. recapture	_____	_____
13. dissolve	_____	_____
14. reorder	_____	_____
15. unfinished	_____	_____
16. disbelieve	_____	_____
17. nonstandard	_____	_____

3a Prefix Group Work

Write down five words that start with these prefixes. (For **ex–**, **e–**, and **ef–**, write three examples for each.) Next, deduce the definition of each prefix. Save your list because it is your study-guide for the test.

1. **pre–** _____
   _____ Definition: _____

2. **de–** _____
   _____ Definition: _____

3. **mis–** _____
   _____ Definition: _____

4. **ex–, e–, ef–** _____
   _____
   _____ Definition: _____

5. **pro–** _____
   _____ Definition: _____

6. **trans–** _____
   _____ Definition: _____

7. **super–** _____
   _____ Definition: _____

8. **anti–** _____
   _____ Definition: _____

9. **counter–** _____
   _____ Definition: _____

10. **mid–** _____
    _____ Definition: _____

3b First Set of Prefixes

pre–	before		**trans–**	across, through
de–	away from, down, reverse		**super–**	above, beyond, over
mis–	wrong, bad		**anti–**	against
ex–, e–, ef–	out, outside		**counter–**	against, opposite
pro–	forward, favoring		**mid–**	middle

Highlight the words you can read in the box. Then write each word next to its definition.

antibiotic	predict	extreme	precede	evacuate	deodorant
supervisor	proceed	misplace	devalue	counterfeit	transmission
misbehave	midday	propeller	translate	antiaircraft	supertanker

1. A weapon against airplanes _____
2. It keeps odors away _____
3. In the middle of the day _____
4. To speak about an event before it happens _____
5. To act badly _____
6. A person who is above the workers and manages them _____
7. To interpret from one language across to another _____
8. To move forward, to go ahead _____
9. To go before _____
10. To put in the wrong place _____
11. To copy money, which is against the law _____
12. To bring down the value of money _____
13. To get out of a building because of danger _____
14. A ship that is above average in size _____
15. A drug that fights against bacteria _____
16. It moves a small airplane forward _____
17. A car part that causes the gears to shift from one across to another _____
18. Out of, or far from average _____

3c The First Set of Prefixes

pre–	before	trans–	across, through
de–	away from, down, reverse	super–	above, beyond, over
mis–	wrong, bad	anti–	against
ex–, e–, ef–	out, outside	counter–	against, opposite
pro–	forward, favoring	mid–	middle

Highlight the words you can read and use them to complete the puzzle. Write in pencil.

> exporter   deleted   supersonic   progress   mistreatment   excommunicate
> defender   mistrust   antifreeze   midtown   prefabricate   transatlantic
>   transcript   counteract

Across:
1. The middle area of a city
2. To manufacture in a factory before the product is assembled
3. A flight from the US across to Europe
4. A liquid used in an engine to guard against cold temperatures
5. Bad treatment
6. Above or beyond the speed of sound
7. A person who ships products abroad

Down:
1. Not to trust
2. To move ahead, to improve
3. To take action against someone else's behavior
4. A certificate that shows your grades
5. Removed, thrown away in the trash
6. A protector who keeps enemies away
7. To throw someone out of a church or a faith

336

3d Vocabulary Test

Write two words that start with each prefix (for **ex–**, **e–**, and **ef–**, write one word for each). Make sure you choose words that clearly illustrate the meaning of the prefix. Next, write the definition of the prefix.

1. **pro–** _____

   Definition: _____

2. **trans–** _____

   Definition: _____

3. **counter–** _____

   Definition: _____

4. **ex–, ef–, e–** _____

   Definition: _____

5. **de–** _____

   Definition: _____

6. **pre–** _____

   Definition: _____

7. **anti–** _____

   Definition: _____

8. **mis–** _____

   Definition: _____

9. **super–** _____

   Definition: _____

10. **mid–** _____

    Definition: _____

4a Prefix Group Work

Write down five words that start with these prefixes. (For **sub–**, **suc–**, and **sup–**, write three examples for each.) Next, deduce the definition of each prefix. Save your list because this is your study-guide for the test.

1. **sub–, suc–, sup–** _____
   _____
   _____ Definition: _____

2. **post–** _____
   _____ Definition: _____

3. **mal–** _____
   _____ Definition: _____

4. **semi–** _____
   _____ Definition: _____

5. **multi–** _____
   _____ Definition: _____

6. **uni–** _____
   _____ Definition: _____

7. **mono–** _____
   _____ Definition: _____

8. **bi–** _____
   _____ Definition: _____

9. **tri–** _____
   _____ Definition: _____

10. **quadr–, quad–** _____
    _____ Definition: _____

11. **cent–, centi–** _____
    _____ Definition: _____

4b The Second Set of Prefixes

sub–, suc–, sup–	below, under	uni–	one (Latin)
post–	after	mono–	one (Greek)
mal–	bad, evil	bi–	two
semi–	half	tri–	three
multi–	many	quadr–, quar–	four
		cent–, centi–	one hundred, one hundredth

Highlight the words you can read and use them to complete the sentences:

> unicorn   trilingual   century   submerge   multinational
> bilingual   malicious   posterity   semiweekly   monotheism
> quarters

1. A person who speaks two languages is _____.
2. One hundred years is a _____.
3. A company that has branches in many countries is _____.
4. Generations that come after you, your children and your grandchildren are _____.
5. A person who speaks three languages is _____.
6. Something that happens every half week, which actually means twice a week _____.
7. A religion that worships only one god: _____
8. A mythical animal with only one horn is a _____.
9. To do something out of pure meanness is to be _____.
10. To put something completely under water is to _____ it.
11. It takes four _____ to make one dollar.

Unscramble these words. Read the hints carefully.

stonepop   _____   You change it, so it will happen afterwards, not now.

ficboals   _____   Two, they help people see.

4c Second Set of Prefixes

sub–, suc–, sup–	below, under	uni–	one (Latin)
post–	after	mono–	one (Greek)
mal–	bad, evil	bi–	two
semi–	half	tri–	three
multi–	many	quadr–, quar–	four
		cent–, centi–	one hundred, one hundredth

Create words by combining a prefix and a base word, which may also have a suffix. Write the words on the lines. One base word will be used twice.

sub–	angle	1. _____
multi–	circle	2. _____
tri–	marine	3. _____
semi–	plication	4. _____
cent–	function	5. _____
uni–	ennial	6. _____
mal–	versity	7. _____
quadr–		8. _____

Highlight the words you can read and use them to complete the sentences.

> tricycle   monotonous   bicentennial   unicycle   multipurpose
> subway   malnourished   semimonthly   bicycle   postoperative
> quadruple

1. When we were little, we used to ride a _____.
2. Most of us learned to ride a _____ when we were about six or seven.
3. Very few of us will ever learn to ride a _____.
4. In the _____ room students eat lunch, meet for P.E. classes, and attend assemblies.
5. After an operation, the patient needs _____ care, usually in a hospital.
6. In New York City most people go to work on the _____.
7. In 1976 our country celebrated the _____.
8. The magazine is published _____.
9. Many children in poor countries are _____.
10. Because the speaker never varied his tone of voice, he was _____.
11. To multiply a certain quantity by four is to _____ it.

4d Second Set of Prefixes

sub–, suc–, sup–	below, under	**uni–**	one (Latin)
post–	after	**mono–**	one (Greek)
mal–	bad, evil	**bi–**	two
semi–	half	**tri–**	three
multi–	many	**quadr–, quar–**	four
		cent–, centi–	one hundred, one hundredth

The prefix **sub–** is an absorbed prefix. It has five other common forms. Highlight the following words you can read. On the line write a list of the variants for this prefix.

successful	suffix	suggest	support	suspicion
succulent	sufficient	suggestion	suppose	suspect
succinct	suffer	suggestive	supply	suspend

_____

Use a dictionary to copy two more words for the absorbed variants you listed. Because **sug–** only occurs in *suggest, suggestion,* and *suggestive,* you do not need to look it up.

_____

_____

Another variant for the prefix **sub–** is **sur–**, but it only occurs in these two common words: **surrogate** and **surreptitious**. There is another prefix, **sur–**, which means above. It occurs in words 1-8:

Highlight the words you can read.

1. surrender
2. surname
3. surprise
4. surcharge
5. surpass
6. surmise
7. surface
8. surreal

4e Vocabulary Test

Write two words that start with each prefix (for **sub–**, **suc–**, and **sup–**, write one for each.) Make sure you choose words that clearly illustrate the meaning of the prefix. Next, write the definition of the prefix.

1. **multi–** _____
   Definition: _____
2. **cent–, centi–** _____
   Definition: _____
3. **sub–, suc–, sup–** _____
   _____
   Definition: _____
4. **uni–** _____
   Definition: _____
5. **semi–** _____
   Definition: _____
6. **tri–** _____
   Definition: _____
7. **post–** _____
   Definition: _____
8. **mono–** _____
   Definition: _____
9. **bi–** _____
   Definition: _____
10. **mal–** _____
    Definition: _____
11. **quadr–, quar–** _____
    Definition: _____

5a Prefix Group Work

Write down five words that start with these prefixes. (For numbers 8 and 9, write two for each.) Next, deduce the definition of each prefix. Save your list because this is your study-guide for the test.

1. **fore–** _____
   _____ Definition: _____

2. **tele–** _____
   _____ Definition: _____

3. **inter–** _____
   _____ Definition: _____

4. **a–** _____
   _____ Definition: _____

5. **bio–** _____
   _____ Definition: _____

6. **per–** _____
   _____ Definition: _____

7. **auto–** _____
   _____ Definition: _____

8. **in–, im–, il–, ir–** _____
   _____
   _____
   _____ Definition: _____

9. **con–, com–, col–, cor–** _____
   _____
   _____
   _____ Definition: _____

5b Third Set of Prefixes

fore–	before, earlier, in front of	per–	completely, intensely
tele–	distant, from afar	auto–	self
inter–	between	in–, il–, im–, ir–	not, into, within
a–	on, in, toward, without	con–, col–, com–, cor–, co–	together, with
bio–	life		

The prefixes **in–** and **con–** are absorbed prefixes. This means their last letter sometimes changes to the beginning letter of the base word, **in–** + regular = irregular, **con–** + mission = commission. In some words, the last letter of the prefix changes to a letter that sounds better with the base word, **in–** + balance = imbalance, **con–** + pass = compass; however, in many words **in–** and **con–** don't change. We use **co–** in front of vowels or h, *coerce, cohort*.

Choose the correct prefix to make the words mean **not**, **into**, or **within**.

1. ____perfect
2. ____visible
3. ____resistible
4. ____literate
5. ____jection
6. ____digestion
7. ____polite
8. ____legible
9. ____regular
10. ____valid
11. ____balance
12. ____legal
13. ____replaceable
14. ____mature
15. ____clude

Choose the correct prefix to make complete words. Use **con–, com–, cor–, col–, co–**.

1. ____ruption
2. ____quest
3. ____promise
4. ____lision
5. ____sider
6. ____lect
7. ____bine
8. ____operate
9. ____tact
10. ____relation
11. ____mittee
12. ____respondence
13. ____incide
14. ____education
15. ____tinue

1. What prefixes do we use in front of the letter **l**? _____
2. What prefixes do we use in front of the letters **m, b,** and **p**? _____
3. What prefixes do we use in front of the letter **r**? _____
4. We use **in–** and **con–** in front of all the other letters.

Make real words by matching the prefix with a base word.

1. **per–** ception
2. **tele–** cussion
3. **inter–** graphy
4. **bio–** vision
5. **auto–** cast
6. **a–** mission
7. **fore–** biography
8. **per–** round
9. **inter–** fathers
10. **bio–** graph
11. **tele–** mission
12. **fore–** logy

5c The Third Set of Prefixes

fore–	before, earlier, in front of	**per–**	completely, intensely
tele–	distant, from afar	**auto–**	self
inter–	between	**in–, il–, im–, ir–**	not, into, within
a–	on, in, toward, without	**con–, col–, com–, cor–, co–**	together, with
bio–	life		

Highlight the words you can read and use them to complete the sentences:

automated	impatient	conversation	invisible	along
interrupt	invitations	foreshadows	illegal	biopsy

1. The music in movies often _____ what's going to happen next.
2. In many states it is _____ to ride a bicycle without wearing a helmet.
3. When we're embarrassed, we'd like to become _____.
4. Fortunately, the _____ of my uncle's tumor proved that it was benign.
5. Teachers try very hard not to be _____.
6. We stopped at the bank's _____ teller machine to get some money.
7. It is rude to _____ other people's _____.
8. My parents agreed to let my friend come _____ on our vacation.
9. My mother sent one hundred _____ for my older sister's wedding.

Draw lines from the prefixes to the base words to make new words. Write them on the lines.

tele–	head	1.	_____
fore–	gram	2.	_____
con–	divisible	3.	_____
in–	tempt	4.	_____
per–	act	1.	_____
inter–	mobile	2.	_____
com–	fume	3.	_____
auto–	degradable	4.	_____
bio–	passion	5.	_____

5d Third Set of Prefixes

Highlight the words you can read and use them for the crossword puzzle:

> corporation   foresight   perfect   combination
> biographer   conclude   televise forewarn
> constitution telescope   asleep   communicate
> interstate   intercept   permit   incredible
>   coincidence

Across:
1. An instrument that shows objects from far away
2. A business that has many owners
3. The supreme law of the land
4. To form an opinion based on evidence
5. The best results, 100%
6. Not believable
7. To grant permission for certain actions
8. Between two states
9. To broadcast from far away

Down:
1. To keep people or objects from reaching their destination
2. To talk with another person
3. Two things that happen at the same time
4. Two or more things are brought together to form a set or unit
5. The ability to envision future problems
6. Opposite of awake
7. To caution about future events
8. A writer who tells about a person's life

346

5e Vocabulary Test

Write two words that start with each prefix. Make sure you choose words that clearly illustrate the meaning of the prefix. Next, write the definition of the prefix.

1. **in–, il–** _____

    Definition: _____

2. **bio–** _____

    Definition: _____

3. **per–** _____

    Definition: _____

4. **inter–** _____

    Definition: _____

5. **im–, ir–** _____

    Definition: _____

6. **con–, com–** _____

    Definition: _____

7. **tele–** _____

    Definition: _____

8. **a–** _____

    Definition: _____

9. **fore–** _____

    Definition: _____

10. **auto–** _____

    Definition: _____

11. **col–, cor–** _____

    Definition: _____

6a Prefix Group Work

Write down five words that start with these prefixes. Next, deduce the definition of each prefix. Save your list because this is your study-guide for the test.

1. **ab–** _____
   _____ Definition: _____

2. **ad–** _____
   _____ Definition: _____

3. **ac–** _____
   _____ Definition: _____

4. **ap–** _____
   _____ Definition: _____

5. **en–** _____
   _____ Definition: _____

6. **em–** _____
   _____ Definition: _____

7. **ob–** _____
   _____ Definition: _____

8. **op–** _____
   _____ Definition: _____

9. **syn–** _____
   _____ Definition: _____

10. **sym–** _____
    _____ Definition: _____

6b Fourth Set of Prefixes

ab–	away from	em–	in, into, to become
ad–	to, near	ob–	opposite, against
ac–	to, near	op–	opposite, against
ap–	to, near	syn–	at the same time, together, with
en–	in, into, to become	sym–	at the same time, together, with

What is an absorbed prefix? _____
_____

Study the list above, and copy the absorbed prefixes (**ab–** is not absorbed):
_____

Choose these prefixes to make real words: **ad–, ac–, ap–, ob–, op–, syn–,** and **sym–**.

Use **ad–, ac–, ap–**   Use **ob–** and **op–**   Use **syn–** and **sym–**

1. ____point   9. ____pose   17. ____ptom
2. ____vance   10. ____noxious   18. ____chronize
3. ____praise   11. ____jection   19. ____onym
4. ____company   12. ____press   20. ____bol
5. ____just   13. ____stacle   21. ____pathy
6. ____credit   14. ____ligation   22. ____drome
7. ____prove   15. ____posite   23. ____phony
8. ____count   16. ____serve   24. ____thetic

Make real words by drawing lines from the prefixes to the word endings. The prefix **em–** is a variant of **en–**.

	list		power
em	breviate	em	rasion
ab	blem	ab	roll
en	sent	en	pathy
	grave		velope
	brace		olish

349

6c Fourth Set of Prefixes

ab–	away from	**em–**	in, into, to become
ad–	to, near	**ob–**	opposite, against
ap–	to, near	**op–**	opposite, against
ac–	to, near	**syn–**	at the same time, together, with
en–	in, into, to become	**sym–**	at the same time, together, with

The absorbed prefix **ob–** has two other common variants: occupy, occur, occasion offer, offend, office. What are the other two variants? _____

The absorbed prefix **en–** changes to **em–** before base words that start with **b**, **m**, and **p**.

With the help of a dictionary, find three words with each of the absorbed prefixes **oc–**, **of–**, and **em–**. Write them on the back of this sheet.

Highlight the following words you can read and use them to complete the expressions:

symptom	obstruction	absent	emperor	enchilada
absolute	appearances	emotion	opposites	admiration
enemies	offense	offer	accident	enforcement

1. The best defense is a good _____.
2. A law-_____ officer
3. The _____-minded professor
4. _____ attract.
5. Mutual _____ society
6. The whole _____
7. _____ of justice
8. With friends like these, who needs _____?
9. His voice was full of _____.
10. _____ are deceiving.
11. _____ power corrupts absolutely.
12. The _____ has no clothes.
13. This is an _____ waiting to happen!
14. He made an _____ we couldn't refuse.
15. This is just a _____ of a deeper problem.

6d Fourth Set of Prefixes

ab–	away from	**em–**	in, into, to become
ad–	toward, near	**ob–**	opposite, against
ap–	toward, near	**op–**	opposite, against
ac–	toward, near	**syn–**	together, with, at the same time
en–	in, into, to become	**sym–**	together, with, at the same time

The prefix **ad–** is an absorbed prefix. You have already studied the two variants **ac–** and **ap–**. It has seven other common forms. Highlight the following words you can read. Then write a list of the additional variants for **ad–** on the line.

affection	aggravate	alliance	announce	arrive	assembly	attire
afford	aggression	allergy	annex	arrange	assume	attempt
affix	aggrandize	allocate	annul	arrest	assign	attribute

_____

Use a dictionary to copy two more words for each absorbed variant of **ad–**:

_____

_____

_____

_____

Review: Highlight the words you can read and try to figure out when we use the absorbed prefix **em–**.

1. emboldened 2. embattled 3. embark 4. empower 5. employment

We use **em–** in front of what letters? _____

Review: The prefix **ob–** is an absorbed prefix. You have already studied its variant **op–**. The prefix **ob–** has two other variants. Highlight the words you can read and write the variants on the line. Next, answer this question? When do we use the other two variants?

1. occupation 2. occur 3. occasion 4. official 5. offense 6. offer

_____

351

6e Vocabulary Test

Write two words that start with each prefix. Make sure you choose words that clearly illustrate the meaning of the prefix. Next, write the definition of the prefix.

1. **em–** _____

   Definition: _____

2. **ad–** _____

   Definition: _____

3. **sym–** _____

   Definition: _____

4. **en–** _____

   Definition: _____

5. **ab–** _____

   Definition: _____

6. **ob–** _____

   Definition: _____

7. **ap–** _____

   Definition: _____

8. **syn–** _____

   Definition: _____

9. **op–** _____

   Definition: _____

10. **ac–** _____

    Definition: _____

CHAPTER 14
Latin and Greek Roots

Note to Instructor

Chapter 14 introduces eighteen Latin roots and seven Greek combining words. The primary reason for studying these roots is to expand students' vocabulary. For example, when students learn that **spect** means *to see*, they will more easily remember the definitions of such words as *perspective*, *introspection*, and *retrospect*. It is important to point out to students that many definitions of Latin/Greek roots translate somewhat loosely. Point out that Latin is over 2000 years old and Greek is approximately 3000 years old, and thus, many vocabulary words of the two languages have changed over time. Introduce the term **etymology**, the study of the history of words, where words originated, and how they have changed to their present-day meaning. Explain that the meaning of many English words has changed in ten or twenty years. Examples of such changes are *rap, hip, jet, rock,* and *net*. Ask your class if they can think of other examples.

Reminders:
1. **Have students reread all the words in every lesson once they have completed the exercises.**
2. Help students create a new section in their Decoding Binders, entitled Latin and Greek Roots. Ask students to write each new root in this section. After the entry, include the phonetic spelling, definition, and four examples of words with the particular root. Review this section of the binder **once a week.** Continue reviewing previous sections as necessary.

The ensuing lessons will be difficult for students in grades 4 and 5; therefore, consider teaching the worksheets as whole class activities for younger children.

Chapter 14 covers the following Latin roots: 1. **script/scribe** 2. **press** 3. **port** 4. **form** 5. **struct/stru** 6. **spect/spec** 7. **dict** 8. **vis/vid** 9. **duct/duc/duce** 10. **sist/stit/sta** 11. **tain/ten** 12. **ject** 13. **tract** 14. **vent/ven** 15. **rupt** 16. **aud/audi/audio** 17. **nom** and 18. **fac/fact/fect**. Latin roots are bound morphemes. This means that they usually occur with prefixes and or suffixes. The criteria for choosing these particular roots, was the number of derivatives they comprise. Most of them occur in twenty words or more. Compared to Latin and Greek suffixes, these roots have fairly good sound/symbol correspondence. Many Latin roots such as **scrip** appear most often with the additional letter **t**.

As was mentioned in earlier chapters, many Anglo-Saxon words combine two base words to form a compound word. Unlike Latin, Greek also combines words. The term *combining form* refers to one part of Greek compound word; however, these lessons will continue to use the term *root* instead of *combining form*. These Greek roots are covered: 1. **phon/phono/phone** 2. **nym** 3. **photo** 4. **graph** 5. **gram** 6. **chron/chrono** 7. **metr/meter**.

Every lesson consists of two parts: (a) You will introduce the root; there is no worksheet for this part. (b) Students complete the worksheet.

Lesson 1a: Introduce the root **script** with its variant **scribe**. They derive from the Latin verb **scribere**, which means **to write** and from the noun **scriba**, which means **secretary** or **keeper of accounts**. When **scrip** is followed by the letter **t**, it derives from **scriptum**, which is the Latin past participle of **scribere**. Write these words on the board/overhead: *description, describe, transcribe, subscribing, inscription, scribe, conscript*. Ask students to do these tasks: 1. Pronounce the words individually if possible, otherwise in unison. 2. Figure out what the roots are, how to pronounce them, (**scrĭpt, scrībe**), and what they mean, (**to write or writing**). 3. Write the roots with marked vowels, the definitions, and four examples in the Decoding Binders, Latin/Greek Roots Section.

Lesson 1b requires students to select listed words, which are used to complete sentences. For added clues, every sentence is prefaced by a code, for example: prefix + root + suffix.

Lesson 2a: Introduce the Latin root **press**, which is easy because our English cognate is the same, with the same meaning **to press**,   . Write these words on the board/overhead: *impression, pressure, compress, suppress, depression, irrepressible, oppress*. Next, follow the steps outlined in **Lesson 1a**.

Lesson 2b: Students read twenty words and use certain ones to complete expressions or sentences.

Lesson 3: Tell students that they will be studying the Latin root **port**. Aside from this comment, there is no other introductory activity. This lesson requires students to compose words from a list of prefixes and suffixes with the Latin root **port**. Because this is a challenging exercise, you might allow students to work in pairs or in groups. Offer dictionaries so they can check the words for accuracy. **Port** has two derivations. The more common one occurs in such words as *support, transport, import* and derives from **portare**, which means **to carry**. The second definition derives from **portione** or **portio**, which means **part**. After students have completed the worksheet, write the word categories on the board/overhead (for example: root + suffix, or prefix + root). Ask one member of a team to write all of the generated words for the first category on the board/overhead. The second team's volunteer adds words that the first team didn't include in the first category. Next, he/she starts the second category. The third team adds words to category one and two and starts the third category. You could set this up as a contest. You may need to modify these directions to fit your class. Next follow the directions from **Lesson 1a**.

Lesson 4a: Introduce the root **form**, derived from the Latin verb **formare**, which means **to shape**. The noun, **forma**, means **a shape**. Write these words on the board/overhead: *formation, conform, transform, nonconformist, formulate, formless, misinformation*. Then follow the directions outlined in **Lesson 1a**.

Lesson 4b: The first exercise directs students to highlight words they can read and use them in a sentence completion activity.

Lesson 5a: Introduce the root **struct** with its variant **stru**, pronounced **strŭct** or **strōō**. They are derived from the Latin verb **struere**, which means **to build**. Write these words on the board/overhead: *instruction, destruction, destructive, constructive, restructure, construe, instrument*. Then follow the directions from **Lesson 1a**.

Lesson 5b presents a list of prefixes, suffixes, and the root **struct** with its variant **stru**. Given synonyms, students will follow specific directions to create words from the listed word components.

Lesson 6a: Introduce the root **spect** or **spec**, pronounced **spĕct** or **spĕc**. It is derived from the Latin verbs **spectare** and **specere**. **Spectare** means **to behold** and **specere** means **to see** or **to look at**.

Write these words on the board/overhead: *spectator, spectacles, inspector, retrospective, respected, perspective, suspecting*. Next, follow the directions from **Lesson 1a**.

Lesson 6b is a crossword puzzle that uses words consisting of prefixes, suffixes, and the root **spect** or **spec**.

Lesson 7a: Introduce the root **dict** or **dic**, pronounced **dĭct** or **dĭc**. It is derived from the Latin verb **dicere**, which means **to say**. Write these words on the board/overhead: *unpredictable, dictation, contradiction, valedictorian, vindicated, diction, indictment*. Please point out **long i, silent c** in the word **indictment**. Next, follow the directions from **Lesson 1a**.

Lesson 7b requires students to read words with the roots **dict** or **dic** and to use them in sentences with related derivatives.

Lesson 8a: Introduce the roots **vis** and its variant **vid**, pronounced **vĭs, vĭd,** or **vĭsh**. They are derived from the Latin verbs **visere** or **videre**, which mean **to see**. Write these words on the board or the overhead: *visit, visual, invisibility, visualization, revision, visionary, evidence, evidently*. Next, follow directions from **Lesson 1a**.

Lesson 8b provides an exercise with synonyms and antonyms and the roots **vis** and **vid**.

Lesson 9a: Introduce the root **duct** or **duc** with its variant **duce**, pronounced **dŭct, dŭc,** or **do͞os**. They are derived from the Latin verb **ducere**, which means **to lead**. Write these words on the board/overhead: *producing, introduce, introductory, conduct, conducive, aqueduct, educate, education, induct*. Next, follow the directions from **Lesson 1a**.

Lesson 9b: Given a list of prefixes, suffixes, and the roots **duct, duc,** or **duce**, students will compose words to fit prescribed patterns and definitions.

Lesson 10a: Introduce the roots **sist**, pronounced **(sĭst)**. It is derived from the Latin verb **sistere**. **Sistere** means **to stand**. Write these words on the board/overhead: *persistent, consistent, insisting, insistent, resistance, desist, subsist*. The root **sist** has three variants: 1. **sta** as in *stand, understand, distant, distance, constant, instant, stance* 2. **stat**, as in *status, statue, station, stationary, statistics, estate, establish* 3. **stit**, as in *constitute, constitution, substitute, substitution, institution, restitution, superstition*. Ask students to write all variants of **sist** and four examples for each in their Decoding Binders and follow the directions outlined in **Lesson 1a**.

Lesson 10b: (No worksheet) Introduce the root **tain** with its variant **ten** pronounced **(tān)** and **(tĕn)**. They are derived from **tenere**, which means **to hold**. Write these words on the board/overhead: *contain, container, maintaining, detained, entertainer, obtain, attainable*. Explain that the root **tain** is usually part of a verb. When it is used as a noun or an adjective, it often changes to **ten** *detain, detention, maintain, maintenance, sustain, sustenance, tenant, tenacious*. Next, follow the directions outline in **Lesson 1a**.

Lesson 10c is a crossword puzzle that uses words consisting of prefixes, suffixes and the roots **sist, tain,** and **ten**.

Lesson 11: (No introductory lesson) Tell students that they will be studying the Latin root **ject**. This lesson requires students to compose words from a list of prefixes, suffixes and **ject**, pronounced **jĕct**. Because this is a challenging exercise, you might consider allowing students to work in pairs or in groups. **Ject** derives from the Latin verb **iacere**, which means **to throw**. Next, follow the directions outlined in **Lesson 3** and in **Lesson 1a**.

Lesson 12a: Introduce the root **tract**, pronounced **trăct**. It is derived from the Latin verb **trahere**, which means **to pull**. Write these words on the board/overhead: *attract, distracting, subtraction, extract, extraction, tractor, contract*. Next, follow the directions outlined in **Lesson 1a**.

Lesson 12b asks students to read a list of words that contain **tract**. The second activity requires students to use these words to complete expressions or sentences.

Lesson 13a: Introduce the root **ven** or **vent** pronounced **věn** and **věnt**. It is derived from the Latin verb **vinere**, which means **to come**. Write these words on the board/overhead: *venture, convention, reconvene, adventure, intervention, avenue, eventually*. Next, follow the directions outlined in **Lesson 1a**.

Lesson 13b provides an exercise with synonyms, antonyms and the roots **ven** and **vent**.

Lesson 14a Introduce the root **rupt**, pronounced **rŭpt**. It is derived from the Latin verb **rumpere**, which means **to break**. Write the words on the board/overhead: *disruption, disrupting, interruption, abrupt, erupting, corruption, corruptive*. Next, follow the directions outlined in **Lesson 1a**.

Lesson 14b: A list of prefixes, suffixes, and the root **rupt** are presented. Given related synonyms, students will follow specific directions to create words from the lists.

Lesson 15a: Introduce the Latin root **aud** with its two variants **audi** and **audio**, pronounced **aud**, **audē**, **audēō**. They are derived from the Latin verb **adire**, which means **to hear**. Write these words on the board/overhead: *audience, auditorium, applaud, audible, audition, audiologist*. Then follow the directions outlined in **Lesson 1a**. This lesson also includes the Greek root **phon** with its two variants **phone** and **phono**, pronounced **fŏn, fōn, fōnə**. They are derived from **phono**, which means **sound**. Write these words on the board/overhead: *homophone, megaphone, telephone, phoneme, headphones, symphony*. Finally, follow the directions outlined in **Lesson 1a**.

Lesson 15b: Students are asked to insert **aud/audi/audio** or **phon/phone/phono** to complete words.

Lesson 16a: Introduce the roots **nom**, pronounced **nŏm** with its variant **nym**, pronounced **nĭm**. **Nym** is derived from the Greek word **onuma** and **nom**, pronounced **nŏm**, is derived from the Latin word **nomen**. Both mean **name**. Write these words on the board/overhead: *synonym, anonymous, antonym, homonym, denominator, nominate*. Then follow the directions listed in **Lesson 1a**. This lesson also includes the root **photo**, which means **light**. It has three pronunciations: **fōtō, fōtə,** and **fətŏ**. Write these words on the board/overhead: *photo, photography, photographer, photocopy, telephoto, photojournalist*. Finally, follow the directions listed in **Lesson 1a**.

Lesson 16b lists 26 words with the roots **nom/nym** and **photo**. Students highlight the words they can read and later use certain ones to solve the crossword puzzle.

Lesson 17: (No introductory lesson) Tell students that they will be studying the roots **graph** and **gram** pronounced **grăf** and **grăm**. They are derived from the Greek verb **graphein**, which means **to write**. This exercise requires students to compose words with various prefixes, the roots **graph** and **gram**, and four suffixes. Because this is a challenging exercise, you might allow students to work in pairs or in groups. After students have completed the worksheet, write the word categories on the board/overhead (root + suffix, or prefix + root). Then follow the directions outlined in **Lessons 3** and **1a**.

Lesson 18a presents words that contain the Greek roots **chron/chrono** and **metr/meter**. **Chron** and **chrono**, pronounced **crŏn crŏnə crənŏ**, are derived from the noun **chronus**, which means **time**. Write these words on the board/overhead: *chronicle, chronicling, chronological, chronic, synchronize, anachronism*. The prefix **syn–** was introduced in Chapter 13. It means *together, with* or *at the same* *time*. Then follow the directions outlined in **Lesson 1a**. This lesson also includes the root **metr**, pronounced **mētr**, with its variant **meter**, pronounced **mētər** or **mĕtər**. They are derived from **metron**, which means **to measure**. Write these words on the board/overhead: *geometry, diameter, perimeter, odometer, altimeter, symmetry, metric*. Then follow the directions outlined in **Lesson 1a**.

Lesson 18b: Students are asked to highlight the words they can read, answer questions, and look up certain words in the dictionary.

Lesson 19a: Introduce the Latin root **fac** with its three variants, **fact**, **fect**, and **fic**. They are derived from **facere**, which mean **to make**. Write these words on the board/overhead: *artifact, artificial, infected, effective, facilitate, factor, factory, faculty*. Next, follow the directions outlined in **Lesson 1a**.

Lesson 19b: Students are asked to insert **fac**, **fact**, **fect**, and **fic** to complete words.

There are many other Latin and Greek roots to explore. You could easily use the format shown in **Lessons 3**, **11**, and **17** and do these exercises on the board or on the overhead. Write the prefixes on the left, the root in the middle, and the suffixes on the right.

1. The Latin root **fer**, which means **to bear**: defer, ferry, fertile, fertilizer, offer, offering, prefer, suffer, suffering, transfer, transferable, odoriferous, etc.

2. The Latin root **vers** or **vert**, which mean **to turn**: advertise, advertisement, averse, aversion, controversial, conversation, converse, convert, diversion, diversify, extrovert, introvert, reverse, etc.

3. The Latin roots **pend** or **pens**, which mean **to hang**: depend, independent, independence, suspend, suspense, impending, pending, pendant, pendulum, expend, expensive, dispense, etc.

4. The Latin roots **mot**, **mov**, and **mob**, which mean **to move**: motor, motorcycle, motorboat, move, movie, removal, movement, automobile, automotive, mobilize, mobilization, mobile, etc.

5. The Latin roots **anni**, **annu**, and **enni**, which mean **year**: annual, annually, anniversary, semiannual, centennial, triennial, bicentennial, millennia, millennium, etc.

6. The Latin roots **voc**, **vok**, and **voke**, which mean **to call** or **voice**: vocal, advocate, vocabulary, vocation, vocational, provoke, provocation, provocative, revoke, irrevocable, etc.

7. The Greek root **path**, which means **to feel, suffering, emotion, disease**: sympathize, sympathy, empathize, empathy, pathology, pathologist, sociopath, apathy, apathetic, pathogen, etc.

8. The Greek root **psych**, which means **mind** or **soul**: psyche, psychiatrist, psychologist, psychosocial, psychotherapy, psychotic, psychosis, psychopath, psychodrama, etc.

9. The Greek root **phil**, which means **love**: philosophy, philosopher, philanthropist, philanthropy, Philadelphia, philanderer, philandering, etc.

10. The Greek root **para**, which means **beside, near**: paragraph, parallel, parallelogram, parade, paradise, parachute, paradox, paralyze, paralysis, paraplegic, parameter, paratrooper, paraphrase, parasite, etc.

Recommendation: These books will give you guidance if you're interested in teaching more Latin roots and Greek combining forms:
1. *Unlocking Literacy* by Marcia Henry (see references) 2. *Words Their Way*, Donald R. Bear, et al, (see references).

1b Latin Roots *script* or *scribe*

Highlight the words you can read and use them to fill in the blanks. Study the prefixes, roots, and suffixes to make your choice.

transcript	descriptive	prescription
nondescript	scriptures	conscription
inscribed	subscriber	postscript
	scribbled	

1. Prefix + root + suffix: When you subscribe to a magazine you are called the _____.
2. Prefix + prefix + root: The suspect was hard to describe because she had no memorable features. Her looks were _____.
3. Prefix + root + suffix: My doctor prescribed a new medication. I was able to fill the _____ at the pharmacy.
4. Root + suffix + suffix: Before the printing press was invented, scribes copied the _____ by hand.
5. Prefix + root + suffix: The inscription on the historic monument was very moving. I wonder who _____ it.
6. Prefix + root + suffix: The author of the cookbook wrote mouthwatering descriptions of her recipes. Her writing was very _____.
7. Prefix + root: After you have finished writing a letter, you realize you forgot to mention an important detail. At the bottom you write a _____.
8. Prefix + root + suffix: A soldier's _____ means he was drafted, or conscripted into the armed forces.
9. Prefix + root: As part of a college application, a _____ from the applicant's high school is required.
10. Root + suffix + suffix: Before I left home, I _____ a quick note to let everyone know where I was going.

What do the roots **script** and **scribe** mean? _____

2b The Latin Root *press*

Highlight the following words you can read and try to figure out the definition of **press**. Choose appropriate words to complete the expressions or sentences below.

1. impressive	6. express	11. unimpressed	16. oppressive
2. compress	7. suppression	12. pressure	17. impressionable
3. expression	8. depressing	13. oppress	18. expressive
4. unexpressed	9. oppression	14. depressant	19. pressed
5. impression	10. compression	15. suppress	20. irrepressible

1. If you'll pardon the _____.
2. They are at an _____ age.
3. This heat is _____!
4. You don't get a second chance to make a first _____.
5. They _____ the panic button.
6. If you want a package shipped fast, use _____ mail.
7. As usual, the news is _____.
8. Peer _____ is a problem at any age.
9. During the long lecture, he tried to _____ a yawn.
10. Her _____ enthusiasm inspired the group to complete the project.
11. You need to _____ your sleeping bag into this stuff sack.

Study the list in the box and write down all of the derivatives for these words:

impress: _____

_____

oppress: _____

express: _____

_____

What does the root **press** mean? _____

3 The Latin Root *port*

Using the prefixes, root, and suffixes from the categories below, create as many words as possible. Follow the syllable patterns. This is very challenging. If you can get twenty words, you're doing great! If you can get twenty-five, you're the champion!!

Prefixes	Root	Suffixes	
un		tion	
pro		ant	ance
re		able	ly
com	port	ate	
ex		er	
sup		ive	
im		ment	
de		ation	

root + suffix: _____

_____

prefix + root: _____

_____

prefix + root + suffix: _____

_____

_____

_____

prefix + root + suffix + suffix: _____

_____

prefix + prefix + root + suffix: _____

_____

4b The Latin Root *form*

Highlight the following words you can read and try to figure out the definition of **form**. Choose appropriate words to complete the sentences below.

1. formation	6. conform	11. nonconformist
2. informal	7. performed	12. uniformity
3. uninformed	8. preformed	13. transformation
4. formality	9. uniform	14. formidable
5. performance	10. misinformed	15. misinformation

Use words from the box in the following sentences:

1. Addressing the judge as "your honor" is an important _____, if you want to win your case.

2. Pablo Picasso was a _____ who created new trends in modern art.

3. Many rumors are based on _____ that can ruin a person's reputation.

4. The vice-principal announced that _____ attire was recommended for the Sweetheart Dance.

5. Kids in drama class, band, and choir gave a flawless _____ of "West Side Story".

6. Soldiers marched in perfect _____ during the military parade.

7. There is no excuse for making an _____ decision.

8. Makeup, a new hairstyle and outfit caused an amazing _____ in my tomboy sister.

What does the root **form** mean? _____

Write all of the derivatives for **perform**: _____

Write all of the derivatives for **conform**: _____

Write all of the derivatives for **inform**: _____

_____

5b   The Latin Root *struct* or *stru*

Use the prefixes, the root **struct** or **stru**, and the suffixes to create words as directed.

Prefixes	Root	Suffixes
in		ment
ob		or
sub	stru	tion
de	struct	ive
infra	stry	ible
con		ture
re		

1. Add a suffix to **struc** to change its meaning to *building*: _____
2. Add a prefix to the previous word to change its meaning to *foundation or basement*: _____
3. Add a different prefix to the first word to change its meaning to *water, power, sewer, and telephone lines*: _____
4. Add a prefix to **struc** to change its meaning to *build*: _____
5. Add a suffix to the previous word to change its meaning to *the trade or work of building*: _____
6. Add another prefix to word # 5 to change its meaning to *the process of building again*: _____
7. Use the last word, but delete its suffix and add a new suffix to describe *surgery after an accident* or *surgery to rebuild*: _____
8. Add a prefix to **struct** to change its meaning *to teach*: _____
9. Add a suffix to the previous word to change it to *teacher*: _____
10. Add a prefix and a suffix to **struct** to change its meaning to *the act of destroying*: _____
11. Add two prefixes and a suffix to **struct** to mean *not able to be destroyed*: _____
12. Add a prefix to **struct** so it means *to get in the way, or to block* _____
13. Add a prefix and a suffix to **stru** so it means *an object that makes music*: _____

What do the roots **struct** and **stru** mean? _____

6b The Latin Root *spect* or *spec*

Highlight the words you can read and use some of them to solve the crossword puzzle. Write in pencil and do the easy ones first. What does **spect** or **spec** mean? _____

a. suspect	e. prospective	i. spectator	m. introspection
b. respect	f. unsuspecting	j. inspector	n. perspective
c. aspect	g. spectacular	k. inspection	o. disrespectful
d. special	h. retrospect	l. spectacle	p. specialist

Across
1. Depth perception
2. Not aware of wrongdoing
3. One factor of the whole thing
4. An amazing, unusual sight
5. A person who oversees the quality of products
6. A person who watches sports
7. The act of looking within oneself

Down
1. Describes behavior that shows lack of respect
2. A view of past events
3. Describes something that looks great
4. The likely culprit
5. The act of quality control
6. To view another person with high regard
7. Likely to become or be, expected to happen

7b The Latin Root *dict* or *dic*

Highlight the following words you can read and use them to fill in the blanks in sentences 1-10. The related words will give you clues.

indicted	dictates	vindicate	unpredictable	dictator
indictment	indicate	vindication	valedictorian	addiction
predict	dictation	predictable	contradictory	dictatorship
predictions	contradict	indicator	addicted	indication

1. A country that is ruled by a dictator is called a _____.
2. Even though no one can predict the future, scientists make _____ based on their research.
3. The student with the highest GPA who gives a valedictory speech at graduation is called the _____.
4. A statement that contradicts itself is _____.
5. A factor that indicates or shows certain trends is called an _____.
6. Evidence that vindicates or clears someone of wrongdoing constitutes a _____.
7. A person who is addicted to drugs is suffering from an _____.
8. A formal accusation when a person is indicted (long **i**, silent **c**) for criminal activity in a court of law is called an _____.
9. A dictation exercise often occurs in an English class when the teacher _____ spelling words.
10. A highly reliable person whose behavior can be predicted is said to be _____.

What does the root **dict** mean? _____

Write the derivatives for these verbs:

dictate: _____
predict: _____
indicate: _____

364

8b Latin Roots *vis* or *vid*

Highlight the following words you can read and use them in the exercises:

1. vision	4. evidence	7. visibility	10. advisability	13. advise
2. invisible	5. revised	8. provider	11. supervisor	14. visitor
3. visualize	6. vista	9. advisor	12. improvised	15. visor

An antonym is a word that means the opposite of a given word. From the above list, find antonyms for these words. Make sure the parts of speech stay the same.

1. visible _____
2. resident _____
3. unrevised _____
4. advisee _____
5. planned _____
6. child/dependent _____
7. inadvisability _____
8. invisibility _____

Synonyms are words that have the same or similar definitions. From the above list, find synonyms for these words:

1. counselor _____
2. edited _____
3. a sun shield _____
4. facts _____
5. sight _____
6. to picture _____
7. a view _____
8. boss _____

Write the verbs for these nouns:

1. provision _____
2. revision _____
3. supervision _____
4. vision _____

What does the root **vis** or **videre** mean? _____

Find the words for these literal translations:

1. looked at again _____
2. unable to be seen _____
3. able to be seen _____
4. ability to be seen _____

9b Latin Roots *duct, duc,* and *duce*

Use the roots **duct, duc,** or **duce** with the listed prefixes and suffixes to create words.

Prefixes	Root	Suffixes
ab		
aque		er
con	duc(t)	ible
de		ive
intro	duce	or
pro		(t)ion
re		

1. prefix + root + suffix: *the director of an orchestra* _____
2. prefix + root + suffix: *The beginning of a book* _____
3. prefix + root: *To take an amount off a bill, to lessen a charge* _____
4. prefix + prefix + root + suffix: *A copy of a work of art* _____
5. prefix + root + suffix: *A person who finances and supervises the making of a movie* _____
6. prefix + prefix + root + suffix: *able to be copied easily* _____
7. prefix + root: *A canal that transports water from rivers to farms or cities* _____
8. prefix + root + suffix: *The transfer of heat through metal.* _____
9. prefix + root: Noun: *fresh vegetables,* verb: *to create, to make* _____
10. prefix + root: *A kidnapping* _____
11. prefix + root + suffix: *Describes a person who gets a lot done* _____

What do the roots **duct, duc,** and **duce** mean? _____

Write four verbs that have a prefix and the root **duce**:

_____

Change three of the above verbs to nouns:

_____

10c Latin Roots *sist, stit, sta, tain*

The roots **sist**, **stit**, and **sta** mean **to stand**. The root **tain** means **to hold**. When it becomes a noun, it changes from **tain** to **ten** (*detain, detention*).

Highlight the words you can read and use them for the crossword puzzle. Write in pencil.

container   maintained   subsistence   pertaining   exist   resistant
establish   persistence   obtainable   assistance   station   substitute
insistent   irresistible maintenance   detention   attain

Across:
1. To start or set up something permanent
2. Perseverance
3. Well taken care of property
4. A place where people catch a train
5. Available and held in stock
6. Regular upkeep and repair
7. To live
8. Punishment for misbehavior in school
9. The act of staying alive with little food
10. Help

Down:
1. Relating or referring to something
2. So desirable that one cannot resist
3. Box, bowl, or bottle that holds something
4. Standing against direction or change
5. The quality of stating or demanding
6. To hold a goal and achieve it
7. A person who takes the place of a teacher

11 The Latin Root *ject* or *jec*

Create words with the prefixes on the left, the root **ject**, and the suffixes on the right. Several words will not have any suffixes and a few will have two suffixes. The words must make sense. Use a dictionary when you are not sure. This is very challenging. If you can get 17 words, you're doing great! If you can get 20, you're the champion!!

Prefixes	Root	Suffixes
in		
sub		tion
ob		or
e	ject	ly
ad		able
pro		ive
inter		
re		

prefix + root (7) _____

_____

prefix + root + suffix (12) _____

_____

_____

_____

prefix + root + suffix + suffix (3) _____

_____

What does the root **ject** mean? Since this is not obvious, you may consult a good dictionary. _____

368

12b The Latin Root *tract*

Highlight the following words you can read and use certain ones to complete the expressions or the sentences. Do the easy ones first.

1. contract	5. extract	9. attract	13. retraction
2. distraction	6. contractual	10. distracts	14. detract
3. subtract	7. tractor	11. attraction	15. abstract
4. attractive	8. distractible	12. retractable	16. contractor

1. The coming _____
2. Vanilla _____
3. Opposites _____.
4. A _____ trailer
5. To balance a checkbook, all you have to know is to add or _____
6. Management and the union held _____ negotiations.
7. After winning the libel lawsuit, he demanded a full _____.
8. _____ art
9. He/she _____ the class.
10. They had a _____ agreement.
11. She was driven to _____ by the complicated directions.
12. Don't _____ from her accomplishments.

What does the root **tract** mean? _____

Write the related words from the box next to numbers 1-4.

1. retract: _____
2. attract: _____
3. contract: _____
4. distract: _____

13b The Latin Root *vent* or *ven*

Highlight the following words you can read and try to deduce the meaning of **vent** or **ven**.

1. reconvene
2. invent
3. eventually
4. souvenir
5. scavenger
6. adventure
7. prevent
8. inconvenient
9. inconvenience
10. inventory
11. convention
12. unconventional
13. vengeful
14. adventurous
15. nonintervention
16. event
17. avenge
18. avenue
19. solvent
20. eventful

An antonym has the opposite meaning of a given word. Select antonyms from numbers 1-20 for the following words. Be sure to match the parts of speech.

1. convenient   _____
2. misadventure   _____
3. boring   _____
4. intervention   _____
5. conventional   _____
6. insolvent   _____
7. unadventurous   _____
8. peaceful   _____

Synonyms are words that have the same or similar definitions. Find synonyms from numbers 1-20 for these words or phrases. Some words have been used before.

1. a hassle, a bother   _____
2. to assemble again   _____
3. later   _____
4. to take revenge   _____
5. to avert, to hinder _____
6. a meeting   _____
7. street   _____
8. to create   _____
9. memento   _____
10. a happening   _____

What does the root **ven(t)** mean? _____

Find words that fit these literal translations:

1. come together again   _____
2. not coming between   _____

14b The Latin Root *rupt*

Use the root **rupt** or **rup** along with these prefixes and suffixes to create words.

Prefixes	Root	Suffixes
in		ly
ab		or
bank		tion
cor	rup(t)	ive
inter		ible
dis		ture
e		cy

1. Add a suffix to **rup** to change its meaning *to break apart* _____.
2. Add a prefix to **rupt** to change its meaning *to burst from below* _____.
3. Add a suffix to change the previous word to a noun _____.
4. Add a different prefix to **rupt** to change its meaning *to divert attention from a lesson* _____.
5. Add a suffix to change the previous word to a noun _____.
6. Add a different suffix to the fourth word to change it to an adjective _____.
7. Add a prefix to **rupt** to change its meaning to *without money to pay debts* _____.
8. Add a suffix to change the previous word to a noun _____
9. Add a prefix to **rupt** to change its meaning to *break into a conversation* _____.
10. Add a prefix to **rupt** to change its meaning to describe *an official who takes bribes* _____.
11. Add a prefix and a suffix to the previous word to describe *a person who cannot be bribed* _____.
12. Add a prefix and a suffix to **rupt** to change its meaning to an adverb that describes *behaving in a sudden, rude, unceremonious manner* _____.

What does the root **rup(t)** mean ? _____

15b aud(io) and phon(o)

The roots **aud/audi/audio** are Latin, whereas **phon/phone/phono** are Greek. Try these two roots or their variants on the following lines to create words. Reread them to be sure they make sense. Feel free to consult a dictionary.

Use **aud, audi, audio** and **phon, phone, phono**.

1. _____it
2. sym_____y
3. _____ence
4. ear_____s
5. in_____ible
6. appl_____
7. homo_____
8. defr_____
9. mega_____
10. _____-visual
11. tele_____
12. _____tory
13. _____ible
14. head_____s
15. _____eme
16. _____itorium
17. saxo_____
18. _____tion
19. _____ologist
20. _____tic

What does the root **aud** and its variants **audi** and **audio** mean?
_____

What does the root **phon** and its variants **phone** and **phono** mean?
_____

Accent patterns often shift, depending on the position of the root. Place accent marks in the following words:

1. sym pho ny
2. au di tor
3. phon ics
4. in au di ble
5. au di tion
6. pho net ic

The root **phono** probably derived from the ancient Phoenicians who invented alphabetic writing. Earlier civilizations, like the Egyptians and Mesopotamians, recorded events by using pictographs, drawn pictures, which represented words. The alphabetic method was adopted by the Greeks and later the Romans whose language was Latin. We adopted alphabetic writing from the Romans.

16b *nom, nym,* and *photo*

The roots **nom** (Latin) and **nym** or **onym** (Greek) have the same meaning.

Highlight the following words you can read and get help with the rest. You will use certain ones for the crossword puzzle. Write in pencil.

a. synonym
b. nominee
c. antonym
d. misnomer
e. nomination
f. homonym
g. mnemonic
h. anomaly
i. anonymous
j. anonymity
k. pseudonym
l. venomous
m. phenomenon
n. synonymous
o. denominator
p. nominate

What do the roots **nom** or **nym** mean? _____

The root **photo** also derives from Greek. Highlight the following words you can read and get help with the rest. You will use some of them for the crossword puzzle.

a. photograph
b. photocopy
c. photography
d. photojournalist
e. photofinishing
f. photosynthesis
g. photocopying
h. photogenic
i. photographic
j. telephoto
k. photographer
l. photocopier

What does the root **photo** mean? _____

Across:
1. The number in a fraction, naming the size of the piece
2. Something extraordinary that excites interest
3. An incorrect name
4. A picture taken with a camera
5. A mental device that helps in remembering facts
6. A type of lens used in taking pictures from afar
7. Published or given without name
8. A word that has the same meaning as another word

Down:
1. A person who takes pictures
2. To suggest someone for an election
3. The person who was suggested for an honor or to run for an election
4. A copy made by a machine
5. A word that means the opposite of another word

373

17 The Greek Forms *graph* and *gram*

Create words with the prefixes on the left, the roots **graph** and **gram**, as well as the suffixes on the right. Several words will not have any suffixes and a few will have two suffixes. For some words you will use two prefixes. The words must make sense. Consult a dictionary if you are not sure.

bio			
auto			
tele	**graph**	y	
di(a)		er	al
geo	**gram**	ic	
topo			
mono			
photo			

Prefix + root _____

_____

Prefix + root + suffix _____

_____

_____

_____

Prefix + root + suffix + suffix _____

_____

Prefix + prefix + root + suffix _____

Prefix + prefix + root + suffix + suffix _____

What do the roots **graph** and **gram** mean? _____

What is the language of origin for **graph** and **gram**? _____

18b The Greek Forms *chron* and *metr/meter*

Highlight the words you can read and underline the root:

1. chronic	4. chronicle	7. chronology	10. synchronize
2. chronically	5. chronicling	8. chronological	11. synchronizer
3. anachronism	6. anachronistic	9. chronologically	12. synchronistic

What is the root and what does it mean? _____

Here is a hint from Greek mythology: The god Chronus is the god of _____.

Do you remember the absorbed prefix **syn–**? It is Greek and means *the same* or *similar*.

What does the word **synchronize** mean? _____

Look up the words **anachronism**, **chronic**, and **chronology** in the dictionary and write the definitions in your notebook.

Highlight the words you can read in 1-24 below and underline the roots. Then answer the questions.

1. thermometer	7. meter	13. geometry	19. symmetry
2. speedometer	8. metric	14. geometric	20. symmetrical
3. odometer	9. millimeter	15. diameter	21. symmetrically
4. altimeter	10. centimeter	16. diametric	22. asymmetry
5. barometer	11. decimeter	17. diametrically	23. asymmetrical
6. optometrist	12. kilometer	18. perimeter	24. parameter

Write the two different ways of spelling the root in numbers 1-24 above.

_____

What does this root mean? _____

The variant form of the absorbed prefix **–syn** is **–sym**. Explain what the word **symmetrical**

means _____

The prefix **a–** can mean **not**. Write the definition of **asymmetrical** in your notebook.

In your notebook write a short definition of words 1-6 (bottom list) and look up the ones you don't know.

Draw a millimeter, a centimeter, and a decimeter in the margin below.

375

19b Latin Roots *fac, fact, fec, fect,* and *fic*

The root **fac** has four variants: **fact, fec, fect,** and **fic**. All four of these roots are related and have the same meaning.

Use **fac, fact, fec, fect,** and **fic** to create meaningful words. Pay special attention as to whether the letter **t** is needed. Reminder: the **t** in the suffixes **–tion** and **–ture** comes from the root, as in *defect, defection*. Therefore, when you see **–ion**, you will probably need to use **fact** or **fect**.

1. _____or
2. dif_____ult
3. dif_____ulty
4. ef_____
5. ef_____ive
6. in_____ion
7. in_____ious
8. disin_____ant
9. _____ion
10. _____ion
11. non_____ion
12. _____itious
13. certi_____ate
14. manu_____ure
15. per_____
16. per_____ion
17. satis_____ion
18. satis_____ory
19. of_____e (soft c)
20. of_____er (soft c)
21. signi_____ant
22. signi_____ance
23. insigni_____ant
24. af_____ion

What do the roots **fac, fact, fec, fect,** and **fic** mean? _____

Do you remember the suffix **–fy** or **–ify**? It is a verb ending that has the same meaning as **fac, fact, fect,** and **fic**.

Highlight the following words you can read. Then write the verbs for these nouns:

1. identification _____
2. clarification _____
3. specification _____
4. falsification _____
5. magnification _____
6. unification _____
7. notification _____
8. satisfaction _____
9. classification _____
10. simplification _____
11. modification _____
12. qualification _____

Go back over the last twenty words and mark the accented syllables with a highlighter.

Where does the accent fall in the verbs? _____

Where does the accent fall in the nouns? _____

Answer Key

Chapter 1

2a (top) 1. Closed syllables have only one vowel 2. The vowel is closed in by one or more consonants on the right side. 3. The vowel is short.

(middle) bat, cat, hat, mat, pat, sat, bad, dad, fad, had, mad, pad
can, man, ban, fan, ran, pan, tan nag, rag, sag, tag, wag
gap, lap, map, nap, sap, tap, zap

2b (top) The underlined words are without blends, the red words are with blends.

1. hat	5. scam	9. mad	13. pan	17. had	21. clam
2. crab	6. tag	10. swam	14. clap	18. scan	22. cab
3. map	7. blab	11. grab	15. brag	19. glad	23. snag
4. plan	8. flag	12. sat	16. tap	20. drag	24. cram

First set: 1. glad 2. slab 3. slap 4. snap 5. trap   Third set: 1. crag 2. crab 3. bran 4. brag 5. span
Second set: 1. clan 2. clam 3. scan 4. scab 5. scam 6. blab

2c (top) First set: land, hand, band, brand, stand   Fourth set: last, past, cast, fast, blast
Second set: rant, grant, plant, slant, scant   Fifth set: ramp, lamp, damp, clamp, stamp
Third set: task, mask, bask, cask, flask

(bottom) 1. handbag 2. handstand 3. backpack 4. craftsman 5. catnap 6. bandstand

2e (top)
1. ă   4. ă   7. ô   10. ô   13. ô   16. ô   19. ô   22. ă
2. ô   5. ô   8. ă   11. ă   14. ă   17. ô   20. ô   23. ô
3. ô   6. ă   9. ô   12. ô   15. ô   18. ă   21. ô   24. ô

(bottom) The vowel **a** says ô when it comes after the letter **w** or is preceded by the letter **l**.
1. walk 2. balk 3. stalking

3a (top)
1. ĭ   6. ă, ĭ   11. ĭ   16. ĭ
2. ă, ĭ   7. ă   12. ă   17. ĭ
3. ă, ĭ   8. ĭ   13. ă, ĭ   18. ĭ
4. ĭ   9. ĭ   14. ă, ĭ   19. ă
5. ă, ĭ   10. ă   15. ĭ   20. ĭ

(bottom) 1. windmill 5. halfback
2. lipstick 6. install
3. catnip 7. napkin
4. pinball

3b (top)
1. sh   6. ch   11. ch/sh   16. sh
2. ch   7. sh/ch   12. ch/sh   17. ch
3. sh   8. sh/ch   13. ch   18. sh
4. ch   9. sh   14. sh   19. sh
5. sh   10. ch   15. ch   20. ch

(bottom)
1. căt-fĭsh   6. mĭsh-măsh
2. ăt-tăch   7. pĭc-nĭc
3. flăsh-băck 8. chĭt-chăt
4. brăn-dĭsh   9. vĭc-tĭm
5. chĭp-pĭng   10. dĭsh-păn

Chapter 1, page 2

3c (middle) 1. blank   2. fling   3. slang   4. crank
             5. swing   6. drink   7. fang   8. blink

1. rank, rink   5. sing, sang   (bottom) blink, drink, link, mink, pink, rink, brink, wink
2. rang, ring   6. blank, blink   hang, fang, pang, rang, sang, slang, tang
3. sank, sink   7. drank, drink   bring, cling, fling, sing, sting, string, spring
4. slang, sling   8. cling, clang   blank, drank, rank, sank, crank, tank, shrank

3d First set: 1. thing   Second Set: 1. slang   Third Set: 1. spring
accept answers 2. bath   2. slam   2. thrash
in any order   3. bang   3. fifth   3. thrift
                4. cling   4. thrill   4. whip
                5. whiz   5. whim   Puzzle: dishpan

3d continued: (top) bash, cash, crash, dash, flash, gash, mash, rash, sash, stash, trash

Crossword puzzle: **Across**: 1. sandwich   4. inkling   **Down**: 1. bathmat   4. fabric
                              2. withstand 5. grandchild   2. whiplash
                              3. within   6. signal   3. thrilling

3f (top) 1. ī   7. ĭ   13. ī   19. ī   Unscrambling puzzle: flashlight
          2. ĭ   8. ī   14. ī   20. ī
          3. ī   9. ī   15. ī   21. ī   1. bright, fight, fright, light, might, night, sight, slight
          4. ĭ   10. ī 16. ĭ   22. ī   2. bind, blind, find, hind, kind, rind, wind
          5. ī   11. ĭ 17. ī   23. ĭ   3. child, mild
          6. ī   12. ī 18. ĭ   24. ī

4a (top) 1. ĕ   5. ĕ   9. ĭ   13. ĕ   17. ĕ   (bot.) 1. express 6. entrench   1. extract
          2. ĭ   6. ĕ   10. ĕ 14. ĕ   18. ĭ   2. exit   2. expand
          3. ĕ   7. ĭ   11. ĭ 15. ĭ   19. ĕ   3. exact   3. extinct
          4. ĕ   8. ĕ   12. ĕ 16. ĕ   20. ĭ   4. enlist   4. enchant
                                                      5. enact   5. entrust

4b (top) 1. stall   5. spill, spiff   9. swell   (mid.) 1. fill   6. call
             staff   6. dress   10. press   2. wall   7. fall
          2. class   7. fill   11. frill   3. dress   8. wills
          3. jazz   fizz   frizz   4. miss   9. class
          4. bell   8. sniff   12. cliff   5. shells 10. cliff

    (bottom)   First set: chill, dill, drill, fill, frill, hill, kill, mill, pill, sill, spill
               Second set: call, fall, hall, mall, stall, tall, wall
               Third set: chess, cress, dress, fess, guess, less, press,
               Fourth set: cliff, miff, sniff, stiff, tiff

4c (top) 1. catch   6. scratch (bott.) 1. branch   2. glitch   3. drench   4. scratch`
          2. deck   7. fetch   5. peck   6. drink   7. quick   8. snack
          3. click   8. brick   9. sketch 10. track   11. quench 12. trick
          4. stretch   9. itch
          5. check   10. stick
          6. scratch   11. stitch

Chapter 1, page 3

4e (top) Please see 2a
    (middle)
1. ĕx-pănd
2. ĭn-věnt
3. ăf-fĕct
4. hĕl-mĕt
5. ĕx-pĕct
6. ĭn-tĕnd
7. ĭn-sĕct
8. trĕs-păss
9. fĭsh-nĕt
10. ĭn-jĕct
11. ĕm-bĕl-lĭsh
12. ĕs-tăb-lĭsh

(bottom) drawings of
short a= an apple
short i= an igloo
short e= an elephant

5a (top)
1. ŏ
2. ŏ
3. ĕ
4. ŏ
5. ŏ
6. ŏ
7. ŏ
8. ŏ
9. ŏ
10. ĕ
11. ŏ
12. ĕ
13. ŏ, (ĕ)
14. ĕ, (ŏ)
15. ŏ, (ĕ)
16. ĕ, (ŏ)
17. ŏ
18. ŏ
19. ŏ
20. ŏ
21. ŏ
22. ĕ
23. ŏ
24. ĕ

(middle)
1. clock
2. shop
3. socks
4. hop
5. doll
6. strong
7. dots
8. log
9. boss
10. lost
11. pop
12. lock

(bottom)
1. bog, cog, dog, fog, frog, hog, jog, slog
2. dock, flock, jock, lock, mock, knock, rock,
3. cop, chop, crop, hop, mop, pop, shop
4. cot, dot, got, hot, jot, lot, pot, rot, tot

5a, p. 2 (top)
1. band, bind, bend, bond
2. champ, chimp, chomp
3. lift, left, loft
4. chap, chip, chop
5. stack, stick, stock
6. mass, miss, mess, moss
7. last, list, lest, lost
8. bland, blind, blend, blond
9. flap, flip, flop
10. flack, flick, fleck, flock

(middle) ff, ll, ss, zz, ck, tch

5a, p2 (bottom)
1. ō
2. ŏ
3. ō
4. ŏ
5. ō
6. ŏ
7. ō
8. ō
9. ō
10. ō
11. ō
12. ŏ
13. ō
14. ō
15. ō
16. ō

The vowel **o** has a long vowel sound in closed syllables when it is followed by the letters **l** or **st**.

5c crossword p: **Across**
1. crisscross
2. compacts
3. crosswalk
4. chopsticks
5. snapshot
6. liftoff
7. goblet
8. softball
9. eggnog

Down
1. watchdog
2. hopscotch
3. stopwatch
4. cobweb
5. slingshot
6. bobsled
7. bottom

6a (top)
1. ŭ
2. ŭ
3. ŏ
4. ŭ
5. ŭ
6. ŭ
7. ŭ
8. ŭ
9. ŭ, ŏ
10. ŭ, ŏ
11. ŏ
12. ŭ
13. ŏ
14. ŭ, ŏ
15. ŭ, ŏ
16. ŭ
17. ŭ
18. ŏ
19. ŭ
20. ŭ
21. ŭ
22. ŭ
23. ŏ
24. ŭ

(bottom)
1. hŭn-drĕd
2. hŭs-bănd
3. gŭm-drŏp
4. ŭn-păck
5. trŭm-pĕt
6. pŭmp-kĭn
7. sŭb-trăct
8. cŏn-dŭct
9. ŭn-plŭg

6a page 2 (top) Beginning blends consist of two consonants that precede a vowel.
Ending blends consist of two consonants that follow a vowel.
Clusters are three consonants that come before or after a vowel.

(bottom)
1. adult
2. chipmunk
3. album
4. chopsticks
5. misspell
6. rubbish
7. exact

1. stump	2. clump	3. slump	4. grump	5. trump
1. trunk	2. chunk	3. skunk	4. plunk	5. sunk
1. blunt	2. grunt	3. stunt	4. brunt	5. shunt
1. stung	2. clung	3. swung	4. strung	5. sprung

Chapter 1, page 4

6b (top) please see **Lesson 1a** (middle) Crossed-out consonants are in red.

1. A, k	5. A, g	8. A, w	12. G	15. A, k	19. G
2. A, k	6. A, w	9. G, ph=f	13. A, k	16. A, g	20. G, ph=f
3. A, w	7. G, ph=f	10. A, k	14. A, w	17. G, ph=f	21. A, w
4. G, ph=f		11. G, ph=f		18. A, k	

7

	How many vs?	How many syls?		How many vs?	How many syls?
1. think	1	1	8. Atlantic	3	3
2. drumstick	2	2	9. dentist	2	2
3. attic	2	2	10. tent	1	1
4. camp	1	1	11. inventing	3	3
5. absent	2	2	12. ticket	2	2
6. swim	1	1	13. sprint	1	1
7. Thanksgiving	3	3	14. establishment	4	4

8 (top)
1. nŏn-stŏp
2. sŭb-jĕct
3. ĭm-prĕss
4. ĭn-spĕct
5. chĕck-ŭp
6. sŭp-prĕss
7. pŭb-lĭsh
8. dĭs-pătch
9. chĕst-nŭts
10. mŏl-lŭsk

(bottom)
1. admit
2. zigzag
3. travel
4. insect

1. contrast
2. relish
3. suspect
4. basket
5. kickoff

9 (top) The vowel **e** says the schwa sound (ə), which sounds like a short **u**.

1. thankful	5. watchful	9. helpless
2. thankless	6. thickness	10. mindful
3. spotless	7. selfless	11. mindless
4. kindness	8. helpful	

(middle)
1. thanklessness
2. thankfulness
3. spotlessness
4. watchfulness
5. selflessness
6. helpfulness
7. helplessness
8. mindfulness
9. mindlessness

(bottom) **–ful** means *with much, full of,* **–less** means *without,*
–ness changes an adjective to a noun.

11 (top)
1. boxes
2. dogs
3. brushes
4. stamps
5. dresses
6. catches
7. taxes
8. glasses
9. stretches
10. dishes

(middle)
2. He lost his tickets.
3. My wishes were granted.
4. The foxes run up the hill.
5. The sandwiches are in the bag.

(bottom)
1. He/she watches a tennis match on t.v.
2. He/she brings six pens to class.
3. He/she munches on a snack.
4. He/she cashes a check at the bank.
5. He/she asks for help.

12a (top)

1. n,o	6. o	11. a	16. ha
2. o	7. o	12. a	17. i
3. o	8. o	13. a	18. i
4. o	9. o	14. i	19. wi
5. o	10. total change	15. ha	20. wi

(bottom)

1. can't	6. wasn't	11. I'm	16. I've
2. don't	7. aren't	12. you're	17. it's
3. didn't	8. hasn't	13. we're	18. what's
4. doesn't	9. haven't	14. he's	19. I'll
5. isn't	10. won't	15. he's	20. we'll

Chapter 2

2 (middle)
1. mādé vce   5. stămp cl   9. blādé vce   13. snăck cl   17. brāvé vce
2. măd cl   6. shāpé vce 10. flăsk cl   14. blāzé vce 18. scrāpé vce
3. băck cl   7. plāté vce 11. skāté vce 15. plănt cl   19. scrăp cl
4. bāké vce   8. ănts cl   12. snāké vce 16. quāké vce 20. strănd cl

(bottom)
cl	in-flate	vce	vce	blame-less	s
vce	take-off	cl	vce	shame-ful	s
vce	stale-mate	vce	pref	ex-hale	vce
cl	hand-made	vce	vce	make-shift	cl
pref	en-grave	vce			

cave, crave, gave, pave, rave, save   bake, brake, fake, lake, make, quake, rake
ate, date, fate, gate, hate, mate

3a (top)
1. crīmé vce   4. flĭp cl   7. splĭt cl   10. spīné vce
2. shīné vce   5. brībé vce 8. strīpé vce 11. spĭn cl
3. shĭn cl   6. spīté vce 9. chīmé vce   12. glīdé vce

(middle)
vce-vce	cl-vce	vce-cl
1. snakebite	1. sunshine	1. sidewalk
2. likewise	2. capsize	2. lineman
3. pinecone	3. pinstripe	3. wiretap
4. lifetime		

(bottom)
1. ī   4. ĭ   7. ī   10. ī
2. ī   5. ī   8. ī   11. ī
3. ĭ   6. ī   9. ĭ   12. ī

4
1. ēvé-nĭng   vce-cl   7. cŏn-crēté   cl-vce   13. lātè-ness vce-s
2. ăth-lēté   cl-vce   8. nāmé-less   vce-s   14. ăt-mŏs-phēré cl-cl-vce
3. hēré-ĭn   vce-cl   9. ex-pĕct   pref-cl
4. ăd-hēré   cl-vce   10. dĭs-crētè   cl-vce
5. ex-trēmé   pref-vce 11. stăm-pēdé   cl-vce
6. māké-ŭp   vce-cl   12. căsh-mēré   cl-vce

(bottom) 1. They all have two vowels. 2. The first vowel is followed by a consonant and **e**.
3. The first vowel is long. 4. The **e** is silent.

5a (top) We use **k** before **e, i,** and **y**, otherwise use **c**.

(middle)
1. clap   5. kiss   9. kids   13. sake   17. crib
2. cake   6. clock   10. cram   14. cop   18. snake
3. kick   7. kite   11. cut   15. skill 19. close
4. kit   8. cloth   12. king   16. take   20. skid

We use **ck** after short vowels.

(bottom left)
1. brake
2. stick
3. cake
4. neck
5. quick
6. strike

(bottom right)
1. like, lick
2. deck
3. quake, quack
4. bike
5. snake, snack
6. stake, stack

5b (top) Use **k** before **e** and **i**. The letter **c** says **s**. The letter **c** says **s** when it is followed by **e, i,** and **y**.

(middle) Hard c: act   Soft c: citrus
               crate   civil
               cost   cell
               expect   since
               cake   space
               cross   fence

(bottom)
1. 2   7. 2   13. 1
2. 1   8. 3   14. 3
3. 2   9. 2   15. 2
4. 1   10. 1 16. 1
5. 2   11. 2 17. 3
6. 1   12. 2 18. 2

The symbol ə is called a schwa sound. It says ŭ.

Chapter 2, page 2

5c (top)
1. grass g
2. gymnast j
3. gem j
4. twig g
5. range j
6. game g
7. gel j
8. age j
9. grove g
10. sponge j
11. fringe j
12. glide g
13. page j
14. globe g
15. genes j

(middle)
1. rĭdge
2. plĕdge
3. pāge
4. bĭnge
5. hūge
6. brĭdge
7. hĭnge
8. āge
9. slĕdge
10. grŭdge
11. stāge
12. plŭnge

(bottom) 1. badge 2. rage 3. edge

6 (top)
1. chose
2. broke
3. globe
4. floss
5. stock
6. stoke
7. throne
8. cross
9. choke
10. block
11. stone
12. strobe
13. flock
14. close
15. gloss
16. shone
17. boss
18. froze

(middle)
1. pothole
2. suppose
3. enclose
4. rosebud
5. likeness
6. oppose
7. pinhole
8. dispose
9. disclose

(bottom) bone, cone, drone, hone, lone, prone, shone
choke, broke, joke, poke, smoke, spoke, stoke
close, hose, nose, pose, prose, rose, those

7a (middle)
1. o͞o   6. ū   11. o͞o 16. o͞o
2. ū   7. o͞o   12. ū   17. o͞o
3. ū   8. ū   13. o͞o 18. o͞o
4. o͞o   9. o͞o   14. ū   19. o͞o
5. ū   10. o͞o   15. o͞o 20. o͞o

(bottom)
cl   con-fuse   vce
vce   rude-ness s
pref en-dure   vce
vce   pure-bred cl
cl   pol-lute   vce
vce   juke-box   cl
pref ex-cuse   vce
vce   use-ful   s
cl   in-clude   vce

8a (top)
ō
stove clove
cove   rove
strove grove
wove   drove

ŭ
shove love
above cover
glove shovel
grovel hovel

o͞o
prove
move

ŏ
novel

9 (bottom)

	How many vs can you see?	How many vs can you hear?	How many syllables?
1. hopeful	3	2	2
2. spoke	2	1	1
3. sideswipe	4	2	2
4. crisp	1	1	1
5. reptile	3	2	2
6. atmosphere	4	3	3
7. basement	3	2	2
8. incomplete	4	3	3
9. watch	1	1	1
10. imbalance	4	3	3
11. likewise	4	2	2
12. closeness	3	2	2

10a (top)
1. ex-pīrɇ   pref-vce
2. stāgɇ-hănd   vce-cl
3. dĭs-trĭct   cl-cl
4. ăd-vīsɇ   cl-vce
5. fīrɇ-plācɇ   vce-vce
6. en-twīnɇ   pref-vce
7. stālɇ-mātɇ   vce-vce
8. cŏm-pĕn-sātɇ cl-cl-vce

Across
1. instruct
2. trumpet
3. limestone
4. address
5. explode

Down
1. confiscate
2. complete
3. combine

382

Chapter 2, page 3

11a (top)
1. sănd-blăst cl-cl
2. trăns-grĕss cl-cl
3. lănd-slīde cl-vce
4. crŏss-chĕck cl-cl
5. grănd-chīld cl-cl
6. ĭn-scrībe cl-vce
7. stōve-pīpe vce-vce
8. ĭl-lŭs-trāte cl-cl-vce
9. săt-ĕl-līte cl-cl-vce
10. sīde-trăck vce-cl
11. trăns-plănt cl-cl

(middle)
1. hand cl   4. home vce   7. bush cl   10. shake vce
2. whole vce 5. grave vce 8. fire vce   11. sick cl
3. brush cl   6. rose vce   9. stone vce 12. sale vce

chart:
cl-vce	vce-vce	vce-cl
handshake	wholesale	homesick
brushfire	gravestone	rosebush

12a (top) 1. hike 2. hiked   (middle) Adding –ed to root words changes a verb to the past or to past tense.

(bottom)
1. əd   5. t   8. əd   12. əd   15. əd   19. t
2. d   6. d   9. t   13. t   16. d   20. əd
3. əd   7. d   10. d   14. d   17. d   21. t
4. t   11. t   18. əd

12b (top) –ed makes these three sounds: d, t, and əd

(middle)
ed=d	ed=t	ed=əd
shined	waxed	rested
buzzed	trapped	ended
planned	poked	prodded
pulled	packed	trotted
jogged	slipped	chatted
inflamed	stuffed	funded

When –ed says əd, it is preceded by the letters **t** or **d**.

1. grĭp – grĭpped   6. scrāpe – scrāped   11. grāde – grāded   16. ăsk - ăsked
2. shrŭg – shrŭgged   7. stŏp – stŏpped   12. slăm – slămmed   17. mĕlt – mĕlted
3. līke – līked   8. hŭm - hŭmmed   13. smīle – smīled   18. cămp – cămped
4. plăn - plănned   9. hŏp – hŏpped   14. thănk - thănked   19. chīme - chīmed
5. spŏt – spŏtted   10. hōpe – hōped   15. drĭft – drĭfted   20. trĭm – trĭmmed

1. The consonant must be doubled.   2. Drop the **e**, and add –ed.   3. No changes are needed.

12c (top)
1. When the first vowel is short, followed by one consonant, double the consonant before adding **–ed**.
2. When the first vowel is long, followed by a consonant and silent **e**, drop the **e** and add **–ed**.
3. When the first vowel is short, followed by two consonants, just add **–ed**.

(middle)
1. hiked   5. drummed   9. joked   13. grinned
2. stepped   6. hired   10. drifted 14. blinked
3. tested   7. sulked   11. based   15. scrubbed
4. tugged   8. strapped 12. wilted   16. pruned

Chapter 2, page 4

12c cont'd (bottom)
1. rise - rose
2. cut - cut
3. sink - sank
4. drink - drank
5. bite - bit
6. drive - drove
7. hide - hid
8. ride - rode
9. make – made

13 (top)
1. lighten
2. widen
3. flatten

(middle)
1. driven
2. written
3. stolen, hidden

(bottom)
1. safest
2. coldest
3. slimmest
4. finest
5. biggest

6. reddest
7. latest
8. grimmest
9. hottest
10. widest

1. sadden
2. dampen
3. rotten
4. spoken
5. gotten

Adding –est makes an adjective mean *the most.* This is called *the superlative.*

14a
1. swĭm – swĭmming
2. slĭp – slĭpping
3. shŏp – shŏpping
4. tŭg – tŭgging
5. gĕt – gĕtting
6. scrŭb – scrŭbbing
7. drīve – drīving
8. blāme – blāming
9. strīke – strīking
10. grīpe – grīping
11. hōpe – hōping
12. shīne – shīning
13. shĭft – shĭfting
14. ăct – ăcting
15. squĭnt – squĭnting
16. bŭmp – bŭmping
17. hĕlp – hĕlping
18. blĭnk – blĭnking

15 (top) The prefix **a–** says the schwa sound (ə).
1. ungrateful
2. misspell
3. disconnect
4. nonfat
5. unkind
6. mistake
7. distract
8. nonstop

(middle)
1. dislike
2. unhappy
3. misplaced
4. unlisted
5. nonsense
6. misbehave
7. unsafe
8. nonstick

The prefixes **un–**, **dis–**, and **non–** mean *not;* **dis–** also means *the opposite of* or *without.* The prefix **mis–** means *wrong, bad.*

Chapter 3

2 (top)
1. cl	4. cl	7. op	10. op	13. vce	16. vce
2. op	5. vce	8. vce	11. cl	14. cl	17. op
3. vce	6. vce	9. cl	12. op	15. op	18. cl

(bottom)
1. pī-lŏt op-cl
2. hē-rō op-op
3. mĕd-ĭc cl-cl
4. rō-tāte op-vce
5. răp-ĭd cl-cl
6. cā-nīne op-vce
7. mĭm-ĭc cl-cl
8. lī-lăc op-cl
9. vŏl-ūme cl-vce
10. mĕm-ō-răn-dŭm cl-op-cl-cl

5a (middle)
1. po/lite op-vce
2. Ve/nus op-cl
3. trav/el cl-cl
4. lem/on cl-cl
5. e/lect op-cl
6. spin/ach cl-cl
7. mel/on cl-cl
8. o/mit op-cl
9. pho/to op-op
10. do/nate op-vce
11. tu/lip op-cl
12. van/ish cl-cl
13. fin/ish cl-cl
14. pro/file op-vce
15. com/ic cl-cl
16. mi/nus op-cl
1. vol/ca/no cl-op-op
2. syn/o/nym cl-op-cl
3. an/to/nym cl-op-cl
4. pan/to/mime cl-op-vce
5. to/ma/to op-op-op
6. mon/u/ment cl-op-cl
7. e/quip/ment op-cl-cl
8. dis/lo/cate cl-op-vce

(bottom) 1. re/fuse op-vce   ref/use cl-vce   2. pre/sent op-cl   pres-ent cl-cl

5b (top)
Across: 1. defense 2. evacuate 3. react 4. bright 5. microscope 6. develop 7. revive 8. violin 9. placemat
Down: 1. frequent 2. album 3. giant 4. isolate 5. potato 6. document 7. revolve 8. prohibit

6a (top) The prefix **re–** means again, anew

prefix	base	w. suffix
1. pre	fix	
2. pre	write	ing
3. pre	shrunk	
4. pre	tend	ed
5. pre	test	

pre means before

prefix	base	w. suffix
1. de	frost	
2. de	grade	ing
3. de	duct	ed
4. de	throne	
5. de	press	ing

de: away from, down

6a, p. 2

prefix	base	w. suffix
1. pro	file	
2. pro	pose	ing
3. pro	test	ed
4. pro	gram	
5. pro	long	ing

pro: forward, ahead, in place of

6a, p. 2
A) expel, explode, eject, erase
B) excuse, expire, erupt, evaluate
C) express, extreme, elastic, elapse
D) expand, expect, elect, event

The prefix **en–** means *into* or *onto*.
The prefixes **ex–** and **e–** mean *out of, on the outside*.

6b (top)
Prefix:	Base W:	Suffix:
co–	host	ing
co–	ed	
co–	exist	ing

1. compose 2. collect 3. commute 4. contribute 5. combine 6. collapse 7. compact 8. commit 9. collide 10. contract 11. compass 12. complete

Use col– before **l**. Use com– before **b, m,** and **p**.
Use co– before vowels and **h**. These prefixes mean *together* and *with*. The **o** says ə.

ə ŏ ə ŏ ə ŏ
1. combine 2. conflict 3. confuse 4. comprehend 5. collapse 6. concentrate

Chapter 3, page 2

7 (middle)
1. to-tal   op-cl
2. fig-ure   cl-vce
3. trib-ute cl-vce
4. lo-cal   op-cl
5. fe-male   op-vce
6. top-ic   cl-cl
7. ri-val   op-cl
8. hu-man   op-cl
9. i-tem   op-cl
10. pan-ic   cl-cl
11. do-nate op-cl
12. ed-it   cl-cl

(bottom)
1. le-gal-ize   op-cl-vce
2. tab-u-late   cl-op-vce
3. i-dol-ize   op-cl-vce
4. il-lus-trate cl-cl-vce
5. re-in-vent   pref-cl-cl

8 (top)
1. ĭn-vīte   cl-vce
2. sī-lĕnt   op-cl
3. crī-sĭs   op-cl
4. wīre-tăp vce-cl
5. re-sĕnt-ful pref-cl-s
6. stĭm-ū-lāte cl-op-vce
7. hū-mĭd   op-cl
8. ĭn-spĕct-ed cl-cl-s
9. e-văl-ū-āte pref-cl-op-vce
10. ăl-lō-cāte cl-op-vce
11. re-lī-ance pref-op-s
12. ăc-cū-mū-lāte cl-op-op-vce

(bottom)
pref. pro/vide vce
cl   man/date vce
op   ti/rade   vce
pref. re/mind   cl
pref. com/plex cl
pref. de/mand   cl
pref. e/rase   vce
op   va/cate   vce
op   du/et   cl

9 (top)
1. de-fend-ed   5. pre-scribe   9. dis-grace-ful   13. knot-ted
2. un-twist-ing 6. re-fresh-ing 10. de-scrib-ing   14. scrub-bing
3. pre-shrunk   7. de-frost-ed   11. mis-quot-ed   15. drop-ping
4. pro-long-ing 8. re-strict-ed 12. re-mind-ed   16. strut-ted

1. 4, 3, 3   6. 3, 3, 3
2. 3, 2, 2   7. 4, 3, 3
3. 4, 3, 3   8. 4, 2, 2
4. 5, 4, 4
5. 4, 3, 3

10a (middle)
1. ī   6. ē   11. ī   12. ē
2. ē   7. ī   12. ē   17. ē
3. ī   8. ē   13. ē   18. ī
4. ē   9. ē   14. ē   19. ē
5. ē   10. ī   15. ē   20. ē

(bottom)
1. shaky   6. poppy
2. drafty   7. hazy
3. lacy   8. crispy
4. skinny   9. baggy
5. foggy   10. spicy

10a, p. 2 (top) At the end of a one-syllable word, **y** says $\bar{\text{i}}$.
At the end of a multisyllabic word, **y** says $\bar{\text{e}}$.
1. slop→py   4. mud→dy   7. wind→y   10. laz→y
2. dust→y   5. dad→dy   8. nos→y   11. fun→ny

(middle) Adding the suffix **y** to base words means that it is like the base word or has the quality of it.
1. wavy   3. silky   5. crabby   7. nutty
2. choppy   4. shady   6. smoky   8. grubby

(bot)
1. likely   4. nicely   7. clumsily   10. openly   13. mostly   16. kindly
2. brightly   5. bodily   8. lately   11. cagily   14. lazily   17. calmly
3. angrily   6. highly   9. safely   12. hugely   15. finely   18. luckily

Since –**ly** starts with a consonant, no changes are needed, just add –**ly** to the base word; however, if the base word ends with **y**, you must change the **y** to **i** before adding –**ly**.

10c (top)
1. sup-ply'   ī   5. com-ply'   ī   9. fluf'-fy   ē
2. re-ply'   ī   6. bul'-ky   ē   10. im-ply'   ī
3. tren'-dy   ē   7. de-fy'   ī   11. snap'-py   ē
4. de-ny'   ī   8. Ju-ly'   ī   12. oc-cu-py' ī

Chapter 3, page 3

10c (middle)
1. justify
2. testify
3. falsify
4. classify
5. intensify
6. humidify
7. solidify
8. notify
9. purify
10. nullify

(bottom)
1. e 3. le 5. ity 7. t
2. ic 4. al 6. ity 8. ity

10e (top)
1. myth ĭ
2. crystal ĭ
3. style ī
4. hymn ĭ
5. hybrid ī
6. synonym ĭ
7. rhyme ī
8. analysis ĭ
9. system ĭ
10. hydrant ī
11. pyramid ĭ
12. tyrant ī
13. lyrics ĭ
14. nylon ī
15. syllable ĭ
16. rhythm ĭ

short i
oxygen
homonym
bicycle
cyst
lynx

physical
onyx
gym
antonym
sympathize

long i
byte
cycle
type

unicycle
hydrate
cyclone

11a (top)
1. āte 4. ət 7. āte
2. ət 5. āte 8. ət
3. āte 6. ət 9. āte

1. īte 4. ət 7. īte
2. īte 5. īte 8. ət
3. īte 6. īte 9. ət

Across:
1. satellite
2. palate
3. tabulate
4. climate

Down:
1. accurate
2. equate
3. invite
4. polite

12a
1. nā-tion op-s
2. mō-tion op-s
3. e-mō-tion pref-op-s
4. pro-mō-tion pref-op-s
5. e-lĕc-tion pref-cl-s
6. de-vō-tion pref-op-s
7. ăc-cū-sā-tion cl-op-op-s
8. frăc-tion cl-s
9. ĭn-vĕn-tion cl-cl-s
10. pre-scrĭp-tion pref-cl-s

(bottom)
1. inspection 6. disrupt
2. motivation 7. hesitate
3. instruction 8. attract
4. creation 9. predict
5. migration 10. donate

(middle)
1. reflection, reflect
2. collection, collect
3. eruption, erupt
4. selection, select
5. locate, location
6. calculate, calculation
7. hesitate, hesitation
8. vacate, vacation

The word ending **ate** turns into the first two letters of **ation**. The letter **e** needs to be dropped.

12a, p. 2 (top) sion=zhən
explosion
invasion
occasion
illusion
division

sion/s-sion=shən
tension
expulsion
extension
pension
mansion

(middle)
1. divide
2. invade
3. decide
4. extend
5. erode
6. explode

(bottom)
1. discuss
2. confess
3. impress
4. admit

When a vowel or **r** comes right before –sion, it says zhən.
When a consonant comes before –sion, it says shən.
Usually after consonants, particularly **n** and **l**.

When a verb ends with **d** or **de**, the noun goes to –sion.

1. expression, express
2. possession, possess
3. transmission, transmit
4. oppression, oppress
5. omission, omit
6. submission, submit
7. compression, compress
8. depression, depress

(bottom)
1. discussion, discuss
2. confession, confess
3. impression, impress
4. admission, admit

When a verb ends with **ss** or **mit**, the noun goes to **–ssion**.

387

Chapter 4: In this chapter, students will mark r-controlled vowels by circling the vowel and the r. The answer key will show them in red.

2a (top)
				(middle)	
1. rc ar	7. vce ā, ℯ	13. rc ar	19. cl ă	1. market	7. harness
2. cl ă	8. rc ar	14. cl ă	20. rc ar	2. harmful	8. darling
3. rc ar	9. cl ă	15. rc ar	21. rc ar	3. disarm	
4. vce ā, ℯ	10. rc ar	16. rc ar	22. vce ā, ℯ	4. depart	
5. rc ar	11. rc ar	17. vce ā, ℯ	23. rc ar	5. partly	
6. rc ar	12. vce ā, ℯ	18. rc ar	24. cl ă	6. carpet	

(bottom) far, tar, star, jar, spar, scar, char   bark, hark, lark, park, mark, stark, shark

2a, p. 2 (top)
				(middle)	
1. ar	6. ar	11. âr	16. âr	1. fare	6. stair
2. âr	7. âr	12. ar	17. ar	2. fair	7. pare
3. âr	8. âr	13. âr	18. âr	3. flare	8. pair
4. ar	9. ar	14. âr	19. ar	4. flair	
5. âr	10. âr	15. ar	20. âr	5. stare	

(bottom)

3a (top)
1. or	7. ō, ℯ	13. or, ℯ	19. ō, ℯ	Explorer, far, North, exploring, area, Afterwards
2. ŏ	8. or, ℯ	14. ō, ℯ	20. or	informed, world, part, large, North, Before,
3. or	9. or	15. or	21. or	started, organized, exploring, party, hardy
4. ō, ℯ	10. ŏ	16. ŏ	22. or	departed, port, York, port, support, enormous,
5. ŏ	11. or, ℯ	17. or	23. ŏ	effort, March, North, carried, short, darkness,
6. or	12. or	18. ŏ	24. or	harsh, storms, remarkable, party, history

recorded, North

3a, p. 2 (top)
1. course   8. bored
2. coarse   9. hoard
3. hoarse   10. horde
4. horse   11. soar
5. boar   12. sore
6. bore   13. morning
7. board   14. mourning

(bottom)
1. or	4. ûr	7. or	10. ûr
2. ûr	5. ûr	8. ûr	11. or
3. or	6. or	9. or	12. ûr

wore and *sword* do not follow the rule.

4a (top)
1. rc, ir	6. rc, ir	11. vce, ī, ℯ	16. rc, ir	rc	first/hand	cl
2. cl, ĭ	7. rc, ir	12. rc, ir	17. rc, ir	pref	con/firm	rc
3. rc, ir	8. cl, ĭ	13. cl, ĭ	18. vce, ī, ℯ	rc	whirl/wind	cl
4. vce, ī, ℯ	9. rc, ir	14. rc, ir	19. cl, ĭ	rc	skir/mish	cl
5. rc, ir	10. cl, ĭ	15. rc, ir	20. rc, ir	pref	re/birth	rc
				cl	black/bird	rc
				rc	birth/stone	vce
				cl	af/firm	rc
				rc	stir/rups	cl

(bottom)
1. rc	5. cl	9. cl	13. rc
2. cl	6. rc	10. rc	14. cl
3. cl	7. rc	11. rc	15. rc
4. rc	8. cl	12. cl	16. cl

5a (top)
				(middle)			
1. er	5. er	9. ĕ	13. er	1. cor-ner	rc-rc	5. for-mer	rc-rc
2. er	6. ĕ	10. er	14. ĕ	2. or-der	rc-rc	6. serv-er	rc-rc
3. ē, ℯ	7. er	11. ē, ℯ	15. er	3. per-form	rc-rc	7. ŏb-serv-er	cl-rc-rc
4. er	8. ē, ℯ	12. er	16. er	4. ex-pert	pref-rc		

Do not mark incorrect if students divide 6 and 7 between r and v.

(bottom) 1. interrupt 2. liberate 3. federal

Chapter 4, page 2: Students will mark r-controlled vowels by circling the vowel and the r. The answer key will show them in red.

				(middle)		(bottom)	
5c (top)	1. n	5. n	9. c	1. shimmer, glimmer	1. ī, ë, timer	5. ă, chatter	9. ō, ë joke
	2. n	6. c	10. n	2. twitter, flutter	2. ă, wrapper	6. ō, ë broker	10. ŭ, shutter
	3. c	7. n	11. n	3. fender, bender	3. ĭ, printer	7. ă, camper	11. ī, ë, liner
	4. n	8. c	12. c	4. skipper, clipper	4. ā, ë scraper	8. ŏ, dropper	12. ĭ, flipper
				5. better, letter			

5c, p. 2 (top)
1. ĕ, pepper　　7. ŭ, drummer　　(middle) 1. critter's litter　　7. runner, winner
2. ō, voter　　　8. ō, closer　　　　　　　 2. pitter, patter
3. ā, safer　　　 9. ĭ, shipper　　　　　　　 3. sister, brother
4. ī, finer　　　 10. ŏ, stopper　　　　　　　4. pitcher, catcher
5. ĭ, slipper　　11. ă, scanner　　　　　　　5. mutter, chatter
6. ŏ, logger　　12. ī, miner　　　　　　　　 6. silver, copper

6a (top)

	1. ur	6. ur	11. ur	16. ur	rc-rc	cl-rc	rc-vce	rc-cl
	2. ur	7. ŭ	12. ŭ	17. ŭ	surf/er	oc/cur	sur/prise	cur/rent
	3. ū, ë	8. ur	13. ur	18. ur	burn/er	sun/burst	sur/vive	
	4. ŭ	9. ū, ë	14. ur	19. ŭ	per turb	in/cur	turn/stile	vce-rc
	5. ū, ë	10. ur	15. ū, ë	20. ur	sun/burn			race/horse

6d, p. 2 (top)
1. dis-t**or**-tion, pref-rc-s　　6. ex-c**ur**-sion, pref-rc-s　　1. ūrë　6. ur　11. ir　16. ir
2. t**ur**-pĕn-tīnë, rc-cl-vce　　7. re-ĭm-b**ur**së, pref-cl-rc　　2. ur　7. ir　12. īrë 17. ir
3. c**or**-ner-stonë, rc-rc-vce　　8. ĭn-j**ur**-y, cl-rc-s　　　　3. ūrë 8. īrë 13. er 18. īrë
4. co-**or**-dĭn-ate pref-rc-cl-s　9. sc**or**n-ful-ly, rc-s-s　　　 4. ur　9. īrë 14. ērë 19. ērë
5. re-frĭg-**er**-ate, pref-cl-rc-s　10. f**ur**-ther-morë, rc-rc-rc　5. ōō 10. ir　15. īrë 20. er

(bottom) The missing letter is **h**. Silent **e** causes the **a** to say âr.

6d (top) 1. entire　2. admire　3. empire　4. require　(bottom)1. ū　4. ĕ　7. âr　10. âr
　　　　 1. endure　2. secure　3. obscure　4. figure　　　　　2. ur　5. ur　8. ĕ　11. ur
　　　　 1. explore　2. restore　3. encore　4. ignore　　　　　 3. ī　6. ĕ　9. ĕ　12. ŏ
　　　　 1. software　2. hardware　3. silverware　Ar says **âr** when **a** is followed by double **r**.
　(bottom) 1. ûr　3. ēr　5. ûr　7. ûr　　The **ur** in bury says âr.
　　　　　2. ēr　4. ûr　6. ēr　8. ûr

7a (top)　Across:　1. importer　6. exploring　Down: 1. cooperation 6. advertise
　　　　　　　　　2. porcupine　7. wilderness　　　　2. cucumber　　7. hibernate
　　　　　　　　　3. harmonize　8. generation　　　　3. perspire　　 8. supervise
　　　　　　　　　4. surrender　9. prehistoric　　　　4. enterprise　 9. northern
　　　　　　　　　5. start　　　　　　　　　　　　　5. argument

8 (top)
1. A　　7. L+G　13. L+G　(bottom) 1. advisor　7. factor
2. L+G　8. A　　14. A　　　　　　2. jogger　　8. scanner
3. L+G　9. L+G　15. L+G　　　　　3. equator　 9. tractor
4. L+G　10. A　　16. A　　　　　　4. swimmer　10. creator
5. A　　11. L+G　17. L+G　　　　　5. actor　　 11. educator
6. L+G　12. L+G　18. L+G　　　　　6. locator　 12. elevator

For rule see Chapter 3, 11a. The word that doesn't fit the rule is *visitor*.
The suffix **–or** means *a person or thing that does…*

9
1. be ware' yes　　7. in quire' yes　　13. sev'er al no
2. there'fore yes　 8. var'y yes　　　　14. ver'y yes
3. nu'mer al no　 9. fed'er al no　　15. min'er al no
4. per'ish yes　 10. pre pared' yes　 16. com pared' yes
5. con spire' yes　11. gen'er al no　　17. re tired' yes
6. car'a way yes　 12. re quire' ment yes　18. mar' a thon yes

Chapter 4, page 3

10 (top)

1. imperfect	6. indigestion	11. improper	1. Use **im–** before b, m, and p
2. insecure	7. impolite	12. illogical	2. Use **il–** before l
3. irresistible	8. illegal	13. irreverence	3. Use **ir–** before r
4. illiterate	9. irregular	14. immature	4. Use **in–** before all other letters
5. imbalance	10. invalid	15. indirect	

These prefixes mean *not*. (bottom) These prefixes can also mean *in, inside, within*.
The prefixes **con–, com–, col–, co–**, and **cor–** mean *together* or *with*.

11 (top) 1. əd-věn′-chər   2. Adventure is a noun
3. (1) An undertaking or enterprise of a hazardous nature (2) An exciting experience
4. The word adventure originated in Latin and came to English from French.
5. chər   6. The two words at the top of the page are called guidewords. The one on the left is the first word on the page. The word on the right is the last word on the page.

12 (top) **–al** says əl.

				(middle)	(bottom)
1. personal	5. signal	8. herbal	12. approval	1. national	1. margin
2. arrival	6. tribal	9. removal	13. cultural	2. natural	2. digit
3. proposal	7. natural	10. global	14. rehearsal	3. emotional	3. refuse
4. rental		11. frontal		4. structural	4. refer
				5. optional	5. center
				6. fictional	6. number

13 (top) The name of the symbol ə is the schwa sound. It sounds just like a short u.

1. constant, adjective   5. merchant, person   The suffixes **–ance** and **–ence**
2. occupant, person   6. recent, adjective   say **əns**.
3. current, adjective   7. frequent, adjective
4. servant, person   8. contestant, person

(middle)

		(bottom)			
1. distance	5. presence		1. **mənt**	4. **mənt**	7. **ənt**
2. attendance	6. residence		2. **ənt**	5. **ənt**	8. **ənt**
3. importance	7. confidence		3. **mənt**	6. **mənt**	9. **mənt**
4. fragrance	8. innocence				

14a (top) The suffix **–en** says **ən**.   (middle)

1. ən	5. ən	8. ən	12. an	15. an	19. ən	jail: dungeon, prison
2. ən	6. ən	9. on	13. ən	16. ən	20. on	fabrics: cotton, nylon
3. ən	7. on	10. ən	14. on	17. ən	21. ən	shapes: hexagon, pentagon
4. on/ən		11. ən		18. ən		

(bottom)

–ənt	–ən	–mənt
current	cannon	argument
agent	person	attachment
instant	orphan	investment
resident	pelican	retirement
exuberant	cotton	compartment

14b (top)

1. warrior, **ēər**	8. nutrient, **ēənt**	**–ian** and **–ion** means *a person who does…*		
2. interior, **ēər**	9. jovial, **ēəl**			
3. champion, **ēən**	10. radiant, **ēənt**	**ēāte**	**ēənt**	**ēəl**
4. librarian, **ēən**	11. obedient, **ēənt**	radiate	gradient	tutorial
5. exterior, **ēər**	12. memorial **ēəl**	infuriate	variant	burial
6. scorpion, **ēən**	13. ingredient, **ēənt**	alleviate	recipient	trivial
7. comedian, **ēən**	14. material, **ēəl**	mediate	expedient	imperial

Chapter 5

Students will circle the vowel+r in r-controlled syllables. The answer key shows them in red.

2a (top) The first vowel is <u>long</u>, the second vowel is <u>silent</u>. They say long **a**.

1. tra(i)n vv	7. scrāpe̸ vce	13. frāil vv	19. trāit vv	Use **ai** in the beginning or middle
2. quāil vv	8. ch(ar)t rc	14. stāy vv	20. fāint vv	of words. Use **ay** at the end.
3. plāne̸ vce	9. prāy vv	15. drāin vv	21. m(ar)ch rc	1. sail 2. pail 3. bail 4. mail
4. swāy vv	10. pāint vv	16. shāpe̸ vce	22. clāim vv	5. nail 6. fail 7. tail 8. rail
5. (ar)ch rc	11. sprāy vv	17. strāit vv	23. strāight vv	1. main 2. pain 3. rain 4. vain
6. trāy vv	12. sh(ar)p rc	18. strāin vv	24. strāy vv	5. gain 6. brain 7. chain 8. stain

(bottom)

2a, p.2 (top)
1. ăc-clāim cl-vv
2. en-t(er)-tāin-er pref-rc-vv-s
3. rāil-wāy vv-vv
4. fĭng-(er)-nāil cl-rc-vv
5. dis-plāy pref-vv
6. pō-ny-tāil op-op-vv
7. ŭn-d(er)-pāy cl-rc-vv
8. t(er)-rāin rc-vv
9. p(or)-trāy rc-vv
10. re-māin-d(er) pref-vv-rc/s

1. shirttail 6. detain
2. bridesmaid 7. highway
3. Thursday 8. hangnail
4. payday 9. betray
5. detail 10. mermaid
(also accept hightail)

3a (top) It says long **e**, the first vowel is <u>long</u>, the second vowel is <u>silent</u>. 1. ēa̸t 2. tēa̸ 3. sēa̸t 4. dēa̸l

1. neat	6. streak	11. trail	16. clean
2. beam	7. cheap	12. cheat	17. frail
3. pain	8. squeak	13. stream	18. smear
4. dream	9. stain	14. paint	19. sprain
5. speak	10. tweak	15. scream	20. squeal

(bottom) Eastern, easy, reach, near clear, clean, stream, heat, releases, steam, season, year, eager, beavers, leap, stream, appear, retreat, fear, heal, disease, great, treat
Great does not follow the rule.

3b (top) It says short **e**. It says long **a**.   (bottom)

(middle)
ea=ĕ	ea=ĕ	ea=ē	ea=ē	
sweat	meant	preacher	increase	1. steak
instead	threads	uneasy	sneaky	2. Great
threat	breath	hear	breathe	3. they
dread	spread	plea	queasy	break

4a (top) It says long **e**. First v. is long, second v. is silent. kēe̸p   **cl-vv**   **vv-vce**

(middle)
1. deed	6. chain	11. sneeze	16. sweep	sixteen	beehive
2. sway	7. sleep	12. snail	17. jeep	indeed	cheesecake
3. deep	8. cheeks	13. freeze	18. claim	upkeep	peephole
4. reef	9. stray	14. geese	19. sweet	**vv-cl**	**vv-vv**
5. creek	10. queen	15. trail	20. sheet	feedback	weekday

see, tree, fee, flee, spree, knee; speed, deed, seed, need, bleed, greed   kneecap   screenplay
                                                                                                                          treetop   freeway

4a, p. 2 (top)
1. fee 2. flee 3. free 4. tree 5. three 6. glee 7. spree 8. knee
1. feed 2. seed 3. weed 4. deed 5. greed 6. bleed 7. freed 8. creed
1. seen 2. teen 3. keen 4. green 5. sheen 6. screen 7. spleen 8. queen

1. re-en-ter pref-pref-rc
2. pro-cēe̸d pref-vv
3. re-e-văl-ū-ate pref-pref-cl-op-s
4. pre-ĕmpt pref-cl
5. căn-tēe̸n cl-vv

6. re-ĕd-ū-cate pref-cl-op-c+s
7. twēe̸z-ers vv-rc-s
8. pre-ex-īst pref-pref-cl
9. re-e-lĕct pref-pref-cl
10. re-en-ăct pref-pref-cl

4b (top) The letter **e** is long, the **y** is silent
1. jockey
2. jersey, volley
3. valley
4. money
5. honey
6. donkeys
7. alley
8. monkey
9. kidneys
10. turkey
11. chimney

The vowel-vowel team **ey** says long **a**.

Chapter 5, page 2

4d (top) y says long e.
   (middle)
		(bottom)			
1. stories	5. cherries	1. ladies	5. pennies	1. pays	5. applies
2. keys	6. daisies	2. turkeys	6. valleys	2. studies	6. says
3. puppies	7. chimneys	3. essays	7. hobbies	3. delays	7. replies
4. plays	8. ponies	4. parties	8. tardies	4. strays	8. tries

5a (top)
   1. ē   5. ē   9. ē   13. ē   (middle) The vowel team **ie** says long **i**, at the end of a
   2. ī   6. ē   10. ē 14. ī   one-syllable word and long **e** at the end of a two-syllable
   3. ē   7. ī   11. ī 15. ē   word.
   4. ī   8. ē   12. ē 16. ē

   (bottom) Verbs: lie, tie, die, vie / lied, tied, died, vied, lying, tying, dying, vying

6a (top)
   1. cōal vv   7. gōat vv   13. sp**or**t rc   19. rōad vv
   2. rōde vce   8. fōe vv   14. grōan vv   20. c**or**k rc
   3. glōat vv   9. thrōat vv 15. stŏck cl   22. dōe vv
   4. rōam vv   10. flŏss cl 16. spōke vce   23. pōach vv
   5. Jōe vv   11. st**or**k rc 17. brōach vv 24. rōast vv
   6. glŏss cl   12. flōat vv 18. brōke vce   25. cōach vv

   (Students must circle r-controlled vowels.
   They are shown in red on the answer key.)

   (6a, middle)
vv	coast/er	vv
vv	oat/meal	vv
cl	tip/toe	vv
vce	scape/goat	vv
pref	en/croach	vv
vv	toast/er	rc
vv	sea/coast	vv
vv	coal/mine	vce
vce	life/boat	vv
cl	ap/proach	vv
vv	road/side	vce

   (bottom) coat, float, goat, moat, bloat, gloat
             boast, roast, toast

6a, p. 2 (top)
   1. soak, seek   5. sail, seal   9. groan, green, grain
   2. boast, beast   6. foal, feel, fail 10. croak, creek, creak
   3. poach, peach   7. moat, meat, meet 11. boat, beet, beat, bait
   4. float, fleet   8. moan, mean, main 12. road, read, reed, raid

   (bottom) 1. oars, overboard   2. hoarse   3. soar, roar, boars   4. coarse   5. hoard

7a (top) The vowel team **ue** says long **u**. The first vowel is marked long; the second one is crossed out.
   ū: rescue   venue   o͞o: due   fruit
       avenue   queue   sue   cruise
       imbue   miscue   suit   true
       argue   revenue   glue   clue
       barbecue   continue   bruise pursuit

   The vowel team **ui** always says o͞o. We use o͞o after the letters **r, l, s, t,** and **d**.

7a, p. 2 (top) 1. flu/id   2. cru/el   3. ru/in   4. flu/ent   5. in/flu/en/za
   1. rescued, rescuer, rescuing   2. subdued, subduer, subduing   3. pursued, pursuer, pursuing

   (bottom)
   1. coast   4. coat   7. clean   10. break   13. dream   16. cream
   2. pursuit 5. teeter   8. heat   11. blues   14. keynote 17. toe
   3. dreams   6. sea, sea 9. free   12. moaned, groaned 15. esteem

8a keep, explain, away, steep, feelings, speedy, retreat, each, dream, true, sweet, maiden, sleep, defied, wait, seek, wee, each, coaxed, dismay, eager, meet, complied screamed, pain, they, tried, feet, meantime, sweeping, cleaning, pail, soapy, approached, mean, disdain, pay, heed, treat, maid, prevailed, beseeched, tee, beaming, knees, pleaded, tears, cheeks, replied, sweetly, faithful, someday, queen   The word **said** does not follow the pronunciation rule, but it could be included. Grade flexibly because this should be fun.

Chapter 5, page 3

9 (top) 1. Every syllable must have one vowel sound. 2. It cannot have more than one sounded vowel. 3. Silent vowels don't count. 4. A word has the same number of syllables as sounded vowels.

(middle)
1.	3, 1, 1	6.	4, 1, 1	11.	4, 2, 2
2.	4, 2, 2	7.	2, 1, 1	12.	5, 3, 3
3.	4, 2, 2	8.	4, 2, 2	13.	4, 3, 3
4.	3, 2, 2	9.	5, 4, 4	14.	5, 4, 4
5.	4, 3, 3	10.	4, 2, 2		

10 (top)
1. gōal-kēep-er   vv-vv-s
2. re-e-lĕc-tion   pref-pref-cl-s
3. frēe-lōad-er   vv-vv-s
4. cōast-līne   vv-vce
5. in-con-grū-ent   pref-pref-op-s
6. māin-tĕn-ance   vv-cl-s
7. un-pro-tĕct-ed   pref-pref-cl-s
8. en-crōach-ment   pref-vv-s
9. strēam-līne   vv-vce
10. un-ex-plāined   pref-pref-vv-s

(middle) 1. Mastering word patterns makes you a great reader. 2. The coach of the Oakland Raiders praised his team after the defeat of the Tampa Bay Buccaneers.

11 **Across:** 1. toasty 2. squeamish 3. skirmish 4. blueberry 5. strengthen 6. arboretum 7. career   **Down:** 1. scribbler 2. arcade 3. constrain 4. committee 5. leadership 6. squeegee

12a (top)
1. crē-ā-tion   op-op-s
2. sēam-strĕss   vv-cl
3. bē-trāy-al   op-vv-s
4. ăv-ĕn-ūe   cl-cl-vv
5. ăc-quāint-ance   cl-vv-s
6. vŏl-ŭn-tēer   cl-cl-vv
7. en-dĕav-or   pref-vv-s
8. fēa-ture   vv-s
9. pī-ō-nēer   op-op-vv
10. dis-ăp-pēar-ance   pref-cl-vv-s
11. mis-de-mēan-or   pref-pref-vv-s
12. dis-con-tĭn-ūe   pref-pref-cl-vv

(bottom) 1. maintain 2. mainstream 3. detain 4. decrease 5. upload 6. upstream 7. overload 8. contain 9. unload 10. entertain

13 (top) 1. item 2. custom 3. tender 4. modern 5. winter 6. motor 7. symbol 8. real 9. final 10. organ 11. civil 12. human

(middle) 1. memorize 2. harmonize 3. agonize 4. sympathize 5. summarize 6. fantasize 7. economize 8. colonize

1. formalize 2. verbalize 3. normalize 4. personalize 5. capitalize 6. centralize 7. legalize 8. localize

14 (top) 1. absent 2. honor 3. escape 4. enlist 5. detain 6. refuge 7. evacuate 8. nominate 9. trust 10. train 11. retire 12. refer

The suffix **ee** means, "One that receives or benefits from a certain action."

(middle) 1. ĭv 2. ĭv 3. īve 4. ĭv 5. īve 6. īve 7. ĭv 8. ĭv 9. ĭv 10. ĭv 11. īve 12. ĭv

(bottom) 1. include 2. explode 3. exclude 4. offend 5. decide 6. divide 7. defend 8. evade 9. expend 10. intend 11. intrude 12. corrode

It should read, "What is the last <u>sound</u> of the base word?" The last sound is **d**.

Chapter 6

2 (top) 1. saddle 2. cuddle 3. bundle 4. griddle
5. tattle 6. kettle 7. turtle 8. startle
9. ripple 10. sample 11. dimple 12. temple

(bottom) huddled, maple, couple, little, speckled, struggle, nibbles, gobbled, jostled, squabbled, Snuggles, startled, little, trembled, battle, rattled, puddle, Snuggles, tangle, scuffle, scuttled, chuckled

3a (top)
1. shŭt-tle cl-cle
2. cŭd-dle cl-cle
3. stā-ble op-cle
4. ăp-ple cl-cle
5. bū-gle op-cle
6. hŏb-ble cl-cle
7. rī-fle op-cle
8. tŏp-ple cl-cle
9. mĭd-dle cl-cle
10. crā-dle op-cle

(bottom)
1. settle 7. cattle
2. riddle 8. smuggle
3. giggle 9. pebble
4. puzzle 10. bubble
5. bridle 11. title
6. maple 12. bottle

4 (top)
1. pickle 5. tickle 9. sparkle
2. crackle 6. chuckle 10. knuckles
3. twinkle 7. buckle 11. wrinkle
4. trickle 8. sprinkle 12. speckle

(middle)
1. hăck-le cl-le
2. frĕck-le cl-le
3. tăck-le cl-le
4. bŭck-le cl-le
5. shăck-le cl-le

(bottom)
1. knucklebones
2. unbuckle
3. honeysuckle
4. dismantle
5. reshuffle

6a (top)
1. gur-gle rc-cle
2. nĕs-tle cl-cle
3. re-kĭn-dle pref-cl-cle
4. un-ā-ble pref-op-cle
5. crŭm-ble cl-cle
6. thĭs-tle cl-cle
7. lā-dle op-cle
8. jŭn-gle cl-cle
9. wrĕs-tle cl-cle
10. ex-ăm-ple pref-cl-cle

(bottom)
1. double, trouble 6. giggle, chuckle
2. stumble, fumble 7. sparkle, twinkle
3. handle, candle 8. mumble, grumble
4. single, jingle 9. cuddle, snuggle
5. tackle, huddle

7 (top)
1. străn-gle-hōld cl-cle-cl
2. bŭm-ble-bēe cl-cle-vv
3. sĕt-tle-ment cl-cle-s
4. ~~re-kĭn-dle~~ pref-cl-cle
5. mis-hăn-dle pref-cl-cle
6. tā-ble-clŏth op-cle-cl
7. em-bĕz-zle cl-cl-cle
8. căn-dle-hōld-er cl-cle-cl-s
9. mĭd-dle-man cl-cle-cl
10. en-cir-cle pref-rc-cle

Across
1. rustle
2. comprehend
3. correspond
4. cockroach
5. wrestler

Down
1. pickles
2. reporter
3. atmosphere
4. steeple
5. drizzle

9 (top)
1. miracle 5. particles 9. cuticles
2. clavicle 6. vehicle 10. tentacles
3. article 7. barnacles 11. spectacle
4. obstacle 8. cubicles 12. pinnacle

(bottom)
long v: vehicle, cubicles, cuticles
short v: clavicle, obstacle, tentacles, spectacle, pinnacle
The vowels in unaccented syllables say the schwa sound.

10 (top)
1. payable 5. sensible 9. adorable
2. washable 6. sizeable or sizable 10. advisable
3. distractible 7. useable or usable 11. terrible
4. taxable 8. convertible 12. horrible

(bottom)
1. disposable 5. preventable
2. refundable 6. comfortable
3. remarkable
4. dependable

Chapter 7

1a (top)
1. oil
2. convoy
3. poise
4. voice
5. cowboy
6. point
7. joist
8. ploy
9. soy
10. ointment
11. corduroy
12. moist
13. joy
14. rejoin
15. foil

Use **oi** in the beginning or the middle of words; use **oy** at the end of a word or a syllable.

(middle) 1. coil 2. coy 3. spoil 4. toy 5. coin 6. void 7. overjoy 8. hoist **(bottom)** 1. employ 2. poison 3. appointment

1a, p. 2
1. busboy
2. avoid
3. thyroid
4. deploy
5. invoice
6. decoys
7. enjoy
8. employer, loyal
9. choices
10. spoil
11. coins
12. annoy
13. hoist
14. destroyed

2a (top) Use **ou** at the beginning or in the middle of words. Use **ow** at the end of words. Use **ow** before the letters **n** and **l**, and before **er** and **el**.

2b

ou as in out		ou=ô (ought)		ou=ŭ	
amount	mountain	bought	brought	young	cousin
couch	sprout	thoughtful	fought	rough	country
counter	scout	wrought	cough	enough	trouble
grouchy	announce	sought	trough	touch	tough

The words **cough, trough, rough, enough,** and **tough** do not follow the rule **gh** is silent.

2c (top)

ou=o͞o		ou=ur		ou=or	
group	soup	journey	courage	fourth	concourse
youth	cougar	nourish	adjourn	course	court
through	coupon	courtesy		pour	resource
souvenir		journal		source	

(middle) Ou says long **o**. **(bottom)** 1. though 2. dough 3. shoulder, boulder 4. thoroughly, poultry 5. Although

3a (top) Ow says the long **o** sound.

show	ow=ō	stow	ow=ō	flow	ow=ō	1. yellow	8. arrow
now	ow=owl	fellow	ow=ō	brow	ow=owl	2. marrow	9. wallow
grow	ow=ō	plow	ow=owl	sparrow	ow=ō	3. borrow	10. narrow.
know	ow=ō	swallow	ow=ō	mellow	ow=ō	4. shadow	11. meadow
vow	ow=owl	crow	ow=ō	throw	ow=ō	5. hollow	12. tomorrow
shallow	ow=ō	allow	ow=owl	anyhow	ow=owl	6. sorrow	13. bellow
						7. widow	14. burrow
							15. follow

4a Use **au** in the beginning or middle of words, use **aw** at the end of words. Use **aw** in the middle of words when a single **l**, **n**, or **k** follow it.
1. haunt
2. gawk
3. crawl
4. gaudy
5. yawn
6. launch
7. sprawl
8. pause
9. aunt
10. dawn
11. gaunt
12. paunch

4a, p. 2 **Across:** 1. sausage 2. autobiography 3. Australia 4. taunt 5. automatic 6. audit 7. saucer 8. vault **Down:** 1. authority 2. faucet 3. auditorium 4. automobile 5. audible 6. autograph 7. autumn

Chapter 7, page 2

5
1. enjoy, show
2. owl
3. tough, tough
4. applause
5. Join
6. fault
7. fought
8. Tomorrow
9. royal
10. spoiled
11. through
12. announcements
13. enough
14. coin
15. point
16. thrown
17. showers, flowers
18. flawless
19. straws
20. automatic

6a (top)
1. o͞o   8. o͝o   15. o͝o
2. o͝o   9. o͝o   16. o͞o
3. o͝o, o͝o   10. o͝o   17. o͝o, o͝o
4. o͞o   11. o͝o   18. o͞o
5. o͝o   12. o͝o   19. o͞o
6. o͞o   13. o͞o   20. o͞o
7. o͞o   14. o͝o   21. o͞o

(bottom)
1. honeymoon   8. tablespoon
2. barefoot   9. yearbook
3. afternoon   10. Hollywood
4. proofread   11. roommate
5. bridegroom   12. broomstick
6. whirlpool
7. seafood

7a (top) We use **oo** in the beginning or middle of words, we use **ew** at the end of words.
(middle) 1. feud ū   2. feudal ū   3. neutral o͞o   4. neutron o͞o   5. neurology ū
(bottom)
1. o͞o   5. o͞o   9. ū   13. o͞o
2. ū   6. ū   10. o͞o   14. o͞o
3. o͞o   7. ū   11. ū   15. ū
4. o͞o   8. ū   12. o͞o   16. o͞o

8 (top)
1. răc-coon   cl-d
2. jour-nal-ĭst   d-n+s-cl
3. com-pound   pref-d
4. tur-quoise   rc-d
5. lawn-mow-er   d-d-s
6. a-loof-ness   pref-d-s
7. mois-tur-iz-er   d-s-s-s
8. ăs-trō-naut   cl-op-d
9. dew-drŏps   d-cl
10. pro-nounce   pref-d

(bottom) farmer, goose, laid, each, first, astounded overjoyed, filled, greed now, goose

9a (middle)
ei = long a
veil
rein
weight
eighty
reign
feint
freight

ei = long e
receive
conceited
weird
perceive
deceit
seize
deceive

ie = long e
believe
thief
priest
shriek
niece
shield
pier

(middle) either, neither, weird, seize, leisure
(bottom) height, sleight = long i
forfeit, counterfeit = short i
friend, foreign, sovereign = short e

9b **Across:**
1. eighteen   5. relieve
2. neighbor   6. sleigh
3. cashier   7. ceiling
4. deceive   8. brief

Down:
1. conceited   5. eighth
2. achieve   6. receipt
3. perceive   7. believe
4. thieves   8. grieve

10
1. har-poon   rc-d
2. au-thor-ize   d-rc/s-s
3. pow-er-house   d-rc-d
4. dis-ăp-point   pref-cl-d
5. in-sur-mount-able   pref-rc-d-s
6. un-em-ploy-ment   pref-cl-d-s
7. dis-bē-lief   pref-op-d
8. au-thĕn-tĭc   d-cl-cl
9. re-triev-er   pref-d-s
10. boo-mer-ăng   d-rc-cl
11. an-nounce-ment   cl-d-s

pref ex-haust d
d boy-cott cl
cl with-drew d
pref dis-count d
pref de-coy d
d scoot-er s
d draw-back cl

11. 1. They had to think carefully about what they brought because they were in the wilderness.
2. Getting too close to the tidewater glaciers is dangerous because big pieces can fall off and cause a tidal wave.   3. The bears were spooked because rocks were bouncing towards them. They were worried because the trio was six hours late in getting back to camp

Chapter 8

1 (top)
				hard c	soft c
1. cost	6. crying	11. space	16. lacy	(bottom) clutter	grocery
2. city	7. decide	12. doctor	17. twice	crunchy	cinema
3. close	8. coffee	13. mascot	18. reflect	subject	mercy
4. center	9. closet	14. discuss	19. citizen	crumble	perceive
5. spicy	10. price	15. fancy	20. crime	direct	decision

(middle) C says **s** when the letters **e, i,** or **y** come right after it.

1, p. 2 (top)
				(middle)	
1. s	6. s	11. s	16. s	attendance	privacy
2. k	7. s	12. k	17. k	balance	absence
3. k	8. s	13. s	18. s	vacancy	residence
4. s	9. k	14. k	19. s	entrance	truancy
5. k	10. k	15. s	20. s	fluency	secrecy
				policy	difference

2 (top)
1. circulate
2. confidence
3. concept
4. occurrence
5. civic
6. concert
7. commerce
8. democracy
9. recycle
10. excellence
11. concern
12. conference
13. clearance
14. circle
15. circus
16. bicycle

(middle) The first **c** says **k**. The second **c** says **s**. **Sc** says **s**.

(bottom) 1. accept 2. vaccine, scientific 3. accident, resuscitate, successful
4. science, fascinating 5. scenery, reminisce

3 (top)
1. ace	5. əs	9. ace	(middle)	1. notice əs	7. sacrifice ice
2. əs	6. ace	10. əs		2. price ice	8. justice əs
3. ace	7. əs	11. əs		3. office əs	9. solstice əs
4. əs	8. ace	12. ace		4. advice ice	10. prejudice əs
				5. practice əs	11. entice ice
				6. service əs	12. apprentice əs

(bottom) 1. race, place 2. spice, nice 3. prejudice, justice 4. price, slice 5. notice, service

5 (top)
1. golden	6. angle	11. gasoline	16. age	(bottom) guess	ranger	baggage
2. huge	7. angel	12. giant	17. golf	glitter	agent	geography
3. gallon	8. gloomy	13. gentle	18. governm.	garden	sponge	gigantic
4. ginger	9. danger	14. glow	19. change	recognize	magic	engage
5. gym	10. gallon	15. grape	20. margin	organize	engine	luggage
				wagon	energy	language

G says **j** when the letters **e, i,** or **y** come right after it.

5, p. 2 Across:
1. gymnastics
2. refrigerator
3. gorgeous
4. enlarge
5. digest
6. governor

Down:
1. engagement
2. ginger
3. garbage
4. gargle
5. tragedy
6. grudge

7. guitar

Chapter 8, page 2

6 (top)
1. general
2. generate
3. gender
4. generic
5. generalize
6. generator
7. generally
8. generous
9. genetic
10. genocide
11. gentle
12. gentleman
13. agent
14. agency
15. agenda
16. urgent

(bottom)
manage
radiology
postage
anthropology
advantage
bandage

apology
village
damage
geology
ecology
package

7 (top)
1. bridge
2. edge
3. cage
4. charge
5. huge
6. pledge
7. plunge
8. smudge
9. page
10. lodge
11. grudge
12. large
13. stage
14. ridge
15. cringe
16. judge
17. rage
18. hedge
19. merge
20. trudge
21. forge

(bottom)
1. nudge
2. hinge
3. wedge
4. sage
5. bulge
6. budge
7. wage
8. verge
9. lunge
10. dodge
11. gorge
12. sledge

9 (top)
1. ch
2. k
3. ch
4. k
5. k
6. ch
7. ch
8. k
9. k
10. ch
11. ch
12. k
13. k
14. k
15. ch
16. k
17. k
18. ch, ch
19. ch
20. k
21. k

(bottom)
1. chauffeur
2. chartreuse
3. chef
4. charades
5. parachutes
6. chalets
7. chandelier

Comprehension Questions:
1. Switzerland became a nation in 1291.
2. The Swiss people became enraged because the Hapsburgers oppressed them and taxed them very heavily.
3. The representatives swore allegiance to each other and decided to wage war to gain their freedom.
4. The Swiss people chose a democratic form of government.
5. Both countries waged war to gain their freedom from kings who oppressed them and imposed very high taxes. Both countries chose a democratic form of government.

Chapter 9

1
1. de part
2. bas ket
3. re quire ment
4. sup ply
5. spark plug
6. ad mire
7. free way
8. big gest
9. pen cil
10. Eng lish
11. de pos it
12. Sep tem ber
13. un der stand
14. art ist
15. teach er
16. af ter
17. pre dict
18. fast
19. ra di o
20. to ma to
21. re cov er

2 (top)
1. dol' lar
2. in flate'
3. bi' cy cle
4. a gree'
5. la' bel
6. skate' board
7. mu' sic
8. mis take'
9. ac count'
10. free' dom
11. mem' ber
12. ex plode'
13. al' bum
14. per fume'
15. li' on
16. al low'
17. trum' pet
18. sup pose'
19. sud' den
20. ad vice'

(middle)
1. com put' er
2. grand' moth er
3. im po lite'
4. tel' e phone
5. rep re sent'
6. e lec' tric
7. buf' fa lo
8. um brel' la
9. vid' e o
10. lib' er ty

(bottom)
1. en ter tain' ment
2. in ter rupt'
3. ed u ca' tion
4. e lec tron' ics
5. dis trib' ute
6. bar' be cue
7. val' en tine
8. his' to ry
9. re fer' ral
10. a part' ment

3a (top) The underlined vowel says the schwa sound (ə).

1. chăn' nel (ə)
2. at tĕnd' (ə)
3. moun' tain (ə)
4. chĭl' dren (ə)
5. ad mīre' (ə)
6. vow' el (ə)
7. a round' (ə)
8. pĕn' cil (ə)
9. strĕngth' en (ə)
10. com mănd' er (ə)
11. ăb' sent (ə)
12. sĕv' enth (ə)
13. com plēte' (ə)
14. per' son al (ə ə)
15. thou' sand (ə)
16. el' e phant (ə ə)
17. sea' son al (ə ə)
18. ŭn der stŏŏd' (ə ə)
19. fĭsh' er man (ə ə)
20. A mĕr' i can (ə ə)

The schwa sound occurs in unaccented syllables.

3b (bottom)
1. so' da (ə)
2. tu' na (ə)
3. ex' tra (ə)
4. par' ka (ə)
5. com' ma (ə)
6. del' ta (ə)
7. i de' a (ə)
8. so' fa (ə)
9. pan' da (ə)
10. scu' ba (ə)
11. a ro' ma (ə ə)
12. ar' e a (ə ə)
13. stan' za (ə)
14. piz' za (ə)
15. dra' ma (ə)
16. cam' er a (ə ə)

5a (top)
1. re– again
2. pre– before
3. de– away from, down
4. pro– forward, ahead
5. co– together, with

a says the schwa sound. The accent falls on the base word or the second syllable.

(middle)
1. car' pet
2. mar' gin
3. far' mer
4. pup' pet
5. cam' er a
6. cal' en dar
7. mo' ment
8. val' en tine
9. nar' row
10. wes' tern
11. jour' nal ist
12. por' cu pine

The accent falls on the first syllable in two and three syllable words.

(bottom)
1. a bove'
2. pre vent'
3. de tect'
4. pro long'
5. con trol'
6. a miss'
7. pro duce'
8. re ply'
9. pre dict'
10. de glaze'
11. re act'
12. pro ceed'

The accent falls on the base word in words with a prefix and a base word.

Chapter 9, page 2

5b (top)
1. nonsense
2. dishonest
3. unarmed, disarmed
4. nonfat
5. discover, uncover
6. unexpected
7. nonstop
8. dislocate
9. uncertain

(middle) **Dis–**, **un–**, and **non–** mean *not.*

(bottom) The accent falls on the first syllable in words with two or three syllables. The accent falls on the base word in words with a prefix and a base word.

(middle)
distracted	unfocused
undefeated	unbeaten
unfortunate	unlucky
disconnect	unplug
disagreeable	unfriendly
unreachable	unavailable
disarray	disorder
uncertain	unsure
disagreement	dispute
distasteful	disgusting

6 (top) The prefix **in–** means *in, into, inside*

(middle)
1. illegal
2. imperfect
3. incorrect
4. irregular
5. irresponsible
6. immoral
7. inhuman
8. illogical

1. commute
2. correct
3. connect
4. committee
5. collect
6. compare
7. commit
8. copilot

In–, **im–**, **il–**, and **ir–** also mean *not.*
Con–, **co–**, **col–**, **cor–**, and **com–** mean *together* or *with.* The **o** says the schwa sound.

(bottom)
1. arrange
2. afford
3. attract
4. account
5. appoint
6. allocate
7. address
8. assume

The prefix **ad–** and its absorbed forms mean *toward, near.*

8 (top)
1. hand' ful
2. teach' er
3. part' ly
4. crowd' ed
5. camp' er
6. kind' ness
7. frost' y
8. roast' ing
9. po' ny
10. tall' est
11. sense' less
12. soft' en

The accent falls on the base word.

(middle)
1. in tense' ly
2. un fair' ness
3. pre tend' ed
4. de fend' ing
5. at trac' tive
6. com plain' er
7. re gard' less
8. pre pay' ment
9. com plete' ly
10. un luck' y
11. pre serv' er
12. non smok' ing
13. pre vent' ed
14. im port' ed
15. un worth' y

The accent falls on the base word in words with a prefix, a base word, and a suffix.

(bottom)
1. thinking
2. away
3. kitchen
4. pulling
5. shoulder
6. different
7. helping
8. meeting
9. bushy
10. minding

9 (top)
1. con' duct, con duct'
2. per' mit, per mit'
3. in sult', in' sult
4. sus pect', sus' pect
5. pre' sent, pre sent'
6. ob ject', ob' ject

1. In verbs, the accent falls on the base word or the second syllable.
2. In nouns, the accent falls on the prefix.

10 (top) Please see Note to Instructor (middle) All of the red vowels say the schwa sound.

11 (top)
1. voter
2. stomping
3. hopped
4. hoped
5. planning
6. drummer
7. stepped
8. strapping

(middle)
1. prof it + ed, profited
2. e quip + ed, equipped
3. re bel + ing, rebelling
4. em bed + ed, embedded
5. de vel op+er, developer

Chapter 9, page 3

11, continued

6. vis it+ed, visited
7. per mit+ing, permitting
8. be gin+er beginner
9. ad mit+ed, admitted
10. hap pen+ed, happened
11. gal lop+ing, galloping
12. com mit+ed, committed
13. car pet+ed, carpeted
14. lim it+ing, limited
15. oc cur+ed, occurred
16. com pel+ing, compelling
17. pro pel+er, propeller
18. cred it+ed, credited
19. pre fer+ed, preferred
20. riv et + ing, riveting

12 Comprehension Questions

1. Walt helped the three riders by hauling their food and camping gear. He also found motels or campgrounds.
2. The riders raised money for Hope Hospice.
3. The radio station KKIQ broadcast updates of their trip every Friday for the duration of the trip.
4. Riding through Nevada and Utah was difficult because it was very hot.
5. The Continental Divide is a ridge that separates rivers flowing in a westerly direction to the Pacific Ocean from those flowing in an easterly direction to the Atlantic Ocean or the Gulf of Mexico (Webster's New World Dictionary). (Give credit if students show any signs of comprehending this concept.
6. Riding through Missouri and Kentucky was tough because of the constant up and down.
7. The three women rode 3,850 miles and raised $ 10,000.

Chapter 10

1 (top)
1. flipper 1. crabby 1. dampen 1. hottest 1. chatted 1. hoping
2. shopper 2. hazy 3. ripen 2. finest 2. stepped 2. jumping
3. timer 3. trendy 4. flatten 3. slimmest 3. lifted 3. scrubbing
4. blender 4. rosy 5. spoken 4. strongest 4. scraped 4. quoting

(bottom)
1. slip 5. swim 9. fog 13. chat
2. cute 6. price 10. strut 14. wave
3. shake 7. rot 11. red 15. bump
4. chop 8. slice 12. shine 16. shake

2 (top)
1. drop 4. pack 7. book 10. star These suffixes mean *a small amount of…*
2. ring 5. snip 8. leaf 11. cover
3. helm 6. cabin 9. lock 12. wave

(middle)
1. rocket 4. market 7. Musketeers 10. bonnet
2. pockets 5. racket 8. hatchet 11. budget
3. ticket 6. basket 9. blanket 12. carpet

3. **Across**
1. straightened 5. leakiest
2. happening 6. entered
3. oxygen 7. droplet
4. shiny 8. recovery

Down
1. quietest 5. banners
2. locket 6. kitten
3. toughen 7. early
4. steepest 8. emboldened

4a (top)
1. happier, happiest 6. prettier, prettiest
2. curlier, curliest 7. funnier, funniest
3. angrier, angriest 8. bulkier, bulkiest
4. juicier, juiciest 9. luckier, luckiest
5. grayer, grayest 10. sloppier, sloppiest

(middle)
1. lazy 7. crazy
2. carry 8. foggy
3. shaky 9. tiny
4. baggy 10. rainy
5. sunny 11. smoky
6. spicy 12. muddy

(bottom)
1. replies, replied, replying
2. denies, denied, denying
3. supplies, supplied, supplying

5a (middle)
1. ən 6. ər 11. ən
2. ər 7. ər 12. ərs
3. ər 8. ən 13. ər
4. ən 9. ər 14. ən
5. ər 10. ən 15. ər

(middle)
1. advisor 5. narrator
2. prison 6. sugar
3. calendar 7. ventilator
4. professor 8. canyon

1. major 5. liberator
2. supervisor 6. circular
3. honor 7. veteran
4. urban 8. uncommon

5c
1. warrior ēər
2. librarian ēən
3. historian ēən
4. interior ēər
5. comedian ēən
6. scorpion ēən
7. guardian ēən
8. exterior ēər
9. champion ēən
10. superior ēər
11. Canadian ēən

6. custodian ēən

ē   ē   ē   ē
1. ruffian 2. barbarian 3. mammalian 4. Australian

Chapter 10, page 2

5c (bottom) ar/or = ər   –iar/–ior = ēər   –ion/–ian = ēən
             regular   familiar   criterion
             popular   inferior   Italian
             grammar   peculiar   amphibian
             conductor   ulterior   median
             instructor   Indian

6 (top)
1. car′ pet   5. bas′ ket ball   9. free′ hand   13. gadg′ et
2. al′ ler gy   6. loos′ en   10. clean′ est   14. flow′ ers
3. gold′ en   7. tall′ est   11. brace′ let   15. nois′ y
4. fol′ low er   8. stock′ bro ker 15. brave′ er y   16. i′ vor y
The accent falls on the first syllable.

1. de scend′   5. pre serve′   9. in tact′
2. un sure′   6. re port′   10. pre scribe′
3. pro claim′   7. con tempt′   11. im pose′
4. dis arm′   8. de rail′   12. re act′
The accent falls on the base word.

1. re cord′ er   5. un luck′ y   9. con duc′ tor
2. im plant′ ed   6. mis tak′ en   10. ac count′ ing
3. un pack′ ing   7. in hu′ man   11. un eas′ y
4. pre vent′ ed   8. un like′ ly   12. de light′ ed
The accent falls on the base word.

8b (top)
1. troublesome   4. threesome   7. likelihood   10. parenthood
2. wholesome   5. worrisome   8. womanhood   11. livelihood
3. bothersome   6. meddlesome   9. brotherhood   12. knighthood

13. forcefully   18. personally   23. snobbish   27. sluggish
14. angrily   19. luckily   24. babyish   28. stylish
15. probably   20. possibly   25. grayish   29. ticklish
16. happily   21. incredibly   26. Scottish   30. boyish
17. carefully   22. legally

9b (top)
1. partnership   4. hardship   7. sideward   10. upward
2. friendship   5. penmanship   8. downward   11. homeward
3. censorship   6. guardianship   9. afterward   12. outward

1. freedom   16. stardom   19. slug   24. greed
2. boredom   17. kingdom   20. clan   25. plenty
3. wisdom   18. chiefdom   21. silly   26. penny
                                    22. live   27. sister
                                    23. play   28. equal

11a (top)
1. nā′-tion-hood (op-s-s)   7. bore′-dom (rc-s)
2. mĕm′-ber-ship (cl-rc-s)   8. un-whōle′-some (pref-vce-s)
3. Scŏt′-tish (cl-t+s)   9. thănk′-ful-ness (cl-s-s)
4. awk′-ward-ly (d-s-s)   10. re-lā′-tion-ship (pref-op-s-s)
5. mēan′-ing-less-ness (vv-s-s-s) 11. ăd-vĕn′-ture-some (cl/ pref-cl-s-s)
6. re-spĕct′-ful-ly (pref-cl-s-s) 12. grāte′-ful-ly (vce-s-s)

Chapter 10, page 3

11 (bottom) usually, cheerful, lovely, sadness, hopeless dreadful, quickly, neighborhood, afterwards, fortunately, handsome, instantly, happily

12 Across:
1. forgiveness
2. falsehood
3. masterful
4. frequently
5. accomplish
6. boyhood
7. distrustful

Down:
1. noiselessly
2. gracefully
3. tenderness
4. quarrelsome
5. indirectly
6. workmanship

14

	base word	pref	suf	suf		base word	pref	suf	suf
1.	yellow		ish		10.	whole	un	some	
2.	lead		er	ship	11.	wild		er	ness
3.	order	dis	ly		12.	perfect	im	ly	
4.	self	un	ish	ness	13.	own		er	ship
5.	down		ward		14.	care		less	ness
6.	mother		hood		15.	grace	dis	ful	ly
7.	fool		ish	ness	16.	wise		dom	
8.	light	de	ful		17.	child		hood	
9.	chief		dom		18.	sight	in	ful	

15

1. The term sound/symbol correspondence means that one sound is represented by one letter.
2. The Angles, Jutes, and Saxons conquered England in the 5th century A.D.
3. The conquerors came from the area of today's Germany and spoke German.
4. The Vikings conquered England in 1013 A.D. They spoke Danish.
5. William the Conqueror conquered England in the year 1066.
6. The new king and his followers spoke French.
7. Anglo-Saxon (also give credit for Old English) and French became all mixed up.
8. We have to learn spelling rules from Anglo-Saxon, Danish, French, Greek, and Latin.

Chapter 11

1b (top)

1. garment	5. scientist	9. investment	1. Department
2. organic	6. plastic	10. soloist	2. aerobic
3. organist	7. announcement	11. economic	3. violinist
4. pavement	8. static	12. economist	4. enforcement
			5. cyclists

1c (top)

1. scenic	1. adjustment	1. stylist	6. erratic
2. academic	2. government	2. flutist	7. measurements
3. heroic	3. enjoyment	3. botanist	
4. basic	4. replacement	4. therapist	
5. economic	5. appointment		

(middle)

1. <u>pun</u> ish ment   3. <u>ar</u> gu ment   5. <u>or</u> na ment   7. de <u>rail</u> ment   9. in <u>vest</u> ment
2. <u>gov</u> ern ment   4. <u>state</u> ment   6. <u>pay</u> ment   8. com <u>mit</u> ment   10. de <u>vel</u> op ment

The accent falls on the first syllable. If there is a prefix, the accent is on the root word.

1. <u>den</u> tist   3. <u>tour</u> ist   5. <u>ter</u> ror ist   7. <u>sci</u> en tist   9. re <u>serv</u> ist
2. <u>hy</u> gien ist   4. <u>fi</u> nal ist   6. <u>op</u> ti mist   8. <u>or</u> gan ist   10. de <u>feat</u> ist

The accent falls on the first syllable. If there is a prefix, the accent is on the root word.

1. re <u>pub</u> lic   3. a <u>tom</u> ic   5. dra <u>mat</u> ic   7. bar <u>bar</u> ic   9. O <u>lym</u> pics
2. e <u>las</u> tic   4. <u>fab</u> ric   6. vol <u>can</u> ic   8. me <u>chan</u> ic   10. <u>pan</u> ic

The accent falls on the syllable right before **ic**.

2b

1. vigorous and strenuous
2. nervous and anxious
3. hilarious and humorous
4. hazardous and dangerous
5. treasonous and traitorous
6. jealous and envious
7. gorgeous and glamorous
8. boisterous and rambunctious
9. venomous and poisonous
10. fabulous and tremendous

2c

The vowels before –ous are long.

1. contemptuous choo-əs
2. virtuous choo-əs
3. deciduous joo-əs
4. tumultuous choo-əs
5. assiduous joo-əs
6. anxious shəs
7. incredulous jə-ləs
8. tortuous choo-əs
9. sumptuous choo-əs
10. obnoxious shəs
11. arduous joo-əs
12. presumptuous choo-əs

The accent falls on the syllable before the connectives.

2d (top)

ē-əm	ē-əs	ē-ən	ē-ər	ē-ə	ē-āte
stadium	curious	librarian	inferior	bacteria	retaliate
premium	victorious	guardian	interior	criteria	humiliate
aquarium	various	median	superior	suburbia	abbreviate
gymnasium	mysterious	comedian	exterior	insomnia	appreciate

The accent falls on the syllable before the connective **i**.

3b (top)

1. limousine, gasoline
2. nectarine, tangerine
3. vaccine, medicine
4. feminine, masculine

(middle)

5. margarine, sardines
6. engine, machine
7. magazine, caffeine
8. routine, trampoline

Across: 1. determined 2. submarine 3. discipline 4. adrenaline 5. pristine 6. destined

Down: 1. examine 2. imagine 3. famine

Chapter 11, page 2

4b (top)
1. justify
2. fortify
3. modify
4. typify
5. diversify
6. purify
7. notify
8. testify
9. humidify
10. intensify

(middle)
1. class
2. horror
3. beauty
4. solid
5. person
6. false
7. simple
8. sign
9. syllable
10. example

(bottom)
1. unified, unifying
2. satisfied, satisfying
3. certified, certifying
4. terrified, terrifying
5. specified, specifying
6. gratified, gratifying

5b (top)
1. chər
2. chər
3. shər
4. zhər
5. chər
6. zhər
7. chər
8. zhər
9. chər
10. chər
10. shər
11. zhər
12. chər
13. chər
15. zhər

(middle)
1. yər
2. zhər
3. yər
4. yər
5. jər

6b box

double cons.		two cons.	r.c.	diphthong/digraph
cottage	villages	advantage	storage	sausages
luggage	message	salvaged	coverage	footage
cabbage	rummage	percentage	average	
			discouraged	

Exceptions: damage, manage, savage

6c
1. damage, salvaged, coverage
2. sausages, cabbage
3. message, luggage
4. percentage, discouraged
5. advantage
6. shortage, villages
7. rummage, storage
8. seepage, drainage

(bottom)
1. entourage
2. garage
3. camouflage
4. corsage

6d (top)
1. fa mous
2. se ri ous
3. nerv ous
4. slan der ous
5. cour te ous
6. en vi ous
7. fu ri ous
8. poi son ous
9. con tin u ous

1. nur ture
2. cul ture
3. sig na ture
4. per jure
5. treas ure
6. ag ri cul ture*
7. de par ture
8. dis clo sure
9. re cap ture

1. hos tage
2. bro ker age
3. lan guage
4. foot age
5. pil-grim-age
6. rough age
7. bag gage
8. her i tage
9. hem or rhage

The accent falls on the first syllable. If the first syllable is a prefix, the accent falls on the root word. *ag'ricul'ture has a secondary accent.

1. pro cure
2. ob scure
3. se cure
4. in sure
5. en dure
6. bro chure (bro shoor)
7. ma ture

The accent falls on the second syllable

1. clar i fy'
2. sat is fy'
3. mag ni fy'
4. u ni fy'
5. tes ti fy'
6. am pli fy'
7. in ten si fy'
8. ex em pli fy'

The primary accent is on the first syllable. If the first syllable is a prefix, the accent falls on the root word. The secondary accent is on the suffix –fy'.

Chapter 11, page 3

Students must circle the vowel+r in r-controlled syllables. The answer key shows them in red.

7b (top)   in any order: unbreakable, undeniable, unusable, unreliable, disposable, disagreeable, immovable, inexcusable

(middle) in any order: indigestible, inflexible, irresponsible, irresistible

(bottom)
1. digest	4. dispense	7. reverse/verse	10. permit
2. afford/ford	5. control	8. deduct/duct	11. flame
3. forgive/give	6. redeem/deem	9. destroy	12. divide

7d Across:
		Down:	
1. avoidable	5. portable	1. available	5. convertible
2. noticeable	6. terrible	2. impossible	6. sensible
3. reversible	7. adorable	3. enjoyable	7. treatable
4. incapable	8. eligible	4. achievable	8. edible

8b (top)   The connectives ti and ci say sh. The suffixes –tion and –cian say shən.
1. lō-cō-mō-tion op-op-op-s
2. for-mā-tion rc-op-s
3. mū-sĭ-cian op-ŏp-s
4. dis-crĕ-tion pref-ŏp-s
5. con-ver-sā-tion pref-rc-op-s
6. rĕv-ō-lū-tion cl-op-op-s
7. pŏl-ĭ-tĭ-cian cl-ŏp-ŏp-s
8. e-lĕc-trĭ-cian pref/op-cl-ŏp-s
9. com-plē-tion pref-op-s
10. in-stĭ-tū-tion pref-ŏp-op-s

(middle)   1. a, o, u   2. i, short   3. a person who performs a job/profession   4. i   5. e

1. inject	6. correct	The **t** in 1, 6, and 9 comes from the verb
2. educate	7. admire	or the root.
3. invite	8. irritate	The **at** in 2, 8, and 10 comes from the verb
4. define	9. reflect	ending **ate**.
5. expire	10. graduate	

9b (top)   The suffix –sion usually says zhən, but sometimes also shən.

1. reaction	6. infection	
2. division	7. vacation	These word endings go to **–tion**: ct, ate
3. operation	8. persuasion	There is a vowel before –sion=zhən.
4. decision	9. graduation	
5. television	10. direction	

(bottom)
1. suspend	5. comprehend	It follows **n** and **l**.
2. extend	6. expel	
3. expand	7. compel	
4. apprehend	8. repel	

10b (top)   The suffix s-sion is pronounced shən. The suffixes –tion, –cian, and sometimes –sion also say shən.

7. transmission	11. discussion	When a verb ends with **mit, ss, cede,** and
8. submission	12. depression	**ceed**, the noun goes to s-sion.
9. omission	13. confession	The vowel changes from long **e** to short **e**.
10. expression		

(bottom) 3. procession 4. concession 5. secession 6. intercession

Chapter 11, page 4

10d (top)   The suffix –ous says əs. They say sh.

(middle)
1. gracious, delicious, nutritious
2. obnoxious and rambunctious
3. predacious and ferocious
4. cautious, infectious
5. suspicious, fictitious
6. superstitious

(bottom)
1. spacious
2. precious
3. cautious
4. ambitious
5. repetitious
6. delicious

The syllable directly before **ci** and **ti** is accented.

10e

vocation	animation	eligible	vulnerable
aggression	decoration	charitable	profitable
graduation	configuration	seasonable	damageable
possession	conversation	manageable	perishable
legislation	explosion	measurable	applicable

These five suffixes follow the rule: the syllable right before the suffix is accented: –ic, –tion, –cian, –sion, s-sion. Otherwise, the first syllable is accented. If there is a prefix the root is accented.

12
1. făn-tăs-tic cl-cl-t+s
2. en-ter-tāin-ment pref-rc-vv-s
3. gĕn-er-ous cl-rc-s
4. ex-cur-sion pref-rc-s
5. con-cĕn-trā-tion pref-cl-op-s
6. in-dĭs-pĕn-sable pref-pref-cl-s+s
7. de-ter-mine pref-rc-s
8. voy-age d-s
9. or-thō-don-tist rc-op-cl-t+s
10. de-par-ture pref-rc-s
11. dis-clō-sure pref-op-s
12. au-tō-măt-ic d-op-cl-s
13. pro-fĕs-sion pref-cl-s
14. mu-sĭ-cian op-ŏp-s

(bottom)
1. terrific
2. conclusion
3. tremendous
4. reversible
5. refreshment
6. storage
7. incredible
8. qualify
9. measure
10. anthropologist
11. delicious
12. identify
13. structure
14. permission
15. imagine

13 (top)

1. equalize, equalizer
2. organize, organizer
3. energize, energizer
4. vaporize, vaporizer
5. moisture, moisturizer
6. pressure, pressurizing

1. classify, classification
2. notify, notification
3. falsify, falsification
4. justify, justification
5. purify, purification
6. fortify, fortification

1. package, packaging
2. envious, enviously
3. pleasure, pleasurable
4. profitable, profitably
5. remarkable, remarkably
6. advantage, advantageous

The first syllable is accented in words with these suffixes: –able, –ible, –age, –er, –fy, –ify, –ing, –ize, –ly, –sure, –ture. If the word has a prefix, the accent is on the root word, usually the second syllable. The syllable before –tion and i=ē is accented, (also **ti**, **si** and **ci**, not covered in this lesson).

Chapter 11, page 5

14a (top) Since the following words are very challenging, be somewhat lenient in correcting the syllabication. What's important is that students can pronounce the words correctly.

1. en-gāgé-ment   pref-vce-s
2. or-gan-ic   rc-cl-s
3. těch-nĭ-cian   cl-ŏp-s
4. sī-mŭl-tā-nē-ous-ly   op-cl-op-op-s-s
5. non-re-new-able   pref-pref-d-s
6. em-běz-zlé-ment   pref-cl-cle-s
7. im-prěs-sion-able   pref-cl-s-s
8. con-scious-ly   pref-sci+s-s
9. re-per-cŭs-sion   pref-rc-cl-s
10. scī-ĕn-tist   op-cl-t+s

14 a, cont'd.   Across: 1. extreme   Down: 1. deny
2. favor   2. therapy
3. range   3. serve
4. satisfy   4. form

15b

	root word	prefix	suffix	suffix
1. deductible	duct	de	ible	
2. unemployment	employ (ploy)	un, (em)	ment	
3. nectarine	nectar		ine	
4. expressionless	express/press (ex)		sion	less
5. noninfectious	infect	non	tious	
6. indefensible	defense	in	ible	
7. allergic	allergy		ic	
8. objectionable	object		tion	able
9. laboriously	labor		ious	ly
10. perfectionist	perfect		tion	ist
11. ungraciously	grace	un	cious	ly
12. disclosure	close	dis	sure	
13. artistic	art		ist	ic
14. postage	post			age
15. nonpoisonous	poison	non	ous	
16. disagreement	agree	dis	ment	
17. unspeakably	speak	un	able	ly
18. contemptuously	tempt	con	tuous	ly

Grade somewhat flexibly. Give credit if students show thoughtful answers.

16 Comprehension Questions

1. The trekkers decided to visit Nepal over winter vacation because they wanted to avoid the monsoon rains.
2. It was quiet in Lukla because there are now roads, therefore, there was no traffic noise of any kind.
3. The symptoms of altitude sickness are: headache, nausea, racing pulse/pounding heart.
4. The trekkers learned about Nepalese culture, religion, and geography.
5. Nuru's friends and relatives invited the trekkers to spend the night.
6. The trekkers reached an altitude of 18,450 ft (5623 meters).
7. The trekkers shared their culture with the Nepalese at Christmas.
8. The trekkers felt enriched by the beauty of Nepal and the new experiences they had. They also missed the company of their new friends.

Chapter 12

1b (top)
1. personal
2. original
3. proposal
4. arrival
5. seasonal
6. signal
7. natural
8. denial
9. marginal
10. colonial
11. global
12. memorial
13. approval
14. cultural
15. rehearsal
16. optional

(bottom)
1. clerical
2. emotional
3. mythical
4. structural
5. national
6. natural
7. radical
8. fictional
9. agricultural
10. classical

1c (top)
1. initials
2. impartial
3. special
4. official
5. financial
6. potential
7. facial
8. social
9. crucial

The combinations **ti** and **ci** say **sh**.

(bottom)
1. mūchooəl
2. vĭshooəl
3. ĭndĭvĭjooəl
4. spĭrĭchooəllē
5. ŭnūshooəl
6. ăcchooəlly
7. grăjooəlly
8. făcchooəl
9. həbĭchooəl

Grade 1-9 flexibly. Also accept chū for choo.
The **i** is short when it precedes these phonograms.
The accent is on the syllable right before **ci** and **ti**.

2b (top)
1. active
2. effective
3. secretive
4. expensive
5. objective
6. attractive
7. creative
8. assertive

(middle)
1. explode
2. include
3. defend
4. corrode
5. divide
6. decide
7. offend
8. conclude

The letter **s** changes to **d** or **de** in root word.

(bottom) For the last column, accept –ible or –able.
1. detect, detection, detectable
2. digest, digestion, digestible
3. collect, collection, collectable
4. divide, division, divisible
5. expand, expansion, expandable
6. prevent, prevention, preventable

The word **passage** can attach all of the suffixes.

3b
1. quantity
2. equity
3. majority
4. identity
5. security
6. publicity
7. Opportunity
8. popularity
9. Familiarity
10. formality
11. Necessity
12. maternity
13. eternity
14. immunity
15. curiosity
16. density

The syllable right before –ity is accented.

3d (top)

	Root Word	Suffix	Suffix		Root Word	Suffix	Suffix
1.	form	al	ity	7.	person	al	ity
2.	act	ive	ities	8.	create	ive	ity
3.	norm	al	ity	9.	music	al	ity
4.	common	al	ity	10.	exclude	ive	ity
5.	impulse	ive	ity	11.	object	ive	ity
6.	origin	al	ity	12.	nation	al	ities

The plural is –ities. The accent falls on the syllable directly before –ity.

(bottom) critical, mentality, captivity, medical, sensitivity
festivity, vertical, generality, classical, passivity

3f (middle)
1. capability
2. feasibility
3. plausibility
4. availability
5. eligibility
6. legibility
7. livability
8. portability
9. reliability
10. vulnerability

(bottom)
1. social
2. employ
3. sense
4. vary
5. admit
6. deduct
7. apply
8. irritate

The accent shifts from the first syllable to **bil** in –ability or ibility –.

410

Chapter 12, page 2

4b (top)   ĕrē: January   secondary   ərē: salary   elementary
          sanctuary stationary   glossary anniversary
          dictionary   boundary

    1. or din **ary** ĕrē   5. **nec** es **sary** ĕrē   9. in **fir** mary ərē
    2. **pri** mary ərē   6. **mo** men **tary** ĕrē   10. doc u **men** tary ərē
    3. **sug** ary ərē   7. **bur** glary ərē   11. **vol** un tary ĕrē
    4. **mil** i **tary** ĕrē   8. **tem** po **rary** ĕrē   12. **budg** et **ary** ĕrē.

With the ĕrē ending, the primary accent is on the first syllable; the secondary accent is on ĕrē.
Across: 1. sugar 2. document 3. bound 4. second **Down**: 1. station 2. budget 3. moment

5b (top)
1. ərē   5. orē   9. orē   13. orē
2. orē   6. orē   10. ərē   14. ərē
3. ərē   7. ərē   11. ərē   15. orē
4. ərē   8. orē   12. orē   16. ərē

5b continued: The suffix –ory has a secondary accent when it says orē.

    1. man da tory (ə)   4. pred a tory (ə)   7. ex plor a tory, explore (ə)
    2. cir cu la tory, circulate (ə)   5. au di tory (ə)   8. mi gra tory, migrate (ə)
    3. ac cu sa tory, accuse (ə)   6. de rog a tory (ə)   9. ex plan a tory, explain (ə)

(bottom) The unscrambled word says **directory**.

6c (chart)
1. persistent persistence   6. existent existence
2. dependent dependence   7. recurrent recurrence
3. excellent excellence   8. resident residence
4. different difference   9. indulgent indulgence
5. insistent insistence   10. divergent divergence

(middle)
1. occurrence – incident   5. transparent – translucent
2. evident – apparent   6. equivalent – identical
3. proficient – competent   7. belligerence – hostility
4. recurrent – frequent   8. lenient – indulgent

(bottom)
1. ascent – descent   3. disappearance – appearance
2. dependence, independence   4. presence – absence

7b (top) 1. private 2. intricate 3. accurate 4. adequate 5. literate 6. delicate
All of the adjectives ended with the suffix **–ate**. The letters **te** were dropped.

(middle)
1. intimacy   4. obstinacy   (middle) 1. agency   5. confidence
2. piracy   5. candidacy   2. turbulence   6. independence
3. advocacy   6. democracy   3. decency   7. nonviolence
    4. insistence   8. currency

(bottom)
1. emergent, emergency   4. resident, residency
2. absorbent, absorbency   5. president, presidency
3. urgent, urgency   6. solvent, solvency

7c   The vowel **i** says the short **i** sound before **ci**, **ti**, and **si**.
    The accent falls on the syllable directly before **ci**, **ti**, and **si**.
    The two ways of spelling shənt are **tient** and **cient**. (Also give credit for **sient**.)

Chapter 12, page 3

R-controlled syllables are highlighted in red on the answer key; students will circle the vowel + r on their worksheets.

7c, continued: The two ways of spelling shəns are **cience** and **tience**, The suffix **ciency** says shənsē.

8c (top)   The suffixes –ent and –ence have the same pronunciation as –ant and –ance.
  1. ŏc-cū-pant   cl-op-p+s
  2. ăm-bū-lance cl-op-l+s
  3. de-fĕn-dant pref-cl-d+s
  4. ex-or-bĭ-tant cl-rc-ŏp-t+s
  5. tŏl-er-ance cl-rc-s
  6. in-hăb-ĭ-tant pref-cl-ŏp-tant
  7. en-dū-rance pref-op-r+s
  8. im-por-tance pref-rc-t+s
  9. de-scĕn-dant pref-cl-d+s
  10. ăp-pēar-ance cl-vv-s

8c (bottom)
  1. rādiant   4. vāliant   7. ingrēdient   10. expērience
  2. vāriant   5. nūtrient   8. ōriental   11. obēdient
  3. vāriance   6. recīpient 9. lēnient   12. obēdience

8d (top) 1. attendant, attendance   2. defiant, defiance 3. informant, information
  4. expectant, expectancy, expectation
  5. resistant, resistance 6. reliant, reliance 7. hydrant, hydration
  8. occupant, occupancy, occupation
  9. vacant, vacancy, vacation   10. consultant, consultation
  11. hesitant, hesitancy, hesitation 12. applicant, application

8d (bottom) 1. relevance   2. excellency   3. competence   4. adolescence
  5. negligence   6. significance

8e (top)
  1. flore(s)cent   5. deter(j)gent   9. signifi(g)(k)(s)cance 13. re(k)(s)cent
  2. va(k)can(s)cy 6. a(ks)ccent   10. a(ks)ceptan(s)ce   14. magnifi(g)(s)(s)cence
  3. appli(k)cant   7. ur(j)gen(s)cy 11. adoles(s)cent   15. reminis(ks)(s)cent
  4. negli(g)(j)gent 8. inno(s)(s)cence 12. extrava(g)gant   16. a(ks)(s)cceptance

Use –ant/–ance/–ancy before hard **g** and **c**. Use –ent/–ence/–ency before soft **g** and **c**.
Across: 1. detergent 2. applicant 3. innocence 4. recent 5. adolescent
Down: 1. magnificence 2. vacancy 3. significance 4. urgency 5. accent

9.   A) 1. **stu** dent   2. **dom** i nant   3. **ev** id ence   4. **am** bul ance   5. **fre** quen cy
Accent the first syllable in words with the suffixes –ent/–ence/–ency and –ant/–ance/–ancy.
B) 1. de **ter** gent   2. in **tol** er ant   3. de **fi** ance   4. in **sis** tence   5. con **sis** ten cy
If there is a prefix, accent the second syllable or the root word.
C) 1. **gen** er al   2. **dig** i tal   3. **cap** i tal   4. **hos** pi tal   5. **per** son al
Accent the first syllable in words with the suffix –al.
D) 1. non **ver** bal   2. re **ver** sal   3. dis **loy** al   4. re **fer** ral   5. ap **prov** al
If there is a prefix, accent the second syllable or the root word.
E) 1. **se** cre tive   2. **rel** a tive   3. **neg** a tive   4. **pos** i tive   5. **dec** o ra tive
Accent the first syllable in words with the suffix –ive.
F) 1. pro **tec** tive   2. dis **rup** tive   3. con **clu** sive   4. im **press** ive   5. pre **dic** tive
If there is a prefix, accent the second syllable or the root word.

Chapter 12, page 4
Students will circle r-controlled vowels; the answer key will show them in red.

9. F) 1. pro tec tive   2. dis rup tive   3. con clu sive   4. im press ive   5. pre dic tive
    If there is a prefix, accent the second syllable or the root word.

11a (top) 1. dis-crĕp-ancy pref-cl+s   5. fī-năn-cial op-cl-ci+s
           2. cor-rĕs-pŏn-dence pref-cl-cl-d+s 6. dis-crē-tion-ary pref-ŏp-s-s
           3. ăd-vī-sory cl-op-s+s   7. fēa-sibility vv-s+s
           4. sŭb-ver-sive cl-rc-s+s   8. bĕl-lĭg-er-ent cl-cl-rc-s
   Across: 1. ignorance 2. temporary 3. universal 4. dependent 5. voluntary
   Down: 1. secretive 2. formality 3. reference

12a (top) 1. sign   6. deceive   11. clear
           2. prefer   7. recognize   12. sufficient or suffice
           3. horizon   8. nation   13. product or produce
           4. vision   9. circle   14. repeat
           5. receive   10. please   15. comprehend
   Unscrambling 1. salary 2. president 3. activity

13 (top) Words 1-12 are difficult, please grade leniently.
           1. sū-per-fĭ-cial op-rc-ŏp-ci+s   6. au-thĕn-tic d-cl-t+s
           2. sĭm-plĭs-tic cl-cl-t+s   7. au-thĕn-tic-ity d-cl-cl-s
           3. sĭm-plĭc-ity cl-cl-s   8. sănc-tū-ary cl-op-s
           4. con-fĭ-dĕn-tial pref-ŏp-cl-ti+s   9. că-sū-al-ly ŏp-op-s-s
              also give cr: cŏn-fĭd-ĕn-tial   10. sŭb-stăn-tial-ly cl-cl-ti+s-s
           5. ē-vĕn-tū-al-ly op-cl-op-s-s

   (bottom) 1. cavity   6. definition   11. residency   16. typical
            2. security   7. official   12. destructive 17. extensive
            3. sanity   8. publicity   13. description 18. electricity
            4. gravity   9. toxicity   14. admission   19. vacancy
            5. clarity   10. variability 15. categorize   20. explosive

14

	root word	prefix	suffix	suffix		root word	prefix	suffix	suffix
1.	pulse	im	ive	ity	9.	expense	in	ive	ly
2.	odor	de	ant		10.	suit	un	ibility	
3.	respond	un	ive	ness	11.	product	non	ive	
4.	appear	dis	ance		12.	depend	in	ent	ly
5.	rely	un	ability		13.	avail	un	ibility	
6.	serve	con	ancy		14.	person		al	ity
7.	accurate	in	cy		15.	respond	ir	ibility	
8.	observe	non	ant						

15. 1. The group had to descend before nightfall because Herb dropped his pack and had no survival gear.
    2. Cecil-Anne fell because a foothold broke off.
    3. Cecil-Anne stayed on top of Mt. Whitney because her foot was broken and she couldn't walk.
    4. She wrapped John's down jacket around her legs and did arm exercises.
    5. The mysterious person was a ranger.
    6. The ranger had brought a sleeping bag for Cecil-Anne and made her tea and soup.
    7. A helicopter came to rescue Cecil-Anne.

Chapter 13

1   Students will circle the prefixes and suffixes; they are highlighted on the answer key.

	root words		root words
1. prehistoric	history	9. impulsive	pulse
2. unusable	use	10. misgivings	give
3. mistaken	take	11. contributor	tribute
4. disagreement	agree	12. department	part
5. unnoticeable	notice	13. irresponsible	response
6. indifferent	differ	14. nonexistent	exist
7. replaceable	place		
8. reaction	act		

2   Do not grade students' guesses, but discuss them in a supportive format.

	root words	definition		root words	def.
1. nonfat	fat	not	10. unfocused	focus	not
2. unsafe	safe	not	11. nonfiction	fiction	not
3. disprove	prove	not, opposite	12. recapture	capture	again
4. resupply	supply	again	13. dissolve	solve	not, opposite
5. disorder	order	not, opposite	14. reorder	order	again
6. unhealty	health	not	15. unfinished	finish	not
7. displease	please	not, opposite	16. disbelieve	believe	not, opposite
8. replacement,	place	again	17. nonstandard	standard	not
9. nondairy	dairy	not			

3a   Responses will vary. For your convenience, possible word choices are listed in Note to Educator. See worksheets for definitions.

3b
1. antiaircraft
2. deodorant
3. midday
4. predict
5. misbehave
6. supervisor
7. translate
8. proceed
9. precede
10. misplace
11. counterfeit
12. devalue
13. evacuate
14. supertanker
15. antibiotic
16. propeller
17. transmission
18. extreme

3c   **Across**
1. midtown
2. prefabricate
3. transatlantic
4. antifreeze
5. mistreatment
6. supersonic
7. exporter

Down:
1. mistrust
2. progress
3. counteract
4. transcript
5. deleted
6. defender
7. excommunicate

4b top
1. bilingual
2. century
3. multinational
4. posterity
5. trilingual
6. semiweekly
7. monotheism
8. unicorn
9. malicious
10. submerge
11. quarters

bottom:
Unscrambling puzzles:
postpone
bifocals

4c top
1. submarine
2. multiplication
3. triangle
4. triennial
4. semicircle
5. centennial/triennial
6. university
7. malfunction
8. quadrangle

middle:
1. tricycle
2. bicycle
3. unicycle
4. multipurpose
5. postoperative
6. subway
7. bicentennial
8. semimonthly
9. malnourished
10. monotonous
11. quadruple

414

Chapter 13, page 2

4d suc–, suf–, sug–, sup–, sus–   Dictionary words will vary.

5b top
1. imperfect
2. invisible
3. irresistible
4. illiterate
5. injection
6. indigestion
7. impolite
8. illegible
9. irregular
10. invalid
11. imbalance
12. illegal
13. irreplaceable
14. immature
15. indirect

1. corruption
2. conquest
3. compromise
4. collision
5. consider
6. collect
7. combine
8. cooperate
9. contact
10. correlation
11. committee
12. correspondence
13. coincide
14. coeducation
15. continue

1. We use **il–** and **col–** in front **l**.
2. We use **im–** and **com–** in front **m**, **b**, and **p**.
3. We use **ir–** and **cor–** in front of **r**.
We use **in–** and **con–** in front of all the other letters.

bottom:
1. perception/percussion
2. television
3. interception
4. biography
5. autobiography
6. around
7. forecast
8. permission
9. intermission
10. biology
11. telegraph
12. forefathers

5c top
1. foreshadows
2. illegal
3. invisible
4. biopsy
5. impatient
6. automated
7. interrupt, conversation
8. along
9. invitations

(bottom)
1. telegram
2. forehead
3. contempt
4. indivisible

1. perfume
2. interact
3. compassion
4. automobile
5. biodegradable

5d top: **suc–, suf–, sug–, sup–, sus–**   middle: words will vary.

5d **Across:**
1. telescope
2. corporation
3. constitution
4. conclude
5. perfect
6. incredible
7. permit
8. interstate
9. televise

Down:
1. intercept
2. communicate
3. coincidence
4. combination
5. foresight
6. asleep
7. forewarn
8. biographer

6b An absorbed prefix matches its last letter to the first letter of the root word or puts in a letter that sounds better with the first letter of the root word.
ad–: ac–, ap–   **en–: em–**   **ob–: op–**   **syn–: sym–**

1. appoint
2. advance
3. appraise
4. accompany
5. adjust
6. accredit
7. approve
8. account
9. oppose
10. obnoxious
11. objection
12. oppress
13. obstacle
14. obligation
15. opposite
16. observe
17. symptom
18. synchronize
19. synonym
20. symbol
21. sympathy
22. syndrome
23. symphony
24. synthetic

Chapter 13, page 3

6b bottom:
    emblem   empower
    embrace   empathy
    abbreviate   abrasion
    absent   abolish
    enlist   enroll
    engrave   envelope

6c The two variants of **ob–** are **oc–of–**.

1. offense
2. enforcement
3. absent
4. Opposites
5. admiration
6. enchilada
7. Obstruction
8. enemies
9. emotion
10. Appearances
11. Absolute
12. emperor
13. accident
14. offer
15. symptom

6d top The other five absorbed prefixes of **ad–** are **af–**, **ag–**, **al–**, **an–**, **ar–**, **as–**, and **at–**.

middle: words will vary.

We use **em–** in front of the letters **b** and **p**.

Two other absorbed prefixes of **ob–** are **oc–** and **of–**. We use them before root words that start with **c** and **f**.

416

Chapter 14

1b
1. subscriber
2. nondescript
3. prescription
4. Scriptures/scriptures
5. inscribed
6. descriptive
7. postscript
8. conscription
9. transcript
10. scribbled

The roots **script** or **scribe** means *to write* or *writing*.

2b
1. expression
2. impressionable
3. oppressive
4. impression
5. pressed
6. express
7. depressing
8. pressure
9. suppress
10. irrepressible
11. compress

impress: impressive, impression, unimpressed, impressionable,
oppress: oppression, oppressive   express: expression, unexpressed, expressive
The root **press** means *to press*.

3 Root + suffix: portion, portable, porter, portly
Prefix + root: report, comport, export, support, import, deport
Prefix+root+suffix: proportion, reporter, reportable, comportment, exportable, exporter, exportation, supportable, supporter, supportive, important, importable, importer, importation, importance, deportable, deportation,
Prefix+root+suffix+suffix: proportionate, supportively, importantly
Prefix+prefix+root+suffix: unimportant, unimportance, unsupportive, unsupportable

The root **port** means *to carry*.

4b
1. formality
2. nonconformist
3. misinformation
4. informal
5. performance
6. formation
7. uninformed
8. transformation

perform: performance, performed
conform: conformist, nonconformist
inform: informal, uninformed, misinformed, misinformation

The root word **form** means **to form**, or **to shape**, also **a shape**.

5b
1. structure
2. substructure
3. infrastructure
4. construct
5. construction
6. reconstruction
7. reconstructive
8. instruct
9. instructor
10. destruction
11. indestructible
12. obstruct
13. instrument

The root **struc(t)** means **to pile up** or **to build**.

6b The root **spect** or **spec** means **to see** or **to look at**.

Across:
1. perspective
2. unsuspecting
3. aspect
4. spectacle
5. inspector
6. spectator
7. introspection

Down:
1. disrespectful
2. retrospect
3. spectacular
4. suspect
5. inspection
6. respect
7. prospective

7b
1. dictatorship
2. predictions
3. valedictorian
4. contradictory
5. indicator
6. vindication
7. addiction
8. indictment
9. dictates
10. predictable

The root **dict** means **to say**.
dictate: dictation, dictates, dictator, dictatorship
predict: prediction, predictable, unpredictable
indicate: indicator, indication

Chapter 14, page 2

8b (top)
	(middle)	(verbs)
1. invisible 5. improvised	1. advisor 5. vision	1. provide
2. visitor 6. provider	2. revised 6. visualize	2. revise
3. revised 7. advisability	3. visor 7. vista	3. supervise
4. advisor 8. visibility	4. evidence 8. supervisor	4. visualize

The root **videre** means **to see**.

(bottom)
1. revised   3. visible
2. invisible   4. visibility

9b
1. conductor   6. reproducible   11. productive
2. introduction   7. aqueduct   The roots **duct** and **duce** mean **to lead**.
3. deduct   8. conduction   (bottom) introduce, deduce, produce, reduce
4. reproduction   9. produce   ~~abduction~~, deduction, introduction, production,
5. producer   10. abduction   reduction

10c **Across:** 1. establish   6. maintenance   **Down:** 1. pertaining   6. attain
           2. persistence 7. exist   2. irresistible 7. substitute
           3. maintained   8. detention   3. container
           4. station   9. subsistence   4. resistant
           5. obtainable   10. assistance   5. insistent

11   prefix + root: inject, subject, object, eject, project, interject, reject
     prefix + root + suffix: (grade flexibly because this is difficult)
        injection, injectable, subjective, objection, objector, objective, ejection, adjective, projection
             projector, projective, interjection, rejection
     prefix + root + suffix + suffix: subjectively, objectively, objectionable
     The root **ject** means **to throw**.

12b
1. attraction   7. retraction   The root **tract** means **to pull**.
2. extract   8. abstract   1. retract: retractable, retraction
3. attract   9. distracts   2. attract: attractive, attraction
4. tractor   10. contractual   3. contract: contractual, contractor
5. subtract   11. distraction   4. distract: distraction, distractible, distracts
6. contract   12. detract

13b
1. inconvenient   5. unconventional   (bottom) 1. inconvenient/inconvenience
2. adventure   6. solvent   2. reconvene   6. convention/event
3. eventful   7. adventurous   3. eventually   7. avenue
4. nonintervention 8. vengeful   4. avenge   8. invent
                                                5. prevent   9. souvenir
                                                                10. event/convention

The root **ven(t)** means **to come**.
(bottom) 1. reconvene 2. nonintervention

14b
1. rupture   5. disruption   9. interrupt   The root **rupt**
2. erupt   6. disruptive   10. corrupt   means **to break**.
3. eruption   7. bankrupt   11. incorruptible
4. disrupt   8. bankruptcy   12. abruptly

15b
1. audit   6. applaud   11. telephone   16. auditorium
2. symphony   7. homophone   12. auditory   17. saxophone
3. audience   8. defraud   13. audible   18. audition
4. earphones   9. megaphone   14. headphones   19. audiologist
5. inaudible 10. audio-visual 15. phoneme   20. phonetic

Chapter 14, page 3

15b The roots **aud(i)** and **audio** mean **to hear**.
      The roots **phon(e)** and **phono** mean **sound**.

1. sym' pho ny
2. au' di tor
3. phon'ics
4. in au'di ble
5. au di' tion
6. pho net' ic

16b **Across:**
1. denominator
2. phenomenon
3. misnomer
4. photograph
5. mnemonic
6. telephoto
7. anonymous
8. synonym

Down:
1. photographer
2. nominate
3. nominee
4. photocopy
5. antonym

The roots **nom** and **nym** mean **name** or **word**. The root **photo** means **light**.

17b Prefix + root: autograph, telegraph, telegram, digraph, diagram, monogram, photograph

Prefix + root + suffix: biography, biographer, biographic, telegraphic, geography, geographer, geographic, topography, topographer, topographic photography, photographer, photographic

Prefix + root + suffix + suffix: biographical, geographical, topographical
Prefix + prefix + root + suffix: autobiography, autobiographic,
Prefix + prefix + root + suffix + suffix: autobiographical

The root **graph** means **to write** or **written**. The language of origin is Greek
The root **gram** means **written thing** or **writing**. The language of origin is Greek

18b The root is **chron**. It means **time**. The god Chronus is the god of Time.
The word **synchronize** means to equalize time as for example set your watches to the same time.
The root has two forms: **metr** and **meter**. It means **to measure**, or **measure**.
Symmetrical means **the exact same shape**. **Asymmetrical** means **not having the same shape**.

19b
1. fact or
2. diffi cult
3. diffi culty
4. eff ect
5. eff ective
6. in fec tion
7. in fec tious
8. disin fect ant
9. fact ion
10. fict ion
11. non fict ion
12. fict itious
13. certi fic ate
14. manu fact ure
15. per fect
16. per fec tion
17. satis fact ion
18. satis fact ory
19. off ice
20. off ic er
21. signi fic ant
22. signi fic ance
23. insigni fic ant
24. af fec tion

1. identify
2. clarify
3. specify
4. falsify
5. magnify
6. unify
7. notify
8. satisfy
9. classify
10. simplify
11. modify
12. qualify

The roots mean **to make** or **to do.**
In verbs, the accent falls on the first syllable with a secondary accent on **fy**.
In nouns, the accent falls on the syllable before **tion**.

419

Glossary

assimilated (absorbed) prefix: A prefix that changes its last letter to the first letter of a Latin root: **con–** + lect = collect, **in–** + mature = immature. Additionally, the last letter may change to a letter that sounds better with the Latin root: **con–** + pile = compile, **in–** + possible, impossible.

bound morpheme: A root, prefix, or suffix that doesn't occur by itself. Most Latin base words, called *roots*, are bound morphemes; they require prefixes or suffixes to become meaningful words.
free morpheme: A base word that can occur by itself and make sense without any prefixes or suffixes *(place, read, fly)*. A free morpheme can add prefixes or suffixes *(replacement, reading, flyers)*.

breve: The curved mark above a vowel that indicates a short vowel sound (ă, ĭ, ĕ, ŏ, ŭ).

diacritical marks: Marks above vowels that show how they are pronounced (ă, ĕ, ē, ō, â, ô, û).

digraphs: Two letters that make a single sound, **sh, ch, th, wh, ph, aw, au, oo, ew, ie, ei**.

diphthongs: Glides that begin with one vowel sound and change to another vowel sound within the same syllable. The common diphthongs are: oi, oy, ou, and ow.

etymology: The study of the origins of words and how they have changed over time in pronunciation and meaning.

homograph: Two or more words that have the same spelling but a different meaning and sometimes a different pronunciation *(tear, separate)*.

homophone: (same as homonym) Two or more words that are pronounced alike but have a different spelling and meaning *(road, rode, mail, male)*.

macron: A horizontal line above vowels that indicates a long vowel sound (ā, ē, ī, ō, ū).

morpheme: A morpheme is the smallest unit of meaning. For example, the word **unlikely** consists of a base word, **like**, which is modified by the prefix **un–** and the suffix **–ly**. The word **unlikely** has three morphemes or three units of meaning.

multisensory method: A method of teaching that uses the visual, auditory, kinesthetic, and oral modalities simultaneously.

phoneme: A phoneme is one spoken sound.

phonogram: A phonogram is a written representation of a speech sound.

red word: A word that is difficult to read or spell because it does not fit a regular spelling pattern.

root: A Latin base word that usually requires prefixes or suffixes. See **bound morpheme**.

schwa (ə): An unstressed vowel sound that occurs in unaccented syllables. It sounds like short **u**.

syllabication: The process of separating words into syllables.

syllable: A unit of spoken language that consists of one vowel sound and/or consonants that precede or follow it. Please see Appendix, *Seven Types of Syllables*.

Proposed Spelling Activities

For lists entitled **Reading and Spelling for Mastery**: **Students must read the spelling words <u>every day</u>**, preferably before they start the two activities.

The instructor chooses two appropriate activities for daily practice.

1. Copy the list of words twice (on two separate sheets of paper). One list should be taken home; the other is to stay in the classroom for daily practice. Copy the red words in red pencil or red pen in all activities.

2. Write a sentence with each word. (No more than two words per sentence.) This activity might be assigned as homework.

3. Draw two columns on a sheet of paper and write these categories on top: first column **Short Vowel Sound**, second column **Long Vowel Sound**. Write the words according to the first vowel in the word. (After students have progressed to **R-Controlled Vowels**, add another column. After students have studied diphthongs/vowel digraphs, add another column.)

4. Write words in syllables.

5. Print and outline each word.

6. Word crosses: find words that have one letter in common. First word is written horizontally, second word is written vertically.

7. Write the words once, with vowels in a different color.

8. Write the words in alphabetical order.

9. Write the list once in black, once in blue, and once in green (or whatever colors are available). The red words should be written with a red pen or pencil on all three lists. This activity might be assigned as homework.

10. Write a rhyming word next to each spelling word.

11. Write the root word next to each spelling word and mark the vowels.

12. Read, cover, write, check. Read each word, cover it with one hand, write it, and check it.

13. The teacher selects one or two pages from a textbook. Ask students to copy all of the words that fit the particular pattern they are studying. This could be set up as a contest.

Seven Types of Syllables

Closed Syllable: (cl) 1. Closed syllables have one vowel. 2. The vowel is followed by one or more consonants on the right side. 3. The vowel is short.

    Examples: lock, sled, in, stamps

Vowel-Consonant-e Syllable: (vce) 1. The vowel is followed by a consonant and the letter **e**. 2. The first vowel is long. 3. The **e** is silent.

    Examples: ate, cute, stripe, spoke

Open Syllable: (op) 1. Open syllables have one vowel. 2. The vowel is at the end of the syllable. 3. The vowel is long.

    Examples: me, so, she, I, go

R-Controlled Syllable: (rc) 1. The vowel is followed by the letter **r**. 2. **ar** as in *car*, **or** as in *sport*, **er** as in her, **ir** as in girl, and **ur** as in turn. 3. This pattern is marked by circling the vowel + **r**.

    Examples: start, porch, her, stir, burn

Vowel-Vowel Syllable: (vv) 1. Two vowels are next to each other. 2. The first vowel is long. 3. The second vowel is silent.

    Examples: aim, stream, boat, blue

Consonant-le Syllable: (cle) 1. This syllable occurs at the end of words. 2. One or two consonants precede the letters **le**. 3. The **e** is silent. 4. The consonant-le syllable is divided before the consonant that precedes **le**.

    Examples: able, fiddle, pebble, stifle

Diphthong/Vowel Digraph Syllable: (d) 1. Diphthongs are glides that begin with one vowel sound and change to another vowel sound within the same syllable. 2. The common diphthongs are: oi, oy, ou, and ow. 3. Vowel digraphs are vowel pairs that can't be sounded out; they must be memorized. 4. The common vowel digraphs are: au, aw, oo, ew, eu, ie, ei. They are not marked.

    Examples: spoil, boy, proud, cow, cause, draw, spoon, threw, brief, seize

Syllabication Rules

First Rule of Syllabication
Every syllable must have one vowel sound. A word has the same number of syllables as the number of sounded vowels.

Second Rule of Syllabication
A word that has two consonants between two vowels is divided between the consonants.

Third Rule of Syllabication
A word that has three consonants between two vowels is often divided after the first consonant because the other two may form a blend. When the first syllable ends in a blend or digraph, divide after the second consonant.

Fourth Rule of Syllabication
Divide a vowel-consonant-e syllable after the silent **e**.

Fifth Rule of Syllabication
Divide a compound word between the words that create it.

Sixth Rule of Syllabication
A word that has four consonants between two vowels is often divided after the second consonant. This doesn't always work. Look for beginning or ending consonant blends, digraphs, or clusters. Then decide where to divide.

Seventh Rule of Syllabication:
A word that has one consonant between two vowels is often divided after the first vowel. This means the first syllable is open and the vowel is long. Sometimes, the word is divided after the consonant. This means the first syllable is closed and the vowel is short.

Eighth Rule of Syllabication:
Divide a word after a prefix and before a suffix and keep the base word intact, if possible.

Ninth Rule of Syllabication:
Divide a word that ends in a consonant-le syllable before the consonant that precedes **le**.

Bibliography

American Heritage Dictionary 2000. Houghton Mifflin, Boston, MA.

Bear, D.R., Invernizzi, M., Templeton, S., & Johnston, F. 1995. *Words Their Way: Word Study for Phonics, Vocabulary, and Spelling Instruction.* Prentice Hall, Upper Saddle River, NJ.

Bertelson, P. 1987. *The Onset of Literacy: Cognitive Processes in Reading Acquisition.* MIT Press, Cambridge, MA.

Gillingham, A., & Stillman, B.W. 1997. *The Gillingham Manual: Remedial Training for Students with Specific Disability in Reading, Spelling, and Penmanship.* Educators Publishing Service, Cambridge, MA.

Greene, V.E. & Enfield, M.L. 1984. *Project Read - Reading Guide* (Phase I - Volume 1). Bloomington Public Schools, Bloomington, MN.

Henry, M.K. 2003. *Unlocking Literacy: Effective Decoding & Spelling Instruction.* Paul H. Brookes Publishing Company, Baltimore, MD.

Johnson, K., & Bayrd, P. 2001. *Megawords.* Educators Publishing Service, Cambridge, MA.

Langer, J.A. 2001. Beating the odds: Teaching middle and high school students to read and write well. *American Education Research Journal* 38: 837-880.

Lyon, G.R. 1995. Research initiatives in learning disabilities: contributions from scientists supported by the National Institute of Child Health and Human Development. *Journal of Child Neurology* 10: S120-126.

Lyon, G.R. 1999. In celebration of science in the study of reading development, reading difficulties, and reading instruction: The NICD perspective. *Issues in Education: Contributions From Educational Psychology* 5: 85-115.

Moats, L.C. 2000. *Speech to Print: Language Essentials for Teachers.* Paul H. Brookes Publishing Company, Baltimore, MD.

Money, J., & Schiffman, G. 1967. *The Disabled Reader: Education of the Dyslexic Child.* Johns Hopkins Press, Baltimore, MD.

National Reading Panel. 2000. *Teaching Children to Read: An Evidence-Based Assessment of the Scientific Research Literature on Reading and its Implication for Reading Instruction* (NIH pub. 00-4754). U.S. Government Printing Office, Washington, DC.

Stanback, M. L. 1992. Syllable and rime patterns for teaching reading: Analysis of a frequency-based vocabulary of 17,602 words. *Annals of Dyslexia* 42: 196-221.

Steere, A., Peck, C.Z., & Kahn, L. 1971. *Solving Language Difficulties.* Educators Publishing Service, Cambridge, MA.

Webster' II New Collegiate Dictionary. 1995. Houghton Mifflin, Boston MA.

White, T.G., Sowell, J., & Yanagihara, A. 1989. Teaching elementary students to use word-part clues. *The Reading Teacher* 42: 302-308.

Index

a, vowels, phonograms and sounds,
    a, pronounced ô, 8, 15, 16
    a, short, 8, 12-15, 50
    a_e, 50-51, 53
    ai, ay, 132, 136-138, 146
    au, aw, 175, 186-189
accented and unaccented
    syllables, 217-230
    how to accent words with
        prefixes, 218, 224-227
    how to accent words with
        suffixes, 218, 227
    Webster's accent rule, 218, 230
Anglo-Saxon, free morphemes, 75, 235
Anglo-Saxon suffixes, 235-258, see
    Suffixes
assimilated (absorbed) prefixes, 77
    86-87, 104, 125, 226, 329-331,
    334-352
auditory discrimination exercises, 3
auditory modality, 2, 3

base word, 9, 24, 39, 48, 64, 67, 75, 77,
    78, 85, 86-87, 92, etc.
beginning blends, 13-40
bound morphemes, 75-76, 86, 261, 299
breve, 8

c, soft, 55-56, 201-205, 207, 319
Closed Syllable, 7, 11
code, 3, 10, 40, 47, 66
compound words, 14, 17, 52, 58, 65
consonant digraphs, 18-23
    ch, 18, 21, 23, 213
    ph, 35-36
    sh, 18
    th, 20-21, 23
    wh, 20-21, 23
consonant doubling, 9, 25, 47-48, 68-73,
    93-94, 103, 115-116, 162, 167, 169,
    235-236, 240-241, 250, 265, 278
Consonant-le Syllable, 161-171
consonants, beginning blends, 13-40
consonants c and k, 54, 203
consonants, ending blends, 14-40
consonants, short-vowel signals,
    ck, 26-27, 36, 54

    ff, ll, ss, zz, 25, 27, 36
    tch, 26-27
    dge, 56-57, 211
contractions, 42-43

Decoding Binder, 4, 7, 45
diacritical marks, 8
dictation exercises, 2, 3
dictation lists, 3
digraphs, vowel, 131-160, 175-176
    186-200, see specific vowels
diphthongs, 173-174, 177-185,
    see specific vowels
    see Vowels, diphthongs

e, vowel, phonograms and sounds
    e, short, 9, 24-28
    e_e, 53
    ea, 132, 139-141
    ee, ey, 132, 142-146
    ei, 175, 193, 195-196
    eu, 175, 192
    ew, 175, 192-193
Eighth Rule of Syllabication, 77, 92
ending blends, 14-16

First Rule of Syllabication, 17, 37, 62
Fourth Rule of Syllabication, 46, 50, 52
Fifth Rule of Syllabication, 47, 58, 62
free morpheme, 75-76, 261, 235, 299

g, soft, 56, 201-202, 208-212, 319
Greek combining forms, 353, 356, 357,
    372-375
    chron, chrono, 356, 375
    gram, 356, 374
    graph, 356, 374
    meter, metr, 356-357, 375
    nym, 356, 373
    para, 357
    path, 357
    phil, 357
    phono, 356, 372
    photo, 356, 373
    psych, 357

hard and soft c, 55-56, 201-205, 207, 319

hard and soft g, 56, 201-202, 208-212, 319
high frequency words, 2, 4
history of English language, 239, 259-260
homograph, 5, 7, 45, 46
homonym, 5
homophone, 5, 7, 9. 45

i, vowel, phonograms and sounds
    i, short, 8 17-23, 51-52
    i, long in closed syllables, 9, 22-23
    i_e, 46, 51-52
    ie, 147, 175, 193, 195-196

kinesthetic modality, 3, 4

Latin roots, 75, 86, 87, 353-372, 376
    anni, annu, enni, 357
    aud, audi, audio, 356, 372
    dict, dic, 355, 364
    duct, duc, duce, 355, 366
    fact, fect, fic, 357, 376
    fer, 357
    form, 354, 361
    ject, jec, 355, 368
    mot, mov, mob, 357
    nom, 356, 373
    pend, pens, 357
    port, 354, 360
    press, 354, 359
    rupt, 356, 371
    script, scribe, 354, 358
    sist, stit, sta, 355, 367
    spect, spec, 354, 363
    struct, stru, 354, 362
    tain, ten, 355, 367
    tract, 356, 369
    vent, ven, 356, 370
    vert, vers, 357
    vis, vid, 355, 365
    voc, vok, voke, 357
Latin suffixes, see suffixes, 99, 103,
    123, 260, 261-295, 299-326
long vowels, (vce), 45-66,
    vowel teams, 131-157

macron, 8, 45
modalities, 2, 3
    auditory, 2, 3
    kinesthetic, 2, 3
    oral, 2, 3
    visual, 2, 3
morphemes, 2, 3, 75-76, 86, 235, 261, 299
multisensory approach, 2, 3

Note to Instructor, 1, 7, 45, 75, 101

    131, 161, 173, 201, 217, 235, 261,
    299, 329, 353

o, vowel, phonograms and sounds,
    o, short 29, 58
    o_e, long, 47, 58, 60
    oa, 148-150
    oar, 149
    oe, 148-150
    oi, oy, 174, 177-179, 189
    oo, 175, 190-192
    ou, 174, 180-183, 189
    ow, 174, 180, 184-185, 189
Open Syllable, 75-92
open-syllable prefixes, 77, 85-86

phonograms, 2, 4, 5, 7, 45, 76
plural, –es, 41
plural, –s, 41
prefixes,
    a–, 224, 331, 343-347
    ab–, 331, 348-352
    ad–, (ac–, af–, ag–, al–,
        an–, ap–, ar–, as–, at–),
        331, 348-352
    anti–, 330, 334-337
    auto–, 331, 343-347
    bi–, 330, 338-342
    bio–, 331, 343-347
    cent–, (centi) 330, 338-342
    con–, (co– col–, com–), 87
        (cor– 125), 226, 331, 343-347
    counter–, 330, 334-337
    de–, 85, 224, 330, 334-337
    dis–, 74, 225, 333
    em–, 331, 348-352
    en–, 24, 58, 64, 331, 348-352
    ex–, 24, 86, (e–86), 330, 334-337
    fore–, 331, 343-347
    in–, (il–, im–, ir–), 125, 226,
        331, 343-347
    inter–, 331, 343-347
    mal–, 330, 338-342
    mid–, 330, 334-337
    mis–, 330, 334-337
    mono–, 330, 338-342
    multi–, 330, 338-342
    non–, 74, 225, 333
    ob–, (oc–, of–, op–), 331, 348-352
    per–, 331, 343-347
    post–, 330, 338-342
    pre–, 85, 224, 330, 334-337
    pro–, 86, 224, 330, 334-337
    quadr–, (quar–), 330, 338-342
    re–, 85, 224, 333

semi–, 330, 338-342
sub–, (suc–, suf–, sug–, sup–),
    330, 338-342
super–, 330, 334-337
sym–, 331, 348-352
syn–, 331, 348-352
tele–, 331, 343-347
trans–, 330, 334-337
tri–, 330, 338-342
un–, 74, 225, 333,
uni–, 330, 338-342

R-Controlled Syllable, 101-124
r-controlled vowels:
    ar, 102, 106-108
    âr, 102, 107-108
    er, 102, 103, 114-116
    ir, 102, 112-113
    or, 102, 109-111
    ur, 103, 117-118
    ûr, 103, 110, 120
Reading and Spelling for Mastery, 3-4
red words, 4, 7, 45, 76
Rules of Syllabication
    First Rule, 1, 10, 14, 17, 37, 52 62
    Second Rule, 8, 18, 28, 37, 77, 290, 322
    Third Rule, 10, 33, 37, 77
    Fourth Rule, 46, 50, 62
    Fifth Rule, 47, 58, 62
    Sixth Rule, 47, 65
    Seventh Rule, 76, 80, 83
    Eighth Rule, 77, 92
    Ninth Rule, 161, 164

schwa, 39, 67-68, 71, 87, 98, 221-223, 229
Second Rule of Syllabication, 8, 18
    28, 37, 77, 290, 322
Seventh Rule of Syllabication, 76, 80, 83
short vowels, 7-40, see specific vowels
short vowel signals,
    9, 25, 47-48, 68-73,
    93-94,103, 115-116, 162, 167, 169,
    235-236, 240-241, 250
Sixth Rule of Syllabication, 47, 65
spelling activities, see Appendix
spelling, Reading and Spelling for Mastery,
    4, 8, 9, 10, 15, 23, 27, 31, 36, etc.

suffixes,
    –ability, 301, 310
    –able, 172, 265, 281-283, 288
    –ace, 206
    –age, 210, 265, 278-279, 280
    –al, 127, 299-300, 304-305, 320
    –an, 129, 246-247

–ance, 55, 204-205, 303, 313, 317-320
–ancy, 303, 317-319
–ant, 128, 303, 313, 317-320
–ar, 123, 246-247
–ary, 301, 311, 313
–ate, 98, 302
–cian, 266, 284, 289
–cy, 204, 302, 315-316, 320
–dom, 238, 251
–ed, 47-48, 67-70, 230, 240
–ee, 160
–en, 71, 240 -241
–ence, 55, 204-205, 302, 313-316
–ency, 302, 315-316
–ent, 128, 302, 313-316
–er, 103, 113, 115-116, 240-241
–est, 71, 240-241
–et, 241-242
–fication, 291-292
–ful, 39, 236, 249, 252
–fy, 96, 264, 276
–hood, 237, 250
–ibility, 301, 310
–ible, 172, 265, 281-283, 288
–ic, 262, 269-271
–ice, 206
–ine, 263, 275
–ing, 72-73, 230, 240
–ion, 99-100, 266-267
–ish, 237, 250
–ist, 262, 269-271
–ite, 98
–ity, 300, 306, 308-309
–ive, 160, 300, 306-307, 320
–ize, 159, 291
–less, 39, 236, 249, 252,
–let, 242
–ly, 94, 249-250
–ment, 128, 262, 269-271
–ness, 39, 236, 252
–ology, 210, 323
–on, 129, 246-247
–or, 123, 246-247
–ory, 301, 312, 313
–ous, 263, 272-274, 287
–s, es, 41
–ship, 238, 251
–sion, (ion), 99-100, 266-267,
    282, 285-286, 288
–some, 237, 249-250, 252
–sure, (ure), 264, 277, 280, 282
–tion, (ion), 99-100, 266, 282,
    284-285, 288
–ture, (ure), 126, 264, 277, 280, 282
–ure, 264, 277, 280, 282

-ward, 238, 251
-xion, 267
-y, 93-95, 240-241, 244-245

Third Rule of Syllabication, 33

u, vowel, phonograms and sounds,
    u, short 33-34, 36
    u_e, long, 47, 59-60
    ue, ui 151-152, 192-193

v, ending, 61
visual modality, 2, 3
vowels,
    digraphs, in order of presentation
        ai, ay, 136
        ea, 139-140
        ee, ey, 142
        ay, ey, plural, 146
        ie, 147
        oa, oe, 148
        ue, ui, 151
        au, aw 186-189
        oo, 190-192, 197
        ew, eu, 192-193
        ei, ie, 195-198
    diphthongs,
        oi and oy 177-178, 189
        ou and ow 180-185
    long, (vce), 45-66, see specific vowels
    (open syllable, 75-92,
    r-controlled, 101-124, see r-controlled vowels
    short, 7-40, see specific vowels
Vowel-Consonant-e Syllable 45, 49, 62-66
Vowel-Digraph/Diphthong Syllable, 173-197
vowel-r-e, 119-120
vowel-r-vowel rule, 124
Vowel-Vowel Syllable, 131-158

y in accented syllables, 78, 96
y, in the middle of words, 35, 78, 97
y, sounds of y, 78, 93-97
y, suffix, 78, 93-95

IMAGES OF FRANKSTON &
MORNINGTON PENINSULA

WRITTEN BY
Alexandra Stevens

PHOTOGRAPHED BY
Barry Stevens

WITH AERIALS BY PETER BARKER PHOTOGRAPHY, SKYPICS, MORNINGTON

GIPPSTAR INTERNATIONAL

*We gratefully acknowledge the support of the
following organisations*

Frankston City

Mornington Peninsula Shire Council

Mornington Peninsula Vignerons Association (MPVA)

Lindenderry of Red Hill

Moonah Links

Peter Barker Photography, SKYPICS, Mornington

Peninsula Radio 3RPP

Visitor Publications

Published by
Gippstar International Pty Ltd
PO Box 10 Yallourn North, Victoria 3825
Telephone 03 5167 1110   Mobile 0427 842 316
Email: gippstar@vic.australis.com.au
Orders can be made direct to the publishers

ISBN NO: 0-646-42852-7

Recommended retail price $28.50
(Limited edition hard cover $49.00)

Publisher GippStar International Pty Ltd. and their staff whilst making every effort to ensure accuracy of material gathered and supplied within the publication, excepts no responsibility to the authenticity or accuracy of all material contained within. No claims will be recognised for errors or omissions of material supplied or collected. All material contained within this publication is protected by Australian Copyright laws and cannot be reprinted or reproduced (including photocopying) without the written consent of the publishers.

Frankston
on the bay

Visit **www.frankston.vic.gov.au**
for more information
or call **(03) 9784 1988**

Stay in Frankston and you are within easy reach of Victoria's most popular attractions:
The wineries and coastal national parks of the Mornington Peninsula, the Dandenong ranges and the fairy penguins of Phillip Island.

Frankston offers its visitors:
10km pristine beaches and coastal habitat for boating, sailing and fishing, lush bushlands and walking tracks, gracious historic homes, theatres, conventions and exhibitions, regional shopping centres and restaurants all close at hand.

Accommodation to suit all pockets:
Camping grounds, bed and breakfasts', motels and apartments.

Major events:
From October to April, there are a large range of events to enjoy and experience including the International Guitar Festival, Festival of Lights, Sea Festival Spectacular, Travelling Film Festival, Melbourne Marathon along with a variety of sporting events.

Introduction

Such is the allure of Frankston and the Mornington Peninsula that many visitors come for a day and stay a lifetime, seduced by the region's uncluttered lifestyle. Its residents have the best of both worlds, close enough to metropolitan Melbourne to enjoy the sophistication of the city, and yet still be surrounded by the intrinsic beauty of a region where comfort, peace and repose can be found. The Peninsula is nature's creative water feature in Melbourne's back yard and any visit can be a dashing country escapade, a historical and cultural indoctrination, or a dreamy seashore adventure.

The area stretches over the locations of Frankston City and the Mornington Peninsula Shire, encompassing a province of diverse natural beauty. The boot-shaped promontory is bounded on three sides by water, dividing the magnificence of Port Phillip Bay and Western Port Bay, giving access to Bass Strait and providing 190 kilometres of unspoiled, ultra scenic coastline. The placid jewelled tones of Port Phillip Bay's beaches contrast vividly with the wild surf and rugged coastline of Western Port and the verdant valleys and imposing slopes of the hinterland. It is all readily accessible – travelling from Melbourne, the Nepean Highway, the Moorooduc Highway and the Frankston-Flinders Road, are the escape routes to perfect peace – entering a world that is steeped in Aboriginal folklore, where Victoria's modern history began and much of the Peninsula's pioneer past has been preserved for visitors to explore.

A city, and over forty charming country villages and scintillating modern towns, offer everything that is essential for a break from the reality and stress of our busy, work-weary lives. The region has a recorded history in hospitality, stretching back to its earliest European occupation. The towns and villages draw on this wealth of experience, welcoming visitors with the ambiance of coming home. It draws visitors out of life's normal direction, enriches, rejuvenates and renders the wanderer a bowl of surprises. The complimentary words used to illuminate this region are not just a literary illusion. There is no slogan that can aptly describe the lucent water, unsullied beaches, verdant hinterland and multivious pursuits on, in and off the water that it confers.

What makes the Mornington Peninsula so great? It's a melting pot, with magnificent beaches at the front and back door and a green belt running down its spine. Inhabited by multi award-winning wineries and golf clubs, top-flight galleries and antique shops, magnificent English and Australian gardens, market gardens and farm-gate produce, unique accommodation and world-class restaurants, clubs and pubs.

The region is a breeding ground for art. Many of the country's most talented artists reside here; their work is visible in galleries all over the Peninsula. Vignerons produce an amazing diversity of excellent cool-climate wine that can be sampled from a plethora of cellar doors. In recent years the region's topography has been recognised as perfect for traditional links golf courses. Country clubs, resorts and courses have sprung up, and been so successful in their pursuit of excellence that the Southern Peninsula has become known as the 'Golf Coast', with over half of the area's 20 golf clubs located there. All this, combined with sailing, fishing, swimming, water skiing, scuba diving and surfing from bayside beaches that are a dreamy technicolour panorama of sunsets and seascapes. Adventure and romance is created with dashing horse rides on far-flung beaches, swimming with dolphins and interacting with some of Australia's endangered animals, or 'taking the waters' in the hot springs. All merge to create a superb multi-seasonal holiday destination.

Everything exists in harmony with nature; some of Victoria's most loved National Parks and marine reserves are to be found on the Peninsula. Internationally renowned wetlands and coastal areas provide homes for migratory birds, endangered animals and marine life. This magnificent peninsula was fashioned by nature, largely without the help of man. It has taken many millions of years to create, and is a delicately balanced eco system. So on any visit enjoy, don't destroy, and leave a legacy for those who are to follow.

The elements that make up the Mornington Peninsula are unique and varied. The enjoyment and *joie de vivre* to be found here starts off as a trickle and ends up a flood – unforgettably pleasurable.

You're about to discover what our locals have always known …

… the magnificence of the Mornington Peninsula.

We made that discovery a long time ago. That's why we're committed to keeping it just like it is … for now and for the future.

Mornington Peninsula Shire – caring for the Mornington Peninsula and its diverse communities

Private Bag 1000, Rosebud 3939, Vic
Ph: 1300 850 600 Fax: 03 5986 6696
mornpen.vic.gov.au   custserv@mornpen.vic.gov.au

Besgrove St, Rosebud; Queen St, Mornington;
Marine Pde, Hastings; Edward St, Somerville
Open: 8.30 am – 5.00 pm

MORNINGTON PENINSULA Shire

COMMITTED TO A SUSTAINABLE PENINSULA

Contents

Frankston City — PAGES 9–42

Seaford | Seaford Foreshore Reserve | Seaford Wetlands | Carrum Downs & Skye | Frankston | Frankston Foreshore | Bunarong Park | Beauty Park | The George Pentland Botanic Gardens | Ballam Park & Homestead | Frankston Arts Centre | Frankston Guitar & Music Festival | Monash University Peninsula Campus | Langwarrin | The McClelland Gallery + Sculpture Park | Langwarrin Flora and Fauna Reserve | Dame Elisabeth Murdoch Arboretum | Mulberry Hill | Baxter | Sages Cottage

MORNINGTON PENINSULA

Northern Peninsula — PAGES 43–74

Port Phillip Bay | Mount Eliza | Somerville | Mornington | Mornington Park | Schnapper Point | The Mornington Racecourse | Mornington Peninsula Regional Gallery | Moorooduc | Mornington Railway Preservation Society | Moorooduc Coolstores | Mount Martha | Mt Martha Foreshore Reserve | Briars Park

Western Port Bay — PAGES 75–116

Pearcedale | Moonlit Sanctuary, Pearcedale Conservation Park | Tyabb | Westernport Airfield | Yaringa Marine National Park | Yaringa Marina | Hastings | Bittern | Crib Point | Stony Point | HMAS Cerberus | Somers | Coolart Wetlands and Homestead | Balnarring | Merricks | Merricks Beach | Point Leo | Shoreham Flinders | Cape Schanck | Cape Schanck Lighthouse.

The Hinterland — PAGES 117–136

Tuerong | Red Hill | Red Hill South | Main Ridge | Arthurs Seat State Park | Seawinds

 ### Peninsula Wineries Feature — PAGES 137–192

Southern Peninsula — PAGES 193–240

Safety Beach | Dromana | Heronswood | McCrae | McCrae Homestead | Rosebud | Fingal | Tootgarook | Rye | Blairgowrie | Sorrento | Portsea | The Mornington Peninsula National Park | Gunnamatta Beach | St Andrews Beach | The Park at Point Nepean.

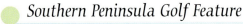 ### Southern Peninsula Golf Feature — PAGES 212–221

Listings — PAGES 242–255
Credits — PAGE 256

Frankston City Listings

SEAFORD: Two Cans Antiques P.14-15/242. Riviera Hotel P.16/242. The Victorian Climbing Centre P.16/242

FRANKSTON: The George Pentland Botanic Gardens P.20/242. Ballam Park.P22-23. Frankston Arts Centre P.22/242. Jenny Pihan, Kananook Creek Boathouse Gallery P22-24/242. Richard Linton Maritime Art P 24/242. Aussie Collections P26. John Crowder & Sons P26. Monash University Peninsula Campus P28-29/242. Daveys Bar & Restaurant P30 /33/36/242. Kananook Creek Boathouse Restaurant P30/33/242. Perovics P30/33. Shakespeares' Bar & Restaurant P30/31/33/242. Siddhartha Indian Restaurant P32/33/242. Via Mare Ristorante P32/33/242. Flanagans at the Pier Hotel P34/35/242. Frankston R.S.L.Club P34/35/242. Ambassador Motel. P36/243. Frankston International Motel P36/243. The Frankston Motel P36/243. Frankston Motor Inn P36/242.

LANGWARRIN: Beratta's Langwarrin Hotel P38/243. McClelland Gallery+Sculpture Park 38-39/243. Mulberry Hil P40-41/243

BAXTER: Sages Cottages 42/243

Frankston Arts Centre

Frankston City opening page: Frankston from the air
Centre-spread background: Sunset over Frankston Pier

FRANKSTON CITY

Frankston City is home to more than 115,000 lucky Australians. The picturesque region covers an area of 130 square kilometres, located on Melbourne's southern doorstep. It shares boundaries with the City of Kingston, the City of Casey, City of Greater Dandenong and Mornington Peninsula Shire. Known for so many years as a suburb of the state capital and the 'gateway to the Mornington Peninsula', the region is finally being recognised for its own potential, embracing and excelling in its role as a stay-put, vibrant holiday destination that has it all. Residents welcome visitors to sample their enviable lifestyle, a mixture of bayside bliss, country casual and city chic.

Frankston City Council is recognised as innovative; it was the first council in Australia to prepare and adopt a local action plan for greenhouse gas reduction, participating in the International Cities for Climate Protection program. It works closely with local community groups to maintain a sustainable environment for the future, providing a clean, green existence for residents.

Healthy activity is encouraged; the City maintains many leisure and recreational facilities. They include the indoor Jubilee Park Aquatic Centre on Hillcrest Road, Frankston, and the outdoor Pines Forest Aquatic Centre on the corner of Forest Drive and Lehmann Crescent, Frankston, open from November to March. The City also maintains the public 18-hole Centenary Park Golf Course on McClelland Drive, which has first-class greens and an up-to-the-minute pro shop.

Nothing has been overlooked in this dynamic region with clubs, pubs, restaurants and hotels meeting a very high standard. Cultural events and annual festivals have become a key element in attracting the limelight from Melbourne, enticing visitors to sample the area's attractions. Put together with wide open parklands and legendary shoreline, the City provides an intriguing mix for the ultimate vacation.

Seaford is a sparkling gem languishing on the bay four kilometres north of Frankston. It has the best of both worlds: a quiet location with close ties to both metropolitan Melbourne and Frankston.

The small town is fringed by five kilometres of idyllic coastline that makes up the eye-catching Seaford Foreshore Reserve. It provides a relaxing atmosphere, a perfect beach with a wide spectacular expanse of golden sand backed by wave-shaped dunes, covered in coastal vegetation. The old wooden pier provides a picture perfect setting for that prolific species – pier fishers. It was built in 1931 as a means of flushing Kananook Creek. A steel pipe 100 centimetres in diameter ran along its side and a 100-horsepower electric pump sucked water from the sea, causing a head of water to build up in the pipe to around 70 centimetres. At low tide the water was released, flushing out the silt that had accumulated at the head of the creek, thus allowing boats to pass through. Pumping was discontinued during WWII and as a result the pipe corroded. It was last used in 1953 and dismantled soon after.

A raised picnic shelter behind the pier opposite the Seaford Life Saving Clubhouse is shaded by slatted wooden umbrellas and overhangs the beach. It creates a unique space to revive the seaside tradition of 'eating fish 'n' chips out of a paper bag'. Of course the repast is accompanied by a cacophony of seagulls as they duck, weave and jostle begging for leftovers.

The **Seaford Foreshore Reserve** is peppered with shady picnic spots and secluded walking tracks. It contains one of the rare areas of pre-European vegetation still visible on the bay, with many significant flora and fauna species, which makes the reserve regionally significant. Informative signposts are interspersed along the tracks, helping wanderers understand more about the surrounding habitat.

The well-known **Seaford Wetlands** is a stunning 303-hectare nature reserve that has earned its place on the Register of the National Estate. The reserve is a vestige of the massive Carrum Carrum Swamp that extended from Mordialloc to Frankston and Dandenong. Work began in the 1870s to drain the region, the Patterson River was created and much of the swampland was turned into rich farmland. Only a few swamp areas still exist the largest being Seaford and Edithvale Wetlands.

Since its inception, the wetlands have been enhanced by the addition of more lagoons and an extensive regeneration programme. The reserve is a work in progress, with plans to revegetate dry areas that are covered in pasture grass. A shared bicycle path and walking track that traverses part of the way around the outer limits of the wetlands will, at a future time, surround the reserve. The track is a favourite route with joggers, walkers and cyclists who enjoy the tranquil outlook over the lagoons. For the more serious ornithologist, there is a raised bird hide available for public use at Seaford Primary School and also a viewing platform in Austin Road.

The wetlands create a sanctuary for multiple bird life, some rare and endangered and some migratory specimens coming from as far afield as Siberia. Over 130 varieties of our feathered friends have been noted reaping the benefit of the refuge the wetlands offer. The vantage points overlooking the lagoons provide good viewing areas, showcasing the more common of the waterfowl, while some of the more timid examples can be heard but not seen, preferring to take shelter in the rushes and reeds around the water.

The woodland contained on the periphery of the reserve holds some significant specimens of ancient river red gums that predate European settlement; some estimated to be 300 years old. Scarring on a few is evidence that their bark was stripped for use by the Bunwurrung people in times long past. The reserve presents visitors with an open and natural setting where nature reigns.

Seaford's beachfront shopping strip runs for approximately a kilometre along the Nepean Highway and is full of surprises.

Above: Seaford Foreshore Reserve   Right: Seaford Jetty

Two Cans Antiques on the southern outskirts of the town has become a celebrated destination for serious collectors and lovers of heirlooms. Its distinctive harlequin logo has become synonymous with quality and style. Upon entering the showrooms, clients are introduced into a world filled with fascinating and beautiful European and English pieces and the occasional Australian gem dating back to the 19th century, all restored with warmth and understanding.

Carole and John Watts bought the established business in 1985 and with patience, perseverance and passion have taken it to new heights. In the early years of the business, the couple along with their baby daughter lived in the residence attached to the former bakery that houses their store, but soon found the business encroaching on their living space.

Today, casual browsers and seasoned searchers wander through room after room bursting with exclusive top-of-the-range antiques and Victorian baubles. The Watts, on occasion, helped by their daughter Kate, now grown up and studying for a Batchelor of Arts in Ballarat, provide a knowledgeable service displaying the antiques in an authentic setting, allowing clients to perceive how they would appear in a home. The former bakery makes an appealing showroom; it lends itself well to the display of the period pieces. When built in 1911 the building played an important role in the village and the local stables was its next-door neighbour. The façade is deceptive and the quantity of antiques on view inside is something of a surprise. A warehouse in Cumberland Drive has been set up to house the overflow of stock that can be viewed between 10am and 4pm each Saturday, or by appointment. In recent years Two Cans has gained a reputation for providing unusual architectural antiques. A range of wonderful doors, windows and stonework can also be viewed at the warehouse.

At one time Two Cans displayed many Australian antiques but in recent years they have become more and more scarce due to a surge in popularity and the fact that not many pieces were produced. Carole travels thousands of kilometres through Europe and the United Kingdom to source the European and English pieces displayed in the shop and warehouse. This is where a discerning eye is essential. The items she collects are mostly run down and sad but with her extensive knowledge and love of the trade, plus her energetic imagination, she knows their worth and can picture them restored to glory. However, Carole does admit on her first buying trip she was like a "kid in a lolly shop" and bought what she called, "Carole's folly". This turned out to be a full size, Doctor Zhivago-style, wooden sleigh, a wonderfully romantic thing beautifully decorated with cane swirls and weaving. It has yet to be restored but once completed Carole would like to sit it on the roof of the antique store for all to survey – it would certainly add a unique feature to the Nepean Highway. It can, at the moment, be seen hanging from the rafters in the warehouse.

The fruits of Carole's regular travels are shipped by container to Australia and delivered to the warehouse. This has become an occasion of some excitement to longtime clients and those in the know as one and all are invited to view the new deliveries in their unrestored condition as they are unpacked from the container and allowed first choice of the quality pieces.

Behind the shop on the Nepean Highway you will find a hive of industry. John, along with an apprentice French polisher and a master French polisher, are hard at work, carefully dismantling and lovingly restoring pieces of history. The work is very involved, an art in itself. John is careful to ensure that the wonderful old pieces retain their stylistic characteristics, signs of age and the glowing patina the years have endowed. He goes to great lengths to match wood grain and colour. Both Carole and John are romantically involved with each item, trying to envisage the people and time they belonged to. Some pieces present intriguing mysteries. An Eastern European amoire bought on one of Carole's trips was badly in need of some TLC and as John started to dismantle the solid old piece of furniture he discovered a bullet hole - with the bullet still embedded in it! As we know, amoires are mostly kept in the bedroom - that leaves plenty of room for speculation. John kept the bullet as a souvenir.

Two Cans Antiques glows with the aura of yesteryear, offering collectors a vast array of period pieces representative of a time when furniture was crafted by hand to withstand the years and grow old with dignity.

Left & right: Two Cans Antiques

South of the village, the Riviera Hotel has seen many changes since it was built in 1885. Initially named the Long Beach Hotel, it was given a new identity in the early 1920s. Its original design incorporated a tower topped by a flagpole that made the structure visible for kilometres around. A later design provided accommodation on the upper level that now acts as the administration hub of the hotel. Decades and many changes later, the building sports a modern attractive façade that houses the seaside community's most popular local haunt.

At one time a giant horseshoe-shaped bar dominated the interior; it has gone making room for an attractive 90-seat bistro and separate spacious sports bar. The bistro is open for lunch and dinner seven days a week serving a wholesome menu offering 400 gram juicy steaks and succulent seafood. A children's playroom, extensive wine list and a restful view over a lush fernery complements the bistro's attractive art deco décor, providing a stress-free area for families. The extra large Sports Bar has a TAB facility with big-screen television and provides the added luxury of hearty counter meals served from the bistro's extensive menu.

The hotel's position opposite the beach on the Nepean Highway is an added bonus for beach goers looking for a wholesome meal or end of day drink in the small intimate lounge that leads into the Riviera's modern gaming room. Manager Steve Nicholls is very experienced in the hospitality industry and feels the historic hotel has something to offer everyone, good food and friendly service, in a comfortable atmosphere.

The Victorian Climbing Centre on Harnett Drive was the first facility of its kind in Australia. It provides a unique indoor pastime that has become increasingly popular in the past decade. Indoor rock climbing is an "off the wall sport" that was invented in Eastern Bloc countries and has proved so popular there is now a championship circuit that culminates in a World Champion title. The Victorian Climbing Centre in Seaford is a popular venue for both novices and experienced climbers from the very young to the very old, providing a platform for learning the important use of legs during a climb and tricky moves in the centre's controlled environment.

Trained instructors are part and parcel of every climb; the centre is run on the Belay System. This means every climber is strapped into a harness that is attached by ropes to a pulley and anchored by a belayer (a human helper that secures the rope). The belayer slackens or tightens the rope as the climber ascends or descends, creating as safe an environment as possible. The walls are constructed to offer different degrees of difficulty with different inclines and surfaces; many outdoor climbing fanatics use the indoor facilities to keep up their levels of strength, flexibility and endurance. Ladders and ropes suspended from the ceiling create their own kind of fun and make an attractive option.

Indoor climbing is an easy to learn, very social, fun pastime that both adults and children love; the centre even caters for birthday parties that give a different perspective to a traditional celebration. The centre has been operating 11 years and has been owned for the last three years by Grace and Les Williams who are keen about the sport organising exciting outdoor expeditions into the real world of climbing, creating situations to experience the exhilaration of abseiling, the wonder of caving and the unbelievable sensation of hanging in the stratosphere searching for hand and footholds when climbing rock faces in some of the most beautiful places in Victoria.

Carrum Downs and Skye sit side by side in the region's hinterland, a pool of suburbia surrounded by magnificent countryside. The area was originally settled in the 1930s but it is only since the 1970s, that the region has seen significant development with young families taking advantage of its country location and sizeable industrial area to the west of Dandenong-Frankston Road. The suburbs still contain relatively large parcels of undeveloped land, providing residents with a relaxed, rural lifestyle. Skye especially has remained mostly pastoral, with verdant fields and rolling hills setting an idyllic scene. The modern shopping precinct, Carrum Downs Regional Shopping Centre, in Hall Road, services both suburbs.

Frankston is the Peninsula's premier city, a vibrant bustling hub for education and industry and the centre of administration for Frankston City Council. The largest of the Peninsula towns and the only city on the bay, it is a mere 40 kilometres from the state capital, making the energetic metropolis a desirable commuter address for many of Melbourne's workers. Because of its close proximity to the capital city, it is considered part of Melbourne – but that's where the comparison ends.

This is a country town at heart, with a fashionable face and a bubbling vivacious attitude, nestling on 10 kilometres of Port Phillip's exhilarating coastline. It stands alone as a tourist destination. Located in the north of the region, it also makes the perfect base for exploring the fascinating dimensions of the Mornington Peninsula.

The land around Frankston has had European settlers since 1836, but it was not until 1854 that a settlement took shape at the mouth of Kananook Creek, around an already established pub. In the beginning the settlement was no more than a handful of fishermen who sold their catches in Melbourne and the surrounding area living in tents and humpies on Frankston's foreshore.

A trail established by early pioneers was utilised by the fishermen to take their wares to market and became known as the Fish Track. This rough thoroughfare was later to become the 160-kilometre Nepean Highway. In the era of early settlement, if you were lucky enough to be travelling in good weather, a one-way trip to Melbourne would take six hours. As the area developed, in 1857 a pier was erected with additions continuing until 1866. Buildings and facilities slowly appeared. A school was built in 1874 and a bank opened in 1881, then with the arrival of the railway in 1882, Frankston was established as a holiday destination.

Above: Victorian Climbing Centre
Right: Frankston / Baxter trail sculptures

There was more than one settler of prominence named "Frank" in the city's early history but it is generally believed that the owner of the original pub at Kananook Creek, Frank Stone, gave rise to the city being named Frankston.

The city has many picturesque open spaces and lookouts within its boundaries of Karingal, Frankston Heights, Frankston Central, Frankston North, and Frankston South. Olivers Hill just south of the CBD watches over the glittering city and provides a spectacular vantage point, presenting panoramic views of the bay to Melbourne and the Dandenong Ranges. The hill was originally named Old Man Davey's Hill after James Davey, who arrived with his father in 1839 and owned huge holdings in the area. (Other namesake sites are Davey's Bay and Davey Street). Later, a name change for the hill commemorated fisherman John Oliver. In the early 1800s this carpenter-cum-fisherman built a cottage at the top of the hill. He would watch for shoals of fish out in the bay from its high point. His son James succeeded him. He too lived on the hill and worked in the same professions as his father, dying at an extreme age in the mid-1920s. Residents followed Oliver's lead and by the late 1800s holiday homes had sprung up on the hill's slopes taking advantage of the expansive views.

Today the original settlement's location at Kananook Creek and the surrounding foreshore is an attractive reserve that covers 43 hectares and stretches north from the mouth of the creek in Frankston travelling 7.5 kilometres, linking the city with Seaford. The reserve is criss-crossed with relaxing walking tracks. The main trail is a 12-kilometre picturesque return walk that follows the creek north running parallel with the foreshore. The track wends its way through tea-tree scrub and banksia woodland, passing close to stands of swamp paperbarks and floodplain swamps, returning via the vibrant foreshore; or for the less robust it can be accessed from several other points along the route.

A variety of birds display themselves: more than 60 species have been identified. The reserve's prolific banksia is a magnet for honeyeaters, parrots and lorikeets. Water birds are a common sight wading, fishing and diving; they account for 30 per cent of the reserve's feathered fauna.

The creek is a favourite fishing, canoeing and boating location that exudes a restful beauty, especially in its more isolated upper reaches. The trip covers 7.5 kilometres from the creek mouth to the Eel Race Drain. It entails a laid-back journey of approximately two hours of easy paddling. The way leads past fragrant bush in the Kananook Creek Reserve, passing under the creek's bevy of famous bridges. The largest and oldest of these is Mile Bridge that has carried the Nepean Highway over the creek since 1861. A new bridge was built in 1936 and upgraded in 1976. Landings for launchings are strategically placed at the creek mouth on the east bank, and Fiocchi Avenue in Frankston and at Eel Race Road, Riviera Street, Station Street and McCulloch Avenue, Seaford.

At one time the creek contained freshwater. In the 1800s the draining of the surrounding swampland that fed the waterway resulted in the creek's mouth being relocated a short distance north, thus opening its length to the bay and its tides. The effect however is regulated by the flow from a pumping station that transfers water from Patterson Lakes into the Eel Race Drain, providing canoeists and boating enthusiasts with many leisurely hours of "messing about on the water".

For the old salts among us looking to the bay for our boating experiences, boat-launching facilities are situated near the mouth of the creek that can be accessed off the Nepean Highway just south of Davey Street.

Frankston Foreshore is having a face-lift. The Pier development already under way, is to include a safe boat harbour facility and marina just north towards Davey's Bay containing 300 berths and five public launching ramps, effectively turning Frankston into a major sailing destination. Included in the plan are an entertainment bowl and a pier forecourt restaurant development. There is even talk of a ferry terminus with a service to run to and from Docklands in Melbourne.

When accomplished, this ambitious enterprise will make Frankston Foreshore the envy of all other tourist destinations. Already a boardwalk climbing to Olivers Hill and an innovative, well-equipped children's playground have been completed. Also ready for use is a uniquely designed picnic precinct, furnished with electric barbecues, attractive benches and tables sheltered by a roof mimicking the undulating waves that break on the adjacent shore. Further along the beach the Frankston Life Saving Club has moved into sparkling modern premises. The building also houses a 120-seat restaurant.

The old footbridge that spanned the mouth of Kananook Creek has been replaced. Today bridges have to be not only functional but also aesthetically pleasing; some modern structures have gained icon status in the eyes of the world. The new Kananook Creek Bridge forms part of the exhilarating Bay Trail and is already a feature landmark in the area. The four-metre wide bridge was designed by Aspect Melbourne and features cutting-edge lighting for night viewing and inventive glass porthole inserts along its 20-metre length, forming a transparent view through the bridge's floor. Juxtaposed against the horizon it shares the eye's vision with the historic jetty. The striking new bridge's cernuous shape and threaded steel strands create a strong modern sculpture that highlights the solid imbedded beauty of the wooden pylons that cradle the enduring old pier.

Bunarong Park located just south of Cranbourne Road, with its main entrance and car park at the end of Wattle Tree Lane, is named after the Aboriginal people who lived in the area for thousands of years prior to European settlement. Discovery of stone implements in the 1940s indicate that the area was once a Bunarong Bulluk clan campsite. The location of the site has been recorded by the Victorian Archaeological Survey and placed on the register of archaeological sites.

Above: Kananook Creek hire boats
Right: Kananook Creek entrance to Port Phillip Bay

Sitting 90 metres above sea level, the park's higher points offer some exceptional vistas of Frankston and the bay. The park has many walking tracks snaking through its length and breadth leading from three main avenues. They wend through eucalypt groves and climb to heathland that is a carpet of flowers from mid-winter to early summer. There are over 100 species of plants for budding botanists to identify, including seven types of orchid. With such a wealth of flora, it is to be expected that on any sojourn through the reserve, wanderers will be rewarded with melodic calls and flashes of colour as over 50 species of birds, including parrots, go about their daily business.

Beauty Park is a quiet oasis in the middle of town bounded by Baxter, Young, High and Yuille Streets. The park's grounds have been put to many uses over the years. Perhaps the most famous was the 1934 Scouting Jamboree in association with Lord Baden Powell. A large man-made lake is the park's central feature with two raised platforms that overhang the water. These platforms make a wonderful stage from where visitors can get close up and personal with the sea birds and ducks that inhabit the park; they are always willing to be fed. Indigenous trees and shrubs stretch down to the lake that is fringed with all manner of grasses and reeds. A dry creek bed, strewn with huge boulders and river pebbles, traverses grassed picnic areas shaded by a canopy of trees. Australian artist Deborah Halpern has created an attractive semi-abstract sculpture from hand-cut ceramic mosaic. In shape and colour, the work resembles a group of Russian babushka dolls and makes a bright splash on the lake's edge.

The George Pentland Botanic Gardens, named for a highly respected, retired shire secretary and director for local government in Victoria, was opened in 1997 and has quickly become one of the city's preferred outdoor areas. It is much more than just a public park. As with other botanical gardens, it is designed primarily for passive recreation and contains a scientifically maintained collection of plants. It is a place of peace and serenity, covering an area of 7.5 hectares that was previously the first four holes of Frankston's original nine-hole golf course, established in 1938. The club closed in 1974 because the developing area had come too close to handle flying golf balls. A main feature of the park is the areas of luxuriant rolling lawns that were once the golf club's greens.

The impressive main entrance is on the corner of William and Foot Streets and leads the way over lawns to various tracks and seating areas. A fern gully contains a glade decorated with wooden carvings depicting indigenous birds and animals, and different plant groups around the park are explained on information boards. A large lake is a central feature and home to all manner of ducks. The heritage of the Bunwurrung people and the life and work of George Pentland is acknowledged in a project titled "Under the Southern Cross". Adjacent to the main gate a large children's playground and several electric barbecues and picnic benches set among shady trees provide a popular family area. The park is centrally located within walking distance of the CBD and a stone's throw from the Monash University Peninsula Campus.

A stroll around town is also a colourful, rewarding experience. Frankston is a city with many faces. Old stands shoulder to shoulder with new; historic icons appear when you least expect them. The gates at the entrance to Frankston Oval that sits high on Bay Street South, running off the Nepean Highway, were obtained from the Old Melbourne Gaol. Transported to Frankston during WWII and hung between imposing supports built of random rubble (a form of medium-size boulders locally mined) they create an imposing entrance. Maybe a fitting watchword to hang above the relics would be "abandon hope all ye who enter here", as a dire warning for the opposing teams that come to play Frankston's favourite sons, the Peninsula Dolphins, on their home ground. Embedded in the pillars a small bronze plaque informs readers that the gates also mark a much earlier historic site that was once "the watering place used by the early settlers". The oval itself contains an impressive wooden grandstand built in 1942.

St Paul's Anglican Parish of Frankston, situated on an elevated position on Bay Street South, was the settlement's first church. Its grounds contain the first burials between 1854 and 1874. It also housed the first school from 1856 to 1874. Built in 1854, the original building was destroyed by fire and rebuilt in 1935. The present church has magnificent stained glass windows.

Frankston Memorial Park, located on Cranbourne Road, dates back to the late 1800s and is the final resting place of many of Frankston's early pioneers, including many of the area's leading citizens.

Ballam Park Playground in Cranbourne Road, Karingal, just east of Frankston, is a popular attraction and full of fun things to do. It sits in front of what is left of Ballam Park estate that contains one of the area's most visited historic houses. Fredrick Evelyn Liardet built the historic homestead of Ballam Park in 1855. He was the son of Wilbraham Fredrick Evelyn Liardet, the founder of Port Melbourne. The Liardet family were descended from French aristocracy and had fled France after the Huguenot massacre. Wilbraham's mother, a descendant of English diarist John Evelyn was, at one time, lady-in-waiting to Queen Victoria.

The family arrived in Australia in 1839 and established themselves as innovators in the region. Wilbraham with his sons set up the first pier and hotel in the Sandridge area. They constructed the first road from Sandridge to Melbourne, establishing the first carriage service along the road. The family initiated, and for 18 years operated, the earliest postal service in Victoria. Fredrick with his brother Frank instigated the public movement that resulted in the building of Frankston pier.

Although built by Fredrick, Ballam Park was utilised by the entire family as a holiday residence. In naming the homestead Liardet derived an Aboriginal word for "butterfly".

Above & right: George Pentland Botanic Gardens

The residence was the first brick house to be built in the area. Constructed of bricks made on the property, it was erected by Thomas Cogger Allchin with the help of Fredrick's two sons and convict labour. Bricks manufactured on the Ballam Estate went into many of Frankston's early buildings. Fredrick sold Ballam Park in 1863 to wealthy Melbourne chemist Daniel Rutter.

Generations of wear and tear had taken their toll on the homestead when Frankston City acquired it. Now restored to its original splendour, the double storey French colonial residence sits in the remaining 64 hectares of the Liardet estate. Many of the homestead's earliest fittings remain: a magnificent cedar and mahogany staircase with intricate carving and leadlight sashes and windows that were brought over from France still grace the elegant building. Frankston Historical Society is to be commended for the thoughtful interpretations displayed in the rooms with life-like mannequins dressed in period costume, some painstakingly copied, some original, bringing alive a vivid picture of the genteel Victorian lifestyle of the more affluent early settlers.

During the family's residence it was the custom each night to hang a lantern in the window of an alcove room on the upper level of the house. We are told the light acted as a beacon for travellers and bullock wagons travelling to Frankston across Carrum Downs. A central feature of the kitchen is a large iron stove. Made in Boston, U.S.A., in the 1880s, it originally graced the American consulate in Melbourne. There are many rarities and relics to view in the homestead that will advise and amaze the curious.

Open to the public most Sundays, the homestead is classified by the National Trust and is the headquarters of the Frankston Historical Society. Members of the society are on hand to guide and relay the history of the house, the grounds and the region. A magnificent oak tree of great age is a feature of the attractive property. Although not proven, it is the opinion of many tree specialists that it may well be the largest of its genus in the Southern Hemisphere. An oak tree, along with a planting of olive trees behind the residence, and a magnificent carob tree adjacent the building, are all as old as the homestead and Heritage listed. The carob tree is of particular interest. A rarity in Australia, it is not only a decorative addition to the gardens with its artistic limbs, but its fruit, that resemble coffee beans, produce a chocolate substitute and each individual pod, no matter what size or shape, weighs exactly 1 carat.

A museum is housed in what was a brick garage built in 1944, replacing the original stables that were destroyed by fire. It holds many Liardet family artefacts and interesting relics and memorabilia of the Frankston area and Victorian era. It can be accessed through tearooms, where almost everything is homemade and Devonshire tea and hospitality are specialities. Visitors are invited to enjoy their repast either in the bright atmosphere of the café or in the courtyard surrounded by the attractive grounds that have been planted to recreate the sweet-smelling, flower-filled, cottage gardens of the 1800s. A number of age-old rose bushes still flourish in the garden and are cosseted to ensure they continue to overpower visitors with their fragrance and beauty.

Frankston is the cultural heart of the region and the building of the Daryl Jackson designed **Frankston Art Centre** on the corner of Young and Davey Streets in 1996 provided a focal point. The stimulating multi-venue complex stages a diverse program of outstanding classical and contemporary theatre, both amateur and professional, attracting top line artists from every genre. It hosts large or small community, social and corporate events and is the scene of many festivals and expositions. An 800-seat theatre and 190-seat flexible performance space are state-of-the-art, enhanced by several function and meeting rooms furnished with a full range of technical and audio-visual equipment. Among its merits is a professional catering facility and parking for 300 cars. On any visit to the region it is worth checking the centre's program of events.

The complex sits adjacent **Cube 37**, a new and innovative multimedia community arts facility. It has a number of areas that are the stage for new media art displays, local art exhibitions, programs and workshops, as well as smaller scale theatre and dance productions. This facility presents enormous opportunities to explore new dimensions in multimedia artforms. The most prominent feature of the building is the glass studio designed for the projection of digital and photographic images on screens behind its glazed exterior that are dramatically visible from the street.

All disciplines of the arts are catered for in this cosmopolitan city and one of the most highly regarded curators of all artistic styles is Jenny Pihan of Jenny Pihan Fine Art @ The Kananook Creek Boathouse Gallery. Jenny has a natural eye for recognising talent. She has "Art Smarts". To those in the know her name has become the hallmark for excellence. Propelled by an extraordinary energy and enthusiasm she presents an impressive collection of artists ranging from established veterans to talented newcomers. She presents them both in her permanent position on the Nepean Highway and in Jenny Pihan-organised exhibitions hosted by many of the Peninsula's most prestigious venues, including the beautiful Morning Star Estate. Her dedication to introducing quality works of art to the public has earned her the acclaim of collectors and admiration and respect of many of the country's finest artists.

The quaint 1930s weatherboard house that hosts the five-roomed gallery has led a chequered life, having been at one time a bordello. With typical sense of humour Jenny says; "the passion's still here – it's just changed direction." The cottage has metamorphosed into a comfortable viewing area with a special feel and is centrally located opposite Office Works on the Nepean Highway. Many first-time visitors to the modest art space are surprised. This is no mundane craft shop; there is not a single coat hanger or lavender bag inside the charismatic cottage. Instead it houses paintings of dynamic structure, many produced by recognised artists, whose works are sought after for their investment potential, who exhibit in London, New York and other major Australian city galleries.

Above: Ballam Park playground
Right: Ballam Park Homestead

Jenny campaigns tirelessly for her artists, showcasing their work in displays within the gallery's rooms that provide the onlooker with a sense of being there. Her fine art company is now a recognised name in the Australian art world. Comprehensive experience garnered over years in exhibition planning now sees Jenny as consultant to several annual art shows. Seasoned collectors and eager neophytes seek out her expert opinion and artistic eye when looking to purchase a painting or make a corporate investment. Jenny Pihan Fine Art has evolved into one of Victoria's most innovative galleries that is worthwhile to experience and a pleasure to relive.

Richard Linton's Maritime Art Shop on Beach Street is a gallery that features a master at work. Richard is renowned worldwide as a maritime artist whose work is distinguished by naturalism and rigorous attention to detail; he will on instances use a single hair artist's brush and magnifying glass to create a meticulous, lifelike effect. He is a self-taught artist who in his youth served an apprenticeship in the printing trade as a photolithographic etcher. At an early age he became immersed in the technical study of sailing ships and his love affair with these romantic swan-like structures has never waned. His work mainly depicts historical maritime events and results of such events with realism and perception that comes from intense study of each and every situation that at times takes years to complete. The finished paintings can consume as many as 4,000 hours each.

During his career the limited edition lithographs that are printed from his work have won multiple gold, silver and bronze medals in the Australian Printing Industry Awards. These lithographs and his original artworks are represented in collections worldwide. Examples are displayed at the gallery along with nautical artefacts and maritime gifts. Born in Caulfield, Victoria, in 1935, Richard created his first series of paintings when he was 20 years of age and has never looked back. He has fashioned a niche and a style unique in today's art world and his intimate knowledge of his subject, teamed with his intricate use of light, captures the imagination, pulling the viewer within. Linton is one of a few artists commissioned by the Franklin Mint to have his paintings reproduced at the famous House of Moulot in Paris by the old method of hand lithography; putting him in the company of previous greats, Chagall, Matisse and Picasso.

On visiting the gallery we were privileged to see Richard working on a piece that has taken 30 years of research and design, the original of which he says, will never be sold. The massive three-metre long masonite work depicts the British tea clipper *Thermopylae* at anchor in Foochow harbour, 40 kilometres up the river Min in China. This harbour is famous for the elaborate designs displayed on the bow of the local Chinese junks and Richard has painted one of these highly decorated ships in intricate detail in the foreground of his work. *Thermopylae* is a historic clipper that holds the record as the fastest sailing ship between England and Australia. There is already a waiting list for the lithographic reproduction of this mammoth work.

It is only natural that a city as dynamic as Frankston would attract the best in festivals and events. Its full calendar of events brings the city alive with music, entertainment, culture, colour and performance. A uniquely different event held over four days in March is the **Frankston Guitar and Music Festival**. The seventh annual event was held in 2003. The festival attracts melomaniacs of the guitar genre from Australia and beyond. The promoters have covered every aspect of guitars: playing, buying, building and enjoying the mellifluous sound of the heavenly instrument. A highlight of the festival is the search for the 'Young Guitarist of the Year' that uncovers a high degree of skill in the younger participants. There are workshops to attend and concerts held in a bevy of venues all over the city, including outdoor performances on the foreshore. The concerts have something to suit all tastes held throughout the day, into evening and the wee hours, emphasising the versatility of the feature instrument and showcasing legendary international and Australian artists.

The imposing Frankston Arts Centre is the central pivot of festival activities housing an exposition, art display and providing the venue for some spectacular performances and clinics. A unique concept of the 2003 festival, complementing the artistic 'Guitar Exhibition' was The 'Mighty Twang', the building of the world's biggest portable guitar. Constructed under the public eye in the window space of Cube 37, participating artists grappled with a swag of components that should have daunted the most creative soul. Bamboo, fabric, paper, sticky tape, chewing gum, paint, bits and bobs and anything else that came to hand went into the production of the colossal guitar and provided a talking point throughout its production. The Guitar Exhibition held in Cube 37 showcased intuitive works of art from invited artists. The exhibition contained highly imaginative sculptures and vibrant paintings all with a guitar theme.

The festival's Guitar Expo is the only one of its kind in the Southern Hemisphere catering only for the guitar, displaying the intricacies of the ancient instrument. On entering the exposition hall of the 2003 festival, visitors were aware of the buzz in the air. There was a hushed babble, emulating the atmosphere in a theatre full to capacity, the sound of subdued conversation over-ridden by the orchestra tuning up ready for the overture.

The collection of world-renowned businesses and craftsmen offered everything from guitar straps and cases to the pliable timber needed to build your own. But the stars of the show were the instruments themselves. Displayed like glistening gems were acoustic guitars and electric guitars of all shapes and sizes, all colours and finishes, some with a beginner's price tag and others that would only be played by the best of the professionals.

Left: Richard Linton
Right: Jenny Pihan Gallery artwork

Tactile feel-good instruments, some crafted by hand, some manufactured by machine, some created from rich gleaming wood and others from man-made products, were all engineered to produce seductively beautiful music. Roland Barthes, philosopher, said; "Plastic can be made into buckets or jewels." He forgot to mention guitars. Potential customers plucked and played the instruments on show as famous faces mingled with enthusiastic amateurs all looking for that special magic to be found in the guitar, while on the mezzanine level curious novices were offered free guitar lessons.

During winter in Frankston, the Winter Arts Program lights up that darker time of year and the Melbourne Marathon in spring gets the city moving again. Come summer the area celebrates its greatest asset, Port Phillip Bay, with the Sea Festival. This spectacular occurs each January (usually the third weekend). Locals and visitors to the region participate in a weekend of light-hearted fun, celebrating the sea. The foreshore area makes a stunning stage for the proceedings, re-establishing its value as a community asset. The program involves a large number of community organisations and includes an emergency services parade. There are a multitude of activities to try, multi-cultural entertainment to enjoy, environmental displays to learn from, workshops to become involved in, and coastal exploration to experience. Kids love to get involved in the 'kids' fishing day' and there's all the fun of the fair with rides and stalls.

Frankston is a shopper's paradise, the third largest regional shopping precinct in Australia with more than 700 retail outlets ranging from large department stores to speciality shops and services. It is a busy, bustling centre with a major public transport interchange located in its heart on Young Street. "If you can't get it here its not available anywhere!" is an oft-heard statement and the multitude of stores and businesses brimming with a splendid variety of choice attest to the town's growing cosmopolitan reputation.

A modern shopping complex and an attractive mall enhance Frankston's traditional shopping precinct. Station Street Mall in the heart of the city holds some interesting stores. Standing out among them is Aussie Collections. Established in 1989, the store has occupied its spot in the mall for the past four years. The only store of its kind in the area, it provides a helpful service to Frankston's visitors, taking on the role of an unofficial tourism information centre, keeping brochures and details on all the region's many attractions. It is also the booking office for French Island Eco Tours, an award-winning company that provides a guided day trip to the unspoiled island in the middle of Western Port Bay.

The attractive store is filled with Australia's most coveted labels; Akubra hats, Drizabone jackets and coats and R.M. Williams boots and jeans, in company with a range of clothing and quality knitwear. There is an extensive collection of tempting knick-knacks that make the perfect gift or a cherished reminder of a visit to the region. Aussie Collections is much more than a store, it is a wonderful place to spend some time soaking up the fair dinkum atmosphere surrounding a business that showcases the best of Australia.

John Crowder & Sons, in their 51st year of business, are agents with a long and distinguished history on the Peninsula. John Gordon Crowder and his son, Ian, opened the first of their offices in 1952 in tiny premises on railway land in Young Street, Frankston. The agents wouldn't lease him an office so he built his own. Another son, Geoffrey, joined the firm in 1958, then later two of his sons, Michael and Tom, together with Ian's sons, Philip and James.

They grew to eight offices covering most of the Peninsula, but after Ian's untimely death in 1993, they decided to downsize to three. "It was the best thing we could have done, back in control, giving much more personalised service and, frankly, doing better than ever," said Geoffrey, who is now managing director. "We have our head office in Frankston, branches in Mt Eliza and Carrum Downs, and handle all facets of real estate".

More recently the company opened its board to include Hugh Gillespie as non-working chairman of directors, and Rosemary McKechnie, who has been with the company for 18 years and manages the huge commercial/industrial property management department.

Frankston has been undervalued for years, but things are changing rapidly. "We have everything down here. There are 23 golf courses on the Mornington Peninsula, top wineries, private schools, some of the best shopping facilities in Melbourne and, of course, our magnificent beaches and boating facilities," said Geoff. "There is a new air of confidence in Frankston and massive commercial and residential developments to take place over the next few years. This is a great place to live, enjoy, and invest. You can't go wrong."

Left: Frankston Sea Festival

Right: Geoff Achison performing at the Frankston Guitar & Music Festival

Frankston is home to two major tertiary education and research facilities – Chisholm Institute of Technical and Further Education (TAFE) and Monash University. Monash is Australia's largest university and is internationally recognised as a leader in teaching and research. It has campuses conveniently located in Frankston, and in nearby Clayton and Berwick.

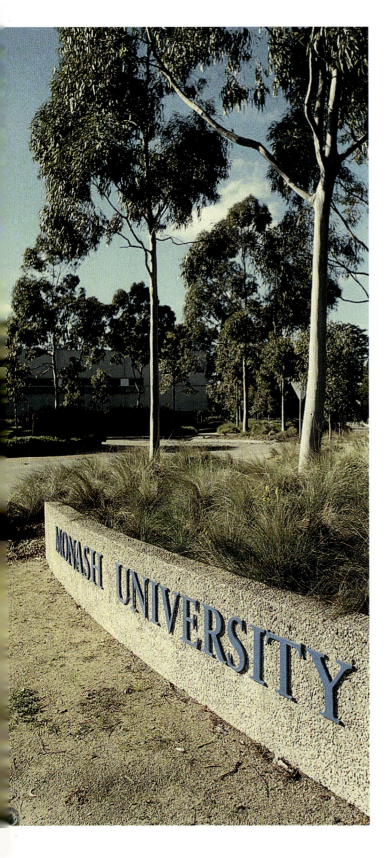

Monash University Peninsula Campus is the region's pre-eminent education facility. It attracts students from around the country and overseas. It is the home to as many as 3,000 students at any one time offering a unique and innovative curriculum for degrees in the major academic areas of business and economics, education, network computing and nursing. The campus also offers courses in health management and ambulance paramedic training.

The Peninsula Campus is conveniently located an hour's drive from Melbourne and students live both on and off site. Occupying an elevated position, on McMahons Road in Frankston South, the campus is a 15-minute walk from the city's heart and the beach. It provides a wide range of facilities that include the George Jenkins Theatre (428-seat), an ideal venue for plays, dances, concerts and conferences. The campus also contains the only all-weather hockey pitch in the Frankston area: it is well utilised by the three hockey clubs in the region. Students are exposed to a caring and supportive educational environment that is enhanced with on-campus accommodation, faculty buildings and facilities attractively displayed within a 12-hectare property set among old trees and gardens, creating a serene village-like atmosphere.

The beauty of the campus is undeniable and stems from the history of the original property dating back to 1896 and 29 acres of crown land that was utilised as an orchard. The land, owned by Mrs Jane Unthank eventually, in 1957, became the Frankston Teachers College then in turn the State College of Victoria and finally the Chisholm Institute of Technology and Monash University Peninsula Campus. The Unthanks were local orchardists and the name is well known on the Peninsula. Unthank Park in Somerville commemorates the family.

A strong feature of the campus is Struan House; history is veiled as to when the house was built. It is known that there was a residence mentioned in 1902 and a Mr Rudolph Werner of Richmond, an engineer who owned a refrigeration and air conditioning company in Melbourne, purchased the property in 1920 containing a house that by then sat within an 18-acre estate. In 1924 he either built a new house or carried out extensive renovations to the old building, but he is credited with constructing the house as it now stands as a holiday home for his family. The small mansion was a showpiece in its day containing 21 centrally heated rooms and a large freezing chamber and cold room. It was Dr Frank Vincent who purchased the estate in 1951 that named the house Struan after a family property in Naracoorte, South Australia. His wife Edna started the volunteer group known as the "Pink Ladies" at the Frankston Hospital. In 1957 when the estate, plus several other properties in the area – including a two-acre chicken farm that adjoined the Struan property – were purchased by the Education Department, Struan House became Frankston Teachers College specialising in Primary Teaching.

The beautiful old mansion (minus the refrigeration plant and cool room) still services the university, housing security and PhD students. It adds grace and character to the campus that surrounds it, highlighted by trees planted in the 1800s endowing a timeless beauty that hopefully imparts a sense of constancy to the students of the Monash University Peninsula Campus.

Left: Monash University Peninsula Campus
Right: Struan House, Monash University Peninsula Campus

Dining out in Frankston takes on many forms, from a bevy of gourmet coffee shops to haute cuisine served in trendy restaurants. No matter what your craving the city provides a culinary adventure with flavours from around the world.

Daveys Bar and Restaurant has pride of place in the middle of Frankston. Its elevated position on the foreshore gives views over the beach, the mouth of Kananook Creek and Port Phillip Bay that are best appreciated from the restaurant. It is a character-filled modern venue that sparkles with stylish comfort. It is one of the area's most popular restaurants and entertainment lounge bars. Most say the atmosphere alone is worth the visit.

The restaurant's moderately priced a la carte menu specialises in modern Australian cuisine with Mediterranean influences featuring flavoursome seafood; the Davey's Locker Seafood Platter is delectable. The restaurant's wine list offers a wide range of local Mornington Peninsula wines, and should guests wish to take a bottle home, the venue's bottle shop also keeps a range in stock. The 160-seat restaurant has been skilfully designed and decorated. Tiered areas featuring exclusive booths surrounding elegant groups of tables and chairs sectionalise the large room. A large outdoor deck is popular for summer repasts, setting the scene for wonderful sun soaked lunches and romantic evenings under a canopy of stars. Open seven days a week for lunch and dinner, the room takes on a different persona for each event. Daylight fills the restaurant with a light, bright, contemporary ambiance, allowing diners to appreciate the relaxing vista created by the closeness of the bay and the picturesque scene created by one of Kananook's quaint bridges and boats berthed at the mouth of the creek, while evening patrons enjoy a sophisticated atmosphere with subdued lighting adding elegance to the meal.

The Lounge Bar at the front of the venue is a casual, comfortable place. A large galley shaped bar divides the room into open plan sections with private booths and large, comfortable easy chairs and settees creating fashionable conversation nooks. Large windows shaded by jungle greenery overlook a sports corner complete with pool table and big screen television and a canvas-shrouded sun deck leads off the lounge through French doors. The lounge is popular with Frankston's night owl set, the scene of Friday and Saturday weekly live performances starring a wide variety of entertainment. Sunday afternoon at Daveys is a special laid-back experience that attracts a jovial host of devotees with jazz on the menu. The popular venue hosts many festivals and special wine evenings and plays a major role in the annual Frankston Guitar and Music Festival.

Kananook Creek Boathouse is centrally located on the Nepean Highway. It sits serenely on the banks of its meandering namesake waterway providing a picturesque setting and a stress-free atmosphere in which to sample good food and fine wine. The purpose-built restaurant offers a layered selection of dining areas. The mezzanine level provides treetop dining. It looks out into textured greenery, down to the creek below through 15-metre high glass doors that neatly concertina, allowing the ground floor area to flow from indoors to out onto a wooden balcony. On the garden level a large jetty and a gazebo have a nautical air. Surrounded by manicured gardens and shaded by tall trees they are well patronised during summer months, while an open fireplace indoors provides a cosy nook for winter repasts.

Debbie and Joe Weinbach acquired the restaurant in its infancy and Joe has stamped his own brand of superior cuisine into the menu. Within the modern Australian fare old favourites take on new guises with each passing season and regular patrons eagerly await Joe's innovative new dishes laced with international influences. In four years Debbie and Joe have created a 60-seat restaurant that is recognised as one of the best on the Peninsula, but fame always has a price – it is advisable to book to avoid disappointment. The restaurant is a local favourite and definitely provides a bright medium where lovers meet, friends congregate and the food is legendary.

Perovics is one of Frankston's newer fine dining restaurants. The exceptional food is augmented by the venue's central position and off-street parking. It is quickly gaining a reputation in the city for good food and friendly service in a comfortably sophisticated atmosphere. Situated on the Nepean Highway close to the Frankston arts precinct, its menu takes patrons on a journey through sumptuous breakfasts to luscious lunches and gastronomic evenings. It is the perfect spot for pre- or post- theatre food and drinks or a cocktail from the bar. An eclectic ever-evolving menu possesses a multitude of flavours highlighting fresh local produce and Peninsula wines at their best.

Soft lights, glistening tablecloths and sparkling accoutrements set the scene for romantic dinners and friendly gatherings. Patrons appreciate the caring and attentive, yet unobtrusive, service that so enhances business lunches and corporate dinners. Perovics is an elegant 60-seat restaurant with a memorable ambiance enhanced by live weekend entertainment that features a wide range of talent and musical styles. It is not hard to relax and enjoy the essence of Perovics, where they take their food seriously and serve it with a smile.

Shakespeare's Bar and Restaurant is a character-filled venue that is well placed for theatre patrons before and after performances as it sits on Young Street directly round the corner from the prestigious Frankston Arts Centre. The popular inner city haunt has been family owned and run since 2001 by David and Beverly Lockett; guests can also meet the couple's two sons and daughter helping out on the premises. The cosy bar is reminiscent of an old English alehouse and the resemblance is carried through to the great English brews and wide range of imported beer on sale at reasonable prices. Guests are invited to pop in at lunchtime and experience the delicious counter lunches or for a less casual repast, choose the ambiance of the venue's attractive restaurant that has a refined but relaxed air.

Above: View from Olivers Hill
Right: Seagull perched on Bruce Armstrong's 'Sentinel' sculpture

The restaurant is housed on the upper level and provides undisturbed fine dining from a modern Australian menu. It also doubles as an intimate function centre that can accommodate up to 70 guests. Shakespeare's is a popular spot with tasty competitively priced lunches and dinners. Patrons are treated to live entertainment most weekends and the venue is also the home of the Peninsula Folk Club. The club meets on the first Sunday of each month and the bar is set ablaze with the multisonant repertoire of a dozen different musical instruments. Anyone is welcome to join in the jam session – even mine host gets into the act. David is an avid player of the banjo, mandolin and guitar. The stirring sound of Irish jigs, Scottish reels, English ballads and Australian bush music gets toes tapping and fingers snapping, an evening the "Bard" would be delighted to attend.

For anyone who thought Indian food consisted merely of curry and rice, a visit to the Siddhartha Indian Restaurant on the Nepean Highway is a must. Over 20 years ago Devendra and Shashi Singh brought the flavours and ancient art of Indian cuisine to Frankston, building up a faithful following in the city, with returning patrons including third-generation family members.

The restaurant is named for Buddha who was born Prince Siddhartha. It is set back off the highway in an attractive cottage elegantly furbished with a regal colour scheme of cream and burgundy. The glass-walled kitchen is a feature of the dining area and guests can witness the intricacies of cooking with one of the world's most ancient ovens, the tandoor. This cylindrical kiln opens from the top and is engineered of unglazed ceramic bricks; it is fired by charcoal, reaching temperatures of between 600 and 700 degrees Fahrenheit. A speciality of the house is rotiyan, Indian bread that is baked in these ovens, trapped on the walls by the intense heat. The bread, of course, can be ordered plain but it also comes flavoured with garlic, olives, spiced cottage cheese, minced lamb or spiced potatoes. There is even a sweeter version stuffed with cherries, dry fruits and nuts - simply scrumptious.

Devendra has exerted tremendous effort into presenting patrons with some of the most unique and rare delicacies that were once served at feasts given by India's past nobility. An extensive, creative bill of fare has been devised specialising in tandoori and Northern Indian cuisine. At the restaurant's inception, determined to recreate these authentic flavours, Devendra took a chance on Bhagwati Prasad, a chef he had never met but who came highly recommended. He arranged passage for the chef all the way from Lucknow, India. Bhagwati did not disappoint: he still presides over the Siddartha kitchen, helped nowadays by Narender Singh, who is also a master in the art of tandoor.

It isn't often you visit a downtown restaurant with its own winery up in the hills. Wildcroft Wines are made by Devendra and Shashi (see wine section) the wines are well represented on the Siddartha wine list and enhance the flavours of the rich, aromatic food. The restaurant is fully licensed and an alternate wine list is also available. A 60-seat function room attached to the 75-seat restaurant provides an elegant venue for special events and guests can be assured of a banquet fit for a king.

Undeniably Via Mare Ristorante Bar and Café is one of the finest Italian restaurants in Victoria, with an outstanding reputation for good food, good wine and a warm creative atmosphere. Located close to the CBD on the Nepean Highway the restaurant is a credit to owners Robert and Lisa de Santis. Robert grew up around good food and successfully run restaurants. He has followed the family tradition, now owning Via Mare and a partnership in The Rocks, a popular Mornington restaurant.

The elegant restaurant holds no resemblance to the old, double-storey property purchased by the couple in the early 1990s. They have remodelled with style and flair, creating a palace dedicated to fine Italian dining. An intimate upstairs function area accommodates 26 and enhances the main ground floor restaurant with indoor seating for 80. Patio settings on both levels make lunch or dinner even more special on warm sunny days and balmy summer evenings. The restaurant is a celebration of Italian flavours encompassing all regions, mirrored by an extensive Italian wine list. Executive chef Des Betinsky has designed the restaurant's menu since 1994; he enjoys the challenge of creating new dishes and visits the markets personally to ensure the best ingredients. Des honed his craft while learning the subtleties of Italian cooking in some of Melbourne's most exclusive restaurants.

Legendary favourites of the Via Mare menu are the flavoursome "la pasta e risottos" and the succulent seafood platter. Daily chef's specials and delicious desserts further augment the wide-ranging bill of fare. Patrons enjoy the restaurant's annual Italian Wine Appreciation Dinners that runs over three evenings and includes a seminar introducing the complexity of Italian wine. Robert and Des believe that consistency and listening to your customers holds the key to a successful restaurant and with this philosophy they have created a premier dining experience laced with all the romance and rich, exotic flavours of Italy.

Left: Via Mare Restaurant

Opposite:
Top left: Siddhartha Indian Restaurant
Centre left: Davey's Restaurant
Bottom left: Perovics Restaurant
Top right: Kananook Creek Boathouse Restaurant
Centre right: Shakespeare's Restaurant
Bottom right: Via Mare seafood banquet

Frankston, like any city, has a thriving club scene and visitors have a wide choice.

The Pier Hotel on the banks of Kananook Creek has been an icon of the city since 1875. Built by Mark Young, who must have been one of the earliest entrepreneurs to recognise Frankston's potential as a holiday destination, he maximised the hotel's attraction by creating landscaped gardens at the rear of the building plus a suspension bridge over the creek, giving easy access to sea baths that he constructed on the beach. In its heyday the Pier was a lively place and today has its own resident ghosts. The grand old property is the home of one of Frankston's most popular establishments.

Flanagans at the Pier Hotel gives patrons a taste of two eras. Extended to suit its modern-day purpose, the oldest part of the hotel remains constant. Consisting of several interconnecting areas, its ambiance and character are enhanced with old-world fixtures and fittings, completed by the creak of century-old wooden floors, bestowing a touch of blarney magic to Flanagans. Leather Chesterfield lounges and chairs add to the solid feel of the warm wood, and private corners lend some romance. Bulbous chandeliers cast a subdued street lamp effect over the rooms and a cubby hole acts as a library, made more convincing by shelves stacked with old books. The gracious old bar serves, among other things, Guinness, Kilkenny and Harp Irish Lager, all adding to the Irish flavour. A range of entertainment is provided Thursdays to Sundays each week, when the bar exudes a raffish charm.

The complex has been extended to contain a large modern gaming area with many up-to-the-minute machines. A casual lounge bar is comfortably furnished and boasts a big screen television; it is the perfect spot for some quiet time out. For the more energetic the 21st Century Dance Club delivers a power-packed evening. Originally built as the Frankston Bowling Alley in the early 1960s, it became part of the hotel complex in the mid-1970s. During this era its walls reverberated to acts like Johnny Farnham and Sky Hooks, whose autographed tour poster can still be seen in the classy Pink Pelican Bar. The signature feature of the 1600-capacity nightclub is a massive revolving dance floor that has proved ever popular since it was installed in 1986. Open Friday and Saturday nights until late featuring top class DJs, the 21st rocks.

The Frankston RSL is perhaps one of Frankston's most distinguished clubs with a long prestigious history. Chartered in 1925 with premises originally in Thompson Street, the present club opened in 1976 in its new location on Cranbourne Road and has set high standards with the facilities on offer. It is only one step away from country club status featuring three bowling rinks, an 18-hole golf putting green, a billiard room with three full size billiards tables and areas to play darts and chess; with organised social groups competing in each league. They even have their own pipe and drum band and, of course, a cosy gaming room and separate TAB.

The club's attitude is very much steeped in the origins of the RSL still working towards helping members and their families and the Frankston community in general. The Women's Auxiliary plays a big role in helping raise an amount in excess of $100,000 that the club donates to charity each year. Every area of the large premises is given over to remembrance, with vast collections of unique museum-quality,memorabilia displayed in cabinets and cases throughout the club. Of particular interest is a 1914-18 pack saddle featured in the club's attractive lounge. It is one of only three privately owned in Australia. Major Max Armstrong (retired) donated the Australian Light Horse Cavalry saddle displayed in the foyer. Born in 1910, Major Armstrong served in the armed forces during WWII and is one of the club's oldest active members. For many years until the death of his mount, Major Armstrong led the ANZAC Day parade in Melbourne on horseback.

The club's attractive restaurant has an Aussie-style menu with an affordable price tag. The restaurant is named in honour of Raphael Oimbari OBE, one of the "Fuzzy-Wuzzy Angels" to whom so many Australian servicemen fighting in Papua during WWII owed their lives. A pictorial story of their heroism decorates the restaurant walls. Regular cabarets and live shows are performed in the Simpson Function Room. Again, this room is named and decorated to commemorate an Australian hero Private John Simpson Kilpatrick who was a member of the Australian Field Ambulance Corps killed at Gallipoli. He gained fame by entering the battle zones with his donkey to rescue the wounded, becoming known as "Simpson and his Donkey". Frankston RSL has so much to offer members and visitors. It is a warm friendly club that honours and celebrates an Australian tradition.

Left: Frankston Gates   Top: Daveys Bar & Restaurant;
Bottom left & bottom right: Flanagans Irish Bar at the Pier Hotel;
Centre right: Frankston RSL

A wide range of accommodation in Frankston offers travellers to the region a multitude of choices.

The Ambassador Motel is centrally located on the Nepean Highway providing 24-hour check-in and undercover parking. It is Frankston's largest hotel, with over 100 rooms. The keynote is relaxed comfort. Quality and affordability combine to provide well-designed accommodation that covers many different configurations and tariffs that include something for most tastes and budgets. The spacious rooms, suites and self-contained apartments are tastefully furbished, nestling within a unique architectural design characterising a picturesque village.

Cobbled undercover alleyways connect accommodation areas leading onto garden walkways and through courtyards filled with textured greenery and water features. A large central courtyard provides an exclusive outdoor area where guests can relax. It leads off some of the accommodation and is surrounded by double storey, ivy dressed walls. Outdoor seating, a barbecue and gazebo are surrounded by a large pond and unique fountain with statues, gardens and a gigantic stone urn delivering a Mediterranean background to the restful spot.

Built in 1980, the hotel is a strong feature of the Nepean Highway. Evenings transform the façade as a fusion of brilliant colour emanates from huge leadlight windows characterized throughout the hotel's public areas and function rooms. The hotel specialises only in large functions with sumptuous menus, catering for 100-plus guests. One of the function areas even has its own chapel with access to a sunken garden complete with cascading waterfall that makes a great backdrop for any photo. An attractive restaurant is conveniently contained within the complex. It delivers first-class food and quality service, rounding off an experience that makes the Ambassador Hotel an attractive alternative when visiting the area.

Frankston International Motel is on the Nepean Highway, centrally located so that visitors can park the car and forget about it for the rest of their stay. A five-minute walk in any direction delivers guests to all that Frankston has to offer. Recent renovations to the property have resulted in bright, spacious, superior rooms and luxurious suites, elegantly decorated and all furnished with attractive private balconies. Thirty-nine of the 43 units are equipped with corner spas and all rooms have queen size beds and business fittings.

When Phil and Lynda Jones purchased the property in 2001 they saw the potential to restore the motel to its former glory as the premier establishment in Frankston. With diligence and innovative ideas they have raised the hotel's standard to new heights of comfort and style. Phil has managed hotels all over Australia and has drawn on his extensive knowledge of the industry, turning the hotel into a corporate haven for work-weary executives and a stylish retreat for Frankston's visitors.

Taggart's Café & Bar is located adjacent to the marble enclosed reception area and has a modern, vibrant atmosphere enhanced by large wraparound windows that embrace views of the garden. Taggart's menu continually evolves, presenting generous meals that are fresh and creative. Sizzling man-sized steaks and innovative international menu items are always featured.

Two function rooms on the hotel's upper level are popular venues for any special occasion. The Panorama Room is flooded with natural light and has 180-degree views of the surrounding area. Seating 100, it has an attractive horseshoe bar and dance floor. It is ideal for corporate functions, weddings and other important occasions. The smaller Liardet Room is also a light-drenched area that is ideal for more intimate functions of up to 60 guests. The hotel is beautifully presented and pleasantly priced.

The Frankston Motel is set back off the highway on the corner of the Frankston-Flinders Road and Bartlett Street. It belongs to the highly respected Budget Motel chain and owners Liz and Barry Sauer have set out to prove that the word budget does not mean second best. The dimensions of the wide-open landscaped gardens that surround the motel are echoed within the spacious, beautifully presented 24 ground floor units that can cater for between one and six guests. The attractive tariff includes a continental breakfast or, should guests prefer, cooked breakfasts can be ordered at an additional charge.

The 2.5-hectare property has plenty of parking spaces for that extra car or boat and the grounds feature a 45-metre attractive in-ground pool and barbecue area set within a decorative garden. A full-size floodlit tennis court is an added bonus. There is no charge to guests for the use of the court and, should they be needed, racquets can be hired from the office for a minimal charge and balls are free.

The motel is centrally located on the south side of Frankston close to Monash University Peninsula Campus, four kilometres from the CBD and close to all the region's attractions. Liz and Barry are experienced moteliers and have turned the motel into a welcoming retreat and offer mid-week golf and winery tour packages. But, no matter when guests visit, an enjoyable stay is assured.

The Frankston Motor Inn, formerly the Colonial, is one of the city's affordable boutique-style motels set back in a quiet location, marked by huge palm trees easily distinguished along the Nepean Highway. The 30 double-tiered units look onto a central paved lamp-lit courtyard fringed by well-kept gardens. A balcony services the upper level, running the length of the building, decorated with wrought iron balustrades that create an old-world village atmosphere. Ample parking is provided and the spacious rooms come in all configurations, some with spas. They are warm and inviting, comfortably furnished in an attractive eclectic country style.

The property is fringed by well-maintained gardens. An enclosed barbecue area is at the disposal of guests and a sparkling pool and spa, complete with water maiden, forms a restful oasis surrounded by palm trees and shrubs. It plays an enticing alternative to the beach that is situated only 150 metres away. Manager Alan Tinner takes pride in Frankston Motor Inn's reputation offering 24-hour check-in and friendly, cheerful service. Night manager Chris Lothian can always manage a smile and a cheery word no matter how late the hour.

Above: Frankston entrance of Kananook Creek
Right: Frankston foreshore

They have a wealth of knowledge on what is happening around town and can help visitors make the most of their time in Frankston. 'Perovics', one of the area's newest restaurants, is attached to the inn and serves hearty breakfasts. With the added bonus of an address that is at the centre of all the action, this property makes a great base for any holiday.

Langwarrin can be found five kilometres inland from Frankston. The history of the region goes back to the early settlers. The township of Langwarrin is relatively new, growing up over the last 20 years. The region is going through a period of growth with attractive, modern housing springing up and infrastructure being set in place for the expected rise in population.

Beretta's Langwarrin Hotel sits opposite the shopping centre on Cranbourne Road. Owner Peter Beretta has shaped the business with a philosophy matching the developing area, providing a family-oriented venue delivering value for money in the reasonably priced meals and beverages on offer. In the coming year it is planned to enlarge the extensive 150-seat bistro utilising the large outdoors area to provide an even more appealing dining venue. The restaurant is a busy, popular local haunt, open for lunch and dinner seven days a week. An extensive rotating wine list complements the continually developing menu that features established Australian favourites with daily chef's specials. Peter's values carry over into the kitchen and chefs use only superior produce in every dish, presenting diners with quality and value - a scarce commodity these days. A children's playroom adjoins the bistro allowing grown-up family members to enjoy a carefree dining experience and soak up the friendly atmosphere.

The hotel's gaming lounge has the distinction of being the number two Tabaret venue in the state. It has 34 up-to-the-minute machines set in a friendly, exclusive area with its own bar and attractive conversation corners. For the racing public the TAB facilities cater for all tastes. A main area located within its own race viewing bar provides a more traditional setting and a separate elegant TAB lounge enclosed by frosted glass walls leads from the gaming area and comes complete with several televisions and an automatic totaliser.

The family-run business is a leading employer in the area with a roll call of 53 staff. The workforce are a youthful, vibrant bunch headed by Jonathon Couch, the hotel's young enthusiastic manager. Peter is a hands on owner who believes in the future of the area and is well known for his philanthropic ways, donating much to local charities, schools and sporting bodies.

The McClelland Gallery+Sculpture Park located three kilometres east of Frankston City, in McClelland Drive off the Frankston-Cranbourne Road, opened in 1971. The gallery complex is beautifully framed within a natural eight-hectare bush setting housing three temporary exhibition galleries, sculpture courtyards, a multi-purpose room, an education and storage wing, plus a licensed café and gift shop.

Nan McClelland was the benefactor whose largesse initiated the complex. Renowned in her lifetime for her philanthropic undertakings, on her death she gifted monies and the property "Studio Park" to establish an art gallery and cultural centre in memory of her younger brother Harry McClelland, as "a lasting legacy for the community".

The McClellands lived in Flemington during the late 1800s and early 1900s, owning large amounts of property in Melbourne. Around 1916 they bought a beachfront property on Long Island in Frankston and some time later Nan, Harry and their widowed mother made the property their home. Both Nan and her brother were lovers of the arts. She wrote poetry and broadcast the first ABC children's programs. Harry was an avid artist with a flair for design, planning much of the gardens and buildings on their property. His passion for painting led him to purchase 40 acres at Langwarrin. He built a studio on the land, going into seclusion for long periods of time to paint. He named the property "Studio Park".

Entry to the McClelland Gallery+Sculpture Park is by donation. The gallery hosts an impressive calendar of exhibitions that are enhanced by a permanent collection created by some of the country's most prominent artists. Situated within the grounds are over 30 major sculptures, including many works representing the *Centre 5* group.

An interesting annex of the gallery contains portraits of both Nan and Harry McClelland. W.B. McInnes, who was a resident of the area, painted Harry's portrait on canvas. McClelland and McInnes were members of the local Scottish pipe band and the portrait depicts Harry in the full highland regalia of a drum major. The work won McInnes the 1930 Archibald Prize.

Harry's Café, contained within the gallery complex, is a blissful place for a delicious lunch or just that well deserved cup of tea. The glass façade overlooks a large lake, creating a bright relaxed venue. The small licensed restaurant is a great meeting place either on a visit to the gallery or just to take a break in the middle of a busy day – the food is worth it.

The gallery's Sculpture Park and Collection is one of the most important compilations in the country. It contains over 30 major works of Australia's finest sculptors. Many of these extraordinary pieces are displayed in the picturesque "Sculpture Park" surrounding the gallery. The grounds invite exploration and are beautifully presented with picnic facilities and walking tracks. The lake is a central feature that provides a natural setting for some of the sculptures. Contemplation benches under shady trees invite visitors to spend time in reflection, surveying the tranquil scene.

Nature has imitated art, dotting the landscape with elegant trees that the hand of master sculptors could have crafted, and plantings of shrubs and flowers adds softness to the man-made art on display. Beyond the "Tarax Play Sculpture", an impressive abstract of large gleaming white balls toppling over one another in playful profusion by renowned artist Peter Corlett, lies the modest stone studio that was so favoured by Harry McClelland. It is tucked away in a woodland setting where nothing disturbs the tranquillity but the sound of birds. The whole McClelland experience is one of beauty and serenity. A peaceful sanctuary that is not encroached on by the nearness of the modern arterial road that runs past the gates of historic Studio Park.

Above & right: McClelland Gallery+Sculpture Park

A professional team at the gallery works tirelessly to boost the gallery's reputation, working to bring exhibitions featuring amazing sculptural masterpieces in all media to an appreciative public. The newly instigated biennial McClelland Survey and $100,000 McClelland Award for contemporary outdoor sculpture is destined to become a major event on the national artistic calendar. The McClelland Gallery+Sculpture Park is an ideal destination for art and nature lovers alike.

Langwarrin Flora and Fauna Reserve is also situated on McClelland Drive, a short distance from Frankston City and is a place of harmony. From 1886 until 1980 the reserve had a military use, being utilised as a military reservist training camp and rifle range. It was converted into a POW camp during WWI then transformed into a hospital to treat veterans returning from Europe with communicable diseases. At the end of its military service most of the buildings were dismantled. All that remains of its past history are some earthworks, building foundations, drainage and a cricket pitch that is located near the car park on McClelland Drive.

In 1985 the 214-hectare site was declared a reserve. It is now one of the few remaining areas south of Melbourne that supports indigenous plants and animals and is managed by Parks Victoria. Ninety-four bird species live within its boundaries and a network of tracks allow easy access to its solitude. The park is a haven for some flora that is near extinction on the Peninsula. Open stands of stringybark forest line the walking tracks, scarce in the region because of land clearance, and tufted blue lilies, wedding bush, rabbit-ears orchids and short purple flag all rare to the area, can be found here.

Koalas and swamp wallabies live in the reserve, sharing their habitat with brown bandicoots and the rare New Holland mouse. The park is an ideal location for walking and observing the beauty of the region, but because of conservation values no facilities are provided.

Dame Elisabeth Murdoch is a highly regarded resident of Langwarrin, living on her "Cruden Farm" property in Cranbourne Road since she and her husband, newspaper tycoon, the late Sir Keith Murdoch, purchased the property in the 1930s. Langwarrin CFA's first truck was a former *Herald* vehicle, converted into a water tanker, donated by the Murdochs. A great patron of the arts, Dame Elisabeth's name appears on many of the dedication plaques in local galleries and the **Dame Elisabeth Murdoch Arboretum** is of course named in her honour.

The arboretum is a 1.13-hectare garden, situated on the Frankston-Cranbourne Road. This attractive park features more than 1,100 plants, both native and exotic. It is an ideal educational facility for tree lovers and both the experienced and inexperienced gardener. The gardens, complete with a rotunda, are very picturesque and the facility can be booked for weddings and all manner of celebratory functions. Vehicles are not permitted to enter the gardens but there is off-street parking available at the arboretum's Edward Street entrance.

Mulberry Hill on Golf Links Road, Langwarrin South, is an American colonial style house built in 1926 by Sir Daryl and Joan (Lady) Lindsay, incorporating an original 1880s cottage. Upon their death the house and a large collection of art and antiques was bequeathed to the National Trust of Victoria.

Sir Daryl was born Ernest Daryl Lindsay in 1889 at Creswick, Victoria, a member of the talented Lindsay family. He was the second youngest of 10 children born to Doctor Robert Lindsay, who travelled to Australia as a ship's doctor. Growing up, Daryl loved the land and became an accomplished horseman. It was his intention to become a station manager. Enlisting in the AIF in 1915 he served in France with the war artist Will Dyson, (his brother-in-law), but was transferred to the Queen Mary Hospital, Sidcup, Kent, in 1917 to work as an artist for the plastic surgeons. During 1917 he met Henry Tonks, Slade Professor of Fine Art, and spent some time in 1918 studying drawing under Tonks at Slade. Upon returning to Australia in 1919 he became a freelance illustrator and painter. He revisited London in 1921, where he met and married Joan in 1922. Lindsay used his time in London to hone his talents as a watercolourist, later drawing many portraits of ballet dancers. The couple returned to Australia on their marriage.

Joan was born Joan a'Beckett Weigall in 1896 at Baxter, Victoria, and became a renowned visual artist and journalist. She studied art at the National Gallery School and exhibited with the Victorian Art Society, Melbourne, and the NSW Society of Artists. After her marriage, she developed her own talents as a writer, producing a number of books, winning international acclaim for *Picnic at Hanging Rock*, which was made into a movie. With Daryl's appointment as director of the National Gallery of Victoria, Melbourne in 1940, Joan became involved, assisting her husband in his work. In 1956 Daryl was a founding member of the National Trust and became the trust's first chairman; he was knighted that same year. Throughout their lives the energetic couple worked tirelessly to bring art and culture to the fore in Australia. Sir Daryl died in 1976, followed in 1984 by Joan.

The Lindsays purchased Mulberry Hill in 1925. The property is part of the original leasehold Carup Carup owned by Benjamin Baxter. The existing four-roomed cottage was included in the design of the attractive country house, created initially as a holiday home.

Above: Sir Daryl Lindsay's studio at Mulberry Hill
Right: Mulberry Hill

The historic kitchen remains, but two of the rooms were opened up to provide a large airy studio, which became the hub of the Lindsays' existence. The room today is just as they left it, with both their own and work of other famous artists adorning the walls. Of all the rooms in the house this is the place that visitors can most feel the presence of the past owners. Daryl had remained a devoted horseman all his life. He kept his saddle and tack just inside the studio door, where it can still be seen. A hand-written list with Joan's personal telephone numbers, that contains the local cab company and her hairdresser, is still pinned to the wall above an antiquated telephone. The room is full of books. A painting by Lindsay rests on an easel. It features Joan, the housekeeper's small daughter and himself astride his beloved mount Pompeii, sitting on the saddle and wearing the hat that resides by the studio door.

The Lindsays were avid collectors of Australia's most accomplished artists. The elegant dining room features one of Joan's favourite pieces, an impressive oil on canvas, 'Woman in Red Tights' by Constance Stokes. Joan has coloured the room deep burgundy, thus compelling the eye to the gold-framed work. A magnificent John Percival, made unique by its dimensions, titled 'The Pool' hangs in the entrance hall and Arthur Boyd's 'Hampstead Heath', a study of winter in black and white, adorns the master bedroom. These are just a few of an amazing collection.

The garden surrounding the house is a peaceful zone, disturbed only by the plaintive tolling of bellbirds. Contoured slopes and a walled garden invite exploration. A sea of agapanthus cover a woodland walk that is divided from the house by a wide lawn, semi-circled by a huge cypress hedge that was planted around the time the house was built. Since Joan's death many brides have utilised this perfect setting. Mulberry Hill's gardens are available for functions and the house is open to the public Sunday afternoons but closed the entire month of July.

Baxter is named for its first European settler, Captain Benjamin Baxter. The town was originally known as Mornington Junction but was renamed in 1911. Like many of the inland areas Baxter's early settlers planted orchards on their land but in recent times the area has garnered a reputation for its fertile market gardens that annually produce a cornucopia of fruit and vegetables. Situated 50 kilometres from Melbourne, Baxter sits astride the Frankston City and the Mornington Peninsula Shire borders. It is a peaceful town that adjoins the Langwarrin Flora and Fauna Reserve.

The historic town still holds some semblance of days gone by. Baxter schoolhouse has survived the years. Originally built in 1890 on a site in Golf Links Road opposite Mulberry Hill, it was moved to its present site in Warrandyte Road in 1955 and is still currently in use within the school system.

One of the Peninsula's most prominent historical homes also sits within Baxter's boundaries. **Sage's Cottage** on Sages Road is a well-preserved example of early European settlement. Built by John Edward Sage in 1856 on a section of land he purchased that was previously part of Carup Carup, the leasehold of his father-in-law, Captain Benjamin Baxter. He named his farm "Eurutta". The farm was divided in 1944 but the cottage and remaining land belonged to the Sage family until 1976 when the Victorian Conservation Trust bought the cottage and surrounding grounds.

The outbuildings and cottage are typical of their time, constructed of timber slabs with shingled roofing; however, the shingled roofs have been replaced with galvanised iron. The cottage stands out in the district as the only known original vertical timber slab-constructed dwelling to have survived the years. Sage's Cottage has been classified by the National Trust and has been restored as near as possible to its original specifications. The property mirrors the life of a pioneer family who will be remembered not only for the cottage they left behind but for the longevity of their blood line: each of them, mother, father and siblings, using most of their four score years and ten.

In 1989 Anne Jukes became part of Sage Cottage's history, taking over an already existing restaurant at the homestead. She has added her own special allure to the Baxter Provender Restaurant, turning it into a restaurant and function centre of distinction. Anne's persona suits her surroundings; old-world charm and her obvious love of the property enter the room with her like a warm wind. She offers a menu that reflects the history of the homestead with delicious country-style food that she expertly prepares in the cottage's updated historic kitchen.

Three rooms of the original cottage provide a character-filled dining ambiance surrounded by images of the past, and a large open fireplace creates special warmth in winter. A kitchen courtyard with outdoor seating under a canopy of wisteria and roses leads through a rustic gate overhung by fragrant angel's trumpets to an orchard with 20-metre high century-old pear trees. John Sage is believed to have planted the trees and they still produce huge quantities of fruit that, along with the property's other crops, make delicious jams and pickles that can be purchased on any visit.

Patrons are encouraged to explore the property. Three resident peacocks (all named Andrew) strut around the extensive gardens that contain the properties historic buildings. What was the blacksmith's shop peeks out from behind a massive age-old peppercorn tree and a lavender run, bordered by catnip, lines the way to the old stables that have been lovingly restored to house a unique function room. The stables had more or less collapsed when Anne turned her attention to them. With the help of Heritage Victoria and Friends of Sage Cottage she has recreated a part of the area's history. The stables open onto a weatherproofed patio and overlook a large lake and restful woodland scene. It makes the perfect spot for any special occasion and a wonderful venue for a wedding. A bridal changing room is made available within the historic cottage in a character-filled bedroom. The restaurant is open Friday through Sunday each week for lunch as well as morning and afternoon teas, with group bookings available at other times.

Above: Sage's Cottage

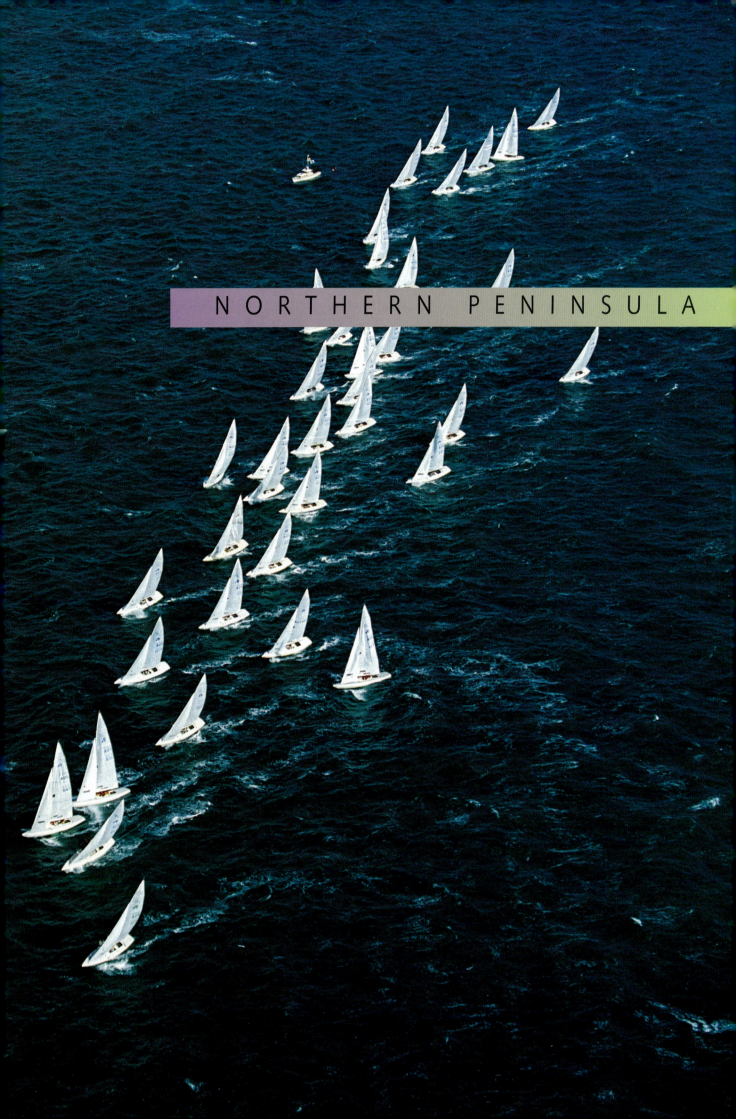
NORTHERN PENINSULA

Northern Peninsula Listings

MOUNT ELIZA: Manyung Gallery P46-47/243. Lintons Garden & Home Centre P48-49/243.

MORNINGTON: Mornington Main Street Markets P50/243. Mornington Central P50/243. Sail Mornington P52/243. Beaches of Mornington P54/243. Boyz 4 Breakie P54.57/243. Peninsula Indulgence Restaurant P54/56/57/244. Rocks Restaurant P 56/57/243. Schnapper Point Kiosk P56/57/243. Bay Hotel P58/244. Grand Hotel P58-59/244. Kirkpatricks P58/61/244. The Royal Hotel P60-61/244. Tanti Hotel P56/60/244. Mornington Racing Club P62-63/244. Mornington Peninsula Regional Gallery M.P.R.G. P64-65/244. Bally Vista B&B P64/244. Canterbury By The Bay P 64/244. Mornington Motel P 66/244. The Ranch Motel P66/244. National Antique Centre P 66 /244.

MOOROODUC: Mornington Railway Preservation Society P 66/67. Boutik Regional Wine & Art Centre P68-69/244. TV World P68-69. The Peninsula Lounge P68-69/244. Bottom Drawer Antiques P68/70/244. Gooseberry Hill Cottages B&B. P70/244.

MOUNT MARTHA: Mt. Martha Beachside Bistro P70-71/245. Briars Historic Park P72-73/245. Perfumed Garden & Roseraie. P72-73/245. Josephine's at the Briars P72-74/245. Briarswood Cottages P74/245. Mt Martha B&B By the Sea P74/245. Original OZ Gallery P74/245.

Mornington's famous Cup Day atmosphere

Northern Peninsula opening page: Racing fleet
Centre-spread background: Mornington Cup racing

NORTHERN PENINSULA

Port Phillip Bay was discovered in January 1802; sighted by the crew of the 'Lady Nelson' commanded by Acting Lieutenant John Murray. It was explored later that month by the ship's first mate William Bowen, who described the bay as, "a great and noble sheet of water." Murray spent a further three weeks exploring the bay, landing at Point King and hoisting the British flag, taking possession of Port King (later named Port Phillip) for the British Government.

Thousands of years ago, what is now the floor of the bay was a lush valley, criss-crossed by the Yarra River and its tributaries on their way to the sea. Rising waters at the end of the last Ice Age flooded the valley.

The bay has only one entrance, through a narrow treacherous channel via Bass Strait that separates the Mornington and Bellarine Peninsulas. Named the Rip, the narrow channel is less than three kilometres wide and ranks among the world's most hazardous harbour entrances; it holds a sailor's every anathema. Flanked by dangerous reefs that create underwater ravines, the bay's tides are at the Rip's mercy. Incoming and outgoing water battles for right of passage in the narrow conduit, at times creating whirlpools and massive perpendicular walls of water that surge to the heavens in their titanic clashes for supremacy; a truly awesome sight.

Lying immediately inside the entrance, on the bay side of the Rip, await the much shallower waters of Port Phillip Sands, 260 square kilometres of constantly shifting sand banks that are now part of the Port Phillip Heads Marine National Park. The Great Sands are in fact remnants of the Yarra estuary. It is of course inevitable that such a devil's cauldron would have claimed many victims. Aided by the inhospitable coastline around the Heads, the Rip has wrecked over 100 ships since the early 1800s, with many lives lost.

An interesting phenomenon of the Great Sands is the exposed section of Mud Islands that are listed on the Register of the National Estate. The reserve lies 10 kilometres inside the bay, a short six kilometres northeast of Portsea. Four small islets have formed on an outcrop of dune rock. The low-lying islands are covered in dune shrubs and salt marsh vegetation with thick, succulent leaves and stems. Covering an area of 100 hectares, they encircle a placid lagoon that provides a natural sanctuary for all manner of sea birds, including endangered species and migratory varieties.

In complete contrast to the turbulent passage the Bay has an amorphous, mirrored surface with chromatic water that covers an area of 1,950 square kilometres, an area of approximately 60 by 65 kilometres. It is almost surrounded by land, the south-east of which contains some of the Mornington Peninsula's most prestigious towns.

The bay is a watery wonderland stunningly fringed with golden sands lapped by placid sparkling waters. This cocktail has proved to be a lure that visitors cannot resist and few fail to return again and again.

Mount Eliza is considered Melbourne's most southern suburb. The town occupies a sharply elevated outcrop that overlooks Canadian Bay backed by a sprawling prestigious residential area that blends effortlessly into the hillside.

The area has been a popular 'get-away' for Melburnians since the late 1800s, with many building imposing holiday homes on the mount. Some of these spectacular homes still snuggle among the trees overlooking the bay from the cliff tops.

A wealth of beaches front the town and the old Moorooduc Quarry (access from Alison Road) has been reclaimed as the Mount Eliza Regional Park. A 1.5-kilometre walking track meanders through the park, complete with lookout points, around the edge of the quarry. It provides good views across the Moorooduc Plains. Picnic facilities are provided at Two Bays Road.

The town's close proximity to Frankston and Mornington in no way detracts from its high profile; in fact it enhances the village atmosphere to be enjoyed in Mount Eliza Village. Excellence is stamped on the businesses to be found within its boundaries; as well as offering quality merchandise in their chosen field, many have become tourism icons in their own right.

Manyung Gallery on the Nepean Highway opened its doors in 1968, a new location on a historic site that dates back to the original goat farm of 1890. It is easy to find, located in an eye-catching imaginative castle-like structure, complete with ornamental moat and drawbridge with just the hint of a portcullis overhead. Entry to the gallery is gained through a sun-dappled courtyard over hung by a massive ancient oak tree, surrounded by a profusion of ferns and lilies that offset some amazing sculptures, creating a restful spot to linger.

Purpose built, the structure enfolds a vast art space that is not obvious from its façade, containing an eight-gallery complex of uniquely designed rooms, incorporating what was the original farmhouse. It houses a masterful display of oil and watercolour paintings, enhanced by strong contemporary sculpture, jewellery, furniture and ceramic pieces. Purchased three years ago by sister and brother partnership Nicole and Stuart Allen, during what was a low ebb in the gallery's history, the duo have breathed new life into the complex, returning it to its roots and concentrating their efforts on new and mid-career artists. Over the gallery's long existence, in their early years, almost all Australia's artists who gained fame have had exhibitions at Manyung. The reputation of the gallery has spread: it has not only clients but also sightseers who spend hours browsing the exhibits. The business won an Australian Tourism Excellence Award and was a finalist in the hospitality award category in recent years. The gallery has an ever-changing face and is a congenial place to spend some time. Nicole and Stuart piqué their clients' interest by presenting a new exhibition each month.

Left: Manyung Gallery at Mt. Eliza
Right: Sculpture 'Flight' by Bruce Clayton, at the Manyung Gallery

Lintons Garden and Home Centre is a flower-filled oasis on the corner of the Nepean Highway and Canadian Bay Road. Voted the 'Best Large Garden Centre in Australia' on two different occasions, the latest in 2003, it is the biggest garden centre on the Peninsula. Lintons is not just a garden centre, it is a destination for garden lovers that attract visitors from far and near.

In 1937 Michael Linton's father, Bill, began what has become a Mornington Peninsula tradition, but the family's horticultural experience goes back to Michael's grandfather, Harry, who grew flower and vegetable seedlings, which his five sons sold door to door. Michael has carried on the family tradition of getting bigger and better, moving the business to its present premises in 1986. Under his direction, Lintons Garden and Home Centre has steadily grown from a small family nursery to a large garden centre that has won multiple national and state awards, gaining an Australia wide reputation for excellence.

Set back off the highway on an elevated 2.5 acres, the main building is a shimmering limestone and glass atrium that resembles the Crystal Palace. It houses many exotic plants and a range of creative home, kitchen and giftware, unique items sourced from both Australia and overseas. The atrium opens out onto a wonderland of courtyards, pergolas, groves and a Rippon Lea-inspired shade house.

There is a pandemonium of pots to choose from – glazed pots and stone pots, terracotta and painted pots, pots that add style to the elegant plants on display. The soothing sound of water trickling over rocks, spouting from stone figures and cascading down horizontal sculptures creates a restful medley. Pools of colourful flowers and elegant greenery abound in Eden-like profusion and a rose garden, when in full flower, creates a riot of colour and fills the air with a fragrance that overwhelms you. Not to be outdone, a full spectrum of native plants and trees is also on display, producing that aromatic scent so characteristic of the Australian bush in their corner of the nursery.

The garden centre occupies land that was once utilised by a squatter family; their cottage built in 1871 has survived and is believed to be one of the oldest of its ilk on the Peninsula. Reinvented as the Cottage Tearooms, it is located in a raised position at the rear of the property and serves lunches and snacks that can be enjoyed inside the renovated cottage or in the surrounding courtyard. It is the perfect spot to linger, overlooking the centre's multitude of plants and trees. An enclosed playground is adjacent the cottage, providing an interesting distraction for younger visitors.

If so far your forays into the garden have been mostly a question of learning by trial and error, then the staff at Lintons are just the people with whom you need to talk. Michael extols their virtues and insists the business's success is because of their enthusiasm. They are a friendly bunch, with the knowledge to help dispel the mystery of gardening and will prove that you don't have to be born with a green thumb. But if you just want to wander around, that's all right too, as all plants are named, priced and tagged with instructions.

For those of us with plenty of everything except time, Lintons can have a garden designed and planted for you by experts – they have been known to transport full-grown trees and plant them with the use of a crane. They provide full gardening support with an on-site gardening consultation service, but customers receive the same helpful advice whether purchasing the smallest seedling or the largest tree. Gardens can be an artistic extension of your home and here at Lintons they have everything you need to turn your backyard into a colourful, decorative, wonderland.

Somerville is a peaceful inland settlement on the eastern perimeter of the Moorooduc Plains that abuts Watson's Creek as it wanders through the district towards Western Port Bay. Its elevated hillside position makes it stand out from the surrounding countryside. Established in 1859, some of its historic buildings still line the streets. The hotel on the corner of Edward and Station Streets was built in 1904 and retains most of its original facade, and the Mechanics Institute, built in 1891, once the heart of the community, is now the headquarters for the Somerville and Tyabb Heritage Society.

The Stony Point railway line divides the town in two, with commercial and shopping areas that contain a good range of shops and businesses on either side. The line has encouraged the residential growth of the town in recent years, as an alternative lifestyle for Melbourne workers

Mornington is a sparkling bayside town, situated on Port Phillip Bay 55 kilometres south-east of Melbourne. It is a modern scintillating centre that throbs with subdued energy. The town's population of approximately 30,000 explodes in the summer months. It has so much to offer, and has been appropriately dubbed 'Marvellous Mornington'.

The town evolved from the original European settlement begun in the 1840s at Schnapper Point. Matthew Flinders was the area's first European visitor, arriving in April 1802 during his expedition to accurately map Australia's coast. His maps were the first to endorse Australia as a continent. So accurate was his cartography that his charts were still in use 150 years later. He took 18 months to complete the journey around Australia. However, it was some time before he returned to Britain. On the journey back he was taken prisoner by the French in Mauritius and held for six years. Flinders was the first to advocate that the continent be named Australia in place of the previously adopted 'Terra Australis'.

For some years after Mornington's inception the area could only be reached by land.

Above & right: Linton Garden and Home Centre

Road travel in the 1800s was a tiring, trepidant time-consuming affair. The main road from Melbourne came only as far as Mordialloc; the journey thereafter was extremely hit and miss, traversing a circuitous route on inadequate, roughly hewn tracks. When a jetty was built in 1857, it created a deep-water port that was the perfect entrée, establishing an important link with the capital for the emerging region. With the commencement of a steamer service between Melbourne and Mornington in the late 1800s, access to the town was simplified. The small community reaped the benefits and flourished as a holiday destination or day trip for Melbourne's growing community.

This era gave rise to many of the elegant hotels and buildings that grace Mornington's streets today. Melbourne's leading families favoured the town and built grand mansions that have endowed it with an enduring genteel elegance. Remnants of the past can be found on every street. The two-cell lock-up gaol, at the foreshore end of Main Street, was built in 1860 and proclaimed a gaol in 1862. It is in complete contrast to the modern police station that sits adjacent to the historic site. The cells lie directly behind the historic courthouse, which now acts as a tourist information office and the headquarters of the Mornington Peninsula Chamber of Commerce. The old building still contains the judge's bench, the clerk of court's box and wooden railings that sectioned off the public area. It makes browsing among the brochures an interesting experience. The courthouse and cells were extended in 1866; they remained in use until 1988. The courthouse is both the oldest courthouse and oldest public building on the Mornington Peninsula.

For a walk through nostalgia, pick up a copy of the Mornington Historic Walk pamphlet. It details buildings of historic interest around town. As mentioned, the Mornington Peninsula Historical Society is located in the town's original post office, circa 1861, located at the corner of Main Street and The Esplanade. It is a treasure trove of historic information with many interesting artefacts on display.

Shopping in Mornington's traditional retail area, which runs off the Nepean Highway, is a pleasure to be savoured. The birth of Main Street dates back to the town's settlement. It is an extremely attractive avenue that gently inclines to the bay, ending at the small, visually stunning harbour. The historic shopping thoroughfare and the adjoining streets are lined with a bevy of boutiques and a gaggle of galleries and gift shops, where avid shoppers can indulge their innermost passion. In recent years, the streetscape has been enhanced by clusters of sidewalk seating spilling out from a melange of new age coffee houses that are so popular with the caffe latté sipping devotees - setting the scene for long lazy days, when it is permissible to do absolutely nothing.

An alternate shopping experience is provided for visitors each Wednesday along Main Street. Commencing in 1979, it is the longest-running street market in Victoria. The bustling market complements the quality already displayed by the sophisticated Main Street retailers. Market day is a casual, outdoor, festive occasion that captures the diversity of the region's produce and artisans. Main Street's footpath becomes the medium for a colourful, titillating bazaar that attracts convoys of buses from far and wide overflowing with eager consumers, only some of the quarter of a million visitors that the market attracts each year. The Mornington Chamber of Commerce expertly manages the event and on any given Wednesday, between one and two hundred stalls set up on the strip. Their wares are home made and home grown, all produced with flair and a high degree of skill. An equally diverse market is held on the second Sunday of each month at the Mornington Racecourse.

Mornington's shopping area has of course outgrown the original main thoroughfare and has expanded into the modern equivalent of main street, 'The Mall'. The concept of an undercover shopping precinct came out of America, first unveiled to the world in 1956 in Minneapolis. This innovative idea opened up a whole new world to shoppers, providing them with 365-days shopping a year, fair weather or foul. Mornington's residents and visitors are fortunate to have two of these esteemed establishments right in the heart of town.

Mornington Central, situated on Mornington's western edge, running parallel to Main Street, is conveniently located and the larger of Mornington's two shopping complexes. It offers shoppers comfort and convenience in a bright spacious area, designed for effortless shopping. An ample assortment of retail establishments, from shopping giants Coles/Liquorland and Target to small boutiques and services, display and provide a full range of merchandise and assistance, colluding to meet every need. The centre is designed to cater for the physically impaired, and the convenience of ample parking on the doorstep makes it easy to arrive and depart with the minimum of fuss.

The Village Shopping Centre at the top of Main Street was Mornington's first shopping complex; it creates what its name implies, a close-knit, double-tiered community of distinctive speciality stores and services headed by Safeway Supermarket. Both floors can be accessed from street level and escalators make it easy to go from one to the other. The centre is wheelchair friendly and has an open, airy atmosphere. Undercover parking makes it a good all-weather complex. The village environment is enhanced Wednesdays, when the centre opens its doors to the Mornington Market. Stallholders overflow into the complex and add a touch of carnival to the everyday.

Mornington Chamber of Commerce was established in 1942 and over the years the members have learned the value of promoting the effervescent town. Known colloquially as the 'party town', the chamber makes sure it lives up to its name, organising an event in every month of the year. One of the most eagerly awaited is the Wine and Food Festival, organised by a committee made up of Mornington business people. It takes over the entire length of Main Street for one day in October, attracting over 26,000 visitors.

Above: Main Street Wine & Food Festival
Right: Aerial view of Mornington Harbour

The Mornington Chamber of Commerce is continually looking for ways to make any visit to the area stress-free, so to find your way around town, simply find your way to one of the 3-D map and directory signs that are being set up at strategic points along Main Street; they will point you in the right direction and help you on your way.

Mornington's foreshore has much to offer families, dotted with picturesque barbecue and picnic areas overlooking the beaches and bluffs. **Mornington Park** is the town's historic gathering place. As early as 1863 Alexander Balcombe had the Legislative Assembly set aside the Mornington coastline and the park area for 'promenade and recreation'. The park has seen many gatherings over the years. At one time it was used by the Fire Brigade as a training track and was also utilised as the cricket and football ground. In the early 1900s trees were planted for shade. A band rotunda and a pavilion for cricket and football spectators was built and a running track developed.

Many works picnics were held within its confines and it remains today a popular picnic venue. Children love to visit the park that now boasts an interactive playground with a good selection of swings and apparatus that includes a large as life wooden replica of a three masted schooner that in young fertile minds plays alternate roles as a pirate ship and a British Man O' War. Three impressive stone archways give access to the park. Built in 1932 during the Depression, they were constructed as part of the unemployment relief project.

Adjacent the park's eastern gate, a stone memorial erected in 1892 is a poignant reminder of what is Mornington's worst boating disaster – the drowning of an entire football team returning from an away game against Mordialloc. Fifteen young men lost their lives in the seas around Pelican Point, Mount Eliza. The family hardest hit was that of Reverend Caldwell of the Presbyterian Church, who lost three of his four sons.

The Mornington Pier, that was built after a Parliamentary Enquiry and responsible for bringing the town to prominence in its early years, is still used by the scallop fishing fleet. Recreational fishers too have discovered its magic and put the sturdy platform to good use all year round, hauling good catches of schnapper and squid in season and garfish and whiting in winter. For the more romantically inclined, the pier makes an extremely stimulating walking platform, open to the elements surrounded by the serenade of the bay.

Schnapper Point, the elevated position from where Mathew Flinders made his first survey of Port Phillip Bay, towers over the pier and surrounding beaches. A monument commemorating the historic event rises from its peak and boardwalks follow the ridge along the foreshore, providing wonderful views. Flinders didn't have the luxury of boardwalks when, carrying all his surveying equipment, he followed the cliff line kilometres to Schnapper Point from his landing site at Bird Rock.

To see Port Phillip Bay from a different perspective take a trip with Sail Mornington. You will find them centrally located berthed on the Mornington Pier. With the owners at the helm, any adventure is possible; long, short or extended overnight voyages, business functions or bareboat training. Budding sailors can even join in and crew during the Thursday night Twilight Sailing Race organised by the Mornington Yacht Club throughout the summer months. This is a fun night – and the Sail Mornington crew has actually powered the boat to victory on occasion. The boat can carry up to 12 passengers; well-behaved children are welcome but would count in the total number on board and must wear the life jackets provided. Trips can be custom designed to suit the occasion, and can also include catering.

Enthusiastic owners, newlyweds, Sandra Watt and Stuart Maconachie are sailing aficionados. Stuart has been sailing all his life, performing the task of Sailing Master on racing boats for many years and can regale guests with many a salty tale. Sandra was brought up in the Snowy Mountains, where she learned to sail on the reservoirs and lakes, in an area where, says Sandra, "one half of the populace went to church on Sundays and the other half went sailing." She took a break for some years but on meeting Stuart the passion was rekindled and now she races on the bay with the best of them. The love of their life is 'Grace' a beautiful name for a beautiful lady. She is a Beneteau Oceanis 400 built by a world-renowned company whose expertise dates back to 1884. The sleek lines allow a smooth ride, the bow slicing through the bay with minimal water displacement, proudly riding the waves. Below deck the Beneteau's traditional rich wooden interior glows warmly and brass accessories glint in the subdued light. 'Grace' is an artistic masterpiece and a pleasure to sail in and has, say her owners, "her own personality."

During trips passengers are encouraged to take a turn at the wheel. There is a no more exhilarating experience than being in control of this exotic machine. Since Sail Mornington's inception in 2002 many satisfied customers have spent many happy hours sailing on and swimming off 'Grace'. She includes snorkelling gear among her equipment and Stuart knows all the best diving locations. An abundance of wildlife can often be seen, such as dolphins, seals and fairy penguins. When asked what were the most common and uncommon things that passengers requested, we were told the boat's very first charter had been a funeral to scatter ashes at sea and, since the motion picture 'Titanic'; the 'Titanic Pose' on the bow of the boat had become something that people were compelled to do!

Mornington's coastline is a scalloped stretch of golden sand and secluded beaches, dotted with colourful beach huts, divided by points and bluffs. Red Bluff creates a vivid splash of colour between Mills Beach and Scout Beach. The town's main beach lies adjacent to the pier. Suitably named Mothers Beach, its protective length is well placed in the centre of town. It is serene and scenic, with rippling, shallow water and a high backed foreshore, topped by tall cypresses that provide the perfect picnic canopy.

Above: Sailing in Mornington Harbour

Right: Views from Schnapper Point and Matthew Flinders memorial, Mornington

Fossil Beach, located along the Esplanade, close to Bensons Road and Bird Rock – the original landing spot of Matthew Flinders – was the site of one of Mornington's largest lime-burning operations. The lime-burning site was cemented over in 1879 and turned into a picnic area. Road access was added in 1927 and fireplaces in 1941. When the site was operational, it contained a large and a small firing kiln, a horse-operated crushing wheel and numerous storage pits. Toilet facilities now stand where the storage pits once filled and emptied. Remains of the kilns, plus parts of the crushing wheel and storage pits, can still be found on the site, discarded where they fell, now covered with years of coastal shrubbery and regrowth. It makes an interesting day searching them out.

In recent years, a riot of restaurants has sprung up in and around Mornington's Main Street, creating a district reminiscent of Lygon Street in Melbourne.

Beaches of Mornington on Barkly Street is the one great restaurant that every town has, where you're greeted with a smile on your first visit and by name on the second. The winner of the Best Restaurant Award four years in a row and Best Business in 1999, the multi award-winning venue is an experience not to be missed. Locals have dubbed their favourite haunt the 'Cheers Bar'; a reputation that owner John Crossin is very proud of. Beaches is many things to many people. A cosy bar, an excellent restaurant and a top line live entertainment venue that is open for lunch and dinner seven days a week.

John has owned the restaurant since 1997. It occupies what was the church hall of the adjacent deconsecrated St. Andrews church and has been refurbished to mirror a casual, comfortable and convivial ambiance. The relaxed surroundings reflect Mornington's seaside position, with memorabilia sourced from boats and the ocean. A mezzanine level, with its own rowboat, overlooks the restaurant and is perfect for private functions. During the early evening cheerful staff, guided by John's daughter Rebecca, serve an expansive menu of sensational food that includes, mouth-watering steaks, succulent Queensland mud crabs and King Island crays, expertly prepared by Chef Paul McLean who trained at the Melbourne Oyster Bar. As the night gets older new customers drift in, the atmosphere changes to one of expectancy and soon the party begins.

Beaches is renowned for presenting world-recognised musicians and fostering up and coming talent. Many of Australia's top artists have started out on the venue's intimate stage. Every night, bar Monday and Tuesday, different artists feature on the entertainment menu. Wednesday nights are special with Bill Dettmer, award-winning songwriter, compering 'Muso Night'. The venue is aimed at a 25+ age group; "somewhere to come and feel comfortable," says John. In this writer's opinion, when in search of a great meal and a rollicking evening, stop in at Beaches and spread your wings.

Boyz 4 Breakie, located at the bottom end of Main Street, is only a cooee from Mornington's foreshore. However, don't be fooled by the name – the restaurant serves a mean lunch, brunch and dinner, as well as everything in between. An extensive wine list complements the menu, with a local wine featured each month. In the two years since its inception the restaurant has become a Mornington institution, where lovers tryst and friends meet and a full menu is served all day.

Business partners for six years, owners Jon Nicholls and John Inserra successfully opened their first restaurant together in Melbourne, but the move to Mornington has proved advantageous. They are passionate about the quality of food, with special attention paid to the coffee they serve; all staff must attend coffee school. The duo exude enthusiasm and are intent on sharing their love of the culinary arts. To this end they run a weekly cookery class in the restaurant's mezzanine level. When this area is not full of eager students, it doubles as a funky function room that has been expertly designed with things that pull up and things that let down, transforming it from an attractive function space into a well equipped teaching area.

The spacious ground floor contains a kitchen boutique, displaying a selection of Meyer equipment that is used by the chefs in the restaurant's kitchen, plus brands of coffee and tea, along with knick-knacks of the culinary genre. The main restaurant shares the gift shop space and customers can relax and enjoy mouth-watering dishes and pastries, served in an area decorated with imagination and flair. The atmosphere is warm and bright, the service is cheerful, and seating overflows onto the sidewalk, where hours can be spent, casually sipping coffee or a glass of wine while watching the world go by. However, if you have your heart set on breakie, then throw caution to the wind and order the 'Breakie 2 Die 4'; a slab of chargrilled sour dough bread topped with layers of spinach and tomato, bacon, mushrooms and eggs drizzled all over with hollandaise sauce – simply scrumptious.

Peninsula Indulgence Restaurant is architecturally designed and artistically decorated with plenty of off-street parking. Located on Barkly Street, the sparkling of wood and the attractive décor surrounds patrons in a bright welcoming atmosphere. Draped canvas sails soften the high ceiling and tall doors open onto tiered decking for summer dining. A conversation corner with couches provides a less formal cup of coffee or relaxing drink and is part of new owner Cassie Scott's aim to encourage, "people to come in and be pampered." Cassie bought the already established restaurant but has totally remodelled the business and everything you experience is her personal signature. She revels in the new and improved attitude that she has created.

Above: Beaches entertainment venue
Right: Sunset at Red Bluff, Mornington

The restaurant is an all-day venue serving gourmet breakfasts, delicious light lunches and succulent dinners accompanied by bread baked on the premises. Patrons are encouraged to pop in for coffee at any time and experience the Peninsula Indulgence appeal. The menu reflects modern Australian cuisine made with fresh local produce where possible and although the venue is fully licensed it also caters for guests who bring their own wine. Sunday Jazz fills the room with sizzling sounds: this is just one of many 'happenings' that Cassie has planned for the future. Full or half-day adventures with a difference are offered by Peninsula Indulgence Personalised Tours that are aimed at assisting visitors to the area to explore its wineries and hidden delights. Available for any size group from couples up providing a choice of wineries and vehicles including menus tailored to suit. Imagine a romantic tour for two in a Rolls Royce!

The 100-seat restaurant is large enough for private chitchat yet small enough to retain a cosy intimacy. This innovative eatery is open from Wednesdays through Sundays. Catering can be arranged for functions with weddings a speciality and corporate events can be tailored to suit. The Peninsula Indulgence is a comfortable contemporary restaurant with a dynamic young owner and staff who aim to please.

Sea air is known to increase the appetite, and there is no better place to assuage it than at The Rocks restaurant in Mornington. The restaurant has an exhilarating waterfront location overlooking the Mornington Pier and all points north, east and west that sets the scene for a memorable dining experience. Patrons can arrive on foot, they can arrive by car or boat. There is ample car parking in the adjacent car park, and a phone call will secure a boat mooring in the Mornington Yacht Club marina that is just a step from the restaurant. The 140-seat licensed restaurant is a much-loved meeting place and a great function venue; its popular weather-proofed deck is perfect for breakfast, lunch and dinner or a quick snack in between.

The restaurant has gained in popularity over the seven years since its inception, due to the dedication and enthusiasm of partner husband and wife teams, Rocco and Patricia Cirillo and Robert and Lisa de Santis, all members of the de Santis restaurateur family. Their inaugural aim, to present quality fine dining in a relaxed atmosphere, has been realised. How could they fail? Their staff is hospitable and well trained, the Mediterranean-influenced cuisine that features the freshest seafood is superb and skilfully presented by international award-winning chef Michael Hoare and is served in a heart-easing, inspirational setting. The reasons are many that will draw you back to The Rocks. Perhaps it's the unusual treats concocted by the in-house pastry chef, who creates mouth-watering treats like citron tarts, that make morning coffee and afternoon tea special; or the time taken to source new and unusual fresh products like tangy thirst-quenching Sicilian mandarin juice; or simply to sit on the deck watching the changing moods of the bay and sip a glass of chardonnay.

Schnapper Point Kiosk has occupied its place on the point since the early 1950s. It served fast food to many thousands of hungry customers through the window of a small shack. The idea is still there but the goal has changed. Nowadays patrons are drawn to a much larger sparkling sea-view café, housed in a charming structure that resembles a row of bathing boxes on the beach. The expanded premises invites diners to linger longer, choosing a table either within the bright interior or on the sun-soaked outdoor deck, taking time to appreciate the wonderful aspect overlooking the bay, the pier and the yacht club marina.

Charles Morgan and his wife Elise, who made the move from St. Kilda to enjoy the Peninsula's unmatched lifestyle, own the kiosk. Now only dabbling in the property development market that he left behind, Charles runs the kiosk with the help of a group of dedicated staff who include mother and daughter teams. "Owned by one family and run by many," says Charles.

Schnapper Point Kiosk has a great location and a reputation for good food that represents good value, it is the perfect choice for a casual lunch. A cosmopolitan all-day menu begins with breakfast and goes through to late afternoon tea, seven days a week, closing only on Christmas Day. A speciality of the house is the ribbon sandwiches, filled with creative layers of the freshest ingredients. The ever-changing wharfside scenery adds a dash of excitement to any repast, with boats coming and going, watched from the pier by fisher folk of every age and children who frolic in the shallow water of Mothers Beach. The colourful atmosphere entices diners to dally over lunch and order yet another cup of delicious coffee.

Above: Tanti Hotel, Mornington

Right:
Top– The Rocks restaurant;
Bottom left– The Boyz 4 Breakie;
Centre right– Schnapper Point Kiosk;
Bottom right– Peninsula Indulgence Restaurant

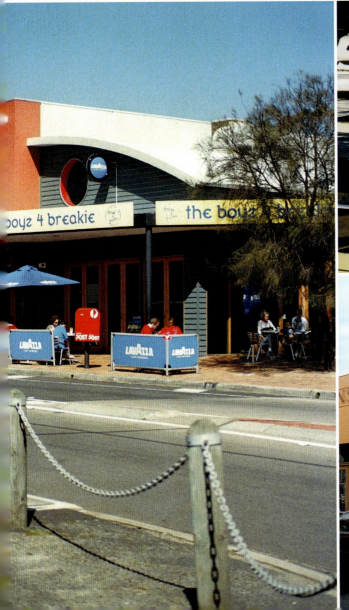

Mornington's historic aura is personified when dining and drinking in its famed old hotels. Each has a tale to tell, contained within century-old walls that have listened to the woes and goes of generations of Mornington citizens.

The Bay Hotel was built in 1890 to house the Commerce Bank. The solid double-storey limestone building would, no doubt, have held an aura of security for the settlement's 500 residents of the time. It survived as a bank until 1986 when, what was by then the National Bank, moved to new premises; at this time the old bank was transformed into a restaurant. In 1998 present owner, businessman Paul Cameron, purchased the fledgling restaurant taking the historic building's hospitality role one step further by creating a venue that holds something for everyone no matter what age.

The building's Main Street position is perfect for its new function. Creative remodelling has retained many of its original features – the massive steel door that once opened into the vault is still functional behind the bar. A newer attraction has been added in the form of French doors opening onto sidewalk seating, presenting a comfortable fair-weather platform to enjoy the outdoor ambiance. Its cosmopolitan aura does not detract from the solid maturity of the grand old building. The restaurant and lounge bar occupy the ground floor. High ceilings, exposed brick and urns of flowers set the scene for the enjoyment of culinary delights. Original fireplaces have been retained and are interspersed among the dining and seating areas, adding a glow of warmth and character to winter outings. The luxury of genuine leather Chesterfield chairs and sofas highlights several comfortable conversation nooks creating intimate areas for friends or lovers to enjoy a quiet drink or dynamic conversation. Live lounge entertainment nightly with the exception of Mondays and Tuesdays creates a festive atmosphere and entertains patrons with a wide range of performers.

The Bay's Mediterranean menu with Australian influences is seasonal and utilises the region's fresh produce whenever possible. Paul believes in showcasing local products: the extensive wine list features most of the Peninsula's leading wines. The hotel's upper floor once contained the bank manager's residence. Now it is the trendy Red Nightclub that opens Friday and Saturday nights until late. Plans include utilising the nightclub for live theatre, shows and comedy evenings. There is always something happening at the hotel; it is a favourite local haunt, famous for its 'After Cup Party', held following the running of the Mornington Cup. Paul grew up in Mt. Eliza and although he also has a design business in Melbourne his first love is the hotel. His enthusiasm is reflected in the attentive staff and the welcome afforded guests at The Bay.

The Grand Hotel on Main Street is a hotel with a past - and celebrates it. Built in 1889, it replaced an earlier hotel, the Cricketers Arms, that had occupied the site next door. The new hotel was originally named the Grand Coffee Palace and was designed by a renowned architect of the era, William Pitt. The hotel is still a strong feature of Mornington, its historic tower is visible from most angles in the heart of town. Over the years the tower has been rebuilt three times. The original was destroyed by fire and not replaced until after WWI. The owner of the day removed the second in 1937 due to its instability and because it would have cost 50 pounds more to repair as opposed to dismantle. Once torn apart it was unceremoniously taken to the tip, leaving The Grand Hotel without its hat for the next 50 years. Present owner Bernie Taylor replaced the tower in 1987, rejuvenating the building's original distinctive French Renaissance revival form and recreating an important part of the town's history. Bernie, who was born in San Francisco, USA, purchased The Grand in 1976 and has become a Mornington identity. He takes his position in the community seriously, giving much to local organizations and charities.

Although the hotel has been remodelled, the interior has been sympathetically refurbished and extended to fit its modern role. The high ceilings have been retained and the rooms opened up to create several spacious areas. A large stylishly furnished relaxing bar and bistro at the front of the hotel houses a baby grand that has been expertly tinkled by resident pianist Bob Couchman for over 20 years. An extensive wine list complements the bistro's menu that offers delicious European cuisine using local produce wherever possible. A Sports Bar is in a separate section of the hotel and a newer section of the hotel leading off the bistro contains a small bar and elegant gaming room. For a more energetic night out, the Cruz Club is located on the upper level, accessed by a stairway that covers what was in the 1800s a carriageway that went through to the rear yard and Swifts Stables. A Blue Light Disco is held the first Friday of the month in the Cruz Club that operates at other times from Wednesday to Sunday nights and provides an energetic night out.

Kirkpatricks Hotel is one of Mornington's earliest historic hotels. Built around 1873, it has stood the test of time. In the 1950s its beautiful original wrought iron balustrades were dismantled and the building's Victorian façade redesigned in favour of a more modern art deco look and the character of the interior was all but destroyed. Purchased in 1999 by present owner Ross Gregory, the old hotel had fallen into friendly hands that immediately went about restoring the historic hotel's Victorian interior.

Ross has gained extensive experience in the role of a publican, spending many years in the industry owning pubs and hotels both in Australia and England. He has worked tirelessly to restore the historic hotel to something like its former glory. The establishment that is fondly called 'Kirks' by the locals now has a main bar that gleams with the warmth of wood, and the large windows once more frame picturesque scenes of the bay in all its moods. Decorated with character and style, holding all the cheerful atmosphere of an old English pub, the original fireplaces on either side of the galley-shaped bar add to the ambiance and create pools of cosy warmth during colder months. Meals are served cocooned in this cordial setting overlooking the bay.

Above: Mornington's Bay Hotel

Right: The historic tower of The Grand Hotel, Mornington

The hotel is popular for the European cuisine that dominates the menu, featuring great steaks and fresh seafood that comes with a deliciously affordable price tag.

Kirks is an all-weather venue, with an attractive grassed beer garden facing the sultry bay. It's a complex that has something for everyone, showcasing a number of events. Sportsmans Nights and Trivia Nights are held in the spacious Sports Bar, Sunday jazz sessions provide a laid back afternoon's entertainment and you can always try your luck in the cosy gaming room with up to the minute machines located in the middle of the hotel. On the upper level, accessed by the original grand old staircase, the Balcony Lounge makes a marvellous venue for private functions. Any celebration is made special in this old-world setting and from its elevated position the lounge provides magnificent uninterrupted views of Mornington's most loved feature, Port Phillip Bay

The Royal Hotel on the Esplanade has a proud history. Built in 1857, it has weathered the years virtually unscathed. Once known as the Schnapper Point Hotel, the name was changed in 1876 after Queen Victoria's second son, Prince Alfred, Duke of Edinburgh, stayed there. A novel attraction offered in the 1800s was to take an invigorating hot seawater bath. In the cellars, huge iron tubs with claw feet were filled with seawater pumped up from the bay via a windmill erected on Royal Beach and warmed to a comfortable temperature.

The hotel today is just as innovative, delivering a refreshing blast of nostalgia that is encountered and encouraged within and without. Massive stained glass windows grace the interior doors of the atrium and the entranceway to the Victoriana Room. They fill the area with defused light, creating a regal setting for dining. Throughout the hotel antique chandeliers and light fittings add lustre to any meal. And the Victoriana Room provides an elegant venue for functions. Weddings for up to 80 have that added touch of romance engulfed in the opulent splendor of yesteryear. The room was the scene in 1920-21 of a civic reception held in honour of Prince Edward, later to become the Duke of Windsor, during a state visit. The graceful hotel remains what it was then – an elegant venue for genteel travellers.

Classified by the National Trust, the hotel was purchased almost two years ago by Mark Torcaso, a member of a business and hotelier family that between them own some of the most elegant, historic hotels in Australia. Mark is enthusiastic as to the regard in which the hotel is held, he goes to great lengths to ensure that all fixtures and fittings are authentic antiques of the era. As a trained chef he has elevated the creativity and taste of the bistro's menu. The kitchen boasts four, five-Star trained chefs, and Mark proudly states: "We can serve everything from tortellini to truffles." The bistro's wide-ranging menu includes many Aussie favourites. Mark is quick to point out the award-winning hotel's success is due mainly to the enthusiasm of his well-trained staff.

The Tavern Bar has a raffish charm and features the original massive open brick fireplace. Still used in colder months, it creates the perfect setting for any winter's day. The scene of weekly entertainment, the tavern has been refurbished with stone and wood reclaimed from the original hotel or sourced from old boats, providing an authentic alehouse atmosphere. Doors open onto the Beer Garden and veranda with picture perfect views of the bay. Canvas parasols shade tables and ivy-draped walls add softness to the scene. Another dimension is added on summer nights when insect repellent flares are lit, turning the courtyard into a glittering wonderland. The hotel still takes in weary travellers, offering several levels of accommodation; some with en-suites some with shared bathrooms, some with bay views, some without – they even have a bridal suite. All rooms are comfortable and attractively furnished and you can almost taste the sense of history.

The Tanti Hotel occupies the site of the first ever hotel in Mornington, built in 1852 to service townsfolk and travellers on the highway. The Cobb and Company coach service was an integral part of life in the region until 1889 and the arrival of the railway. The Tanti was an important stop on the coach's route between Melbourne and Sorrento. Like many wooden buildings of the same vintage, the original hotel burned to the ground but the sparkling new premises that now stands in its place still welcomes and entertains travellers and townsfolk alike.

Allan and Gail Shepherd are putting their stamp on the premises, having recently purchased the hotel, and are full of plans to create an even more attractive venue for locals and the countless visitors to the area. Floor to ceiling windows in the extra spacious open-plan bistro and bar area create a bright airy atmosphere. Diners have plenty of choice from the delicious cosmopolitan menu and daily chef's specials that are perfectly prepared and promptly served. A comfortable Sports Bar and TAB adjoins the restaurant. The Shepherds have plans to add a new decked al fresco cafe that will lead from this area where lazy summer days can be spent sipping a cool wine or cleansing ale. A cosy gaming room offers patrons a chance to try their luck on the up to the minute machines completing a well-rounded facility where cheerful service and good times go hand in hand.

Left: Royal Beach, Mornington
Top right: The historic Royal Hotel *Bottom right:* Kirkpatrick's Hotel

The Mornington Racecourse is hailed as one of Victoria's premier racing venues. Expansive tailored lawns and landscaped gardens create a park-like setting for some of the best equine entertainment staged anywhere in Australia. It is the home the Mornington Racing Club that received the coveted Victorian Country Racing Club of the Year award for 1999-2000. The club takes pride in presenting "city racing with a country feel".

The first race meeting was held on the 24th May 1899 at Baxter's Flat and was the start of a long distinguished history. Meetings continued at this venue until 1903. After a hiatus of six years, racing was resumed in 1909, and in 1911 the venue moved to its present site in Tyabb Road, Mornington. During WWII the sport of kings was suspended and the course handed over to the military for use as a training camp. It was with some trepidation that the club's management surveyed the scene when the course was handed back after the war. It was in ruins! No longer resembling a racecourse. Thanks to their dedication, and the support of Sir Reginald Ansett, founder of Ansett Airlines, the club flourished once more and racing recommenced in 1947.

Early in the club's history a day at the races became popular with summer visitors. Trains full to capacity would bring racegoers from the city to enjoy the magic of Mornington and its racetrack. So began a tradition that continues to this day, with happy bands of racing enthusiasts filling the trains, escaping from the city to sample country racing at its best.

In 1996, at huge cost to the club, the racecourse went through a massive upgrade. Now jockeys wax lyrical about the track's cambered turns and excellent drainage. Hand in hand with its decorative gardens and relaxed atmosphere, the new facilities are first rate, with a modern grandstand and an undercover betting ring. Excellent snack and bar areas ensure easily accessible food and drink, while the comfortable Winning Post restaurant provides that more relaxed dining atmosphere. The Panorama Room, part of the members' grandstand, is aptly named, providing an excellent vantage point with its glassed façade overlooking the racecourse. All of the course's areas, indoor and out, are available for functions and special events.

Not only the racegoing public appreciates the exceptional facilities at Mornington. The club is the third largest training centre in the state, catering to a number of the country's top trainers. In excess of 550 horses work out on the Mornington track. The list includes many notable champions past and present.

A day at the races always provides exciting entertainment for young and old. Mornington Racing Club holds 20 meetings annually, with several feature races among them. But none is more eagerly awaited than the Mornington Cup, held in February each year. Cup day features a nine-race programme that includes the Carlton Draught Mornington Cup, with prizemoney of $150,000, and the Hareeba Stakes, with prize money of $100,000, constituting the richest prize pool in country Victoria for a cup meeting.

The atmosphere at this year's cup was electric. Happy racegoers arrived by the thousand – thirteen thousand to be exact. They came by train and by car, on foot and by horse and jinker. Groups were even ferried in on a London double-decker bus, all eager for the day's festivities, all intent on having a good time. Marquees, to cater for the expectant hordes, had sprung up on every flat vantage point of the course and groups of picnickers created islands of merriment on the manicured lawns.

The horses picked up on the crowd's excitement, pawing the ground, pricking their ears and tossing their magnificent heads. The jockeys gleamed in their brightly hued silks, creating a fluid ribbon of colour as they thundered past the posts, their progress producing screams of delight from the crowd cheering them on. Elegantly dressed ladies added a touch of glamour to the proceedings, competing in the Mornington Chamber of Commerce-sponsored and run – 'Fashions on the Field'. The parade is a showcase for Mornington's Main Street traders, without whose generous sponsorship it would not survive. The fashionable pageant was run between races with a number of categories and attractive prizes.

The whole day was a spectacular success, with highlights between races. A fly-past of the local Mornington Peninsula Aero Club brought forth oohs and aahs from the onlookers, music lingered in the air, adding to the party atmosphere and the crowd's enthusiasm.

Steeples Tabaret is a newer addition to the racing complex. A joint venture between Mornington Racing Club and Sale Turf Club, it opened in 1998 and is listed in the top ten Tabaret venues in the state. The club has become a popular meeting place, where visitors and locals can enjoy a drink with friends. Located near the corner of Mornington-Tyabb Road and Racecourse Road, it has a friendly, relaxed atmosphere. The bistro serves delicious meals and the modern gaming room is the heart of a very hospitable club.

Above: Cup Day fashions
Right: Scenes from Mornington Cup Day, 2003

Art plays an important role on the Mornington Peninsula and artists of every medium and style have made this diverse and extraordinary region their home. Arthur Boyd, one of Australia's most celebrated artists, spent many summers at his grandfather's cottage in Rosebud. It is therefore not surprising to find that one of the country's top twenty public galleries has taken root here. The highly regarded **Mornington Peninsula Regional Gallery** (MPRG), an impressive art space opened in 1990 sitting on an elevated position on the Civic Reserve off Dunns Road, has come a long way from its inception. Born of an idea conceived in 1968, a dedicated group of volunteers led by Alan McCulloch – the gallery's founding director and long time art critic with the *Herald* – staged the first of the gallery's exhibitions in the Shire Council Chambers. An old weatherboard house on Vancouver Street was then donated by the council and renovated to provide an art precinct for the public. From these humble beginnings the gallery has emerged to become one of Victoria's leading and most respected regional galleries.

Since its 1990 opening the gallery has been remodelled to international museum standards by Andrew Andersons and Peddle Thorpe, who designed the recent extension for the Art Gallery of New South Wales. The spacious exhibition area provides three light and airy inter-flowing spaces plus a large foyer and can easily house two or more exhibitions at any given time. The work involved in sourcing and curating exhibitions can be a long, drawn-out process and the gallery's program of exhibitions is set two to three years in advance. Director Andrea May Churcher's vision has taken the gallery to new heights and through the efforts of its informed and committed staff the gallery offers an extensive range of exhibitions throughout the year designed to both stimulate and entertain.

In 1999 the MPRG's major exhibition, *The artists' retreat: Discovering the Mornington Peninsula 1850s to the present*, first brought to wide public attention the rich cultural significance of the region and the impressive roll call of nationally significant artists who have lived, worked, and produced art in response to the Mornington Peninsula. Recent exhibitions featuring the work of Fred Williams, Arthur Boyd and Janet Cumbrae Stewart, have continued to build on this important legacy.

The MPRG's annual National Works on Paper award has become a coveted prize among artists. Arguably one of Australia's most prestigious awards in the medium, it aims to support and promote contemporary Australian artists who work with paper. Alan McCulloch was instrumental in beginning a specialist collection of prints and drawings on paper and the gallery's extensive collection now boasts work from the nineteenth century through to the present day by such Australian icons as Sydney Nolan and Russell Drysdale.

On visiting the gallery we were overwhelmed to view Lucian Freud's controversial painting *After Cézanne* 1999-2000, on loan from the National Gallery of Australia as part of its 'Out and About' touring exhibition to commemorate the NGA's twentieth anniversary. This major work, purchased in 2001 for $7.1 million, is the most expensive painting to date purchased by an Australian public gallery. Also on show was the inspired work of landscape artist and two-time Archibald Prize winner William Robinson. The gallery is renowned for the quality of its exhibitions and for a very small entry fee the beauty on show is within the reach of everyone.

Accommodation in Mornington is of a very high standard from unique historic hotels and houses to cosy centrally located motels and wonderful bed and breakfast establishments.

Bally Vista Bed & Breakfast on Wilson Road welcomes guests to a world where they awake each morning into a milieu that refreshes and rejuvenates the soul. The spacious ten square, one-bedroom fully serviced, self-contained accommodation, leaves nothing to be desired. Accessed by its own entrance, that also leads through onto a private courtyard complete with barbecue, the upper level apartment showcases the bay through large windows that embrace the living quarters and open out onto a sun-drenched balcony. The beautifully furnished apartment has a well-equipped kitchen that is stocked with all the ingredients necessary for a sumptuous breakfast.

Hosts Andrea and Keith Ford attach importance to making guests feel at home. They have created a place that can fit any criteria; perfect as a romantic getaway, a comfortable base to set out from and return to each day or a sanctuary to soak up the therapy of the Peninsula. The apartment is located only three doors from the beach and a short stroll from Mornington's famous Main Street. The panoramic views from the deck and living area are inspiring, the perfect spot to watch the evening shadows creep over the bay and enjoy a cocktail at *fin du jour*.

Canterbury by the Bay is set in a secluded location just off the Esplanade – a slipslop slap from the beach. The two-bedroom retreat is fully self-contained and equipped with every possible amenity. A short stroll brings guests into the heart of Main Street and likewise to the wonderful walks and scenery around Schnapper Point and the foreshore reserve.

The cottage's décor reflects the gold and blue of the bay, enhanced by high ceilings with windows everywhere. It radiates an extremely cheerful, bright ambiance that is a pleasure to wake to each morning. Two very private paved courtyards at the front and back of the property are filled with flower boxes, shrubs and established trees; they provide wonderful barbecue and breakfast nooks. A lock up garage is accessed from a the rear of the property and back courtyard. Owners Pam and Russell Marsham have welcomed guests for the past five years to this eminently inviting getaway. The travel experience gained over 20 years by Pam in her role within Ansett Airlines (the last name the airline traded under) has been incorporated into this exceptional cottage.

Above: Entrance to the Mornington Peninsula Regional Gallery
Right: MPRG acquisition – 'Susie Quinlan in a blue dress' c.1918. Pastel on paper, by Janet Cumbrae Stewart

The Mornington Motel, set in a quiet location right on Main Street, is family owned and operated, providing attractive accommodation in the heart of the Peninsula. Helen and Charles Hona have owned the premises for four years and have created a peaceful village-like atmosphere within the complex. Twelve single storey well-maintained units are beautifully furnished and creatively decorated to match the region's surrounding seascape. They open on to flower-bedecked car spaces and overlook the grassed area of a dazzling solar heated bathing pool and undercover barbecue.

The units can house varying numbers of guests. A recently refurbished 3-bedroom house on the property has been decorated and furnished with flair and makes a perfect home away from home for larger groups or family get-togethers. The motel is perfectly placed within walking distance to all Mornington's midtown attractions and beach, plus it's only a short drive to everything else. This motel represents great value; continental breakfast is included in a tariff that will suit most budgets

The Ranch Motel, on the corner of the Nepean Highway and Bentons Road, sits on Mornington's border with Mt Martha and is handy to either town's attractions. Thirteen units of various configurations, some self-contained, are tastefully decorated with a nautical theme and all are furnished with queen size beds. Also available for larger groups, attractive and spacious Benambra Cottage is fully self-contained with three bedrooms. It accommodates groups of up to 6 and contains little extras like DVD, video and CD players, TV to master bedroom, heating/cooling (open fire place), BBQ facilities and undercover parking.

The quiet motel has a pretty face with flowers spilling out of quaint window boxes. An attractive pool and spa surrounded by lawn and barbecue area creates the perfect spot for that end of day drink or daytime break. The motel is family owned and operated and enjoys a relaxed, friendly atmosphere. It is centrally located, close to the Mornington Racecourse, next door to the Black Angus Steakhouse and only a short walk to the Dava Hotel, Bentons Square shopping centre and the beach, providing a good base for any holiday

Mornington cannot been overlooked when on the antique trail. The National Antique Centre, located on Tyabb Road at the edge of Main Street, is housed in a massive open span structure that was built as a factory in the 1930s. At that time, with over 60,000 square feet under its tin roof, the structure was deemed the largest building of its kind in the Southern Hemisphere. Today the old factory features a restaurant and bar, auction rooms, a restoration centre and a wonderland of trash and treasure that emanates a strong magnetism, attracting antique dealers from near and far as well as private collectors. The centre is a cooperative, showcasing the merchandise of 150 traders it is a landscape full of the ordinary and the extraordinary, the mundane and the magnificent, and is well worth a visit.

Moorooduc was once a region full of orchards; situated in the northern plains it has the perfect climate for growing fruit and grain crops. Today this attractive locality is the arena for some of Victoria's most successful thoroughbred horse and cattle breeding farms and advertises its pride in being the home of Olympic Gold Medal-winning Debbie Flintoff King. Vignerons have discovered the area with its drier climate ideal for growing grapes, especially pinot noir. The area name was first used on official plans in 1854 and is derived from the Aboriginal word *Murraduk*, maning 'dark' or 'flat and swampy'.

In May 1981 the last passenger train was run on the Frankston to Mornington railway line. It was the passing of an era began in 1880 that had opened up so much of the Peninsula to Melbourne's citizens.

Its closure, however, allowed a group of steam train enthusiasts the opportunity to form a society devoted to providing a historical re-enactment, introducing the steam train ride to a new generation and a walk down memory lane for another. The Mornington Railway Preservation Society was formed in 1984 to restore and operate the Baxter to Mornington line as a tourist railway.

It was not until 1991 that the society was given the go-ahead. The government had simply abandoned the line and in the ensuing seven years nature had reclaimed the train route. Pine trees, blackberries and rampant greenery covered the once glistening tracks. It took the volunteer staff many man-hours to clear the debris. In 1992 a section was opened for trolley rides and in April 1999 the Mornington Tourist Railway was opened, running a service from the original Moorooduc Station to Yuilles Road, Mornington, making a stop en route at Tanti. But the line is still a work in progress, with the society determined to open the line all the way to Baxter.

The journey is a stirring mixture of smell, sight and sound; enthusiastic adults and wide-eyed children board the train for a journey with a different perspective. The line runs past farm houses and stands of pine trees: the swaying of the carriages, the metallic clanging of the couplings, the clickety-clack of the wheels and the mournful call of the whistle have a mesmerising effect. Children call and wave as the train passes cars standing patiently at level crossings, their drivers returning the salute with looks of bemused wistfulness.

The society relies on volunteers to fill all facets of railway administration. All engineers are trained to regulation standard and carriage and station staff are a wealth of information. Their flagship Engine K163 was built in the Newport Workshops and can reach speeds of 73 kilometres an hour. The four railway carriages were built in the early 1900s and the compartments have been lovingly restored. The train runs on designated days and makes a worthwhile family outing. The locomotive and carriages are available for private functions and provide a great venue for birthday parties.

Above & right: Mornington Tourist Railway, Moorooduc Station

On the Moorooduc Highway a pocket of diverse and unique attractions are based in what was the Moorooduc Coldstores. Once housing the surrounding countryside's fruit crops, the attractive buildings have been sympathetically renovated, retaining all of their charm to form a small village-style complex with oodles of parking.

The most recent business to settle in the complex is the Boutik-Regional Wine and Art Centre. The brainchild of Casper Pieters and Alieska Manintveld, their innovative company has added style and culture to the historic buildings by furnishing a one-stop tasting room and cellar door showcasing a wide range of Mornington Peninsula wines including cleanskins. The region provides wine lovers with numerous wineries to visit. Many open only once a month, presenting a daunting task when trying to sample them all. Boutik provides the opportunity to make a purchase of the smaller, less accessible wineries' produce, and plan any future visits, all under one roof. A unique service offered by the centre entails the design and production of 'while you wait' personalised wine labels using personal photos, words or both. One label or a hundred plus can be produced at a very reasonable cost and add a touch of class to any special gift, celebratory function or corporate meeting.

The wine and art centre has a special ambiance decorated with panache and artist in residence Alieska's vivid art. The wine is presented in stylish wine racks, which embrace the bright attractive room that gleams with the lustre of polished wood. Garden seating provides a novel spot for pleasant repose in the company of friendly alpacas surrounded by sculptures and ceramic works.

Alieska is a very talented artist and examples of her work can be seen in several of the Peninsula's leading galleries. Born in the Netherlands, she studied Fine Arts at the University of Utrecht. She has a very individual style, working with strong magnetic colours utilising free, fluid strokes that create bold aggressive works. Her creative approach has no set plan and she generates her masterpieces seated on the floor, using large unmounted canvases, and lets her imaginative genius flow. Her works are for sale at the centre. Other regional artists will also be on show at the centre. Boutik-Regional Wine and Art is a great place to start any regional wine tour, helping shape the travelling public's perception of what gems are to be discovered among the rolling hills of the Mornington Peninsula wine region.

TV World is an interesting attraction, also located in the Coldstores Complex. This Australian Museum of Modern Media is a fascinating mix of film, television and radio memorabilia. Put together by Bob Gordon and Judy Banks, it is in fact all facets of reporting and entertaining dating pack to the industry's electronic inception. Judy, herself a television personality, is well known as the principal of the Judy Banks School of Television and Dramatic Art.

The collection has been sourced from around Australia, with exhibits and film from some of the country's best-loved entertainers and television shows. As well as a huge collection of photos, film, props, equipment and working models of television and radio studios, the 'Rock Candy Store' an extensive, nostalgic, collection depicting the history of rock 'n' roll, keeps visitors enthralled. Open throughout the year, a visit to the museum is both rewarding and refreshing.

The Peninsula Lounge, one of the region's most happening places, holds pride of place in the Coldstores facing the highway. The brand new venue replaces a restaurant that occupied the location for some years. When taken over by hospitality guru Brent Manning, the out-of-date premises was transformed into a sparkling venue with lots of snap-crackle-and-pop.

Roquets bistro provides dining of international quality with a large restaurant that is an elegantly casual space. Santa Fe colours and décor blends magically with ultra-modern couches and seating arranged strategically in cosy conversation corners close to a stylish oval bar. A glassed façade overlooks wooded slopes and diners are treated to an extensive menu headed by very affordable and expertly cooked succulent 600-gram steaks.

A large character-filled Sports Bar provides enthusiastic pool players with six full size billiard tables and a massive big screen television complete with Foxtel for up-front viewing. The venue is highly geared for functions and to this end a 'big top' has been added to the entertainment space at the Peninsula. The Marquee Lounge is a large paved area under the purpose made canvas. It provides a very special function room that seats 100 guests and is the stage for many top line artists ranging from top bands and cabaret acts to comedy stars.

It is the management's aim not to be one-dimensional when it comes to the performers presented at the Peninsula Lounge. Energetic venue manager Ben Johnstone oversees the trendy new premises and is the Lounge's entertainment expert. His extensive knowledge of the industry allows him to know who's hot and what's not. The venue caters for a wide range of age groups and tastes: in recent months Billy Thorpe performed at the lounge, attracting 600 guests.

For those who choose to indulge their curiosity, the Bottom Drawer Antique Centre, situated midway between Mornington and Tyabb on the corner of Mornington-Tyabb and Derril Roads, provides collectors of curios with an intriguing package. The complex has been a fixture of the landscape since the early 1900s, servicing the area as a general store with adjoining farm buildings. For the last 25 years the historic building has housed the antique centre featuring over an acre of distinctive interconnecting areas full of the unusual and the unique.

Since 1993 proprietors Margaret and Bob Morgan have expertly showcased the 45 independent dealers who source the multitude of fads, frills and follies to be found here. Margaret has a background in gold and silver smithing and both she and Bob have been collectors all their lives, and as you would expect from two people with such a long

Above: Bottom Drawer Antique Centre, Moorooduc
Right: The Peninsula Lounge, Boutik Regional Wine & Art Centre, Studio City TV Museum, Moorooduc Cool Stores

history in the trade, the complex has gained a reputation as a destination not to be missed on the antique trail. It holds a treasure trove of the traditional and exotic, a huge range of collectables, bric-a-brac of all varieties, old wares, jewellery and antiques. It is open Thursday to Sunday each week and all public holidays with the exception of Good Friday and Christmas Day.

In the heart of the complex 'The Tearooms' is gaining a reputation as a cosy lunch spot or relaxing nook for a shopping break. A light seasonal lunch menu featuring wholesome homemade dishes is served in a cheery relaxed atmosphere. Delicious cakes are all home made, but Devonshire tea is a speciality with the scones made on the premises tempting the taste buds as the aroma of baking floods the air. Fossickers can easily lose a day within this magic centre and emerge clinging to an item of great worth or little consequence but something precious that without the help of The Bottom Drawer Antiques would take a lifetime to find.

Moorooduc has its share of unique accommodation. Gooseberry Hill Cottages have a choice of self-contained, self-catering accommodation in different areas on the Peninsula. They are owned and run by Rosemary and Roger Redston, who initially bought the charismatic Gooseberry Hill property 11 years ago merely to enjoy it. They have found that the invigorating country air and the closeness to Mother Nature does strange things to the system. Feeling the need to grow something, they planted an olive grove. Now with their first crop harvested, they are making mouth-watering products. Roger, as well as being a practising physician, takes his olives seriously and is President of the Mornington Peninsula Olive Association.

The property is situated in the heart of Peninsula wine country on Graydens Road. It is conveniently located to Devilbend Reservoir and the public golf course abutting one of the area's most spectacular vineyards, The Garden Winery, whose proprietors not only produce great wine but have also created a garden full of exuberant colour and design that is an inspiration for gardens everywhere. The olive grove shares the property with a spacious two-bedroom cedar cottage that is available for holiday rental. The cottage has a charming lounge with a wood fire for winter comfort. A vine-covered veranda and private garden delivers peaceful views over an idyllic valley that adds ambiance to a very special country retreat. Privacy is guaranteed in this peaceful haven that is perfect for family holidays or get-away-from-it-all weekends – even well behaved pets are welcome.

In Mornington the Gooseberry Hill Beach Cottages comprise a sunny, spacious two-bedroom ground floor unit in Wilsons Road plus a bright two-bedroom townhouse in Canterbury Place. Both are a stone's throw from the beach and a short walk from the middle of all the action that Mornington has to offer. Both are tastefully furnished with all mod cons and attractive outdoor barbecue areas.

Mount Martha rises 152 metres above sea level, a granite outcrop that bestows on visitors clear air and panoramic vistas. The peak's picturesque hamlet, situated 60 kilometres from Melbourne, four kilometres south of Mornington, nestles on the cliff line and is simply heaven for those of us in search of stylish tranquillity.

The beach is picture perfect, made exclusive by the outcrops of Balcombe Point and Martha Point. A cluster of beach huts contributes a colourful splash on the golden sands that are lapped by crystal water. A sloping foreshore backs the sand and is topped by tall trees, which generate restful shade; it could be a world away from the busy Esplanade that runs along its ridge. A number of scenic parks and reserves surround the village with walking tracks and picnic areas. The beach reserve has a boat ramp and leads onto the Balcombe Creek Wetlands. Balcombe Creek is the area's main waterway that joins the bay at Mount Martha; a boardwalk traverses some way along its length and provides a tranquil look at the wetlands habitat and its inhabitants.

Off the Esplanade a cluster of quality shops facilitate the beach community, servicing an area that contains the best of accommodation and the most flavoursome of restaurants.

The Bistro is located just south of the shopping precinct. The bistro is a well-known landmark on the Esplanade. It has occupied its plot since the 1930s, serving the beachgoing public as a food and beverage kiosk. The original building plus its successor burned to the ground, but like the phoenix they were reborn. Rosemary and Frank Monro have owned the most recent, more up-to-date version, for the past five years and serve up gourmet tit-bits to an appreciative public. Open seven days for lunch and afternoon tea and coffee, six nights for dinner, and breakfast at weekends, the bistro caters for all gastronomic occasions. Sensational varieties of wood-fired pizza, juicy steaks and succulent seafood are part of a modern Australia menu accentuated by delicious pastas. The bistro is fully licensed but also caters for diners who prefer to bring their own.

Mt. Martha Beachside Bistro is one of those casual seaside gems that combine good food with the special atmosphere that only comes from close proximity to the sea. Situated directly opposite Mt. Martha South Beach, an overwhelming view of the bay can be enjoyed from all areas of the restaurant. Patrons have the choice of comfortable café-style interior dining, with a wood fire creating a warm welcome in winter, or an outdoor ambiance in the flower bedecked weatherproofed courtyard. Evening at the restaurant displays brilliant sunsets, as the sun kisses the Peninsula goodnight, slipping below the horizon in a burst of vermilion and gold. Rosemary has been inspired by the nightly fireworks, and, as an amateur photographer of some ability, has decorated the inner restaurant with special shots of the nightly spectacular.

Mt. Martha's refined historic past is evident throughout the community in the surviving elegant homes. Mt Martha House, currently owned by the Mornington Peninsula Shire, is one example. Built in 1891 the house was originally part of the Mt. Martha Estate and began life as the Mt. Martha Hotel. It has been used for many purposes through the years, the most prominent being as a 76-room guest house.

Above: Views of vineyard and olive grove from Gooseberry Hill Cottages
Right: Windsurfing at Mt Martha. *Inset:* Mt Martha Sunset

Briars Park sits at the edge of the village on the Nepean Highway. It is one of the region's oldest properties. The restored house is surrounded by 225 hectares of the original 2,000-hectare property, purchased by the Mornington Peninsula Shire in 1976 from Alexander Balcombe's great-great grandsons. They also presented the homestead and remaining eight hectares of gardens, jointly, to the Shire and the National Trust of Victoria.

In 1840 Captain James Reid was the first owner of the 2,000-hectare estate that he named *Tichin-Gorouke*, Aboriginal for 'voice of the frogs' that was also the ancient name for Balcombe Creek. Alexander Balcombe purchased the estate in 1846 and between 1848-1851 constructed the earliest section of a 12-room homestead, which was added to in 1866. The homestead is constructed from bricks made on the property. He named his estate 'The Briars', in reverence for the home he had left behind on the island of St Helena, a British colony in the Atlantic Ocean. A collection of antiques that belonged to the family are showcased in the house and include magnificent pieces presented to Alexander's father by Napoleon during the French tyrant's imprisonment on St. Helena.

Briars Park makes a wonderful excursion for both children and adults. Wide open spaces and sweeping lawns provide perfect picnic spots. The original driveway to the house is lined with ancient oak trees, elms and Canary Island pines that are believed to have been planted around the time the homestead was built; they still make an impressive impact. Alexander, also planted two vineyards totalling 100 acres between 1865-1869; these were the first vines to be planted on the Peninsula. Briars Park at one time had its own label. Unfortunately the original vineyard was destroyed by disease, but two vines have survived the ravages of time and are to be found thriving among the hawthorn hedge. A new generation of vines is now grown in the park, looked after by Red Hill Estate. They make a statement most times of the year, but their autumnal colours are spectacular, spreading a gleaming, golden-red mantle over the hillside.

The park contains both woodland and wetland walks. The Wetland Walk is a 1.4-kilometre return journey. It traverses the flood plain areas of Balcombe Creek with many lagoons that are home to a large variety of birds. A boardwalk runs the entire distance and is equipped with unobtrusive bird hides. The woodland boardwalk is a return journey of 1.5 kilometres, passing through areas of pasture grasses and stands of Eucalypt.

A visitor's centre was built on the property in 1988. It was designed to replicate a wooden slab hut that the original owner, Captain James Reid, occupied during his lease. A huge aquarium dominates the main room. It contains eel, fish and long neck tortoise. Watching their antics enthrals children and absorbs adults. A large one-way window overlooks a wetlands lagoon; relics and information boards decorate the walls, telling the story of the history, birds and animals that make the park their home.

During the year Briars Park hosts many festivals and events. It is open daily with the exception of Good Friday and Christmas Day and is free to the public.

Contained within the park is The Perfumed Garden and Roseraie, an independent nursery that is dedicated to exceptional beauty, form and fragrance. Filled with abundant plantings of the world's most romantic flower, the garden makes a poetic statement to the rose. Sophie Adamson is the creator of this living canvas. By profession a teacher, she has lived her life enamoured of the fragrance of flowers; her obsession has always been gardening.

The Perfumed Garden was responsible in the early 1980s for introducing the David Austin rose collection to Australia, and, remains the registered collection of David Austin roses for the OPCAA (Melbourne Botanical Gardens). The collection is constantly being updated: over 100 varieties, most with multiple plantings, are now on display in Sophie's garden.

Moving to her present site at the Briars three years ago, Sophie has splashed colour over what was originally a two-acre paddock of undistinguished landscape. She has created a, 'walk-through-and-wander' display with wide pathways that can easily accommodate wheelchairs, paths that meander through arched walkways of fragrant climbing roses, formal walled gardens and a hillside of Old Roses that include: gallica, damask and tea. There are rarities to be viewed, like the Maltese Cross and the Chinese winghorn, prized for its young thorns that are a translucent red. In her garden she dramatises the beauty and brilliance of the rose against the colour and texture of other beautiful plants and blooms.

The garden is full of innovative ideas and a wide variety of planting styles and structures. Sophie employs the splendour of her garden to inform and educate visitors and customers, helping them to plan and select the varieties most in harmony with their garden and vision. Her knowledge has become so extensive that she is a widely sought-after speaker and prolific writer on all things horticultural, also running workshops and guided tours of the garden. The Roseraie is a rewarding, fragrantly exquisite place to visit when exploring the region.

Josephine's at the Briars is a restaurant that has it all. The historic building that contains the restaurant was built in 1849, by Alexander Balcombe, high on the brow of a hill, a short distance from his elegant homestead. The old shearing shed makes a charismatic restaurant, with 20-metre high vaulted ceilings, exposed beams and age-old brickwork, coming together in a rustically elegant venue. Patio dining in a large weatherproofed area adjoining the main building exploits the restaurant's elevated position, delivering a vista of serene and gentle beauty over the estate and surrounding countryside. Sunsets from the patio are especially stunning, providing a front row seat as the charcoal shadows creep across the sky and the descending sun's rays create patterns of three-dimensional vivid colour.

Above: Briars Park Homestead

Right: Briars Park observation centre, Homestead interior, Josephine's Restaurant, Briar's Perfumed Garden & Roseraie

The food at Josephine's is as impressive as the setting; with daily, light a la carte lunches and man-sized dinners served Friday and Saturday nights through winter and from Thursday to Sunday in the summer months. The restaurant's rustic casual flair in daylight gives way to evenings enhanced by a more sophisticated, romantic ambiance surrounded by historic architecture, linen tablecloths and glistening accoutrements. Guests are invited to choose from a very affordable seasonal menu and daily blackboard specials that feature international cuisine laced with a country flavour, all prepared from local produce.

Owner Lyn Taulla admits that when she bought the restaurant in 1997, she was a novice to the industry. Her philosophy of, "looking after people the way you would like people to look after you" has paid off. Armed with the knowledge that staff can make or break a restaurant, she has collected a group of dedicated professionals that add flair to the Josephine's dining experience. Special celebrations for 100-plus guests are expertly catered for in this ideal setting with weddings an in-house speciality.

Accommodation in this idyllic part of the Peninsula is just as special as anywhere in the region. Briarswood Cottage is Heritage Listed, it dates back to the late 1930s but on crossing its threshold you would swear that it was an original 16th century Tudor residence. Now run as a bed and breakfast, the cottage sits opposite peaceful Craigie Beach on the corner of the Esplanade and Craigie Road in Mt. Martha. For most of its life the cottage was a private residence, designed to resemble the genuine article named Briarswood that stood in Norfolk, England. Present owners Ann and Ian Duncan purchased the property in 1999. Although previous occupants had kept the property's authenticity over the years, when purchased by the Duncans the house and grounds had fallen into disrepair.

Over a period of eighteen months Ann and Ian created a delightful seaside retreat, enhancing the charm of the character-filled property by furnishing the rooms with antiques that they have collected over many years – beautiful pieces that appear to have been chosen with Briarswood in mind. The landscaped gardens surrounding the cottage retain old trees and provide an idyllic resting place. Three upper level bedrooms offer a haven for the workweary and the attractive tariff includes a sumptuous cooked breakfast served in the dining room. The original gardener's cottage nestling at the back of the property has been reinvented as a self-contained hideaway and is perfect for a romantic weekend away from it all, or a very special honeymoon.

Contentment reigns at Mt. Martha Bed and Breakfast By The Sea. The double-storey modern colonial sandstone house, complete with wrought iron balustrade, sits serenely directly opposite the beach on the Esplanade, just north of Mt. Martha village. Pam and Robert Beveridge, who bought the property in 2000, purpose-built the bed and breakfast in 2002 and have left nothing to chance. Two spacious ground floor guest suites were designed with privacy in mind and offer their own dining and sitting areas and an a la carte breakfast menu. A choice is available of queen, king or large single size beds and ensuite with spa. Both rooms are exquisitely furnished with large windows overlooking a profusion of heavenly perfumed David Austin roses in hues of vanilla and burnt orange, wonderful views of the bay and glorious sunsets. One suite is designed to cater for guests who are physically challenged and is wheelchair friendly. A large comfortably furnished guest lounge is contained in a picturesque atrium that leads out to a wonderful private garden complete with barbecue; a fully equipped kitchen is also at guests' disposal. This exclusive hideaway represents value for money adding to the property's ambiance of peace and repose.

The bed and breakfast shares the one-acre block with property's original 1926 beach house that Pam and Robert have renovated with style and grace. The fully self-contained cottage exudes old-world charm. It is enhanced by; three open fireplaces, its own private entrance, large living area, five bedrooms and three bathrooms with an expansive, secluded, country-style back yard. The beach house is available for larger groups of up to 10 guests. Both properties have access to the beach via a pathway that lies directly opposite the accommodation, providing yetanother feature that makes Mt. Martha Bed and Breakfast By The Sea perfect for that get-away-from-it-all vacation.

Off the Esplanade a cluster of quality shops facilitates the beach community. Original Oz, contained in the Mt. Martha Village arcade, Lochiel Avenue, is one of the most original and diverse galleries on the Peninsula. The successful gallery has been in existence for five years. It is owned and expertly run by husband and wife team, Peter and Christina Nolan. The couple do not put on individual exhibitions, but the pieces on show are updated monthly, offering a new and ever changing face. Established artists from around Australia are represented; confident in the knowledge their work will be presented with integrity

Peter is Irish by birth and Christina is Greek; they have always been captivated by the strong, vibrant and unique qualities that flavour Australian artwork. This captivation led them to develop an art gallery dedicated to exposing Australia's talented artists. Their love of the subject is evident; they have a wide knowledge of each piece and artist on display.

The gallery is a bright cheerful medium that delivers impact, a blaze of colour and light. The Nolans have sourced an impressive group of artisans, established artists, local professionals and award winning interstate artists. Works by Bernie Walsh, Australia's most exported artist in print, are featured in the gallery. Until now, Bernie only sold prints of his colourful pieces. At Original Oz, patrons can purchase his original works. Angelo Quabba, a legendary artist, winner of many of the most presigeious awards, is also showcased at Oz. Works by David Chen, Maryanne Holmes, Mary Hennekam and local Mt. Martha artist, past artist of the year, Rodney Summers, in the company of other greats, can all be found at Original Oz. Outstanding glass glistens in the light, crafted by the best glass artists from around the country, adding yet another dimension to this amazing gallery.

Above: Mornington Peninsula beach scene at Oz Gallery, Mt Martha

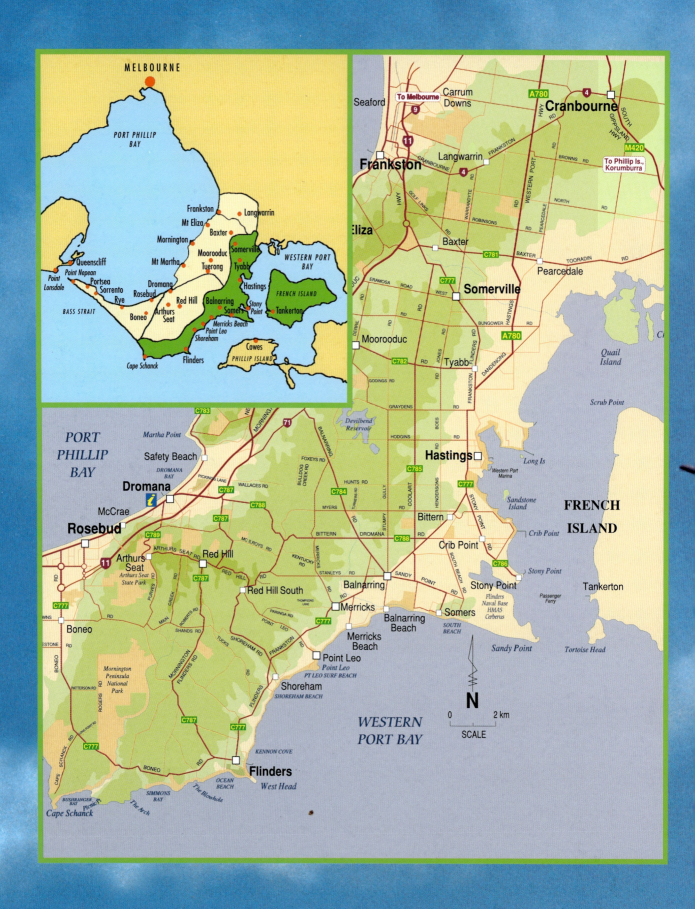

Westernport Bay Listings

SOMERVILLE: Moonlit Sanctuary P.78-79/245. Bembridge Golf Course P.78/245.

TYABB: Tyabb Packing House Antiques P.80-81/245. Tyabb Craft Village P.80-81/245. Tyabb Antique Centre 82-84/245. Luton Hatters Gallery P 82/245. Tack Box Saddlery P.82/245. Peninsula Motor Inn P.84/245. Eldon Park Retreat P.84-85/246.

YARINGA: Yaringa Boat Harbour & Marina P.86-87/246. Yaringa Boathouse Restaurant. P.86-87/246. Yaringa Chandlery P.86-88/246.

HASTINGS: Westernport Hotel P.90-91/246. Anchorage Restaurant P.90-91/246. Harbour View Motor Inn & Victoriana Restaurant P.90/246. Marina View Van Village P.90-91/246.

BITTERN: Summerfields Country House. P 92-93/246.

FRENCH ISLAND: French Island Eco Tours P.92-94/246.

HMAS CERBERUS: HMAS Cerberus Museum P.94-96/246.

SOMERS: Coolart Wetlands & Homestead P.98-99/246.

BALNARRING: Rain Hayne & Shine P.100/246. Balnarring Village Motor Inn P.100-101/246. Heritage 3095 Tavern P.102/246.

MERRICKS: Murranna Herbs & Cottages P.102-103/246.

SHOREHAM: Ashcombe Maze P.104-105/247. Shoreham Beachside P.104/247. Le Pavillon P.104/247.

FLINDERS: Flinders Hotel P.106/247. Beast Creations P.108-109/247. Flinders Fine Art 108-109/247. Transference Antiques & Décor P.108/247. Flinders Village Café P.109-110/247. Salty's Restaurant P.108-110/247. Cipriani's Flinders Country Inn P.110-111/247. Flinders Cove Motor Inn P110/247. Nazaaray P.110-111/247. Ora Banda B&B P.110-112/247. Papillon B&B P.111-112/247. Flinders Golf Club P.112-113/247.

CAPE SCHANCK: Cape Schanck Lighthouse P.114-116/247.

Late afternoon tranquil scene at Hastings

Western Port opening page: Pair of black swans on lake at Coolart Wetlands
Centre-spread background: Historic aircraft at Tyabb Airshow

The Western Port side of the Mornington Peninsula is an unspoiled natural paradise. Visitors get a front row seat for Nature's tour de force with exhilarating walks, world-significant wetlands and rugged coastline, highly scenic beaches, bluffs and coves, fringed by verdant valleys and wooded hills. Surgeon George Bass first explored Western Port Bay in 1798. He named the bay that gave him asylum, Western Port, being the most westerly point he reached on his epic journey, exploring the coast south of Sydney. Bass and six sailors completed a journey full of hardship. They rowed a flat-bottomed 27-foot 8-inch whaling boat from Port Jackson with enough rations for only six weeks. They survived the journey by eating swans, ducks and other birds, as well as fish and seals. Bass was a colourful character with adventure in his blood, a member of the renowned scientific 'Linnean Society' that still functions today. He disappeared on a journey from Sydney to South America in 1803; his fate remains a mystery. Mathew Flinders best summed up Bass's journey when he wrote of the voyage; "a voyage expressly undertaken for discovery in an open boat and in which six hundred miles of coast, mostly in boisterous climate, was explored, has not perhaps its equal in the annals of maritime history."

Western Port is one of the most biologically diverse bodies of water in Australia. Unlike Port Phillip Bay it has deep channels – the main shipping channel has depths of up to 33 metres. It has a wide tidal range and massive seagrass beds and is home to a host of rare and endangered marine life. Two of the most rare are Lamp Shells and Brooch Shells, species that have survived for over 600 million years. In 1854 a report commented upon the extraordinary giant sponges that can still be found in the area. Due to the wide range of habitats within the bay, marine life is prolific and includes dolphins and the occasional visit from humpback and southern right whales. The bay's vast meadows of seagrass are not only vital to the water's purity but act as a nursery for myriad species of young fish and baby prawns.

Pearcedale is located two kilometres off the Monash Highway, three kilometres from Western Port Bay. It is the first village on the Peninsula that visitors from Melbourne will encounter. It is a 'green and pleasant land', full of market gardens, horse breeding farms and quaint country lanes lined by age-old trees.

Moonlit Sanctuary, located in the Pearcedale Conservation Park on the Tyabb-Tooradin Road, allows city folks the opportunity to get close up and personal with some of Australia's unique, rare and endangered nocturnal animals in the wild. Each evening at dusk, armed with lanterns, trained guides escort groups on 90-minute walks through the Australian bush, introducing curiosities as well as the more common of our furry and feathered neighbours.

It is a magical experience and an opportunity too good to miss. The walk is set up to appeal to all age groups as well as being wheelchair and stroller friendly. On any given visit you can witness a night in the lives of bettongs and potoroos, rare Eastern Quolls and pademelons not to mention dunnarts, tiny squirrel and feathertail gliders, also dingoes, kangaroos, emus and the endangered masked owl. Some may even honour visitors by eating out of their hands. The park contains the world's largest feathertail glider exhibit and has one of only two captive colonies of the tiny, very endangered, New Holland Mouse.

The sanctuary has been set up for the conservation and breeding of some of Australia's most endangered species in an orchestrated environment within the natural bush. A fox-proof fence encloses the entire bush area of the sanctuary, allowing some of the animals to run free. Others are contained in enclosures to control breeding. A window that covers a complete wall in the sanctuary's café overlooks a wetland area. It makes an interesting backdrop for a cup of coffee or light lunch and the large café is the perfect venue for birthday parties. Since the park opened in 2001 the park's fame has spread. The walk through the fragrant Australian bush at dusk and the knowledge acquired on the way, plus the personal contact with wild things that could never be encountered without the help of the sanctuary, creates a very special memory to draw on.

Any time is a good time to play golf and the staff at the nine-hole (5 par 4 and 4 par 3) Bembridge Golf Course welcomes players with open arms. It is a privately owned, intimate facility where members pay only green fees and the course is open to the public. The course is named in memory of Bembridge, a town that was part of the area until 1953 when the last of its buildings, the schoolhouse, was removed.

Bembridge owners Steve and Ronda and Melinda and Mathew have a zest for life. They established the club during a midlife swerve in 1991. Steve has lived on the property most of his life and worked in the family market garden. The cosy licensed clubhouse where players sit on the weatherproofed terrace, in the shade of an ancient oak, overlooking waterways and the 5th and 9th holes, was originally Steve's family home. It is a great place for a snack-style lunch or relaxed break even if you don't play golf. Weddings and functions, corporate meetings and training days, can also be expertly catered for within the club's picturesque surroundings.

At most golf clubs you could make a career out of trying to get a tee-off time, but this club is a golfer's dream: no bookings, no long tee-off times and a friendly, relaxed environment. The tailored fairways and greens are a treat to play on and offer a challenge without steep hills - although the scenic waterways have claimed a ball or two. There is a pro shop on the premises and if your tee shots are starting to fall short, the club's pro can coach you back onto par. During summer, weekly twilight games are well patronised and winter brings its own highlight. Around the full moon each month a night game is played amid great hilarity, when as many as 60 golfers chase their glow balls around the course. This is a club where golfers and non-golfers choose to come for enjoyment that is well priced and a friendly, easy game of golf.

Above: Teeing off at Bembridge Golf Course
Right: Nocturnal animals at the Moonlit Sanctuary, Pearcedale

Tyabb was once the heart of the Peninsula's apple producing country. In 1861 the town was situated in the area now known as Old Tyabb and fishing was its main function. All that remains of Old Tyabb can be seen at the Tyabb Cemetery circa 1862-66 that is located in Cemetery Road on Tyabb's boundary with Hastings, often called Hastings Cemetery. The town's history goes back to the 1840s when the district was part of the region's first pastoral holding, 'Bungunyan', granted to Martha Jane King, the region's first permanent settler, in 1845. Martha operated the cattle run with the help of her son, as her husband had died en route to Australia. Her holdings covered much of what are now Hastings, Tyabb and Somerville, plus Sandstone Island. Tyabb is a derivative of the Aboriginal word for tea-tree; the small town is located on the Stony Point rail line in close proximity to Hastings and Somerville. The arrival of the railway in 1889 determined the location of the present town. The township has progressed from its roots as a farming settlement with many thoroughbred horse farms and cattle studs taking over yesterday's orchards.

Antiques have become serious business in Tyabb, with the town gaining a reputation as Victoria's pre-eminent antiques centre. Antique stores decorate the main street and on the Mornington-Tyabb Road. The old Tyabb Packing House and Coolstore, circa 1914, has been reinvented as a one-stop antique precinct, sharing the seven-acre property with the Tyabb Craft Village. The exciting complex is the brainchild of Sheila and Gerard Martland. The couple purchased the derelict property in 1992, taking six months to refurbish it, fitting it out to house what has become the largest collection of antiques and collectables under one roof in the Southern Hemisphere. The huge building covers over 500 square metres and houses 35 individual dealers, specialising in quality and the hard-to-find, trading in, as one dealer said, "everything from watering cans to coffins." It is a town in miniature and a fun place to wander through, where you can choose from hundreds of constantly changing items, both beautiful and bizarre.

There is jewellery that would make a sultan's wife swoon, lace that is as fine as a spider's web, furniture and silver that gleams with the patina of age and a book store that rivals the National Library. Clothing that has seen fashion come and go is intermingled with collectables that will astound you and an attractive licensed café and restaurant provides a serene spot for lunch. There are specialised dealers with unique collections of organs, crystal and linen. We saw curios that ranged from a gigantic Jar Jar Binks effigy (of Star Wars fame) standing 20 hands high, won by a family in a competition, to Turks turban pumpkins. The dealers are a friendly bunch: get chatting and you never know what you will discover.

On our way round we discovered in one shop that among other things specialised in cameras, a Robert Prenzel carving, 'Kookaburra', 1935 and a pair of binoculars inscribed to the commander of Australia's first warship, Captain Henry J. Feakes, who became Rear Admiral H. Feakes CBE. In 1925 Feakes was superintendent of the Department of Training (HMAS Cerberus). The binoculars were presented to him by the President of the United States in recognition of his part in the rescue of the master and crew from the American sloop, 'Helen B. Stirling'

Many of the dealer's visitors meet have run their business from the coolstore since it opened, speaking volumes for the expertise with which Sheila and Gerard conduct business. The Tyabb Packing House gives new meaning to an old pastime – shopping.

Tucked away behind the Packing House, the Tyabb Craft Village is a reminder of another era. So much of Australia's past has been all but obliterated by the pace of modern living; it is like a breath of fresh air to discover a place where the goods on display are made by hand by the craftsman that sell them to you after you watch them being created. The village's mood and design allows for relaxed marketplace browsing. Most of the artisans in the village specialise in the unusual and if they haven't got the exact something, then they can probably make it especially for you.

Many crafts are featured in the village and hours can be spent exploring its length and breadth. Children too enjoy the visit with a miniature train ride on 'Timothy at Tyabb' that travels past exotic places like the Eiffel Tower and the Leaning Tower of Pisa. A toddlers' play area on the village green also distracts the small bundles of energy, allowing parents to relax with a snack from the village's kiosk.

Sue Goodall is the creator behind 'Down Under Glazed Mud Pottery'. She shapes beauty on her potters' wheel, turning extraordinary pots and dishes with both terracotta and glazed finishes. Being extremely artistic, she allows her expression to flow free when creating her wall plaques, dishes and pots, not working to any set design. Sue says she has 'pottered around' most of her life – and she does it very well. Giving something back to her craft, Sue, conducts very affordable lessons in pottery at her workshop in the village.

Jewel of the Nile is a very special jewellery shop, showcasing the work of a very special craftsman. Sammy is a third generation jeweller who has worked with precious metals and gems for almost as long as he can remember, starting at his father's side in Cairo when he was 11 years old, learning a trade that he has turned into an art. He creates jewellery with a price to suit all budgets and one-of-a-kind-jewellery at down-to-earth prices. A dazzling array of rings, necklaces and earrings are on display. In addition, Sam is a master at remodelling old pieces and will also purchase unwanted items.

Tyabb Village Woodturning has a tactile collection of hand-crafted giftware and household items. Specialising in Australian timber, the pieces are crafted from exotic recycled wood such as: Tasmanian Blackwood, Jarrah, Cherry, Red Gum and Oak. The artistic wooden pieces make perfect gifts that will be treasured for generations. A window looking into the workshop from the rear of the premises allows a peek at the craftsman at work.

Tyabb's main shopping precinct on Flinders Road is not to be overlooked when on the antique trail. The Tyabb Antique Centre in the heart of town is a well-established, well-patronised store, owned by Peter McDonnell who is a distinguished name in the antiques trade. The centre is housed in one of Tyabb's historic buildings, 'Pott's Modern Cash Store'; the haberdashery store was built in the early 1900s and advertised 'less than city prices'. Peter purchased the building 19 years ago from the daughter of the original owner, R.A. Potts. Indeed, Potts daughter, Nancy Ludgate, now well into her eighties, is still a resident of the town.

Above: Display at Tyabb Antiques
Right: Tyabb's famous Packing House antiques centre and craft village

Peter learned all about antiques from his mother and previously ran his business in Somerville. He has had a lifetime in the trade and has an eye for quality, specialising in mainly Victorian furniture, Jacobean oak with some French and an occasional Australian gem, dating from the 1860s to the 1920s. There is a wonderful range on display and the large showroom is sectionalised to create rooms that showcase the gleaming pieces of history to perfection. He also offers collectors a restoration service with three French polishers on staff.

The centre is a complex with three levels of antiques, top of the range, lesser quality and what is labelled 'The Junk Shed'. But in actuality this is where small, lesser, unrestored pieces are held for sale - albeit in a 'Steptoe' kind of way. At the rear of the main showroom the original Potts family home is now a home-style restaurant. The Colonial Cottage Restaurant has great food, a good atmosphere and attractive courtyard seating.

Luton Hatters Gallery is also domiciled in Tyabb's main street. It is a curiosity rarely seen today; a store dedicated to hats. Susan and Andrew Morris have re-established "Luton Hatter's" that has been a tradition from the 1930s, importing and distributing hats made by the milliners of Luton in England. With the dictates of fashion going against the humble hat, the factory that had been set up in Sydney in 1938 finally closed in 2001. But the tradition lives on in Tyabb's main street. On display in the gallery are hats of every denomination; hundreds of Akubras, men's and ladies' straw hats, felt hats, feathered, sequined and faux fur hats; Greek fishermen's hats, tweed caps, deerstalkers, Sherlock Holmes' and bowler hats. The stock on display will defy the most selective shopper. The gallery showcases a collection of antique and distinctive headdresses; even one that has gone to tea with the Queen, and a unique display of hat moulds and machinery that were used in the Luton factories.

Should you have a hat that doesn't fit too well or could do with a bit of dressing up, the gallery offers customers the added service of stretching and remodelling. As well as hundreds of hats, this individual store also offers a range of super-fine woollen knitwear, leather gloves, knitted and woven scarves and a selection of Driza-Bone merchandise. And if your taste runs to art, the Hatter Gallery's walls provide a unique exhibition space for well-known local artist Ray Barnard-Brown's pastels and watercolours.

The Tack Box on the main strip is a country store with an exclusive rural atmosphere where the rich, strong aroma of leather assails the senses as you walk through the door. Located in the heart of equine country that boasts 10 pony clubs, with longer than long waiting lists, plus dressage and show jumping clubs, the Tack Box provides a much-needed service. This is the place where young hopefuls and veteran equestrians go shopping. It is a horse and owner boutique that sells everything for the health and beautification of magnificent animals and the paraphernalia that their owners need to do them justice; in fact everything that the well-groomed horse and jauntily dressed rider could possibly need.

The business is owned and expertly run by Marion and Ken Van De Beek who, with horses of their own, are knowledgeable in the trade. The store carries a large range of saddles plus woollens, brand name clothing and riding boots. As well as a pre-loved saddle and clothing department, the Tack Box provides a rug mending service and is renowned in the area for the hand-made rugs designed and produced on the premises.

There always seems to be something going on in Tyabb and in March each year the sky comes alive as a barrage of small aircraft take to the air during the Tyabb Airshow. The show has become an honoured tradition of the Peninsula Aero Club, who organise the event in aid of worthy charities. Westernport Airfield in Tyabb is a private strip owned by the members of the 40-year old aero club. It is world renowned for its collection of historic aircraft that is named as the largest collection in the Southern Hemisphere. Most of these unique aircraft are on paraded at the show.

The club has a distinguished past, with one of its early protagonists, Bill Vowell, instigating the 'Angel of Mercy' helicopter service that was the world's first fully equipped air ambulance. The Peninsula Aero Club shouldered the responsibility of raising funds for the air ambulance that today is known as the Southern Peninsula Rescue Service. The community-minded club has continued to raise funds and help local services in any way that they can. At no cost to the community the club allows all state emergency services 24-hour access to the airfield plus its amenities, utilising a new all-weather runway that has improved the airfield's safety facilities. The club's award-winning flying school is open all year round, providing future aviators with flying training. Or, if you want to sit back and relax, they run a charter service and take passengers up on joy flights.

The 2003 air show was a special event celebrating a milestone in aviation history, commemorating 100 years of flight. The Wright brothers made their pioneer flight in December 1903, starting mankind on a trail that led to the stars. The event is a great family day out that educates and entertains, displaying a multitude of machines both on the ground and in the air. The prestigious program included waterbirds, aerobatics, vintage aircraft, ultra-lights, military vehicles, veteran cars and a host of stalls to browse among. Special features of the show are an Australian-built Mustang; a P40 Kittyhawk that saw action in New Guinea, and a Spitfire. All three aircraft flew in defence of their country: both the Spitfire and the P40 Kittyhawk are the only one of their kind still flying in Australia; an added bonus was a 1910 Bleriot also flown at the show.

Next door to the airfield visitors to the area can be assured of a warm welcome at the family owned and run Peninsula Motor Inn, situated on the corner of the Mornington-Tyabb and Stuart Roads. The double storey inn is set well back from the road with ample parking. It is in a central position to all the area's attractions and directly opposite the Tyabb antique village. The Motor Inn is a complete function and convention complex, specialising in weddings and conferences with excellent accommodation and entertainment facilities. This property has it all; four spacious conference rooms with state of the art equipment, a large comfortable games room and the fully licensed Tyabb Fly Inn Restaurant and function room that seats 150 guests comfortably with plenty of room for dancing.

Above: Skydiving demonstration in front of appreciative Tyabb Airshow crowd
Right: Display of historic aircraft on the ground and in the air at the Tyabb Airshow

A feature of the Peninsula Motor Inn is the 12-metre heated swimming pool complete with spa and sauna, housed in a bright and airy glass and brick building, a wonderful place to relax after a busy day – it is a favourite spot for children's birthday parties. To complete the picture, large trees shade a relaxing barbecue area surrounded by spacious grounds and attractive gardens.

One of Tyabb's more unique accommodation opportunities is located on Graydens Road. Set up to renew, refresh and revitalise your routine, Eldon Park Retreat is a place eminently suited as a base from which to enjoy the magnificence of the Mornington Peninsula, and in particular the Western Port region. Two large self-contained cottages that sleep up to 20 guests between them are ideal for leisure getaways, celebrations, seminar workshops, team building, career respite, carer respite and support and special needs groups. Many individuals and groups have enjoyed the possibilities of the park, from carers and special needs groups to musicians, artists, sporting, corporate and church workshops and respite. Day, weekend or extended stays are available with self-catering or bed and breakfast options at very reasonable prices. Full catering may be organized on request

The cottages are comfortably furnished, and include a spacious in house gymnasium. Owner, physiotherapist Elizabeth Byrne, ably assisted by former Boxing, Commonwealth Medallist and Olympian, Des Duguid, can help you regain body rhythm and coordination to a musical beat. Acquire expertise with fit-ball, speedball, focus pads, and light weights, helping to equip your body for an active lifestyle. Your whole visit can be spent limbering up on the full-size tennis court or sharpening your skills on the golf, basketball, volleyball and badminton practice nets. Or, if a restful return to sanity is what you are looking for, indulge in a relaxing massage and experience the quiet solitude and therapy afforded by the surrounding environs.

The cottages are set apart on a 200-acre horse stud and farm amongst natural bush and heavily treed plantations, which attract an abundance of bird life. Elizabeth and husband Don, a Gynaecologist, began to develop Eldon Park 25 years ago as a recreational hobby and a means of pursuing the latter's interest in thoroughbred horse breeding. Now one of the longest established studs on the Mornington Peninsula, Eldon Park has turned out many champion racehorses.

Currently it has an impressive list of three stallions with impeccable bloodlines, headed by Portland Pirate, a son of Zabeel, by the mare Spirit of Kingston. The stud has the unique distinction of having bred three individual race winners of the 2000 Caulfield Cup Day program.

The horses are a decorative attraction to the views from the smaller three-bedroom cottage and guests are invited to walk or cycle along the timber railed laneways, enjoy the property and indulge in some "horse talk". The extremely spacious five-bedroom cottage enjoys expansive views over a rural scene to Western Port Bay and is linked to the smaller cottage by a pleasant walk, flanked by grazing animals and shady trees. The entire Eldon Park experience is one of perfect tranquillity, enhanced by a setting in harmony with nature.

The Mornington Peninsula has long been associated with the thoroughbred racing industry. Eldon Park Stud is not alone in utilising the Peninsula as its base. A leading Victorian stable recently established by the Freedman brothers, on their Markdel property at Rye, adds yet another focus to the massive racing industry on the Peninsula. As well there is the famous Yulgibar quarter horse stud at Elgee Park, where the Myer family have been breeding many of the industry's finest for many years amidst the vines. One of Australia's most famous champion racehorses, the Great Kingston Town, is buried at Kingston Park, Merricks North, where he was raised. The famous T..J. Smith trained thoroughbred was the only horse in racing history to win the Cox Plate three years running.

The industry thrives on the lush pastureland of the region that once held orchards and market gardens. This is particularly prevalent on the Western Port side of the Peninsula. These days the rationalisation in the racing industry, and particularly the studs, has seen the numbers of studs in the area diminish to a handful of successful operations. This has been due in no small means to the massive escalation of property values in recent years. Today the land is almost too valuable to be used for thoroughbred studs.

There are also a number of pony clubs operating in the area. Hundreds of participants take their horses to regular events, and the showing and training of these magnificent animals has led to an expanding equestrian circuit.

Red Hill Agricultural Society's annual show has been for many years one of the premier country shows in Victoria. Held over a weekend, the Sunday is devoted entirely to horse and rider. The Peninsula also boasts a number of polo clubs, with events hosted throughout the year, particularly during the warm summer months. It's difficult to put a value on the amount invested and spent on the associated thoroughbred and standard-bred industry for the region, but one can safely say it would be many millions of dollars.

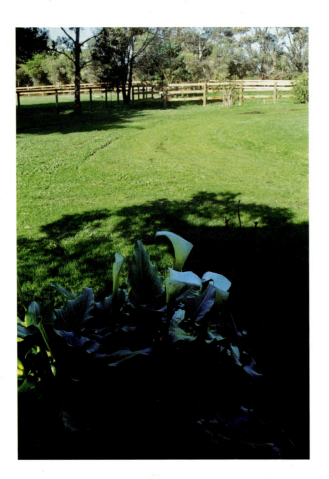

Above: Serene countryside at Eldon Park Retreat
Right: Views of Eldon Park thoroughbred stud. Inset: Champion stallion, Portland Pirate

Discovering **Yaringa Marine National Park** and Yaringa Boat Harbour and Restaurant, often described as one of Melbourne's best-kept secrets, is as easy as taking a short, pleasant drive down a country lane. Simply follow the signs off Westernport Highway at Bungower Road, Sommerville, midway between Frankston and Hastings, and you are there!

What you will find at the end of this sealed access road, on the shores of Watsons Inlet, is as amazing as it is surprising: a marine national park; a deepwater marina and slipway; extensive boat servicing centre; self-drive hire boats; fishing charters, bait and tackle suppliers; nautical gift shop, chandlery and boat brokerage and a sensational waterfront restaurant, overlooking Yaringa Marina across the water to Quail Island, French Island and Phillip Island.

Covering 1,000 hectares of Western Port Bay and declared a marine park in 2002, Yaringa Marine Park lies adjacent to Quail Island Nature Conservation Reserve and is of considerable national zoological significance. The park has international listing for its distinctive confluence of wetlands and coastal bushland, feature that provides protective mangrove, salt marsh and tidal habitat for waders and waterbirds along with many varieties of fish and other significant marine species. Yaringa is a popular destination for bird watchers. Nestled alongside this park, amongst eucalyptus and mangroves, is the tranquil boat harbour from which Yaringa Marine Park takes its name.

Yaringa Boat Harbour and Marina nudges the low-lying foreshore of Watsons Inlet at the top end of Western Port Bay. Started in the mid-1980s by owner Stefan Borzecki, a locally born engineer and Western Port boating enthusiast, Yaringa has since evolved as a well protected 'home' for over 400 boats. In itself it is a place of great interest for those who enjoy coastal features and even more so for those interested in looking at boats.

Yaringa also offers delightful waterfront dining in a unique setting. Established in 2002, Café Yaringa, also known as Yaringa Boathouse Restaurant, is extremely popular with lovers of delicious food and wines, already earning rave reviews and restaurant award nominations. Spectacular views by day and an enchanting outlook after nightfall, Café Yaringa is fully licensed and open all year round for lunch and dinner and great coffee in-between. The restaurant has a captivating design and nautical atmosphere. (Mind your head as you pass under the ship's prow when entering the restaurant!) A log fire gives warmth and atmosphere, complementing hearty winter menus. In summer, air-conditioned comfort or open balcony dining is your choice. Local Peninsula wines are served by the glass or bottle

Don't assume you will always find a vacant table if you wander into Café Yaringa, especially at weekends. Popular chef Bernard Ricca has a widespread reputation; regulars know that it is wise to book ahead. For freshness of ingredients and variety of choice, expect changes to be made daily to the menu. The cuisine is eclectic Australian, featuring European flair and an exotic hint of Asian and Moroccan influences. Fresh seafood, grain-fed eye fillet, vegetarian dishes and mouth-watering homemade deserts are specialities of proprietors Bernard and Sally Ricca. Fresh local produce is used whenever available.

Unique views from all tables, friendly efficient service and reasonable prices all complement the outstanding meals, making it well worth including a lunch or dinner at Café Yaringa in any holiday itinerary. Patrons have front row seats as the harbour comes alive on weekends. A fleet of 30 or more yachts can often be seen flying colourful spinnakers as they compete in the Yaringa Yacht Club's Winter or Summer Series races. During the main fishing season, from early October to the end of April, it is not uncommon to see the Yaringa Fishing Boat Club boats returning to weigh in their catches after a weekend competition.

The best way to enjoy Yaringa Marine Park is by water. Yaringa Boat Hire has a fleet of Marine Board-approved boats for up to six people, fully equipped with safety gear. Fitted with weather protective canopies, boats are available for hire at very reasonable rates seven days a week all year round. No boat licence is needed; just a driver's licence, appropriate clothing for the weather conditions and, preferably, a mobile phone.

Yaringa staff will fully explain safety procedures and provide handling instructions and maps. Viewing the scenic vegetation and wild life from the water rivals the famous mangrove estuaries of the Daintree, and you don't have to travel to Far North Queensland! Known locally as the Yaringa Everglades, you can cruise peacefully past swans, ibis, cormorants, pelicans terns and Pacific gulls - without giving crocodiles a thought!

Should you prefer to try the rich fishing grounds of Western Port you can purchase, or hire, fishing gear from Yaringa Bait and Tackle and head out to the estuary entrance for whiting, salmon and flathead. For the more adventurous, proceed to the open waters around Eagle Rock for snapper, gummies or elephants (of the fish variety!). Before departing on your fishing trip, check with Phil or Merrilyn, owners of Yaringa Chandlery, on what and where fish are biting, which bait to use and Victorian bag limits.

Phil and Merrilyn also conduct fishing charters aboard their luxurious cruiser 'Reel Adventure'. Book in advance by calling Yaringa Chandlery. While in the chandlery, check out the art, craft and gift section for a fascinating range of local nautical handcrafts – they make great souvenirs or gifts for friends. If contemplating or dreaming of buying a boat it's worth browsing through the new and pre-loved boats at Yaringa Boat Sales. They have an exciting range of new diesel-powered boats at Magnit Marine, where proprietor Graeme will be happy to chat about your dream boat.

Left: Boat models at Yaringa Chandlery
Right: Aerial view of Yaringa Boat Harbour & Marina.
Right inset: Afternoon light at Yaringa Boat Harbour & Marina, and Yaringa Boathouse Restaurant

Perhaps the biggest surprise of all in discovering Yaringa Harbour is the size and extent of the Yaringa Boat Servicing Centre. An extensive cluster of shipwrights, boat builders and repairers, a fibreglass manufacturer, spars and rigging specialist, marine diesel outboard and stern drive mechanic, marine electronics specialist, canopy maker, boat detailer, trailer manufacturer and repairer, all operate from on site premises within the servicing centre, some open seven days.

All this tucked away at the end of a country lane amidst native bushland by the peaceful shores of Western Port. A 'best kept secret' indeed – but one you must discover for yourself!

Hastings until the 1860s was known as Star Point or King's Creek. It was renamed Hastings in honour of the Marquis of Hastings. It is today a modern progressive town, a bustling centre forming the commercial capital of Western Port. The original small settlement was established in the 1840s and took shape along the banks of King's Creek as a farming and fishing community, making an early industry out of wattle bark stripping. The modern town is now home to over 6,000 people. In the 1960s, with the discovery of oil in Bass Strait, Hastings' natural deep-water harbour along Hastings Bight attracted corporate giants Esso and BHP, confirming the town as the Peninsula's industrial heart. The presence of big business has not, however, prevented the town from retaining its vibrant natural beauty. Its spacious waterfront location has unimpeded views of the mangrove-skirted shoreline of Western Port Bay, with mystical French Island and minuscule Sandstone Island completing the seascape.

This is a seafaring town and a Mecca for 'yachties', a fact that is celebrated with the Western Port Festival held each March and September. The harbour is a vision during the Hastings Ocean Yacht Race.

From the 1850s Hastings has been lauded as an unrivalled base for anglers and nothing has changed! Every day, in all weather, eager fishers can be seen lining the jetty. Hastings foreshore has picnic and barbecue facilities and a walk along the shared cycle/walking track is a relaxing experience. The area is well patronised by seagulls, who wheel and dart in happy disorder, teetering along the footpaths like elegant ladies in high-heeled shoes. Pelicans, too, look for any tit-bit that comes their way. They are the jumbo jets of the bird world, magnificent feathered creatures with a wingspan of over 250 centimetres. Comedic on land and incongruous when taking to the air with a series of hops, ungainly when landing with their webbed feet angled out in front, slicing through the water like jet skis, settling on the water with a sassy quiver of their tails. Their enormous beaks take up the majority of their faces and appear too heavy for their leathery necks to hold aloft. A truly magnificent bird!

The area abounds with some of the region's easiest, most vibrant walks, many starting on the foreshore. The most popular of these is Jack's Beach walk, which can also be explored by bicycle. It links Western Port Marina with Bittern. The full journey is an eight-kilometre return trek, or a shortened version to the halfway lookout is three-kilometres there and back. Boardwalks pass a stand of white mangroves growing in their most southern extremity in the Southern Hemisphere, providing food for an abundant range of bird and marine life. The walk passes through a wide variety of habitats, allowing glimpses of over 35 species of birds and providing the wanderer with wonderful coastal scenes. Jacks Beach derived its name from the Jack brothers, bark cutters and fishermen, who in the 1840s built stone tanning pits on the beach. Remnants of the pits can still be seen.

The Mornington Peninsula Shire has added a new dimension to the Hastings foreshore, at the Hastings Jetty, by replacing the old 1938 still-water pool that in its time was the first in Victoria. Its successor, the new Pelican Park Aquatic Centre, due to open in late 2003, is an indoor facility that is one of the largest of its kind in the state. It contains: an eight-lane multi-purpose pool, a leisure pool, a toddlers' pool, spa and steam sauna. A fully equipped gymnasium is also a feature, with various multi-purpose rooms and a child minding facility.

A uniquely intriguing attraction newly opened in Hastings pays homage to one of the most feared war machines ever to set sail – the submarine. In particular the Oberon class submarine one of which, decommissioned 'HMAS Otama', lies in the harbour and is a proposed permanent attraction for the region. Princess Ann commissioned the vessel in 1978. It is number six built of its class and was utilised mainly as a surveillance vessel during its years in service - its voyages known in the trade as 'spooky trips'.

HMAS Otama was purchased with a government grant by the Western Port Oberon Association and it is planned to dry dock the submarine as part of a museum that will include historical reference, memorabilia and artefacts of Australia's naval and merchant marine history. The museum will be open to the public as soon as plans are finalised. As forerunner to the opening, located in Marine Parade, the Information and Display Centre of the Hastings-Cerberus Maritime Memorial Centre has been set up. The Western Port Oberon Association manages the centre, which displays a vast range of nautical memorabilia sourced from all over Australia.

Intricate functional details of the Oberon class submarine are on show, with technical manuals and diagrams along with photographs, equipment and interesting anecdotes like the personal Jolly Rogers that were standard issue to all submarines during WWII, as a sort of 'brag book'. When issued, these flags had only the image of skull and crossbones, but with every enemy encounter a symbol was hand-sewn onto the flag, telling the story of the boat's exploits. The information centre is the proud possessor of the Jolly Roger from 'HMS Unsparing', which, as well as having symbols for confirmed sinkings etc. has a symbol of two figures with hands raised in a row boat, depicting the surrender and capture of two enemy agents trying to infiltrate British lines. Visiting the centre is an edifying experience and the collection showcased is a tribute to submariners past and present.

Above: Submarine HMAS Otama in Western Port Bay
Right: Lone pelican glides across the shimmering waters at Hastings

A number of historic buildings still exist in and around the town and the commercial heart has a bevy of shops that line High Street and adjacent thoroughfares.

One such building is the historic Westernport Hotel in the heart of town, on the corner of Salmon and High Streets. Established in 1895, it is Hastings' oldest hotel. Its façade retains the old-world style and grace of the original building. Upgrading within the hotel has deleted much of the old building's original fittings, but has created a bright and airy, extremely comfortable, top-line entertainment venue and a restaurant that is open seven days for lunch and dinner.

Separate areas allow for different entertainment requirements: an up-to-the-minute TAB and bar with bar menu, retains its old-world charm enhanced by an open fire and exposed brickwork. 'O'Hares Bar' is not exclusively a sports bar with pool tables, but a spacious area that is the scene of live entertainment on Saturday evenings and DJ presentations on Fridays. An overhead projector turns a wall into a three-metre picture theatre, allowing sports fans an 'in your face' account of all the action blow by blow. The atrium style lounge bar attached to the gaming area has a Spanish feel, with ceramic floor tiles and floor to ceiling windows that look out onto the flower-festooned, paved, beer garden, which provides a sun-drenched corner most times of the year. The restaurant is renowned for serving man-size steaks from a bistro style menu and is a favourite local haunt. The 140-seat restaurant is made cosy in winter by a large central fireplace and serves modern fare with many Aussie favourites featuring local seafood.

The Anchorage Restaurant and function centre, situated at Westernport Marina on the corner of Mullet and Skinner Streets, has an enviable setting overlooking the harbour and an array of luxury boats and yachts – 'great by day, magic by night'. The restaurant serves a modern Australian menu, featuring seafood at affordable prices to enjoy in the warm, bright and cheerful harbourside setting or deckside in the beer garden. Spit roasts on Sundays are a local favourite and every second weekend, live music creates a toe-tapping atmosphere. A 'Summer Breeze' concert series and shows are planned, presenting major artists. A kiddies' activity corner caters for younger guests with colouring books and video movies, allowing parents stress-free dining. The complex is purpose designed, built from sandstone, enhanced by stained glass, rich wood and brass features, the ambiance is elegantly casual, the price is affordable, the welcome is warm – and have I mentioned the view!

The character-filled Lady Nelson function room has charm and atmosphere with banqueting facilities for up to 200 persons with space for a dance floor. This is an exceptionally beautiful room with cathedral ceilings and views over the picturesque marina. Brides have been known to arrive by boat and say their vows surrounded by the venue's idyllic garden. A team of experienced event coordinators and chefs are on hand to plan every event, large or small, down to the smallest detail, creating deliciously memorable moments.

Accommodation in Hastings leaves nothing to be desired.

The Harbour View Motor Inn on Marine Parade nestles in the Hastings foreshore reserve; it is set amidst an expanse of waterside parkland and has everything and more required of a four-Star motel. It combines superb city service with classic country chic and has the location, facilities and attractions right on its doorstep. Tom and Rosemary Davies purchased the motel in 2000 and are devoted to the area, providing guests with a high standard of accommodation and a warm welcome.

The 30 ground floor units, sparkling swimming pool and small gymnasium are set on four acres surrounded by a wide expanse of manicured lawns and gardens that bestow a country village atmosphere. The units range from twin share to self-contained apartments, some with spas.

The fully licensed Victoriana Restaurant is part of the motel complex. It offers the best in Australian and international cuisine and serves a range of Peninsula wines. The restaurant and separate function room have a gracious old-world ambiance furbished in rich burgundy tones. The restaurant's atmosphere is accentuated during winter, by the warmth from a large open fireplace. Functions are elegantly catered for and outdoor weddings are made romantically special, held in the garden's gazebo overlooking the bay.

Set on Salmon Street, the small hamlet atmosphere of Marina View Van Village is enhanced by its location overlooking Western Port Bay. A range of accommodation from deluxe four-Star, two-bedroom, fully self-contained cabins, to well grassed sites for caravans and tents, nestle among flower-filled gardens, overhung by shady trees. The quiet relaxed atmosphere provides holidaymakers with an outdoors stress-free environment, while still enjoying up to the minute facilities.

Resident owners Leanne and Floyde Murphy have recently updated many of the cabins and have created an ideal base for sailing, boating and diving in the area. A recreation room on site is equipped with a billiard table, television, table tennis and open fireplace; you can even catch your dinner and cook it on the park's electric barbecue. The village can be whatever you make it – a soulful address for seekers of solitude, a central base for energetic holidaymakers or a comfortable overnight stop for travellers. It is a place where old friends are met and new friends are made, and man's best friend has not been overlooked; well-behaved pooches are welcome.

Bittern is a small pocket of rural Victoria with a placid laid back profile surrounded by fragrant Australian bush and farmland. Established in the 1860s around the area's major waterway, Warringine Creek, it is situated 3.5 kilometres south of Hastings on the junction of Hastings-Flinders and Myers Roads. The hamlet has its own distinctive blend of serenity, thanks to the wooded terrain and dense coastal vegetation between the towns. The area was once part of Coolart Estate and is named after the elusive water bird, the Australian Bittern, whose loud call was attributed by the settlers to the Bunyip! There are several attractive walks in the area including the Bittern Coastal Wetlands Walk; this is a pleasant shared walking and cycling, gravel/boardwalk track that can be accessed from Salmon Street. It leads through mangrove swamps to Jacks Beach, with a lookout and picnic facilities located on the way at the Warrengine Creek Bridge. The Bittern Market livens up the sleepy hamlet; it is a weekly occurrence, held each Sunday in Railway Station Reserve.

Above: Night lights at Victoriana Restaurant, Hastings
Right: View from Anchorage Restaurant, Western Port Marina
Right insets: Left– Marina View Van Village; Centre– Historic Westernport Hotel; Right– Interior at the Anchorage Restaurant and Function Centre

The surrounding countryside holds many beautiful estates, and Summerfields Country House captures the essence of hospitality, beckoning visitors to make the most of its glorious position. The house itself is the property's centrepiece, a glowing high-gabled, Cape Cod style country manor, cocooned in a rural setting, illuminated by a large lake, surrounded by rambling gardens and an arc of olive trees. Hosts Maxine and Leo Janssen purpose-built the dwelling and nothing has been left to chance.

The house is built on three levels, harbouring six spacious suites that include an elegant loft bedroom. Each suite is uniquely different and lavishly appointed with tasteful elegance. Art, antiques and huge flower-filled vases abound and a stately grandfather clock chimes out the hour in heavenly cathedral tones. Gourmet breakfasts and delicious dinners (on request) are served within the light filled conservatory, or on the sun-drenched patio, overlooking the mirrored waters of the lake. The guest lounge is made cosy in winter with an open fire, and huge velvet sofas and chairs provide vortices of comfort. Outdoor pursuits are encouraged by the provision of a full size tennis court and the use of racquets and balls. The estate is a short drive to all the region's attractions yet exudes an atmosphere of peace, quiet and tranquillity.

Adjacent to the house the same attention to detail and wonderful ambiance has been created in the estate's stylish function centre. The Janssens have spent a lifetime in the hospitality industry and can expertly provide for any occasion. The attractive function room is suitable for any special occasion and its significant attractions and surrounding gardens make it an exceptional wedding location.

Crib Point has the navy and the railway to thank for its steady growth. Settled in the 1800s as a fishing village, the arrival of the railway in 1889 brought new prosperity. In 1911 the area was further rejuvenated by the selection of Hanns Inlet for a proposed naval base. The village is named after the cribs, or huts, that the early fishermen built on the foreshore. The hamlet was originally named *Morradoo*, Aboriginal for 'powder and shot'. The town's location is actually two kilometres from its namesake point. It has been going through a period of growth in recent years but has still retained its rural persona.

Stony Point marks the end of the line for the rail trail from Melbourne and the embarking point for the ferry service to French Island and Phillip Island. The small fishing village became known as a port in the 1860s and a wharf was constructed in 1888. The present 'T' shaped wharf built in the 1950s dominates the harbour and creates a sturdy platform for the ferries to tie up to and for fishers to cast in their lines. In the 1900s the village was well known for its commercial cray fishing and in the 1920s 15 crayfish boats worked out of Stony Point. Each trip they would catch as many as 200-300 crayfish per boat.

Mangroves grow in abundance and wherever there are mangroves you can be sure the fishing will be plentiful. Stony Point lives up to its reputation and serves as the jumping off point for the prolific fishing to be found in the waters of North Arm. Boat ramps are located on Stony Point's foreshore.

French Island is Victoria's largest island, resting in the centre of Western Port Bay. It is rich in history; first occupied, so an ancient Aborigine song tells us, by the Bunwurrung people, until a warring Gippsland tribe massacred them, then much later, in 1802, by a French scientific expedition. The island's first settlers were William and John Gardiner in 1850. From 1916 to 1975 a portion of the island functioned as an open prison. Prisoners slept in tents at night and worked on the land during the day. With the acquisition of 186 hectares in 1925, the prison became a self-sufficient farm and wooden huts replaced the tents as living quarters. The surviving buildings were constructed in 1946. The prison became known as 'the holiday camp' because of its coastal setting, golf course, basketball court and gym built for exercise by the prisoners. Chicory became an important crop in the 1890s, with 30 drying kilns operating on the island.

The island is Victoria's only state park to be contained entirely on an island. Parks Victoria manages the state park that now covers over seventy per cent of the landmass. Remaining true to its roots, the island contains neither foxes, cats nor the European rat. Not even our home-grown dingo stalks its forests and beaches. The island's main activities are farming and tourism, offering unspoiled natural bushland and remote beaches.

The unique heart-shaped island covers 17,410 hectares with 144 kilometres of coastline. It provides a sanctuary for unique flora and fauna and its surrounding waters support a plethora of marine life. The island plays host to 230 bird species, including the magnificent white bellied sea eagle, king quail and orange bellied parrot. Zorstera sea grasses growing on the mudflats provide a smorgasbord for 33 species of wading birds. The island supports a diverse range of flora, from unique wetlands to eucalyptus stands where the koalas happily munch their way through the day, to delicate native orchids of which 102 varieties are known to grow on the island.

The sixty local residents find themselves outnumbered twenty-five to one by the island's koala population. Members of the present colony are all descendants of three koalas introduced in the 1880s. The colony is disease free and annual transfers of koalas to the mainland keep the colony numbers stable. Sambur deer and the only population of potoroos in the Western Port area live on the island. The potoroos' survival is due to the exclusion of their deadliest enemy, the fox. These small marsupials belong to the macropod family, along with their larger cousins, kangaroos and wallabies. The word macropod is a Greek term meaning 'large footed'. They resemble miniature kangaroos, weighing no more than 1.3 kilograms. A striking feature of this nocturnal animal is its long pointed nose that has a bald patch above its nostrils.

Above: French Island, famous for its koala colony
Right: Sunset over Stony Point
Right inset: Summerfields Country House, Bittern

In May 2002 the government declared the waters north of French Island a Marine National Park, restricting fishing and other water-based activities. The solitude of French Island is legendary and mangroves grow in abundance. They are not the most beautiful of plants but they do what most other plants cannot – they survive in salt water. Not only do they survive, they are productive food nurseries and crucial to the health of the bay.

These special trees have a network of respiratory roots that stick up several centimetres above water, allowing the trees to breathe. The plants' thick glossy dark green leaves expel salt through their pores. When dropped they are caught in the intricate root system, where they decompose and become a life-giving formula for an abundance of creatures, snails, crabs, fish, prawns, lizards and birds to name but a few, dine off the rich cocktail. This amazing plant also creates land. The root system, aided by the low-slung branches, collects sediment washed in by the tide, slowly building up mud to the stage that it is above water and deemed dry land.

The local slogan for this idyllic island – 'Victoria's Natural Escape' – is an apt description for a very tranquil retreat. Bush-walking, cycling and camping are permitted on limited areas of the island.

Ferries run from Stony Point to the island: the journey takes only twelve minutes. Visitors' cars are not allowed on the island and the only means of travel is by bike or on foot. Guided tours of the island depart from Stony Point, run by the multi-award-winning company, **French Island Eco Tours**. Hosted by partners Allan Chandler or Rod Johnston, the personally narrated tours are both educational and entertaining. A true 'Leyland Brothers' adventure awaits. The coach bumps its way over unmade roads through scenery that has not changed much since settlement days. An eagle eye is kept peeled for koalas feeding in the roadside swamp gums, where you are guaranteed so see many of these unique marsupials - who pay little attention to their admiring public.

A number of tour options allow visitors to cater for their own special interests. Bird watching, wildflower, nature and heritage tours can be organised. The regular, 'Afternoon General Interest Tour', is scheduled for Wednesdays and Sundays (also on Fridays during January) and includes a delicious organic lunch at the old prison, which has been reinvented as the McLeod Eco Farm and also provides budget backpacker style accommodation for visitors in the converted original prison cells. The general tour highlights the amazing environment and fascinating history of the island. The totally absorbing day is tailored as an introduction and showcases the island's isolation and the pioneer lifestyle still lived by the residents. It uncovers the bountiful gifts of nature and the countless myths and legends that surround the island, introducing visitors to sheer scenic beauty and the time capsule that is French Island.

HMAS Cerberus is named for the ferocious, mythical, three-headed dog-like monster with a serpent's tail that guards the gates to Hades, according to Greek mythology. The name, with its suitably frightening connotations, has been utilised by the Royal Australian Navy for over three-quarters of a century. The building of HMAS Cerberus was carried out between 1912 and 1920. It is Australia's largest naval training base: tens of thousands of officers and sailors have completed their training within its confines. Naval training began in Victoria as early as 1855 during the colonial era. Initially carried out on, HMVS Victoria, of the Victorian Naval Force. This naval force, initiated in 1865, became the largest colonial navy in Australia. The Commonwealth Naval Forces was established in 1901 and subsequently the Royal Australian Navy in 1911 trained at Williamstown until the force outgrew the base. In 1920 the Flinders Naval Depot was commissioned as HMAS Cerberus.

Five faculties are housed within HMAS Cerberus. They cover Initial Training, Gunnery, Communications and Seamanship and Survivability, Engineering, Supply and Health and Training Services, making up one of the most diverse training complexes to be found anywhere in Australia. Today on average 5,000 personnel, including approximately 28 percent female recruits, pass through HMAS Cerberus each year, which in turn injects in excess of $50 million annually into the local economy.

The Royal Australian Navy Band – Melbourne Detachment is also domiciled at HMAS Cerberus. It is one of two major detachments of professional musicians stationed at naval establishments. The second detachment is based at HMAS Kuttabul in New South Wales. The Navy Band was established in 1901 and has performed for thousands of audiences within Australia and around the world. A state of the art 300-seat rehearsal theatre is part of the, on base, Southern Cross Cinema. One Wednesday a month the band opens the doors to the public and performs a concert, to the delight of a loyal local following, as they get a sneak preview of the band's latest material. The Southern Cross Cinema is also open to the public and screens up to the minute movies with an occasional opening night, where filmgoers get the chance to view a first-time screening in Victoria of selected films.

The base has a picturesque setting located on an outcrop of land that juts out into Hanns Inlet between Stony Point and Somers on Western Port Bay. It covers 1,500 hectares of land and 1,600 hectares of water. The fully self-sufficient station contains every amenity to be found in a modern township including an intriguing history and its own postcode. Some of the area's oldest buildings are still functional within the base, which contains several unique elements.

Above: Sundial and historic church at HMAS Cerberus
Right: HMAS Cerberus museum exhibition areas and historic Wardroom (officers' mess)

History starts at the entrance gates to HMAS Cerberus. Erected in the early 1930s to replace the original gates of 1919, the central and side pillars are constructed of bluestone that was relocated from the 'Customs House', built in 1853 to deal with the illegal Chinese immigrants, who tried to enter Australia surreptitiously and avoid paying the levy of ten pounds per head imposed on Chinese immigrants during the gold rush era. The only water-driven clock in the Southern Hemisphere sat for many years atop the old Drill Hall, built in 1916. The clock was moved to its present site overlooking the parade ground when the Drill Hall was demolished – and still keeps perfect time.

The Wardroom (Officers Mess) is one of the station's most treasured buildings, constructed in 1915 with additions in 1927 and 1970. Its façade has changed but its heart remains unsullied and contains many historic artefacts. The wood-lined hallway leading to the large dining hall contains individual panels of major Australian timbers and glows with aesthetic warmth. The hall itself is steeped in tradition and reflects turn-of-the-20th-century grandeur. An elevated orchestra balcony is a feature, but the hall's most breath-taking characteristic is the two enormous paintings that cover the entire east and west walls. Painted by father and son partners, Messrs Coleman, in 1929, the east wall painting depicts, 'The Defeat of the Spanish Armada, 1588', and the west wall, 'The Landing of Captain Cook'. Their size and magnificent spectacle dwarfs all other features of the banquet room.

Among the many items of an ornamental nature in the grounds are the imposing Catholic Our Lady Star of the Sea Chapel, circa 1948, and the Protestant Memorial Chapel of St. Mark, circa 1954. St. Mark's is the home of the old King's and Queen's colours, having been 'laid up', in addition to the ensigns of the Royal Navy and the Royal Australian Navy. The first royal colours to be presented to any Australian naval unit were presented to HMAS Cerberus by King George V in 1927; the most recently presented Queen's Colours reside in the Wardroom and were presented personally by Queen Elizabeth II in 1986.

Magnificent stained glass windows, dedicated to various service organizations and associations, highlight the chapel's walls. The Roman Catholic Chapel is unique in that individuals and corporations donated almost every item in the chapel. Bing Crosby donated the confessional stained glass windows! Both chapels are open to the public.

Opposite the chapels lie decorative gardens containing a Japanese garden lantern, one of a pair presented by a ship returning from Japan after WWII, and an unusual bridge that spans an ornamental pond. Depot shipwrights built the bridge in the late 1920s from tea-tree sticks. Station personnel and gardeners also constructed the pond and sundial in the 1920s. The striking gardens are full of all kinds of bird life and are a sanctuary for all manner of water birds that include Cape Baren Geese.

Sitting adjacent to the chapels, one of the largest historic naval collections in Australia is housed in the Museum of HMAS Cerberus. It is contained in one of the station's early buildings, formerly the Supply School, built in 1926. It showcases a wealth of artefacts that tell the story of the significant part played by Australia's navy in the founding and defence of the nation. There have been several attempts to establish a museum in HMAS Cerberus. The first was made at the suggestion of the British Admiralty, who sent 3 ships' figureheads from England in 1927 for display. These superb busts were taken from HMS Pearl, an 18-gun sloop, 1828-1851, HMS Pylades, a 21-gun corvette, 1853-1875 and HMS Encounter a 14-gun corvette, 1873-1889. The figureheads are among the museums most treasured possessions and are only part of a huge collection of relics, photographs, uniforms (dating back to an era when doe skin and gold thread were used as materials), medals and memorabilia that are expertly displayed in the rooms of the old building.

The museum contains the ship's wheel, binnacle bell, personal possessions and wardroom china from the monitor HMVS Cerberus. This was the sixth ship of the Royal Navy, launched in 1868, to bear the name; she was taken over by the Victorian Government as a guardian for Port Phillip Bay. The ungainly iron-clad war ship arrived in Australia in 1871 and was described by one journalist of the time as, 'an elongated gasometre'. The monitor spent more than 30 years at her moorings off Williamstown as a floating fortress and kept Port Phillip Bay virtually impregnable. She remains part of the bay, having been sunk as a breakwater in the 1920s, creating a unique diving attraction in the waters of Half Moon Bay at Black Rock.

Other ships in Victorian naval history are represented in the museum, including the ship's badge and personal items from the state's first ship, the sloop HMVS Victoria. Arriving in Australia in 1856, the historic vessel, among other duties, assisted in the search for Burke and Wills, delivered the first trout's eggs to Tasmania and was dispatched to New Zealand during the Maori Wars. This was the first occasion that Australian military and naval forces were deployed overseas as part of an imperial force. Other relics of extreme interest are items returned to Australia from the expedition of the Naval Brigades, the blue jackets, from the Chinese, Boxer Rebellion in 1890. This is a museum holding items of intense interest; it is open to the public from Wednesday to Sunday each week, with group tours arranged by appointment that include a brief tour of HMAS Cerberus. Entrance fees are minimal and a fully stocked souvenir shop and food kiosk is also on site.

Somers is one of the romantically poetic towns that can be uncovered on Western Port Bay's 'coast of coves' that stretches from Somers to Flinders, a scalloped string of evocatively beautiful beaches

Originally part of the Meyrick pastoral run, Somers was derived from a residential subdivision built in 1925. It was initially called South Beach Estate, then Balnarring East and finally Somers in 1934, honouring the popular Governor of Victoria, Lord Somers. Located 75 kilometres from Melbourne, the hamlet is cradled between Balnarring and HMAS Cerberus. The town is surrounded by prolific woodland, containing banksia, she-oak, blackwood, manna gums and coastal tea-tree, which in turn attract myriad bird life and are home to a large community of koalas that can be espied in the woodland areas, campgrounds and backyards.

Above: Fountain and parklands at HMAS Cerberus
Right: Post-sitting Australian White Ibis at Somers Park

The small community offers residents and travellers a slice of serenity. Residential housing fuses with the surrounding greenery, creating little intrusion on the landscape. It has an unmatched setting of natural beauty, facing the majesty of Western Port Bay, with unblemished beaches screened by sand dunes covered in a profusion of coastal vegetation. The idyllic foreshore can be explored via a network of walking tracks. Merricks Creek flows through the village to its nexus with the bay and at its convergence the creek becomes shallow, creating a relaxed paddling pool for younger family members.

During WWII an RAAF training camp was set up in Somers. The Education Department inherited the buildings and in 1931, at the instigation of Lord Somers and District Scout Commissioner Doctor C.G. McAdam, the Lord Somers Camp, a holiday camp for children, was initiated.

Coolart Wetlands and Homestead – Henry and Alfred Meyrick established Coolart Estate in 1840 but it was Frederick S. Grimwade, who bought the remaining 2,103-acre property in 1895, who built the grand mansion. Post-Meyricks, the property saw several owners including Joseph Hann, who purchased Coolart in 1854, retaining it until 1862. Hanns Inlet was named in honour of Joseph. The Bunwurrung people once occupied the estate's land and 'Coolart' is derived from Colourt or Callert, the Aboriginal word for nearby Sandy Point.

Fredrick Grimwade made his fortune in the pharmaceutical industry as a wholesale druggist. He built the mansion as a family country retreat, with the equally grand main Grimwade residence, 'Harleston', located in Caulfield. Coolart has 27 rooms, with 40-centimetre thick outside walls. It is built of bricks that were brought from Melbourne in ox carts, and has rendered window trims and quoins. The house has a slate mansard roof that is dominated by an imposing lookout tower. Adjacent to the main house, the 'Barracks', built in the 1850s and '60s as the workmen's quarters, pre-date the mansion. They are constructed of hand-made bricks, as are the outhouses. The original roofs of the Barracks and stables were made from split timber shakes that are still visible under the galvanised iron. In the farmyard the century-old machinery shed has recently been restored. It houses some interesting farming implements of the era.

The Grimwade family ran beef shorthorn cattle and Shropshire sheep on the farm and were keen thoroughbred horse breeders. Fredrick kept 100 horses on the property. He was a successful breeder and attended all the major Melbourne race meetings – although he was never known to gamble, not even on his own horses. One of his thoroughbreds, 'Bobadil', sired a Caulfield Cup winner and his offspring were renowned all over Australia. The horses were trained on a track below the house where the present wetlands are situated. Because of Grimwades easy access to pharmaceuticals the Coolart farm manager became the 'vet' for the district and the local racehorse industry, at the Balnarring racecourse, had its beginnings from Coolart.

Due to ill health Frederick Grimwade sold the property in 1907 after which time the estate saw several owners with not a lot known about its history. By the time Tom Luxton purchased the estate in 1937 the property was reduced to 800 acres. The Luxtons were attracted by the prolific birdlife and were instrumental in having the property declared a sanctuary for native wildlife. A shallow, seasonal paperbark swamp was dammed during the droughts in 1958 and later further extended to create a lagoon that covered four hectares. Luxton created small islands to protect the water birds from foxes; which in turn encouraged Australian White Ibis to take up residence. In 1961 six pairs raised their chicks; the numbers have since, at times, increased to over 500 breeding pairs.

The Grimwades left behind a formal Victorian-style garden, established in the early 1900s, with rectangular flowerbeds and geometric paths plus a croquet lawn and tennis court that by now were in poor condition. David Matthews, curator of Footscray Gardens, was commissioned in 1938 to redesign the grounds with Tom's wife Gertrude, who was an avid horticulturist. She was largely responsible for the rose garden that holds over 30 varieties and many of the two dozen exotic trees and plantings that include water hyacinth, louisiana swamp cypress, ginko, algerian cedar, pin oak, walnut, weeping elm, and arbutus, to name but a few, many still to be found around the property.

The homestead plus 87 hectares of the original estate was purchased by the State Government in 1977. A trust has been set up to guide the development of the property while Parks Victoria employ the Ranger-in-Charge and staff plus manage the estate. The voluntary body, Friends of Coolart, provides much of the labour and has helped restore the enduring old mansion to its original beauty, opening the complex daily.

The mansion's ground floor rooms hold the Grimwade and Luxton photographic display and historical records. One of Fredrick's 4 sons, Sir Russel Grimwade, took many of the Grimwade family photographs on display. The memorabilia highlight the era, providing a window into the lives of these two families and echoes of many happy summer days. The grand staircase leads to the upper level that is the scene of constantly changing art exhibitions and craft workshops. The work on show is for sale and showcases a wide range of high calibre Australian artists covering many styles.

The estate contains significant wetlands with several areas of various sizes being added in recent years. An observatory, opened in 1985, was constructed facing out onto the new wetlands below the mansion. Designed with one-way glass in inward-sloping windows, it allows visitors uninterrupted views of the wetlands without disturbing the wildlife. A telescope was donated by Friends of Coolart to provide an even closer look at the wetland's residents. The facility with theatrette-style seating for 200 is also the venue for many concerts and lectures and is available for corporate training days and seminars. A purpose-built visitors' centre was added to the property in 1989. It includes toilet facilities plus a souvenir shop and cafe. Maps detailing the formal gardens, wetlands and woodland walks are available from the centre. The woodland walk has been divided into four loops of different durations and has resident koalas. It meanders along Merricks Creek, through a remnant stand of forest that was never cleared for farming, crossing a footbridge to Balnarring foreshore and an idyllic view of Western Port Bay.

Above: Tree frog, Coolart wetlands
Right: Late afternoon at Coolart Homestead

Barbecue and picnic areas are provided in the grounds and numerous events are held annually on the estate, of which the Coolart Jazz Festival, staged by Hastings Rotary Club, is perhaps the most renowned. As many as 4,000 enthusiasts enjoy a weekend of laid back entertainment. The original entrance to Coolart was via Luxton Avenue but it has been relocated and access can now be gained off Lord Somers Road.

Balnarring is a sparkling bayside town, the second largest in the Western Port region. In recent times it has gone through a period of growth but its European roots go back to before it was settled in the 1860s, when large areas of land were put up for selection. The township itself developed after a post office and general store was added to historic Warrawee Homestead that later became a hotel.

The Balnarring district was originally part of the squatting runs of Tuerong and Colourt and was originally known as Tulum, an Aboriginal word thought to mean 'camp in open space'. The town was renamed after WWII and its location on the intersection of the Frankston-Flinders, Balnarring and Sandy Point Roads has resulted in the development of a range of businesses that service the surrounding district. Orchards sprang up in the town's outlying areas during the 1800s but its main function today is to cater for the holidaymakers searching for the special brand of peace that Balnarring and the Western Port region provides. Merricks Creek meanders through the charming town and located adjacent to the township, walking tracks and boardwalks lead through the Bakbirooroo Wetlands, a natural habitat full of the wonders of life. The wetlands can be accessed from Civic Court.

History has left its mark on the colourful town and early architecture is visible in a number of buildings. St. Marks Anglican Church, opened in 1914, sits quietly on the corner of the Balnarring and Flinders/Hastings Roads, surrounded by tall pines adjacent to the edge of the shopping village. Thirty-three cypresses make up the bulk of the trees. They were planted in 1914 to honour the thirty-three young men who enlisted from the area to fight in WWI. The steep-gabled weatherboard church has a quaint, attractive wooden interior that has lost none of its appeal over the years and is a picturesque wedding venue. The church bell was a later addition, presented by two long-time parishioners in 1961. It is rung each Sunday calling members to prayer.

Coolart Road is the location of the famous Balnarring Picnic Racing Club. The club is a historic identity, formed under the name Hastings and Balnarring Racing Club in 1863. The 62-hectare site is decorated by a sweep of messmate forest that protects the 80-year old clubhouse, originally the Flinders Golf Club clubhouse, and provides a striking backdrop for the 200-metre track.

Balnarring Beach is two kilometres south of Balnarring village. It is a small beach community that lies behind the dune-festooned foreshore and is a wonderland worth exploring. A rocky point divides two small bays where silver sands are washed by three-metre tides that leave behind echoes of the ocean in the rock pools peppering the exposed platforms. Idyllic hours can be spent studying the small creatures that await the returning tide. The beach is a stress-free zone, with lyrical views of Phillip Island and West Head at Flinders. The disciplined surf that curls towards the beach provides a good learning platform for surfers and attracts bodyboarding and surf ski enthusiasts.

An idiosyncratic memory is to be found at the corner of the Mornington-Balnarring Road and Foxy's Road. Now past its best years, Foxy's Hangout, an ancient gum tree, stands as an echo of the past when in the early 1900s fox trappers Jack 'Dodd' Johnson and Lou Connell vied with each other for supremacy in fox numbers killed. They used the tree as a scoreboard, tying their booty to its limbs for later tally; the carcases would sway in the breeze creating a macabre decoration. Motorists collected the tails as car decorations. Dodd unfortunately came to a sticky end, murdered, some say, for his lucky charm, a nugget of gold he found in his home region of Tasmania.

The uniqueness of the town is to be found in many of the businesses that it contains. Unlike many actors, who will not work with children or animals, Sue and Ian Hayne have made it their life's work. The couple have owned and run the 'Rain, Hayne and Shine Farmyard', on Stumpy Gully Road for the last six years plus operated their travelling Petting Zoo for 16 years.

Visitors young and old delight in a day 'down on the farm' surrounded by a bevy of animals who think they are human. City slickers are given a taste of what living on the land entails. During the July school holidays they are shown how to milk a cow or goat and how to churn cream into butter while their senses are bombarded with the aroma of fresh baked bread. Special Christmas celebrations see children transported as they watch pantomimes, with the animals as the actors. The favourite, Sue tells us, is 'The Three Little Pigs', when the family dog gets to star as the villainous wolf. September brings round the Showtime Parade. Children participate in this homespun parade by leading or carrying a veritable 'Noah's Ark' of animals around the property.

The farm is a wonderful place to pop in and roam around. It has a unique diner housed in a 1926 'Red Rattler' train carriage, where visitors can relax with their BYO lunch and free cuppa, and it doubles as the perfect place for a birthday party. Children love the hands-on experience provided at the farm, and the most satisfied customers cry when its time to leave!

The Western Port region is renowned for its accommodation and businesses full of character and comfort, and Balnarring has its fair share of these establishments.

Balnarring Village Motor Inn is a stylish boutique motel that was a finalist in the Frankston and Mornington Peninsula Tourism Awards 2003. The 16 ground floor units, all with kitchenettes, are surrounded by idyllic gardens dotted with palm trees and full of colour, with an occasional koala as a visitor in the tall trees. The accommodation is bright and airy and beautifully presented, each one unique with a character of its own. The configurations are varied, some with spas, from twin share to family units – even large two-bedroom self-contained apartments or, located close by, a three-bedroom house. The motor inn's position on the Frankston-Flinders Road puts it at the centre of everything and only a short walk to the shops.

Owners Margaret and Derryck Rees have a hands-on-approach to their business that enables them to build a rapport with their guests and go that step further in their warm welcome. It is a common occurrence for this hospitable couple to hold a dinner party and invite some of their guests, or host a barbecue in the undercover barbecue area.

Above: Rain, Hayne and Shine Farmyard, Balnarring.
Right: View to Seal Rocks from Shoreham Beach at low tide.
Right inset: Surf shop Point Leo.

Summer sees comfortable chairs and tables decorating the gardens and coloured lights adorn the barbecue courtyard, giving a festive air to an already attractive site.

The Heritage Tavern and restaurant is the village's meeting place, a laid back bar and restaurant that serves good food and good times. The historic building, set back off the Frankston-Flinders road, has been modernised in keeping with its past. It is attractively presented to attract a wide variety of patrons by new owner Glenn Gallagher and his excellent staff. The superb restaurant is complimented by a spacious bar and guest lounge, complete with luxurious Chesterfield sofas and a large open fire that adds to a great winter atmosphere, where comfort is the order of the evening.

During summer months the enclosed rambling deck bar overflows with both locals and visitors soaking up the outdoor atmosphere that extends to the lawns and garden. Regular entertainment from some of Melbourne's finest musicians adds to a memorable total entertainment package. The restaurant is cosy and classy in keeping with the whole experience, and a modern Australian menu with plenty of variety is sure to tempt.

Merricks is a bright light among a constellation of stars, an enchanting place endowed with evocative scenery set on the lower reaches of gently sloping hills. Located between the crests of the hinterland and the beaches of Western Port Bay, it is part of the oldest farming district on the Peninsula, occupying land that was once part of a pastoral run established in the 1840s. The settlement that began to take shape was named for the Meyricks (original spelling) cousins who were among the first settlers in the district. It grew up around a railway service that has since left the district. The township remains today, much as it was then, a sleepy centre servicing the surrounding farms, plantations and, in more recent times, wineries. The hub of the small inland community is the general store built in 1927. Tourism has opened the area up to a newer industry as travellers take advantage of the peaceful atmosphere and magnificent scenery of Western Port.

There is much to enjoy on a visit to the area. **Merricks Beach**, originally named Tulum Sands, is a palette of relaxing colour and an ideal outdoor recreational area with numerous foreshore reserves. Set against a background of abundant coastal shrubbery, stretches of fine textured silver sand are broken at low tide by exposed rock platforms. The miniature oceans created in the crevices are a constant source of delight, allowing a peek into King Neptune's realm. Merricks Beach Village is cocooned within this wonderful setting. It evolved from a sub-division named Manly Beach Estate in 1928. The foreshore has many recreational opportunities and is home to the Merricks Yacht Club.

On Tubbarubba Road, Merricks North, set on 70 acres of undulating treed pastures that slope down to the heavily timbered Tubbarubba Creek, lies 'Muranna Herbs and Cottages'. This glorious spot is the home of Dizzy and Norman Carlyon and they welcome visitors, not only to stay and soak up the peaceful surroundings of the property's two self-contained cottages but to view and experience the heart-easing power to be found within their inspirational garden. Dizzy and Norman have lived on the property for 35 years. Originally their estate encompassed the surrounding farms, on which they ran a very successful thoroughbred horse stud and training stables – with many champion racehorses to their credit. On leaving the industry they sold off some of their land and entered the world of hospitality, utilising existing cottages on the property as self-contained accommodation.

For anyone looking for a change of pace, the cottages are perfect. Set apart in woodland glades surrounded by gently sloping meadows, they are spacious, stress-free and secluded, comfortably furnished with an eclectic mix of antiques and original art. They cater for up to 12 guests and are available for short-term self-catered holidays or overnight bed and breakfast. Facilities at the disposal of guests include a tennis court, croquet lawn, swimming pool and a play area with swings and slides, plus the run of the property that has a bush walk and the serendipitous gardens to explore. Included within the boundaries are two lakes, the larger filled with trout and the smaller filled with yabbies. Guests are free to try their luck catching the residents in either lake, and to lend a helping hand there is a rowboat on the smaller lake and a yabby net in each cottage.

The garden at Muranna is exquisite, and is often referred to as a 'garden of the spirit'. A number of powered areas within the garden are available for functions and a fully equipped pavilion is perfect for meetings and small groups or parties. Wide gravel pathways lead through corridors draped with wisteria, along walls and walks and secret gardens decorated with roses and glades full of lilies. Every turn adds a new dimension; ornamental ponds and lakes covered by drifts of water lilies, wide expanses of lawn, gazebos, a moon gate, a dove house, bronze lifelike statues and sculptures, a bridge leading to a small island, bird-song and peace, heavenly peace.

A themed herb garden is a feature of Muranna. It contains quirky philosophical sayings and an amazing variety of plants, all labelled and grown in raised bow-shaped beds. It is incredible how a few leaves from these plants can promote wellbeing, decrease pain, induce sleep, transform a meal and fill the air with fragrance. Should you wish to take home a reminder of this special place, herbs and plants grown at Muranna are available for sale. Dizzy and Norman are happy to have day visitors, but only by appointment.

Point Leo provides visitors with a beachside location that makes an indelible impression. It is a small coastal community that exists because of the surf that tumbles like quicksilver towards a gleaming beach set against undulating sand dunes that are backed by sloping hills and tall trees. Scenic walks along sparsely treed cliff tops are accompanied by the heavenly chorus of bellbirds.

Left: Wisteria pergola, Muranna Herbs & Cottages at Merricks
Right: Autumn leaves at Muranna Herbs & Cottages.

Early morning walks along Pines Beach provide a magical scenario as the early morning sun backlights the adjacent Seal Rocks and the Nobbies. The local residents you meet have a 'hail fellow well met' attitude to companion wanderers and happily pass on local knowledge of the area.

Shoreham lies in a quiet, exclusive part of the coastline between Point Leo and Flinders just off the Flinders-Frankston Road, on the eastern fringe of the Mornington Peninsula. The small town began in 1870s and was originally named Stony Creek, with a name changed in 1882. It has gone through a period of growth in recent years, but all who live here are careful not to detract from the pastoral setting and natural coastal ambiance that provides views across Western Port Bay to Phillip Island, through the heads to Bass Strait. It's a place where creativity flourishes, people come to gain balance and life is lived at a slower pace.

Some of the region's most unique facilities and attractions are domiciled in and around Shoreham.

Ashcombe Maze on Shoreham Road was the first hedge maze to be planted in Australia in over 100 years. The luxuriant two-hedge structures of Monterey Cypress were planted over 20 years ago and now in their maturity are dense sculptured walls that stand three metres high and two metres thick. The famous Hampton Court Maze in Herefordshire, England, built in 1430, inspired previous owners John and Sally Daly to plant the maze, and the town of Ashcombe, where they stayed during their UK trip seemed the perfect name for their new venture.

The maze sits amid 25 acres of sculpted gardens that have been carefully nurtured, containing relaxing woodland walks, rock gardens, formal fountains, waterfalls and lily ponds. Ten thousand tonnes of rocks were used in the construction of the rock gardens and water features. A rose maze has been designed to complement the traditional hedge maze. Planted in a circular design, it is the first of its kind in the world and consists of 1,200 plants, utilising 217 highly perfumed old-world varieties that make a magnificent spectacle of colour and perfume when in bloom. They are at their best from October through May. Recently opened is the forest of rare and exotic trees. This unique collection of exotica presents visitors with a quiet glade filled with bird song and the sound of water lazily gliding between the seven ponds that are scattered through the area. August through October sees the English woodlands transformed into a sea of purple and blue as 350,000 hand-planted bluebells turn the woodland floor into a springtime fantasy.

Whatever the age, 'there's a reason every season to visit the Maze'. The rotunda is the scene of many concerts and the Hay Shed is the supervised activity centre where children are entertained with a multitude of pursuits. Annual events during school holidays, Easter, Halloween and the Children's Fantasy Festival are directly aimed at family fun. The Ashcombe Maze Restaurant has an outdoor-indoor ambiance contained within a unique arrowhead shape, featuring an outdoor garden deck and a wall of windows stretching up to the high ceilings. Present owner Arthur Ross has been Head Maze Keeper since 1998 and is passionate about his partnership with nature. His many years in the hospitality industry have brought new direction to the fully licensed restaurant and it has become a popular venue for weddings, functions and special events. It certainly makes a restful spot to sit and enjoy lunch or a glass of wine overlooking the maze and a large formal fountain set in the centre of a Celtic cross.

Two of the town's most attractive bed and breakfast establishments belong to Malcolm Nicolson and his wife Lee Collins who have taken the art of owner building to another dimension. 'Le Pavillon', the first of the couple's properties, was inspired by the architecture they experienced on a trip to Provence. The bed and breakfast that it inspired is located in Pine Grove, built from mud bricks, local stone and recycled timber. The villa was designed and erected, beam-by-beam, brick-by-brick and tile-by-tile, by Malcolm. The end result radiates the care and attention to detail that is his signature.

Both Lee and Malcolm have a background in education and Malcolm has completed a multitude of trade courses including an architectural drawing, blacksmithing and metal casting. But what no amount of education can instil is the artistic detail lavished on the villa. There are many outstanding features of 'Le Style Provencal' incorporated into Le Pavillon, the most exceptional being the wood block floor in the living area and the entrance gate. The floor is made out of recycled timber, mostly red gum from a dismantled railway siding. It is a glowing feature that is artistically beautiful and extremely serviceable. The gate is a unique piece of iron art that depicts 'Frilla', an intricate, modern version of a Dreamtime story about the origin of night and day. Indoors is layered with Malcolm's artistic craftsmanship, which adds to the very special atmosphere.

Centrally located yet totally secluded, the two-storey property is self-contained and offers guests three bedrooms that can comfortably accommodate six people. Winter is made snug by a big 'Morso' wood heater. In summer an attractive outdoor area featuring a bronze and stone fountain set in a private paved Mediterranean-style courtyard that becomes part of the living area.

Shoreham Beachside is the couple's second property located nearby in Myers Drive. It is known locally as 'Kiln House' with its design inspiration taken from a local chicory kiln. Again it is totally constructed by Malcolm. Made of cedar and stone, it has high ceilings and plenty of space with expansive windows framing views over a verdant valley towards Western Port. Another exclusive handmade wrought iron gate plus light fittings and kelp-inspired balustrades, along with the use of local Arthur's Seat granite, detailed floors made from reclaimed timbers and inlaid pebble work ('krokalia') make the interior of the cottage as inviting as the location.

With five bedrooms, a full entertainer's kitchen and a barbecue on the deck, the house was designed as the perfect retreat for groups, but is still surprisingly intimate for a couple. The combination of space, light and colour pleases the eye and relaxes the spirit

Above: Iron Gate in courtyard at Le Pavillon, Shoreham.
Right: Stunning views over Ashcombe Maze.
Right insets: Water features at Ashcombe Maze, Shoreham

Flinders is one of Western Port's hidden treasures that will capture your heart. It nestles in a protected bay at the western end of West Head on Bass Strait, sheltered by the cliffs of Kennon Cove, 23 kilometres south-west of Hastings. It combines all the elements of scenery, history and adventure. The headland has majestic views over the Western Passage and Bass Strait, showcasing the confluence of Western Port and the awesome energy and limitless challenge of the ocean. Most of the headland is closed to the public – it is the location of the Naval Gunnery.

Lieutenant James Tuckey of HMS Calcutta, who walked across previously unexplored land from Sorrento in 1803, discovered the site that became Flinders. The Bunwurrung people called Flinders *Mendi-Moke-Moke* meaning 'still waters' but Europeans named it Black Rock, after the black basaltic that makes up West Head bluffs. It was later changed by George Bass in honour of his friend Mathew Flinders. Like the majority of the surrounding area it was originally part of Mantons Creek Run, named for the squatter who first used the area for grazing. Henry Tuck was awarded the first official lease in 1846 and his descendants still own property and live in the area.

Flinders' first settlers are thought to have been a Chinese community of around 110 souls who successfully dodged the immigration levy. They dwelled in tents and in huts left by early sealers on the foreshore, approximately on the site of the present yacht club, where the women and children lived by fishing and market gardening, while the men worked in the gold fields. There is still evidence of the terraced walkways they constructed to climb the surrounding cliffs. Some Europeans also used the village on a seasonal basis, attracted by good hauls of crayfish. Permanent European settlement dates from 1854, when subdivisions were made available. A pier was built in 1864-65 with the first school erected in 1870, replaced in 1884 by a brick building. The hamlet's importance was further enhanced and growth ensured in 1869 when it became the site station for a submerged communications cable that connected Tasmania and the mainland. The cable remained in operation until it was replaced by the telephone in 1936.

Flinders is renowned for its old-world atmosphere and the many pockets of history that decorate its laneways. But its most unique documented feature is the quality of its air! It was recorded by the University of Melbourne as early as 1929 as one of only two sites having the lowest figure of contamination anywhere in the world! It is still of such quality that it is bottled by the CSIRO! It is an area of contradictions, recorded as 10 degrees cooler than Melbourne in summer and 10 degrees warmer in winter. Locals revel in the unbuttoned lifestyle of the coastal community and visitors fall under its spell and wish they could remain. Many renowned Australians have homes in the area, and the local authorities make a point of not stressing the picturesque surrounds with overdevelopment and clutter.

In the late 1800s Flinders gained favour as a holiday destination for Melbourne's affluent society, lured by the promise of health and vitality. Many exclusive guesthouses were built at this time. The only surviving example is the Flinders Hotel, known at that time as Hotel Flinders. It was advertised as the most modern in Victoria with mineral baths in close proximity. Built in 1890, the original building burned down in 1926 and was rebuilt in 1928. It has since been altered to cope with the growing community and is the only hotel in Flinders.

Today the Flinders Hotel, on the corner of Cook and Wood Streets, is the hub of the village, as in the past, the meeting place for all community activities, it is full of character and filled with characters. Among others, we met resident Eric Lucas who was born at Flinders in 1920. His grandfather had the first fishing hut on Flinders beach in 1890. Eric is a mine of local knowledge, and a renowned sailor and fisherman, plus a talented golfer who has scored nine holes in one, six of them on the Flinders golf course. The hotel's front bar has the casual ambiance of the best country pubs and contains the only TAB facility in town. Live bands every weekend and jazz performed by the Peninsula Dixieland Jazz Band on the first Friday of the month initiate a party atmosphere at the hotel. A large wisteria and flower-decorated beer garden provides a relaxed fair weather port, and it is the perfect summer place. Paul and Jenny Wakefield have owned the premises for four years and have become locals in every sense of the word. Having always been beach/bush people, they fell for the small hamlet on sight and have become involved in many of the fund-raising projects to help the region and the community. Jenny says, "its lots of work, but lots of fun."

The hotel's large restaurant is spacious while retaining a natural cosiness and warmth. The modern Australian man-size meals that are served are full of flavour, the blackboard menu features local seafood and boast the best steaks in Victoria. A mural that surrounds the 'Pioneer Room' depicts Flinders' history and was painted by local artist Beth McManus. The hotel is the scene of many functions and can cater from silver service to low-key casual. The original hotel had rooms on the upper level, but times change, and the hotel accommodation now sits beyond the main building adjacent to the beer garden. Nine spacious suites offer value accommodation in a modern motel setting. Like the hotel they are at the centre of everything and a short stroll to the beach.

Flinders has all the quintessential elements that make vacations memorable. There is just so much to do in this small pocket of serenity – fishing, swimming and surfing, with secret inlets and beaches to explore, rock pools to examine and many wonderful, invigorating walks. The Foreshore Reserve can be accessed from the bottom of Cook Street, the village's main thoroughfare. The park has a boat ramp and jetty that extends out into the calm waters of Western Port Bay. An undercover barbecue and shady picnic spots are set amid parkland complete with children's playground. Cook Street itself, and adjoining roadways, hold numerous historical buildings worth exploring. The Pioneers Cemetery at the end of Stokes Road contains graves of many of the early settlers.

Above: View across Western Port Bay to Phillip Island
Right: Aerial view of coastline and bays, looking towards Flinders

Mushroom Reef Marine Sanctuary at Flinders is part of 13 marine national parks and 11 smaller marine sanctuaries created by the Victorian Government to protect Victoria's diverse marine environment for future generations. It is a 56-hectare sanctuary that encompasses the reef and extends offshore to the south for approximately one kilometre. The huge mushroom-shaped platform is exposed at low tide and supports one of the most diverse intertidal rocky reef communities in Victoria. Other reefs lie to the left and right of the mushroom and the exposed ocean area provides a rich variety of microhabitats in a montage of sheltered bays and rock pools. Vivid green seagrass and brown seaweed carpet the rock pools. The fronds are home to a variety of sea creatures including crabs, sea stars and daisy-like anemones. The black and white sea star is an uncommon species; it favours shallow rockpools on basalt, surviving only in Victoria and Tasmania. Fish include saddle wrasse, magpie morwong and box-like cowfish plus colonies of the ethereal weedy seadragon. Diving and snorkelling on the subtidal reef are popular pastimes. There are 60 known wrecks in the bay, 15 of these are well-utilised dives.

The Blowhole Walk (1.2 kilometres return) lies off Boneo Road, three kilometres west of town on the ocean side of Flinders. Set back from the cliff's edge, the hole is an almost perpendicular fissure connecting a sea cave with the surface. The walking track descends to the spot, as well as to a rock-strewn beach and rock pools. Garnets and sapphires were at one time fossicked in the area and can sometimes be found on the beach. The only facilities are a parking area and viewing platform.

The 800-metre Tea Creek – Simmons Beach Walk is an easy jaunt in the national park. It leads across grazing land to the Kerry Green Quarry or Simmons Beach. Kerry Green is a spectacular cove that produces turbulent surf in winter. It lies two kilometres further west of the Blowhole, off Boneo Road. Flanked by vertical bluffs, a sandy dune-backed beach and rock platforms provide an opportunity for beach-combing.

Hang-gliding is an interesting pastime, both for onlookers and participants, and the thermals that accompany the onshore winds often to be experienced on the cliffs facing Bass Strait are a magnet for aficionados of the sport. These daredevils provide a colourful spectacle as they launch themselves into the stratosphere.

The modern face of Flinders is picture postcard pretty with the village's shops and services reflecting this element.

In 2002, two dynamic young businesswomen fulfilled their life ambitions and opened art galleries. At the time the two girls did not know each other. Rebecca Barbour unveiled Flinders Fine Art, a painting gallery, whilst next-door, glass blower Roberta Easton opened Beast Creations, a glass gallery featuring her own hand-blown art glass pieces. Beast Creations and Flinders Fine Art have grown into a synonymous couple, while still retaining their individual identities. The galleries sit side by side on Cook Street in Flinders village and the duo has made the most of a serendipitous event, working together to promote their galleries.

Roberta studied ceramics at Monash University, majoring in hot glass; she graduated with honours in 1995. Her talent explodes in designs that capture a moment in time. She uses vibrant colours and patterns within the contemporary and classical pieces she generates. Her fire series reflect an inferno of heat and flames, tones of red, yellow and orange manipulated into energetic pieces of great beauty. Roberta's gallery also includes several other glass artists, many of whom she has worked with personally over the years. They include glass sculptures by Crystal Stubbs and unique jewellery by Pauline Delaney, and a range of exquisite and unique hand-crafted jewellery by local jewellers Lauren Harris and Nadine Morton. There are also magnificent paintings by Su Lesley Fishpool, which complement the glass perfectly. The space is a sparkling showplace that highlights talent that is gaining recognition throughout Australia.

Next door at Flinders Art Gallery, Rebecca Barbour is a curator with a fine eye for quality artworks. Rebecca has had a long association with promoting artists on the Peninsula and has an in-depth knowledge of the artists she represents, knowing what inspires and drives them. The artists represented in the gallery are both up and coming and established professionals.

The art space is discerningly decorated and superbly lit displaying each piece to its full potential. The subjects include landscape, seascape, still life, figures and wildlife in a traditional and contemporary vein. Many of the artists are local and aspire to capture the beauty of the Mornington Peninsula. The gallery prides itself on having a constantly moving display of new works and hosting regular exhibitions. Also displayed is a wide selection of hand-made jewellery, including paua shell, pearls and semi precious stones made into unique necklaces, bracelets and earrings. The seaside gallery also features John Stromer's signature crystalline ceramics, which include bowls, platters, vases, urns and water fountains. The work presented at Flinders Fine Art remains fresh and very collectable.

Transference Antiques and Décor situated on Cook Street is owned and run by Christopher Neesham. The antique store provides a window to the past that deeds a legacy of splendour, which was formed long ago by craftsmen who had an inherent ability to produce beauty. The salon is brimming with antiques large and small, from the provincial to the classical, ranging from 17th to early 20th century furniture, décor and art. The pieces have been sourced from Australia and Europe. The quest for these treasures, "which," says Christopher, "at times seems more like a crusade," leads him every three months to as many as 12 countries, on three continents, with more than a million kilometres travelled. He tries to satisfy divergent tastes, providing variety and quality.

Christopher holds the pieces of history that pass through his doors in reverence, feeling privileged to have possession of them for no matter how short a time. He feels each piece purchased says something about the person it appeals to and in owning an antique we simply borrow something from history, merely custodians for the future. Transference Antiques is also based in Hampton Street, Hampton, Melbourne, and has a warehouse that holds the overflow plus some amazing antique architectural décor.

Above: Transference Antiques & Decor display, Flinders
Right: Sails on roof of Salty's Restaurant; Peninsula artwork featured at Flinders Gallery; Glass Sculpture at Beast Creations; Totem pole in grounds of Flinders Village Cafe

Eating out is a lifestyle in Flinders and the village contains some unique eateries.

Contained in the old postmaster's residence on Cook Street, circa 1905, Flinders Village Café is a comfortable contemporary restaurant that offers relaxed dining, cocooned in a country cottage atmosphere. Indoors, in winter, roaring fires create warmth around individual and long banquet tables. Delicious coffee and decadent cakes invite patrons to linger, reading some of the many books and magazines provided. Outdoors, paved, weatherproofed (gas warmed in winter) courtyard seating creates a great dining mood. The menu ranges from gourmet light lunches to a simple cup of coffee, all served with panache.

Julie and Lee Everett, who own the business, allowed the café to evolve at its own pace. It actually started out as an antiques and gift shop – indeed, you can still pick up unusual knickknacks at the café. The walls are decorated with the work of (mainly local) artists that you can purchase and take away. The store started to serve coffee, then cakes, then sandwiches and, before long, gourmet lunches. Indoor seating led to outdoor seating ad infinitum. Today the café opens for breakfast as well as all day for lunch and it is one of the most highly recommended BYO cafes in the region. Lee is the last 'cray fisherman' in Flinders, so needless to say the succulent crustacean is a speciality of the house. Reflecting the owners' aura, the mood is fun, the atmosphere is relaxed and the food is excellent.

Salty's Restaurant on Cook Street is known for serving a wide variety of simple yet sensational food in a comfortably casual setting. Owned and run by partners of 16 years, Rod Sprague and Suan Chin, the innovative restaurant has been established for three years and has captured the essence of Flinders. Rod has an inherent ability to turn out good food, and while he cooks up a storm, Suan welcomes guests with his infectious smile and perpetually sunny mood. Layered indoor-outdoors and weatherproofed decking gives a number of ambiance options and provides comfortable all-weather seating. The restaurant is a focal point of Cook Street, sporting huge sails resembling a ship at full speed, with the same nautical theme perpetuated indoors.

An innovative menu presents a delicious decision, featuring modern Australian dishes with Asian and Mediterranean influences that are enhanced by the area's fresh seafood and famous Flinders mussels. The restaurant is open seven days for breakfast, brunch, lunch, afternoon tea and dinner, and has become 'the place', for breakfast on a Sunday morning with patrons travelling from near and far to experience the old-fashioned breakfast and genuine hospitality of Salty's.

Cipriani's Flinders Country Inn, Bed & Breakfast and Restaurant, is an enchanting "Cape Cod" home set on two acres of delightful gardens featuring an ornamental lake. Cipriani's offer superb traditional suites or self-contained accommodation, all with private facilities. The beautifully appointed guest lounges include cosy open fires. Guests at Cipriani's are assured of good old-fashioned country comfort and hospitality, great Italian food and hearty cooked country breakfasts.

Music lovers are also catered for when Cipriani's stage Musical Shows by the lake 'under the stars' during summer months, while in winter, the shows are staged in the restaurant with the grand piano and open fire! They also specialize in boutique weddings and private functions with great attention to detail.

Set in the quaint little township of Flinders on Western Port Bay, Cipriani's is the perfect venue if you wish to be close to all Mornington Peninsula tourist attractions, particularly Western Port Bay and the hinterland.

Flinders Cove Motor Inn is centrally located to all Flinders has to offer and is only a minute's walk to the foreshore. It is a substantial double-tiered motel surrounded by attractive gardens set in a quiet location. The attractive modern inn is affordable quality that represents great value. Extra thought has gone into its design, with all ground floor rooms giving out onto their own intimate courtyards and upper level rooms onto individual private balconies. The rooms come in different comfortable configurations, all doubles with queen size beds. Two spacious family units provide a bright atmosphere with unique lofts as the second bedroom.

An attention-drawing feature of the motel is the large heated indoor swimming pool, spa and sauna complex that provides a relaxing change to the beach in summer and weatherproofed comfort in winter. Conferences, seminars and training days can be fully catered for in the up-to-the-minute conference room that can easily cater for 50-plus persons. Functions too are elegantly accommodated in the 60-seat restaurant with wrap-around veranda adjacent to the motel, surrounded by the idyllic gardens.

Peace and tranquillity are all part of the package at Nazaaray. It is a spacious country retreat in the heart of Nazaaray Vineyard, just out of town on Meakins Road. Built of limestone, the secluded luxury self-contained cottage has an elevated position with uninterrupted views of rolling green meadows and wooded slopes. Sleeping six to eight people, it makes the perfect getaway for two family groups or individual couples with romance on their minds. Wood-burning fires and attractive furnishings and every modern convenience combine to create a perfect hideaway just minutes from Flinders and all the Peninsula's attractions. Hosts Nirmal and Raymun have gone to great lengths to ensure guests can relax in an secluded environment and enjoy the surrounding 50 acres of picturesque hinterland, with its passing parade of kangaroos, friendly cows and Henry, the hospitable donkey.

Sharing the property with a vineyard has its advantages. It means guests don't have to travel far to taste some of the region's exceptional wine. Nazaaray is one of Western Port's most southerly vineyards. The boutique winery produces small quantities of very good quality pinot noir, pinot gris and chardonnay that are all made and bottled on the estate. The winery's unique cellar door is contained in an old railway carriage that provides a novel tasting room.

Ora Banda Bed and Breakfast is situated right in the heart of town on Cook Street, close to restaurants and shops, set back from the road, surrounded by a pleasant country garden full of roses and lavender.

Above: Poolside at the Flinders Cove Motor Inn
Right:
Top left– Cipriani's Flinders Country Inn;
Top right & bottom left– The gardens at Papillon B&B, Flinders;
Centre– Nazaaray B&B and vineyard, Flinders; *Bottom right–* Ora Banda B&B, Flinders;

The name is Spanish for band of gold, and was given to the original property by the previous owner to honour his fisherman father's past. Two totally separate one-bedroom boutique apartments are contained within the renovated fisherman's cottage and offer guests a relaxing getaway complete with every modern convenience. The apartments are pools of elegant style, exquisitely decorated with an eclectic mix of antique and modern furnishings. Each has its own character, with comfortable sitting room and wood-burning stoves for winter romance, plus tea and coffee-making facilities and access to a large veranda for idle contemplation. Located at the centre of everything, guests can park their car and forget it.

Mine host Janet McLean has spent many years as a caterer on the Peninsula and now tempts her guests with sumptuous breakfasts and, on request, dinners or picnic hampers. A number of carefully arranged packages are a delicious treat when Janet brings her full culinary expertise to bear on romantic, decadent, three-course candlelit dinners that never fail to pamper and please.

Papillon Bed and Breakfast is a secret place on King Street hidden behind century-old trees. It offers rest and recuperation to work-weary travellers. Two individual one-bedroom units are named Wanderer and Wood White, after local butterflies, and, as their name implies, nestle in an acre of exquisite gardens. Each unit has its own entrance and the mud brick walls rebuff the heat of summer and capture the warmth in winter providing all-year-round cosy comfort. Large oregon beams support cathedral ceilings and the glowing heat of a wood-burning fire intensifies winter's appeal. Although not fully self-contained, facilities include small kitchens equipped with microwave ovens, electric toasters and electric frying pans, along with the normal tea and coffee-making facilities. Generous breakfast baskets are provided for guests to prepare at their convenience and peace, perfect peace, reigns.

The slightly sloping garden is a work of art, with winding paths and arbors draped in roses, wisteria and jasmine surrounded by a full cast of plants. Among the glory, a gazebo protects a six-person spa, the perfect spot for soaking away the world's woes. The paths link the garden areas to a central lawn, and a shared outdoor area has a barbecue. The restful beauty of this property is unforgettable.

Visitors come to Flinders for many reasons in all seasons, but perhaps the best recorded is the Flinders Golf Club in Bass Street. It is an institution in the region and has the reputation of being one of the most scenic courses in Australia, with exciting coastal views from many holes. It is contained within Bass Park, formed as a 103-acre permanent recreation reserve in 1923. A public road meanders through parts of the course, along the cliff line down to the beach. The club's unique design stretches along the cliff top with deep ravines as hazards. Players must often battle the unrelenting force of the wind that sweeps in from Bass Strait. The club was formed in 1903 by a group of professionals and businessmen who vacationed in the area, led by Sir James Barrett and Mr David Myles Maxwell, who became the club's first chairman and secretary respectively. Maxwell was listed as the first Club Champion of the Royal Melbourne Golf Club. He was secretary at Flinders for 33 years and his wooden driver, wedge and putter are encased in the foyer of the club rooms.

Flinders Golf Club actually started life before 1903 with one hole on Kennon's Cove foreshore. This was increased shortly afterwards, incorporating a green on top of West Head. These early greens became part of a new course layout when the club was officially incorporated. In 1926 Dr. Alistair Mackenzie, a world-renowned Scottish golf course architect, was commissioned to redesign the course. Dr. Mackenzie was reported in the 'Peninsula Post' as saying that he deemed Flinders Golf Course, "equalled by only one other natural course, which is in California." The new club quickly gained fame, and by the 1920s was named as the area's major tourist attraction. The club held its first tournament in 1905 with more than 450 players entering the competition.

The 18-hole par 69 course, covering 5,260 metres, is not one of Australia's longest courses but it does present golfers with a challenge, and is one of only a few links-style courses in the country. The seaward side links are a test for any golfer. The most dreaded is the fourth hole, a short par four, nicknamed 'The Coffin'. It runs along the summit of the cliff. A well-hit tee shot is needed to clear the first deep ravine to set up a precise shot onto the heavily sloping green positioned just beyond another treacherous ravine. It was remarked by McKenzie that if 'The Coffin' had been a hole at a course in Scotland, it would have been world-famous.

Perhaps five times British open winner Peter Thomson summed it up best when he said, "Flinders is one of those unique coastal courses – not quite links – neither is it woodland or marsh, that perches high on the cliff top, making it a distant cousin of Pebble Beach and a relative of Muirfield. It is in a fine family of golf that is always best played in wind on salt-sprayed turf with a view of the blue sea. Flinders course is friendly yet full of surprises and intrigue. Bring all your clubs because you are going to need them and a good understanding of what golf is all about."

The Flinders Golf Club is steeped in history and has spawned many excellent golfers that include one of the earliest, Bill Darley, whose golfing feats on the Flinders course in the 1920s and 1930s are legendary. Gored by a boar when he was seven years old, Darley wore a surgical boot for the remainder of his life and walked with a very pronounced limp. The 'Bill Darley Golf Classic' honours his memory. The club is set up to service its members and their guests, but does welcome visitors to play on the exceptional links. The modern clubrooms feature the same magnificent views as the links, in a place dedicated to an ancient sport, played in the traditional way.

Above: A leisurely round of golf at the Flinders Golf Course
Right: Bird's-eye view of the layout of the famous fairways at Flinders Golf Club
Right inset: Flinders Golf Club clubhouse

Cape Schanck is one of Parks Victoria's most visited destinations. It is the southernmost point of the Mornington Peninsula, just west of Flinders, approximately 12 kilometres south of Rosebud. The promontory extends from one of Bass Strait's most unhospitable sections of coastline and was named *Tunnahan* by the local Bunwurrung people. Lieutenant James Grant named the cape in 1801 in honour of his commander, Captain John Schanck of the British Admiralty, who was later to become an Admiral. Cape Schanck was initially part of the 'Barrabang' pastoral run leased by Charles Campbell in the 1830s, thus making the area one of the earliest settled in Victoria.

The cape is a wildly beautiful bluff overlooking rugged vorpal cliffs, darkly ominous submerged reefs and rock-strewn beaches. It thrusts out into Bass Strait marking the entrance to Western Port Bay. The locality stretches from Bushrangers Bay in the east to Gunnamatta Surf Beach in the west, including the inland sections of the Mornington Peninsula National Park at Highfield and Greens Bush, also covering some rural hinterland.

The surrounding Cape Schanck Coastal Park covers 900 hectares stretching from the cape to London Bridge and Point Nepean. It is interwoven with coastal walks offering breathtaking views and invigorating sea air. A popular walk to Bushrangers Bay begins close to Cape Schanck car park. The three-kilometre signed track wends its way through shady forest glades and grassland, past woodland and along the shoreline. It culminates at Main Creek, where a further extension along the creek provides attractive views. Nectar eating birds can be espied in the tall stands of banksias that line the track.

Bushrangers Bay was named for two desperate bushrangers, 23 year old Patrick O'Connor and 21 year old Henry Bradley. In 1853 they escaped from authorities while working on a chain gang in Tasmania. Hijacking a schooner, they forced the captain to sail to Victoria, where they rowed ashore at a point close to the mouth of Main Creek, thus giving Bushrangers Bay its name. The duo, after a murderous journey, were eventually hanged at Kilmore.

Traversing the boardwalk out to Pulpit Rock from the light station is an exhilarating experience with a breathtaking sheer drop on either side, providing panoramic views as the walkway descends by a series of steps to the beach, sometimes to be greeted by wild and raging water.

Cape Schanck Lighthouse is recognisable by its distinctive red cap and is classified by the National Trust. It sits 130 metres above sea level, built of limestone and iron. The cylindrical lightstation stands an imposing 21 metres high; it has been in constant use since 1859 and is significant because the original mechanisms are still in place. The original lamp was powered by kerosene but was converted to electricity in 1935; a fully automatic system was installed in 1987. The current light is a 12 volt 1,000 watt 'Halogen Tungsten' lamp that is magnified 27,000 times by 'Bulls Eye' lenses emitting rays equivalent to 1.6-million candles or 60,000 car headlights on full beam. Cape Schanck is a Category one lighthouse, which means that the light is always lit. Its beam carries across the water for 51 kilometres and has a 10.8-second flash, the longest signal emitted by a light station on the Australian coastline. A lighthouse's signal is its identification, and like human fingerprints no two are the same!

Novel self-contained accommodation is available in the original Light Keepers Cottages built in 1859 and set within the lighthouse's grassed compound. Four individual cottages with a choice of either three bedrooms or one bedroom have modern facilities and sleep a total of 22. The 'Inspectors Room' with en suite has been renovated and boasts its own entrance onto a north-facing balcony. The grounds surrounding the light station have inspirational views over Bass Strait and it is the perfect spot for a picnic. Picnic hampers are available from the lightstation. Ring ahead to order the 'light keepers selection', a delicious three-course concoction of seasonal produce that includes dessert. Everything needed for a stress-free picnic is contained in the hamper – cutlery, condiments and drink containers. Catered twilight barbecues are another choice for groups of 10 or more, or cook your own on the barbecues provided. There could be no more romantic setting as the sun sinks below the horizon and bathes the scene in wondrous light. The lighthouse is one of the region's most popular attractions; over 150,000 visitors make the pilgrimage to view the spectacular spot each year.

Left: Original lighthouse keeper's cottage – now the Cape Schanck Lighthouse Museum
Right: Historic Cape Schanck Lighthouse at sunrise

Aerial view of Cape Schanck Lighthouse
Insets: Cape Schanck Lighthouse museum and rugged Bass Strait coastline

THE HINTERLAND

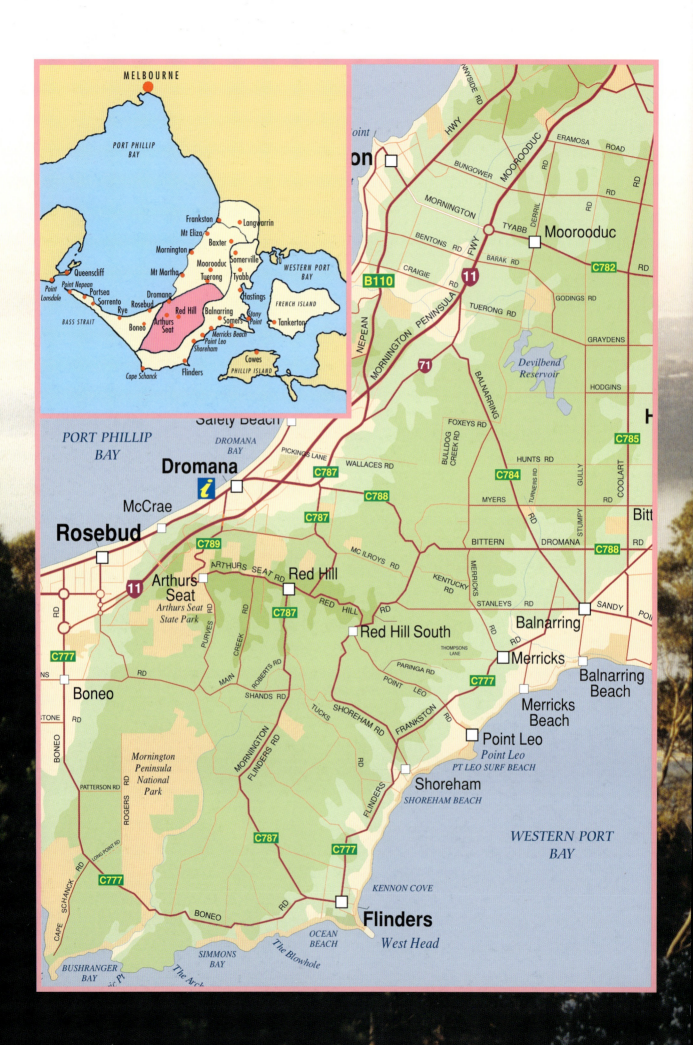

The Hinterland Listings

TUERONG: Nedlands Lavender Farm & Cottage P.120-121/248.

ARTHURS SEAT: Arthurs Seat Maze P.124-127/248. Arthurs Restaurant P.126, 128/248. Arthurs Seat Walk/Seawinds P.124-125.

RED HILL & RED HILL SOUTH: Sunny Ridge Strawberry Farm P.122-123/248. Linden Tree Restaurant P.126,129/248. Poffs Restaurant P.126-129/248. Vines of Red Hill P.128-129/248. Janes Hideway P.128, 131/248. Langdon's of Red Hill P.128, 130/248. Pennyroyal B&B P.130-131/248. Summerfield Farm P.130-131/248. Red Hill Retreat, Red Hill Cheesery P.130-131/248. Red Hill Gallery P.141. Alpacas on the Hill P.132-133/248. Gordon Studio P.132-133/248. Noels Gallery Restaurant & Lavender Farm P.132-133/248. Red Hill Coolstores Gallery P.134-135/249. The Art Shed Gallery P.134-135/249.

DROMANA/RED HILL: Marion Rosetzky Gallery P.132-133/248. White Hill Gallery P.132-133/248.

Mosaic sculpture at Art Shed Gallery, Red Hill

THE HINTERLAND

The roads between the bays on the east and west coasts and the communities in the south take travellers through the Peninsula's spectacular hinterland. It contains one of the area's most impressive landmarks – Arthurs Seat. Travelling inland from the bays the coastal scenery quickly gives way to rolling hills with verdant slopes. The thing that strikes you most when driving through the Peninsula, especially in the hinterland, is the age and character of the trees planted by the early settlers as wind breaks. Their massive trunks and dramatically spread limbs stretch metres into the sky, creating animated patterns on the roadway. They are a strong, unique feature of the landscape.

Areas of meadow and cultivated fields break the drive along the tree-lined, sun-dappled avenues. Many of the region's legendary wineries are based in the area (see wine segment). Rows of vines decorate the slopes in artistic regimentation, bestowing different hues with each passing season.

Tuerong is a region of the hinterland steeped in history, which is today favoured by many of the Peninsula's vignerons, but when visiting don't overlook the area's many other attractions. Nedlands Lavender Farm welcomes visitors to its fragrant fields. It occupies one of the charismatic region's historic farmsteads nestling on Old Moorooduc Road in an area known as Tuerong Junction. The property is an enclave of delicate perfume and transcending beauty, highlighted by a turn-of-the-20th-century ambiance that exudes peace and contentment.

The farm was originally part of 'Tuerong', a 640-acre property purchased in 1858 by Ralph Ruddell. In 1895 William Henry Cornford bought 169 acres of 'Tuerong' naming it 'Hadlow', and in the late 1800s built the present historic homestead. Several years and owners later in 1927, it was purchased by Kenneth Mansfield Niall. He built extensive aviaries for exotic birds, and also pens for the purpose of breeding pheasants. The pens still exist at the rear of the property. Niall made further subdivisions to 'Hadlow' and after his death in 1956 the property housed various owners and over time became dilapidated.

Current custodians Sue and Brian McCarthy purchased the property in 1994, "104 acres of total dereliction." They embarked on a massive rescue mission of the collapsed homestead, restoring the fine old building to its former glory. The couple had restored many houses over the years, but this was a major challenge. Built primarily of brick, the now beautifully restored home has an elegantly simple Victorian design, with a wide attractive wrap-round veranda. It sits on a hill overlooking the surrounding countryside, protected from the wind by stands of mighty cypress and pines. Few of the original mahogany gums that once lined the long driveway have survived, but Sue and Brian have planted 80 Spotted Gums to take their place which, when grown, will once more create an impressive entry to a beautiful property.

The same care and attention to detail has been lavished on what was the farm manager's cottage located some way back from the main house. It now lodges guests who wish to experience the serenity to be found at Nedlands. An interlude in the cottage is a relaxing experience. You arrive to the soft murmur of classical music and a view over sloping pastureland fringed by the Australian bush. When we arrived, as if on cue, a pair of wedge tail eagles soared into our eye-line – a pair, we are told, of only two breeding couples in the area that have honoured Nedlands by making their nest somewhere on the property. The sweeping view often furnishes onlookers with the sight of kangaroos and birdlife feeding in the fields. Decorated in chic country-style and warmed in winter by a wood-burning fire, the two double-bedroom cottage has a unique captivating quality. Fully self-contained it lacks no piece of equipment that could improve any sojourn and the fridge is stocked with produce for a decadently sumptuous breakfast.

As the name would suggest Nedlands Lavender Farm produces crops of one of the world's most ancient herbs. From the moment of arrival the fragrant perfume assails the senses. The history of lavender dates back to the bible, where it was recorded as one of only two herbs blessed by God and taken from the Garden of Eden by Adam and Eve. It was widely used by Egyptians who are believed to have gained knowledge of the herb from the physicians of Atlantis. Tutankhamen's tomb contained urns of lavender oil 'to scent the desert and the dead', and Roman soldiers carried it to rub on their wounds. During the mid 1900s the old-world fragrance went out of vogue, reminding the hip generation of the 1960s of days spent in the company of their grandmothers. In recent years, however, there has been a resurgence in all things natural and lavender has once again been launched into the spotlight. With its evocative perfume the herb has gained a worldwide reputation for toilette water, but this captivating plant can be used for so much more. It can relieve pain and tone the skin, it is a natural insecticide and disinfectant. It induces sleep and can be used as an ingredient in cooking – not to mention the romance and folklore that surrounds it.

In the growing, processing and marketing of Nedlands lavender Sue and Brian have been joined by their youngest son David. His first major contribution to the business was to engineer a device that enabled Sue to strip the lavender mechanically, whereas before she had to perform this tiring, time-consuming function by hand. In the gift shop and tearooms visitors can purchase a large range of products that are produced from Nedlands lavender. Among other things hand-made soaps, a range of body products, lavender oil, incense, candles, biscuits, shortbread, honey, ice cream and tea – plus a range of giftware and crafts that delight the senses and tickle the tongue.

The Tea Room at Nedlands is the perfect location to enjoy the 'tastes of lavender'. Open for delicious lunches plus morning and afternoon tea, the café's indoor-outdoor atmosphere provides an elevated vantage point overlooking spectacular scenery and, in summer, the mystical purple haze that covers the lavender fields. Visitors enjoy wandering the property and discovering the century-old barn where the lavender is processed. During harvest the crop is distilled, or hung to dry from the roof of the barn and later stripped. Any time of year, a visit to Nedlands Lavender Farm is a rewarding experience. It never fails to lift the sprit and rejuvenate the soul.

Above & right: Nedlands Cottage and Lavender Farm, Tuerong

Red Hill and **Red Hill South** nestle in the Peninsula's heartland in the centre of 'The Hills' region, perched on Arthurs Seat ridge, 333 metres above sea level. First settled in 1862 the area came to prominence as the fruit bowl of the fledgling state, with countless orchards making use of the temperate climate and fertile soil. In later years the lush countryside gained fame for its strawberry fields, garnering a reputation as one of Australia's largest strawberry producing regions.

It is a peaceful picturesque hamlet, with pockets of shops and services connected by leafy, tree-lined roadways. The Red Hill Central Store on Arthurs Seat Road (previously Red Hill Road) opened its doors in 1926 and still caters to the surrounding area. It has been upgraded over the years but has retained the look and charm of an old country business, delivering personal service with a smile.

The railway arrived at Red Hill in 1921, but closed in 1954. The old line has been reinvented as Red Hill-Merrick Station Cycling and Walking Trail. On the surface Red Hill is a sleepy hollow still immersed in last century, but this is a fine veil that hides a vibrant energetic community, overflowing with the elixir of life. A number of highly regarded annual festivals are the high spot on many calendars. They include, the Red Hill Garden Festival in October, the Red Hill Music and Truck Festival held in December and The Red Hill Agricultural Show in March. The agricultural show held in the Red Hill Showgrounds on Arthurs Seat Road is one of Victoria's premier rural agricultural shows and is run annually over two days on a weekend in March. The event held in 2003 celebrated its Diamond Jubilee – 75 ears of a show that has become bigger and better each year. The Winter Wine Festival is launched at the showgrounds each June. The three-day event held at several venues attracts thousands of visitors to the region eager to sample the latest vintages from some of the country's best wineries.

Red Hill Market, Victoria's oldest community market, operates monthly from September to May. A visit is highly recommended but it is best to make the market your first stop of the day as it's practically all over by lunchtime. Held in the grounds of the Red Hill Reserve, stallholders make and produce all goods on sale. There is a bonanza of gourmet food available, creating a good excuse to have a picnic lunch. Any region with such a cornucopia on offer is bound to hold many hidden delights – discovering them is half the fun of any vacation.

A day on the prowl around the hinterland uncovers a variety of experiences. The surrounding fruit farms encourage visitors to 'pick their own'. This is an experience to be savoured. The explosive taste of sun-kissed fruit still warm from the tree, and an over-abundance of juice spilling down your chin, dwells in the memory for ages to come.

One such site is Sunny Ridge U-Pick Strawberry Farm on the corner of Flinders and Shands Road, Main Ridge. It is the ultimate strawberry experience where they specialise in flavour, and you can pick your own strawberries, cherries, raspberries, and peas, to mention only a few. Or if you prefer, buy the fresh produce already picked (not half so much fun). The 250-acre property contains 160 acres of strawberries, 10 acres of avocados, five acres of raspberries, three acres of dwarfing cherries and four acres of vineyard, plus a variety of other crops.

The farm is a family business, owned and run by Mick and Anne Gallace. It was started in 1964 by Mick's parents, Peter and Rosa, at first planted mainly with stone fruits, to furnish the family fruit stores in Melbourne with fresh produce. In 1968 strawberries were planted and by 1983 they were the dominant crop. Since then the farm has grown into the largest strawberry producer in Australia, and is extensively involved in research and development with the Department of Agriculture. The farm produces three million punnets of strawberries annually that go Australia-wide and all over the world. They have even supplied Her Majesty Queen Elizabeth II!

The Sunny Ridge Strawberry Farm has slowly developed into a major tourist destination – almost of its own volition – with eager customers turning up unannounced at the door. To cater for demand a cellar door, shop and café were created with indoor and courtyard seating that has become 'the place' to stop for a multitude of reasons. During strawberry season (October through May) the heady aroma of the fruit permeates the air. Huge mounds of freshly picked strawberries piled up within the shop and café area arouse the senses. The luscious fruit is a temptation in itself, but when purchased along with chocolate dipping sauce, or freeze-dried in white chocolate, the decadence scale in the good taste barometer hits new heights.

Wine and liqueurs reflect the Gallace family's Italian heritage, so it was a natural progression to manufacture strawberry wine, fruit liqueurs and strawberry port from fruit grown on the farm. Among others the award-winning wines and liqueurs include a strawberry sparkling and a pinot grigio. Morning and afternoon tea takes on new meaning in the Strawberry Café, with delicious strawberry desserts and Devonshire tea served with farm-made jam that delivers a taste sensation. Even the weight conscious are catered for with icecream sporting only four percent fat and a diabetic sugar-free icecream.

The shop contains a plethora of produce, most with the strawberry as its base. Hand lotion, cream, soap and candles, pickles, chutney, jams and preserves – all produced from the highest quality products straight off the farm. Among the more unique items are soap crayons and pots of soap finger paint! The farm is open seven days, November to April and weekends only, May through October, closed only Christmas Day New Years Day and Good Friday.

Main Ridge is a peaceful rural neighbourhood in the higher reaches of the hinterland, nestling between the more dominant communities of Red Hill and Arthurs Seat, the best known and best-loved landmark of the Mornington Peninsula that can certainly be ranked as one of its top attractions. Called Wonga by the Bunwurrung people, John Murray named the crest in 1802 after a similar shaped hill in Edinburgh, Scotland.

Above & top right: A selection of treats from the Sunny Ridge Strawberry Farm, one of the Peninsula's leading tourist destination
Right below: Scenes from the 2003 Red Hill Show

The area's first settlers were the McCrae family who leased a pastoral run that encompassed Arthurs Seat, but the first European inhabitant is said to have been 'Simon the Frenchman', who could possibly have been Belgian. Initially he lived in the trunk of a hollow tree on the peak's upper slopes. During the period from 1877–1881 he gradually purchased 81 acres that stretched up the mountain from Boundary Road. He was a man of enormous strength and is accredited with growing the region's first grapes and making the region's first wine. Simons Creek is named after him.

In 1929 the construction of the first proper graded road access to the summit was less of an expedition and more of an experience, and Melburnians by the thousands took advantage of it. The road was widened and sealed in 1962 to allow for the droves of cars and buses carrying eager sightseers, intent on experiencing the tremendous scenery at the top of the mountain. It is estimated that 200,000 visitors each year make the pilgrimage to the top. A lookout tower was added in 1934 to commemorate the opening of the road. It stands 16 metres high and has 83 internal stairs leading to the top. During its construction the base of the original trig station built in 1853 was uncovered.

Standing 314 metres, Arthurs Seat is the Peninsula's highest peak and provides unbelievable views, flaunting the land and sea below in a wide sweep of scintillating light and colour. The summit is equipped with barbecue, picnic and play areas and where better to spend a day feasting and frolicking? A unique feature on the summit is 'Arthurs Seat III' – an enormous, giant-size throne. Constructed of wood and metal the chair is the third of its ilk to grace the spot and makes a fantastic photographic prop.

Arthurs Seat is wonderful in winter, superb in summer, amazing in autumn and sparkling in spring. This special place has a different face for every time of year with myriad walks that embroider the slopes, putting on a show as flowers and plants reflect the changing colours of the season. There is a wide range of attractions on and around the summit of Arthurs Seat; some businesses occupying buildings that have decorated the peak since the 1920s.

Arthurs Seat State Park covers an area of 572 hectares and protects large areas of unsullied bushland. Numerous walking tracks criss-cross the slopes, leading through fern gullies, past waterfalls and along creek banks. Birds, animals and reptiles find sanctuary in the park, and due to the different levels of elevation a diverse range of plants flourish that include many wildflower species and rare orchids.

Seawinds is part of Arthurs Seat State Park managed by Parks Victoria. It is a 34 acre property on Purves Road, originally owned by George Chapman who was the peak's only resident at that time. He was employed as a gardener during the late 1800s at Heronswood, an historic mansion that is located in Dromana. Chapmans Point was named in his honour. Each day he would walk to and from Heronswood, roughly following the same path that now makes up the Two Bays Walk. He built a small wooden shack on the property and created a very special garden to complement the stupendous views of Port Phillip Bay and the Bellarine Peninsula, to be savoured from the properties elevated position. Some of the cypresses he planted have survived and are over 100 years old.

Sir Thomas Traverse, an eminent Melbourne surgeon, purchased the property with a view to building a mansion. A small cottage was built but the mansion never came to pass. However, Sir Thomas and Lady Traverse did plan and start work on the garden that was to surround their mansion, and for that visitors are forever appreciative. The couple planted a number of elm, ash and maple trees that have survived. They built a walled garden and lagoon where they featured five ceramic sculptures by renowned Melbourne born artist, William Ricketts. Ricketts frequently lived with the Pitjantjatjar and Arrente people in the Northern Territory and his exquisite, mystical work is an integration of the European Christian tradition and the ethnicity and culture he shared with the Australian Aborigines. The Victorian government bought the property in 1975 and Parks Victoria has continued to cultivate the restful garden areas within its boundaries. In spring under plantings of freesias paint the landscape in colour, superseded by exotic flora and fragrant roses in summer that provide yet another reason to visit this inspiring place.

Arthurs Seat Maze on Purves Road has got to be experienced to be believed and creates a lasting impression. It's a fun place for children, yet contains many elements that appeal to adults. The sheer magnitude of the design and structural elements of the ever-changing features within the gardens and maze components is overwhelming.

In 1993 Sally and Michael Savage took 15 acres of vacant paddock and began a process that is still developing today. A decade later the area contains three traditional hedge mazes, 20 themed gardens, a Sculpture Park, miniature mazes, an animal farm and the annual Maize Maze. The Maize Maze covers three acres of the property and is replanted each year in an intricate new design that is always a real mind bender. At every twist and turn the three hedge mazes are filled with innovative features that give an added dimension to the journey through the lofty green corridors, and delight the children. The gardens are full of works of art, some that have been commissioned and many that Sally has acquired specifically to create a new feature in the garden. Some of these pieces are truly magnificent, like the metre-high marble sculptures that she purchased in Vietnam.

Left: William Rickett's sculptures at Seawinds
Right: Entrance way to Seawinds, Arthurs Seat State Park

The Savages have adopted a process of systematic change and have created the Artists in Residence program to nurture new creative talent. Artists are invited to sculpt, paint and carve on the grounds to the delight of onlookers. From this innovative idea the Sculpture Park has evolved; carved out of recycled Macrocarpa cypress rescued after being felled on properties throughout the Peninsula. Set on five acres the Sculpture Park contains amazing giant tree sculptures and highly decorated Aboriginal burial poles that honour the energetic spirit of the Aboriginal people and celebrate their heritage. It shares the area with the Blue Gum Gallery which features artwork brought back by Michael and Sally from 'Maningrida', a remote Aboriginal settlement in the Northern Territory, whose people have developed an extensive artistic community quoted as a commercial and creative adaptation of existing cultural practices. A sensor-activated sound system adds a touch of drama to the air, sending out the reverberating sound of a didgeridoo and Aboriginal chanting. There is just so much to take in. Rocks from the property have been utilised in a waterfall feature. The Conifer Garden contains 100 species of conifer with some rare varieties. Even the vegetable garden is a feature and the produce is used in the property's restaurant.

The 100-seat licensed Solair Restaurant and function centre can be accessed from the main road and sits high over the park. Wide windows open onto decking that has views over the park. It is an eminently appealing venue for lunch and a perfect spot for any special occasion. The artistic theme adopted by Sally and Michael throughout the park is present in the décor of the bright cheerful venue and the restaurant's mascot is a bronze, metre-high Great Dane named Chester.

With such an abundance of fresh organically grown produce on the doorstep it is not surprising that the quality of the restaurants in the hinterland is second to none, attracting some of the country's best chefs.

Arthurs Restaurant is perched on the roof of the hinterland at the peak of Arthurs Seat. It is contained in an art deco building that survives from the mountain's heyday when the city's elite would travel from Melbourne and party at the top of the mountain. The intriguing development was built in the early 1930s, named 'Hollywood Gardens of the Moon'. The complex was styled on an American theme park with a swimming pool on the roof, a ballroom with underwater swimming pool views and innovative amusements well ahead of their time.

Today's owners, the Wyllie family, have recently embarked on a total refurbishment of the premises, employing the entrepreneurial and managerial skills of Ray and Jill Johns. The food is matched only by the view. Position, position and position, allows patrons to dine in an unmatched setting. It is the perfect spot night or day with Port Phillip Bay and the towns of the southern peninsula spread out in all their majesty. The recently restyled, glass-enclosed restaurant now contains a step-up lounge area with large comfy sofas, providing a stage for musical nights, a relaxed drink and laid-back jazz. The mood is elegantly casual and the service gracious and personal.

The breathtaking views can be savoured either in the relaxed dining atmosphere of the restaurant or from the Terrace Café on the lower level. Indoor-outdoor seating at the licensed café makes it a popular venue any time of year and the casual menu is a special treat, full of fresh local produce, gourmet pies, soups, winemakers platters and sinful cakes and pastries. An exceptional function venue has been created out of the building's original ballroom with a wide expanse of windows, gracious terraces and a backdrop that will enhance any special memory. It is a sought-after venue for weddings, where brides radiate within the exceptional surrounds. The historic complex is as special now as it was when it was created – and just as much fun.

The Linden Tree Restaurant at Lindenderry of Redhill, on the corner of Andrews Lane and Arthurs Seat Road, Red Hill is one of the region's foremost fine-dining establishments, contained within the region's premier hotel and function centre and surrounded by its own vineyard. It is an elegantly beautiful restaurant overlooking the vineyard, nestled within a glade of tall trees. It takes patrons from early morning to late night every day and is open for breakfast, lunch and dinner, plus morning and afternoon tea – welcoming day visitors as well as hotel guests.

It makes the perfect spot for; the celebrated 'long lunch', the indulgent 'high tea' or the stylish 'intimate dinner' that can be served cocooned within the sophisticated restaurant, or al fresco in a flower-filled courtyard. During summer guests may find a tapas menu being served in the courtyard and be serenaded by the passionate Latin mood of a classical Spanish guitarist. Evening dining is made even more special by the glint of flickering candlelight, the scent of fresh flowers and the murmur of subdued music. Expert service is friendly but unobtrusive, and an open fire in winter adds to the appeal.

One of Australia's finest chefs, Andrew Blake, who has had one of the most celebrated careers of any modern Australian chef, designs the menu for Linden Tree. His culinary expertise is renowned and his masterpieces emulate the restaurant's elegant surrounds, full of natural flavours. Dishes are prepared in an innovative modern Australian style, featuring Peninsula produce, matching the superb estate and regional wines as well as award-winning wine from all over Australia. The vineyard's calendar of events incorporates master classes with Andrew, wine dinners and other festive occasions for lovers of good food and fine wine.

Occasionally you come across a restaurant that serves food so intoxicating that each mouthful delivers a gastronomic explosion to the senses. Poff's is one of these. Owner/Chef, Sasha Esipoff, is a culinary master. His Russian background permeates the dishes he prepares with rich exotic flavours, taking diners on a delicious adventure. Sasha's interest in the culinary arts began in his grandmother's kitchen. He trained both internationally and in Australia in renowned restaurants, headed by 'La Popotte', Melbourne's only 'real' French restaurant in the 1960s. He met and married Lorraine while performing with the Karasieve Russian Dance Company. She was a dancer and teacher studying Russian dance. Finally in 1992 the dream of a lifetime was realised when the couple opened Poff's, and for over 10 years they have held court high on a ridge surrounded by an evocative landscaped cottage garden, overlooking vine-covered hills and verdant dales, backlit by the shimmering illusion of Western Port Bay.

Above & right: Aerial views of Arthurs Seat Maze with feature Maize Maze on right which changes annually

The restaurant is special for many reasons and is highly recommended by locals. The Esipoffs have realised their dream of bringing fine dining to the Peninsula at a realistic price, with not only a fully stocked bar serving many Peninsula wines, but also allowing dinners to BYO should they prefer.

The peaceful ritual of dining is made special at Poff's with a choice of seating in the bi-level restaurant or outdoors on the wide decked veranda. Wonderful views are shared through long stretches of windows, and vaulted ceilings add space and light to the scene. A variety of international dishes decorate the menu but the house speciality has been self nominated by a loyal following – a riot would ensue if it ever disappeared from the menu! 'Siberian Pelmeni': little dumplings of lamb in thin dough, boiled and served on a soy sauce, spiked with garlic and chilli, topped with sour cream and parsley. It is a Russian tradition to drink a shot of vodka with Pelmeni and the flavour of the vodka and the dish create a gastronomic fusion of pure bliss.

Most of the vineyards in the area list themselves as vineyards that include a restaurant. But Helen, Geoff and daughter Jessica Graham, who own 'Vines of Red Hill' on Red Hill Road, prefer to think of themselves as owning a restaurant which has the added bonus of being happily situated in a vineyard on 20 acres – and what a situation it is! An Italianate staircase flanked by mass plantings of lavender sweeps down to the architect designed, modern Tuscan-style restaurant. Relaxing gardens dotted with massive apple gums and vines surround the building that nestles into a slope which rolls down to a natural creek-fed lake. The restaurant's glass façade looks out onto a paved terrace providing views from every table, overlooking the lake and a panorama of gentle sloping countryside fringed by tree-lined ridges.

The restaurant comfortably seats 60 and an open fire in winter radiates warmth. A modern Australian menu with European influences is changed weekly to allow guests the optimum in choice. Wonderful dishes that include crisp duck with beetroot jam and poached pears with home made cinnamon icecream, tempt the tastebuds. Steve Davidson, a London trained chef, plus a team of young vibrant staff is professionally led by Jessica. It is the perfect spot for any celebratory occasion. Weddings are made romantically special with expert planning and a superb backdrop. The restaurant is open for most public holidays and for lunch Fridays, Saturdays and Sundays plus dinner Friday and Saturday evenings, with extended summer trading

The vineyard has equal plantings of chardonnay, pinot noir and pinot gris, plus a small amount of gewurztraminer. The cellar door is open each weekend and tastings are held in the unique tower atop the restaurant. The restaurant is fully licensed and the extensive wine list features Vines of Red Hill wines and also includes styles from other regions in Australia and overseas. Some time in the future it is planned to add accommodation to the estate, which will create an all-round experience at Vines of Red Hill.

Like everything in the hinterland, the quality of accommodation is exceptional and comes in a variety of properties each with its own individual appeal.

Jane's Hideaway is readably accessible on Shoreham Road, Red Hill village's main street. Its façade has the high gables and trimmings of the gingerbread house ensconced in childhood memories. The purpose-built accommodation is surrounded by country-style gardens and exudes old-world charm, peace and tranquillity.

There are two (soon to be three) separate apartments with separate entranceways. Both are decorated with flair and style. The feel is light and airy with leadlights, polished floors and gas log fires, each with its own, private, garden courtyard and barbecue. The design of the cottages is unique with open plan, fully-equipped kitchens and cosy loungerooms. Open-loft bedrooms are romantically furnished with opulent four-poster beds and indulgent bathrooms complete with generous corner spas. The cottages are furnished with antiques and original artworks, some of which have been skilfully created by host, Jane Stinchcombe, who is a trained artist with a degree in visual art.

Although of the same design, each cottage has an individual character. The name for the 'Granger' cottage comes from Jane and husband Daniel's English ancestors. This quintessentially romantic cottage is decorated with an English rose theme; it provides today's luxury in a yesterday setting. The 'Hannoy' cottage is also an echo of mine hosts' past. Pronounced 'Anoire', it comes from the couple's French heritage. Guests are given the royal treatment within this cottage that has the feel of a mini chateau, surrounded by rich fabrics, gilded mirrors and opulently-decorated walls. A sumptuous breakfast hamper is included in the tariff, and the old-world ambiance is enhanced with all the modern conveniences of today.

Langdon's of Red Hill is located in picturesque seclusion on Arthurs Seat Road. It is full of atmosphere, screened by tall trees and surrounded by a rambling garden, part of an old 1900s property that was once known as Pickle Cottage. The bed and breakfast is perfect for lively group getaways, or relaxing individual sojourns. Centrally located, the property is within 15 minutes to everywhere.

Four queen-size bedrooms lead off a large central dining area. They are individually decorated in period style, each with its own romantic ambiance, en suite and private verandah. The massive communal banquet table in the dining room provides the perfect spot for the sumptuous gourmet breakfasts served, and a convivial place to plan the day's adventures. Breakfasts feature local produce, with tea, coffee and treats always available. The character-filled room is the heart of the house, the perfect stage for romantic meals for two, or group dinner parties, which can be arranged on request. Or for a more relaxed repast, cook your own in the garden barbecue courtyard.

A central glass-walled conservatory joins the dining room with the guest drawing room. It provides a quiet nook for a refreshing afternoon interlude overlooking relaxing views of the peaceful garden that has both native and formal areas. The drawing room is a cosy corner with an old-world feel, well stocked with reading material, games and an open fire for winter comfort. The stylishly restful retreat allows visitors to unwind in a location that specialises in quality and extends a warm welcome.

Above: The Vines of Red Hill Restaurant
Right:
Top: View from Arthurs Restaurant
Centre left top: Linden Tree Restaurant
Centre left bottom, and centre right: Poffs Restaurant
Bottom: View over The Vines of Red Hill Restaurant

On Main Creek Road at Main Ridge, a sweeping driveway guides you to Pennyroyal, an exquisite bed and breakfast set within a 9.5-acre garden that demands admiration. The property is as special as its name and delivers a sense of space and seclusion Guest can choose from a studio or a two-room suite, which are separated by the main house, each with its own entrance and private patio. The house is designed to resemble an historic homestead, built of stone and furbished with architectural antique gothic windows and doors and recycled timber. The rooms are exquisitely furnished and the tariff covers a cooked country-style breakfast and includes snacks to accompany tea and coffee. The trees and shrubs surrounding the outdoor patios are alive with birdlife: parrots and honeyeaters put on a show for an admiring public. Val and Roger Gould purchased Pennyroyal in 1999 and are steadily leaving their mark on the property. Val is an artist who takes inspiration from her garden and Roger is a renowned international photographer. Examples of their work decorate the apartment walls.

The signature of the property is a marriage of nature and comfort. Any visitor cannot help but become enamoured of the garden. A number of defined spaces linked by informal pathways create garden rooms for quiet contemplation. Each space has its own enchantment; curtains of roses hang from stone arches and sculptures and birdbaths give substance to garden beds full of textured greenery and vibrant colour. Adjacent to the house mass plantings of lavender and iceberg roses create waves of colour, climbing to a folly draped in clematis and roses.

Structured gardens give way to tree-strewn parkland that slopes down to the creek, and a massive Chinese elm's drooping branches create a secret reading room. Furnished with a table and chairs it provides a cool sanctuary away from the summer heat, or a secluded picnic spot.

Tucked away down a country lane you will find a picturesque and quaint bed and breakfast called Summerhill Farm. Set on 10 peaceful acres it is located off Barkers Road, Main Ridge. Visitors have a choice of accommodation. The Edwardian Suite with one or two bedrooms is contained within the 1920s homestead awash with all the romance of that era. The suite has everything needed for a relaxing sojourn: modern conveniences, queen-size beds and elegant antique furnishings. A bay window with stylish leadlighting provides a charming dining nook where generous country breakfasts are served, overlooking a restful view of rolling pastureland and attractive gardens with a preponderance of lavender and carpet roses.

Adjacent to the main house, Butterfly Cottage, circa 1940s, is fully self-contained. The one-bedroom farm cottage is comfortably furnished and has the added warmth of a wood-burning stove to tackle winter's chills. Its picturesque setting includes a frog pond overhung by a twisted willow and butterfly-attracting buddleia bushes. An elevated position provides tranquil views down to a stream that joins Main Creek. All this is set against neighbouring slopes covered in olive trees and vines. For the last three years Beverley Baker has welcomed guests to this delightful property, providing a quiet retreat that is conveniently located amidst the Mornington Peninsula's many attractions.

On the outskirts of Red Hill in a secluded forest valley, where native birds provide the perfect wake up call, a unique bush retreat with a country-house feel awaits discovery. Red Hill Retreat, owned by Trevor and Jan Brandon, merges into the scenery, built of mud bricks individually made and initialled by the Brandon family. Once the family home, the comfortable house has been refurbished to provide two self-contained romantic suites, privately situated at either end of the old homestead. Each suite has a private entrance through the exotic garden. The Forest Suite has one king size or twin and one queen-size bedroom and the Orchard Suite has one king-size or twin bedroom with en suite. A cooked breakfast is served in the privacy of each unit. Menus vary with the season to take advantage of the organic produce grown on the property.

The accommodation shares the eight-acre property with an orchard, magnificent garden, organic vegetable patch and one of Red Hill's most famous attractions – Red Hill Cheese. Trevor and Jan established their small boutique award-winning Cheesery and Cellar Door in April 2000, producing distinctive handcrafted regional cheeses that compliment Peninsula wines. They were first inspired by farmhouse cheesemaking in Europe, and draw upon Trevor's experience as a Food Microbiologist.

Only the best ingredients and vegetarian rennet are used, and are free from genetically-modified organisms, artificial stabilisers and preservative. Slow processing and gentle handling help preserve the raw qualities of the clean rich milk, resulting in cheeses with character and great depth of flavour with unique taste and aroma. Most of the notable restaurants in the region use Red Hill Cheese. Its name has become synonymous with flavour and structure. Their youngest son, Burke, has joined the Brandons in the business so it has become a family affair. Tastings and sales are available daily at the cellar door and cheesemaking workshops are held regularly, teaching eager novices the secrets of this ancient art. It is an unforgettable experience, but bookings are essential.

Left: Interiors of Langdons B&B (top) & Janes Hideaway (below)

Right:
Top: Aerial view of Pennyroyal
Centre left: Red Hill Retreat & Cheesery
Centre right: Janes Hideaway
Bottom: Summerhill Farm B&B

The exceptional beauty of the hinterland inspires artists of every discipline. Depicted on canvas, in sculpture in words and in song, their work can be seen in the area's many galleries contained within the region's flourishing art trail.

Red Hill Gallery 141 on Red Hill Road, Red Hill South, is an art space dedicated to fine crafts and talented artists covering many mediums. Owned by Deidre and Geoff Bruton, the gallery is set off the road, cocooned within the surrounding hills of a 10-acre property. It is picture-postcard pretty, set within a country cottage entered from a rose and vine-draped verandah. The gallery is a series of interconnecting rooms, including a coffee nook that delivers views over the treed slopes and rolling pastures. The Brutons have attracted a prestigious stable of artists from both the Peninsula and around Australia, allowing them to present regular fresh and vibrant exhibitions, showcasing the likes of Joan Denner, Jeff Gilmour, Raelene Sharp, Patricia O'Gready, Helen Badcock, and Jill Bygott who sculpts amazing flowerpot containers and birdbaths.

Deidre and Geoff run a gallery within a gallery, having added the unique element of 'Alpaca on the Hill' to their property, with an alpaca room just off the main gallery. The room is full of colourful, tactile designer garments, shawls, jumpers, hats, socks and gloves with some wonderful throw rugs and wall hangings, plus knitting yarn.

Having always had an interest in animals, the Brutons decided to farm alpacas. Why? "Well," says Deidre, "they do minimal damage to the environment, they make you part of the herd – and they talk to you! The ancient Incas believed the animals were a gift from God, and when you spend time with them you understand."

Indeed these curious, outlandish creatures with 'Bette Davis eyes' do indeed talk to you. Originating from South America, the males are called machos, the females hembras and the young crias, who, unlike lambs that gamble around the paddock, play by pronking! Their pads cause minimal damage to the land and they graze gently, allowing faster pasture regrowth. Alpaca fibre is hollow; this structure gives it high durability, tensile strength and it resists pilling and shrinking. It is also lightweight and suitable to allergy sufferers. Its natural colours are easily enhanced with dye and it mixes well with other natural fibres such as silk or wool.

Alpaca on the Hill is one of more than 800 alpaca breeders that belong to the Australian Alpaca Cooperative, established in 1995. It is a breeder-driven organization, which on behalf of its members markets products that are manufactured and designed in Australia from Australian-grown alpaca fibre. The Cooperative, in conjunction with its members, is working to create an Australian alpaca brand identity and logo that will be associated with softness, warmth, luxury and durability. Brand name fashion houses worldwide are discovering the delights of alpaca fibre and utilising it in a range of designer products. The Alpaca Room at Red Hill Gallery 141 proudly displays a range of these sumptuous garments made from a fibre that was once the exclusive property of Inca royalty.

Gordon Studio Glass Blowers are expected to set up shop mid 2004 in the area, on the corner of Red Hill and Dunns Creek Road, Red Hill, relocating from their present site on the Nepean Highway at West Rosebud. In 1990 Eileen Gordon established Gordon Studio Glass Blowers in Numurkah in northern Victoria. Moving to Rosebud eight years ago she was joined in the business by her husband Grant Donaldson, who had helped establish her original success.

Eileen grew up with the art. Her parents are renowned glass engravers, Alasdair and Rish Gordon, and both her brothers also work in the medium. Grant's background was on the land. He was inspired to the art in the 1990s. The pair has become known for their vibrant work, Eileen's depicting bright energetic contemporary colours and Grant's reflecting his rural background in rich evocative Australian landscape tones.

A visit to their studio not only provides a display of exceptional beauty, but also allows a window into the ancient process of glass blowing. It is a fascinating experience to watch the creation of vases, bottles and platters out of, what looks to the layman, like a pile of sand, manufacturing the molten glass into intricate shapes that are both tactile and beautiful. The process requires strength as well as creativity, taking up to four people manipulating the rods to create some of the large vases on display. The large vases were first commissioned by Crown Casino and make a wonderful receptacle to offset floral displays. Pieces on display range from small perfume bottles and glass animals to small and large platters and various size vases and bowls – the graceful curves of the sculpted glass shimmering with translucent colour.

Noel's Gallery Restaurant and Lavender Farm has an idyllic setting on the Mornington-Flinders Road in the farmhouse of a historic property. The 103-year-old building has been extended over the years but the gallery still retains what was the original cottage, transported from England onto the site in the late 1800s. Noel's is one of the area's longest established galleries. It changed ownership last year and now husband and wife team, Gai and Les Clough, have breathed new life into the established business. The art space features many of Australia's best-known artists and rolling exhibitions ensure an ever-changing face. Highly decorative craft, ceramics and metal work complete an eclectic mix to suit all tastes.

The restaurant at the rear of the gallery has become as much a destination for locals as it is for visitors. Fully licensed, the menu has international flavours and is complemented by a decadent array of cakes and pastries. Breakfast is becoming a weekend institution at Noel's when old-fashioned breakfasts are savoured and lingered over by an appreciative public. The bar and restaurant is open Wednesdays through Sundays for long, drawn-out lunches and relaxed dinners, or just a casual drink. The balcony-style restaurant has indoor and outdoor seating that provides a mesmerising view over rolling pastureland and a sea of heavenly lavender. An old Brazilian honeysuckle drapes the verandah. When in bloom, its giant flowers emit a hypnotic perfume that wafts through the restaurant enhancing the evocative atmosphere.

Above: Alpacas On The Hill, Red Hill
Right: Top left- Noel's Gallery, Restaurant & Lavender Farm;
Top right- Marion Rosetzky Gallery; *Centre–* Gordon Glass Studios;
Below: Gallery 141

THE HINTERLAND

The Marion Rosetzky Gallery is set in a woodland glade, surrounded by nature, on the Mornington-Flinders Road at Red Hill. It presents decorative and beautiful work that adds dimension to any personal space. It is one of the region's most sought-out galleries where visitors can meet the artist in residence, Marion Rosetzky. Her hand-painted designs on ceramic tiles are colourful and intricately decorated, in an elaborate Islamic style. She captures the beauty of renaissance Middle-Eastern art and provides an affordable opportunity to own something quite unique and timeless.

Marion has worked with clay for over 20 years, working as a potter for some time before developing her current range of hand-painted tiles. The inspiration for the tiles grew from a series of renaissance-style tiles she was invited to produce for an exhibition at the National Gallery in Canberra. Marion has evolved three repeating patterns, created fundamentally with dots and vivid colour combinations. She has created an abundance of variations on these patterns, of which she says, "There is a meditative quality in the doing and in the end result when the tiles are viewed en masse." This is certainly true when surveying the impact created by the patterns as displayed on tabletops. Marion has expanded her gallery to include a range of art by artists she admires that include paintings, jewellery, glass and pottery. Visitors are tempted to linger over a cup of coffee, listen to relaxing music and absorb the ambiance of this unique working gallery.

The Red Hill Cool Stores Emporium and Art Gallery on Shoreham Road is an art space with a point of difference. It is not just an exceptional gallery full of fabulous things and fun ideas, but is contained within a heritage-listed building, erected in the early 1920s beside the now defunct railway line. The emporium brings together history, gourmet food art and wine – all the things that Red Hill is famous for. It continues on today as an integral part of the community where orchardists, vignerons and artists display their goods in a manner reminiscent of the old general stores that were the heart of every Australian settlement.

Owner Gillian Haig is herself an artist of some repute. A variety of her eclectic work is on display at the cool stores, along with a range from local painters, potters, craft artists and sculptors. Gillian sources product and art regionally and has gained a reputation for specialising in work that is more unusual and unique. The Red Hill Cool Stores' attraction lies in offering visitors a complete taste of the Peninsula all housed beneath one roof, and the individual artist and mixed artists' exhibitions she stages are eagerly awaited.

Only the freshest organically-grown produce graces the cool stores barrels, along with a range of hand-made cheeses, superior farm-made jams pickles and chutneys plus a display of hot to very hot Hells Breath chilli chutney and local olive oil. Wine tastings held each weekend are a crowd-pleaser. The cool stores carries over 30 Mornington Peninsula wines that include the less accessible labels from the region's smaller producers, and a range of clean skins. The heady smell of roast coffee permeates the air in the cool stores. It emanates from Red Hill Roast, contained at the rear of the emporium, where visitors can take time out for some freshly-roasted coffee and cake. This unique gallery holds something for every one, Driza-Bone fashion, jewellery, art and accessories plus food and wine – a delightful mish-mash where visitors are sure to find a treasure to keep or a perfect gift to give.

White Hill Gallery shows a variety of contemporary and classical-style paintings, ceramics and woodwork by both established and emerging Australian artists. It is the aim of gallery owners Rick and Carol Hayllar to promote these artists, who demonstrate excellence in their field. The gallery is becoming well known for showcasing outstanding art works from many art disciplines. Paintings, both traditional watercolour and oil, are juxtaposed with thought-provoking modern works and botanical studies.

The gallery allows private and corporate collectors, connoisseurs and novices alike to view some of the Peninsula's most accredited artists. The ever-changing collection appeals to a wide range of aficionados as the display also features sculptures, leather and fabric wearable art and intricate jewellery. Regular exhibitions, dedicated to individual artists or groups of artists, keeps the excitement in the work on show. Exhibitions are of a high standard, showcasing talent such as Margaret Lourey, Mike McMeekan and Barbara Stuart. Musical renderings are often included to highlight the prestigious exhibition openings.

The art space is a quintessential country gallery full of character and charm, set within two acres of gardens in White Hill Road, on Dromana's border with Red Hill. Birdbaths and sculptures decorate the garden creating a relaxing spot to stay awhile, relax, and enjoy a cup of coffee and a snack from the gallery's coffee shop.

The Art Shed Gallery on Arthurs Seat Road at Red Hill South is run by Marion Trevellyan, strongly supported by partner David Harrison. The building was originally an apple coolstore and packing shed. But thanks to David's expertise, it has been transformed, utilising its aesthetic focal points, into a chic art space that has become a local haunt. The two large rooms, with their high ceilings, and the sunny north-facing verandah, are perfect areas for displaying the Art Shed's range of constantly changing, stimulating and unusual exhibits from its stable of more than 50 artists. They include sought-after works from Stewart Westle, Catherine Hamilton, John Hunt and Margaret Metcalf, enhanced by wooden sculptures by Jean Sheridan and highly-prized metal sculptures from Vince Green. The gallery is renowned for its displays of contemporary sculptures and its philosophy of encouraging emerging artists. It presents approximately six exhibitions a year, showcasing works in various media. The Art Shed's popular, signature exhibition, "The Garden Party", falls annually on Melbourne Cup weekend, highlighting gardens and gardeners, with contributions by more than 30 of the gallery's regular artists. The art space isa relaxing place to visit; visitors contemplate with awe its glittering mascot – two large, distinctive mosaic figures – which can be seen from Arthurs Seat Road. The three-metre tall linked sculptures, by Jenny Compton, are based on New Guinean fertility figures. Beside the gallery is the complementary nursery, containing many interesting sculptural plants, both native and exotic, plus garden ornaments.

Above & bottom right: White Hill Gallery
Right:
Top: Art Shed Gallery
Centre: Red Hill Cool Stores Emporium & Art Gallery
Bottom left: Marion Rosetzky Gallery

Port Phillip Bay sunset, from Arthurs Seat

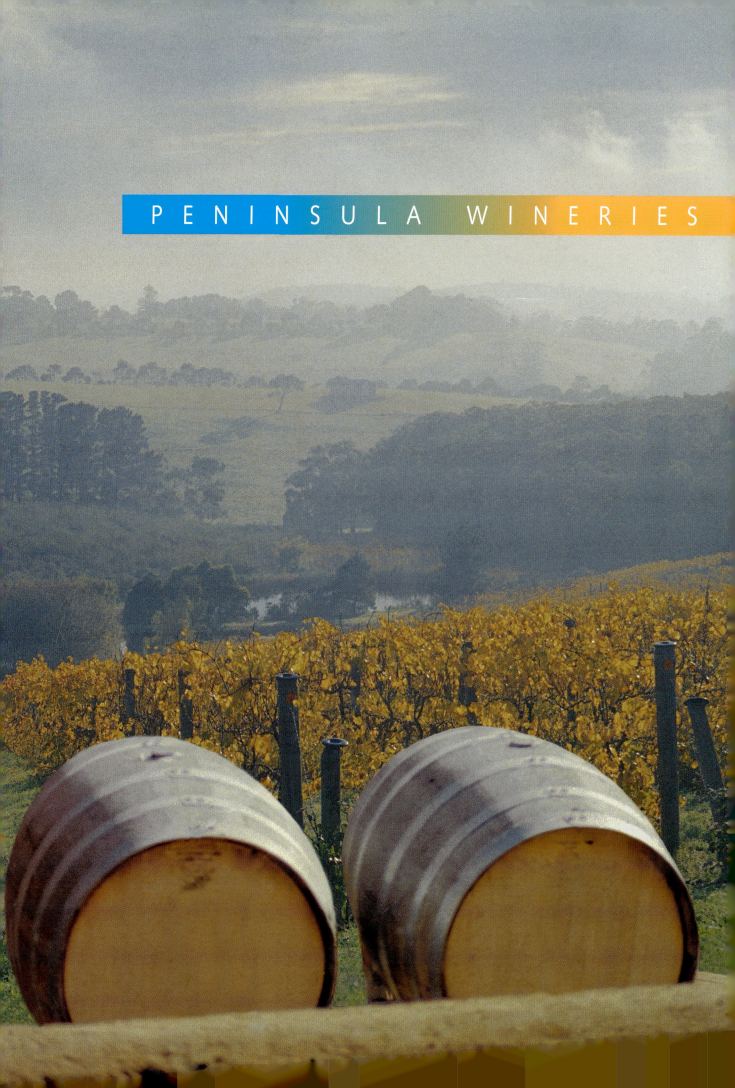

Wine Touring Map

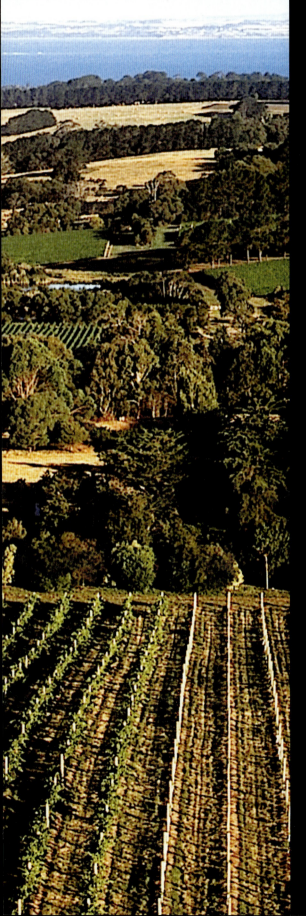

Information is obtained from the Mornington Peninsula Vignerons 2003 Wine Touring Map. This map is updated annually and is available on www.mpva.com.au or phone MPVA for a free map (03) 5989 2377

1. Barak Estate. Lot 4 Barak Road, Moorooduc, 3933. Mel Ref: 146 F8 Tel: (03) 5978 8439. Open Every Weekend and Public Holidays 11am-5pm.

2. Barrymore Estate. 76 Tuerong Road, Tuerong, 3933. Mel Ref: 152 C2 Tel: (03) 5974 8999. Open every day 11am-5pm.

3. Bayview Estate Winery. 365 Purves Road Main Ridge 3928. Mel Ref: 171 F8 Tel: (03) 5989 6130. Open Every Day 12 noon - 5pm. Restaurant and Tavern open till 11.30pm.

4. Box Stallion Wines. 64 Tubbarubba Road, Merricks North. Mef Ref 152 E12 (Near "Foxey's Hangout") Tel: (03) 5989 7444

5. Charlottes Vineyard. 26 Kentucky Road Merricks North, 3926. Mel Ref: 191 H1 Tel: (03) 5989 7266. Open daily 11am-5pm.

6. Darling Park Winery. 232 Red Hill Road, Red Hill. Mel Ref: 191 F3. Tel: (03) 5989 2324 Open every weekend, public holidays and throughout January 11.00am to 5.30pm.

7. Dromana Estate. 25 Harrisons Road, Dromana 3936. Mel Ref: 160 J6 Tel : (03) 5987 3800

8. Elan Vineyard & Winery. 17 Turners Road, Balnarring, 3918. Mel Ref: 162 K5 Tel: (03) 5983 1858. Open First Weekend of the Month. Public Holidays 12 noon-5pm & by appointment.

9. Eldridge Estate of Red Hill. Arthurs Seat Road (formerly Red Hill Road) Red Hill, 3937 (100m east of Andrews Lane). Mel Ref: 190 K4 Tel: (03) 5989 2644. Open every-day week days 12 noon-4 pm, Weekends 11am-5pm.

10. Elgee Park. Enter from Wallaces Road, Dromana, 3936. Mel Ref: 161 G3 Tel: (03) 5989 7338. Open by Appointment Only - Contact Laurence Tedesco.

11. Ermes Estate. 2 Godings Road, Moorooduc, 3933. Mel Ref: 147 A11 Tel: (03) 5978 8376. Open every weekend and Public Holidays 11am- 5pm, except Christmas Day and Easter Sunday.

12. Frogspond. 400 Arthurs Seat Road, Red Hill. Mel Ref: 190 D2. Tel: (03) 5989 2941 Open by appointment only.

13. Garden Vineyard. 174 Graydens Road Moorooduc. Mel Ref: 152 J2. Tel: (03) 5978 8336. Open to visitors every weekend from January through to Easter and the first full weekend of other months from 11am-5pm, closed June, July and August.

14. Hickinbotham of Dromana. 194 Nepean Hwy, Dromana 3936. Mel Ref: 160 K2. Tel: (03) 5981 0355. Open every day 11am - 5pm Weekdays, 11am - 6pm Weekends.

15. Hurley Vineyard. 101 Balnarring Road, Balnarring 3926. Mel Ref: 193 A1 Tel: (03) 5931 3000. Open first weekend of the month and public holidays 11.00am-5.00pm & by appointment.

16. Karina Vineyard. Harrisons Road, Dromana, 3936. Mel Ref: 160 J7 Tel: (03) 5981 0137. Open Every Weekend - Public Holidays and Every Day in January 11am - 5pm.

17. La Campagna Vineyard. 176 Rogers Road, Cape Schanck 3939. Mel Ref: 253 H9 Tel: (03) 5988 5350. Open every weekend 10am to 5pm.

18. Lindenderry Country House Hotel, Restaurant & Vineyard. 142 Arthurs Seat Road. Mel Ref: 190 K4. Tel: (03) 5989 2933

19. Main Ridge Estate. 80 William Road, Red Hill, 3937. Mel Ref: 190 C4. Tel: (03) 5989 2686. Open every day weekends 12 noon-5pm, weekdays 12 noon-4pm. NO BUSES.

20. Mantons Creek Vineyard. 240 Tucks Road, Main Ridge, 3928. Mel Ref: 255 F1. Tel: (03) 5989 6264. Cellar Door Wine Bar opens every day 11.00-5.00.

21. Maritime Estate. Tucks Road, Red Hill. 3937. Mel Ref: 190 E9. Tel: (03) 9848 2926 or (03) 5989 2735. Open every weekend, public holidays and every day Dec 27 - Jan 27.

22. Merricks Creek. 44 Merricks Road, Merricks, 3916 (cnr Yal Yal Road). Mel Ref: 192 D6. Tel: (03) 5989 8868. Email: merricksceek@ozemail.com.au Website: www.pinot.com.au Sales by mail order and appointment only.

23. Merricks Estate. Thompsons Lane, Merricks, 3916. Mel Ref: 192 B9. Tel: (03) 5989 8416. Open first weekend of the month, everyday 27-31 Dec. Every weekend in January and public holiday weekends, 12 noon - 5 pm.

24. Miceli. 60 Main Creek Road, Arthurs Seat 3936. Mel Ref: 190 A4. Tel: (03) 5989 2755. Open First Weekend of the Month, Every Weekend in January, Special Events 12 noon - 5pm and by appointment.

25. Montalto Vineyard and Olive Grove. 33 Shoreham Road, Red Hill South, Mel Ref: 256 B2. Tel: (03) 5989 8412. Open daily from 11-5 & until 11pm on Friday and Saturday.

26. Moorooduc Estate. 501 Derril Road, Moorooduc, 3933. Mel Ref 152 H2 Tel: (03) 5971 8506. Open Every Weekend 11am - 5pm.

27. Morning Star Estate. 1 Sunnyside Road, Mt Eliza. Mel Ref: 105 A7 Tel: (03) 9787 7760. Open Every Day 10am - 4pm except Christmas Day.

28. Mt. Eliza Estate. Cnr Sunnyside Road & Nepean Hwy, Mt. Eliza, 3930, Mel Ref: 105 A6. Tel: (03) 9787 0663. Open Every Day 11am-5pm.

29. Myrtaceae. 53 Main Creek Road, Red Hill 3937, Mel Ref: 190 A3. Tel: (03) 5989 2045 Open first weekend of every month and public holidays 12-5pm.

30. Northway Downs Estate. 437 Stumpy Gully Road, Balnarring. Mel Ref: 163 D6. Tel: 0417 050 627. Open First Weekend of the Month 11am - 5pm and Festival weekends.

31. Osborns Harwood Vineyard. 166 Foxeys Rd, Merricks North, 3926 (formerly Ellerina Rd). Mel Ref: 152 B11 Tel: (03) 5989 7417. Open First Weekend of Month, Public Holidays and by Appointment.

32. Paringa Estate. 44 Paringa Road, Red Hill South, 3937. Mel Ref: 191 D9 Tel: (03) 5989 2669. Open Every Day 11am-5pm. Restaurant- Lunch: Wed-Sun, dinner: Fri-Sat.

33. Phaedrus Estate. 200 Mornington-Tyabb Road, Moorooduc, 3933. Mel Ref: 147 E9. Tel: (03) 5978 8134. Open every weekend, except July - open by appointment.

34. Pier 10. 10 Shoreham Road, (formerly Red Hill-Shoreham Road) Shoreham Vic 3916. Mel Ref: 256 E5. Tel: (03) 5989 8848. Open every weekend & Public Holidays 11am-5pm and by appointment.

35. Poplar Bend Winery. 465 Main Creek Road, Main Ridge, 3937. Tel: (03) 5989 6046. Area Open Every Weekend (except July/August) and Public Holidays 12 noon-5pm.

36. Port Phillip Estate. 261 Red Hill Road, Red Hill South, 3937. Mel Ref: 191 G2 Tel: 5989 2708. Open every weekend, public holidays and every day in December and January 11am-5pm.

37. Red Hill Estate. 53 Shoreham Road, Red Hill South, 3937. Mel Ref: 190 K12. Tel: (03) 5989 2838. Open every day 11am-5pm (except Christmas Day).

38. Stonier Wines. 362 Frankston-Flinders Road, Merricks 3916. Mel Ref: 192 F9. Tel: (03) 5989 8300. Open every day 12 noon-5pm, Summer 11am-5pm.

39. Stumpy Gully Vineyard. 1247 Stumpy Gully Road, Moorooduc, 3933. Mel Ref: 147 D10. Tel: (03) 5978 8429. Open Every Weekend. 11am-5pm.

40. T'Gallant Winemakers. Cnr Mornington-Flinders and Shands Roads, Main Ridge, 3928. Mel Ref: 190 E12. Tel: (03) 5989 6565. Open Every Day 10am-5pm.

41. Tanglewood Estate. Bulldog Creek Road, Merricks North 3926. Mel Ref: 151 K12. Tel: (03) 5974 3325. Open Every Day 12 noon-5pm.

42. Ten Minutes By Tractor Wine Co. 111 Roberts Road, Main Ridge, 3928. Mel Ref: 190 B12. Tel: (03) 5989 6084. Open every weekend. Hours: 11am-5pm.

43. The Duke Vineyard. 38 Paringa Road, Red Hill South, 3937. Mel Ref: 191 D9. Tel: (03) 5989 2407. Open Every Weekend, Public and School Holidays 12 noon-5pm.

44. Tuck's Ridge. 37 Shoreham Road, Red Hill South 3937. Mel Ref: 256 B2 Tel: (03) 5989 8660. Open Every Day 12 noon-5pm

45. Turramurra Estate Vineyard. 3km up Wallaces Road, Dromana 3936. Mel Ref: 161 G3. Tel: (03) 5987 1146. Open first weekend of the month 12 noon-5pm. By appointment for groups of 6 or more.

46. Wildcroft Estate. 98 Stanleys Road, Red Hill South. Mel Ref: 191 H5 Tel: (03) 5989 2646 Open Monday - Sunday 11am-5pm.

47. Willow Creek Vineyard. 166 Balnarring Road, Merricks North 3926. Mel Ref: 162 H8 Tel: (03) 5989 7448. Restaurant Tel: (03) 5989 7640. Cellar Door Open Every Day 10am-5pm.

48. Yrsa's Vineyard. 105 Tucks Road, Main Ridge. Mel Ref: 190 F9. Tel: (03) 5989 6500

49. Marinda Park Vineyard. 238 Myers Road, Balnarring. Mel Ref: 163 A7. Tel: (03) 5989 7613. Open daily 11am-5pm

- Open every day
- Open every weekend
- Open first weekend of every month
- Open by appointment only

For additional detail winery information, see Listing section at the back of the book

Overview and History of Winemaking in the Mornington Peninsula Region

Walk pristine beaches or spectacular cliff tops, catch a wave, paddle a sea kayak, tackle the fairway at Cape Schanck, or even sail Port Phillip Bay – and feel the difference…when you visit the Mornington Peninsula. Some call it Melbourne's playground, others home: either way, it is a special place that for almost 50 years has had a powerful attraction – especially to the region's winemakers and vignerons.

On any sunny day you might meet John Mitchell of Montalto in a couta boat race off Sorrento, Lindsay McCall from Paringa catching whiting off Flinders, or the Stonier cellar hand in the surf off Point Leo. They and their wine industry colleagues work and play on the Mornington Peninsula – a unique maritime wine region where vines thrive in the cool climate and sheltered valleys.

Less than an hour's drive southeast of Melbourne, the region now hosts 175 small-scale vineyards and more than 45 cellar door outlets. The growth of the area's wine industry is remarkable when you consider that the very first Mornington Peninsula wine was made less than 50 years ago by noted Melbourne wine merchant Douglas Seabrook.

The earliest vines were reputedly planted by Seppelt but most consider the true foundation stone rests with Elgee Park, established by Baillieu Myer, an estate now renowned for its exceptional viognier. Hot on his heels were Nat and Rosalie White of Main Ridge Estate, who in 1975 produced the district's inaugural commercial wines from their sheltered hillside block in Red Hill, the harbingers of a thriving industry.

Other early seachangers were Brian Stonier and his wife Noel, who planted in the Merricks area in 1978, and Garry Crittenden, whose first five acres became Dromana Estate in 1981.

These founding vignerons foresaw both the lifestyle and the viticultural potential of the region, which is bounded on three sides by the sea – Port Phillip and Western Port Bays and Bass Strait.

Visitors to the Mornington Peninsula encounter their first sight of vines in Mount Eliza or Moorooduc, a carpet of neat rows that alternate from tones of bright green to autumnal red or bare brown canes, depending on the season. It 's a landscape that signposts the existence of one of Australia's most compact and unique cool climate wine regions.

The Peninsula's vineyard plantings currently constitute 775 hectares, an area that has almost doubled since 1996. The predominant grape varieties are pinot noir and chardonnay, with smaller plantings of shiraz, cabernet sauvignon, merlot, pinot gris, sauvignon blanc, riesling and semillon.

Climate, terroir and the local winemakers' passions have gradually combined to nurture the Peninsula's undisputed flagship varieties – pinot noir and chardonnay, Burgundian grapes that have adapted well to their southern hemisphere maritime home.

In recent years the foundation labels have been joined by nationally recognised brands including Red Hill Estate, T'Gallant and Tucks Ridge, plus a bevy of smaller, innovative quality producers led by Kooyong, Scorpo and Ten Minutes By Tractor.

The Peninsula is also recognised for pioneering top quality, personality-packed pinot gris (T'Gallant), and increasingly for its elegant, spice-driven shiraz (take a bow Paringa and Turramurra Estate).

Be they originators or recent arrivals, there is one characteristic that unites the vignerons of the Mornington Peninsula – they are all innovators and individualists with strong passions and commitment to a quality lifestyle – yours and theirs!

That's possibly why there are so many top-quality winery restaurants on the Peninsula – led by Max's at Red Hill, Montalto, Jill's at Moorooduc Estate, and Salix at Willow Creek – which take pride in featuring regional and seasonal produce. Naturally, relaxed dining is ideally accompanied by nurturing, and comfortable vineyard-based accommodation – and many of the vignerons and their neighbours offer that too.

Wake with the birds, enjoy a hearty seasonal breakfast, then plot your cellar door explorations followed by a swim or 18 holes at one of the Peninsula's world standard golf courses. In summer, quench your thirst with a chilled bottle of chardonnay, or warm up those gentle misty, winter days with a velvety, voluptuous pinot noir – and taste that Mornington Peninsula difference! It's the seachange you've been promising yourself for ages…

Mark Rodman (Marinda Park Vineyard)
MPVA President

The first Mornington Peninsula wine was made by Douglas Seabrook of the famous wine merchant family about 1956 (though there was an earlier vine planting by Seppelt). I dismissed the wine of the only bottle I tasted as grossly oxidised while thinking of the adage that merchants should stick to selling while oenologists make the wine.

It was David Wynn of Coonawarra Estate fame who suggested to Bails Myer that he plant grapes on his 800-acre horse stud Elgee Park, which Bails duly did in 1972 – in a small way. His first vintage was in 1975 when, again on Wynn's suggestion, he retained me as the consulting oenologist.

That grape crop was so small that we had to use beer industry barrels, mainly to protect the new wines from the air, but also for 'pumping' purposes as we used gas to force wine from one container to another, including through a filter. The barrels were made of protective stainless steel.

In 1978, I could not get the desirable secondary bacterial fermentation to start. Stephen our eldest son (deceased) was working for Seppelts at Great Western where he introduced pinot noir to their Great Western 'Champagne'.

He had returned from Bordeaux University and explicated my problem as due to the considerable natural acidity of the cabernet sauvignon being more than the Australian norm because the Myer vineyard was the most southerly on the mainland. After adding selected bacteria from Bordeaux University, the natural acid softening malo-lactic fermentation duly went to conclusion. Even so, such was the thinking of the period; it was a Seppelt who said to Stephen, "Why do you want to make battery acid?" He also introduced French oak barrels, which I had avoided because of the eternal problem of protecting a small quantity of wine from oxidation.

When Andrew, our second son, returned from Dijon University he diagnosed viruses (for which there is no cure) as the cause of the declining grape yields at Anakie and after experiencing the drought and terrible 1983 bushfires we decided to search for green fields and chose the Mornington Peninsula. Andrew and his wife Terryn, who happens to be a botanist, searched for two years for the ideal site – adjacent to the highway to facilitate selling from a cellar door – and planted our first vines in 1988.

During those years they worked as consulting viticulturists and undoubtedly because of his Burgundy education, Andrew physically introduced pinot noir and pinot meuniere in 26 vineyards! This was at the time when clones of the classic varieties (first documented about 600AD) were just being imported to this continent. They included mariafeld, which had already been dismissed for Australia because it made wines too light in colour. Andrew, because of his vintaging stint in Burgundy, knew it would prove to be ideal when grown in a cool climate and on the soils of his beloved Mornington Peninsula.

Another important reason why we chose the Peninsula was the coming official defining of Australia's vineyard regions. We realised it would be easy to define the Mornington Peninsula with one boundary whereas elsewhere controversy has been sustained. Thus, after 30 years of such argument and altercation, disastrously, Chianti could only be defined as inner and outer Chianti.

Bails Myer's initiative has been vindicated: incredible as it may seem today, I remember the teasing and criticism he endured within the industry for his folly of daring to plant a vineyard and make Mornington Peninsula wine just 28 years ago. Further, he deserves to bask in the acclaim accorded his Elgee Park Viognier, having been the patron of this new variety on this continent.

Ian Hickinbotham
Oenologist, Wine Writer

View from Main Ridge Estate

Barrymore Estate is one of the Peninsula's exciting young wineries, but its fields are steeped in the tradition of agriculture, begun in 1845. In the 1840s a huge area in the Tuerong Valley formed the historic Tuerong Station, first settled by William Thomas. Six hundred and forty acres of this was taken over by Ralph Ruddell in 1852. Barrymore Estate covers 165 acres of the original property.

The idyllic estate, established in 1997, sits within a very special part of the Peninsula, high on a hill, a short way off the Moorooduc Highway (left at the old Moorooduc Road exit) along a well-maintained gravel road, enveloped in the heart of the verdant valley on Tuerong Road. Listed as number 2 on our wine touring map, a visit to the estate is well worth the extra effort to get there.

The vineyard, planted in 1998, contains 26 acres under vine and the young vines are cosseted by the estate's northerly aspect. The profile of the land is very picturesque, embracing aromatic bushland, historic wetlands, and some of the most productive pastureland on the Peninsula. So it is no surprise that the rich soil, combined with Tuerong's microclimate, produces superior grapes that create outstanding wine.

Barrymore makes five varieties of handcrafted wines that reflect the site. Every aspect in the process of making the wine is carried out on the estate, including the bottling. Barrymore Pinot Noir is maturated in 30% French oak barriques, has aromatic cherry, plum characteristics and a balanced, supple texture. Barrymore Pinot Gris is created in a classical style with delicate honeysuckle characteristics. Barrymore Sauvignon Blanc is their most floral wine, exhibiting gentle passionfruit and melon like bouquet and a balanced lingering palate and Barrymore Chardonnay from 'Mendoza' clone plantings, fermented in French oak, is a wine of balanced complexity with a lingering fresh citrus finish. Pinot Grigio and Rosé will be added in 2003.

The estate released its first vintage in 2001 and already the wines are garnering acclaim. At the Red Hill Cold Climate Wine Show in 2003 the 2001 Pinot Gris was voted top wine in its class. Renowned wine writer James Halliday praised Barrymore Pinot Gris 2001 in the Wine Companion 2003 edition as 'quite aromatic with ripe apple, pear/dried flowers and hay aromas. The palate has abundant flavours. An impressive example of the variety'.

Peter Cotter was the man with the vision that shaped Barrymore Estate. Peter was raised on a farm on the Mornington Peninsula and winemaking was a natural progression from his love of agriculture plus a background in food technology and manufacturing. His aim is simple – "to produce premium quality wines which are enjoyed with food and which reflect our special part of the world."

The Cotter family were all involved in the project. Their forefathers originated in Ireland from County Cork and interestingly enough the Ruddell family, owners of the estate in 1852, embarked for Australia from County Cork. The ancient name for County Cork is 'Barrymore' and even more coincidentally this name was engraved on a brass plaque that rested above the door of Peter's grandparents' home during initial schooling in Melbourne. So it was decided that this was a fitting name for the Cotters' new venture.

Barrymore Estate's distinctive logo also has family connotations. The ancient Cotter family crest depicts three lizards over an azure background. The name Cotter evolved from the family names of Ottir and McOttir who travelled to Ireland from Scandinavia in 800AD. The crest is thought to have originated from serpents that decorated the prow of Viking longboats. An adaptation of the serpent illustration has been engineered to fit the Australian image and the dramatic label, with its native emblem, is much admired and well received by the company's export market. In Aboriginal folklore, lizards are symbolic of regeneration and seasonal rebirth, and this too reflects the annual cycle of the grape.

The Cotter family have a strong connection with the land and are committed to environmentally friendly agriculture, using sustainable practices, including connection to a water re-use scheme for summertime irrigation. They take what the vineyard provides and keep the process as natural as possible. A revegetation scheme has been embarked upon, with 500 indigenous trees and shrubs already planted and plans to eventually restore a nature corridor to the property's frontage along Devil Bend Creek and the surrounding wetlands.

The view from the Barrymore cellar door showcases the spellbinding beauty of Port Phillip Bay and the undulating Tuerong Valley and creek. Age-old trees surround the tasting room that is contained in a quaint 1930s stone cottage, which was at one time utilised as stables. A paved courtyard provides a serene respite that will enhance your wellbeing, away from the world's woes, away from crowds and traffic, overlooking a stunning vista that provides a magnificent backdrop and adds to the enjoyment of a glass of wine. In the colder months an open fire within the cottage provides a cosy corner against winter chills and promotes a warm, intimate atmosphere.

The cellar door is usually open seven days a week with light seasonal lunches available on specially designated weekends in the form of: dip platters, gourmet foccacias and hot soups. The estate lends itself well to special festive events and functions, large or small, with plenty of room to spread out. Devotees should keep track of the regular winery functions and special purchases. Barrymore Estate is a boutique winery that is hard to fault, a stunning location that evokes the spirit of the earth and its bountiful harvest, where visitors can sip and sup, and enjoy a relaxing day in the country

Box Stallion Wines, the Mornington Peninsula's leading producer of varietal wines, was established by the Zerbe, Wharton and Gillies families in 2000. Working with winemaker Alex White, their aim is to make a range of wines that best express the distinctive nature of the grape varieties and of the region.

Box Stallion produces nine varietal wines: chardonnay, pinot noir, pinot meunier, sauvignon blanc, arneis, moscato, dolcetto, shiraz, and tempranillo, as well as several blends. The handsome property at Merricks North (number 4 on our wine-touring map) includes a spacious cellar door that was once a stallion barn (fully renovated, of course), and includes a café so that visitors can relax and enjoy the beauty of the vineyard.

Chardonnay and pinot noir are now well established as premium varieties in the Mornington Peninsula, with its long ripening season. Sauvignon Blanc and Shiraz are less often grown in the region.

Box Stallion's Pinot meunier is one of a handful made in Australia. The variety is often used as a component in champagne, but also makes an attractive medium-bodied red table wine. Arneis, dolcetto and moscato are three north west Italian varieties, rarely grown in Australia. Tempranillo is a Spanish red variety that is gaining increasing attention from winemakers and consumers for its distinctive fruit characters.

The vines are grown on two sites. One is at Bittern, on a property that was an orchard from 1959 until 1995 and was known for its quality fruit production. The soil is largely ironstone buckshot with heavy orange clay at a depth of 1-1.5 metres. The other vineyard site is at Merricks North, around the Box Stallion cellar door 10 minutes from the Bittern vineyard.

Both sites are in a unique microclimate. "It's very special in the Peninsula," Garry Zerbe says. "It's ideal for vines because it is maritime, which means virtually no frosts and mild temperatures; it's north-facing and is well protected from the southerly winds that are the nightmare of the Peninsula; the soils are clay loam." For him, the proof of the excellence of the two vineyard sites is that they can always ripen shiraz. Not only does it ripen consistently well, but it has already made an award-winning wine. The 2001 Box Stallion Shiraz won triple trophies including Best Wine Of Show at the National Cool Climate Wine Show in 2002.

Good wine does not occur by accident. Everything is done to ensure the quality of the grapes: the trellising (mainly Scott-Henry) allows for optimum light exposure: vines are leaf-plucked by hand to ensure light and air during the growing season, and, where necessary, the crop is thinned to ensure the best quality fruit. Winemaker Alex White says that one of the attractions of Box Stallion was the wide range of grape varieties in the two vineyard sites. "A number of varieties are grown on both properties, which gives me the chance to see how they perform on both sites, how the flavours differ. It also enables us to make wines of greater complexity," he says. "It's an unusually wide range for a small company," he observes. "It's possible here because the ripening period is very long, enabling later ripening varieties, such as moscato and dolcetto, to develop good flavour. And it's still cool enough to produce intense varietal flavours in the early ripening vines, such as tempranillo and arneis."

He is the one who turns the grapes into wine. Thirty years' experience in winemaking in southern Victoria has established him as a leader in the field. His expertise is acknowledged in the wine industry, his wines have won countless trophies and medals over the years.

He says he liked the challenge of the Italian varieties. "The other thing I liked about Box Stallion was the proposal to plant gewürztraminer, one of my favourites," he says. Gewürztraminer will soon join the range.

Box Stallion Wines takes its name from the horse stud that used to exist at its location in Tubbarubba Road. The former life of the property is evident in the clipped cypress hedge that borders the driveway to the cellar door, in the formal layout, and in the wide open spaces around the architect-designed Red Barn, as the cellar door is called, sited to take best advantage of the view over the spectacular property. The horse connection is also recalled in the lively logo.

The property has a much longer history. In the late 1800s it was a grazing property called Glengala, it had only two owners before it took on a new life as a vineyard. Garry Zerbe knew its history, and also knew how good the property would be for vines.

He himself comes from generations of orchardists. "I wanted something to grow that wouldn't walk around, moo, or jump fences." Vines were the answer. They fascinate him – "so much more responsive than apples."

He is well aware of the virtues of the vineyard sites, partly because he has owned the Bittern site since 1959. It was one of the family orchards, growing apples and pears.

For Stephen Wharton, Box Stallion represented an opportunity to fulfil a dream. "The vineyard was a family ambition for some time. I've been interested in wine for over 30 years. My father was passionate about wine and I have continued with the love of the grape. I wanted something on the Mornington Peninsula because I like the place, and from a business perspective, it's an hour from Melbourne – it's not difficult for people to visit the cellar door. We'd researched the site, we were sure it was good for vines. And it's a beautiful property."

John Gillies has worked together with Stephen for many years and shares a similar passion for wine. He and his family have been involved in the Box Stallion adventure from its early planning.

For them, as for others, it hasn't all been plain sailing. There have been challenges with planning permits, neighbours, finances, and marketing. "It's very hard work," they admit.

They are enjoying the consolidation and growth, and are bringing their professionalism and experience to bear on new opportunities, and a change of focus. "We're old dogs learning new tricks," Garry says, roaring with laughter.

They have made conscious decisions about the Box Stallion style. There are dozens of wineries on the Mornington Peninsula, and many of the smaller ones are open only at weekends, or on certain weekends of every month. Box Stallion is open daily, and offers a range of light lunches. "There may be a greater emphasis on the food in time, but whatever happens the wines will always be the main event," says Stephen.

Some of those visitors have returned with special requests – bookings for special functions such as birthdays, social outings, even weddings.

Garry is proud that his daughter Alexis is the vineyard manager, the sixth generation of the family to be involved in horticulture in Victoria. His son Matthew is also involved in the family business, handling the marketing. Members of the three families all regularly assist at the numerous cellar door functions. Together they make up a strong and committed team.

A row of weathered mailboxes sits at the beginning of Junction Road, an unassuming dirt thoroughfare in Merricks North. It is lined with gracefully shaped snow gums and leads to an exquisite Mornington Peninsula property, containing one of the most exclusive wineries.

They say the problems of the world can be solved over lunch, and many innovative ideas have seen the light of day after the odd bottle of wine. In early 1972 at a lunch held on Baillieu (Bails) and Sarah Myer's property, Elgee Park, a seed was planted in Bails' mind by David Wynn, who verbalised over the estate, admiring its suitability for grape growing. His opinion was backed up by fellow wine guests from Bordeaux. The seed, once planted, has grown into a vineyard of 10,000 vines with an annual yield of 1,800 cases of wine.

The transition, of course did not happen overnight. Expert advice was sought from Allan Antcliffe of the CSIRO, and later Ian Hickinbotham. This amalgamation of minds culminated in the first plantings in 1972 of cabernet sauvignon and riesling. This produced the first crop in 1975, thus creating the first vineyard planted on the Peninsula in modern times. In the early years vintages were small. Today – although more prolific – the estate still retains its exclusivity, producing lusty reds including, cabernet sauvignon, merlot, pinot noir and a small amount of shiraz, and crisp whites chardonnay, riesling, pinot gris and the lesser-known variety, viognier (vee-ohn-yea). The viognier is a specialised grape that is hard to grow, providing viticulturalists with the ultimate challenge. The clone was introduced by the CSIRO in 1968 from an ancient grape variety that dates back to the Crusades. The resultant wine is a golden, fruity elixir with apricot, clove and cinnamon aromas retaining its character with a dry, soft finish. Always the innovator, Elgee Park was the first winery on the Peninsula to release wine in magnums and in 1992 released their first cuvée brut.

Initially the winery was established to provide wine for family and friends. The theory hasn't changed, except the amount of wine produced from the five hectares under vine has grown in proportion and can now be purchased in selected restaurants and wine outlets or through Elgee Park Cellar Club. The vineyard provides Bails with a sanity patch and he personally oversees the annual harvest. Whenever time permits in his busy schedule, he makes for the vineyard, helping out, pruning and carefully tending the vines he planted so long ago. His hands-on approach is what makes the Elgee Park label such a prestigious one. Bails has a lifelong association with wine. He served some time as president of the French Chamber of Commerce and was the founder of the great Burgundian Confrerie des chevaliers de Tastevin, in Australia. (A highly regarded worldwide wine drinkers club.) He was also involved in the setting up of the Mornington Peninsula Vignerons Association that was convened at a meeting in Elgee Park's old winery.

Bails and Sarah never treat their vineyard as a business, more like a hobby that provides a lifestyle and interest for its owners. The estate is open to the public one day a year, on the Sunday of the Queen's Birthday Weekend in June. Upwards of 1,000 visitors enjoy the annual gala day. Food, wine and entertainment are all on the menu as well as an invitation to enjoy the spectacular grounds.

Elgee Park is an extremely beautiful estate with views extending across Port Phillip Bay to the Melbourne skyline. The vines are planted on the northern face of a natural amphitheatre, with a heavily wooded ridge protecting their back from prevailing winds. The Myer family are collectors of art and have turned their property into a sculpture park. A gazebo rests like a rustic 'temple of Vesta' in the middle of the vines, manicured gardens decorate the slopes and hand-hewn posts and rails line the pathways. The whole scene is one of total harmony. The couple bought the estate that was originally part of the 1850s crown grant Jamison's Run, in 1960. It was at that time the property of one L.G. Trumbul – hence the name Elgee Park.

The vines at Elgee Park share the property with elegant mares and stallions of one of Australia's oldest quarter horse studs - Yulgilbar. Yulgilbar Station is the name of the historic Myer family property in northern New South Wales where many magnificent Santa Gertrudis cattle are bred. The name is thought to mean, 'place of the platypus'. The historic property is the subject of a book by Janet Cannon titled 'Yulgilbar 1949-1999'.

The stud was established in 1954 at Retford Park, Bowral, by Sarah's father, the late Sam Hordern (Snr), who, together with King Ranch Australia, imported the first four registered quarter horse stallions into Australia. The Horderns retained 'Mescal', one of the four – a gift from King Ranch. Today, the stud is owned by Sarah and Bails and was moved to Merricks North in 1976. The classic quarter horse bloodlines are still represented in the current broodmare band, together with outcrosses to later imported lines.

The current senior sire is 'Playboy Roy', the sire of some of Australia's most successful quarter horses. Sarah and Bails are passionate owners and continue to breed horses in the tradition set down by Sarah's father 'breeding foals with a future from horses with a past'.

Baillieu Vineyard is committed to producing quality wine from exceptional fruit. Charlie and Samantha Baillieu established the 10-hectare vineyard in 1999 on their beautiful 64-hectare property, 'Bulldog Run'. Situated in the heart of the Mornington Peninsula at Merricks North, with boundaries on Tubbarubba and Myers Roads, the property is afforded protection from the west by an adjacent bush block, which has abundant wildlife.

Bulldog Run takes its name from Bulldog Creek, a small perennial creek that originates on the property. It winds its way through adjoining Elgee Park that is Samantha's family home.

The vineyard is planted with exquisite traditional rose bushes at each end of the vine rows, and a recently established riparian corridor along Bulldog Creek was planted, using indigenous vegetation. A large spring-fed dam near the vineyard contains some amazingly life-like wetland bird sculptures and – closer to the homestead – a wonderful ornamental lake has an island refuge for several species of ducks and geese. Contented and colourful fat Hereford cattle graze alongside family ponies, all of which are the subject of a stunning painting by talented artist, Julie Ellery, that has been reproduced on the vineyard's wine label.

Grape varieties grown on the estate include chardonnay, pinot gris, pinot meunier, pinot noir and shiraz. All grapes used in Baillieu Vineyard wines are 100 percent estate grown. Baillieu Vineyard and Elgee Park wines – whilst each retaining their individual labels – have recently combined resources in order to streamline vineyard management.

At present, the Baillieu Vineyard cellar door is open only once a year for a special event. In 2003 it will be on Sunday 7th December for a Baillieu Vineyard Gourmet Summer Lunch, featuring scrumptious food, wine, live music and Samantha's superb old-fashioned roses. This is a chance to sample both Baillieu Vineyard and Elgee Park Wines, plus handmade local cheese, in spectacular surroundings.

Visits at other times are by appointment only. The vineyard's wines are also available through their cellar club, which gives members exclusive access to pre-release wines, limited releases, special functions, cellar club discounts and vineyard newsletter. The wines are also available from selected wine stores.

Darling Park is a Peninsula winery with a point of difference, located in the heart of Red Hill on Red Hill Road. (Number 6 on our wine-touring map.) It is a boutique, family owned vineyard of the highest standard, producing handcrafted, sophisticated, top quality wine. Their range of wine is made from grapes sourced from the finest vineyards in Australia and presented under their unique 'Art of Wine' logo. These Limited Release wines are made using traditional winemaking methods, with pride, passion and scrupulous attention to detail.

The images on the Masters Collection label features reproductions of old masters, produced with the permission of the trustees of the Wallace Collection, London. Images include masterpieces by Jean-Honore Fragonard, Pieter Pourbus and Jane Steen. These wines represent the very best that the Mornington Peninsula has to offer. A more recent release depicts paintings by Arthur Boyd. They are of Limited Release covering an Australia-wide range of wines. Boyd's paintings give recognition to these special wines and are highly collectable, featuring works that are regarded as Australian icons. The paintings come from the private collection of Darling Park's owners and have been selected as a visual expression signifying the outstanding quality of these wines. With an affordable price range these exclusive wines are available only from the estate's cellar door, selected wine retailers and premium restaurants.

There is a wide range of wine on offer, including the 'Madhatters Sparkling' a methode champonoise that will be appreciated as a wine for every day enjoyment, chardonnay – a limited release hand crafted wine of sheer excellence, querida rose – a voluptuously rich wine with a relaxed Mediterranean style that is perfect for lovers, te quiero – the name means 'I love it' in Spanish, and you will, pinot noir – subtle yet seductive made with attention to detail, merlot – displays great structure and depth with an elegant rich palate and finally a cabernet sauvignon – matured in oak for 20 months, a great example of cool climate red wine.

Darling Park cellar door is contained in a castle-like building that is reminiscent of a French chateau; it is the venue for many laid back lazy days. Cocooned in a friendly relaxed atmosphere it is surrounded by tall trees and colourful gardens with outdoor decking for summer lounging and a warm fire for cosy winter days. An innovative menu includes mouth-watering dishes; dip platters, tarts flambee and Red Hill Cheese and Papas that all complement the Darling Park wines. Visitors are encouraged to explore the grounds and picnic among its attractive surrounds. The cellar door is open every weekend and public holidays.

Garry and Margaret Crittenden purchased their 11-hectare site in Harrisons Road, Dromana in 1981. It was destined to become Dromana Estate, one of the Peninsula's leading wineries. (Number 7 on our wine-touring map.) Garry's name is spoken with respect among Mornington Peninsula's vignerons, acknowledged as one of the region's pioneers, a trendsetter and, an all round good bloke! He was one of the first to recognise the Peninsula's suitability for growing grapes and has helped many of his neighbouring vignerons realise their potential while building up the Dromana Estate label. Established in 1982, the estate has expanded its horizons and now offers a large range of award winning wine, covered by four labels. Grapes are sourced from both the original Dromana Estate and other vineyards, situated in other regions, both on the Peninsula and around Australia, now under Dromana's umbrella.

In the 1990s Garry became enamoured of the characteristics to be found in grapes grown in Northern Italy. Once again he was at the fore, experimenting with these vines to produce an authentic taste of the Italian grapes. His success can be sampled in his range of Italian varietals under the Garry Crittenden 'i' label. All Dromana wines can be sampled at the cellar door that is open daily. The Critendens' son, Rollo, has followed his father's lead, training as a winemaker, already gaining recognition by becoming a 'Young Winemaker of the Year' finalist in 2001.

Total peace and quiet surround this exquisite vineyard. A wide-open space, enhanced by a large picturesque lake and acres of vines, provides the perfect place for a relaxed lunch. The sweeping lawn is furnished with a barbecue area and sports a trampoline, totem tennis and swings, providing an interest for younger party members. Margaret Crittenden has developed the estate's café style restaurant into a fashionably rustic, contemporary casual destination, blending perfectly with the surrounding vista. Lunches and functions are catered for with a high degree of expertise. The menu is as laid back as the atmosphere, offering a seasonal selection of soups and dips, fresh epicurean salads, gourmet pies, ploughman's platters, Victorian cheeses and a decadent dessert board skilfully created from fresh local produce. Daily, more substantial specials are exactly that – special, offering dishes such as smoked salmon and crispy wonton stacks, layered with avocado and wasabi crème fraiche, surrounded by a lime and dill vinaigrette – delicious. Patrons have a choice of interior or al fresco dining on a large deck. From either area the view can't be missed. All positions overlook the placid lake and dreamy surroundings to the hazy hills beyond.

When you purchase wine from Eldridge Estate of Red Hill you buy passion in a bottle. Although David and Wendy Lloyd have a keen sense of humour, their serious side shows through in the passion displayed when creating and crafting their wine. The couple purchased the already established vineyard in 1995, containing 10-year-old vines. With eight acres under vine the estate is classed as a small producer, specialising in classic chardonnay and pinot noir from fruit grown on the estate.

Their chardonnay is a stylish wine, portraying a complex mixture of flavours with a characteristic long finish. The estate pinot noir has a spicy oak finish with a seductive, silky soft texture and a long lingering palate. The estate also produces small amounts of sauvignon blanc - keenly awaited, and quickly sold and merlot that displays a palate with grip and the flavours of mushroom and plum, and finally gamay, a light red wine that has a richness that is often associated with warmer climate wines. The Lloyds decided from the start that their vineyard would contain gamay. Being both lovers of beaujolais, and having also visited the region, directed their passion in that direction. Renowned wine critic, James Halliday, called Eldridge Estate Gamay "Australia's finest". Indeed, all Eldridge Estate wines have gained recognition with a total to date of five trophies, 12 gold medals and many silver and bronze. The first pinot noir produced by David in 1997, won gold.

David describes his love of winemaking as, "a hobby that got out of hand." The Lloyds' background is in education, with David resigning in recent years as head of science at the Peninsula School to devote his life to his obsession. He has made a success of his chosen path and the Eldridge Estate wines are the expression of a single vineyard, its soil, the climate and its management.

The couple spent two years searching for the perfect patch for their vineyard, immediately falling under the spell of the estate located on Arthur's Seat Road (formerly Red Hill Road), number 9 on our wine-touring map. The spot they have chosen clings to a steeply sloping hillside. The view from their cellar door is as heady as their wine. Alluring vistas of vine-draped hillsides and azure sky (most of the time) – an idyllic place to visit and a difficult spot to leave.

Darling Park

Dromana Estate

Eldridge Estate

For a real Italian-style welcome you can't go past Ermes Estate on Godings Road, Moorooduc, number 11 on our wine-touring map. Ermes and Denise Zucchet are well known names on the Peninsula; they established their estate in 1989 on an old property that had been put to many uses, among them a piggery. For years they scoured the Peninsula before settling on the Moorooduc property, looking for the perfect site to grow grapes and make perfect wine – an occupation that is close to both their hearts. As qualified property developers they have accrued great acclaim in the region and as exceptional winemakers they have accumulated awards and accolades. There is a high degree of professionalism behind the relaxed façade of this vigneron couple. Ermes gained his winemaking knowledge from his father, as did his father before him, handed down over the generations in the Veneto town of Pradolino where he was raised. At Ermes Estate he retains charge of the basket press, barrels and beakers, helped at every stage by Denise, who is a trained winemaker, at the moment studying an Associate Degree at Charles Sturt University.

When other vignerons on the Peninsula were ripping out their cabernet sauvignon vines, denouncing them as unsuitable for the region the Zucchets were industriously planting the sublime red. Their optimism has paid off, with their cabernet sauvignon winning numerous awards. Today half the 13-acre vineyard is given over to the variety. Ermes was one of the first vineyards to plant pinot grigio, originally to supply Denise's love for the variety, which she had become familiar with on visits to Italy as a young bride. The wine became so popular that expansion was inevitable and the estate is now renowned for its individual style. Also available for tasting at the cellar door: Ermes chardonnay, riesling, merlot and the blended variety fresco.

The cellar door sits on a hill overlooking the vines across layers of picturesque countryside to the crest of Mt. Martha. It was originally the piggery and has been reinvented as a rustically quaint tasting room. It is open every weekend and public holidays, but a date on the monthly calendar that loyal followers flock to comes around every third Sunday, when Denise prepares a genuine 'casalinga'. This delicious light Italian lunch includes mouth watering antipasto, lasagne and woodfire pizza. Served within the cantina atmosphere of the tasting room or on the paved patio, the lunch is a monthly celebration of an Italian tradition –flavoursome food, excellent wine, entertaining company and overwhelming hospitality!

Over one hundred years of history makes Hurley Vineyard special, situated two kilometres north of Balnarring Village, on Balnarring Road; number 15 on our wine-touring map. William Hurley, orchardist (thought to be the first in the district) and farmer, settled the property in the mid 1800s. He built the existing cottage in 1884, where he lived with his wife Johanna and their 13 children, naming the wattle and daub homestead 'Hazel Grove'. The home remains listed as a historic house. Present owners Kevin Bell and Tricia Byrnes are restoring the home to reflect its history. The Hurley family owned the homestead and surrounding acreage until 1988.

Kevin and Tricia chose the 19-acre estate as their vineyard for much the same reasons as the Hurley family, its climate protected, sloping position and good soil, perfect for growing pinot noir grapes. The couple are dedicated to the craft of producing quality pinot noir inspired by the best Burgundian traditions. They practice very careful viticulture, including low yields and non-irrigation, to allow the grapes to express the terroir of the site. It is a single estate vineyard and the wine is hand crafted during each step of the winemaking process.

Kevin is completing an Applied Science (Wine Science) degree at Charles Sturt University, but by profession is a Queen's Counsel in Melbourne. Tricia is a family law partner with the Melbourne law firm, Howie and Maher. They moved to the property on a full time basis in 2002, along with the youngest of their three children, Imogen. The couple have a deep connection with the land and practise a philosophy of minimum impact. Kevin and Tricia enjoy the hands on approach and perform most of the labour on the nine acre vineyard, helped by family, local contractors and a devoted band of volunteers. The Hurley Vineyard is very picturesque. It wraps around the north eastern crest of a small sheltered hill. A substantial landscaping and renewal program of replanting indigenous plants is under way, adding to its charm.

The vineyard's first vintage was bottled in 2001 and released in 2003 along with the opening of the cellar door in September of that year. Hurley Vineyards offers wine to its mailing list customers and is open on the first weekend of the month and public holidays (more often in the summer months) and by appointment. Kevin and Tricia have a business ethic that cannot be faulted: respect for country, tradition and community.

Main Ridge Estate is where it all started; it was the first piece in the jigsaw that makes up the Mornington Peninsula wine region's commercial history. Established in 1975 by Nat and Rosalie White, the couple proved to the country that the Mornington Peninsula was a viable region for growing grapes and making good wine, worthy of tables anywhere in the world. The Red Hill site's rich red volcanic soil and 230-metre elevation first attracted Nat and Rosalie. They caught their passion for wine through travel – Spartan travel at that, on a very strict budget. Eight months in Europe in 1965, "footloose and poverty-stricken," where wine was cheaper than soft drink, saw the start of the love affair. But, it was in Burgundy where they fell under the spell of the bewitching pinot noir. On their return to Australia, after a housekeeping period that lasted some years, they finally realised their dream, planting vines that began their search for the most enigmatic of wines, the perfect pinot. The Whites' favourite quote came from a French general, who, when seduced from his military campaign in Burgundy explained, "the wine, is like the Lord himself in velvet pants."

The enthusiastic duo started from scratch. There wasn't even a track to the property's entrance from the road. They carved out a dirt road and physically planted posts and vines by hand. The 12-acre site chosen for their vineyard has an idyllic setting on a sunny north-facing slope, protected by the ridges of the central Peninsula from coastal elements. They focused their attention on pinot noir and chardonnay, cool climate wines that have become the region's signature. Theirs is a high quality product, adhering to a philosophy of making the best possible wine from grapes selected from their own vineyard. Nat is a trained winemaker, holding a wine science degree from Charles Sturt University. He allows the site's characteristics to be fully expressed through the use of natural yeasts and bacteria. The French word 'terroir' is used to describe the influences on a wine from a particular vineyard; it is the terroir of Main Ridge Estate that controls the very special wines produced here.

The cellar door sits high above the estates eight acres of vines and provides a serene venue for tasting the excellent wine and sampling Rosalie's innovative Sunday lunch menu. Main Ridge hosts many special events but any weekend, lazy Sundays can be spent nibbling on antipasto platters, prawns from the wok, butterflied quail, Sichuan chicken or pasta alla puttanesca, all rounded off with friendly conversation and Main Ridge Estate's celebrated chardonnay and perfect pinot noir. The vineyard can be found off the beaten track on William Road, Red Hill; number 19 on our wine-touring map.

Ermes Estate

Hurley Vineyard

Main Ridge Estate

The word is out. The Garden Vineyard (number 13 on our wine-touring map), nestling in the heart of the Mornington Peninsula on Graydens Road, Moorooduc, in a secret valley, beside Devil Bend Creek, provides a picture that even the brush of Monet would find hard to replicate. Wine connoisseurs come to taste the excellent pinot noir and pinot gris that has gained the winery fame and find themselves surrounded by glory.

Di and Doug Johnson left town to find space where they could indulge their passion – gardening. What started, as a dream has become a driving force that is as natural to the couple as breathing! It must have taken a lot of imagination to visualise a flourishing garden when the Johnsons bought the six hectare property in 1994. A small 1970s house surrounded by wattles and rampant Banksia, which were intent on engulfing the building, a leaky dam and virtually non-existent topsoil was their legacy. In the ensuing nine years they have sculpted, out of cow paddocks, a skilfully designed series of garden areas. Yes, there is the romantic English garden, complete with all its sense and sensibility. But there is also the Italian Garden, the Grey Garden, the Walled Garden, the Vegetable Garden and a dramatically beautiful Native Garden.

Planned to perfection, the garden has composition, contour, colour and contrast, a living canvas that develops with every season. In the long borders bright perennials intermingle with silver and green contrasting foliage. Dramatic purple salvia, pastel pink sedums and cheerful yellow yarrow are backed by hedges of Portuguese laurel and accentuated by the wonderful plumes of grasses such as Miscanthus sinensis.

The garden's interconnecting areas have many delightful surprises. Rounding the corner from the long borders the mood changes with the restrained silver elegance of clipped westringia, artemisia and helichrysum beneath lemon scented gums. Wide avenues of lush lawn and gravelled pathways lead to a courtyard full of fragrance and beauty. With a small legacy left to Di by her army father she has created a lasting tribute to him that has been named 'Bernard's Steps'. The grand Italianate stairway is fit for any triumphant Roman general to descend.

Junipers stand sentinel along its length and agapanthus with umbels of delicate white flowers point the way to a circular planting of pink Pennisetum orientale, mauve flowering oregano and agapanthus that blend into a protective surrounding for a decorative bird-bath.

In recent times the Johnsons' daughter, Jenny, has planted a native garden. It is full of the aroma of the Australian bush, proving that our indigenous plants have a lot to offer even the most formal garden. Jenny has labelled all her plants and selected them with care and patience, resulting in inspirational plant groupings. The bright silver leaves of Acacia binervia are beginning to form one of the main focal points behind a grove of Eucalyptus lencoxylon and stately kangaroo paws form vibrant stands of, gold, crimson, and green. The gravel paths are artistically bordered with: hakeas, grevilleas, thomasia, hibbertia and homoranthus to name but a few.

On initially clearing the land Di and Doug discovered that the view from the house was panoramic, consisting of picturesque layers all the way to the ridge of Mt. Eliza. House extensions and a paved patio have taken advantage of this attribute and added a new dimension to the property. The dam was rebuilt and enlarged, to provide the many litres of water that the beauty of such an enterprising garden requires.

First came the garden, then came the grapes! Not completely true, as there was already an acre under vine when the Johnsons purchased the property. A further three acres were planted to enable the vineyard to produce a commercial quantity of wine.

The Garden Vineyard specialises in the Peninsula's popular pinot varieties, the much-favoured pinot noir and pinot gris. The latter is also confusingly termed pinot grigio – the names correspond to the origins of the varieties. In the Alsace region of France the wines are called pinot gris and the style is rich, with a dense complexity, often with some level of residual sweetness. In Italy the wine is called pinot grigio and is light and dry with a higher acidity that lends itself well to food. In Australia, the term pinot gris is used interchangeably and The Garden Vineyard has a fine example of each style.

The early maturing nature of the pinot noir grape is ideally suited to the Mornington Peninsula's cooler climate. The grape is universally recognised as one of the noble wine grape varieties. It produces a wine with a rich velvety structure that has longevity. More than any other variety, the region in which the grape is grown will affect the wine. The Garden Vineyard has produced good examples with style, balance and character. Di and Doug have found that the vines on their land respond better to low cropping and produce a high quality harvest. At The Garden Vineyard, visitors have the added advantage of tasting these two varieties over a number of different vintages, which demonstrates the subtle variations in flavour that can be achieved by winemaking techniques and vineyard management.

Visitors to the vineyard are encouraged to explore the garden and perhaps bring a picnic to enjoy, either in the garden or on the terrace. Plans for the future include the sale of olive products provided by Gooseberry Hill Olive Grove located on the next property. Olives and wine have been teamed up for centuries and this new venture is bound to be a delicious success. The cellar door terrace, which overlooks the charming vineyard, makes a seductive spot to sip a glass of wine while soaking up the tranquility. The Garden Vineyard is an exclusive boutique vineyard and does not widely distribute their wine, so a visit to the garden will provide an edifying look at an outstanding horticultural achievement and the chance to acquire an excellent drop of Mornington Peninsula wine.

They are a hospitable bunch at Hickinbotham of Dromana, and it comes from a long history in winemaking and the hospitality industry. Three generations of exceptional wine makers have placed the families name on the 'who's who' of Australian oenologists. Family tradition dates back to the early 1940s when 'Hick' (Alan Hickinbotham), grandfather of present wine maker Andrew Hickinbotham initiated the first scientific wine making course in Australia at Roseworthy Agricultural College.

He was emulated by his son Ian, who himself is now an icon, adding further accolades to the family name. Ian was the founder of Kaiser Stuhl in the Barossa Valley where he created some of Australia's best-loved wines. His piece de resistance during these early years was the famous 1952 Wynns Coonawarra Dry Red – a legend to this day. He is the first Australian oenologist awarded an honorary life membership of the American Society of Oenology and has been instrumental in developing and promoting innovative technology that is now standard winery equipment. In the early 1980s, the family teamed up, leasing a vineyard at Mt. Anakie in the Geelong district. During this successful venture they were instrumental in launching such brands as Elgee Park, Stoniers and Meadowbank, with their expertise utilised by other labels from all over Australia. So began a dynasty that has made Hickinbotham of Dromana what it is today.

The decision to move to Dromana was made to take advantage of the perfect climatic conditions to be found on the Peninsula, so necessary for the Burgundian grape varieties, pinot and chardonnay. The relocation made the family pioneers of the nebulous wine industry on the Mornington Peninsula, setting standards as one of the region's first full time wineries.

At 74 years of age, Ian has handed over the winemaking reins to his son Andrew, who is ably helped by his wife Terryn. However, Ian is still active in the industry as a wine educator and raconteur, hosting seminars at the estate; he is also feature writer for the Australian Society of Wine Educators Quarterly.

Andrew Hickinbotham needed no urging to follow his father and grandfather into the heady world of wine. His love of his profession is obvious in his exuberant attitude and passion for the grape. He too is sought out by other wineries, recently taking up the gauntlet to help Flinders Island make wines of distinction. A 2000 vintage he made for yet another winery won international acclaim in San Francisco at the International Wine Challenge.

Hickinbotham of Dromana has 15 acres under vine of a 40-acre estate and produces six varieties of wine from grapes grown on the Peninsula: chardonnay, pinot noir, cabernet sauvignon, merlot, shiraz and taminga, producing exceptional wines from all varieties. 'Taminga' is Aboriginal for ' Place of White Gums'. The grape is an exotic fruit, a hybrid of the guwurztraminer and riesling grapes developed by the CSIRO for Australian conditions. It produces a crisp, slightly spicy, aromatic wine with some residual sweetness. Among the winery's new vintages is Cab Mac, an old favourite that was initially developed by Ian and eldest son Stephen (deceased) at Mt. Anakie and has proved constantly popular. Fermenting the berries within their own skins results in a lighter style spicy red and produces this soft easy to drink wine.

Andrew and Terryn have definite views on the right approach to viticulture, adopting environmental responsibility and sustainability. Recognized as a 'Waste Wise Business', they recycle everything, and significantly decrease the use of pesticides by, among other things, mulching vines with compost made from the estate's waste. Andrew, like his father, is becoming known as a technological innovator, having invented the FermentaBag that is revolutionising the industry. The bag provides a less expensive method, allowing a longer post-ferment maceration process without having to take up scarce tank space. The technology has already been embraced by wineries all over the world, even by the doyens of winemaking in France and Italy.

The winery can be found on the old Nepean Highway close to Dromana; number 14 on our wine-touring map. Any visit to Hickinbothams is made special by the welcome extended at the cellar door, hosted by Terryn. The family have gone to great lengths to create an area in keeping with the country atmosphere and relaxed medium of the grape. The tasting room and café look as if they have stood since early European settlement. Great care has been taken to source materials from the old buildings recycling their antique bricks, timber and doors. In winter an open fire glowing in a Tintinara slate fireplace, rescued from an old Brighton beach house, warms the room that is decorated with memorabilia of another era and the paraphernalia of winemaking. An added attraction at the cellar door is the 'Wine Cave'. This Hickinbotham museum of wine highlights wine making development over the past 50 years and provides visitors with the chance to taste some great old wines, like a 20-year-old cabernet from Tasmania, a superb 10-year-old, ripe riesling from Ballarat or perhaps a rich 11-year-old sparkling pinot. The cellar door specialises in the sale of older wines plus wines not available at other locations.

The Hickinbotham Café is a special experience. Seating is set within the tasting room and in a paved weatherproofed courtyard that tames the elements and provides relaxing views over the estate. The casual ambiance is enhanced by a light gourmet lunch menu headed by a delicious Winemakers Platter featuring bread made with the yeast left over from the winemaking process – it is splendiferous. The restaurant makes a great function and wedding venue and guests can be assured of a memorable event provided by a winery where they are always looking to 'do things a bit different'. The winery and café are open daily and there is weekly, weekend entertainment, plus wide-open spaces and a children's wine barrel cubby hut (rescued from a Corio distillery!) to keep the younger generation amused.

The Hickinbotham love of good times is mirrored in the expansive annual program of events. There is always something spectacular on the horizon and it pays to keep in touch. Easter weekend has become an institution at the winery, with the fun, frolics and entertainment being staged for a different charity each year and the inaugural Blessing of the Vintage was so well received this year that it is likely to become an annual event. But every day is a very important occasion at Hickinbotham of Dromana and every visitor a very important one.

Karina Vineyard in Harrisons Road, Dromana is conveniently located close to the Mornington Peninsula Freeway, only five minutes from the Dromana turnoff, number 16 on our wine-touring map. The small family business is owned, run and loved by Gerard and Joy Terpstra. It is one of a handful of estates on the Peninsula that cultivate their product from grape to goblet.

Before moving to Australia Gerard spent many years travelling the world setting up dairy food plants mostly in third-world countries. He trained as a food technologist and was born on the land in the Netherlands, the son of a farmer. He gained a Batchelor of Science in Food Technology at Bolsward College of Food Technology in Holland and an MBA from Newport University California. On a sailing holiday in Turkey he met English born Joy, who was to become his wife. Joy is multilingual, and at the time was working in the Netherlands as the personal assistant to a Japanese judge attached to the United Nations International Court of Justice in The Hague, better known as "The Peace Palace".

Gerard had gained some experience in wine making when working for a Dutch food company early in his career and while studying at Bolsward. So in 1998 during a working vacation to Australia, when the opportunity to enter the world of viticulture was presented, the couple purchased Karina Vineyard and along with their two sons have embraced their new life with vigour and zeal.

Established in 1984 Karina is one of the earliest wineries on the Peninsula, planted at a time when viticulture was still very experimental in the region.

The vineyard sits amid 25 gently-sloping acres with eight acres under vine backed by patches of very old native trees. No grapes are imported from other properties for the making of Karina wines. Being dependant on the quality of the estates vines for their entire crop the Terpstra's give the 7,000 vines personalised attention with particular thought paid to viticultural practices. All fruit is hand picked and the vines hand pruned to particular bud numbers thus ensuring that overcropping does not occur and flavour and ripeness is maximised. They are trained to a vertical vine canopy system and planted in a north-south aspect. This method allows for easier harvesting and gains the fruit full exposure to the sunlight thereby increasing flavour and sweetness levels. The winery produces approximately 2,000 cases per year, most of which is sold at cellar door.

The vineyard can be characterised as low yield/high quality that fits in with the Terpstra's philosophy of producing premium quality wines that sell for a realistic price. Their perseverance has been rewarded with a swag of commendations. Karina Sauvignon Blanc and Chardonnay both won gold medals at the Victorian Wine Show. Their Cabernet Merlot picked up the 'Best of Victoria' title from Winestate Magazine and the Devine Magazine Wine Challenge: Best Victorian Riesling.

Karina is one of the only vineyards on the Peninsula to grow and produce a classic riesling with any success. Although suited to cooler climates, this is a temperamental grape that is among the most difficult to grow. The slightest error can destroy the wine. When grown in the cooler regions the wine has greater potential for ageing, but it needs care and attention and cool fermentation to protect its delicate flavours. Karina's unique aromatic variety is light golden in colour and has an intense lemon/lime bouquet, with a fine crisp finish. It provides the winery with its 'point of difference' and complements the estate's Burgundian style, oak matured chardonnay that is barrel fermented in Vosges oak. The finished wine has lively melon and peach flavours and the mouthfeel is soft, yet full. It will age gracefully for many years. The Karina's crisp sauvignon blanc is one of the finest examples of this style available! The bouquet is of tropical fruit with some herbaceous overtones. Passionfruit and lychee flavours dominate the palate; whilst subtle yet beautifully balanced acids provide a crisp, clean finish.

Merlot makes up only a small percentage of the grapes grown in the vineyard and they are combined to perfection with the cabernet sauvignon to produce rich raisin and dark chocolate flavours. The deep crimson elixir is brought to maturity in French oak hogsheads that enhance the flavoursome wine's structure. Karina also produce the Peninsula's signature wine, pinot noir, and have crafted a well-structured variety giving great flavour intensity with a clean, long finish.

Gerard, using the most up-to-date winemaking equipment, blends Karina wines and the best French oak is used for maturation. The lower altitude and northerly position of the estate, sheltered by the surrounding peaks of Arthurs Seat and Main Ridge, provide Karina Vineyard with a warmer position than that experienced by the majority of the Peninsula wineries. It lends itself well to the later ripening grape varieties of riesling and cabernet sauvignon that do not thrive in the region's higher altitudes.

The winery is a pleasant place to visit, accessed by a sweeping driveway past rows of vines headed by fragrant rose bushes. Manicured lawns and attractive gardens surround the tasting room and cellar door that is contained within the immaculate winery. Gerard has a wealth of knowledge and delights in explaining the intricacies of wine producing to the uninitiated. The winery is open throughout the year on weekends and public holidays and daily from Boxing Day until the end of January.

Gerard and Joy take pleasure in welcoming visitors to their estate and invite guests to stay awhile and enjoy the beauty and tranquility of Karina's impeccably maintained vineyard, the serenity of the gardens and imbibe a taste of the Mornington Peninsula that they have captured in a bottle.

Lindenderry at Red Hill was opened in 1995. It is a magnificent 40-room stay-put, 5-Star Country House Hotel, a celebration of the good life where guests are pampered in a style that is fast disappearing from the hospitality map. Cradled in the heart of the Mornington Peninsula wine region, the estate also produces two of the Peninsula's most successful cool climate wine varieties. Positioned on the outskirts of Red Hill village on the corner of Andrews Lane and Arthur's Seat Road, it is easy to find; number 18 on our wine-touring map.

A gently sloping tree-lined drive leads visitors to the country house hotel past chorus lines of vines, high kicking their way over the hills in military precision, decorating a scene that produces medal winning wines. The meandering hotel presides over a captivating landscape, that covers 12 sprawling hectares of gardens, decorated by a tree fringed lake, towering eucalypts, Japanese maples, Linden trees, roses, shrubs and vines, offering guests a feast of facilities. Rooms and suites are attractively angled, delivering maximum privacy, providing attractive views of the vineyard or manicured gardens, natural bush or the sunken herb garden. Every room is superbly finished with the finest fabrics from Europe complemented by an eclectic mix of modern and antique furnishings. Works of art from Australian painters and sculptors adorn the gardens, rooms and hallways, enhanced by immense displays of fresh flowers. An invitation awaits guests on arrival to sample the estate's wines and partake of canapés before dinner. Special care is taken each evening to turn down beds, turn on lamps and leave a chocolate on the pillow, creating a soft welcoming ambiance for the occupants return.

If rest and recuperation is your aim you need never leave the property. A large glass enclosed, heated swimming pool opens onto green lawns and is complemented by a spa and sauna that promote physical wellbeing while providing a relaxing time out. Fresh air environs abound, with floodlit tennis courts at the visitors' disposal, secluded walks within the property's boundaries that lead along bushland tracks lined with camellias and rhododendrons. The gardens are perfect in every season, full of incandescent colour. Mountain bikes are available and picnic baskets can be ordered for adventures further a field. Indoor activities are catered for with a well-equipped games room and library. Comfortable guest lounges and reading areas are a magnet in winter with vast open wood-burning fires and conversation nooks, furnished with large, comfortable leather sofas, empowered by expansive views over the gardens and surrounding bushland. Any time spent here is over too soon. Bring your camera, bring your paint box, bring a friend and you'll never want to leave!

Holistic health is catered for with spa therapy that combines the touches and philosophies of Western and Eastern cultures. Full body polish, customized massage, aromatherapy facial and pedispa are offered to guests and day visitors in Lindenderry's Endota Retreat Spa. The therapies are designed as a vibrant experience of total relaxation and invigoration. It is intended to extend the spa's program to include a series of aromatherapy, yoga and naturopathy workshops as well as holistic health programs. Endota has created its own signature treatment by integrating relaxation, healing and the ancient techniques of the Indian head and shoulder massage. During the treatment oils such as rosemary are used to rejuvenate hair and stimulate mental clarity.

Lindenderry also encourages corporate Australia's use of their multifarious facility for meetings and retreats. They believe "that excellence is the only starting point," and they always aim to exceed any expectations. Groups are allocated a totally private conference area, which incorporates a light and airy meeting room and a separate indoor recreation room. Syndicate rooms and numerous other areas are available for breakout groups or private contemplation. The same attention to detail is adhered to when planning weddings and celebratory functions, either with fanfare or low-key intimacy. The gardens, full of sculptural works of art, pools of colour and textured greenery, create the perfect backdrop to any special event.

Of course the region is full of first class attractions to woo guests from the luxury of Lindenderry. The hotel's friendly staff are well informed and more than happy to organise day trips or suggest activities to further enhance a visit.

Lindenderry's restaurant, the Linden Tree, is an elegantly beautiful place, overlooking the vineyard surrounded by tall trees. It is open all day for breakfast, lunch and dinner plus morning and afternoon tea. Welcoming day visitors as well as hotel guests, it makes the perfect spot for the 'long lunch', the 'indulgent afternoon tea' or the stylish 'intimate dinner', cocooned in the elegant restaurant or al fresco in a flower filled courtyard. During summer, guests may find a tapas menu being served in the courtyard serenaded by the passionate Latin mood of a classical Spanish guitarist.

One of Australia's finest chefs, Andrew Blake, designs menus for Lindenderry that emulate the restaurant's elegant surrounds; full of natural flavours. Dishes are prepared in an innovative modern Australian style, featuring Peninsula produce, matching the superb estate and regional wines as well as award winning wine from all over Australia. Lindenderry has an annual program of events that includes master classes with Andrew Blake and wine dinners. For food and wine lovers everywhere it pays to keep informed.

The estate's 10-acre vineyard was established in 1991. Award winning wines are produced under the Lindenderry at Red Hill label. A newer addition to property is the cellar door that sits adjacent to the restaurant. It is nestled in a clearing, dwarfed by a stand of massive trees in a picture perfect setting. Visitors are invited to sample the excellent pinot noir, chardonnay and pinot blanc. The Lindenderry varieties are available over a number of vintages that like everything here at Lindenderry make an elegant statement.

Lindenderry at Red Hill

The Mornington Peninsula Winter Wine Festivall

Merricks Estate is located on Thomsons Lane, number 23 on our wine-touring map. Established in 1977 it is recognised as the second of the Peninsula's commercial vineyards. Originally a dairy farm, George and Jacquellyn Kefford purchased the Merricks property in 1975, but George was sure of one thing, he was not cut out to care for bovine! He consulted with Ross Brown (Brown Brothers wines), an old acquaintance, initially meeting him as a customer during Brown Brothers inaugural years, standing out from the crowd by buying wine not by the bottle but by the barrel!

The Keffords planted 50 vines as a trial. In 1979 they got serious and planted 100 vines each of cabernet sauvignon, shiraz and chardonnay, topping the list in 1980 with pinot noir. So began a vineyard that today has an outstanding reputation, producing good wine at a good price. George admits to early mistakes, but with expert advice from wine consultant Alex White, quality increased. The 1984 shiraz won a gold medal at the Victorian Wine Show and regularly receives outstanding acclaim from show judges and wine critics. The shiraz shows intense black pepper, spice and cedar in perfect balance.

Merricks Chardonnay offers a complex and fascinating bouquet. Malolactic fermentation adds richness to the palate that is soft and finely textured. The cabernet sauvignon is blended with merlot in the classic French style, producing wine of rich colour and subtle depth of flavour. The pinot noir is full-bodied; it won a trophy at the Royal Melbourne Show and gold medal at the Victorian Wine Show. The vineyard holds back some of each year's vintages that are released in moderation at the cellar door.

George and Jacquellyn chose the vineyard's distinctive label from a collection of lithographs by de Sainson, illustrator with the French expedition of Nicholas Baudin, that were published in Paris in 1823. It shows a sealers' camp on Western Port. The rustic cellar door is open the first weekend of each month, every weekend during January and public holidays, serving tastings and wine by the glass that can be enjoyed in the rose-bedecked courtyard. Visitors can explore the picturesque property that has extensive views over Western Port Bay to the Nobbies, Seal Rocks and Phillip Island. There are two natural lakes, the larger of which has picnic facilities and a barbecue plus a boardwalk that leads around the lake's edge. The Keffords are part of Melbourne Water's Healthy Waterways program and are revegetating a tributary of East Creek that flows through their property. The couple have planted 10,000 trees over the years and eventually intend to complete a shelter belt that will extend around the estate. They have created a place of serenity that is a joy to visit.

Merricks Creek on Merricks Road, Merricks (number 22 on our wine-touring map), is a specialist two-hectare pinot noir vineyard whose owners belong to that breed of pinot noir fanatics who are preoccupied with making good pinot.

Specialising in pinot noir, five estate pinot noirs are produced each year including a bottle fermented Vintage Pinot Noir Sparkling. Merricks Creek achieved a 5 star winery rating in "James Halliday's Australian Wine Companion" 2004 edition. Three of the winery's Pinot Noirs also achieved individual five-star ratings. Different trellising styles, a variety of clones plus variations in oak treatment (20%-100%), all combine to enable this boutique vineyard and winery to produce interesting and evolving pinot noirs.

Merricks Creek has a close-planted section modelled on the Burgundy tradition of low one-metre high trellising. Vines are closely planted at 500-millimetre spacing with the fruit positioned approximately 15 centimetres above ground level. This encourages competition amongst the vines for nutrients and water, thus forcing the roots to go down into deeper layers of the soil, adding dimensions to the quality of the fruit. Closeness to ground level also facilitates maximum ripeness through the effects of radiant heat.

The vineyard was established with the best available clones in Australia (MV6, 114, 115, 777 & D2V6). Merricks Creek has also imported the most highly regarded clones that have been used in the U.S.A. and New Zealand. The prized 667 clone was due to be released from quarantine in July 2003.

Jeni Port pointed out in her article 'On the Nose' (The Age Epicure 15/04/03) that we "haven't got to know pinot the way we have chardonnay or shiraz, that is, starting with the wine cask or a $10 bottle over dinner. We have skipped that stage."

Within the bounds of the costly exercise of growing pinot, Merricks Creek is attempting to introduce "that stage". Merricks Creek's vintage 2003 (to be released late 2004) will include an $18 entry point pinot noir which has been created from clean, healthy, ripe and hand picked fruit using pre and post maceration, a long 21 day ferment with wild yeast in small one-ton vats followed by malolactic fermentation and barrel maturation in the finest new French oak. Merricks Creek Winery and Cellar Door is open by appointment only and wine is also available by mail order.

Miceli is a small vineyard with a growing reputation on Main Creek Road; number 24 on the wine-touring map. The estate is located in the higher, cooler southern part of the Peninsula's wine region, situated close to the summit of Arthurs Seat, where grapes are picked three to four weeks later than the rest of the Peninsula, producing fruit with complex flavours. The winery is owned and operated by Tony and Pauline Miceli, with lots of help from their four children, Lucy, Olivia, Iolanda and Michael.

Anthony's background is in medicine, a busy general practitioner in Hastings, he has found time to graduate from Charles Sturt University Wine Science course and is being recognised as a winemaker of some ability. The Main Creek Road property was devoid of vines when purchased in 1989, but it was for the express purpose of growing grapes that Anthony and Pauline selected the site. They planted the vineyard in 1991 with the aim of establishing a small premium vineyard and winery to make and bottle wine under its own label on the premises. The label is a strikingly colourful one, representing the variations in the soil found on the property.

Don't be fooled as you drive into the winery. Only the family home is visible from the road, the low-key atmosphere is deliberate but the welcome is immense. The winery sits high on a shelf on the brow of a steeply sloping vine-decorated hill and overlooks the hills and valleys of adjoining properties. The estate has two labels, 'Miceli' and their premium wines named after the Miceli children: 'Lucy's Choice' pinot noir – rich and complex but fine, with great pinot fruit and lovely oak length; 'Olivia's' Chardonnay' – not over oaked or dulled by malolactic, falls into the 'fine' rather than 'fat' category; 'Iolanda's' pinot grigio – a flavoursome and savoury white wine with distinctive Pinot Grigio characters, lovely freshness and long-lasting flavours. Until recently Michael, the only son, was the only sibling without a namesake wine. Tony has taken care of that by producing a simply delicious dry sparkling wine that is to be named 'Michael's' methode champenoise. These wines, over the last few years, have taken out two trophies and a number of gold, silver and bronze medals, along with high praise from the industry.

All Miceli wines express delicate flavour characteristics with particularly long palate length, and relatively slow ageing. This is a direct result from the combination of good soil, cool and even temperatures and lack of severe water stress. Over ripe and jammy characters are never encountered, even at maximum ripeness. The cellar door is open the first weekend of the month, every weekend in January and for special events. Cheese platters are available to munch on and the Miceli wines are worth sampling. The vineyard may be small but their wines make a serious statement.

Merricks Estate

Merricks Creek

Miceli

Montalto Vineyard and Olive Grove is set within 50 acres of undulating countryside in a stunning natural amphitheatre. The vineyard's buildings blend into the brow of a hill, overlooking a panorama of wooded slopes, well-tended vines and open green spaces. The aura is enhanced by glimpses of shimmering Western Port Bay melding with the horizon, framed between the encircling knolls' softly rounded peaks. The serenity is almost palpable, rising from the valley floor like a heavenly mist. John and Wendy Mitchell purchased the original acreage in 1997, complete with established vines planted in 1986. They added to its dimension a short time later, purchasing an adjoining property, creating one of the most scenic estates on the Peninsula.

John travelled extensively in Europe during his corporate career that included a term as regional director for Nabisco. He became enamoured by the beauty of the vineyards and the romance of the grape, envying the *Vena Amoris* relationship the Europeans had with wine. On his return to Australia he set about courting a parallel lifestyle. He enrolled in a viticulture course at Dookie Agricultural College and his fate was sealed on first viewing the land that was to become Montalto Vineyard and Olive Grove. The property is easily accessible on Shoreham Road; number 25 on our wine-touring map.

The Mitchells nurture a cornucopia of crops on their property. Their dedication to making the best use of their natural resources led to the creation of a natural wetlands, the planting of 1,500 olive trees, extensive kitchen gardens, a fruit and nut grove and berry gardens, as well as the 30 acres of cool climate grape varieties. The 13 different varieties of olives grown by Montalto are available from the cellar door in a medley of delicious dishes and oils. This herbaceous fruit is a versatile little number and is hailed as a preventative medicine necessary in any diet for a healthy heart. It is an ancient food that has been associated with wine for centuries. Montalto olive oil can be tasted at the cellar door and is delicious as a dipping agent with the freshly baked olive bread that can also be purchased. Montalto is not just a vineyard and olive grove – it is a total experience, a salute to the finer things in life, stylishly presented in an architect designed area that includes, a restaurant, cellar door and processing rooms embracing a sun-soaked piazza. The man-made structures have a distinct Tuscan flavour and settle into the hillside with natural ease. The restaurant was opened in 2002 with a high standard set by French chef Philippe Mouchel. Present chef James Redfern has taken the restaurant on to bigger and better things, receiving the prestigious Chef's Hat in the 2003 and 2004 Age Good Food Guide. Guests are exposed to the panorama of hills, framed by recycled wooden beams set in the restaurant's glassed face, backed by the natural texture of rammed earth walls.

The chef's distinctive culinary style brings French provincial cuisine to the Peninsula, featured in exquisite dishes with flavours that tingle on the tongue. High quality ingredients, including produce grown in the estate's organic fruit and nut grove and kitchen and berry gardens, accent the gastronomic creations. What can't be grown on the estate is sourced locally. Lunch can be enjoyed daily at Montalto with dinner on Friday and Saturday evenings. During the warmer months, midweek dinners are also served. The restaurant is a striking venue for functions, and a private dining room is available for intimate gatherings of up to 24 guests. Degustation dinners and cooking classes are run monthly and offer an educational point of view combined with a night out. Themes range from wine and olive releases to seasonal produce.

For a function with a difference, designer picnics are a speciality of the vineyard. Several designated picturesque picnic spots within the property's sweeping lawns and wetlands area can be booked for an outdoor celebration or a romantic secluded rendezvous. Gourmet picnic hampers are packed with a wealth of delicacies that can comprise a variety of dishes including the house cured and marinated salmon, grilled meats and salads. All cutlery, crockery and glassware is supplied and stylishly laid out at your picnic spot - a truly decadent way to spend an afternoon.

John and Wendy have been joined in the family business by their daughter Heidi. The obvious love of the region and natural environment is evident in the family's philosophy of minimal intervention. The property's wetlands area is a place where nature is celebrated and encouraged to flourish, it provides a relaxing oasis filled with indigenous flora and fauna. A spring fed stream meanders through the wetlands, connecting four tranquil lakes and dams. Visitors are encouraged to explore a walk that has been engineered along sensitive viewing paths and leads past magnificent trees and ferns. Part of the walk passes a rosary planted by Wendy containing 250 fragrant rose bushes.

A stroll round the property uncovers another of the Mitchell family passions – art. They have turned the grounds into an outdoor gallery, full of unique and unusual pieces. A sculpture exhibition is held in the grounds of the estate each year. The exhibition attracts a diverse range of high quality artists hoping to win the Montalto Acquisition Sculpture Prize that is judged from the exhibits. The winning sculpture becomes an integral part of the Montalto collection.

The cellar door provides a stylish venue for tasting some of the vineyard's excellent wines. It also offers visitors a lower key dining experience ensconced on the piazza and kitchen gardens surrounded by invigorating outdoor environs. The menu advertises simple, seasonal delicacies that can be imbued with a glass of wine or an aromatic cup of coffee.

The Montalto label's first vintage burst onto the wine scene in 1999 presented under two labels. The 'Reserve Montalto' label covers three wines: riesling, chardonnay and pinot noir, the mainstream label, 'Pennon', covers five wines: riesling, sauvignon blanc/semillon, pinot meunier, pinot noir and rosé. Gourmet Traveller Wine Magazine awarded five stars to the 2001 Pennon Pinot Noir. All are excellent examples of cool climate wines reflecting the best of the Mornington Peninsula region, produced with the same dedication and presentation that goes into all areas of the Montalto experience.

Myrtaceae Vineyard has been established on the Peninsula since 1985, placing it among the oldest vineyards in the region. Things are afoot at the property, located on Main Creek Road, Red Hill, number 29 on our wine-touring map; a new cellar door has emerged onto the wine trail. The small vineyard is owned by John and Julie Trueman and is situated in a secluded valley close to Arthur's Seat. The couple believe in single vineyard wines that are grown and made on the property. They appreciate the individual wines that can be produced this way and work hard to build on their knowledge and experiences that will enhance the wine and produce the highest possible quality.

Prior to 1997, all grapes grown at the vineyard were sold to local vignerons, thus allowing the Truemans time to fine-tune their crops. The couple make a good team: John is in charge of the vineyard and Julie is the winemaker. Their operation is very hands on, keeping in mind traditional methods while incorporating recent innovations. They are aiming their product at the top end of the market and will only attach their label to the best.

The winery specialises in pinot noir and chardonnay. The chardonnay is fermented and aged in oak while the pinot noir macerates on its skins after initial fermentation and is then aged in wood. All Myrtaceae wines undergo full malolactic fermentation in barrels.

Julie's great-grandfather, Clements Langford, was renowned for the buildings he left behind. He built the Herald Sun building, the Queen Victoria Hospital, Myers, the spires of St. Paul's Cathedral and many early Melbourne buildings. Julie and John, with nephew Ross, are doing some building of their own with their purpose-built cellar door and surrounding landscaped gardens. The tasting room, with its embedded glass floor, is decorated with the unique art of local artist April Nutter, and shares the space with future vintages stored in French oak barrels; adding to the authentic winery experience as the pinking sound of the wine fermenting and aroma fills the air. Large doors give out onto a sunken flower-bedecked, courtyard with extensive views over hills and valleys and the classified Land for Wildlife bushland. Myrtaceae has one of the highest elevations of all the vineyards: it gives birth to Main Creek, which meanders through the property, journeying to Cape Schanck. Open on the first full weekend of each month, Myrtaceae is another exciting find on the Peninsula wine trail.

Northway Downs Estate on Stumpy Gully Road, Balnarring (number 30 on our wine-touring map), offers yet another unique international experience on the Peninsula's wine trail. Sigi and Pauline Schindler have brought a touch of Austria to the region. Their family-operated vineyard was established in 1996 and released its first vintage in 2000, offering good examples of cool climate pinot noir and chardonnay that can be sampled at the cellar door. The vineyard is open on the first full weekend of each month and public holidays, when visitors find themselves transported into the middle of an October Fest.

Locals as well as travellers have discovered the authentic wholesome Austrian food that is served, and the toe-tapping oom-pa-pa atmosphere delivered on Sundays in the warmer months, when the entertainment is live and lusty. Sigi, with the help of his family serves up dishes he remembers from his childhood that feature smallgoods from the vineyard's own smokehouse. The cellar door has gradually expanded to include a casual eating area that seats 75 people, with all the character of a German beer hall. Uncovered at the cellar door is another of Sigi's passions – antiques. On display is a 1,000cc 1920 Harley Davidson, in working condition. He admits to being an avid collector and purchased the machine, in awful condition, from the original owner in Tasmania. It took two years to restore.

The grounds surrounding the cellar door are very picturesque, with a large lake as a central feature. The Schindlers' daughter Tammy is to be commended for the thought and planning that has gone into the garden and wetlands area. The panorama of the garden and vines can be enjoyed from the cellar door, large patio or gazebo. To complete the scene an Austrian style chalet has been built on the property. The attractive four-bedroom house makes the perfect vacation address. It is Austrian inside and out, beautifully furnished with large queen size bedrooms, solid furniture, a wood-burning fire, and a pool table plus a huge living area and kitchen and massive wrap round balcony. Guests are also invited to make use of the full size tennis court that sits adjacent to the house.

Osborns Harwood Vineyard is one of the Peninsula wine country's boutique gems, open only on the first weekend of each month, holiday weekends and festival periods, or by appointment. It can be found on a protected north-facing slope on Foxeys Road at Merricks North, number 31 on our wine-touring map. Pam and Frank Osborn together with their son Guy purchased the property in 1998 as part of a post retirement plan. Frank was due to retire after a busy lifetime in the mining industry and the vineyard, with its attendant physical activity, was seen as a healthy alternative that would provide a new pursuit and social activity. The name chosen for the venture is made up of family names shared by the Osborns and their children.

The vineyard totalling six hectares comprises chardonnay and pinot noir plus smaller areas of cabernet sauvignon, merlot and shiraz. Frank works closely with winemaker Richard McIntyre of Moorooduc Estate and tends to the wine during its maturation stage in the barrels. When not tied up in the marketing end of the business, he can be found tending the vines and manning the cellar door. He is dedicated to expanding the Peninsula as a wine region and is a past president of the Mornington Peninsula Vignerons Association.

The property is immaculate with park like gardens and well-tended vines that put on a show any time of year. The driveway descends to the cellar door, contained in the barrel room. Although classed as a small producer, Osborns wines are contenders for the industry's awards. They have taken out their share of trophies, gold, silver and bronze medals, with the stars being the winery's pinot noir and chardonnay.

The oaked chardonnay is fermented in French barriques. The fruit comes from mature vines and the resultant wine has a tight, fresh, well-concentrated and supple texture. The pinot noir is fermented in open fermenters and relies on wild yeasts, matured in French barriques. The wine has a ripe raspberry flavour, subtle tannins and a mouthfeel which shows all the complexity and layers of a pinot noir made with the greatest attention to detail. The cabernet sauvignon is memorable, with intense colour and a fine and lingering finish. The shiraz is a vibrant spicy mouthful. Visitors are made very welcome at the cellar door with a complimentary cheese board to nibble on. The vineyard and its products can truly be characterised as "Elegant"

Myrtaceae Vineyard

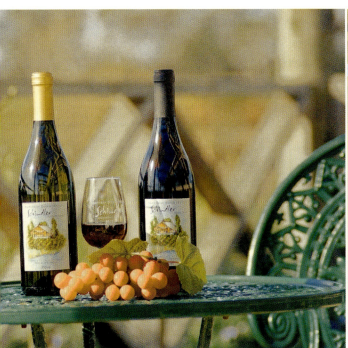

Northway Downs Estate

Osborns Harwood Vineyard

Moorooduc Estate is an eight-hectare property with a five-hectare vineyard, a small winery and a spectacular restaurant/accommodation complex. An idyllic oasis nestled among the softly undulating hills of Moorooduc, it can be found off the beaten track on Derril Road - number 26 on our wine-touring map. One of the Peninsula's oldest wineries, Jill and Richard McIntyre found this particular piece of land in 1982, after a long and intensive search.

The original vineyard of two hectares was planted in 1983. The first wine was made in 1986, with subsequent plantings of three hectares. Experience has shown that the site is best suited to the early ripening varieties chardonnay and pinot noir, but is warm enough to successfully produce small quantities of cabernet and shiraz.

Richard and Jill believe in the idea of "terroir", the French term referring to the unique characteristics of a particular vineyard being reflected in its wine. They also believe that their Derril Road vineyard has special characteristics, identifiable in the wine they produce.

Richard has taken to his life on the land with zeal and delights in his role as a winemaker, a far cry from his background as a surgeon. In 1983 he knew very little about winemaking, but has mastered the art to such a degree he now produces wine for other vineyards in the region as well as for his own estate. He has confidence in the potential of the Peninsula to become one of Australia's top wine producing areas. He says, "Site selection is very important in this marginal climate. We have aspirations to grow and make table wines that not only reflect individual vineyard sites but are of the very highest quality."

Chardonnay and pinot noir are produced on three levels. A wine that reflects the 'terroir' of the Derril Road site, 'The Moorooduc' is sourced from only the best Derril Road fruit and is therefore produced in very small quantities. The chardonnay displays great richness and complexity. Typically, more new wood is employed in this reserve wine and a greater proportion is fermented on solids. The pinot noir is mainly taken from the 114, 115 and low-yielding MV6 clones. It is an intense, highly structured wine and demands greater time in the bottle to develop.

Wines under the 'Moorooduc Estate' label, which include chardonnay, pinot noir, shiraz and cabernet, are made from grapes sourced from the Moorooduc sub region that also includes the Derril Road vineyard. They express the relatively warm, dry climate of the sub region, generally being rich and full-bodied. Consistently a high quality wine, the chardonnay has richness, sophisticated complex flavours and great length. The pinot noir has flavours in the plum and dark cherry spectrum, often with earthy and mineral characters. The cabernet is an elegant wine that is a blend of cabernet sauvignon, merlot and cabernet franc, a wine of purity and length. Moorooduc Estate shiraz displays the classic, cool climate characteristics of plummy fruit with spicy overtones, soft velvety tannins and good natural acidity.

'Devil Bend Creek' chardonnay and pinot noir are wines that reflect the Mornington Peninsula as a region, with fruit sourced from viticulturally different parts of the Peninsula. The chardonnay is a stylish, high quality wine that, as well as reflecting the Mornington Peninsula character is deliciously affordable. The pinot noir produced under this label demonstrates that the Mornington Peninsula is a region suited to this difficult but seductive variety.

The winemaking philosophy is to allow the wine to reflect the origin and quality of the fruit as well as to employ techniques which encourage the development of secondary aromas and flavours, structure and mouthfeel, achieving wine with a subtle complexity, middle palate richness, structure and length. This high quality can only be achieved if the vineyard delivers the best possible fruit through intensive management of the canopy, keeping yields low and giving the fruit good exposure to light.

The cellar door and winery are contained within a complex of rammed earth and timber buildings, fitting beautifully into the elevated north and west facing hillside. Visitors are welcome each weekend to sample the estate wines and relax in the courtyard.

The buildings also house one of the area's most elegant restaurants and stylish retreats. It is an amazing development with jutting angles, soft arches and expansive windows. Designed by Melbourne architect Gregory Burgess, with its earth and timber walls and lofty ceilings, the complex is in harmony with the subtle beauty of this fine piece of land.

'Jill's at Moorooduc Estate', contained within the main body of the complex, is a formal but relaxed restaurant that seats a maximum of 35 guests within a spacious dining area. The room is furnished with family antiques that blend with modern sofas set in front of a large open fire for cosy winter warmth. The setting is elegant and the service impeccable, creating a dinner party atmosphere where culinary masterpieces can be enjoyed in an architectural work of art. A vaulted ceiling that mimics the soft, undulating hills of Moorooduc highlights the restaurant's inspired interior and a wall of windows showcase magnificent views over the vines, down to the Moorooduc valley. The food created by Jill McIntyre is influenced by the provincial cuisine to be found in the rural areas of southern France and Italy, full of character, flavour and freshness. Whenever possible, local, seasonal and organic produce is used. Open for lunch on Saturday and Sunday and for dinner on Friday and Saturday evenings, guests are assured of a delicious experience.

The estate is adjacent to the Devil Bend Golf Course, is within walking distance of the Devil Bend Reservoir, with its surrounding bushland, and is only a short drive to all the other attractions of the area. Overnight guests can witness God showing off, staging a "spectacular" each morning and evening, as the sun rises and sets over this stunning property. Four luxury suites are understated yet elegant, amalgamating all the best elements of style. Japanese-inspired screens and either a king-size bed or twin single beds furnish intimate rooms looking out onto sunken gardens and private patios. An inspired breakfast menu featuring home produced free-range eggs as well as other treats is included in the tariff. This is a winery retreat that offers peace and secluded bliss – and a high degree of comfort.

Morning Star Estate is a property that has the WOW factor. The very name suggests an elegant flight of fancy where visitors gain a rich experience that indulges the senses. Situated on Sunnyside Road off the Nepean Highway, it is number 27 on our wine-touring map. The estate is cradled between the shores of Port Phillip Bay and Mt. Eliza, surrounded by manicured gardens containing an exultation of roses, tinted every colour on an artist's palette. Three hundred varieties pull the eye and fill the air with fragrance. It would be no surprise to see the 'Queen of Hearts' from 'Alice in Wonderland', pompously strolling through the grounds, crying; "off with their heads," or the 'White Rabbit' calling, "I'm late, I'm late," but his haste and her infamous cry would be totally out of tune with the panoramic vista and relaxed atmosphere, created by the magnificent gardens and close proximity of Port Phillip Bay.

The history of Morning Star Estate has been a long and chequered one. Francis Gillett built the stately Tudor gothic Victorian mansion in 1867, naming it 'Sunnyside'. It was a home of some distinction and he developed the property, planting extensive gardens. The estate belonged to the Gillett family until 1922 but was administered by a trust after the death of Francis Gillett's widow in 1909. The distinguished old home has, in its time, been the 'Morning Star Boy's Training Farm' that was run by the Franciscan Fathers as a rehabilitation centre for wayward young men and a Catholic Church Retreat. The Catholic Church retained ownership for 45 years, adding several wings and a chapel during their occupancy. However, the original mansion survived unchanged and remains the central feature of the estate. The property reverted to private hands in 1976 and during the 1980s operated as a horse stud before being purchased in 1993 by present owner Judy Barrett.

Moving from her home on Oliver's Hill in Frankston, Judy took possession of a sadly neglected estate. She and her family are totally committed to their role as custodians for the future of this grand old property and have dedicated the interim years to restoring it, reinstating its grandeur and re-establishing its reputation as one of the most highly acclaimed estates on the Peninsula.

The inviting gardens that surround the magnificent old mansion have been designed and planted by Judy. She has powered a lifetime of her love of growing things into the estate's masses of roses, with all specimens individually named. Hundred-year-old monkey-puzzle and pine trees decorate the grounds. The ancient trees shade an outdoor theatre area with a permanent stage that is regularly the scene of operas, recitals and concerts, hosting celebrity performers. Art exhibitions presented by Jenny Pihan Fine Art are also regular events at the vineyard, usually held in the character-filled old chapel.

Unique accommodation has been fashioned from what was the dormitory wing of the boys' home. The original 30 cell-like rooms have been converted into a boutique hotel by adapting every second room to provide two ensuites. As a consequence of the historic content, the dimension of the rooms are 'undersized' to what many guests may anticipate from a four-Star establishment, but, they are extremely comfortable and elegantly furbished. The hotel has standard double rooms, standard queen rooms plus an executive suite with a spa bath. A range of attractive packages has been devised, allowing guests a titillating sample of the estate's allure.

In recent times, the exclusive Melbourne catering company 'Table Matters' has been commissioned to run the estate's restaurant and functions. They have put their personal stamp of quality on the premises. Master chef David Bruguera-McLaren presents a creative focus on food, with a fusion of flavours in an international menu that complements Morning Star Estate's wines. The casual yet elegant restaurant occupies what was the boys' home woodwork shop. Stylish chandeliers now encase the outlets that once housed the sockets for power tools. The wooden floor gleams with a warm patina and the intimate interior gives way to a weatherproofed terrace that is ideal for al fresco dining. In any other restaurant the quality of the food would be enough to satisfy customers, but the one impression that every diner at Morning Star Estate will forever remember is the incomparably serene setting, with views to Melbourne and the Bellarine Peninsula on a fine day. In the foreground, masses of Iceberg roses lead the eye over a fringe of green vines towards the spellbinding beauty of Port Phillip Bay, witnessing sun and shadows playing a glittering tattoo on the water, backlighting the horizon like a neon sign.

The 'Chardonnay Function Room', one of six function rooms, sits directly above the restaurant and is blessed with the same vista, but with greater impact. Its elevated position allows wedding parties and function guests to totally appreciate the gardens and the bay from a bird's eye perspective. It is of course, a popular venue for special occasions. 'Table Matters' are master caterers, who can plan special occasion from A-Z, tailor made to personal needs. The estate can stylishly cater functions from 30 guests to 260 guests with ease. The gardens provide a fairytale setting for wedding ceremonies, either in the sunken garden, the rose arbour or with the grand Italianate cascading water steps as a backdrop. For a more traditional approach, the elegant historic chapel built during the Catholic Church's residency is a splendid alternative.

The estate's 30 acres of vines produce two distinct vintages that are bottled under separate labels. The Morning Star Estate label contains wine made from some of the oldest vines on the Peninsula, planted on the property over 30 years ago and the 'Sunnyside' label covers a range of wine from grapes planted by the Barrett family. Tastings and sales are available from the cellar door that is contained in the old school house.

All wine aficionados started off just liking the taste of wine and if you are in this category then the region to further educate and stimulate your palate is in the wine region of the Mornington Peninsula, and Morning Star Estate will truly delight you.

Poplar Bend Winery resides in a classic woodland glade, surrounded by century-old trees, on Main Creek Road, Main Ridge; number 35 on our wine-touring map. The vineyard was established in 1987 by no less a celebrity than wine critic and columnist Keith Dunstan. For 30 years Keith terrorised vignerons through his assessment of their wines within the pages of the Melbourne Sun. The winery is probably one of the smallest producers on the Peninsula but its signature label is one that is hard to forget. It depicts the infamous, risqué painting, 'Chloe', that for 100 years has taken pride of place above the bar in that legendary drinking hole, Young and Jacksons, on the corner of Swanson and Flinders Streets, Melbourne.

Owners Cathie and Peter Wallace are a bit bemused to find they own a winery. For years they had owned a holiday home on the Peninsula and were often in the area. On one such weekend, as old customers of Poplar Bend, they looked in on the vineyard's auction and, with no previous intention of participating, bought the property. Once the deed was done the couple jumped in with both feet. After all, Peter has a background in accounting and wanted to see a return for their money. Well this story has a happy ending; the Wallaces' son Paul joined the team and is training as a winemaker under David Lloyd of Eldridge Estate. The family is quickly learning what it takes to produce top quality fruit and have dispelled the myth that you should invest only in the things you understand. Their first vintage has been well received and shows good characters. They are concentrating their efforts on pinot noir, pinot gris, shiraz and semillon, which are all available at the cellar door that is open every weekend and public holidays with the exception of July and August, other times by appointment.

This is an intimate vineyard with all the romance of the species. Cathie usually looks after the small rustic cellar door, but Peter is usually around somewhere. The family has proved that scale is unimportant – the magic is in the size of the welcome.

Port Phillip Estate stands out from the crowd for many reasons, not the least being the Blue Peter, their eye-catching symbol representing the estate. Sailors among you will be familiar with this image: the nautical flag represents the letter 'P' in the international code of signals and is hoisted when a boat is about to sail. Of course whist players will say it is the call for trumps, but the reason it was chosen as the vineyard's embodiment is the former. A symbol of the region's maritime influences, the first initial of the winery's name and an indication that their wines are sailing on to bigger and better things. The winery's name signifies the closeness of Port Phillip Bay, dear to owner Giorgio Gjergja. Being a passionate sailor, he enjoys sailing on the bay and has sailed in the Sydney to Hobart Yacht Race. The award-winning vineyard can be found on Red Hill Road, Red Hill; number 36 on our wine-touring map.

The vineyard was established in 1987 and owners Giorgio and Dianne have expanded the area under vine to 20 acres. In addition to the recognition afforded Port Phillip's chardonnay and sauvignon blanc, the vineyard flagship wines, pinot noir and shiraz are much sought-after. Port Phillip wines have collectively won a multitude of awards, most recently the 2001 Pinot Noir. They won gold respectively at, the 2002 Victorian Wines Show, Southern Victorian Wine Show and National Wine Show. The Reserve Pinot 2000 received the trophy for 'Best Boutique Pinot Noir' at the Boutique Wine Awards, Sydney. The 2000 Reserve Shiraz was listed in the James Halliday Top 100 and the Top 100 wines in the Sydney International Wine Competition 2003, also winning gold medals at the National Wine Show in 2001 and 2002 plus the Southern Victorian Wine Show 2001.

In recent years it would appear that Bacchus, the Roman god of wine, has taken over the Peninsula and an ancient Roman adage describes Port Phillip Estate's success, 'Bacchus amat colles', (Bacchus loves the hills). The vineyard is set in a sheltered natural amphitheatre with north and east-facing slopes providing excellent drainage and fruit exposure. Its elevated position also provides the cellar door with a touch of magic.

A winding avenue with glimpses of the bay meanders through the vines, leading to the rustic cellar door. It lives in a reinvented old machinery shed that has been decked out, without too much fanfare, to provide a cosy welcoming room with a wood-burning fire to dispel winter chills, and a pleasant patio for summer sipping. Visitors are encouraged to bring a picnic and sit out among the age-old trees that decorate the estate and allow the essence that is the Mornington Peninsula wine country to take over.

Marinda Park on Myers Road, Balnarring (number 49 on our wine-touring map), is the home of fine wines, Mark and Belinda Rodman, and their young sons Simon and Jeremy. It is a bright new spot on the Mornington Peninsula wine trail. The estate was a hive of activity over 2003 getting ready for the cellar door opening in October 2003. The Rodmans purchased the property in January 2000. They chose their vineyard's name carefully to encapsulate their feelings regarding their new home. Marinda, as well as being an anagram of Mark and Belinda, is a derivative of the Aboriginal word 'merindah', meaning beautiful place and this estate is certainly that.

After being corporate nomads for 25 years, and having lived on every continent except Antarctica, the Rodmans had very well defined criteria for the selection of the property they were seeking. They chose the Mornington Peninsula for its beauty and lifestyle, combined with its developing fame as a cool climate wine region.

The estate has been developed on the grey loam that sits atop the famous 'Merrick Mud' clay soil that is responsible for the savoury flavours in Marinda Park's red wine varieties, helping their first vintage to gain acclaim. Wines are crafted by gifted winemaker Sandro Mosele and reflect his inimitable touch. The pinot noir has a deep bouquet that is complex and alluring. Previous plantings of merlot in the area had not, until the establishment of new clones, enjoyed the Balnarring locality, but the Marinda merlot has proved a winner, exhibiting both savoury and earthy overtones, finishing with a persistent length. Marinda Park Chardonnay is crafted in the chablis tradition that includes 100 percent maturation in French barriques. The wine's tight creamy palate is savoury and flinty with a long, clean finish. A complex, clean mineral palate with a long dry finish of fresh gooseberry, green olive and a hint of passionfruit reinforces the aromas present in the estate's sauvignon blanc.

It is obvious that Marinda Park will become a preferred destination to many wine lovers. Care and attention to detail has been meticulously adhered to. The French provincial style café has a rustically comfortable ambiance, with an open fireplace for winter warmth and outdoor grass decking in the shade of tall trees for summer idylls.

Poplar Bend Winery

Port Phillip Estate

Marinda Park

Mount Eliza Estate on the corner of Nepean Highway and Sunnyside Road, Mt Eliza, is exquisitely easy to find; number 28 on our wine touring map. There are no dirt roads to traverse: it is accessed straight off the highway, it is the closest winery to Melbourne. Heading south, follow the road past Flinders Street Station, and keep on going till you reach the pot of gold at the end of the rainbow. Robert and Jenny Thurley and son James, who is studying viticulture, have carved themselves a little piece of heaven out of the Mornington Peninsula countryside. The natural beauty of their plantation leaves visitors breathless. Situated 800 metres from Port Phillip Bay's only optional clothing shoreline, Sunnyside Beach, the views are phenomenal, stretching into the horizon over the bay to Melbourne's castellated skyline. The estate is a symphony of clear air, panoramic vistas, wide-open spaces and majestic wines.

The Thurleys grew up around Mt. Eliza and Frankston and have always had a deep connection with the piece of land that is now Mt. Eliza Estate. They initially purchased the property to raise horses, as Jill has a deep love for the stately animals. Jill still has her horses, but the estates priority is now focussed on the glorious liquid produced from the estates crops each year. First plantings were carried out in 1997 and the vineyard now contains 3,000 vines, planted over 15 hectares, contentedly growing on sunny north facing slopes. The aim says Rob, "is to follow the French and Italian philosophy and become the winery of the precinct. The place where locals go to purchase their wine."

The estate produces seven varieties all made from grapes that are 100 percent grown on the estate – riesling, chardonnay sauvignon blanc, shiraz, pinot noir and magnum maximus pinot noir, cabernet sauvignon and a special 'methode champenoise'. The wines are gaining acclaim with prestigious awards to their names. At the Murrumbateman Cool Climate Show the magnus maximus pinot noir 2000 won gold and the shiraz 2000 and riesling 2000 bronze, The pinot noir 2000 won silver and the sauvignon blanc 2002 won bronze at the Annual Rutherglen Wine Show and bronze at the Victorian Wine Show. At the prestigious le Concours des vins du Victoria Mt. Eliza riesling 2002 received a high commendation.

All Mt. Eliza wines are cultivated and crafted with care. The riesling is a well-balanced, fruit driven wine with a huge mid palate and a creamy, powerful finish. The sauvignon blanc is crisp and clean with good acid balance and a long lingering finish. The subtly flavoured French oak chardonnay is a lively wine, with citrus and mineral characters at the fore, showing a complex bouquet and clean zesty finish. A character filled pinot noir is a jaunty wine, containing spicy nutmeg aromas along with ripe raspberry and plummy fruit. The palate provides the same play between plum, spice and well-integrated oak with a subtle tannin structure, in true Mornington Peninsula style. Magnus maximus 2000 stands head and shoulders above the rest. Made entirely from grapes of the highly prized, very low yielding MV6 clone, the winemaker was compelled to set these five barrels apart, allowing the distinctively divine character of the wine its full expression. The tannins are beautifully soft. This wine is all about texture, which is the essence of great pinot noir. Named for Jenny and Rob's young grandson, the mighty Magnus Barber, as well as the wine, knows how to make his presence felt.

Shiraz is not a widely produced wine on the Peninsula, with few properties having the ideal growing conditions, and along with the Astrid Elizabeth Sparkling Pinot Noir Chardonnay provides Mt. Eliza with a point of difference. Mt. Eliza's shiraz is a seductively elegant wine, showing licorice, spice and plums on the nose. The palate has good length of flavour supported by a subtle tannin structure; it is a delicious deep-coloured red, reminiscent of wines from the Northern Rhone Valley. The Astrid Elizabeth Sparkling Pinot Noir Chardonnay 2001 vintage is a combination of two popular wines made in the traditional age-old method used by the masters in Champagne. It offers a fresh elegant nose, good straw colour, with a soft creamy generous palate and a crisp dry finish. This wine is destined to become a cellar door favourite.

Rob and Jenny see it as a natural progression from wine consumer to wine producer. They feel that the exposure to wine, gained in their world jaunts, not only broadened the mind but also developed the palate, and in their case, kindled a hankering to own their own vineyard by the sea. They set about creating not only a vineyard but also a place of celebration. The cellar door is a comfortably informal place and has become a favourite lunchtime haunt. 'Rillettes Café' excels in light, seasonal lunches providing food with finesse that includes a delicious antipasto plate, full of fresh flavours, and wonderful local bread. Lunch can be served in the fresh air paradise that surrounds the estate, with wonderful views from the patio, or picnic style beneath one of the amazingly shaped age-old trees that form living sculptures on the lawn, or nestled in the weatherproofed courtyard. Plans are afoot to build a restaurant and new cellar door, but the Thurleys promise it will not detract from the estate's exquisite rustic ambiance that visitors so enjoy.

Weekends during summer are special at Mt. Eliza Estate with music, fun and frivolity. Regular special events are staged throughout the year, showcasing top entertainers, themed parties and festivals. The estate creates a very special setting for any celebratory gathering, with its spectacular backdrop and blissful atmosphere. Any occasion can be catered for, tailored to suit the day and delivered with first class expertise.

Mt. Eliza Estate is one of the region's illuminating destinations that make an indelible impression, the perfect setting for viewing things from a different angle, soaking up peaceful country energy and tasting the elixir of life. Who could ask for a more pleasant way to spend a day?

Melbourne Wine Show 2003, a small winery wins two big awards, Most Successful National Exhibitor and Most Successful Victorian Exhibitor. Paringa Estate entered just five wines in the show yet this small Peninsula Winery snared the highest score with outstanding quality across its classes of pinot noir, shiraz and chardonnay. These trophies join a cluster of other awards at Paringa Estate as testament to winemaking still having particular empathy here with a special site. Lindsay and Margaret McCall purchased the 10 acre property at Red Hill in 1985. (Number 32 on our wine touring map). They both have a background in education and a passion for the grape. Lindsay's childhood and adolescence, spent in rural Australia, has endowed him with a deeply embedded love of the land. After earning a degree in economics he spent some years in the education system, returning to his first love on purchasing the Peninsula property. Success has been earned by the McCalls. They started on a shoestring budget, armed with a tenacious will to succeed, but both agree that the sacrifices made in the early years were all worthwhile and are proud of the level their wines have reached over the years.

Lindsay has very definite views on viticulture, believing that the best wines are largely made in the vineyard. In the early years he trialed a number of trellising systems to control the vine vigour and to maximise fruit quality. In 1989 he settled on an elaborate lyre or 'U' trellis system which while not unique to Paringa, it is used by few other vineyards because of its high establishment and running costs. As winemaker, it is his ethic to produce wines with minimal interference, the aim being to maintain as much of the grapes natural aromas and flavours as possible. He must be doing something right – Paringa Pinot Noir and Paringa Shiraz have become nationally acclaimed, winning award after award. Lindsay admits to having obtained his first pinot cuttings from Nat White at Main Ridge Estate. On researching the clone, he found some anomalies in its numbering and is now amused to hear it referred to as the "Paringa Clone".

In 1999, the 1997 Estate Shiraz rocked the industry by taking out the most prestigious trophy of the Sydney International Wine Competition, 'The Chairman of Judges' trophy for 'The Best Wine'. This trophy was made even more special as the Peninsula is not known as a shiraz growing region: very few Peninsula wineries produce the spicy red. Paringa Estate's Shiraz has notched up many wins, starting in 1990 and more recently the 2000 Estate Shiraz has won multiple awards in the 2001 wine shows. At the Southern Victorian Wine Show Paringa Estate's Shiraz and Pinot Noir have won the 'Best Mornington Peninsula Red Wine Trophy' an unprecedented seven times, the latest being in 2002. Awards started flowing early in the winery's existence. From 1992 to 2000 the Estate Pinot Noir has won one or more major trophies each vintage, with the exception of 1996. To date racking up an impressive total of 15 trophies and 22 gold medals.

Of course, the winery makes other excellent wines covered by its 'Estate' and Peninsula Labels. Estate wines are made exclusively from Paringa vineyard fruit while the Peninsula wines are produced from grapes sourced from other vineyards on the Peninsula, three of which are under viticultural management by the Paringa Team. Under the Estate label there is a delicate and aromatic white pinot, a favourite in summer, and also a very fine chardonnay with fusion of citrus, peach and butterscotch characters. The Peninsula Chardonnay, having lighter oak, gives more fruit expression and is quite tropical. 2000 saw the release of Paringa's first Estate Pinot Gris. It is Lindsay's aim to produce pinot gris in the rich Alsacian style with pear and honey characters. In 2003 Riesling appeared in the Paringa line-up, sourced from a nearby vineyard under management. This is floral and limey with a touch of residual sweetness – a popular extension to the range.

The sloping property is very picturesque, situated amid rolling hills. The present winery and restaurant was built in 1998 on the same site as the original small winery shed. The double-tiered building nestles into the hillside and allows for tall storage tanks in the winery that maximise fermentation floor space. The design is set to change yet again with a new cellar door planned in the coming year. The restaurant and present cellar door are on the building's upper level and the elevated position affords patrons a special feast – views are spread out like a banquet, sweeping over the vineyard and sloping hills to the tree lined crests. Floor to ceiling windows bring the outdoors right up to the table and, for summer dreaming, a large deck is a sun-soaked haven for long leisurely lunches. Indoor windows frame the winery providing a bird's eye view of the massive vats and stacks of French oak barrels filled with tomorrow's vintages.

The popular restaurant at Paringa Estate allows visitors to enjoy both current and past vintages of Paringa wines with perfectly flavoured and matched dishes. The cuisine is modern Australian with local produce being the basis for many dishes. Menus have a seasonal flair, accompanied by chef specials to maintain a new and varied experience for diners. Whether it be a casual relaxed weekday / weekend lunchtime meal or a more formal evening dining experience Paringa caters for all these tastes.

Paringa's regular customers eagerly await winemaker dinners. Carefully selected wines are presented for comparison. Food full of flavour is served, each course meticulously matched to the special wine that is presented. At a dinner held in July 2002, when compared, the Paringa Estate 2000 Shiraz was a match for a 1998 Gilles Barge Cote-Rotie 'Cote-Brune'. Participation at these dinners is keenly sought and for those wishing to attend, it is wise to place your name on the Paringa mailing list.

Visitors are lured to Paringa Estate's cellar door, not only to sample the award winning wine, but also because it is the only place to pick a bottle of the estate's reserve wines. These are very special wines, produced from extra special vintages. They are exclusive, with limited availability and the cream of a very select group. Magnums are also on sale and all wines purchased are available in gift boxes. Paringa Estate is a winery that not only gets the seal of approval from experts but also from wine lovers around Australia.

Pier 10 is relatively new on the Mornington Peninsula wine trail, opening the cellar door in January 2003. The attractive vineyard was established in 1996 on a former horse property in Shoreham Road, Shoreham; number 34 on our wine-touring map. Eric Baker and Sue McKenzie planted eight acres of the Peninsula's signature wines, pinot noir, pinot gris and chardonnay on the 11-acre property. Until recently they were absentee owners, visiting and working the property on weekends. But, all that has changed. The plan had always been to make the move from the 'big smoke' to the clean country lifestyle of the Mornington Peninsula, taking on the wine business full time – and finally the plan has been fulfilled.

Sue and Eric met eight years ago, through a mutual friend at a house-warming party. Eric has been a Melbourne businessman for the past 30 years, creating a reputation for excellence in the picture framing business, owning two retail shops (Port Melbourne Prints & Framing and Albert Park Prints & Framing) plus a manufacturing plant in South Melbourne. Sue worked at police HQ in the World Trade Centre in Melbourne. She resigned last year and now administers Eric's Melbourne-based business and Pier 10's cellar door. The couple make a good partnership: they have made their vision to create the ultimate lifestyle and a source of income a reality and have done it with modern flair and panache.

The vineyard had its first small vintage in 1999. A visit to the cellar door of this boutique vineyard, gives visitors the added bonus of comparing several vintages of the same varieties.

Pier 10's 2000 Chardonnay was fermented in French oak and is full of spicy oak characters, gleaned from 11 months' fermentation in quality oak barrels. It has rich yellow golden hues with great structure and a silky soft mouthfeel plus a delicate peach and apricote aroma that makes a classic, cool climate, chardonnay. The 2001 Chardonnay is unoaked, portraying brilliant straw colours with the aroma of ripe stone fruit and peach. It exudes extraordinary power and length. A white wine that is complete and unoaked demands to accompany food to be fully appreciated. The Indian summer of 2002 produced a chardonnay with natural acids and a unique flavour. This is evident in the estate's 2002 Chardonnay, full of classic flavours, rich yellow golden hues and aromas of delicate peach and apricot. It is full of fruit characters and great structure from yeast fermentation in French oak with a silky soft mouthfeel.

The vineyard's Pinot Gris 2001 is unoaked and is a classic v of this cool climate wine. A light straw colour provides a ric creamy palate with great length and a well-balanced finish. It e enticing aromas of honey and hay with just a hint of mushroo cashew. This is a wine for the adventurous wine lover. The Pinot 2000, unoaked, is a stunning wine with deep pink s hues. It is typical of pinot noir with hints of strawberry and berry. This is a rich silky wine and beautiful served chilled, aperitif.

Pier 10 Pinot Noir 2000, oaked, has a wonderful intense red colour. It is an elegant combination of sweet strawberry fru velvet soft tannins; its aroma portrays delicate hints of straw fruit and fungal mushrooms. This wine is a big soft mouthfu a lingering finish, showing characters of violet, rich plun cherry. Pinot Noir 2001, oaked, is a brilliant red wine. It is a enly pinot with a perfume that is guaranteed to seduce, with ripe fruit, cherry plum and strawberry, showing charry over from French oak. It is rich and full-bodied, with hints of cho and spice. A totally satisfying mouthful that will peak and minds and become equivalent to the best of Burgundies. The yard's latest release, Pinot Noir 2002, exudes aromas of won oriental spice with intensity and silkiness. Wonderful on the with ripe stone fruit, cherry and plum, married with quality F oak and exotic oriental spice. It has rich red berry hues and pr a generous weighty palate, with oak influences and spicy over This wine won a bronze medal at the 2003 Cool Climate Wine

The innovative vineyard is becoming known for its 'partie picnics'. The idyllic setting of the spacious, custom-built cellar is not missed by visitors looking for an unusual venue for a ce tory function. Sue and Eric have created a trendy sanc complete with a huge wood-burning fire encircled by lush l sofas, furnishing a haven of warmth and comfort in the months. As to be expected, magnificently framed prints ador walls and a sweeping bar and stylish, café-style tables and complete the indoor scene that opens onto a patio.

Sue has an easy grace that she brings to the welcome v receive at Pier 10. She has become expert at organising small mal wedding receptions, themed parties and special int celebrations; surprising one birthday girl, who has a passion f cakes with a moulded tower of her favourite treats as a bir cake. A picnic hamper can be purchased from the cellar doo taken to the vineyard's lake, located in the middle of the pro where picnic tables surrounded by landscaped gardens provi perfect spot for romance or revelry. The elevated picnic spot i rounded by a medley of pastoral views over the surrounding with vision carried all the way over the Heads to Bass Strait.

Pier 10 takes its name from the small chunk of Flinders h pier that greets visitors to the vineyard. It is a historic mascot modern company. The weekend includes Friday at Pier 10 wh cellar door is open to visitors. Music and entertainment, showe a variety of performers and styles, turns the vineyard into a zone after 2pm on designated Saturdays and Sundays. Inno light food with a seasonal theme is served throughout the da weekend and can be consumed within the cellar door or on the both areas are blessed with stunning views overlooking the vin to the rolling hills. Sue and Eric are fun loving hosts and the door is the perfect venue for that relaxing weekend jaunt or laid-back lunch.

Red Hill Estate is one of the viticultural showpieces of the Mornington Peninsula. It is easily accessed from Shoreham Road, Red Hill South; number 37 on our wine-touring map. The stunning 24 acres of vines nestles on 30-plus acres of a formerly 600-acre historic estate, dating back to the 1860s. James Wiseman, a Scotsman, owned the original estate, from where he ran his blacksmith business, servicing the length and breadth of the Peninsula. The estate has gone through many changes since Wiseman's time, from blacksmithing to thoroughbred breeding to cattle farming and finally to one of the most successful wineries in the region.

Established in 1989 by Sir Peter and Lady Derham, the estate's perfect position produces top quality cool climate grapes. Initially the grapes were sold to other winemakers but the vineyard was soon developed into a winery that has gained in stature and strength with every passing vintage. Of course, it is not just a case of sticking a vine in the soil and watching it grow. Although the estate is blessed with fertile soil, the key to developing cool climate wines is the special techniques needed to manage the subsequent vigorous growth. Red Hill Estate practices careful irrigation strategies to ensure yields of the highest possible quality each vintage. Red Hill Estate has expanded over the years and now manages the historic Briars Park vineyard in Mt. Martha and several other vineyards in Merricks, Moorooduc and Main Ridge. The grapes from these other properties possess slightly different fruit characteristics, further contributing to

the complexity of the wines produced at Red Hill, while still maintaining the integrity of the region. Greater consistency of wine styles is afforded by drawing fruit from these other vineyards as well as providing a bounty of blending options.

Red Hill Estate has three brands of wine produced under the, 'Classic Release', 'Red Hill Estate' and 'Bimaris' labels. This winery has a multivious collection of awards to its name, which grows annually, starting with gold awarded to the 1992 vintage of their critically acclaimed sparkling wine at the Cowra Wine Show. In the last 2.5 years alone, from wine shows all over Australia, the estate's different labels and different varieties have notched up between them 14 gold, 29 silver, 85 bronze medals and five 'Best of Show' trophies, plus the Red Hill Estate Classic Release Chardonnay was given a commendation at the London International Wine Challenge 2002 and Red Hill Estate 2001 Pinot Noir a commendation at the 2003 challenge. Not only Red Hill Estate's wines have been lauded: in 1994 the vineyard was awarded the 'Vineyard of the Year – Award for Excellence' by the Department of Agriculture. In 1997 and 1998 the winery won the 'Victorian Tourism Commission Award for Best Winery'. This was capped in 1998 by winning the national 'Best Winery' prize, beating out prestigious opposition that included giants such as Penfolds.

The cellar door is open seven days and group tastings can be arranged by appointment. In 1992, made by Red Hill's winemaker of the day, Jenny Bright, the estate produced the region's first 'Premium Methode Champenoise'. Current winemaker Michael Kyberd has continued this delicious variety, producing a perfect aperitif with crisp clean bubbles and a subtle fruit overtone. Visitors are amazed at the variety and quality of wine produced by Red Hill Estate, from aromatic sauvignon blanc and fresh, light pinot grigio to gold medal chardonnay, spicy, full-bodied shiraz, velvety pinot noir and cabernet merlot plus a sweet liqueur muscat. All can be sampled at the cellar door.

The winery has one of the most majestic positions on the Mornington Peninsula with heart-easing views over Western Port Bay to Phillip Island's golden fringed, charcoal silhouette. In 1995, to meet popular demand, the Cellar Door Restaurant was added to the estate's attractions.

The restaurant was renamed 'Max's at Red Hill' in honour of the restaurant's innovative owner/chef, Max Paganoni. He is recognised as a culinary innovator; his flamboyant style and masterful amalgamation of flavours are legendary. The bill of fare now offered is a far cry from the gourmet pies and toasted sandwiches that was, pre-Max's, the extent of Red Hill Estate's menu.

The restaurant's cuisine is continually evolving and combines the best of exotic international and Asian influences, using the finest of local produce. Max takes annual trips to Tuscany that provide new stimuli for his creativity, returning with more secrets of the ancient culture's cuisine to incorporate into his exceptional menu. The contemporary international fare is created with Red Hill Estate wines in mind and the union of flavours explodes on the palate. A speciality of the house combines local Flinders' mussels cooked in Red Hill Estate Chardonnay cream sauce, tossed with julienne vegetables and just a touch of sweet chilli – m..m..m..mouth watering.

Max's rests on the brow of a hill overlooking the estate's breathtaking view. The main dining room, which also doubles as a function room for weddings and corporate events, seats up to 100 people. It opens onto a terrace area that can, weather permitting, seat another 60 guests. Open seven days for lunch and Friday and Saturday evenings for dinner, visiting Max's at Red Hill is a culinary adventure. It comes as no surprise that the restaurant was voted, Best Restaurant in Victoria in the 2002 American Express Restaurant Awards and Best Regional Restaurant 2002.

The restaurant is the pivot for a lively calendar of events. The annual 'Burning of the Canes' in August is a celebration of the changing seasons, the end of last year's growth. It involves igniting a large bonfire comprising woody canes pruned from the vineyard – a truly spectacular sight. Guests are invited to warm themselves with fabulous wines, partake of a three-course feast and enjoy live music and pyrotechnic entertainment. But, keep a weathered eye on the up coming events at Red Hill – they often slip in special occasions such as this year's visit of the ladies from the Tutti a Tavola Cooking School in Radda, Chianta. The five lively senoras spent an entire weekend cooking as the Tuscans do, with passion, in Max's kitchen. The extravaganza incorporated a five-course luncheon, containing old traditional family recipes, cooking tips and anecdotes from some of Tuscany's best.

Stonier Wines is centrally located in Merricks on the corner of Frankston-Flinders Road and Thomson Lane; number 38 on our wine-touring map. It is a member of the Mornington Peninsula wine region's reigning royalty, and one of the earliest vineyards in the region. Noel and Brian Stonier established the popular winery in 1977, utilising a 112-acre grazing property they purchased primarily as a holiday home. The property was formerly the Thompson family farming property, established in 1945. On clearing the land around the existing house, the Stoniers were delighted to find a visual feast spread out before them, with stunning views stretching to Western Port Bay and Phillip Island. Noel and Brian planted the first acre of chardonnay vines themselves, by hand, referring to a textbook for their expertise. The success of these vines led to a planting of 600 vines in 1978.

The Stonier family are ex-Melbournians. Brian was a leading publisher, chairman of Pan Macmillan, and admits to being a wine enthusiast at the time, without much knowledge of winemaking. But with the help of other wine pioneers in the region, and expert advice, the mistakes became fewer and the returns greater. Early planters on the Peninsula cooperated and experimented to grow the market and induce the public to visit the region. Stonier Wines have travelled a long way since the first vines were planted. Over the last 25 years the area under vine has expanded and now produces some of the region's best cool climate wines, crushing 400-500 tonnes of grapes annually.

What began as a hobby, that was developed without much thought of expansion, has grown into a multi award-winning winery, comprising several vineyards, covering 155 acres in Merricks, Merricks North, Balnarring, Shoreham and Red Hill. Among the plethora of gold, silver and bronze medals won by the winery, two instances stand out: the gold medal won at the prestigious le Concour de Vins Show 2001, for their 2000 Chardonnay, and a bevy of medals won at the International Wine Challenge 2001 in London; one gold medal each, for their 1999 Reserve Chardonnay and 1999 Reserve Pinot Noir, plus a bronze each for the 1999 Pinot Noir and Chardonnay and trophies for Best White Wine and Best Chardonnay. The 1999 Reserve Chardonnay was described as 'Best White Wine in the World'!

The early vintages from 1982 to 1986 were made for Brian by the late Stephen Hickinbotham, a skilled and creative winemaker, at his Geelong Mt. Anakie Winery. These wines helped to develop and expand the enormous interest that other pioneer vineyards were creating in the Peninsula region in those early days. Subsequent vintages from 1987 have all been made under the direction of the talented Tod Dexter, initially utilizing the Elgee Park Winery of Baillieu Myer, until the Stonier Winery was built in 1991.

In 1998 Stonier Wines became part of the prestigious Petaluma group, but continue their independence with existing management. Brian has surrounded himself with a coterie of experts: chief winemaker Tod Dexter, winemaker Geraldine McFaul, and viticulturist Stuart Marshal, all colluding to, "create wine of great strength and complexity through careful selection of fruit from exceptional vineyard sites."

The original property of Stonier Wines now has 50 acres under vine comprising 20 acres of chardonnay and 30 acres of pinot noir. The grapes from each of the vineyards are vinified separately to ensure the highest standards, with numerous winemaking techniques used in moderation so that no flavour dominates any wine, and a wine of seamless complexity, balance and power is created.

Stonier's range of engaging wines at their cellar door includes Reserve Chardonnay, Reserve Pinot Noir, Chardonnay and Pinot Noir. The company have also introduced their first cuvée. The 1999 Stonier Cuvée is a traditional aperitif-style sparkling wine with a steady bead of tiny bubbles that tingle on the tongue and leave the farewell at the back of the throat. This year saw the release of Stonier Single Vineyard Wines under the Stonier KBS label. 2000 Stonier KBS Chardonnay and 2000 Stonier KBS Pinot Noir are crafted from grapes grown only on the original Stonier property and display the 'terroir' of the estate.

Brian remains enthusiastic about the quality of many of the wines produced on the Peninsula. He has worked tirelessly to promote the region, serving several terms on the Mornington Peninsula Vignerons Association (MPVA) committee, both as secretary and president. The famed Winter Wine Festival, launched in June each year over the Queen's Birthday Weekend, was initiated during his term in office. He is excited about the reception that Australian wines are being afforded internationally and has led Stonier to court the Asian markets. Already on the shelves in the United Kingdom and Europe, Brian sees the Asian region as new and uncharted territory, "a nation of developing palates." In their bid to enter this market, Stonier Wines have won gold medals in the Hong Kong International Wine Challenge.

Everything at Stonier is done with flair and style. Brian commissioned renowned architect Daryl Jackson to design the winery. Travelling extensively overseas, Brian collected information to ensure the design would produce an absolutely, world-class wine facility. The resulting building is a large, bright and well-organised space with an attractive cellar door and patio area, facing sweeping lawns that are the scene of many merry occasions. The winery has become renowned for its weekend hospitality, halcyon days of comfortable informality where good music permeates the air and good wine entertains the palate. There are cheese platters available to nibble on and there is always a member of staff willing to conduct winery tours. A childrens play ground and the great outdoors, provide younger visitors with an entertaining distraction. Stonier has an annual calendar of events that are well patronised. January brings around the St. Onier Day Celebration Feast. St. Onier is the patron saint of bliss and a lunchtime feast, to honour him, is a celebration of enjoyment. After the vintage, Easter weekend is always a good time to visit. Family fun is the order of the day with a petting zoo, a larger than life Easter bunny and lots of seasonal fun. Adults enjoy the day, soaking up the atmosphere, listening to the strains of excellent music, eating excellent food from the barbecue and sipping excellent wine. In June when the vines are asleep and the barrels are gurgling with the promise of next year's vintage, Stonier take part in the Winter Wine Festival, unveiling new vintages, serving toasty winter food and relaxing after a long hard season. Melbourne Cup is also heartily celebrated at Stonier and fun lovers should keep informed of upcoming events at this winery, where the wines are exceptional and the welcome expansive.

Tucked away in the middle of horse country, on Stumpy Gully Road, Moorooduc, number 39 on our wine-touring map, nestles one of the Peninsula's hidden stars. Stumpy Gully Vineyard takes its name from the road it sits on, but that's where the ordinary ends. Wendy and Frank Zantvoort put the 'Z' in pizzazz. They established the vineyard in 1989, on a historic dairy farm that lay unused for half a century, planting some unusual grape varieties along with the more classic types for which the region is better known. This vineyard is truly a family affair, with Wendy and Maitena Zantvoort, (Victoria's only mother/daughter winemaking team) and Ewan Campbell, (husband of Maitena), making the wine, and father and son team Frank and Michael Zantvoort handling the viticulture. You are likely to meet any one of them at the cellar door.

The Stumpy Gully wine list is impressive. White Wine: chardonnay – Full-bodied fruity wine; sauvignon blanc – crisp dry sancerre-style; pinot grigio – intense full bodied Italian style; marsanne – spicy aromatic dry wine developing honey characteristics with age; riesling- full round palate good length and clean crisp acidity; botrytis riesling – by encouraging the botrytis culture on the berries skin the juice is concentrated up to five times, creating a rich, luscious wine. Red wine: cabernet sauvignon – deep red velvet hue complemented by firm natural tannins and toasty oak; merlot cabernet – full bodied dry wine with ripe cassis and spicy oak; merlot – only made in excellent years, well balanced rich and ripe; pinot noir – cool climate fruit driven medium-bodied wine; shiraz – excellent example of cool climate shiraz from Australia; sangiovese – deep brick red colour, aromas of cherry, spice and slightly earthy with persistent palate.

If colour is a source of happiness, the cellar door at Stumpy Gully is Nirvana. It is a celebration of style where colour is used with abandon, highlighting the surrounding environs. A vibrantly coloured logo sets the standard and tactile labels scream 'good taste'. Local Peninsula artist Mary Hennekam's colourful beach scenes have been chosen as the image for the vineyards second label, 'Peninsula Panorama', and marries wine to art. The cellar door is open every weekend; it is attached to the winery and overlooks a garden glade with a paved patio for lazy summer days. Watch for upcoming events – winemaker's dinners and festivals are a common occurrence at the vineyard - where the mood is casual and the good times automatic.

The Ten Minutes by Tractor Wine Company can be found on Roberts Road, Main Ridge; number 42 on our wine-touring map. Just look for the old 'Fergie' tractor. 'Ten minutes to where?' you might ask. Realising that the three vineyards that combined to form this innovative wine company lie approximately 10 minutes apart when travelling by tractor (doesn't everyone!) it seemed a good name to call the new venture. Simple, funky and hard to forget!

The blending of the three family vineyards each located on Main Ridge, the Mornington Peninsula's highest wine producing region, has proved a clever one. The families of Peter and Elizabeth Wallis, Andrew and Vivienne McCutcheon and James and Kerry Judd, pooled the fruit from their individual properties and shared the costs of expensive equipment and professional help. They also engaged experienced winemakers Richard McIntyre and Alex White, who have produced sensational wines from the high quality fruit, enabling the company to surge ahead.

Regional cool climate viticulture throws up challenges that make these vineyards labour intensive. Great care and attention to detail is required at all stages of vine management. But the end result is worth it, producing a range of splendid wines that show the intense lingering flavours of a long, slow ripening season. The vineyards produce a range of award-winning wines under two labels. The '10X<<' label covers a traditionally fermented pinot noir, a barrel-fermented chardonnay an unwooded pinot gris and a sauvignon blanc. The 'Tractor' label includes Single Vineyard and Reserve bottlings of a barrel-fermented pinot gris, a barrel-fermented chardonnay, a traditionally fermented pinot noir and a botrytis chardonnay sauvignon blanc. All wines are available from the cellar door.

The cellar door is open every weekend and regularly features entertainment. It has become an established favourite with the wine touring public for light lunches and wine tastings, rounded off with aromatic coffee and cake. The charmingly casual cellar door is full of quintessential country character made special by the lofty views over the vine-decorated slopes and strawberry fields of neighbouring farms. It is located in the heart of the vineyard and visitors are encouraged to explore the property. A lake sparkles at the bottom of the slope, covered with drifts of waterlilies, imprinting colour and pattern on the water's surface – an absolute vision when in bloom.

The Duke Vineyard on Paringa Road, Red Hill South, number 43 on our wine-touring map, is Lilliputian compared to some of its neighbours, but what it lacks in size it makes up for in quality. First planted in 1989, the vineyard now consists of four acres under vine of the 11-acre property, exclusively planted with chardonnay and pinot noir, including a variety of clones. The wines are made totally with fruit grown on site and are hand-crafted at every stage of the process. Labour intensive? "Yes, but worth it," says Geoff Duke.

Geoff and wife Sue own the vineyard and Geoff teaches viticulture and wine science at Holmesglen TAFE. The couple aspire to produce small quantities of very high quality wine, specialising in chardonnay and pinot noir, using classical varieties, small-scale methods and featuring intensive viticulture. 'Proof of the pudding is in the eating', so they say, and the Dukes were delighted when their 1996 Chardonnay won gold at the 2001 Southern Victorian Wine Show. This renewed Geoff's belief in producing chardonnays that mature well over three to eight years. A range of vintages is available at the cellar door that is open weekends and all holidays, and customers can be assured that the product they purchase has gone from vine to wine to bottle all on the Dukes' premises – even the labelling is done on site!

A new cellar door and winery built specifically for the production of small batches of top-quality wine has recently been completed. The innovative, architect-designed complex, comprising three cement cylindrical buildings, sits on a ledge built into the steep slope of the hillside overlooking East Creek Valley, a panorama of rural perfection. It is a scene of contentment. Wooded slopes and olive groves alternate with open stretches of meadow that hold neighbouring homesteads, resembling miniature doll's houses put in place by a giant hand. The tolling of bellbirds adds to the rhapsody – a wonderful spot to spend the day, sitting on the patio sipping a drop of some very special wine.

Stumpy Gully Vineyard

Ten Minutes by Tractor Wine Company

The Duke Vineyard

Tucks Ridge is one of the big boys on the block, but with all the appeal of the smaller boutique wineries. It can be found on Shoreham Road, Redhill; number 44 on our wine-touring map. Their award-winning brand is synonymous with excellence and elegance. They offer a variety of wines with a wide variety of prices. The estate is family owned and had humble beginnings, starting on a small four-acre vineyard established at Red Hill in 1986. Since its first vintage, in 1999, Tucks Ridge has grown and now makes over 15,000 cases of wine a year that are sold Australia wide and overseas. In addition to fruit grown at the Red Hill vineyard the company sources fruit from 10 other sites across the Peninsula, providing wine with a diverse cross-section of flavours from the regional terroir. Senior winemaker Phillip Kittle has a philosophy of handling all wines in small batches and then blending to ensure that the final wine reflects the region it is grown in. Varieties are packaged under two distinct labels – Tucks Ridge and Callanans Road. Both are available at the cellar door and the range includes, chardonnay, pinot noir, pinot gris and a northeast Victorian shiraz. A range of popular Italian style wines is available only from the cellar door.

The vineyard is part of an old property, and the cellar door is contained in a quaint 1800s bluestone cottage that presides over a picturesque valley. The views are very prescriptive, guaranteed to relax and rejuvenate an overworked body. Any time of the year is a good time to visit. Winter days are made cosy with a large open fire and warmer days can be spent on the patio surrounded by sun-kissed outdoor environs. The winery is gaining fame as the Peninsula 'party place', with a multitude of annual festivals and celebrations. People flock to the winery each year to be 'winemakers for a day' during the 'Pinot Rustica' celebrations, stomping grapes amongst great hilarity and enjoying the ambiance created by good food, great wine and carefree company. The stars of Tucks Ridge culinary success are the Flying Calamari Brothers. They can be found each weekend and public holidays specialising in their unique deckchair dining, headlined by dishes such as seafood chowder, Big Ed's lamb shank ragout with special appearances by Big Al's bangers and mash and of course, calamari rings. The food is realistically priced, uniquely original and – you don't need to book!

On exploring the Mornington Peninsula's wine trail, you continually think you could not possibly find a more beautiful winery than the last, and then you drive along a dirt road and pull up in front of Turramurra Estate Vineyard. Established in 1989 by David and Paula Leslie, it can be found three-kilometres up Wallaces Road in Dromana, number 45 on our wine-touring map. It is open on the first full weekend of each month, or by appointment. The property nestles on the north-facing slopes of the Peninsula, overlooking Port Phillip Bay. It covers 27 hectares of sheer beauty, with 10 hectares of vines, extensive bush reservation and a glistening, natural, 2.5-hectare lake. Turramurra is an Aboriginal word meaning "a high hill" and the estate's distinctive labels represent a hill, a vineyard and the reflection of the waters of the property's magnificent lake. Artist Ken Cato designed a different label for each of the Turramurra wine varieties to illustrate the beauty of the location and high quality of the wine produced.

The winery and cellar door are built to take maximum advantage of the massive lake with a wall of windows looking down over its mirrored, placid surface. The element of water is the focal point, with wooded sloping banks, rocky outcrops, black swans and other waterfowl creating a storybook location. A unique wine walkway allows visitors a bird's eye view of the working winery and outdoor decking provides a platform to bide and imbibe the aural appeal of the surrounding tranquillity.

Paula, an accountant with a passion for horticulture, became the vigneron while David, a medical microbiologist, completed a Batchelor of Applied Science (wine science) degree, left his pathology practice and became a winemaker. Son Andrew has got in on the act and is also part of the winemaking process at Turramurra. The couple initially bought the property to clone orchids, but vines got the upper hand. Turramurra's first vintage was released in 1996 and immediately started earning accolades with, to date, a multitude of trophies and medals to their credit. Britain's 'Decanter' magazine voted their '98 cabernet 'best new release'.

All Turramurra Estate wines are characterized by their excellent balance and elegance, designed to enhance, not subdue, food flavours and augment the cheese and olive snacks available at the cellar door. All wines made at Turramurra are produced from 100 percent estate grown grapes. Their varieties include sauvignon blanc, chardonnay, cabernet sauvignon, pinot noir and shiraz.

Wildcroft Estate is blessed with an exceptional location. Tucked away among the picturesque hills of Red Hill South on Stanleys Road, number 46 on our wine-touring map. The estate has 10 acres under vine and produces excellent varieties of pinot noir, chardonnay, shiraz and cabernet sauvignon. Owners Devendra and Shashi Singh provide the passion and the labour for Wildcroft. Their love of wine was nurtured when they acquired the renowned Siddhartha Indian Restaurant in Frankston and led to the purchase of the established vineyard in 1998. The previous owners named the property. At the time of acquisition they found themselves in possession of a half-constructed house and a few wild-growing grapes. Like its name Wildcroft was untamed and uncultivated. By the time the Singhs took over it provided all that a budding vigneron could hope for.

Shashi has a master's degree in chemistry and at the moment is studying for a Batchelor in Viticulture at Charles Sturt University. She cares for the vineyard with knowledge and dedication. The 14-year old vines produce a consistently high quality harvest. Minimal chemical inputs and no irrigation results in low yielding vines that produce intensely flavoured fruit. Philip Jones at Bass Phillip crafts the wines in the traditional way using wild yeast, no fining and no filtration. The estate pinot noir is an intense earthy wine with plenty of structure; the shiraz reveals white pepper heightened by red ripe fruits and spice; the cabernet sauvignon is well balanced with depth and power and the Chardonnay is rich and structured.

The cellar door is contained in the mud brick winery and is open Thursday through Sunday each week. It provides the perfect stage for the Singhs to introduce yet another of their passions, the aromatically rich Indian cuisine they are famous for. The menu at Café 98 offers modern cuisine with Indian and Middle Eastern influences that complement the Wildcroft wines. The atrium style restaurant brings nature indoors, offering indoor and deck seating that highlights a dreamy, wide expansive view over a vine-strewn landscape, across the valley floor to Western Port Bay. Devendra and Shashi have created a special ambiance in a vineyard where conventions are broken, and a new and exciting style is created: they dare to be different – this is their mantra.

Tucks Ridge

Turramurra Estate Vineyard

Wildcroft Estate

Willow Creek Vineyard is located in an awesome setting, nestling amid Merricks North's gently sloping hills, surrounded by the serene sanity of Peninsula wine country. The property is easily discovered on Balnarring Road, number 47 on our wine-touring map. The vineyard was established in 1989 on land that had served as an orchard and a dairy farm. It is part of an old property dating back to the 1870s. History hovers in the air; the 40-acre estate still contains the original red brick homestead and barns that were part of Willow Creek Farm. The new buildings blend in: built of red brick, they have been designed to mimic history and the original historic outhouses and homestead have been incorporated into the working vineyard.

The Melbourne based families of Knowles, Ball and Harris purchased Willow Creek in 1988, with a vision to mould the mesmerising property into a top-flight winery. During the initial years wine was processed off-site. The vineyard's first vintage was launched in 1992, presenting 1991 varieties of chardonnay and cabernet sauvignon with tastings held in the newly opened cellar door that was contained in the old tractor shed. The vineyard became a winery in 1998 and, with the building of the barrel room, cellar and restaurant that same year, has steadily become one of the Peninsula's preferred destinations.

The Barrel Hall is a grand affair; the rafters in the ceiling came from a munitions factory in Tottenham (near Footscray) and date back to the 1920s. The hall currently stores 400 barrels, each with a total capacity of 228 litres. The timber used to make the barrels comes from the legendary forests of central France. Making barrels is an art: the timber is split, not sawn, into staves, stacked and seasoned for up to three years, then hand-crafted by French coopers and imported into Australia complete. Cellar Door staff can arrange personalised tours of the barrel room, vineyard and winery.

The Cellar Door and tasting room is now a far cry from the old tractor shed. It is an elegantly decorated, wood furbished, gleaming reception area, with indoor windows that make a feature of the Barrel Hall. It exudes a welcome befitting the state-of-the-art winery that it represents. Set on a slightly lower level than the restaurant, it leads through massive glass doors to a secluded veranda overlooking the vine-striped slopes. Less formal lunches and snacks can be ordered from the deck, or from within the cosy comfort of the Cellar Door that has an open fire for winter warmth. The food is scrumptiously prepared and swiftly served, chosen from a seasonal blackboard menu. An investment cellar is a new addition to the winery and visits are by invitation only. The Private Cellar holds some exclusive wines and is heaven for serious wine collectors.

Willow Creek did not take long to become a major player on the Peninsula wine scene. The winery's 1994 pinot noir brought the first of many accolades by winning two trophies; this was the winery's first vintage of the popular variety. The estate produces wines made from 100 percent estate grown fruit.

Winemaker and general manager, Phil Kerney, knows the industry inside out on all levels; he has been with Willow Creek Vineyard since 2001. It is obvious that he has succeeded in his brief, to provide the best wine possible from the vineyard. Phil has extensive vintage and production experience, both locally and overseas. He is sharply focused, totally driven with an uncompromising philosophy and has moved quickly to refine and enhance the Willow Creek style. Crop levels, vineyard practises and wine making methods are determined by one criterion only – optimum quality.

From the 2000 vintage onward the new 'Tulum' reserve range of pinot noir, chardonnay and single vintage brut sparkling will be top-drawer. Willow Creek Pinot Noir has rightly earned a reputation as being among the finest produced, characterised by deep colour, complex dark fruit and spice aromas with a rich, firm, long and finely structured palate. The estate is proud of their excellent variety of this, the most unforgettable of wines. The elegant cabernet sauvignon has cool red fruit, cedar, coffee and blackcurrant notes, supple structure and refined texture. Known to be a difficult variety for the region, Willow Creek's cabernet is unique in its rich, ripe style.

The exclusive Tulum Chardonnay is produced from the estate's oldest vines. The wine is barrel-fermented and matured; it is released only in exceptional vintages and provides a wine of depth and intensity. Phil believes in 'wild' fermentation and takes great care to avoid unnatural intervention in the winemaking process, ensuring Willow Creek wines show the individual character of the vineyard site.

The invitation from Willow Creek is simple – come up the winding driveway, relax, enjoy the view, sip sensational wine and dine on world-class cuisine. The estate is an anthem to good taste and Salix Restaurant is one of the property's main attractions. It is ranked among the most exciting eateries on the Mornington Peninsula, where the food is as impressive as the view. Floor to ceiling windows provide uninterrupted vision of the valley and hills, decorated by parade lines of vines that march over the slopes. Operated by executive chefs Michael and Rebecca Cook, the restaurant has earned a reputation for excellence with many awards to its name, being mentioned repeatedly in the Age Good Food Guide and gaining the coveted chef's hat in 2003.

Inspiration gained by the Cooks from extensive overseas travel gives the regional cuisine various influences, crossing between French and Asian with neither dominating the flavour. Dishes are liberated by fresh local produce, including Flinders mussels and Red Hill cheeses. The menu is redesigned on a regular basis, each dish calculated to enhance and be enhanced by Willow Creek Wines. Lunch is available every day of the week in this special place and dinner is served Friday and Saturday nights. Daytime vistas from the restaurant are exceptional but sunsets are overpowering, with ribbons of colour streaking the sky, creating a scintillating light spectacular. The 70-seat restaurant provides the perfect venue for special functions, weddings and celebratory dinners.

Many special occasions are attributed to the winery. Degustation 10-course banquets accompanied by superior vintage wines are held in the winery, surrounded by the enormous stainless steel vats. The food is matched to the wine and the banquets are enlightening, enriching and an edibly extravagant experience.

The aim is to develop Willow Creek, as close as possible, into the equivalent of a top-flight French chateau, starting on a scale of best and very good and heading into the stratosphere – it has certainly taken a gigantic step towards this goal!

Situated on Tucks Road, Main Ridge, number 48 on our wine-touring map, in the heart of the Mornington Peninsula, Yrsa's Vineyard (pronounced Irsa's) is an easy one-hour drive from the outskirts of Melbourne. As you leave the Mornington Peninsula Freeway and start the journey towards the ridge, departing the tremendous vista of the bay and the city and turn down the gentle gravel road that leads to the vineyard, so too does your head and heart shrug off the confines of metropolis life. It's not hard to imagine what drew owners Marianne and Stephen Stern, who purchased the property in 1993, inexorably to this area that weaves its own spell, and to the property that is a small patch of heaven. The vineyard was established in 1994 and is named after the lady from whom the Sterns acquired the estate. She in turn was named after Yrsa, Queen of Sweden, born in 565, whose story is told in the Norse sagas.

At Yrsa's, grapes grown on the meticulously hand-pruned vines, growing on the gently undulating slopes of the estate, are given the attention they deserve. The clones for the vines were carefully chosen, with several parcels imported from France to match the local climatic and soil conditions. The harvest is carefully hand-picked, to better allow for small lot winemaking using traditional winemaking techniques to bring each vintage of wine to its fullest potential. The 30-acre property contains 14 glorious acres of vineyard. It is planted on the rich red clay soil of Main Ridge, responsible for so much of the character and strength of the wine, oriented with a perfect east-north-easterly aspect, ensuring ample ripening sun. The vineyard consists of almost equal plantings of the trademark chardonnay and pinot noir, for which this region is so well known. Chicory is planted between the rows of vines to guard against excessive vigour of the vines. When in bloom the chicory coats the hillside in a hazy, silvery blue mantle that bestows an old-world atmosphere to the tranquil scene.

The property stretches down to Stony Creek, whose clear spring-fed waters provide the vineyard with its own water supply. Irrigation is used sparingly, except in times of drought, as soil moisture is closely monitored. Yrsa's is not a commercial undertaking in the mould of most vineyards. The owners, managers and staff are all wine enthusiasts and this is borne out by the implementation of the philosophy of producing high quality, ultra-premium wines, (now being offered by some of Melbourne's leading restaurants) rather than focusing on producing quantities for commercial purposes.

The emphasis is purely on quality at every level. Cellar door tastings are very welcome, albeit by appointment only, which thus creates a more personal affair at Yrsa's, in keeping with the philosophy of the vineyard. Tasting guests are seated on a long antique table in the elevated tasting room, affording a splendid view of the vineyard and the ocean in the distance. Guests are treated to a history and wine crafting of each vintage and offered palate-cleansing local cheeses and spring water between varieties. The vineyard wines are presented under two labels, 'Yrsa's Vineyard' and 'Scion', with the former already available in the UK and Italy plus selected Melbourne restaurants, as well as at the cellar door.

Yrsa's Vineyard Chardonnay 2001 is pale yellow/gold showing excellent pristine clarity, lovely aromas of citrus with peach and nectarine stone fruit enveloped with cashew barrel characters, the taste building in the mouth with a long lingering flavour, all this enveloping a spine of fine acids to cleanse the palate. Yrsa's Vineyard Pinot Noir 2001 is a bright cherry red to crimson with aromas of cherry, strawberry and hints of plum, with cherry stone and undergrowth to add spice to the palate. Nuances of mocha and smoky/charry barrel characters add lift on the finish.

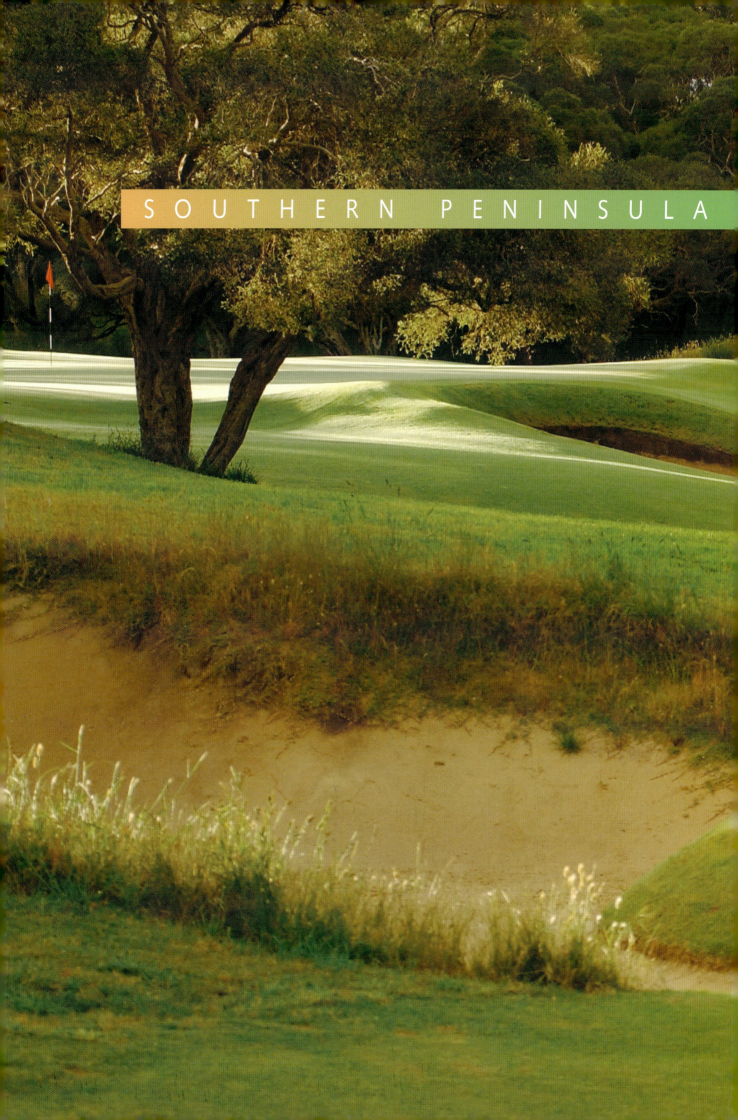

SOUTHERN PENINSULA

Southern Peninsula Listings

SAFETY BEACH: Valley Resort P.196/252. Bluestone Cottages P196/252.

DROMANA: Stellas Dromana Hotel P.198-199/252. Dromana Hub Shopping Centre. P.198-199/252. Dromana Red Hill RSL P.198-200/252. Heronswood P.200-201/252.

McCRAE: McCrae Homestead P.202-203/252.

ROSEBUD: Mornington Peninsula Getaways P.204/252. Amberlee Family Park P.204/252. Nazaaray Beach House P.204-205/253. Rosebud Motel P 206/253.

CAPE SCHANCK / FINGAL: Cape Schanck Shearwater Resort P.206-207/253.

FINGAL: Ace-Hi Ranch P.208-209/253. Ace-Hi Wildlife Park P.208-209/253. Mizu Spa P210-211/253.

SOUTHERN PENINSULA GOLFING FEATURE: Dunes Golf Links P.212-213/253. Eagle Ridge P.212-213/253. Rosebud Country Club P.214-215/253. Rosebud Park Public Golf Club P.214-215/253. Nepean Country Club Resort P.216-217/253. Moonah Links, Peppers @ Moonah P.218-219/253. Shearwater Cape Schanck Golf Club P.220-221/253. Sorrento Golf Club P.220-221/253.

RYE: Rye Sand Sculpting Championships P222-225. Hilltonia Homestead P.224/254. The Rye Hotel P.224-225/254. Gunnamatta Equestrian Centre P.224-225/254.

BLAIRGOWRIE: The Boathouse Resort Motel P.226/254. Coast 2827 Restaurant. P.226/254. Aspects Gallery P.226-227/254.

SORRENTO: Hotel Sorrento P230-231/254. Oceanic Whitehall Guest House P231-232/254. Antipodes Bookshop and Gallery P.232-233/254. First Settlement Gallery P.232-233/254. Peninsula Searoad Transport P.232-234/254. The Wooden Boat Shop P.234-235/254. Moonraker Dolphin Charters P.236-237/254. Polperro Dolphin Swims P.236-237/254.

PORTSEA: Portsea Hotel P238/254.

MORNINGTON PENINSULA NATIONAL PARK P.238-240.

THE PARK AT POINT NEPEAN P.240-241/254.

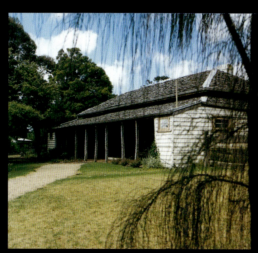

National Trust McCrae Homestead, McCrae

Southern Peninsula opening page: Moonah Links Golf Course, home of the 2003 Australian Open
Centre-spread background: View to Whitecliffs from Cameron Bight foreshore.

Safety Beach is situated four kilometres north east of Dromana in Tassells and Dunns Creek valley. It sits at the beginning of a three-kilometre stretch of gentle coastline running between Arthurs Seat and Mount Martha on the Kangerong Basin. The small community received its name from Tasmanian cattle farmer John Aitken, whose ship ran aground in 1836. The fact that, with the help of some local Aborigines, he was able to save his cargo gave rise to the name. The area's first settler was Edward Hobson, who held a grazing licence in 1837. In recent years a revegetation programme has glamorised the foreshore and the settlement has gone through a period of growth complemented by attractive residential housing. A proposal to build a marina (Martha Cove) will showcase an already attractive seaside resort.

The Safety Beach Sailing Club and the Australian Coast Guard are situated on the beach, along with adequate car parking, picnic facilities, play area and a boat ramp. A two-kilometre return walking track traverses a shingle-strewn beach to the foot of the red cliffs. The protected cove is popular for boating, wind surfing and water skiing.

Safety Beach Country Club on Country Club Drive was developed in 1989 as a nine-hole golf course. Open to the public, the redesigned club now offers an easy walking, unique and challenging 18-hole course that winds through the estate with 500 mature palm trees and 3,000 native trees recently planted. There are 26 beautiful lakes with myriad bird life and views to Arthurs Seat and Mt Martha.

Valley Resort is positioned on the first hole of the golf course, surrounded by the environs that make the country club one of the most visited on the Peninsula. The one, two and three-bedroom, self-contained apartments have been superbly designed by Hoban Hynes Architects of Mornington to reflect the stylish location. They are connected to the country club by a walkway and are protected by sculptured gardens that showcase native trees and bushes side by side with exotics. During summer the feathery golden leaves of Robinia trees add lustre to the palm-studded surrounds.

Your host, Patricia Renouf, built the apartments to complement the vast array of outstanding sporting facilities currently available at Safety Beach Country Club. The development of the luxury up-market accommodation has ensured that the package is now complete. Each unit has been meticulously designed and furnished and includes a quality spa bathroom with glass roof. The units feature a separate lounge and dining room and can sleep between two to six people.

Although situated only seven minutes' walk from a picturesque swimming beach, the complex offers guests the alternative comfort of a solar-heated swimming pool. The attractive, paved pool area also houses a barbecue for lazy relaxed meals. A continental breakfast basket allows guests to arrange their day to suit themselves, although the resort is renowned for its innovative packages, which can be put together on request, allowing guests to make the most of all the Peninsula's attractions.

Bluestone Homestead on Pickings Road is a four-Star retreat that caters for travellers looking for unique bed and breakfast accommodation. It is at the centre of everything – adjoining the Valley Country Club looking onto the lush fairways of the golf course and only a few minutes' walk from a sandy beach. Glynis and daughter Gayner, ably supported by husband John, host this unusual property. It had been a lifelong dream of Glynis and John's to run a bed and breakfast and for the past four years they have concentrated their efforts on providing one of the best properties that the Peninsula has to offer.

Built of darkly hued bluestone, the cottages' colour acts as the perfect foil for the surrounding greenery. Set back from the main house, the cosy cottages are meticulously furnished and decorated. Breakfast is served within the cottages, or for groups in the guest lounge that is contained within the main house. The property's original owner who built the homestead was an avid collector, and his obsession manifests itself in the many highly topical, original fixtures, historic fittings and recycled timber within the main building.

The buildings are surrounded by three-acres of informal gardens with shady corners that ensure a relaxing respite. The swimming pool is a feature of the property, set in an Eden-like oasis edged by a gazebo that makes the perfect breakfast nook or end-of-day resting place. The whole Bluestone Cottages' experience is one of inviting comfort and welcoming hospitality.

Left: View from cliffs at Safety Beach towards Mt Martha
Right: Views of Safety Beach, Dromana

Dromana is an exceptionally pretty town beneath the lofty peaks of Arthurs Seat and Mount Martha. Located 70 kilometres from Melbourne, it is a thriving beach resort, home to over 7,000 people. The wooded slopes of the twin peaks are peppered with residential homes that overlook the bay. The beach rests placidly at the foot of Arthurs Seat, its glittering shore kissed by lips of foam from gentle waves.

Originally named Hobsons Flat, the fledgling community was renamed Dromana in the late 1830s during the short-lived gold rush. The name is thought to mimic that of a town in Ireland honouring the many Irish miners in the area at that time. Like all the Peninsula towns, the building of a 465-metre pier in 1873 opened up the area to trade and visitors. By 1881 Dromana had become an established holiday destination. The pier was the second longest to be built on the bay and helped establish Dromana as the commercial hub for the area.

Camping plays a big role in Dromana's summer visitor statistics. The scenic foreshore comes alive during holiday periods with crowds of happy campers enjoying the laid back atmosphere, revelling in the 'roll out of bed onto the beach' syndrome. The town is ideal for family vacations, with picnic shelters, play grounds and barbecues all close at hand. Wooden and sand boat ramps along the foreshore give easy boat access to the bay.

Dromana's scenic position lends itself well to long meandering walks in the vibrant fresh air. The Two Bays Walking Track is a mighty 30-kilometre signposted trek that follows a bush track from Dromana to Cape Schanck lighthouse, leading through eucalypt groves, 200-year-old grass trees and fern gullies. It can be explored in sections. A hike of 9 kilometres return leads to the summit of Arthurs Seat. The track passes through the Seawinds property. It climbs 500 metres through wooded grassland and open forest, passing rocky outcrops and providing heart-stopping vistas of the bay that seemingly melds with the horizon in a shimmering illusion. The signed Kings Falls Circuit Walk leads off the track at the summit of Arthurs Seat. This walk can be accessed without walking all the way from Dromana – simply follow Arthurs Seat Road to the summit and turn right into Purves Road then right into Waterfall Gully Road. The track's entrance is via a small gravel car park.

The town's shopping strip runs along Point Nepean Road. Outdoor markets are held every Sunday morning.

Dromana Hub Shopping Centre is part of the local community's daily life. The centre has a million-dollar view, being situated directly opposite the beach; it is creatively designed with a seaside persona. The centre occupies one of the town's historic sites; erected on the original location of the 50-room Belmont Guest House, built by James Chapman in the 1890s. It was a familiar Dromana landmark and run by the Chapman family until the 1950s. The large site has provided a spacious car park surrounded by some of Dromana's most utilized shops. Located approximately 70 kilometres south east of Melbourne CBD situated between O'Donohue and Pier Streets the Dromana Hub is an institution in the Dromana area and surrounding environs and has been a part of the community for 20 years.

The original shopping centre underwent substantial renovations in 2002 and now can boast some of the most convenient shopping in the area anchored by one of only seven of the 'World's Best' Ritchies supermarkets. The centre really is your one stop convenient shopping experience, with over 19 specialty retailers. Dromana Hub is a completely different, relaxed shopping experience, you can do your grocery shopping at one of the world's best supermarkets, load up the car, then grab some fish and chips from The Lucky Catch and a bun from either of the bakeries and head to the foreshore directly across the road to relax and unwind.

Stella's Dromana Hotel opposite the Dromana foreshore in the heart of the shopping area has a past, a present and a future. It is a well-loved feature of the landscape, built on a site that has contained a hotel since the 1870s. The oldest part of the present hotel is a Canadian-style building constructed in the 1920s that still retains all of its style and grace.

The hotel contains three acres of entertainment. Its rooms are full of character that is reminiscent of an old English pub with bric-a-brac and décor to match. Rae and Leila Stella became part of the hotel's history in 1986 when they purchased the hotel and have added their unique brand of old-world atmosphere. The pub has seen many owners come and go and has been owned by its share of 'Stars'. Perhaps the most famous in modern times was John Coleman, Essendon Football Club's legendary full forward who was licensee in the 1960s and early 1970s. One of Australia's greatest prime ministers, John Curtin, spent part of his youth in the pub during his father's ownership of it.

The rambling old building has had new sections added that blend in with the old and offers patrons a choice of four bars, a large bistro area attractive gaming room, a TAB that is open each day until the last race and a terrace overlooking the foreshore. A large atrium that will seat 200 is to be unveiled in the summer of 2003; it will add a sparkling new dimension to the premises. The tavern bar is located in the oldest part of the hotel. It is a comfortable area where seating spills out onto the footpath, lighter café-style meals are served and an open fireplace is set in a magnificent feature wall of Dromana granite. The bistro's three dining areas offer fine old-fashioned service with all the culinary delights of a five-Star restaurant without the associated price tag. The menu offers an extensive range to suit all tastes and features local seafood, pasta and woodfired pizzas, complemented by an extensive wine list of both local and other Australian wines. The hotel provides an ideal venue for weddings and celebratory functions for up to 120 guests and a variety of weekly entertainment is featured at the hotel, ranging from classical jazz to modern pop.

Recently refurbished hotel rooms within the historic hotel are spacious, light, bright and airy. They are full of old-world charm and character, furnished in period style with magnificent en suites. New townhouses and motel units have recently been added to the hotel's accommodation completing an all-round character-filled holiday destination.

Above: Dromana/Red Hill RSL Club
Right: Fishing from Dromana Pier at sunset.   *Inset–* Historic Stellas Dromana Hotel

Dromana and Red Hill RSL can be found on the corner of Gibson and Noel Streets, it is an intimate club with a friendly, welcoming attitude. The Dromana chapter was originally established in 1946 and the clubs of Dromana and Red Hill amalgamated in 1984. The club is all about community, immersed in RSL traditions with memorabilia from Australia's military campaigns displayed around the walls. Visitors are made welcome and invited to make use of the club's facilities. The only Victorian chapter of the 'Old Bastards Association' holds its meetings at the club, a caring association set up to help the community.

A comfortable restaurant serves bistro-style quality meals at reasonable prices and is open seven days a week. A large function room is the scene of weekly bingo games and regular entertainment. It is ideal for private functions and meetings, catering for up to 200 guests. The Quarter Deck is a popular oasis in the warmer weather, providing a secluded, palm-decorated enclosed outdoor area, perfect for a quiet drink or al fresco dining. There is always something going on in this cosy club and you can always try your hand at a game of pool or your luck in the small casino room or a quality ale in the members' bar.

The National Trust registered property Heronswood is one of the area's most treasured attractions, located on La Trobe Parade. Not only a historic house, it has been brought to prominence by the cultivation of an extensive garden that is a horticultural masterpiece and home of the renowned 'Diggers Garden Club', established by owners Clive and Penny Blazey in 1978. The club is Australia's largest gardening club, helping gardeners from Hobart to Cairns grow better vegetables and flowers. The Diggers Club has grown to include many thousands of members who gain the benefit from Clive and Penny's two properties – Heronswood, and St Erth in Blackwood, Victoria. Visitors are welcome to both gardens (fees apply) and Heronswood house is open to the public over a four-day weekend in November; during the Melbourne Cup carnival.

Professor William Edward Hearn, who was one of four founding professors of the University of Melbourne, built Heronswood. It was completed in 1871, from a design by Edward Latrobe Bateman. The imposing house has many interesting aspects. Its position on the slopes of Arthurs Seat facing the bay is as close to perfect as one can get, with spectacular views of the bay from its elevated location. Its asymmetrical shape has pleasing contrasts constructed of local granite with southern peninsula limestone dressings and bell-shaped Welsh slate roofs, the design is termed Gothic Revival, describing the shape of the windows, porch and other openings. Originally used as the kitchen, the drop slab timber cottage sitting adjacent the main house was built earlier in 1864. It now houses the property's garden shop, selling plants, seeds and gardening accoutrements with helpful friendly staff who are knowledgeable in all things horticultural.

Clive and Penny have followed Professor Hearn's example and constructed a rammed earth thatched cottage at the rear of the property using natural local materials. Earth from Arthurs Seat was gathered for the walls, and water reeds from the Tootgarook wetlands for the thatched roof. It was the first time in decades that a thatched building had been constructed in Victoria, and it is believed to be the only one of its kind in Australia; the nearest thatchers were located in New Zealand. The cottage houses 'The Thatched Earth Harvest Café' that serves, as much as possible, regional, seasonal, organic food, with flavoursome effect. Australian Gourmet Traveller awarded the café the Jaguar Award for Excellence in 2000. A garden surrounding the café grows many of the organic herbs and vegetables used in the tasty dishes. The plants are picked straight from the garden so that food served in the café is truly fresh.

Heronswood has three main vegetable gardens, two perennial borders, an annual border and a wide expanse of verdant lawns that feature a horizon pool and are decorated by age-old trees. An example is a 130-year-old Moreton Bay Fig that dominates an area at the rear of the house. Visitors enter the property through a dry-climate garden, which shows how to attain a stunning effect with plants that require little if any water. The Blazeys like to experiment and surprise with colour harmonies and unusual plant combinations. They employ the gardens to trial heirlooms and to test the suitability of new varieties for the Australian climate, to supply seeds for listing in the Diggers Club catalogues, and also to provide organic food for the café.

Heronswood's herbaceous perennial border is the pinnacle of artistic and horticultural achievement that is rarely attempted in other gardens. The border peaks during the summer when it becomes a fascinating tapestry of texture and colour. The cut turf parterre is a productive and ornamental garden designed as a wheel in six wedge-shaped segments. Planted with vegetables it shows an innovative and decorative way to grow crops. The cottage annual border uses harmonious colours and ornamental vegetables and the spring and summer border flower from January to March. The perennial border flowers from December to March: its waves of flowers gently edge the historic house with a profusion of pastel shades in a heart-easing display. A garden is like a theatre that each year presents a four-act play, featuring many different actors. Spring, summer, autumn and winter all have their stars and Heronswood contributes the perfect stage.

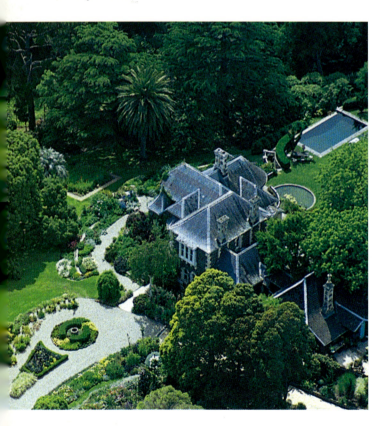

Left & right: The National Trust registered Heronswood, at Dromana

McCrae flourishes within the Arthurs Seat State Park between Dromana and Rosebud, cradled in the foothills. The granite outcrop of Anthony's Nose acts as a demarcation line and gives McCrae a distinctiveness that's all its own. It effectively breaks the long sweep of shoreline stretching from Martha Point. Built in 1854 on the tip of Anthony's Nose, the McCrae Eastern Shore Lighthouse was originally a beacon held within a wooden structure. The wooden frame was moved to Arthurs Seat and used as a lookout tower when it was replaced in 1883. Its successor was built in Birmingham and constructed on site. Made of externally braced riveted steel, it stands 33.5 metres high – the tallest of Port Phillip Bay's lighthouses. A total of 120 steps on an internal spiral staircase leads up the narrow structure to the lantern room that originally contained a dioptric catadioptric and halo photal lens system. The lighthouse is easily accessible, sitting directly opposite the MaCrae shopping strip. Its light guided traffic on the bay until 1994, at which time it was decommissioned and is now owned by the McCrae Foreshore Committee.

Attractive houses cling to the steep western slopes of Arthurs Seat, adding to the appeal of the village. The foreshore reserve contains a shoreline with a gentle profile, endowed with glistening golden sandy beaches and calm rippling water sheltered by a tree-lined foreshore.

The initial McCrae settlement was an independent town named West Dromana; it evolved from the lighthouse keepers and their families who worked a four-week on and off roster tending the light. The hamlet sprang up close to the original pastoral run that was awarded to Andrew and Georgiana McCrae. It was appropriate that the settlement should, in 1934, be renamed McCrae, after the McCrae homestead that survives on the slopes of Arthurs Seat. It pays to explore the highways and byways around Rosebud, there is many an exclusive gem tucked away down a side street, like Gordon Glass on the Nepean Highway, West Rosebud. This innovative company will be situated at this address until the middle of 2004 when they will relocate to Red Hill (see Hinterland section).

The McCrae Homestead on Beverley Road has been fully restored by the National Trust. Built in 1844, it was one of the first homesteads on the Mornington Peninsula and is now one of the oldest surviving historic buildings of its style in Victoria. Constructed with hand-made nails brought from England, hewn slabs of stringy-bark walls and messmate floors plus a stringy bark shingle roof, it was home to Andrew and Georgiana McCrae and their eight children. The homestead was built at the base of the mountain surrounded by the 5,120-hectare property that they named Arthur's Seat Cattle Run, which included the summit of the mountain.

Georgiana was born in 1804, the illegitimate daughter of the Marquis of Huntly, later the fifth and last Duke of Gordon and Jane Graham, daughter of a Northumberland farmer. It was the Gordon family tradition to acknowledge and provide for their numerous illegitimate children so Georgiana was highly educated. Raised by her mother, she attended a convent school in a shabby-genteel suburb of London, run by noble French ladies who had fled the French revolution.

Georgiana became an accomplished musician, artist and diarist. She studied art with John Varley the watercolourist, John Glover, Dominic Serres and the miniaturist Charles Hayter. At the age of 12 her painting, 'View of a Church', was exhibited at the Royal Academy. She lived for some time in Gordon Castle but was living in Edinburgh, supporting herself with her painting, when she married Andrew in 1830. The homestead's detailed restoration has been carried out thanks to her descriptive diaries and detailed sketches. Andrew was a distant cousin of Georgina's; when they married he was a young lawyer with prospects. He travelled to Australia in 1838, followed by Georgina in 1841.

The historic home is furnished with the McCraes' personal belongings and most of their furniture, including the 70 pieces of luggage that travelled to Melbourne with Georgina on the 'Argyle'. The placement of the furniture was made possible by the detailed floor plan of the homestead drawn by Georgina. Family portraits and many reproductions of sketches and watercolours meticulously created by her hang in the museum attached to the visitors centre. The historic couple's descendants have generously donated the household items and artefacts displayed in the homestead and museum. In the decades following the McCraes' departure in 1851, the property went through many changes. The Arthurs's Seat property returned to McCrae ownership in 1961, purchased by George Gordon McCrae, Georgina and Andrew's great-grandson. On George's death in 1970, his son Andrew McCrae sold the property to the National Trust of Victoria.

The modern reception centre that fronts the property was opened in 1996; it contains the only Victorian National Trust property museum. Expertly displayed are many interesting artefacts of the McCrae family's lives and the era they lived in. A glass cabinet contains Georgina's wedding ring and Andrew's elegant pocket-watch, another her first writing book, written in French. In yet another is a child's kilt made by Georgina from a swath of very rare, ancient tartan that was worn at the battle of Culloden – thereafter hidden, as the wearing of the tartan was outlawed in Scotland. The entire property is a delightful experience, surrounded by restful gardens with some of the property's original trees planted by the McCraes. It is run by a team of dedicated, knowledgeable volunteers headed by Lorraine White and is open to the public. The homestead and the museum are a fascinating study, providing a window into the life led by some of the area's founding families and, unlike most historic houses one visits, would be totally recognisable to the original owners, Georgiana and Andrew McCrae.

Left & right: Interior and grounds of historic McCrae Homestead

Rosebud was originally named Banksia Point, acknowledging the profusion of banksia that covers the foreshore. The town was first established in the 1850s and prospered as a fishing village. It was not until a shipwreck in 1855 that the settlement became known as Rosebud. The 'Rosebud' was a two-masted hermaphrodite (square-rigged forward and schooner-rigged aft) vessel. She came to grief off the coast and was washed over the sandbank, coming to rest at Rosebud in June 1855. There is a plaque near Durham Place marking the exact spot.

The locals salvaged her cargo of damask and household goods, with much of her timber going into town buildings. The ship's carcass was a familiar sight on the coastline for many years, giving rise to the declaration, "I'm going down to the Rosebud," that soon became, "I'm going to Rosebud."

Rosebud did not grow as quickly as the neighbouring towns, mainly because of the lack of a deep-water jetty that prevented steamers from docking. A jetty built in 1888 catered mostly for fishing boats and did not reach the deep offshore water. A replacement built in 1940 in a new location opposite Rosebud Parade still did not access the deeper water. Not until 1966 when a new pier was built, utilising the 1888 location, was a longer structure designed giving larger ships and ferries entrée.

In the 1920s and 1930s Rosebud became a favourite camping destination, with Melbourne's families taking advantage of the magnificent beach. The town's forefathers endorsed this image by developing the foreshore to cater for the holiday season's visitors. This forward planning has resulted in Rosebud remaining to this day a much-loved camping haven and all-round holiday getaway. The foreshore and beach are shielded by masses of banksia, sheoak and tea-tree. The beach is further enhanced by sand bars that stretch 200 metres from the shore, providing an idyllic shallow bathing spot.

The town has two shopping areas, Rosebud and Rosebud West. The original shopping area extends along the Nepean Highway in no particular order, brimming with seaside flavour. In recent times Rosebud has found itself identified by the swag of golf courses making use of the nearby picturesque hinterland. (See southern Peninsula golfing segment.)

Mornington Peninsula Getaways is an accommodation reservation service located on the Mornington Peninsula, servicing most areas adjacent to Port Phillip Bay. They specialise in properties on the Mornington Peninsula, Western Port Bay encompassing the wine and golfing regions and across the bay to include selected Bellarine Peninsula properties.

Robyn Chipman saw the need for a central booking service and has developed the business, which began five years ago, drawing on experience gained in handling her own holiday apartments. Thirty years on the Peninsula and a background in property development gave her the intimate knowledge of the area and solid base needed for the business. The free service is designed for people who are too busy, or just not sure where to begin in organising their accommodation requirements, whether it be for a single night, a week or two or even a month or more. Robyn and her friendly, well-informed staff have intimate understanding of all the properties listed in their service and have a large selection of luxurious yet affordable accommodation to make any getaway a memorable experience.

For those on a budget or holidaying with children or pets, they offer a selection of over 280 properties, so it makes sense to let them do the work and organise your stress-free, perfect getaway.

Amberlee Family Park is the preferred holiday address for many Australian families. The Neary family purchased the vacant land over 20 years ago and have expertly designed and built the park to fit the criteria gained from their experience in the industry over many years.

The quality accommodation nestles in a natural bush setting with little or no concrete in sight, surrounded by 20 acres bounded by Jetty and Old Cape Schanck Roads. A variety of lodgings are on offer from powered sites, Family loft villas with spas and three-Star en suite cabins to deluxe four-Star en suite cabins. The on-site facilities are first-class and include a games room. All villas and cabins are self-contained, purpose built and designed to give visitors space, comfort and privacy in a totally relaxed holiday atmosphere.

The caravan and tent sites are well grassed and there is five acres in the park set aside as a personal recreation area for children's activities. Parents have never had it so good; they can unwind in the peace of the surrounding environs while kids make the most of the adventure playground, parkland, tennis court, trampolines, mini golf and a large sparkling pool. The youngsters are even invited to bring their own bikes. The well-established park has everything and more needed for an enjoyable 'stay-put' vacation – or, for the more inquisitive, it is situated close to all the other attractions that the Peninsula is famous for.

Nazaaray Beach House on Murray Anderson Road is a quaint holiday house that belies its humble exterior. The three plus bedroom home sleeps up to six adults or an extended family. It has been meticulously renovated to a level seldom seen in rental properties. Owners, the Ghumman family, have taken the best ideas gained from around the Peninsula and incorporated them into the property, which opened in 2001. The holiday home is 350 metres from the swimming beach and shopping precinct of Rosebud. Fully self-contained with open wood fired or panel reverse cycle heaters, it's perfect for cosy getaways all year round.

A gleaming wooden floor in the dining area is a feature of the cottage with French doors that open onto a deck, the ideal place for al fresco dining under the trees in the warm summer months. The main bedroom features a queen size bed and large adjoining bathroom that is specifically designed to suit those with a disability.

House-trained pets are welcome for those who can't bear to leave their best friends behind. A large secure back yard is the perfect place for playtime with pets and children. Visitors' comments confirm the cottage as a great choice for any vacation.

Rosebud Motel on the Nepean Highway is located opposite the Capel Sound foreshore at Rosebud West. It emits a bright relaxed atmosphere with its painted façade resembling the bright colours of the iconic beach boxes that line the Peninsula foreshore.

Above: The McCrae Eastern Shore Lighthouse
Right: The Rosebud Sound Shell on the Rosebud Foreshore Reserve

Family owned and operated by Don and Kerry Thompson, the motel is located among colourful gardens and boasts twelve modern ground floor rooms incorporating one spa room and two family units that include extras. A grassed picnic and barbecue area equipped with tables and benches surrounds a sparkling pool and a children's play area. The atmosphere is casual and relaxed and the close proximity to the beach makes it an ideal vacation spot.

Next door to the motel, Rosebud House is available for two families or groups of up to eight guests. It is a fully self-contained three-bedroom house with all linen and cooking facilities supplied and includes a dishwasher, microwave and equipped laundry. There is a large spa in the main bathroom and spacious garden area with an outdoor barbecue. The open-plan living area is comfortably furnished with a wood fire for winter warmth. Its nearness to the beach and recent renovations has made this cottage a very desirable holiday address. Don and Kerry specialise in golfing packages that can utilise either of their properties and can be personally tailored to suit individual needs.

Cape Schanck Shearwater Resort is one of the area's best-kept secrets. Located on Boneo Road, Cape Schanck it is set among a landscape of contrasts, both sculptured and wild. The resort sits high upon the rolling escarpments overlooking the Bass Strait, providing a magnificent setting for either a serene and relaxing interlude or an invigorating and entertaining escape.

The luxurious accommodation is as wonderful as the views that stretch over the coastal dunes and golf course to St Andrews and Gunnamatta beaches. Accommodation is available in spacious deluxe king size, terrace rooms, or self-contained two and four bedroom executive suites, all with private en suites and balconies. Every room has breathtaking views engineered to pamper and please. This is the place to watch the sun kiss the Peninsula good night, when evening writes its signature across the sky with charcoal fingers and vivid red and golden hues.

A visit to Shearwater can be whatever you make it – a power-packed adventure or an anthem to relaxation. Apart from being housed and having access to one of the area's premier championship 18-hole golf courses, guests can also indulge themselves in myriad leisure activities. The resort has an outdoor heated 12.5-metre lap pool and adjoining heated spa and sauna. In the recreation room next to the pool billiards and table tennis have their place and three artificial grass tennis courts provide an energetic alternative. Racquets and balls are complimentary. A volleyball course nestles within the golf course and mountain bikes and helmets are available for exploring the area.

A four-kilometre jogging or walking track encircling the grounds provides a scenic adventure. The resort abuts Point Nepean National Park, Victoria's most popular bushwalking destination and home to a vast array of native flora and fauna and great natural beauty. The management at Shearwater is protective of the environment, supporting its own Land for Wildlife scheme and environmental research through the Earthwatch Institute.

As part of the overall service, the resort has its very own on-site activities coordinator. The coordinator's role is a varied one: the task ranges from tour guide around the Mornington Peninsula with activities that include guided national park tours, beach tours, wine tastings and horse riding, as well as conducting beginners golf and tennis lessons, organising table tennis and billiard round robins and social volleyball and water polo tournaments for in-house guests. Other services include an on-site shuttle and disabled facilities.

Elegance, charm and gastronomic gems are the signature of Caspian via Corso, the resort's stylish restaurant. Open to both in-house guests and the general public, seven days a week, it serves indulgent buffet breakfasts, relaxing weekend lunches and sumptuous à la carte dinners. The menu favours the finest in local and seasonal produce, hand selected from the many market gardens and fisheries in the area. The cosmopolitan cuisine is complemented by a wine list featuring premium local and international wines.

Floor to ceiling windows sweep around the restaurant and bring the outdoors right up to the table with dazzling views over the verdant first and tenth holes of the Cape Schanck Golf Course and the surrounding spectacular coastline. Al fresco dining can be enjoyed on the paved patio and evening brings its own intimate ambiance to the restaurant with subdued lighting and easy listening music. In winter a large double-sided open fire is a stunning feature of the room. As an alternative, the Caddy Shack lounge is open daily for a more informal snack.

If as a company you are serious about your conferencing environment then you need look no further than The Shearwater Conferencing Centre. They follow strict criteria to provide a unique, stimulating and professional environment for staging a successful conference and related activities. Shearwater's dramatic natural setting belies its proximity to Melbourne as it is just over an hour's freeway drive from the eastern suburbs. It lies between the traditional resort areas and the emerging wine and food centres of the Mornington Peninsula, making it one of the most flexible and convenient for corporate retreats. The 'Terraces' wing conference area has drawn high praise from the industry, being hailed as, "the best thought out conference facility in Australia."

A range of conference areas allows for flexibility in numbers, from eight to 250, set up in arrangements of U-shape, theatre, classroom and boardroom. Eight syndicate rooms and a library workroom and two lounges are also available as breakout rooms. Full secretarial and state-of-the-art equipment and attention to detail ensure that conferences are efficiently organised, backed up by flexible on-site service. Conferences can be tailored to meet all needs for delegates on and off duty and corporate golf days are a speciality.

Left: Beach box pool at Rosebud Motel
Right: The Cape Schanck Shearwater Resort

The resort holds something for everyone. In the near future the resort will be extended to include a new hotel, bringing the resort's room capacity to 200, an enlarged conferencing centre, a produce centre with cellar door and therapeutic spa that will make use of the Peninsula's hot artesian mineral water. The additions will transform this quality get away into an indulgent escape.

Fingal coastal area is a wildly beautiful stretch of beach that runs across Selwyn Fault, a displacement of rock structures descending to Fingal Beach. The three-kilometre Fingal Coastal Circuit Walk is a flagged walk that traverses a route from the Cape Schanck side of the coast to the Point Nepean side, introducing wanderers to the contrasts between the rugged basalt cliffs of Cape Schanck and the softer sands and limestone stacks of Point Nepean. A steep descent leads to Fingal Beach: it is best traversed at low tide. In fact it is folly to attempt walks between Fingal and Gunnamatta beaches at any time other than low tide.

The environs have given birth to some amazing attractions. Among the most unique is an adventure park that includes Ace-Hi Beach Rides and Ace-Hi Wildlife Park, on Boneo Road at Cape Schanck, only minutes from Rosebud. Owned by partners Ron Neary and Tony Marks and run by Tony, it caters for families, the budget traveller, school camps and group retreats, with facilities to cater for 160 people and day visitors. The park is set within a 200-acre property of rolling green hills. A frontier town inspired by the Old Wild West with themed facilities is at its heart and includes two homesteads, log cabins, a general store, livery stables, a sheriff's office and jailhouse. Not to mention a chapel (adjacent its boot hill) a shearing shed, authentic covered wagons, an old red rattler railway carriage and a farm yard. It's a place that caters for excitement, great for a day or a week's entertainment!

Dormitory style accommodation within the country cabin and railway carriage are perfect for large groups while individuals are made cosy in the fully self-contained cabins. Although rustically picturesque, the cabins contain all of today's modern conveniences and the homesteads have magnificent views over the property. The sandstone chapel has been used for the odd wedding, but it actually houses the park's unique takeout 'licensed' restaurant. High vaulted ceilings with exposed wooden trusses and stained glass windows enhance any meal for groups. A bistro menu is served, with guests seated on pew-style benches at refectory-style tables. The chapel makes a perfect party venue and also has courtyard seating. The large shearing shed is actually a character-filled function hall that caters for up to 100 guests. An open fire and a stage enhance the hall's atmosphere, creating a great venue for any celebratory function. Within the circle of covered wagons a barbecue area makes an imaginative venue for a party, or simply a quaint barbecue spot. In the cooler months a campfire is lit giving added ambiance to the scene. Day visitors are welcome to use both barbecue areas situated within the park.

Ten-acres of the property is devoted to wildlife. The free-range park gives visitors the chance to view and interact with both native and other animals in typical surroundings. It is an opportunity to get close-up and personal with: koalas, wombats, wallaby, deer, dingos, emus and a variety of native and other birds. Most of the animals are human friendly and enjoy a gentle pat.

An adventure park would not be true to its name without exciting activities. At Hi-Ace both children and adults are presented with the challenge of rock climbing, and the exhilaration of the giant swing and flying fox ropes. There is a BMX track and an archery range, which doubles as the rodeo arena during the annual Ace-Hi Rodeo that attracts approximately 5,000 spectators, and then of course there are the horses and pony rides for the children. Special adventure programmes and team-building activities can be tailored to suit visiting groups and a well-equipped games room provides plenty of after-hours entertainment.

Ace-Hi is recognised as a premier horse riding facility. Whether a beginner or an advanced rider the ranch has a horse to suit all capabilities. Before each ride novices are instructed in basic horse riding skills, making sure of the rider's ability to control their horse. The ranch also runs an excellent horse awareness programme.

There is no better way to explore the scenic countryside than to see the sights from the saddle. Each Ace-Hi ride is accompanied by qualified, professional staff who ensure riders have a trouble-free, enjoyable ride. There are several trails to follow, with different degrees of difficulty, of different durations. They traverse scenic and forest routes and include the coastal trail onto St Andrews ocean beach. This is by far the most popular of the trail rides. After travelling through the verdant countryside and coastal bush, the beach stretches out before the riders in an expanse of glistening sand, pounding surf and wild scenic beauty – the rides are great fun, the stuff that memories are made of.

Left: Ace-Hi horse riders on St Andrews Beach
Right: Ace-Hi Ranch and Wildlife Park *Inset–* Centurian Tank rides and picnic areas

Mizu Spa is designed for lovers of relaxation. Located in Fingal (Moonahgai/Rye Ocean Beach) the unique attraction brings to life the knowledge and inspiration of a lifetime of travel by Charles and Yuki Davidson, incorporating over 45 countries including 15 trips on spa research missions. Visits to some 150 baths throughout Japan inspired many of the resort's 13 open-air hot mineral baths, scooped from 370-million-year-old granite. The white washed domed steam rooms utilise Arabic design from Yemen, the land of frankincense, myrrh, mocca coffee and the Queen of Sheba. A cold Russian plunge pool invigorates the body after a hot bath and Indonesian day beds in the accommodations and Arabic tent provide a place to drift off into an afternoon slumber.

Past the United Nations of relaxation, Mizu's most stunning feature is the way it embraces the indigenous environment and culture. In the seven acres of gardens, paths wind their way around the trees rewarding wanderers with a new delight at every turn. A garden mimicking a human body grows herbs in the location of the body they help to heal. A fire pit with huge granite boulders as seats is the perfect story telling location. Local indigenous artist Ben McKewan's art depicts Mizu as a location where people come to meet, rest and rejuvenate. Lanterns crafted by Charles, cut from tea-tree and carved from granite, light the paths at night.

The Mizu story is celebrated in music by Marty and Tom Williams of Cousin Leonard fame, helped by many indigenous and indigenous-minded musicians and artists. The music, inspired, written and produced on-site at the spa, can be experienced in a garden walking tour called 'Songlines of Mizu'. This imaginative musical walk takes you into the seven elements of Mizu Spa's creation: water, space, culture, earth, time, stars and creativity.

The spa centre at Mizu offers treatments utilising Aboriginal massage and healing techniques and the superb Li'Tya range of Australian spa products. Massages, facials, mud wraps and foot treatments take you from the relaxing pleasure of hot mineral baths to another realm of blissful connection. On experiencing the Li'Tya Kodo full body massage offered at Mizu, singer songwriter Sting said, "That was the best massage I have ever had. Quote me on that."

If, after all the relaxation, visitors build up a hunger and thirst, the Juice Bar and café offers freshly squeezed juices, light healthy snacks and Japanese meals. Mizu is fully licensed, so once you have enjoyed a fresh detox juice you can also relax with a retox beer, sake or local wine!! With books in the library, art in the gardens and massage, music and meals, visitors to Mizu lose the passage of time, part of them always refuses to leave. So why leave? Mizu also offers accommodation for groups and couples in the Winery and Spa Lodge, providing a perfect way to bliss out on reaching that floating Mizu state of being.

Mizu Spa, for all its charm and creativity, is but a dream in a larger dreaming of 'Peninsula Hot Springs'. The springs are the inspiration of brothers Charles and Richard Davidson. In 2002, after ten years of planning and research, five years of designs, permits and drilling on their 17-hectare property in Fingal, finally came gushing 47°C natural hot mineral waters. These sodium chloride bicarbonate springs, containing the added health benefits of potassium and magnesium, were assessed by the Japanese Hot Springs Research Institute in Tokyo and the Russian Mineral Water Organisation in Moscow as being ideally suited for bathing and consumption.

The hot springs are the central focus for a future relaxation precinct that will offer private and public hot spring bathing, a massage spa centre, restaurants and function facilities, 150 rooms of accommodation in lodges and cabins, a Wellness centre, food bowl with a barramundi aquaculture fish farm, herb gardens and greenhouses. Also, importantly for stressed parents, a Kids' Club and entertainment centre, planned to let parents rest and rejuvenate while children run, play and learn. The hot springs will enable visitors to the Peninsula to 'take the waters' and enjoy the healing pleasures that only hot mineral springs can provide. Peninsula Hot Springs will be the only location in Victoria where visitors can bathe in natural thermal waters – all other baths in the state, including the famous Hepburn Springs near Daylesford, rely on gas to heat their waters.

What inspired the Davidson brothers to get into hot springs and how were they discovered on the Peninsula? In the winter of 1992, while working in Japan, Charles visited the hot spring town of Kusatsu. While there, lying back in an open hot spring bath surrounded by snow and looking up at the trees and the sky, the dream to bring the wonderful sensation to Australia was born.

Five years later, while working at the Australian Embassy in Tokyo, in a chance conversation with Kevin Knowles from the Victorian State Office, Kevin said, "You know I think there may be hot springs on the Mornington Peninsula." Some quick checking revealed that the Department of Minerals and Energy had conducted test drilling on the Peninsula in 1979 and discovered a hot spring resource. This fired the dream and the rest, as they say, is history.

Asked about the future of hot springs on the Peninsula, Charles responded, "I dream of a day in the next 10-15 years, when there are several hot spring facilities on the Peninsula and the region is known as the bathing and healing capital of Australia. At that time the thermal waters will draw hundreds of thousands of people from all over the world to a bathing, relaxation and wellness experience."

The potential for a long-term sustainable industry in Australia is incredible. In Japan Charles met Professor Sato, chairman of the Organisation for the Preservation of Hot Springs in Japan. Sato's family established and has operated the Daimaru hot spring in Tohoku, central Japan, since 488 AD – over 1,500 years!

Peninsula Hot Springs will open towards the end of 2004. For those unable to wait, give Mizu Spa a try and get a taste of the delightful pleasures soon to come to the Mornington Peninsula.

Above & right: Relaxing at Mizu Spa, Fingal

SOUTHERN PENINSULA • GOLFING FEATURE

Golfing on the Mornington Peninsula has its own special pleasures – and challenges. Ask any golfer and they will tell you that the game is the closest thing to heaven and hell on earth, with magnificent highs and abysmal lows. The Peninsula courses are playable year-round, their 'sand belt' layouts quickly draining water in wet weather. The area has become know as 'The Golf Coast' of Victoria, the scenery is spectacular and the professionally designed courses challenging – what more can any golfer ask?

The Dunes Golf Links has reinvented the face of public golfing facilities, affording VIP status to each and every visitor. They have succeeded in their ambition, "to bring world class golf within the reach of every player." The Dunes course is comparable to many of the world's most revered, and has won a bevy of awards including being voted the country's number one public access golf course.

Set amidst more than 150 hectares of rolling coastal hills on Browns Road, Rye, in 'The Cups' region of the Peninsula, the 18-hole championship course has been designed to exploit the natural beauty of the terrain while providing a true test of skill and judgement for golfers on all levels. Tony Cashmore redesigned the championship course in 1997, presenting golf in the traditional links design with signature mounding that has all the obstacles players love to hate. The abundant charm of the par 72 layout is dramatically enhanced by the technical merit of the course. Covering 6,409 metres, the sloping fairways meander through undulating ridges onto expansive greens that are typically sheltered in a natural amphitheatre or exposed on elevated promontories to the full force of the elements. The trademark natural bunkering and prevalence of native grasses ensure every aspect of a game is relentlessly challenged, with the rough tormenting any player who ventures wide of the fairway.

On the first Thursday of each month players can take on the test of the 'Top Flight Tombstone Challenge', where they play the championship course off the black tees and win some great prizes. Monthly winners are invited back to compete for a spot in the 'MasterCard Masters 2003 Pro-am'. While playing The Dunes, visitors are invited to make use of the outstanding locker rooms that include showers, an extensive range of Cobra rental clubs, hand buggies and a fleet of E-ZGO golf carts. Also visit the golf shop that has an impressive selection of brand name merchandise. For limbering up, the practice facilities include a 280-metre driving range, complete with grass tees and multiple target greens, A large chipping green, sand bunker and putting green.

The Clubhouse restaurant and bar featuring exposed timber and sandstone has been sympathetically designed to meld into the environment. Floor to ceiling windows frame a captivating view, allowing full appreciation of the course's scenic grandeur. It is the perfect spot for an end of play drink, or (Friday and Saturday only) a delicious evening meal in the restaurant.

The scenic beauty of The Dunes has been recognised by prospective brides and grooms. The restaurant is strategically placed overlooking the ninth fairway and green, providing the perfect backdrop. The elegant dining room makes an ideal venue. At The Dunes expert staff help to plan weddings that are tailored to suit individual needs. They provide that unique touch to make the day a perfect one.

Celebrations of any kind, business functions, meetings and corporate golf events are also skilfully handled. For many on the Mornington Peninsula The Dunes is the social venue of choice.

Eagle Ridge Golf Course is an exceptional resort style facility with an American-design championship golf course. The par 72, 18-hole public course is located on Browns Road in The Cups region. Kept green by artesian water, the 80-acre property is a lush emerald island of undulating fairways and greens, dotted with colourful flowerbeds, waterways and picturesque waterfalls. The prestigious Royal Melbourne was Kevin Hartley's inspiration when designing Eagle Ridge championship course. The club opened in 1989 and, with the ongoing alterations, provides a course that is the envy of its peers with raised tee areas and greens that are true. Its playability, difficulty and redeveloped facilities are hard to match.

During 1999, Eagle Ridge underwent many changes to an already impressive establishment. A new clubhouse complex was completed, comprising a formal ballroom, conference rooms, golf shop and spike bar, members' lounge and locker rooms. The magnificent Mount Gambier Sandstone clubhouse is Victorian in style with an awe inspiring formal marble port-cochere entrance. Each area of the interior is lavishly furnished with antiques and the building is backed by a wide verandah that overlooks the course, landscaped gardens and a magnificent ornamental lake. The attractive café and more formal character-filled lounge bar both look out onto this decorative scene. Both are licensed and provide a relaxing oasis after an exhilarating game.

The spectacular ballroom is ideal for conferences, weddings and any special occasion. It is regally furbished, with sweeping views of the course and the bell-shaped gazebo on the lake, which has been the scene of many wedding ceremonies. Weddings are important occasions at Eagle Ridge; the attention to detail makes them an unforgettable experience. Indeed the new-look clubhouse was renovated with weddings in mind, catering for brides with an intimate, elegant bridal retreat and adding the allure of a private garden courtyard.

Eagle Ridge is a major player in the rapidly expanding golf and recreation industry on the Mornington Peninsula. Corporate Australia is discovering the course, lured by the promise of exhilarating corporate golf tournaments, state-of-the-art facilities and the opportunity to tee off in paradise. Everyone is welcome at the course, including green fee players and social clubs. No matter what level of golfer you are, Eagle Ridge will challenge the single digit handicapper and at the same time be quite accommodating for the social player. Every aspect has been covered: golf clinics can be organised on request and five undercover bays provide an opportunity to warm up before a game.

In February 2003, Eagle Ridge was deservedly named by Golf Australia magazine as one of Australia's 'Top 25 Public Access' golf courses. The course was also recently honoured by the local tourism industry with an award for the 'Best Hospitality Venue' on the Mornington Peninsula. These two awards cement Eagle Ridge's reputation as one of Victoria's finest corporate golf and wedding venues.

The Dunes Golf Links

Eagle Ridge Golf Course

SOUTHERN PENINSULA • GOLFING FEATURE

Rosebud Country Club situated on Boneo Road, Rosebud is a superb complex that has it all. At Rosebud Golf Course a group of local businessmen who were regular golfers saw the need for a true members' golf club. This effort established Rosebud Country Club in 1956. They found land, and with the assistance of volunteers and local companies the first course opened in 1962. Today, the club boasts two golf courses, three lawn bowling greens, and up-to-the-minute clubrooms.

The 36-hole golf course covers two distinct layouts, one essentially lined with pines, the other planted with native trees. Both courses are picturesque, attracting bird life and offering superb views up to Arthurs Seat. In 1998 the club enlisted the services of Mike Clayton Design to further enhance both course layouts. The two-time Victorian Open champion and his team worked with the course Superintendent resulting in some exciting changes. A real benchmark for the team's work is the par five ninth on the north course, where the corner of the dogleg is protected by a series of bunkers rather than the pine plantation that used to blanket the green. It is now a super hole for players of all abilities. Over the years Rosebud Country Club has hosted prestigious events including the Victorian and Australian PGA Championships.

Russell Wilson, the club's pro said, "The great features of this complex are its beautiful trees, its big challenging greens and especially its fine couch fairways. If you are on the fairway you can count on the ball sitting up well, giving you more confidence and a better chance of making a great shot."

Over the years the course has developed from a rundown pine forest to its present state – a championship course that can be played by any standard golfer. Putting, chipping and practice areas are within close proximity to the clubhouse, as are fully fitted changing rooms, storage areas, spike bar and pro shop with a large range of golfing equipment and apparel.

An extensive lawn bowls complex has 22 top quality rinks and a separate clubroom. The immaculate greens have year-round playability, made possible by the manicured couch grass. The country club's modern clubhouse was opened in 1999: there members can 'enjoy the exterior from the interior', thanks to floor to ceiling windows that embrace the building. The à la carte dining area and bistro offer panoramic views over the superb golf course. Open seven days a week they serve delicious modern Australian cuisine with many old favourites. The club lounge is a relaxed room reminiscent of a bygone era. It offers an intimate place to unwind and plan tomorrow's adventure or discuss the day's play. Or, if you feel lucky, for some excitement visit the spacious gaming room that has a bevy of up-to-the-minute poker machines

The function room can cater for a variety of celebratory occasions and gatherings, including weddings, official dinners, cocktail parties, corporate functions, meetings and conferences. All of which can be tailored to suit individual needs and expertly organised by the club's experienced staff. The area has been purpose-built to provide total privacy. Depending on requirements it has a function capacity for 200 guests. If you are looking for a prime golfing challenge, friendly service and end of play entertainment – it awaits you at the Rosebud Country Club.

ROSEBUD PARK
Public Golf Course

The history of Rosebud Park Public Golf Club and Recreation Reserve on Elizabeth Drive goes back to 1884, when it was a parcel of grazing land administered by the Victorian Lands Department. After various lessees failed to make a living from the land, it was suggested in 1926 that it be kept as a 'Department Reserve'. In 1927, 158 acres was declared a permanent reserve for use as a public park and recreation area. It was gazetted as Rosebud Park in 1930 under the control of Flinders Shire Council as a committee of management. The land the course is built on now forms part of the State Forest's magnificent property that runs from Arthurs Seat through Sea Winds Park and down to the southern corner of the coastal suburb of Rosebud.

As early as 1939 a move was afoot to develop a golf course on the land, but it was not until 1952 that the course took shape. Mr Morcom of Kingston Heath Golf Course designed the original course: it has subsequently been updated, with considerable improvements under the expert care of Thomson, Wolveridge and Perrett. The course's position on the steeply undulating, lower slopes of Arthurs Seat provides players with a challenge set against a technicolour wonderland of land, sky and sea. The view of the coastline down to Rye, Blairgowrie and Sorrento captures traffic on the bay and the rural greenery of the Mornington Peninsula and is enough to inspire golfers of any ability. The 18-hole course has watered fairways, wonderful putting greens and some extremely challenging holes. Resident teaching professional Tim Silver, is on hand to bring ailing tee shots up to par, and a well-equipped shop carries a large range of equipment and apparel.

The well laid out course's tee areas, quality fairways and large greens provide a less formal alternative for golfers. Many businesses, hotels, sporting clubs and service clubs have formed their own social golf clubs and Rosebud Park specialises in helping these groups enjoy a special day. There are five undercover areas with free electric or wood barbecues nestled within the course, which are also open to the non-golfing public. Many local groups arrange a regular 9-hole or 18-hole competition and, to encourage the social golf clubs, golf balls are donated to them for their competitions when they have in excess of 20 players.

Rosebud Park delivers value for money and gives you change. The paying public plays an estimated 60,000 rounds of golf at the course annually. As there is no membership to guarantee regular players, it is obvious the general public is waking up to the fact that golf need not be an elitist sport and that Rosebud Park has been a well kept secret for far too long.

Rosebud Country Club

Rosebud Park Public Golf Course

SOUTHERN PENINSULA • GOLFING FEATURE

Nepean Country Club Resort on Browns Road at Boneo, only minutes from Rosebud, nestles on 38 scenic acres of landscaped gardens and offers affordable luxury. It is one of Victoria's premier holiday destinations, surrounded by a wealth of on-site and local activities. The fully self-contained units provide the background for indoor tennis courts, squash court, gymnasium, indoor and outdoor swimming pools, spa, and mini golf. Facilities also include children's adventure play area, lawn bowls, sand volley and basketball court, a 2.1-kilometre exercise track (currently under development), games room and barbecue and picnic facilities. A large reed lined lake is a glittering feature of the property and home to many water birds. Canadian canoes are supplied and a relaxed paddle on the picturesque body of water is a soothing pastime.

The resort is dedicated to quality recreational vacations starting with year-round tennis that can be enjoyed in the floodlit undercover tennis courts. A new multi-million dollar leisure precinct contains indoor and outdoor pools, plus a large heated outdoor spa. The indoor swimming pool has a unique beach entry that gradually descends into the deeper water, making it perfect for the physically infirm and the very young. Adjacent to the pool centre, a full size indoor squash court is state of the art and a personal trainer is on hand each morning to take the more dedicated through a personally structured exercise program in the fully equipped gymnasium.

The spacious clubhouse with two pool tables, table tennis and air hockey tables, provides a fun retreat. It comes complete with a kitchen and lounge area, handy for the use of time-share owners, who with ownership are entitled to utilise the resort on day visits as well as yearly stays.

Accommodation at the resort comes in a variety of designs. Motel studio style apartments with limited cooking facilities, queen size beds and large spa baths are perfect for two persons. One and two bedroom fully self-contained apartments can comfortably house a maximum of six persons and a two-bedroom split-level, fully self-contained apartment with separate parents' retreat has the ability to house a maximum of six guests. The apartments are all comfortably furnished, with quality fittings, decorated in modern relaxing tones.

Situated in the leisure complex, Fingal's Poolside Café has a bright atmosphere with both indoor and outdoor seating. Breakfast served in the café is a laid back casual affair, catering from a health-conscious repast through to the traditional fully cooked hearty country-style version. The poolside oasis serves an all-day menu and is a pleasant place to capture some sun and relax with the day's newspapers.

The resort sits on part of one of the area's historic properties and Fingal's Restaurant is contained in the old Fingal homestead that has overlooked the area for at least 120 years – some say complete with ghost. It is a place of great character and charm, sitting on one of the resort's higher points surrounded by shady trees and lush lawn. The large paved Fox Hollow Terrace Garden fronts the window-lined dining room, providing exceptional undercanvas al fresco dining overlooking relaxed parkland. The charismatic restaurant comes complete with an old-world atmosphere and several connecting areas that make perfect private function venues.

The restaurant's à la carte menu provides fine contemporary cuisine for the discerning diner as well as a family menu and is the perfect spot for celebratory diners. Summer features spit roasts and traditional barbecues in the terrace garden, and the lounge bar is the ideal spot for pre dinner drinks or in winter a nightcap round the open fire. The restaurant and bar are open to the public as well as in-house guests.

A wide range of packages can be organised for corporate conferencing that can include team building programs and golf days utilising the magnificent surrounding courses, plus a sample of the Peninsula's many other attractions.

The resort's staff can professionally arrange successful conferences. Three bright attractive conference rooms are located in a quiet position within the grounds and cater from numbers of 30 to 100 delegates, equipped with state of the art apparatus.

The Nepean Resort is perfectly located for corporate conferences, groups, individual or family getaways, just over an hour from Melbourne and within minutes of all the wonders that can be found on the Mornington Peninsula. The facilities on offer are second to none. Guests can choose an energetic sojourn or simply do nothing at all and spend lazy, languid days soaking up the surrounding environs in blissful peace.

SOUTHERN PENINSULA • GOLFING FEATURE

Moonah Links on Peter Thomson Drive (off Truemans Road), Rye is a 196-hectare spectacular development boasting two world-class golf courses set in the heart of 'The Cups' region, an area renowned throughout the world for its suitability for links golf. The sea breeze that rolls over the Mornington Peninsula was part of the initial inspiration for the resort that has been designed to harmonise with the undulating ancient dunes that are near perfect for this style of golf course. Recognised as one of the longest courses in Australia, measuring 6,822 metres, it provides a potent and powerful game of golf, testing the player's ability at every turn. Even the top pros find its length a test of endurance and skill. The Moonah Links Golf Complex and Peppers Moonah Links Resort is the largest tourism development in recent Victorian history. It consists of several components that live up to the label 'The Home of Australian Golf' and provides a heady blend for avid golfers.

Only two years ago cattle were running where golfers now tread. The punishing eighth hole of the Open Course was a vineyard; indeed the vigneron's hut still stands near the hole. Internationally renowned designers Thomson, Wolveridge and Perrett employed this rural landscape to design the resort's championship Open Course. It is a links course that brings out the worst and the best in golfers and utilises nature by exploiting the ever-present wind conditions. The strong airstream cannot be escaped no matter what direction is used and brings an added dimension to the game. The Open Course at Moonah Links has a natural stadium layout with wide undulating fairways of pure couch grass, punctuated with classic Peter Thomson pot bunkers. It leads onto large multi-tiered greens that make this course a true test for all levels of golfers. The 18th has been specifically designed to give a spectacular finish. It is, perhaps, the longest par 5 in the world, a minefield of danger from the first to last shot. It is full of obstacles, with 11 bunkers lying in wait along its length to catch the unwary or the careless.

Moonah's second course, the highly celebrated Legends Course, has a user-friendly layout, in stark contrast to the leviathan that is the Open Course. It takes players on a scenic journey through ancient tracts of Moonah forest and out onto vast open fairways. Panoramic views can be appreciated from raised tees and a host of other unique features combine to make this course a must play for all golfers.

The Moonah Links complex was designed specifically to host Australia's most prestigious annual golfing event, the Australian Open, and create a home for the Australian Golf Union and The Australian Institute of Sport Golf Academy. It is the first course in Australian history to be built specifically to host a national championship. The prestigious event is an institution in Australian golfing. The event, to be held at Moonah in December 2003, will be the Australian Open's ninety-ninth year. It will be the first time that the event has ever been held outside of a private golf club in a major capital city, aimed at making the event more accessible to the general public by holding it in the holiday mecca that is the Mornington Peninsula.

Moonah is tailor made as the ultimate luxury resort and golf experience. The quality practice facilities are designed to AIS specifications and include a driving range and short game area. A team of PGA golf professionals are on hand to structure a coaching package to bring ailing games up to scratch with on course lessons, video swing analysis and links specific tuition programs. The Pro Shop is stocked with a vast range of quality apparel and the latest state-of-the-art golf equipment. Weekend ball competitions and a variety of other opportunities to test a player's skill against the links layouts are a regular weekly highlight. Many other organised challenges also tempt competitors, lured by a vast array of prizes that encourage their best performance.

With the exceptional design and course sophistication present at Moonah Links it is to be expected that the Golf Pavilion will live up to the standard already set. The building's design comes from the collaboration of award winning architects Nation Fender Katsalidis and Synman Justin Bialek. The stunning $40 million resort complex is a benchmark for style, housing a fully integrated golf clubhouse with gymnasium and day spa and includes a world class Pro Shop and lavishly appointed change rooms. It is, however, the café, spike bar and magnificent function and dining area that steals pride of place. Elegance characterises Pebbles Restaurant that carries the Peppers' reputation for superb à la carte cuisine. Floor to ceiling windows embrace the room, providing a perfect picture of the first hole. Spacious decking is built to show off the view and an open fire creates winter ambiance.

Accommodation at Moonah is provided by one of Australia's most highly regarded companies. Peppers' retreats and resorts have a reputation for being the most indulgent escapes throughout Australia and Peppers Moonah Links Resort is no exception. Set amid the rolling fairways of the golf courses, surrounded by the seascape environment, it offers visitors a getaway that will pamper and please.

"For golfers who want to enjoy a unique 'stay and play' experience, Peppers Moonah Links Resort will be the most stylish and comprehensive golf resort in Victoria, offering an invigorating getaway that is hard to beat," says Peppers managing director, Rolf Krecklenberg. Like all Peppers accommodation, the resort is highly individual, taking its character from the local environment. This is enhanced by the company's signature décor, which builds on the property's charm with style, elegance and comfort. At Peppers, every visitor is made to feel special they have the impeccable touch that creates a vacation environment second to none with friendly helpful staff that can organise your day or keep the world at bay.

The entire resort is an inspiring achievement that turns the spotlight on an ancient sport and, if you welcome a challenge, appreciate exceptional service and expect quality course conditioning, it all awaits you at Moonah Links.

SOUTHERN PENINSULA • GOLFING FEATURE

Shearwater Cape Schanck Resort Golf Course is arguably the best shorter course (5,629 metres) you will ever play. The 18-hole par 70 championship course on Boneo Road, Cape Schanck, was designed by Robert Trent Jones Jnr in the early 1980s. 'The Schanck', as it is affectionately known, was one of the first resort courses built specifically to allow public access all year round. Created among rolling sand dunes, surrounded by national park and perched high on one of Australia's most spectacular headlands, it has majestic views over the Bass Strait and Port Phillip Bay.

In his design Jones has proved that a golf course does not have to be a monster in length to be difficult. Accuracy off the tee at Cape Schanck is a must to find the undulating fairways, leaving an approach shot to a heavily guarded green. The large greens are varied in shape and often combine with the diverse bunkering to put a premium on placement of the approach shot for players, to avoid leaving themselves a roller coaster putt.

Although water from both sides of the Peninsula comes into view on several holes there is only one lake on the course. It cuts across the 168-metre par 3 seventh and also just in front of the eighth tee. For first-timers, the back nine is more spectacular, simply for the view on the fourteenth and fifteenth. Both head towards the ocean with stunning views over Gunnamatta and St Andrews surf beaches, stretching all the way down the Peninsula to Portsea.

The course has the most impressive of driving ranges – hitting off grass tees to a long wide fairway, players get the feel of the true fairway surface. Sealed cart paths run the entire course, allowing for year-round cart use and, with their access to recycled water, the manicured fairways stay lush during the summer months, even if water restrictions are in place. The resort course is open to the public seven days a week and has a fully serviced golf shop with golfing apparel and equipment for all golfing needs. The Caddy Shack lounge at the clubhouse is an informal café that is perfect for snacks and after-game drinks.

Accommodation is available in the resort's deluxe hotel-style rooms, or self-contained two and four bedroomed executive suites. all rooms have private en suites, balconies and provide visitors with their very own front row seat for the Peninsula's spectacular sunsets. The resort offers a recreation room with billiards and table tennis, a heated pool, spa, sauna and all-weather tennis courts – and a visit would not be complete without sampling the menu at the resort's world-class restaurant, Caspian via Corso.

Shearwater prides itself on being a premier conference centre, servicing corporate groups of up to 250 delegates with state-of-the-art equipment. Companies wishing to hold corporate golf days need only make the phone call and Shearwater's professional team will custom-build a golf day that includes the use of the resort's 60 golf carts, on-site activities, coordinator and private function rooms.

For your next golfing pilgrimage, whether it is a day or a week, put The Shearwater Cape Schanck Resort high on your list of places to play.

Sorrento Golf Club on Langford Road, Sorrento, enjoys a special reputation within Victoria as one of the premier courses on the Mornington Peninsula. When Melbourne's early stalwarts travelled to the Mornington Peninsula for their holidays, they took their golf along with them. Formed in 1907, the Sorrento Golf Club, then known, as the Sorrento and Portsea Golf Club, became the 'Royal Melbourne of the South', a course built on classic lines borrowed from the original, for the joy and pleasure of golfers good and bad. Since its inception, the club's primary focus has been on developing a golf course that is 'on par' with the best and it has earned its reputation as one of the finest coastal clubs in Australia.

The course has a year-round quality, characterised by a beautifully groomed, hilly course. Densely wooded plantations surround its generous couch fairways and roughs and bent grass greens are moderately heavily to very heavily bunkered. Each picturesque hole has its own distinctive features, providing both challenges and rewards to all handicap golfers, challenging them to a rematch, over and over again. British Open champion Peter Thomson said of the course: "Golf these days is high on my list of pleasures, and I'd rather be here than at Gleneagles, Pebble Beach or Carnoustie." The club hosted its first major tournament, the Victorian Open Championship, in 2003. The competing professional players liked the 'Pro Am' format and were delighted with Sorrento as the chosen venue.

The club's Professional Shop provides every service a golfer could need: clubs hire, clothing and equipment. A number of motorised golf carts are available to make the 18 holes a little less demanding. Brett Parker has been the resident club professional since 1996. Brett is classed in the Australian Professional Golfers' Association's highest membership classification – AAA. He can be booked for lessons through the professional shop.

In 1999 the club completed a major clubhouse refurbishment program and now offers members and visitors facilities of the highest standard, in an environment that preserves and enhances the traditions of dignity, fellowship and understated elegance. The Club Bar and dining room plus the terrace bar is open daily for drinks and light snacks. Facilities for social groups, wedding receptions, special functions and corporate entertaining are extensive. Downstairs, the Terrace Bar is the perfect place for informal occasions, light lunches, barbecues and buffet catering, or just simply sipping cocktails in front of the open fireplace. Upstairs the dining room, with panoramic views over the course, offers something more formal for those special occasions. Catering can range from an intimate dinner party for 20 in the John Baillieu Room to up to 200 guests in the Terrace Bar and Dining Room. Corporate golf days, business seminars and conferences are also professionally catered for.

The Sorrento Golf Club is a wonderful place to mix a little business with a lot of pleasure and invites visitors to share its treasure, enjoy its beauty and record a score they can boast about.

Shearwater Cape Schanck Resort Golf Club

Sorrento Golf Club

Tootgarook by the bay is a secluded holiday village fringed by Port Phillip Bay and flanked by Rosebud West and Rye. It is a small pocket of pioneer history, being part of the original pastoral holding called *Packomedeurrawurra*, awarded to the area's first European settler, Edward Hobson, in 1837. The name Tootgarook is thought to mean 'land of the croaking frogs'.

Although dwarfed by its sprawling neighbours it has managed to retain much of its pioneer charm, with shops and businesses occupying sympathetically restored historic buildings.

Tootgarook's gently sloping beach and shallow water is greatly appreciated by young family members. The gentle curve of sand dunes built up by the sea and banksia growth on the foreshore provides protection from the elements.

Rye sits on the eastern side of White Cliffs and shares many of its attractions with Tootgarook. It sprang to life in the 1840s, populated by lime burners. Lime burning was the region's main industry until the 1860s. During this productive lime-burning era the town was dubbed 'Queen of the Peninsula' with fourteen kilns working in the Rye locality. It was during this time that Whitecliffs, (at that time named Yellow Bluffs) a well-admired landmark today, lost much of its substance as large sections of the cliffs were quarried for burning. A pier was constructed in 1860 to service the local kilns and firewood industry, but it was not suitable for the paddle steamers that brought holidaymakers to the area. Ships would leave laden with local products and return laden with liquid of the alcoholic variety. Not until the 1950s, when motor vehicles became more available to the average family, did the newly mobile public discover Rye. The visitor boom has continued: travellers enthused by the wealth of recreational opportunities on offer and the serendipitous seaside atmosphere have transformed Rye into one of the Peninsula's favourite destinations.

The main shopping area runs the length of the Nepean Highway opposite the foreshore. As well as supermarkets and attractive eateries, the strip contains a diverse range of shops that pride themselves in catering for visitors.

Rye is the first of the Peninsula towns to have the added advantage of a choice of beaches. The main beach is an idyllic place where dreamy inertia comes easy. A wide stretch of golden sand inclines gently towards crystal water, where sandbanks undulate, creating swimming holes of differing depths. Throughout the year the view from the beach is enlivened by sail boarders and wind surfers utilising the offshore airstream to be found in this part of the bay. They duck and weave zealously, chasing the breeze in colourful confusion. The Blow Wave Surfing Classic is held each January in this intoxicating setting.

The pier that juts out from a small point on the coast and the corrugated face of Whitecliffs aesthetically enhances the beach's attributes. A large attractive rotunda is set among shady trees that blend into the grassed foreshore where undercover electric barbecues and picnic areas are popular lunch spots. The pier makes an invigorating walking platform, and to help walk off lunch a walking come cycling track meanders along the foreshore. The Blairgowrie-Rye Recreational Track can be followed on to Rosebud or Dromana. It leads through native coastal vegetation emerging onto the beach in places where the track is incomplete.

At Whitecliffs, on the western end of the beach, a replicated limekiln is a feature of the foreshore. Attractive views of the bay are to be gleaned from taking a walk up the steps and along a track that leads over the cliff's back and gives access to the designated camping areas on Tyrone Foreshore.

Sandy Road via Dundas Street leads to the wild beauty of Rye Back Beach, St Andrews and Gunnamatta beaches located at the town's back door through the rolling hills district named 'The Cups'

Rye's colourful history is evident throughout the bustling town. Rye Cemetery is one of the oldest on the Peninsula, and St Andrews Church, built of local limestone in 1882, can still be seen in Lyons Street. Many houses built during the lime burners era survive, as do many relics of the industry.

The town has a wide-ranging program of annual events. One of the most noteworthy that draws thousands of amazed spectators each year is the Rye Beach Sand Sculpting Championship, held in February/March. Located on the foreshore, the 2003 event was the third annual championship. The theme was 'French Carnival'. Ten huge sculptures were created out of 1,500 tonnes of sand brought in especially for the task.

The current world sand-sculpting champion, American Kevin Crawford, was brought to Rye, together with Australian and international sculptors, to create the giant fun fair replicas. The larger than life exhibits were put together over the championship's twenty-nine days, to the total admiration of a stunned public. The masterpieces were shaped from the top down. Tiered wooden frames allowed the sculptors to work on one section at a time, removing frame upon frame, revealing the finished creation. A sense of humour was evident in the work, with many of the exhibits poking fun at recent topical events.

The event was organised jointly by the Vision Australia Foundation and Rye Beach Action Group. Each weekend, as well as being able to wander through the maze of sand sculptures, children and families were invited to bring to life their own fantasies and legends in the competition pits, and workshops were conducted to initiate the public in the pleasure and problems of creating a work of art out of a pile of sand. The event had a true carnival flavour, with sideshows and rides, hotdogs and coffee and the one thing that no fair is complete without – fairy floss.

Above: Chinamans Creek entering Port Phillip Bay at West Rosebud
Right: Lady Nelson sails from Rye Pier as part of Victoria's bicentenary celebrations

This exceptional area is bound to contain exceptional accommodation and the comfort and elegance that is the signature of Hilltonia Homestead is sure to make the most jaded traveller sit up and take notice. Hosted by Jo-Anne Williamson and Anthony Colles, the property is situated on Browns Road a stone's throw from three of the region's premier golf courses. The entrance drive sets the theme -stress flows from the body on the journey up the extended driveway. The main house, although of modern construction, is designed to resemble the historic mansions that the Peninsula is famous for. A bar and elegant drawing rooms with massive open fireplaces are pools of comfort, and four individual, extra spacious bed and breakfast suites, all with separate character, leave nothing to be desired and tariff includes a fully cooked breakfast. The suites comprise 'The Loft', which takes up the complete upper floor with a private entrance, plus bay views from a private balcony. Two poolside suites overlook the oasis-style pool area and a tennis court lies adjacent the house.

The property covers 38 acres of structured bush. For total seclusion, a stay in one of the five self-contained individually situated wooden cottages is recommended. Each cottage has a different theme and is the ultimate in style. All have views from their elevated position, some of the bay and others of the rolling countryside; all views are serene and soothing. The cottages are beautifully furnished, with large windows and balconies complete with barbecues. Breakfast baskets allow guests totally privacy. The cottages have many attributes to ponder, but perhaps the most unique is the bathrooms, each with raised or sunken double spas looking out over the magnificent views – total indulgence.

The Rye Hotel is an integral piece of the town's history, along with the distric's impressive history of lime burning. The present building was built in 1927 succeeding an older hotel named the Gracefield (circa 1875). So all in all, people have been visiting the same site for over a hundred and twenty-five years to slake their hunger and thirst, make contact with friends and in general relax and enjoy the seaside atmosphere.

The Houghton family have a long history with the hotel, firstly as licensees in the 1950s, returning in 1974 and finally Dorothy and son Peter purchasing the hotel in 1990. With a succession of improvements they have transformed a country pub into a sparkling entertainment and function complex that comfortably caters for every occasion, social or corporate, and stands out as the town's centrepiece.

The award-winning Rye Hotel has a complete range of facilities, starting with the conveniently situated drive through bottle shop, and the attractive gaming room with state of the art machines. Its position opposite the relaxed ambiance of Rye Foreshore with stunning views of Port Phillip Bay enhances meals served in the Bistro Café and al fresco terrace complemented by the garden bar that is popular as a relaxed meeting place. The Main Sail Bar attracts both visitors and locals; it is set in comfortable surrounds, run by helpful friendly staff. Affordable bar meals are served and there is a full TAB facility. Conferences, meetings and seminars can be professionally catered for in the function area with breakout rooms available and state-of-the-art equipment. Weddings, too, find a special venue at the hotel overlooking the bay. A modern contemporary resort-style accommodation development has recently been added incorporating 30 suites (including two disabled suites) complementing an all-round facility catering for visitors every need.

Gunnamatta Equestrian Centre on the corner of Trueman and Sandy Roads is one of Rye's more unique attractions, allowing visitors to live out a fantasy. Even people who have never sat astride a horse before are irresistibly drawn to the exhilaration of galloping down a deserted beach on golden sand, dashing through the shallows, waves breaking around them and spray washing over them, with the thunder of horses' hooves and breaking surf in their ears. But that is where the journey ends, not where it begins.

Budding riders first have to check in with Peter Hurley and Donna Connelly at the equestrian centre and get put through their paces. They are given a short safety demonstration, introduced to their horse and for non-riders taught the basic riding skills needed to control their mounts. Don't be bashful if you don't ride - say so. All equipment is provided and this includes a helmet that must be worn. Qualified staff accompany all rides.

Once the preliminaries are over there are a number of trails to follow. Bush rides allow the relaxed enjoyment of walking the horses along bush tracks, feeling the sway of their languid amble. There are plenty of opportunities during the ride to trot and canter up the long, straight hills. These rides have duration of about an hour and are suitable for all levels, especially young children. The ocean beach ride leads along a bush track to the ruggedly beautiful St. Andrews Beach. The sense of freedom is thrilling, feeling the spray on one's face as the horses canter along the edge of the waves. For the more advanced rider a different route along a more challenging bush track has many more chances to trot and canter. This ride will challenge riders and add to their experience.

Gunnamatta Equestrian Centre has been operating since 1980. It is an award-winning integrated equestrian facility with qualified staff and over 80 quality, well-behaved horses. They offer everyone, of all ages and levels of ability, the chance to participate in the exhilarating experience of horse riding, catering for schools and colleges, day trippers and community groups. The centre not only runs trail rides but also has qualified instructors who give individual riding lessons and equestrian and dressage tuition. During school holidays they hold four-day tutorials culminating in a gymkhana where young riders are encouraged to decorate and dress their horses - needless to say, some of the designs are extremely imaginative. Paul and Donna are passionate about their business and plans for the future include an indoor equestrian arena.

Above: Gunnamatta's famous equestrian centre beach and trail rides
Right: The annual Rye beach sand-sculpting championships

Blairgowrie exudes a quiete restful persona that is a precious commodity in today's hurly-burly world. It is historically linked to Sorrento, with its early settlement following the same path, and was named Sorrento East until the 1950s. Sandwiched between the dynamic towns of Sorrento and Rye, the small village has a gentle profile and a laid back atmosphere. The most prominent historic home in the township has right of passage. It was the original home on the Blairgowrie Estate, built in 1872 by the Honourable Michael O'Grady, a Melbourne physician and Member of Parliament. Built of random-coursed limestone with a slate roof, O'Grady called his holiday home Villa Maria, but it was renamed Blairgowrie House after his death in 1876 by new owner Doctor John Blair. The house is an imposing structure and was built as a landmark, sitting atop a prominent hill on Scott Wynd Street, a gracious reminder of another era.

Holiday homes and accommodation in the township have a prime position, stretching along the foreshore with a magic outlook over both Port Phillip Bay and the turbulent coast of Bass Strait. A small cluster of quality shops provide for the needs of residents and visitors, completely in tune with the seductive village. The foreshore and beach curve in a wide natural sweep of golden sand and coastal vegetation. A protective sea wall at the eastern end creates a breakwater, and a few boatsheds and the jetty add to the attractive seascape. The yachts moored in the Blairgowrie Yacht Squadron's marina endow the scene with the languid anticipation of adventures to come.

The Boathouse Resort Motel, located opposite the marina on the Point Nepean Highway, is four-Star holiday accommodation. It has the perfect position adjacent to the beach and is within walking distance to the Blairgowrie shopping strip. Owned and run by Kate and Ian Diamond, who have spent their lives in the hospitality industry, the 20 double-storey units were originally built as managed apartments. The redesign has created a unique motel, affording extra spacious apartments that are luxuriously appointed, some with double spas.

Upper-level apartments have balconies and the family units have their own private courtyard.

The design of the apartments creates a village-style ambiance with an enticing barbecue area and kidney-shaped pool that makes a good alternative to the beach. An oasis of lawns and palm-studded manicured gardens surround the apartments. They add a serene atmosphere to the first-class complex. The resort has excellent conferencing facilities for small groups, making it an ideal venue for seminars and conferences. Group packages are available for the golfing fraternity and a range of great adventure packages can be organised to complement any conference. Centrally located, the Boathouse Resort Motel is a sought after location and takes the stress out of any holiday.

Coast 2827 is an exceptional restaurant and bar on Point Nepean Road in the heart of the Blairgowrie shopping strip, a haven of relaxed style. This is not surprising considering owners Mark and Shani Anderson are expatriates of Melbourne's fashion industry, where they were involved with the development, design and owned the Scooter children's brand. They moved to the Peninsula for the lifestyle it afforded both themselves and their two young daughters. They have melded with their new environment and on their days off make use of the many golf courses in the area their favourites being Portsea.

Opening Coast 2827 in December 2001 opposite the Blairgowrie foreshore, Shani's expertise in design and Mark's love of the beach is apparent in the Balinese influences incorporated into the restaurant's décor. Glassed concertina doors open up to bring the outdoor deck into the restaurant and parasol shaded pavement-dining gives a cosmopolitan flavour to the streetscape. Winter too has its ambiance made cosy by a wood fire in the restaurant and patio heaters on the deck.

Breakfast is a popular time at Coast. Locals and visitors take time to enjoy the food and the seaside atmosphere. Lunches can be long, drawn-out affairs and dinner has its own special appeal. The menu offers flavoursome modern Australian cuisine with Asian and Italian influences and features the region's wonderful seafood. One of the restaurant's most popular dishes is 'Coast' Seafood Linguini. The menu is enhanced by an eclectic wine list that showcases some Peninsula wines.

Jill Swann has a discerning eye for art that she puts to good use in her Aspects Gallery on Point Nepean Road, Blairgowrie. She has a long history in retail, experience that has been utilised during her two years at Aspects. Jill is the gallery's fifth owner: it is one of the Peninsula's longest established art spaces. The art at Aspects reflects the gallery's seaside position; Jill chooses artists who specialise in large canvases that depict the surrounding environs – vivid canvases that capture the beauty of seascapes and boats, coastal flora and fauna. She presents an eclectic celebrated group of artists who include Marg Hennekam, Charles Bock, Michael Goff, James Uhe, Ian Chisholm, Clive Sinclair and Jayne Henderson.

The gallery also showcases ceramics and imaginative Falco Kooper sculptures. A display of sleek, sophisticated jewellery also keeps the character of the gallery's position, crafted in amethyst and pearls for summer and richly toned amber for winter. Aspects Gallery has a relaxed atmosphere and professionally presents distinctive, timeless pieces. Jill hosts a highly regarded summer exhibition and will introduce an exhibition as part of the First Settlement celebrations in the summer of 2003.

Left: The Coast 2827 Restaurant at Blairgowrie
Right: The Blairgowrie Yacht Club.   *Inset–* Display at Aspects Gallery, Blairgowrie

Sorrento was Victoria's first official European settlement. A British garrison consisting of 50 Royal Marines, under the command of Lieutenant-Governor David Collins, and 460 convicts, settlers and civil officers, arrived in 1803; deployed to prevent the French, who were surveying the area, from gaining a foothold in Victoria. John Fawkner, the founder of Melbourne, together with his mother and father, were among the original settlers.

The settlement was formed on Sullivan Bay, by the perilous mouth of Port Phillip Bay. Its garrison was wild and unruly and the marines undisciplined; three convicts made good their escape. Two were never heard from again but one, William Buckley, survived by living with the Aborigines. After a 30-year hiatus he surrendered in 1835, bringing news of an alleged Aboriginal attack and an amazing story of his life with the tribe. He received a pardon and worked for the government as an Aboriginal interpreter.

The fledgling community's inhabitants suffered numerous privations, with the lack of fresh water a major factor. Their small community was under continual threat of attack from hostile Aborigines. Collins abandoned the site in 1804, moving the inhabitants to Van Diemen's Land and established Hobart Town, where the remnants of the community flourished.

The historic settlement was the scene of many of Victoria's 'firsts'; the first magistrates court, public hospital, postal service, government printing press and water supply and, of course the first wedding, birth and funeral to be conducted in Victoria.

The site of the original settlement is situated on Sullivan Bay's eastern headland, just east of Sorrento off Point Nepean Road and makes an interesting visit. An on-site information centre gives detailed information about the ill-fated settlement. None of the original buildings have survived but a graveyard nestling in a landscaped grove holds four sites believed to contain the remains of 30 pioneers who died during the settlement's short existence.

Much later lime burners and fishermen were the fledgling community's first permanent settlers. It is believed that Sir Charles Gavan Duffy, parliamentarian and local developer, named the town, christening the land he owned after his families estates in Dublin Bay, Ireland.

It was not until the 1870s that Sorrento became an established star, catering for many of Victoria's elite families during their summer vacations. Entrepreneur George Coppin, 'the father of Sorrento', was the first to cultivate the area's natural charm and promoted the region through land sales. Coppin built many of the striking limestone buildings that still dominate the skyline. He constructed sea baths in 1875 and a rotunda decorated with murals situated on the ocean beach with a walking track that follows the cliff line, complete with seats and viewing areas. His grand plan also included the development of a paddle steamer service between bay settlementsand Melbourne (a trip on the steamers from Melbourne to Sorrento entailed a day's travel) and a small steam train that ran from the bay jetty to the ocean beach; the service continued until 1921. Two of Sorrento's most prominent historic buildings are the Continental Hotel, circa 1875 (built by Jack Crawford, it is thought to be the tallest limestone building in Australia) and the Mechanics Institute, circa 1876-77.

The Mechanics Institute has served the community well. It was the heart of the early settlement; it contained the town library and provided the venue for major events. During both world wars the Red Cross utilised its space to assemble comfort packages for troops overseas. To this day it plays a part in the town's culture as the headquarters of the Nepean Historical Society, complete with a museum that has a wide collection of artefacts dating back to the Peninsula's early beginnings. The institute was opened in 1877 with a gala performance at which George Coppin performed. Among this amazing man's attributes was his ability as an actor, patron of the arts, business entrepreneur and parliamentarian.

The Sorrento Rotunda, framed in a picturesque setting on the foreshore, has been the stage for many well-attended performances, hosting bands from visiting ships and the town band (formed in 1888) for which it was constructed in 1903. Originally dubbed 'The Bandstand', as many as three thousand people would settle themselves on the foreshore, participating in what was a popular seaside pastime. The historic Rotunda still functions as a venue in Sorrento's outdoor events and is the arena for bay side performances during the Sorrento Street Festival, held annually in late March. During this festival the streets become a carnival of song, dance and mime, as buskers and musicians from near and far perform for adoring crowds, and gourmet food stalls line the streets.

Coppin's dream for Sorrento has been an enduring one. The town today is a scintillating, thriving community, retaining all of its old-world charm and holiday excitement. Casually elegant holidaymakers bask in the cosmopolitan, laid back atmosphere, browsing the many unique shops, housed in historic buildings, and making the most of the al fresco dining and open natural environment.

Sorrento's shoreline has an exclusive scalloped edge of secluded bays sheltered by outcrops running between Cameron Bight and King Point. South Channel Fort, Victoria's only man-made island, lies 5.7 kilometres north of Point King. It was built in 1888 of bluestone covering an area of 0.7-hectares, the fortress until the late 1990s was off limits to tourists. It is now part of the Mornington Peninsula National Park and is an important bird sanctuary. Visitors are permitted only during daylight hours. Some parts of the historic fort are closed, but visitors are free to explore those sections not sectioned off.

The Sorrento Pier, built in 1870, is a hive of activity most times of the day and fishers make the most of its deep-water access. The historic foreshore is an idyllic place with a wide promenade and shady barbecue areas. **Sorrento Front Beach** is a popular bathing beach within the foreshore reserve. A gentle curve of sand dunes built up by the tides back golden stretches of sand, caressed by aqua-coloured waves. In contrast, **Sorrento Ocean Beach** is an untamed wildly beautiful beach facing Bass Strait. Myriad walks criss-cross its crests and a lookout perched high on a ridge offers awesome views. Portsea Life Saving Club has a clubhouse at the beach and during summer operates a canteen from the premises.

Above: Sorrento's famous foreshore
Right: Sorrento's jettys on Port Phillip Bay

Hotel Sorrento on Hotham Road is an historic icon. Mr J. Martin built the hotel in 1872 on land that was originally owned by Gavin Duffy. It was the town's first hotel and first registered business. At that time there were only 22 dwellings in the Sorrento and Portsea area. The hotel sits on Sorrento's highest point and can be seen from near and far. Its hand-hewn, locally mined limestone walls gleam in the translucent light that surrounds its elevated position. An elegant tower is the building's signature feature and a windsock flies proudly from its peak, directing fishers, surfers and townsfolk alike as to wind conditions on the bay. Its struts were damaged in 2003 and the sock was taken down. The town became so disorientated and demand was so great it had to be quickly replaced.

In 1981 Rob and Anne Pitt purchased the hotel, which by then had seen better days. With loving care over the years, they have systematically upgraded the property until it is once more the premier hotel on the bay, and offers a wide range of facilities. They have modernised the hotel but have been ever mindful of its history, and the result is a sympathetic melding of old with new. At the beginning of the 21st century, Hotel Sorrento still retains the grace and charm of the Victorian era, showcasing elegant staircases, gleaming woodwork and majestic mirrors. Stylish décor and traditional service are the hotel's autograph.

The Australian Hotel's Association voted the Limeburners Bar the best hotel bar in Victoria. Visitors are awed by the bar's aspect, with sweeping views over the bay, and its welcoming atmosphere. Original limestone blocks have been exposed around the walls and wooden floors gleam with rich warm tones. It is not unusual for the bay's dolphins to be seen by guests partaking of a cool drink seated outdoors on the paved sun deck.

Recent renovations have doubled the size of the lounge bar creating interconnecting sectionalised areas in which to relax and enjoy the view. The Pub TAB also has its own exclusive corner in the large lounge and on a lower level beneath the bar a cosy gaming room has up to the minute machines. Weekly entertainment staged in the Limeburners Bar t covers a wide range of styles. Sundays are a favourite with the locals – the hotel puts on a free sausage sizzle and talented musicians take the stage.

The 300 seat award-winning restaurant at Hotel Sorrento also enjoys superb views. It includes a glassed in terrace that overlooks the bay. Open fires in winter add to the ambiance. A feature of the dining room is a magnificent sideboard; elaborately carved, crafted in 1880, the huge antique has been on the premises since the hotel was built, a reminder of the grandeur that was Portsea in the late 1800s. A delectable modern Australian menu deliciously laced with European and Asian influences is served in this wonderful setting, prepared from the freshest produce and featuring delicious wood fired pizzas. Open for breakfast, lunch and dinner every day the restaurant also offers a well-balanced wine list, featuring the best of both local and Australia's most popular wines. Celebratory functions and weddings are also expertly catered for at the Hotel Sorrento.

The fully equipped Beach House Conference Centre is part of the complex, perfect for all corporate needs. It offers natural light, its own integrated restaurant and technical facilities. The centre provides an atmosphere that is relaxed and productive, far enough away from the grind to escape distraction yet close enough for total control. The hotel's team of dedicated professionals can tailor any session to suit small or large groups and create a total package to include work, play and stay.

The original hotel was built to shelter guests, but in recent times a whole range of superb accommodation has been devised on several levels. The three Heritage Suites within the hotel on the upper level have views of either the bay or Sorrento township. The spacious suites are tastefully appointed with tea and coffee making facilities, sitting areas, televisions and en suites, one with a corner spa. Private balconies off the suites provide the perfect spot to relax after a hard day on the beach.

In 1994, 'Sorrento on the Park', 18 stylish, self-contained apartments were added to the hotel. They are located opposite Sorrento Park, a rolling arc of botanic parkland that is beautifully maintained. The park was planned in 1917 by famous botanist, Baron Von Mueller, who planted the magnificent surviving pines as a windbreak for the surrounding area. The double-tiered apartments showcase different features that make them perfect for short or long-term stays. Sorrento Hotel has recently added two family apartments to itslist of accommodation. Exquisitely designed, the ten square metre apartments have two bedrooms and are ideal for either families or two couples. The modern décor has plush suede leather couches and sparkling designer kitchens. They are light and spacious, with spa baths and barbecues on private balconies.

'Sorrento on the Hill', completed in 2002, comprises six ultra-modern apartments perched on the Sorrento cliffs overlooking Port Phillip Bay. These 4.5-Star, AAA rated, luxury apartments have quality furnishings and fabrics, queen size beds and plush suede leather couches. An open gas log fireplace provides a cosy hideaway in winter and spa baths with bay views allow decadent pampering. Complete with all modern conveniences and private balconies these apartments are ideal retreats for a romantic liaison or a luxurious base for the modern traveller.

At the Hotel Sorrento they have turned the pursuit of pleasure into an art form and friendly staff led by energetic young manager Mike Flanagan ensure it. The venue has been delivering excellence for over a century and whether you come for a day or an extended stay, the same attention to detail and dedicated service is its legacy and is sure to be a feature of your visit.

Above & right: Southern Peninsula landmark, Hotel Sorrento

Oceanic Whitehall Guest House on Ocean Beach Road, adjacent to the Mornington Peninsula National Park, has welcomed visitors to Sorrento since 1904. It was purpose-built as a guesthouse, catering for genteel travellers of the era, built by the owner of the Back Beach Coffee Palace that sat directly opposite Whitehall. The Coffee Palace was destroyed by fire in the 1960s and replaced by the Oceanic Motel Units that are once more owned by the proprietors of Whitehall. The motel has been renamed Oceanic Apartments and is being renovated to provide 20 stylish apartment units to complement the grand old guesthouse.

For most of Whitehall's existence it has functioned as a guesthouse, with a break from 1945 to 1949 when it was used by the Commonwealth Government as accommodation for service personnel families. The guesthouse is of historic regional significance, being one of only three intact examples of a large guesthouse still operating in Victoria. Although the building has been sympathetically altered internally, and rear sections added, the street frontage remains the same. The elegant proportions and the recently renovated double-storey timber verandah that has retained the original fine detailing distinguish the building's façade. The sophisticated design of local limestone, together with red brick quoins to corners and openings and elegant gardens, make Whitehall one of Sorrento's most attractive landmarks.

The guesthouse contains 31 rooms of different dimensions and styles. They range from standard accommodation to stylishly renovated luxury en suite rooms or the historic, traditional guestrooms, with open fireplaces and period features, overlooking the grand balcony. The entire guesthouse is furnished in an elegant eclectic style, which perfectly complements the old building, which boasts a grand staircase and high ceilings. A traditional cooked breakfast is served in the magnificent guest dining room that opens onto a walled patio – perfect for summer dining. The dining room is resplendent with large open fire and is also available for private functions, conferences and events.

The spacious grounds are perfect for having fun or sitting back and relaxing after a hard day on the beach. Guest lounges, a salt-water pool, barbecue area and tennis court are included in the guest facilities and Oceanic Whitehall Guest House is only a short walk to the magnificence of Sorrento's Back Beach and all the town's attractions.

Located in Sorrento's popular Ocean Beach Road, Antipodes Bookshop and Gallery offers an enticing selection of carefully chosen books and exquisite art. Sitting between a pair of genuine historic houses built in the very early 1900s; the gallery has been sympathetically designed to fit right in, giving the impression of being of the same era. The bi-level interior resembles a boat shed with bagged and painted brickwork. An impression of space is created by lime-lined vaulted ceilings with exposed trusses. When you step into the gentle vibrancy of the gallery, the ambience is very Zen. The balance between serene music, architecture and natural light heightens the sensory experience of browsing, nurturing both mind and soul.

Glenda Stewart and friends purchased the existing gallery in 1998 and added the extra dimension of books. Almost every possible subject that could be portrayed within the covers of a book is here; an irresistible selection of cookery, architecture and design, recently reviewed releases and even an alcove devoted to children's books. Antipodes' exceptional taste is reflected in the display of works from the studios of their artists, ceramicists, jewellers and craft designers. Inspired ceramics by Chris Plumridge, Gillian Broinowski, Sandra Bowkett and the elegant work of local ceramicist Kerrie Lightbody are enhanced by the glisten of glass from Leisa Wharington and Emma Varga. The gallery holds regular exhibitions, showcasing both local and Australian work, but on any visit Antipodes presents an ever-changing display of contemporary art.

Occupying one of the town's historic houses on Ocean Beach Road, the First Settlement Gallery is a treasure trove of Australian art. The old house was built by a Norwegian boatbuilder named Johannsen in the late 1800s; he named his home Sandarne, in memory of the village he left behind in Norway. The old homestead makes a perfect gallery, full of character with large solid rooms, open fireplaces and wooden floors. Neridah McGaan with her husband Jim bought the existing gallery in 1993; their son Jamie later joined them in the business.

The artists that the gallery represents produce real in-your-face vibrant art of every style, working in every medium. Oils on canvas by such Australian greats as Marshall Williams, who is a master at controlling the dimensional environment, attack the senses, exploding in light and energy. Bright feisty canvases by Janine Daddo and Christine Wellington titillate the imagination. Evocative Australian indigenous scenes by Ted Young, who spends eight weeks each year gathering inspiration for his vivid work, living with Aborigine tribes in the outback, decorate the walls, along with the intricate work of Robert Langley who studied with Boyd and Mirka Mora, and sculptures by Robbie Delves enhance the displays. The gallery reflects Neridah's attitude towards life and is a fun place to browse through. Every piece has a story to tell, and listening to Neridah brings each work of art vividly to life.

Visiting the Mornington Peninsula from the Bellarine Peninsula has been made an effortless sightseeing adventure, thanks to the innovative award-winning company Peninsula Searoad Transport. The introduction of a vehicular and passenger ferry service across Port Phillip Heads in 1987 was the culmination of 30 years of dreaming, planning and lobbying by many people, organizations and government departments, in both communities of the Mornington and the Bellarine Peninsulas.

Long before the formation of the operating company, Peninsula Searoad Transport Ltd (PST), in June 1983, moves were being made and pressure brought to bear for the establishment of a reliable vehicular ferry service that would link the 2 Peninsulas, both economically and socially.

Above: Oceanic Whitehall Guest House on Ocean Beach Road
Right:
Top left: The Antipodes Bookstore & Gallery
Top right: Surf Club and lookout at Sorrento Back Beach
Centre right: Interior of the Oceanic Whitehall Guest House
Bottom: The First Settlement Gallery, Sorrento

After years of extensive research and feasibility studies plus two years of work by Peninsula Searoad Transport to obtain the 17 permits required from government and semi-government bodies, the go-ahead was finally given.

An outlay of $2 million was made to construct a purpose built 35-vehicle vessel at Carrington slips in Newcastle.

Despite scepticism in some quarters about the viability of the service, especially during winter months, from September 1987 the MV 'Peninsula Princess' rarely missed a scheduled crossing until she was replaced in 1993. A ticket office and transit lounge was established at the eastern end of Queenscliff Larken Parade in 1990, and at the end of the Sorrento pier in 1992. In 1993 the MV 'Queenscliff' replaced MV 'Peninsula Princess'. The new ferry was designed in Tasmania by Seward Maritime and built by Port Lincoln Ship Construction Pty Ltd at Port Lincoln, South Australia, especially designed to meet the service's growing needs. The 'Queenscliff' not only more than doubled the vehicle transport capacity of the 'Peninsula Princess' but introduced a new level of comfort and enjoyment for the 700 passengers it is capable of carrying.

Growing patronage, and the company's desire to better serve the business community on both sides of the bay, prompted the construction of an additional 80-car vessel in April 2000. The MV 'Sorrento' took shape at Southern Marine Shiplift in Launceston, Tasmania. The new vessel began operation in March 2001. The Queenscliff-Sorrento car ferries criss-cross the southern end of Port Phillip Bay 24 times a day, every day of the year. The twin-hull vessels are purposely built to operate in all weather conditions. The ferries operate daily, leaving every hour on the hour 7am-6pm, with an extra 7pm trip operating from December 26 until the end of daylight saving. The MV 'Sorrento' is fully equipped to cater for passengers with disabilities, including an internal lift from the vehicle deck to the passenger lounge.

Imagine yourself sitting back in relaxed comfort aboard the MV 'Sorrento' or MV 'Queenscliff' while taking the searoad when you are next visiting the Mornington or the Bellarine Peninsulas. There are many highlights on the 40-minute journey, including unparalleled views of historic lighthouses, at Point Lonsdale and Queenscliff. Look out for the Point Nepean fortifications along the shoreline and navigational features guiding shipping vessels down the bay. Seals and dolphins are often spotted frolicking and performing in the waters; all of these sights are available from the comfortable lounge areas and numerous observation decks. On-board cafes provide delicious light meals, with freshly baked cakes and refreshing drinks. Occasionally, during special Bellarine and Mornington Peninsula festivals, entertainment is included on the journey.

Peninsula Searoad Transport was the proud recipient of the 2002 Victorian Tourism Award for Major Transport and Tour Operator, another richly deserved award that recognises the high standard and professionalism of the company.

Based on the Sorrento foreshore, the Sorrento Sailing Couta Boat Club is responsible for the fleet of over 100 Couta boats oft espied on the bay. Now recognised as a unique class, the club's main regatta is the GANT Portsea Cup, held in January. The first Couta boat race was held at Queenscliff in 1884. The craft's origins are as romantically historic as the area that surrounds the club. They evolved from a small wooden, broad-beamed, centre-plate style of fishing boat that was slung low in the water. The boats originated from Queenscliff and Port Melbourne and soon spread right along the Victorian coastline, then to Perth, Sydney and across Bass Strait to Tasmania. From the outset they were built for speed as the fisherman, catch limit obtained, would sail for home. Others would join in, limit reached or not, therefore ensuring a race. Over the years as fishermen replaced boats the criteria was for more speed.

Fishing amongst the abundance of species to be found close in to the Australian shores, they were ideally suited to the then-plentiful Barracouta, and it is from this fish that the boat is named after.

Today these boats have a sleek style and a champagne price tag, owned by true aficionados and mostly dedicated racers. They are unique in Australian boating and adhere to the ancient craft of wooden boat building. The Couta Boat Association is rigid, ensuring a strong class where no modern fibres such as kevlar, carbon fibre or spectra are permitted. Boats must be made of wood and use wooden block pulleys.

The Wooden Boat Shop, run by Tim Phillips, one of the few masters of the craft still to be found, is based at Sorrento. Couta boats are usually around twenty-six feet long and with the scarcity of suitable timber and the dying craft of wooden boat building, constructing everything by hand using traditional techniques, make the building time about 1500 hours. The sight of these classic wooden boats on the bay with sails unfurled, scudding along in front of the wind evokes a deep feeling of freedom, and a sense of excitement that only a bonding with the elements can incite.

The Wooden Boatshop occupies 2.5 acres on Hotham Road, Sorrento. It has evolved from a purpose-built shop for constructing Couta boats to a complete wooden boat building facility incorporating the construction of the new Nepean displacement motor launches. With three boat-building sheds, a fully stocked chandlery and a team of experienced craftsmen, they have the ability to construct up to 16 new vessels a year. As well as offering traditional boat designs, classic restorations, rebuilds and full maintenance, they have an in-house design team for custom work.

Tim's most recent project is the Cheviot 32, a 10-metre round bilge planing boat, a design reminiscent of the highly successful, proven hull forms of the 'Maine Lobster Boat' – This elegant vessel will soon be seen on the bay and hopefully in Sydney Harbour.

Above: Casting a line from Sorrento Pier
Right: Sorrento Sailing Couta Boat Club regatta

There are over a hundred bottlenose dolphins residing in Port Phillip Bay. These wonderful mammals are a gregarious bunch, the hedonists of their under water domain; they love an audience and show off in front of any cruise boat in the area. It is an awesome sight watching the sleek, glistening bodies leaping in perfect unison out of the roiling waters; a faultless amphibian ballet!

These "ever smiling" dolphins are a promiscuous lot, having many partners in their lifetime. They have no set mating season, giving birth throughout the year, although it has been noted that more calves are born through spring and summer. Females carry their young for 12 months and, once born, calves suckle for up to eighteen months, although by six months they begin to eat fish. Calves will remain with their mothers for five years or more. Adult females give birth only every two to three years and do not begin breeding until they are nine years old. The breed has longevity in its genes, living in excess of 30 years. In fact, some studies have come up with 50 year-old animals.

Bottlenose dolphins are thought to have two distinct groups - inshore populations and offshore populations. The offshore groups migrate each year whereas the inshore groups prefer to stay in one place. Inshore animals are smaller and slimmer than their ocean-going kin. The adult weight ranges from 150 to 650 kilograms and they measure anything from 190 to 390 centimetres. These animals have the uncanny ability to close down one half of their brain at a time, switching from one side to the other at will. They sleep, on the surface, in a semi-conscious state, needing stay alert enough to breathe.

These magnificent creatures have a keen sense of community. The whole pod cooperates in the defence of the group, also baby-sitting and feeding the young. They communicate with body language and sharp broadband pulses of ultrasonic sound referred to as clicks, and measure distance by how long the echo takes to come back. All in all these gracious mammals are highly intelligent and never fail to captivate onlookers with their rollicking behaviour on the surface of the bay.

The Australian Fur Seal is also to be found cavorting in the bay. The waters around the Peninsula were once home to huge colonies of these endearing animals. During the 1800s they were hunted to near extinction. By 1891 the devastation of seal populations in all parts of Australia was acknowledged and seals became the first native animal in Australia to be protected. Numbers are now on the rise, thanks to the work carried out in the marine parks, but are still nowhere near the levels achieved before Europeans came to the area.

Sorrento's seaside position presents a varied selection of seagoing options and Moonraker Charters offers visitors a wide variety of tours, from swimming with dolphins to private charters on beautiful Port Phillip Bay. Passengers can be assured they are in good hands when they book aboard Moonraker. The Mackinnon family have been operating Moonraker Charters since September 1991.

Torie and Sandy Mackinnon own and operate Moonraker Charters from October to April each year. The 70-foot cruiser 'Moonraker' is state of the art, equipped with lounge, shower and toilet facilities plus a fully equipped modern galley, thus providing guests with comfort, safety and professionalism.

The most appealing of Moonraker's organised cruises must certainly be the interaction with dolphins and seals. These tours are designed with the welfare of the animals in mind. Moonraker Charters is an advanced fully accredited company of Eco-tourism Association of Australia and Moonraker's trained crew ensure the experience is a memorable one! At the commencement of each cruise, guests are fully briefed on safety and points of interest aboard Moonraker. An experienced dive master leads each snorkelling excursion and guests are supplied with a full-length wet suit, mask, snorkel and fins.

Nothing can compare to the thrill and excitement of seeing dolphins in their natural habitat, hearing their high-pitched sounds and looking into their intelligent eyes as they swim around you. Being accepted as part of their world – you will never forget your first dolphin encounter!

Polperro Dolphin Swims is a multi-award-winning company, being recognised for their dedication to eco tourism. It is owned and operated by the Muir family. Established in 1986 it was the first commercial dolphin swim company to operate in Port Phillip Bay and conducts environmentally responsible dolphin interactions.

Numbers on the Polperro Swims are purposely limited. This guarantees a high standard of safety, plus customer and environmental care, in keeping with their philosophy of caring for the welfare of the dolphins and their habitat. Polperro Dolphin Swims has shown that success can be achieved within environmental limits, and in recognition of their efforts were awarded Hall of Fame for Environmental Tourism at the Victorian Tourism Awards. Polperro's on-board facilities include change areas, toilet, hot shower and a galley for serving refreshments; all crewmembers possess recognised diving and first-aid qualifications. Wetsuits, masks and snorkels are all supplied. Reef and seal swims are also often part of the trip, allowing passengers to experience much more than the dolphins.

The company provides a wide range of other services including bay cruises, educational and historical tours, fully catered charters or personally tailored trips. During peak summer season, Polperro runs two dolphin swim trips a day, seven days a week, from Sorrento pier and this is by far the most popular of their cruises. Polperro Dolphin Swims offer passengers the chance to experience the marine adventure of a lifetime. There is no feeling on earth that inspires such awe, or provides the rush of adrenalin, as does the close proximity of these hydro dynamically shaped, intelligent animals. When encountered their beauty and elegance and zest for life evokes delight, creating a memory that lives in the mind forever.

Left: Moonraker Charters returning to Sorrento
Right: Port Phillip Bay's dolphin pod at play

Portsea is Sorrento's twin – not identical but linked by a shared history. It is the Peninsula's most westerly town and, if anything, a touch more elegant than Sorrento. It has long been famous for its stylish mansions and decorative gardens but it is also a traveller's playground. Set on the doorstep of Point Nepean, part of the Mornington Peninsula National Park, the town is central to invigorating clifftop walks that provide stunning views and the choice of ocean or bay beaches. A feature of the village is the avenue of cernuous cypress that greets the visitor.

Perhaps Portsea's most famous holiday resident was Prime Minister Harold Holt, who spent time in the town in the 1960s. He had a passion for scuba diving, a sport that Portsea is famous for, and tragically vanished during a dive at Cheviot Beach. His disappearance created a mystery that has never been solved.

Weeroona Bay is Portsea's main bayside beach. It is a restful stretch of coastline decorated by low sand dunes and a pier that is a bustling centre for ferries, fishers and divers. A wide range of fish can be caught from the pier, including snapper, whiting, bay trout, barracouta and the odd shark. At night, squid, garfish and red roughy are known to bite. There is a fish-measuring guide fixed to the pier and of course anyone over the age of 18 needs a fishing licence. A natural phenomenon close to Portsea's surf beach is the unique rock formation London Bridge; it is easily accessed via the car park. It was at one time an arch of dune rock that has over the years become eroded by the elements. A trail to Sphinx Rock can be reached via a track that starts at Portsea

The town hosts a full program of annual events that include The Portsea Swim Classic, held in January each year. The classic is one of the largest open-water swims in Australia and attracts competitors from far and near. The L-shaped 1.2-kilometre course is laid out at Portsea Front Beach off the Nepean Highway near the pier.

Portsea Pier is the spectacular setting for the second leg in an internationally renowned yacht race that is recognised as one of the world's great yachting challenges. The competing yachts in the Tasaki Osaka Cup leave the sheltered haven of Port Phillip Bay for the ominous stretch of ocean that awaits outside The Heads. In the 2003 challenge the yachts were given a riotous send-off, with historic vessels and ferries mingling with a large spectator fleet.

Portsea Hotel has been a landmark on the Point Nepean Road since 1876. It evolved from a cottage built by Alexander Watson, a Scotsman, one of three brothers who arrived in Portsea in 1870. He built the cottage in the 1870s, later adding a bar. In 1927 most of the old Portsea Hotel was demolished and a 'modern' hotel was erected. The years in-between have seen many owners and many changes to the historic property, although its face has remained unchanged. In 1994 the hotel underwent extensive internal renovations, whilst retaining its historic character. The sympathetic renovations exposed the hotel's spectacular views and in 1999 present owners Fraser Island Pty Ltd purchased the hotel and continued to improve upon the success of its earlier metamorphosis.

The hotel's open spaces and three bars let guests take in the superb views. A terrace encircles the bay side of the hotel, allowing al fresco dining in the summer months, or enclosed views in the cooler seasons protected by clear shades that still allow unprecedented views of the bay. The unveiling of the Portsea Deck restaurant above the Nepean Room provided the hotel with an even greater 'WOW' factor. The fine dining restaurant is a blend of exquisite food and breathtaking views all the way to the Bellarine Peninsula. Diners can also enjoy sumptuous meals from a contemporary menu in the bistro; perfectly prepared and promptly served, surrounded by the warm patina of jarrah, serene seaside shades, Sydney blue gum floors and awesome views.

Winter has its own allure with four open fires creating pools of warmth, or on brighter days patrons can capture the sun in the nationally acclaimed beer garden. A wide program of weekly entertainment rounds off a colourful venue. It presents a variety of performers that cater for all tastes and age groups.

Portsea Hotel also offers comfortable country style, seaside accommodation with tariffs to suit all budgets. There is a variety of room types with either en suites or shared facilities. Some of the rooms have second bedrooms, sitting rooms and bay views. Three function areas easily cater for small or large conferences and special occasions. Weddings are made special with the function rooms not only offering superb views but also excellent facilities and professional, flexible staff who ensure groups a memorable event.

The Mornington Peninsula National Park covers a large section of the region, approximately 2,686 hectares round the heel and along the sole and toe of the boot shaped Peninsula. With the arrival of Europeans in the early 1800s the Peninsula's natural resources were soon in danger of being violated. As early as 1876 the government was persuaded by one of the area's initial protagonists, George Coppin, to reserve a section of coastal land as an ocean park.

Situated 80 kilometres south of Melbourne via the Mornington Peninsula Freeway and the Point Nepean Road from Rosebud, the park provides visitors with a multitude of outdoor recreational choices. A ferry from Queenscliff also provides access.

The park's 40-kilometre coastline offers windswept ocean beaches of stunning beauty fringed by glittering sand, washed by translucent emerald waters undulating with the movement of liquid silk. Its beaches are renowned surfing spots with **Gunnamatta Beach** being hailed as the most challenging facing the awesome waters of Bass Strait and particularly renowned for its pounding surf. Its wave action produces tunnels that test the skill of the most experienced surfers. Before 1960 Gunamatta (an Aboriginal word meaning 'beach and sand hills') was known as Paradise Beach, reflecting the raw breathtaking beauty encountered on the Bass Strait beaches. Gunnamatta is also a favourite surf-fishing beach, and provides an inspirational walk, backed by high dunes and fringed by wild, tumultuous surf. It is a dangerous swimming location and should be treated with respect; the Gunnamatta Surf Life Saving Club has been called on to rescue thousands of swimmers since its inception in 1966. A sandbar creates two rips; these channels relentlessly drag tonnes of water back to the ocean. The force of the

Above: Historic Portsea Hotel, c.1876
Right: Wild seas at Shelly beach, Portsea

water knocks swimmers off the sandbar throwing them into the huge breakers that wait offshore. So always swim between the flags. Facilities exist at Gunnamatta in the shape of picnic tables, a car park and toilet facilities. The surf life saving club has a modern clubhouse on the beach and manages a kiosk in the summer months.

St Andrews Beach is a non-swimming beach with wild surf and deadly rips. It is never wise to ignore the flagged swimming areas and directions on these beaches. Bass Strait has a fearsome reputation; its waters are treacherous and should be treated with extreme caution. However the beaches themselves are an unbridled wonderland and provide hours of exhilarating exploration.

The Park at Point Nepean lies at the most westerly tip of the Mornington Peninsula, on the dividing arm between Port Phillip Bay and Bass Strait. It provides a spectacular viewing platform from where the terrifying awesomeness of the Heads and the Rip can be simultaneously experienced. Parts of the point lie within the Mornington Peninsula National Park; the historic Quarantine Station and Fort Nepean are on the Register of the National Estate. The entire area is a gigantic open-air museum with historic tunnels, coastal walks, ocean and Rip views, gun emplacements and the surviving buildings of the fort and quarantine station. The site is unique and is of major archaeological, historical and biological significance.

The fort was built on the point in 1882, part of a defence complex designed to protect the colony of Victoria, at a time when there were fears of a Russian invasion. Much of the fortification was built underground. By the close of the 19th century the installation was reputedly the most heavily fortified military post in the Southern Hemisphere. Its use as a military installation came to an end in 1988.

A quarantine station was established in 1852 when a ship arrived in Port Phillip Bay carrying passengers suffering from typhus; 100 of its 850 passengers had died from the disease. The station was completed by 1859 and continued to operate for 120 years, providing an effective barrier against unwelcome, ship-borne contagious diseases arriving in Australia. The peak of its use came after WWI when it housed more than 11,800 immigrants suffering from the catastrophic worldwide influenza virus that during its year of virility claimed more people than were killed during the entire hostilities of the war, including 12,000 deaths in Australia.

For more than a 140 years Point Nepean was closed to the general public, but is now one of the region's most visited attractions, both for its historic content and its wild scenic beauty. Private cars and buses are not permitted beyond the Gunners Car Park, 2.5 kilometres from the Orientation Centre. Visitors can explore the point in various ways, by hiking, by biking (bikes can be hired at the Orientation Centre) or by taking a ride on the Point Explorer.

The express leaves every half-hour in the peak season from the Orientation Centre, located at the end of Point Nepean Road carrying visitors on transporters that comprise a chain of open carriages pulled by a gigantic tractor – in itself an adventure. During the trip to Fort Nepean an informative documentary gives travellers a look into the past. Passengers can embark or disembark at three points along the route and can explore the area for as long as they like. The Orientation Centre provides general information about the park and houses audio-visual displays that includes video footage of life during the early 1900s on the southern Mornington Peninsula. It also contains a gift shop where drinks and ice creams can be purchased. Picnic tables and benches and electric barbecues are set within the parkland that surrounds the centre.

When visiting the point, set aside at least half a day to investigate its fascinating history and appreciate its stark wilderness features, golden beaches and huge rocks sculpted by wind and waves. An underwater plinth is a poignant reminder of the loss of Australian Prime Minister Harold Holt in 1967 at Cheviot Beach. The waters off the beach are protected in the Port Phillip Heads Marine National Park. At one time the entire point was covered in sheoak woodland, which was quickly stripped by the demands of the limeburners. Now it is carpeted in low-lying brush and coastal vegetation. The feeling of remoteness at the promontory adds to the overall experience.

A cemetery dating back to the point's first occupation is thought to contain around 300 graves, although only 30 headstones have survived. It is linked to early European settlement, quarantine, shipwrecks and defence. The last burial, in the 1920s, was of a man drowned at the point while trying to rescue survivors from a shipwreck. In 1887 eight of a total of 35 people who lost their lives when the steamer 'Cheviot' came aground on Corsair Rock were buried in the cemetery.

Exhilarating walking tracks embroider the slopes of the point and the old fortifications are a warren of tunnels and old gun emplacements, with many observation points that provide sweeping views all the way to Melbourne. The walks lead to many places of interest within the park, to scenic beaches and historic remains. A visit to Point Nepean provides an interesting day out for both adults and children that enriches, entertains and educates, providing a spectacle during any visit.

Left: Sunset over the Heads and Rip at Point Nepean

Right (from top): The old gun emplacement fortifications and rugged coastline at the Park at Point Nepean; Engine house at the Park at Point Nepean; View of narrows dividing Port Phillip Bay and Bass Strait; Sunset over Pt Lonsdale lighthouse from the Park at Point Nepean

LISTINGS • FRANKSTON

SEAFORD

Two Cans Antiques & Decor

Specialising in 19th century French, English & European antiques & decor.

Quality • Character • Style

Open 6 days (closed Sunday)

Showroom:
142 Nepean Highway, Seaford
Warehouse (Sat only):
2/11 Cumberland Drive, Seaford
Ph: 03 9786 7894, 0415 374 213

SEAFORD

Riviera Hotel

Family bistro with indoor playroom, sports-bar, full TAB facilities, Skychannel, Tabaret Gaming Room.
Berettas Liquor Drive-through bottleshop located opposite Seaford beach

30 Nepean Hwy, Seaford 3198
Ph: (03) 9786 5666 • Fax: (03) 9786 2255
theriviera@bigpond.com

SEAFORD

The Victorian Climbing Centre

Indoor Rock Climbing is safe, easy to learn, great for all ages and inexpensive. Birthday Parties and Group Bookings available. Fully supervised. Kiosk facilities available.

1/12 Hartnett Drive, Seaford
Tel: (03) 9782 4222 or Fax: (03) 9782 4333
(Mel Ref: 99 H5)

FRANKSTON

George Pentland Botanic Gardens

Having undergone a stunning transformation in recent years, the Gardens offer visitors examples of native plants from South-Eastern Australia including a fern gully. Picnic & BBQ facilities provided.

Williams St, Frankston
Opening hours: 1 Nov – 31 Mar 7am – 9pm
1 Apr – 31 Oct 7am – 6pm

FRANKSTON

Jenny Pihan Fine Art

Specialising in contemporary & traditional paintings by Australian & internationally recognised artists.
EXHIBITIONS   COMMISSIONS
Tues – Sun 10am – 5pm

The Kananook Creek Boathouse Gallery
368 Nepean Hwy, Frankston 3199
(Mel Ref: 99 D12)   Tel: (03) 9770 5354
Email: art@jennypihanfineart.com.au

FRANKSTON

Richard Linton Maritime Art Gallery

Specialising in Richard Linton's Limited Edition Lithographs of famous Sailing Ships & Marine Historical works.

46B Beach Street, Frankston 3199
Tel: (03) 9783 1246 Fax: (03) 9775 2522
www.lintonmaritimeart.com.au
Email: rlinton@lintonmaritimeart.com.au

FRANKSTON
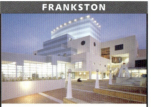
Frankston Arts Centre

• 800 seat Professional Theatre & Program
• Function & Conference Facilities
• Exhibitions & Workshops
• Undercover Parking

Corner of Davey & Young St, Frankston
(Mel Ref: 100A D8)
Box Office: (03) 9784 1060
Fax: (03) 9770 1164
Website: artscentre.frankston.vic.gov.au

FRANKSTON

Frankston RSL

• Wine & dine at Raphael's Bistro 7 days a week
• Tatts Pokies, Keno, TAB
• Watch sport on Foxtel
• Dance the night away to live bands & fabulous floorshows

183 Cranbourne Rd, Frankston 3199
Ph: (03) 9783 2288 • Fax: (03) 9781 2701

FRANKSTON
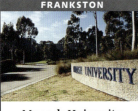
Monash University Peninsula Campus

Internationally recognised institution offering courses in Business, Education, IT, Nursing and Ambulance Paramedic training. Friendly learning environment with broad range of services

McMahons Rd, Frankston
Tel: 61 3 9904 4100 • Fax: 61 3 9904 4190
www.monash.edu.au

FRANKSTON

Daveys Bar & Restaurant

Daveys Bar & Bistro offers alfresco and fine dining, Peninsula wines & ocean views. Quality weekend entertainment from Jazz, Blues to Acoustic. Function facilities available.

510 Nepean Hwy, Frankston 3199
Tel: (03) 9783 7255 Fax: (03) 9783 7018
Email: Daveys.Hotel@fostersgroup.com

FRANKSTON

The Kananook Creek Boathouse

One of the region's most acclaimed a la carte restaurant and tearooms. Superbly presented restaurant with modern Australian cuisine. Dine indoors or in the garden setting. Open 7 days.

366-368 Nepean Hwy, Frankston 3199
Ph: (03) 9770 5330 • Fax: (03) 9770 5332
email: boathouse@boathouse.com.au

FRANKSTON
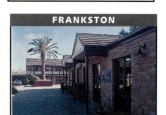
Frankston Motor Inn & Perovics Restaurant

Quiet location in the heart of Frankston. Beachside with pool and 30 air-conditioned rooms with queen beds, spa rooms, and all modern facilities. 24-hour checkin

406 Nepean Hwy, Frankston 3199
Ph: (03) 9781 5544 • Fax: (03) 9781 5886

FRANKSTON

Shakespeare's Bar & Restaurant

Try our classic presentation of fine international cuisine in the restaurant's relaxed, intimate atmosphere or enjoy a drink in the friendly bar and bistro with an extensive selection of European and local beers.

Tel: (03) 9781 2266
101 Young Street, Frankston
(next to Frankston Arts Centre)

FRANKSTON
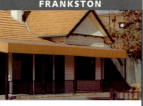
Siddharta Indian Restaurant

Standing the test of time. Superb Indian restaurant featuring Northern Indian, Tandoori, coupled with Peninsula wine from our own vineyard

345 Nepean Hwy, Frankston
Ph: (03) 9783 6382 • Fax: (03) 9783 9469

FRANKSTON

Via Mare Restaurant

Frankston's leading Mediterranean & seafood restaurant. Recommended 'Melbourne Age Good Food Guide' each year. Large selection of local wines available. Mention this ad to receive a complimentary coffee.

Tel: (03) 9770 0111
343 Nepean Hwy, Frankston
www.viamare.com.au

FRANKSTON

Flanagans Irish Bar

Flanagans at the Pier Hotel –
the premier entertainment venue in the centre of Frankston. Relax in the Irish bar or one of the loung areas.
The perfect meeting place.

Cnr Nepean Hwy & Davey St, Frankston 3199
Ph: (03) 9783 9800 • Fax: (03) 9783 2092
pier.hotel@alhgroup.com.au

LISTINGS • FRANKSTON & NORTHERN PENINSULA

FRANKSTON

Ambassador Hotel

Frankston & The Peninsula's landmark hotel. Featuring convention & function facilities, restaurant, landscaped grounds & gardens, private chapel. The region's affordable venue, whilst exploring the Mornington Peninsula

325-335 Nepean Hwy, Frankston 3199
Ph: (03) 9781 4488 • Fax: (03) 9781 4785
email: ambassadorfrankston@bigpond.com

FRANKSTON

Frankston International

Well appointed rooms with spas. Taggarts Cafe & Bar and function facilities available. Northern end of Peninsula, one hour from Phillip Island. Close to shops, beach & cinema. Earn Flybuys/Frequent Flyers.

389 Nepean Hwy, Frankston
Tel: (03) 9781 3444 Fax: (03) 9781 3738
Email: bw97152@bestwestern.com.au
www.bestwestern.com.au/frankstonintl

FRANKSTON

Frankston Motel
★★★☆

24 well-appointed ground floor units. Pool, tennis court, BBQs. Free light breakfast in rooms, ample parking for cars & boats. Gateway to all Mornington Peninsula has to offer

233 Frankston-Flinders Rd, Frankston 3199
Ph: (03) 5971 1233 • Fax: (03) 5971 4375
email: frankston-motel@bigpond.com

LANGWARRIN

Beretta's Langwarrin Hotel

Enjoy the modern family-oriented venue serving modern Australian cuisine, with daily specials in the Bistro. Full TAB facilities, gaming lounge and drive-in bottleshop.
Open 7 days for lunch & dinner

220 Cranbourne Rd, Langwarrin 3910
Ph: (03) 9789 2711 • Fax: (03) 9789 0235
langyhotel@bigpond.com.au

LANGWARRIN

McClelland Gallery

Award-winning facility set in sculpture park which displays works by leading Australian artists. Exhibitions, library, gift shop, air-conditioned cafe overlooking picturesque lake (café hours 10.30-4.30 Fri-Sun). Opening hours Tues-Sun 10am-5pm

390 McClelland Drive, Langwarrin
Tel: (03) 9789 1671 Fax: (03) 9789 1610
Email: info@mcclellandgallery.com

LANGWARRIN SOUTH

Mulberry Hill

Former home of Sir Daryl Lindsay, artist, and Lady Joan Lindsay, author.
Sunday tours 1.30, 2.15, 3pm.
Groups any day by appointment.
Closed July.

Golf Links Rd, Langwarrin South
(Mel Ref: 107 C2) Tel: (03) 5971 4138
Email: tourism@nattrust.com.au

BAXTER

Sages Cottage
RESTAURANT & FUNCTION CENTRE

Historic (1856) cottage in the heart of Peninsula at Baxter. Dine in the kitchen courtyard or cosy historic Baxter Provender Restaurant, then explore the property's grounds & garden.

Sages Rd, Baxter (Mel: 106 F5)
Ph: (03) 5971 1337

MT ELIZA

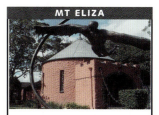

Manyung Gallery

One of the Peninsula's most visited Galleries, displaying a wide range of Australian, and the Peninsula's foremost artists.
Open 7 days.

1408 Nepean Hwy, Mt Eliza 3930
Ph: (03) 9787 2953 • Fax: (03) 9787 2957
stuart@manyunggallery.com.au

MT ELIZA

Lintons Garden & Home

The largest garden centre on the Peninsula Winner of the Best Garden Centre in Australia 1999 & 2003. Tearooms for lunch or refreshments – Bookings 9787 3244 Lintons 'More than just a nursery'.

cnr Canadian Bay Rd & Nepean H'Way Mt Eliza
Tel: (03) 9787 2122 Fax (03) 9787 8555
Email: lintons@lintons.com.au

MORNINGTON

Mornington Chamber of Commerce

— MARVELLOUS MORNINGTON —
The shopping strip with style. Featuring the Wednesday Main Street markets, attracting 250,000 visitors annually

PO Box 40, Mornington 3931
Ph: (03) 5975 4522 • Fax: (03) 5977 1939
email: mcc@satlink.com.au
www.mornington.commerce.asu.au

MORNINGTON

Mornington Central Shopping Centre

• Coles open 24 hours
• Target and 36 specialty stores
• 300 free undercover carparks available

78 Barkly St, Mornington 3931
Ph: (03) 5976 1299 • Fax: (03) 5976 1466
email: carol_white@centro.com.au
web: www.centro.com.au

MORNINGTON

Sail Mornington Luxury Yacht Charter

A sensational and affordable way to discover the delights of Port Phillip in true style, comfort and luxury.
Sailing is an experience to be shared.

Located at the Mornington Pier
Mob: 0418 349 364
www.sailmornington.com.au

MORNINGTON

The Boyz 4 Breakie

Divine Food for Interesting People!
A Mornington tradition –
get hot this summer at the Boyz.
Open 7 days
Mon-Tues 8am-5pm
Wed-Sun 8am to late

1A Main St, Mornington
Ph: (03) 5977 2888

MORNINGTON

Beaches of Mornington

Mornington's most awarded restaurant.
The fun and food centre of the Peninsula, with signature great steaks and seafood dishes.
Enjoy live music till late,
4 nights a week.

1/55 Barkly St, Mornington 3931
Ph: (03) 5975 0966 • Fax: (03) 5977 2974

MORNINGTON

Peninsula Indulgence Restaurant

Mod Australian cuisine. Open seven days, breakfast, lunch & dinner, or we do tailored wine tours. Relaxed climate-controlled atmosphere, great food, wine, and service.

71 Barkly St, Mornington 3931
Ph: (03) 5976 2188 • Fax: (03) 5977 2496
www.peninsulaindulgence.com

MORNINGTON

Come for the food – stay for the view.
Take in the unsurpassed views over Mornington Harbour and Port Phillip Bay, on the deck or in the restaurant.
Breakfast, lunch & dinner, 7 days

1 Schnapper Point Drive, Mornington
Ph: (03) 5973 5599
www.therocksmornington.com.au

LISTINGS • NORTHERN PENINSULA

MORNINGTON

Schnapper Point Kiosk
Relax and soak up the atmosphere of Mornington Pier whilst enjoying a snack or refreshments and local produce. The ideal meeting place on the Peninsula
No. 1 Schnapper Point Drive, Mornington 3931
Ph: (03) 5975 6332 • Fax: (03) 5976 2744

MORNINGTON

- SIDEWALK CAFE
- BAR
- NIGHTSPOT

The Peninsula's funky venue. Open for lunch & dinner 7 days. Weekly entertainment. Function packages available. Cube nightspot Fridays & Saturdays and special events.
62 Main St, Mornington 3931
Ph: (03) 5976 2222 • Fax: (03) 5977 2799
bayhotelmornington@bigpond.com

MORNINGTON
Grand Hotel
A Mornington tradition for over 100 years
124 Main St, Mornington 3931
Ph: (03) 5975 2001 • Fax: (03) 5975 1756
email: grand@zx.net

MORNINGTON

Kirkpatricks Hotel
Fully renovated hotel featuring magnificent bay views from our Bistro, Beer garden and Balcony lounge. Other attractions include Tatts Pokies and Sports Bar.
774 Esplanade, Mornington
Tel: (03) 5975 2007 Fax: (03) 5975 0116
Email: kirkshotel@bigpond.com
(Mel Ref: 104 D10)

MORNINGTON
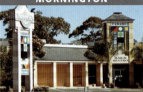
The Tanti Hotel Mornington
Est. 1852
Mornington's oldest hotel boasts friendly staff, the best chefs and finest fare on the Peninsula. Facilities include a family bistro, alfresco cafe, gaming machines, Pubtab and Innkeeper bottleshop.
917 Nepean Hwy, Mornington 3931
Ph: (03) 5975 2015 • Fax: (03) 5977 0678
email: thetanti@bigpond.com

MORNINGTON

Mornington Racing Club
Within an hour's drive of Melbourne the Mornington Racing Club is one of Australia's most picturesque racecourses. The facilities, catering, beautiful lawns & gardens plus exciting racing make a great day's entertainment.
Racecourse Road, Mornington
Tel: (03) 5975 3310 Fax: (03) 5976 0766
Email: info@mrc.net.au

MORNINGTON

Mornington Peninsula Regional Gallery (MPRG)
Let the MPRG unlock the secrets to the art, stories & treasures of Victoria's principal artistic & cultural region. The Gallery has a changing program of nationally significant exhibitions by Australia's leading artists.
Civic Reserve, Dunns Road, Mornington
Tel: (03) 5975 4395 Fax: (03) 5977 0377
Email: mprg@mornpen.vic.gov.au

MORNINGTON
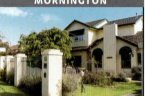
Bally Vista Bed & Breakfast
★★★★☆ self-contained 10-square fully serviced apartment. Magnificent bay views. Three doors from beach. Short walk to Main Street.
18 Wilsons Rd, Mornington (Mel Ref: 104 C12)
Tel: (03) 5977 1525 Fax: (03) 5977 1939
Email: aandk@cinet.com.au

MORNINGTON

Canterbury by the Bay
Bright and cheery fully self-contained two bedroom retreat in the heart of Mornington with a beach theme. Short walk to 'Main Street' shopping, cafes and beaches. Facilities include: linen, air-cond/heating, gas BBQ and garage..
PO Box 84, Mornington (Mel Ref: 104 D10)
Tel: (03) 5974 3136 Fax: (03) 5974 3900
Email: cantbury@satlink.com.au

MORNINGTON

Mornington Motel
AAA ★★★☆
Single, double, twin & family rooms with all amenities. 3-br self-contained unit. Located in main street. Solar heated swimming pool, garden barbeque. The perfect place to base your holiday.
334 Main St, Mornington 3931
Ph: (03) 5975 3711
morningtonmotel@bigpond.com

MORNINGTON

National Antique Centre
Largest range of antiques & collectables in southern hemisphere under one roof.
Open 7 days, 10am–4.45pm.
Browse for hours amongst the displays.
Buy where the other dealers shop!
65 Tyabb-Mornington Rd, Mornington 3931
Ph: (03) 5977 0155, 0408 356 424

MORNINGTON

THE ROYAL HOTEL
Beautiful, Elegant, Romantic... the pearl of the Mornington Peninsula. The Royal Hotel offers quality service, bistro dining and exquisite accommodation. Chosen for all the right reasons.
770 The Esplanade, Mornington 3931
Ph: (03) 5975 5466
email: info@theroyal.com.au

MOOROODUC

Boutik Regional Wine & Art Centre
Largest range of Peninsula wines under the one roof at Moorooduc Coolstores. Personal labelling to your private or corporate requirements. Regular regional art exhibitions. Open Thurs-Mon 11am-7pm
Suite 21, 475 Moorooduc Hwy, Moorooduc 3933
Phone/Fax: (03) 5978 8462
email: info@boutik.com.au

MOOROODUC

The Peninsula Lounge
The Peninsula Lounge at Moorooduc Coolstores has undergone extensive renovations to create a spacious modern venue, offering lounge bars, beer garden, function facilities, Roquets bistro, entertainment, live bands and pool tables, at the gateway to the Mornington Peninsula
990 Moorooduc Hwy, Moorooduc 3933
Ph: (03) 5978 8717 • penlge990@bigpond.com

MOOROODUC
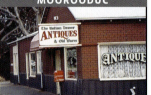
The Bottom Drawer Antique Centre
Antiques and collectables galore. Forty dealers under one roof. Something for everyone. Spend a couple of hours and have lunch or afternoon tea in our cosy tearoom.
Cnr Mornington/Tyabb Rd/Derril Rd
Moorooduc 3933 Mel ref: 146 J6
Ph: (03)5978 8677 • www.thebottomdrawer.com.au

MOOROODUC
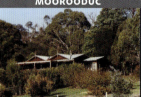
Gooseberry Hill Cottages
The choice is yours!
A two-bedroom cottage on an olive grove, or two two-bedroom units by the beach in Mornington
170 Graydens Rd, Moorooduc 3933
Ph: (03) 5978 8227 • Fax: (03) 5978 8227
email: redston@bigpond.com

LISTINGS • NORTHERN PENINSULA & WESTERN PORT BAY

MT MARTHA
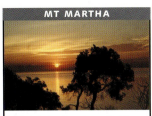
Mt Martha Beachside Restaurant
Views across the Bay.
Choose from our extensive menu in the restaurant or outdoor patio.
Open 7 days. The perfect place to meet and soak up the atmosphere.
464 Esplanade, Mt Martha 3934
Ph: (03) 5974 4443 • Fax: (03) 5974 4446

MT MARTHA

The Briars Park
Explore the Wildlife Reserve along bushland trails, looking for koalas, kangaroos & wallabies. View the wetland birds from observation hides. Visit the 1840's Homestead, renowned for its Napoleonic Collection. Bring your picnic or BBQ lunch.
Nepean Highway, Mt Martha (Mel Ref: 145 D11)
Tel: (03) 5974 3686 Fax: (03) 5974 1167
Email: the.briars@mornpen.vic.gov.au

MT MARTHA

The Perfumed Garden & Roseraie
Specially selected roses for beauty of form & fragrance. Austins, Old World & Australian roses in a stunning unique setting. Expert advice. Garden open Nov–May. Nursery – all year. Proprietor: Sophie Adamson
Nepean Hwy, Mt Martha (Mel Ref: 145 D11)
roseraie@bigpond.com.au
Tel: (03) 5974 4833 Fax: (03) 5974 8455

MT MARTHA

Josephine's at the Briars
The leading Peninsula restaurant. Set in historic Briars Park.
Serving lunch 7 days a week. 10.30–4.30 pm with morning & afternoon teas.
Friday & Saturday evening dinners.
The perfect function venue.
Briars Park, Nepean Hwy, Mt Martha
Ph: (03) 5974 1104 • Fax: (03) 5974 1606
briarsfunctions@hotmail.com

MORNINGTON/MT MARTHA

RACV / AAA ★★★☆
Ranch Motel
Centrally located to all Peninsula attractions and beach. Double, twin family rooms & self-cont. units, with queen beds. All ground floor units. 3 br self-cont. cottage available. Family owned & operated
Cnr Nepean Hwy & Bentons Rd, Mornington 3931
Ph: (03) 5975 4022 • Fax: (03) 5976 2082
email: admin@ranchmotel.com.au

MT MARTHA

Mt Martha B&B By the Sea
One of Mt Martha's best kept secrets, opposite a beautiful, safe secluded swimming beach. Luxuriously appointed with ensuites & spa baths. Includes delicious cooked breakfast. Beach house next door also available. 4-star RACV rated.
538 Esplanade, Mt Martha 3934
Ph: (03) 5974 1019 • Fax: (03) 5974 1022
www.mountmarthabandbbythesea.com.au

MT MARTHA

Briarswood Cottage
★★★★ Traditional B&B, Heritage listed Tudor style cottage. Opposite beach. Perfect for romantic getaway, open fire, guest lounge/dining, two queen bedrooms/bathrooms. One Self Contained cottage for two. Hosts - Ann and Ian Duncan.
559 Esplanade, Mount Martha (Mel Ref: 145 B8)
Tel: (03) 5974 2245 Fax: (03) 5974 8310
Email: enquiries@briarswood.com.au
www.briarswood.com.au

MT MARTHA

Original Oz Art Gallery
A must-see for all visitors to the Peninsula. This gallery shows the best of local professional & interstate painters.
Open 9am–5.30pm 7 days.
Shop 7, 34/38 Mt Martha Village Arcade, Lochiel Ave, Mt Martha 3934
Ph: (03) 5974 8170
email: original@sx.com.au
www.originaloz.com.au

PEARCEDALE
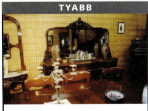
Moonlit Sanctuary
Magical wildlife experience. Meet rarely seen night animals like quolls, gliders, bettongs, pademelons, and many others on our escorted evening walks. Open Wed-Sun & hols. Evening walks start at dusk. Bookings required.
550 Tyabb-Tooradin Road, Pearcedale
Tel: (03) 5978 7935 Fax: (03) 9546 0877
Email: info@pearcedale.com

SOMERVILLE

Bembridge Golf Course
The Peninsula's fun club.
9-hole course in picturesque surroundings, watered greens, club & buggy hire.
Licensed club house, practice greens
125 Tyabb/Tooradin Rd, Somerville 3912
Ph: (03) 5978 6215 • Fax: (03) 5978 7511

TYABB

Tyabb Packing House Antiques
Australia's largest Antique Centre. Everything for the collector, including a unique working craft village. Cafe & licensed restaurant, kiosk, children's play area.
Thurs to Sun and Public Holidays.
Opposite Tyabb Railway Station, Tyabb
Tel: (03) 5977 4414 Fax: (03) 5977 3216
www.tyabbpackinghouseantiques.com.au

TYABB

Tyabb Craft Village
Best-kept secret on the Peninsula at the Tyabb Packing House.
Down Under Glazemud – 5977 3986
Jewel Of The Nile – 5977 3711
Tyabb Wood Turning – 5983 1334
14 Mornington Tyabb Rd, Tyabb 3913
Ph: (03) 5977 3986 • Fax: (03) 5987 2696
email: jgoodall@chisholm.vic.edu.au
www.tyabbpackinghouseantiques.com.au

TYABB
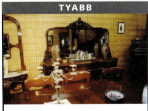
Tyabb Antique Centre
The Peninsula's leading antique centre, specialising in fine-quality furniture & decorative pieces. A lifetime of experience & attention to detail make us unique.
Open 5 days a week
Wed/Sun 10.30am-5pm
1527 Frankston/Flinders Rd, Tyabb 3913
Ph: (03) 5977 4245 • mob: 0414 523 461

TYABB

Luton Hatters Gallery
AUSTRALIA'S BIGGEST HAT SHOP
Right here in Tyabb!
Everything from Akubra's & millinery for the races to cheerful strawhats & sunhats, toppers, bowlers, leather and a large range of caps
1552 Frankston-Flinders Rd, Tyabb
Ph: (03) 5977 4447

TYABB

The Tack Box Saddlery
We provide a wide range of equestrian needs, specialising in saddlery, competition, casual and country clothing.
Your complete saddlery store
1554 Frankston/Flinders Rd, Tyabb 3913
Ph: (03) 5977 3522 • Fax: (03) 5977 3790
email: tackbox@bigpond.com
www.tackbox.com.au

TYABB

Peninsula Motor Inn
Peninsula Motor Inn is a complete holiday venue with 34 suites (some spa), indoor heated pool, spa & sauna, games room, BBQ facility, situated on five acres of gardens
Mornington/Tyabb Rd, Tyabb 3913
Ph: (03) 5977 4431 • Fax: (03) 5977 3208
email: info@peninsulamotorinn.com.au
www.peninsulamotorinn.com.au

LISTINGS • WESTERN PORT BAY

TYABB
Eldon Park Retreat

Offering "a simple path to awareness – body, mind and spirit" with home-style, fully self-contained accommodation for individuals, couples & families or groups of up to 20, with self-catering or B&B options.

74 Graydens Rd, Tyabb 3913
Ph: (03) 5977 4727I • Fax: (03) 5979 4017
email: eldonpark@satlink.com.au

SOMERVILLE
Yaringa Boat Harbour

One-stop boating centre & marina alongside Yaringa Marine Park
• over 400 boats • slipway & on-site boat repairs • boat hire & charters
• boat sales & chandlery
• waterfront restaurant

1 Lumeah Rd, Somerville 3912
Mel ref: 149 K7   Ph: (03)5977 4154
www.yaringa.com.au

SOMERVILLE
Yaringa Boathouse Restaurant

Balcony seating, absolute water front dining. Lunch & dinner 7 days, fully licensed bar. Bookings recommended. Relaxed dining, quality cuisine, great coffee.

1 Lumeah Rd, Somerville 3912
Ph: (03) 5977 3735

SOMERVILLE
Yaringa Boat Sales

Whilst enjoying the hidden jewel of the Mornington Peninsula, come and see Phil & Merilyn, who can cater for all your boating needs – even fishing charters.

1 Lumeah Rd, Somerville 3912
Ph: (03) 5977 3004 • Fax: (03) 5977 3854
email: pwasnig@vtown.com.au

HASTINGS
Westernport Hotel

Westernport's oldest hotel is now fully renovated, offering a range of hospitality options:
Bistro meals, lounge bar, sports bar with TAB facilities, gaming lounge with 40 Tatts machines.

Cnr High & Salmon Sts, Hastings 3915
Ph: (03) 5979 1201 • Fax: (03) 5979 2557

HASTINGS
The Anchorage

Sensational waterfront bar & restaurant featuring modern heritage-style ambiance. Superb food and views of the marina. Entertainment & function centre for every occasion

At Westernport Marina
PO Box 260, Hastings 3915
Ph: (03) 5979 3699

HASTINGS
Harbour View Motor Inn & Victoriana Restaurant

Modern 4-star units in the Hastings foreshore reserve close to wetland walks, beaches, wineries & antiques. A-la-carte restaurant offers international fare & a well balanced wine list. RACV ★★★★

126 Marine Parade, Hastings
Tel: (03) 5979 3333 Fax: (03) 5979 3206
www.victoriana.com.au

HASTINGS
Victoriana Restaurant

Fine dining at an affordable price, with an a la carte menu, featuring Peninsula & Australian wines. A cozy log fire in winter. Weddings, Conferences & groups catered for.

126 Marine Pde, Hastings 3915
Ph: (03) 5979 3333 • Fax: (03) 5979 3206
email: info@victoriana.com.au
www.victoriana.com.au

HASTINGS
Marina View Van Village

Peaceful coastal setting overlooking Westernport Bay and French Island. Deluxe holiday cabins, well-grassed sites, plenty of shade trees and quiet relaxed atmosphere. Close to Peninsula attractions.

38 Salmon Street, Hastings 3915
Tel: (03) 5979 2322 Fax: (03) 5979 4599
Email: enquiries@marinaviewvillage.com.au
www.marinaviewvillage.com.au

BITTERN
Summerfields Country House

Centrally located to the attractions of the Peninsula. The ideal country house for touring the region or simply an indulgent retreat. Enjoy a game of tennis, fish in our lake, or explore surrounding countryside

17 Hunts Rd, Bittern
Ph: (03) 5983 6700
janssen@iprimus.com.au
www.summerfields.com.au

FRENCH ISLAND
French Island Eco Tours

Award winning, wildlife, environmental and heritage tours to French Island for individuals, clubs, schools and universities. Departing Stony Pt and Cowes.

Tel/Fax: (03) 9770 1822
AH: (03) 5980 1210
Mob: 0429 177 532
www.frenchislandecotours.com.au

HMAS CERBERUS
HMAS Cerberus

Visit one of the largest naval historical collections in Australia featuring collection of relics, photographs, uniforms, medals & memorabilia from Australia's naval past.
Open Wed–Sun & most public holidays
10am–12pm 1.30–5pm
HMAS Cerberus, Western Port 3920
Mel: p194.H3
Ph: (03) 5950 7141 • Fax: (03) 5950 7515

SOMERS
Coolart Wetlands & Homestead

A harmonious blending of nature and human settlement set in a delightful garden and wetlands environment perfect for bird watching. Mention this advertisement for 2 for the price of 1 entry (except events).

Lord Somers Rd, Somers (Melways Ref: 193 J9)
For further information Tel: 13 1963
www.parkweb.vic.gov.au

BALNARRING
Rain Hayne & Shine Farmyard

A large variety of friendly farm animals to feed & cuddle. FREE: hay rides, BBQs, tea, coffee. Pony rides $2. Suitable for all ages.
Open daily 10am-4pm (except Xmas Day)
(Extended hours at peak times).
Family accommodation opening soon.

490 Stumpy Gully Road, Balnarring
(Mel Ref: 163 E5) Tel: (03) 5983 1691

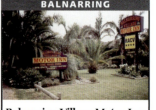

BALNARRING
Balnarring Village Motor Inn

★★★★ Impeccable country-style boutique motel in gardens & palms. Walk to village shops, restaurants. Close to wineries, beaches, markets, attractions. Great service & value. Guest, spa, family self-contained suites.

3055 Frankston Flinders Road, Balnarring
Tel: (03) 5983 5222 Fax: (03) 5983 2549
Email: balmotel@satlink.com.au
www.balnarringvillagemotorinn.com.au

MERRICKS NORTH
Muranna Herbs & Cottages

Beautiful 70-acre retreat; secret gardens; stunning kitchen potager-herb nursery; yabbie dam; kangaroos & bush walks; two separate s/c cottages sleeping 12 people; garden pavilion. Perfect for romantic getaways, family holidays, weddings or workshops

52 Tubbarubba Rd, Merricks North 3926
Tel: (03) 5989 7499 Fax: (03) 5989 7498
mob: 0428 654 630
Email: info@muranna.com.au
www.muranna.com.au

LISTINGS • WESTERN PORT BAY

SHOREHAM

Shoreham Beach House

A self-contained beach house overlooking a farm valley towards Westernport. Handcrafted architectural features, stone open fireplace, entertainer's kitchen, deck with barbeque.

20 Myers Drive, Shoreham 3916
Ph: (03) 5989 8433
www.lepav.com.au

SHOREHAM

Ashcombe Maze & Water Gardens

Australia's oldest & largest hedge mazes • 25 acres of internationally renowned gardens & water ways • the oldest rose maze in the world • relax in our fully licensed cafe. Open Daily from 10 am

Shoreham Road, Shoreham
Tel: (03) 5989 8387 Fax: (03) 5989 8700
www.ashcombemaze.com.au

SHOREHAM

Le Pavillon

A 2-storey mudbrick and stone 'gite', Le Pavillon is a private self-contained cottage handcrafted from a melange of local materials, reflecting "le style provencale".

1 Pine Grove, Shoreham 3916
Ph: (03) 5989 8433
www.lepav.com.au

FLINDERS

Hotel Flinders

Bistro open 7 days lunch & dinner. Extensive menu & wine list. Children's menu & playground. Live bands every weekend. Spacious motel suites. Beer garden, pool tables, Pubtab. Great midweek specials. RACV ★★☆

Cook Street, Flinders
Tel: (03) 5989 0201 Fax (03) 5989 0878
Email: flinders@fox.net.au

FLINDERS

Flinders Fine Art

A leading Peninsula gallery located in Flinders Village. Displaying traditional & contemporary collectable art from the region's most sought-after artists.
Open Wed-Sun 10.30am-5pm

Shop 10, 33 Cook St, Flinders
Ph/Fax: (03) 5989 0889
bec.barbour@bigpond.com.au

FLINDERS

Beast Creations

Gallery hours:
Wednesday to Sunday 10am – 5.30pm
Open daily over school & public holidays

33 Cook St, Flinders 3929
Ph: (03) 5989 0902
email: glass@beastcreations.com.au

FLINDERS

Transference Antiques & Decor
IMPORTERS OF FINE EUROPEAN ANTIQUES

"from the exotic to the sublime"
Quality antiques bought and sold. Local and international sourcing of antiques. Restoration services and antique rental available

65 Cook St, Flinders 3929 Ph: (03) 5989 0507
465 Hampton St, Hampton 3188 Ph: 9597 0471
email: transference@primus.com.au
www.transferencepl.com.au

FLINDERS

Flinders Village Cafe

Flinders meeting & eating place.
Relax and soak up the village atmosphere indoor in our gallery rooms or outdoor on patio areas.
Excellent food & cosy atmosphere

49 Cook St, Flinders 3929
Ph: (03) 5989 0700

FLINDERS

Salty's Cafe

If you have not eaten at Salty's, you have not been to Flinders.
Fresh local seafood our speciality.
Extensive lunch & dinner menu catering to all your needs.

37 Cook St, Flinders 3929
Ph: (03) 5989 0067 • Fax: (03) 5989 1022
mob: 0418 346 067

FLINDERS

Cipriani's of Flinders B&B & Restaurant

Superb accommodation in an enchanting setting. Lounges with open fires and Cipriani's Restaurant overlook lake and gardens for Weddings, and all private functions ★★★★

165 Wood St, Flinders 3929
Tel: (03) 5989 0933 Fax: (03) 5989 0059
Email: cipriani@nex.net.au

FLINDERS

Flinders Cove Motor Inn
★★★☆

Set in the heart of Flinders and surrounded by the region's beaches and wineries. Spacious rooms with queen beds, in-house movies, indoor pool, spa & sauna.

32 Cook Street, Flinders (Mel Ref: 261 K8)
Tel: (03) 5989 0666 Fax: (03) 5989 0906
Email: bw90921@bigpond.com
www.bestwestern.com.au/flinders

FLINDERS

Nazaaray Country Retreat

Experience the luxury and total seclusion of self-contained Nazaaray. Panoramic rural views, 3BR, open fireplace. Sleeps 6-8. Group discount. Close to golf courses, wineries and beaches. ★★★★☆

266 Meakins Road, Flinders (Mel Ref: 260 F3)
Tel: (03) 5985 1138 Fax: (03) 5985 1140
Email: nazaaray@bigpond.com

FLINDERS

Ora Banda
Gourmet Bed & Breakfast

Luxury 4.5-Star accommodation in the heart of Flinders Village. Sample our Candlelit Dinners for two.
Two private stuies in our renovated Fisherman's Cottage. All amenities

39 Cook St, Flinders
Ph: (03) 5989 1150 • Mob: 0401 016 663

FLINDERS

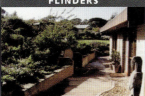

Papillon B&B

2 recently-built mudbrick, spacious, self-contained units in an acre of landscaped gardens; wood fires, outdoor spa and BBQ area. Generous basket breakfast provided
★★★★

15 King St, Flinders 3929 (Mel ref: 261 J7)
Ph: (03) 5989 1071 • Fax: (03) 5989 1073
email: pgerdsen@hotkey.net.au
www.papillonbb.com.au

FLINDERS

Flinders Golf Club

A unique coastoal links course with scenic views from all fairways. Proshop with full hire requirements.
Green fee players welcome.
Undercover gazebo & BBQs.
Trade days & catering welcome.

Bass St, Flinders 3929
Ph: (03)5989 0312 • Fax: (03) 5989 0940

CAPE SCHANCK

Cape Schanck Lightstation

Historic Accommodation. Stay in the spacious, comfortable Lighthouse Keeper's Residence and let the sounds of the ocean lull you to sleep. Daily tours of the Lighthouse.

Cape Schanck Rd, Cape Schanck
Tel: (03) 5988 6184
Accom Bookings: 0500 527 891
Email: capeschanck@austpacinns.com.au

247

LISTINGS • THE HINTERLAND

TUERONG

Nedlands Farm Cottage
Private, luxurious and fully self-contained cottage set on a beautiful, century old 100 acre farm. Air-conditioned, cosy wood fire. Wide verandahs. Glorious rural views. Farm fresh provisions. A relaxing getaway for one or two couples.
500 Old Moorooduc Road, Tuerong
Tel: (03) 5974 4160 Fax: (03) 5974 4161
Email: nedlands@alphalink.com.au

MAIN RIDGE

Sunny Ridge Strawberry Farm
Pick your own strawberries. Enjoy fabulous desserts in our strawberry cafe. Browse through the gourmet produce. Taste medal winning fruit wines & liqueurs. Open 7 days Nov-Apr. Open weekends May-Oct.
Cnr Mornington-Flinders & Shands Rd, Main Ridge
Tel: (03) 5989 6273 Fax: (03) 5989 6363
Email: info@sunnyridge.com.au

ARTHURS SEAT

Arthurs Seat Maze
Get lost in a wonderland of mazes, theme gardens & sculptural creations. Cuddle a baby animal, decorate the kids with temporary tattoos or relax at Solair Café. Australia's only maize maze. Open daily 10am-6pm.
55 Purves Road, Arthurs Seat,
Tel: (03) 5981 8449
(Mel Ref: 159 E12)

ARTHURS SEAT
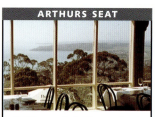
Arthurs at Arthurs Seat
Restaurant– Tavern Bar – Garden Deck – Function Centre
Arthurs has been refurbished, repainted, redecorated, re-landscaped and returned as the Peninsula's user-friendly destination.
Open 7 days
Arthurs Seat Rd, Arthurs Seat
Ph: (03) 5981 4444

RED HILL

Poffs' Restaurant
• The Peninsula's favourite eating place
• classic cuisine with an enticing difference
• choose from the largest range of local wines or take advantage of the only BYO on the hill
164 Arthurs Seat Rd, Red Hill 3937
Ph: (03) 5989 2566
email: ESIPN@C.D.I.com.au

RED HILL

Magnificent Garden Vineyard Restaurant in the heart of Red Hill. Modern Australian menu with European influences & superb country views. Relax in the restaurant or paved terrace courtyard.
150 Red Hill Rd, Red Hill
Ph: (03) 5989 2977 • Fax: (03) 5989 2436
email: jessica@vinesofredhill.com.au
www.vinesofredhill.com.au

RED HILL SOUTH

Jane's Hide-Aways
Beautiful old-world self-contained B&Bs in the heart of Red Hill. Romantic cottages for 2 or larger cottages for up to 8. Antiques, fireplaces, QS brass beds, spa baths, private gardens & balconies. Affordable luxury.
114 Shoreham Rd, Red Hill South 3937
Ph: (03) 5989 2288
Email: jane@hideaways.com.au
www.hideaways.com.au

RED HILL SOUTH

Langdons of Red Hill B&B
In the picturesque seclusion of Red Hill, Langdon's offers a stylish yet tranquil getaway. Enjoy luxury accommodation with homely hospitality and bask in the ambience.
★★★★
52-54 Arthur's Seat Road, Red Hill South
(cnr Mechanics Rd) (Mel Ref: 191 A5)
Tel: (03) 5989 2965 Fax: (03) 5989 2355
Email: langdonsofredhill@bigpond.com

MAIN RIDGE

Pennyroyal B&B
First class self-contained accommodation, close to wineries, golf, beaches & markets.
Set in nine acres of gardens at Main Ridge
555 Main Creek Rd, Main Ridge
Ph: (03) 5989 6564
www.pennyroyalbb.com.au

MAIN RIDGE
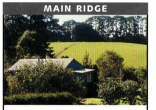
Summerhill Farm B&B
Central to all Peninsua attractions on 10 tranquil acres. Offering comfort and seclusion in the country cottage or the luxurious Edwardian suite in the homestead. A warm welcome, a peaceful stay.
264 Barkers Rd, Main Ridge
Mel ref: 254 K2
Ph/Fax: 5989 6077
email: summerhillfarm@vic.australis.com.au

RED HILL
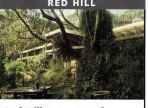
Red Hill Retreat & Cheesery
Country house accommodation; mudbrick suites; native forests; organic farm produce; legendary breakfasts; tariff $150-$200 double. Also handmade cheese tastings & sales. Daily 12-5pm
81 William Rd, Red Hill 3937
Ph: (03) 5989 2035 • Fax: (03) 5989 2427
email: rhr@alphalink.com.au
www.redhillretreat.com.au

RED HILL SOUTH
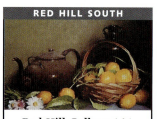
Red Hill Gallery 141
An exhibition gallery with lovely views. Fine art, pottery & sculpture blended with quality alpaca products.
Relax over a coffee or wander around & meet our beautiful animals.
Open Friday - Monday 11am - 5.30pm.
141 Red Hill Road, Red Hill South 3937
Tel: (03) 5989 2614 Fax (03) 5989 2614
Email: rhgal141@satlink.com.au

SOUTHERN PENINSULA

Gordon Studio Glassblowers
A working hot glass studio & gallery. See molten glass made from sand transformed into art by traditional hand blown methods.
Open Mon-Sat 10am-4pm.
3/1591 Nepean Hwy (Mel Ref: 169 J2)
(moving to Red Hill 2004)
Tel: (03) 5986 7044 Fax (03) 5986 7044
Email: gordonstudio@hotkey.net.au

RED HILL

Noel's Gallery Restaurant & Lavender Garden
Nestled in a well established cottage garden C1900, overlooking tranquil rural views. Indoor & outdoor eating, air conditioning & log fire. Known for fine art, fine food, gifts & beautiful lavender nursery.
Mornington Flinders Road, Red Hill
Tel: (03) 5989 2538 Fax: (03) 5989 3105
Email: gaiclough@telstra.com

RED HILL

Marion Rosetzky Gallery
A working studio specialising in the production of unique hand painted tiles. Enjoy a select range of craftworks by leading Australian artists, great espresso coffee, and native bird life, in a gallery surrounded by natural bushland. Open: 11am–5pm most days.
650 White Hill Rd, Red Hill
Ph/Fax (03) 5989 2557 (Melway Ref 160 J11)
http://marion.infotile.com.au

RED HILL / DROMANA
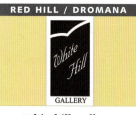
Whitehill Gallery
Australian fine art & craft. Wearable art, jewellery, ceramics and handmade glass features. Changing exhibitions of established artists. Enjoy a coffee in the rural setting.
White Hill Rd, Red Hill / Dromana
(Mel Ref: 160 G9)
Tel: (03) 5989 2483 Fax: (03) 5931 0146
Email: rickhayllar@bigpond.com
www.visitvictoria.com

LISTINGS • THE HINTERLAND & PENINSULA WINERIES

WINERIES TOURING GUIDE – REFER TO PAGES 138-139

RED HILL

The Art Shed Gallery

This beautifully renovated gallery specialises in unusual and stimulating artworks for your home and garden. Open most days 11am - 5pm.

138 Arthurs Seat Road, Red Hill
Tel: (03) 5989 2285 Fax (03) 5989 2285
Email: wordart@vicnet.net.au
(Mel Ref: 190 K4)

RED HILL SOUTH

Red Hill Cool Stores & Art Gallery

A wide range of unique products including Australian made clothing, local art & giftware. Local Peninsula wines, fresh produce, jams & relishes. This is all housed in our 'heritage listed' old apple packing shed.

65 Shoreham Rd, Red Hill South
(Mel Ref: 191 B7) Tel: 59310133 Fax: 59893165
Email: rhcs@pen.hotkey.net.au

TUERONG

Barrymore Estate

Barrymore Estate continues a tradition of agriculture of historic Tuerong Station, ideally suited to the growing of premium cool climate wines of distinctive character. Cellar door open daily 11am-5pm

76 Tuerong Rd, Tuerong 3933
Ph: (03) 5974 8999 • Fax: (03) 97789 0821
pjcotter@barrymore.com.au

TUERONG

Barrymore Estate

76 Tuerong Rd, Tuerong 3933
Ph: (03) 5974 8999 • Fax: (03) 97789 0821
pjcotter@barrymore.com.au

MERRICKS NORTH

Box Stallion Wines

MORNINGTON PENINSULA'S LEADER IN VARIETAL WINES

Discover the Peninsula's best kept secret. Enjoy lunch & tastings at the Red Barn Cellar Door. Classic French & exciting Italian varieties of our estate-grown Peninsula Wines. Open every day 11am-5pm

64 Tubbarubba Rd, Merricks North 3926
Ph: (03) 5989 7444 • Fax: (03) 5989 7688
email: wine@boxstallion.com.au

MERRICKS NORTH

MORNINGTON PENINSULA'S LEADER IN VARIETAL WINES

Box Stallion Wines

64 Tubbarubba Rd, Merricks North 3926
Ph: (03) 5989 7444 • Fax: (03) 5989 7688
email: wine@boxstallion.com.au

MERRICKS NORTH

Elgee Park Winery

The oldest vineyard on the Mornington Peninsula. The picturesque vineyard at Wallaces Road produces superb maritime cool climate wines form the north facing vineyard, with views across Port Phillip Bay

RMB 5560 Junction Rd, Merricks Nth, 3926
Ph: (03) 5989 7338 • Fax: (03) 5989 7338
email: elgee@pac.com.au

MERRICKS NORTH

Baillieu Vineyard

Established by Samantha & Charlie Baillieu. The 10 ha north facing vineyard is bounded by Tubbarubba Rd & Myers Rd. Producing superb cool climate maritime wines

Bulldog Run, Junction Rd, RMB 5560, Merricks Nth, 3926
Ph/Fax: (03) 5989 7622
email: baillieu@pac.com.au

RED HILL

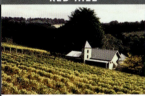

Darling Park Winery

...Where wine & art blend well together. Relax in the beautiful vineyard & its surrounds. Choose from the light & easy menu featuring local produce, while tasting the premium collection of Peninsula wines. Open every weekend, public holidays and throughout January 11am-5.30pm

232 Red Hill Rd, Red Hill (Mel Ref: 191 F3)
Ph: (03) 5989 2324
email: darlingpark@bigpond.com

DROMANA

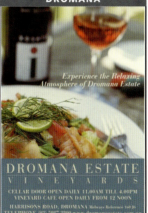

RED HILL

Eldridge Estate of Red Hill

Specialising in classic Chardonnay & Pinot Noir that have a long flavour-packed palate. A delicious fruity gamay, enjoyed chilled over summer. All wines are made from grapes grown on the Estate by David & Wendy Lloyd.

Arthurs Seat Rd, Red Hill 3937
Ph: (03) 5989 2644 • Fax: (03) 5989 2089
email: fizz@eldridge-estate.au

MOOROODUC

Ermes Estate

Ermes & Denise Zucchet invite you to visit and taste their 100% Estate grown Merlot, Chardonnay, Riesling, exciting Pinot Grigio & award winning Cabernet Sauvignon. Open every weekend 11-5 pm

2 Godings Rd, Moorooduc 3933
Ph: (03) 5978 8376 • 0418 357 206
Fax: (03) 5978 8396
email: ermesestate@bigpond.com

BALNARRING

Hurley Vineyard

Historic Hurley Farm (c.1876) is now a specialised Pinot Noir vineyard. Gentle winemaking reveals Pinot Noir that celebrates the individual terroir of the stony red earth & non-irrigated vines. Grown & bottled entirely on site

101 Balnarring Rd, Balnarring 3926
Ph: (03) 5931 3000
email: bell@menzies.aust.com

RED HILL

Established 1975. Peninsula's first winery. Wines 100% grown, made & bottled on the estate.
Classic styles of Chardonnay & Pinot Noir. Lunch every Sunday.
Open daily

80 William Rd, Red Hill 3937
Ph: (03) 5989 2686 • Fax: (03) 5931 0000
email: mrestate@mre.com.au

MOOROODUC

The Garden Vineyard

A glorious one hectare garden - all in a beautiful vineyard setting. Wine by the glass on the terrace surrounded by roses, lavender and wisteria
Cellar door tasting and sales.
Open 11am-5pm: Every weekend Nov-April and by appointment.

174 Graydens Road, Moorooduc
Tel: (03) 5978 8336 Fax: (03) 5978 8343

MOOROODUC

The Garden Vineyard

174 Graydens Rd, Moorooduc 3933
Ph: (03) 5978 8336 • Fax: (03) 5978 8343
email: gardenvineyard@pac.com.au

LISTINGS • PENINSULA WINERIES

WINERIES TOURING GUIDE – REFER TO PAGES 138-139

DROMANA

Hickinbotham of Dromana
Escape the rat race! Relax in the rustic setting of Hickinbotham Winery & Café. Experience our superb wines, gourmet lunches and unique winebreads by the open fireplace. Live music weekends from 1pm. Open 7 days from 11am.
194 Nepean Highway, Dromana
Tel: (03) 5981 0355 • Fax: (03) 5987 0692
www.hickinbotham.biz

DROMANA
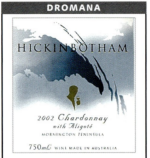
Hickinbotham of Dromana
194 Nepean Highway, Dromana
Tel: (03) 5981 0355 • Fax: (03) 5987 0692
www.hickinbotham.biz

DROMANA

Karina Vineyard
Small, family owned vineyard & winery established in 1984. Owners Gerard & Joy take pride in their 100% Estate-grown & made wines. Visitors can enjoy complimentary wine tastings. Meet the winemaker. Open weekends, public holidays and daily in January 11am-5pm
35 Harrisons Rd, Dromana 3936
Ph/Fax: (03) 5981 0137

RED HILL

Linden Tree Restaurant
Experience the finest in modern cuisine with the Andrew Blake influence, using the best of local produce.
The Linden Tree Restaurant is open daily. Al fresco dining available in courtyard
142 Arthurs Seat Rd, Red Hill
Ph: (03) 5989 2933
Email: info@lindenderry.com.au

RED HILL

Lindenderry at Red Hill
30 acres of gardens and vineyard, with 40 luxurious bedrooms, swimming pool, spa, sauna, tennis courts, retreat spa and cellar door. The Linden Tree Restaurant and courtyard offers lunch and dinner daily.
AAA Tourism ★★★★★
142 Arthurs Seat Rd, Red Hill
Tel: (03) 5989 2933 Fax: (03) 5989 2936
Email: info@lindenderry.com.au

MERRICKS

Merricks Estate
Jacky & George Kefford invite you to taste their award-winning wines including the acclaimed 1999 Shiraz, 1997 Cabernet Sauvignon, 1999 Chardonnay and 2000 Pinot Noir.
Thompsons Lane, Merricks 3916
Ph: (03) 5989 8416 • Fax: (03) 9606 9090
email: gkefford@vic.dbglaw.com.au

MERRICKS
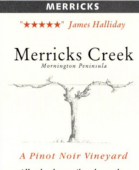
"★★★★★" James Halliday
Merricks Creek
Mornington Peninsula
A Pinot Noir Vineyard
All sales by mail order only. Contact us to join the mailing list.
44 Merricks Road, Merricks 3916
Phone (03) 5989 8868
e: merrickscreek@ozemail.com.au
web: www.pinot.com.au

ARTHURS SEAT

Miceli
Delicate, fine & distinctive award winning wines. Taste 'Lucy's' choice Pinot Noir, 'Olivia's' Chardonnay, 'Iolanda's' Pinot Grigio, methode champonaise White & Rosé. All Estate grown & bottled. Cellar door open 1st weekend of month. Every weekend January. 12-5pm
60 Main Creek Rd, Arthurs Seat 3936
Ph/Fax: (03) 5989 2755

RED HILL
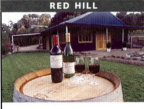
Myrtaceae
VINEYARD & WINERY
Close to Arthurs Seat, Myrtaceae produces classic cool climate wines made exclusively from grapes grown on the property. Taste single vineyard wine at the distinctive winery cellar door.
53 Main Creek Rd, Red Hill 3937
Ph: (03) 5989 2045 • Fax: (03) 5989 2845
email: myrtaceae@alphalink.com.au

RED HILL

MONTALTO VINEYARD & OLIVE GROVE
Fabulous wines, luscious olive oil, gourmet picnic hampers, chef's hat restaurant, stunning wetlands & award-winning landscape building make Montalto the ultimate wine & food experience
33 Shoreham Rd, Red Hill
Ph: (03) 5989 8412
email: info@montalto.com.au
www.montalto.com.au

RED HILL

MONTALTO VINEYARD & OLIVE GROVE
33 Shoreham Rd, Red Hill
Ph: (03) 5989 8412
email: info@montalto.com.au
www.montalto.com.au

BALNARRING
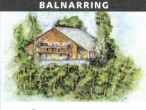
Northway Downs Estate
Established in 1996. The Schindler Family welcome you to enjoy Pinot Noir & Chardonnay whilst enjoying homestyle Austrian cooking & smallgoods from the smokehouse. Outdoor terrace & lake views. Open 1st weekend of the month 11am-5pm & Festival weekends.
437 Stumpy Gully Rd, Balnarring 3926
Ph: 0417 050 627

MT ELIZA
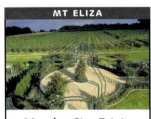
Morning Star Estate
The Estate restaurant open daily for lunch 10am-4pm. Dinner Friday & Saturday from 6pm. Reservations essential. Cellar door & Peninsula produce open daily 10am-4pm
1 Sunnyside Rd, Mt Eliza 3930
Ph: (03) 9787 7760 • Fax: (03) 9787 7160
email: email@morningstarestate.com.au

MT ELIZA

Morning Star Estate
Restaurant – Accommodation
– Functions & Events
– Conference facilities
– Extensive Gardens & Vineyards.
Open 7 days.
1 Sunnyside Road, Mt Eliza (Mel Ref: 105 A7)
Tel: (03) 9787 7760 • Fax: (03) 9787 7160
email@morningstarestate.com.au
www.morningstarestate.com.au

MAIN RIDGE

Poplar Bend Winery
Home of Chloe Wine, established in early '80s by one of Melbourne's best loved journalists, Keith Dunstan. A small family run vineyard, set in picturesque garden. Cellar door open weekends 11am-5pm
465 Main Creek Rd, Main Ridge 3928
Ph: (03) 5989 6046 • Fax: (03) 5989 6279
email: peter@pwallace.com.au

RED HILL SOUTH
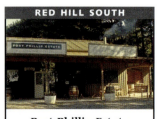
Port Phillip Estate
One of the most scenic vineyards on the Mornington Peninsula, producing award-winning cool climate Pinot Noir, Shiraz, Chardonnay & Sauvignon Blanc. Open every weekend, public holidays, and every day in Dec-Jan. 11am-5pm
261 Red Hill Rd, Red Hill South 3937
Ph: (03) 5989 2708 • Fax: (03) 5989 3017
email: sales@portphillip.net

LISTINGS • PENINSULA WINERIES

WINERIES TOURING GUIDE – REFER TO PAGES 138-139

BALNARRING

Marinda Park Vineyard

238 Myers Rd, Balnarring 3926
Phone/Fax: 5989 7613
email: mark@marindapark.com

MT ELIZA

Mt Eliza Estate

Sunnyside precinct. Gateway vineyard producing superb estate wine focused on local winery conditions.
Cellar door 7 days 11am-5pm

9 Sunnyside Rd, Mt Eliza 3930
Ph: (03) 9787 0663 • Fax: (03) 9708 8355
email: mtelizaestate@telstra.com

MT ELIZA

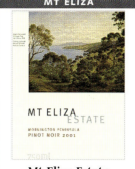

Mt Eliza Estate

9 Sunnyside Rd, Mt Eliza 3930
Ph: (03) 9787 0663 • Fax: (03) 9708 8355
email: mtelizaestate@telstra.com

MOOROODUC

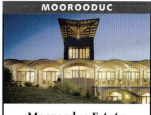

Moorooduc Estate

Jill's Restaurant at Moorooduc Estate offers fine, regional, seasonal food in the striking Gregory Burgess designed rammed earth building. Overnight accommodation in elegant modern suites looking onto the vineyard is also available

501 Derril Rd, Moorooduc 3933
Tel: (03) 5971 8506 / Fax: (03) 5971 8550
email: moorooduc@ozemail.com.au
www.moorooducestate.com.au

MOOROODUC

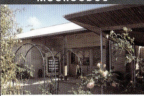

Moorooduc Estate

Moorooduc Estate, established in 1983, is a working vineyard & winery. The complex structured wines are available from the original rammed earth winery.

501 Derril Rd, Moorooduc 3933
Tel: (03) 5971 8506 • Fax: (03) 5971 8550
email: moorooduc@ozemail.com.au
www.moorooducestate.com.au

MERRICKS NORTH

Osborns

Experience the range of our highly regarded wines before or after lunching at one of the many fine restaurants on the Peninsula.
Open first weekend of the month, holidays, and by appointment

166 Foxeys Rd, Merricks North 3926
Ph: (03) 5989 7417

RED HILL SOUTH

44 Paringa Road, Red Hill South
Tel: (03) 5989 2669   Fax: (03) 5931 0135
www.paringaestate.com.au

RED HILL SOUTH

Paringa Estate

44 Paringa Road, Red Hill South
Tel: (03) 5989 2669   Fax: (03) 5931 0135
www.paringaestate.com.au

SHOREHAM

Pier 10 Vineyard

Award winning wines. Innovative light food. Regular live music. Outdoor terrace with stunning views over vineyard. Cellar door Friday, Saturday & Sunday 11am-5pm

10 Shoreham Rd, Shoreham 3916
Ph: 5989 8848 • Fax: 5989 8848
email: wine@pier10.com.au
www.pier10.com.au

SHOREHAM

Pier 10 Vineyard

Award winning wines. Innovative light food. Regular live music. Outdoor terrace with stunning views over vineyard. Cellar door Friday, Saturday & Sunday 11am-5pm

10 Shoreham Rd, Shoreham 3916
Ph: 5989 8848 • Fax: 5989 8848
email: wine@pier10.com.au
www.pier10.com.au

RED HILL SOUTH

Red Hill Estate

Red Hill Estate is a multi award winning winery, restaurant and vineyard. An unsurpassed view, combined with food and wine to match, makes Red Hill Estate the ultimate winery experience

53 Shoreham Rd, Red Hill South 3937
Ph: (03) 5989 2838 • Fax: (03) 5989 2855
email: info@redhillestate.com.au

RED HILL SOUTH

Max's Restaurant
RED HILL ESTATE

Winner of the American Express Restaurant Awards Best Restaurant in Victoria 2002. Max's has sweeping views over Westernport Bay to Phillip Island and an internationally-inspired menu using the finest of local ingredients.

53 Shoreham Rd, Red Hill South 3937
Ph: (03) 5931 0177 • Fax: (03) 5989 2204
email: info@maxsatredhillestate.com.au

MERRICKS

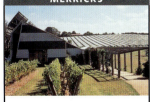

The Stonier Winery

Stonier Wines produces outstanding Sauvignon Blanc, Chardonnay, Pinot Noir & Cabernet. Cheese platters available daily, children's playground & winery tours.

362 Frankston Flinders Road, Merricks 3916
Tel: (03) 5989 8300 Fax: (03) 5989 8709
Email: stoniers@stoniers.com.au
www.stoniers.com.au   (Mel Ref: 192 F9)

MERRICKS

Stonier Wines

362 Frankston-Flinders Rd, Merricks 3916
Ph: (03) 5989 8300 • Fax: (03) 5989 8709
stoniers@stoniers.com.au

MOOROODUC

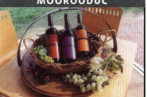

Stumpy Gully Vineyard

Visit the colourful cellar door & be guided through an unforgettable tasting experience with the winemakers or vineyard workers, who double up as cellar door staff.
All within an hour's drive of Melbourne.

1247 Stumpy Gully Rd, Moorooduc 3933
Ph: (03) 5978 8429 • Fax: (03) 5978 8419
email: sgvzant@bigpond.com

MAIN RIDGE

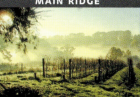

Ten Minutes by Tractor Wine Co.

Enjoy sensational wines & limited individual vineyard varieties form the Wallis, Judd & McCutcheon Family vineyards.
Ten minuites apart in Main Ridge.
Cellar door open weekends 11-5pm

111 Roberts Rd, Main Ridge 3928
Ph: (03) 9589 6084

251

LISTINGS • PENINSULA WINERIES & SOUTHERN PENINSULA

WINERIES TOURING GUIDE – REFER TO PAGES 138-139

RED HILL SOUTH

The Duke Vineyard

The Duke Vineyard, a fascinating minute vineyard and winery, produces Pinot Noir and Chardonnay. All wines are made on the property by the owners.
Open 12pm – 5pm weekends,
Public & Summer Holidays.

38 Paringa Road, Red Hill South (Mel Ref: 191 D9)
Tel: (03) 5989 2407 Fax: (03) 5989 2407
Email: duke@dukevineyard.com.au

RED HILL SOUTH

Tuck's Ridge

Visitors to our intimate bluestone cellar door will experience a range of wines that express the intense fruit flavours of the area.
'Seriously Exciting' Huon Hooke
Cellar Door Open Daily 12 noon – 5pm

37 Shoreham Road, Red Hill South
(Mel Ref: 256 A2)
Tel: (03) 5989 8660 Fax: (03) 5989 8579
Email: cellardoor@tucksridge.com.au

DROMANA

Turramurra Estate

Come and taste our delicious, cool climate wines, grown and produced on the Estate by Paula and David Lellie.
Open first weekend of each month.

295 Wallaces Rd, Dromana 3936
Ph: (03) 5987 1146 • Fax: (03) 5987 1286
email: turramurraest@ozemail.com.au

RED HILL SOUTH

Wildcroft Winery & Restaurant

Nestled cosily into the rolling hills of Red Hill. Sip our spicy Shiraz in our charming mud brick restaurant (Cafe 98) whilst enjoying the modern cuisine with middle eastern & asian influences. Open daily 11am-5pm

98 Stanleys Rd, Red Hill South 3937
Ph: (03) 5989 2646

MERRICKS NORTH
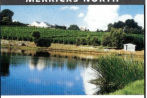
Willow Creek Vineyard

Internationally acclaimed wines. Fine dining at Salix Restaurant. Twenty eight acres of manicured vines and gardens surround the original 1870's homestead in our own hidden valley. Savour the surroundings with all your senses.

166 Balnarring Road, Merricks North
Tel: (03) 5989 7448 Fax (03) 5989 7584
Email: admin@willow-creek.com.au

MERRICKS NORTH

Willow Creek Vineyard

166 Balnarring Road, Merricks North
Tel: (03) 5989 7448 Fax (03) 5989 7584
Email: admin@willow-creek.com.au

MAIN RIDGE
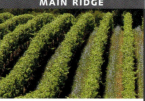
Yrsa's Vineyard

Distinctive cool climate Pinot Noir & Chardonnay from one of the Peninsula's newest wineries.
By appointment only

105 Tucks Rd, Main Ridge 3928
Ph: (03) 5989 6500 • Fax: (03) 5989 6501
email: yrsas@bigpond.com
www.yrsasvineyard.com.au

SAFETY BEACH

Bluestone Homestead B&B

Tucked away on a rural property just minutes from all Southern Peninsula attractions, the secluded garden cottages are the perfect setting for your Peninsula experience. Breakfast in room or in our garden gazebo.

140 Pickings Rd, Safety Beach 3936
Ph: (03) 5981 4073

SAFETY BEACH

Mt Martha Valley Resort

Located on the beautiful Mornington Peninsula, minutes from a picturesque swimming beach.
Built on the 18-hole golf course.
Boutique accommodation at its best.

1-18 Valley Court, Safety Beach
Ph: (03) 5987 3535 • Fax: (03) 5987 3560
email: mail@valleyresort.com.au
www.valleyresort.com.au

DROMANA

Dromana Hub Shopping Centre

Southern Peninsula's modern shopping centre, adjacent to Dromana foreshore and beach.
19 Specialty stores with award-winning Ritchies Supermarket.
Ample car parking

Pt. Nepean Rd, Dromana

DROMANA

Stella's Dromana Hotel

One of the Peninsula's landmark hotels. Featuring extensive Italian-style bistro, streetwalk cafe & light meals. New luxury ensuited accommodation, Tabaret Pokies, Full TAB, Drive-in bottleshop

151 Pt Nepean Rd, Dromana
Ph: (03) 5987 1922
email: dromanah@surf.net.au

DROMANA

The Diggers' Club
- HERONSWOOD -

Visit National Trust classified Heronswood & enjoy stunning gardens, fabulous food, historic buildings. Purchase your Diggers' Club seeds & plants from the nursery bookshop

105 LaTrobe Parade, Dromana
Ph: (03) 5987 1877 • Fax: (03) 5981 4298
email: taleik@diggers.com.au
www.diggers.com

DROMANA

Dromana/Red Hill RSL Club

Situated at the rear of the shopping hub, the Club provides for the welfare needs of the community. It boasts a large bistro, lounge bar, members bar, gaming room, pool room and outdoor deck.
Open 7 days

1-4 Noel St, Dromana 3936
Ph: (03) 5987 2448 • Fax: (03) 5987 2170

MCCRAE
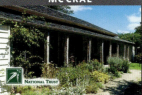
McCrae Homestead

McCrae Homestead National Trust property built in 1844 of drop-slab construction, designed by diarist Georgiana McCrae, contains much original furniture and memorabilia which recreate the life of these Scottish migrants.

11 Beverley Road, McCrae. (Mel Ref: 159 A10)
Tel: (03) 5986 5688   www.nattrust.com.au

ROSEBUD

Complimentary
Accommodation Reservation Service
Self Contained Cottages, Apartments, Houses, Bed & Breakfasts, & Resorts for
Singles, Couples, Families & Groups.
PHONE: (03) 5982 3366
info@peninsulagetaways.com.au
www.peninsulagetaways.com.au
mornington peninsula getaway booking service
melbourne's peninsula getaway luxury
accommodation reservation service.

ROSEBUD

Amberlee ★★★★ Family Holidays

★★★★ Spa Villas or Ensuite cabins.
All fully self-contained. In a unique bush setting with inground pools & spa, trampoline, volleyball, tennis & mini golf.
Playground & BBQs. RACV ★★★★

306 Jetty Road, Rosebud (Mel Ref: 170 F7)
Freecall: 1800 818 587 Tel: (03) 5982 2122
Email: stay@amberlee.com.au

LISTINGS • SOUTHERN PENINSULA

ROSEBUD

Nazaaray Beach House

Stylish s/c house, quiet idyllic location, close beach and shops. Spa, open fire, TV, MW. Child, disabled, dog and cost friendly. One nights welcome.

40 Murray Anderson Road, Rosebud
Tel: (03) 9585 1138 Mobile: 0416 143 439
Email: nazaaray@bigpond.com
Website: www.nazaaray.com.au

ROSEBUD WEST
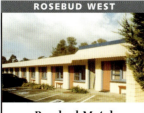

Rosebud Motel

Opposite sandy beach. 12 ground-floor air-conditioned units. Golf packages a speciality with most of the best courses on the Peninsula in close proximity. Relax by the pool and BBQ

1869 Pt Nepean Rd, Rosebud West 3941
Ph: (03) 5985 2041 • Fax: (03) 5985 6626
email: rosebudmotel@bigpond.com
www.rosebudmotel.escape.to

CAPE SCHANCK
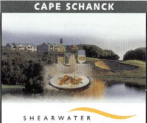

SHEARWATER Cape Schanck Resort

Incorporating the Shearwater Conference Centre, Resort Accommodation & Atrium Restaurant. The perfect corporate or Trade Day venue in the heart of the Mornington Peninsula

Boneo Rd, Cape Schanck
Ph: (03) 5950 8100
www.TheResort.com.au

CAPE SCHANCK
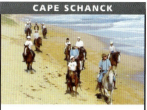

Ace-Hi Beach Rides

• Scenic Trail Rides over 200 acres
• Forest Rides through unique Mornington Peninsula Trails • Ocean Beach Rides •
Also Self contained Cabins • Chapel Restaurant & BBQs. Ace-Hi cater for couples, families, groups & school camps.

810 Boneo Road, Cape Schanck
Tel: (03) 5988 6262 Fax: (03) 5988 6698
Email: ride@ace-hi.com.au

CAPE SCHANCK

Ace-Hi Wildlife Park

• 10 acres, wildlife park & farmyard
• Kangaroo, Wallaby, Koala, Wombat, Dingo, Deer, Possum, Tawney Frogmouth, Peacock, Waterfowl, Parrots & Picnic Grounds. Ace-Hi cater for couples, families, groups & school camps.

810 Boneo Road, Cape Schanck
Tel: (03) 5988 6262 Fax: (03) 5988 6698
Email: ride@ace-hi.com.au

FINGAL

Mizu Spa

Outdoor Japanese style hot baths, Aboriginal relaxation massage, Arabic steam room, Indonesian day bed. Accommodation. Day Spa.
A world of relaxation.

175 Devonport Drive, Fingal
Tel: (03) 5988 6088 Fax: (03) 5988 6099
Email: relax@bathe.com.au
www.bathe.com.au

RYE

Moonah Links

World Class Golf Resort & Australian Open Venue. 2 Championship Links golf courses, Peppers Hotel, conference facility, AGU headquarters, AIS golf academy, Golf Museum & Hall of Fame. The home of Australian Golf is open to the public 7 days.

Peter Thomson Drv (off Truemans Rd, Rye 3941
Ph: 1300 362 386
email: moonah@moonahlinks.com.au
www.moonahlinks.com.au

RYE

Peppers Moonah Links

Stylish accommodation overlooking the golf course or garden. Boasting great facilities, including gym, Endota day spa. Offering superb food & wine. The ultimate resort destination for golf enthusiasts

Peter Thomson Drive, Rye
Ph: 1300 362 386 (Mel. 252 E1)
email: peppers@peppers.com.au
www.peppers.com.au

ROSEBUD

Rosebud Country Club

Centrally located in the heart of the Peninsula. Featuring a 36-hole golf course, lawn bowls, clubhouse & entertainment venue. Modern cuisine restaurant serving lunch & dinner 7 days a week.

207 Boneo Rd, Rosebud 3939
Ph: (03) 5986 1481
www.rosebudcountryclub.com.au

ROSEBUD
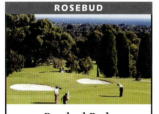

Rosebud Park Public Golf Course

Living up to their motto "Where the view is worth the drive". Great fairways & greens, low green fees, attractive season-ticket plans. Social club & BBQ facilities. Pro shop hire facilities

Elizabeth Drive, Rosebud
Ph: (03) 5981 2833

CAPE SCHANCK
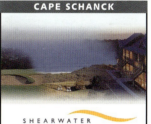

SHEARWATER Cape Schanck Resort

The Peninsula's premier access course •
60 motorised carts • Driving range •
Open 7 days • Resort accommodation & atrium restaurant. Open to public

Boneo Rd, Cape Schanck
Ph: (03) 5950 8100
www.TheResort.com.au

SORRENTO

Sorrento Golf Club

A Unique Golfing Experience, we invite you to share. Sorrento Golf Club enjoys a special reputation within Victoria as one of the premier courses on the Mornington Peninsula. Our staff will go out of their way to make your visit to Sorrento Golf Club a memorable one

Langford Rd, Sorrento 3943
Ph: (03) 5984 2226 • Fax: (03) 5984 4567
email: club@sorrentogolf.com.au

ROSEBUD
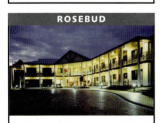

Nepean Country Club

Golf packages to Australia's finest sandbelt courses on the Mornington Peninsula. The ideal destination for the most meticulous & fun-loving holiday makers, conference delegates & business guests

SALES OFFICE LOCATED AT
920 Pt Nepean Rd, Rosebud
Ph: (03) 5981 2011 • Fax: (03) 5981 2188
email: sales@nepeancountryclub.com.au

BONEO

Fingals Restaurant
-AT NEPEAN COUNTRY CLUB-

Central to bay, beaches, wineries & golf courses. Accommodation to cater for all needs. Dining at Fingals Restaurant offers a relaxed, family atmosphere, superior menus & extensive wine cellar. RACV ★★★★☆

205 Browns Road, Boneo (Mel Ref: 169 G12)
Tel: (03) 5986 9800 Fax: (03) 5986 9700
www.nepeancountryclub.com.au

RYE
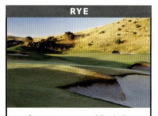

The Dunes Golf Links

The Dunes Golf Links offers not only a world class course but also provides the best in Australian service, facilities, and friendly staff.
Recently voted the number one public access course in Victoria for 2003.

Browns Road, Rye (Mel Ref: 168 G11)
Tel: (03) 5985 1334 Fax: (03) 5985 8305
Email: golf@thedunes.com.au

ROSEBUD
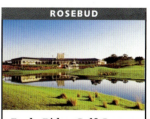

Eagle Ridge Golf Course

Eagle Ridge's professionally designed course offers excellent year-round golfing. The new 1500 sq.m. Clubhouse and Conference Centre caters for all occasions including Corporate and Weddings. You'll be warmly welcomed at Eagle Ridge.

Browns Road, Rosebud (Mel Ref: 169 G12)
Tel: (03) 5988 6341 Fax: (03) 5988 6033
Email: golf@eagleridge.net.au

LISTINGS • SOUTHERN PENINSULA

RYE

Hilltonia Homestead
Exclusive accommodation set on 40 acres offering secluded cottages with views, spas & fireplaces, plus luxurious B&B suites, swimming pool, tennis court and large guest lounge with bar.
Lot B1, Browns Road, Rye (Mel Ref: 169 A11)
Tel: (03) 5985 2654 • Fax: (03) 5985 2684
Email: sales@hilltonia.com.au
www.hilltonia.com.au

RYE

Gunnamatta Equestrian Centre & Trail Rides
Spectacular Ocean Beach & Bush Trail Rides. Enjoy the exhilaration of horse riding with qualified instructors and horses to suit all riding levels. Lessons available. All equipment supplied. Open 7 days 8.00am.
Truemans Rd, Rye
Tel: (03) 5988 6755 Freecall: 1800 801 003
Email: reservations@gunnamatta.com.au

RYE FORESHORE

The Rye Hotel
Experience the multi award-winning Hotel. Family Bistro • Alfresco Cafe • Ryders Playzone for kids • Gaming room • live entertainment • Sportsbar TAB • Garden Courtyard • Private Function Rooms • Drive-thru Bottleshop
2415 Pt Nepean Rd, Rye Beach
Ph: (03) 5985 2277 • Fax: (03) 5985 7710
www.ryehotel.com.au

BLAIRGOWRIE

Coast 2827 Restaurant Bar
With views across the bay, this stylish restaurant bar is well known for its fabulous food & warm atmosphere. Modern Australian menu with influences from Italy & Asia. Best breakfast and coffee on the Peninsula
2827 Point Nepean Rd, Blairgowrie
Ph: (03) 5988 0700
email: coast2827@bigpond.com.au

BLAIRGOWRIE

Aspects Coastal Gallery
Southern Peninsula's leading gallery.
Featuring regional and Peninsula artists.
Open daily 10am–5pm

2843 Pt Nepean Rd, Blairgowrie 3942
Ph: (03) 5988 8876 • Fax: (03) 5988 8871
email: aspects@satlink

BLAIRGOWRIE

Boat House Resort
★★★★ ACCOMMODATION, LICENSED BAR & RESTAURANT
Adjacent to front beach, yacht club & marina. Minutes driving from the Peninsula's finest golf clubs and wineries. Short stroll to restaurants, cafes & shops. Swimming pool, BBQ facilities. Group rates available.
2871-2875 Point Nepean Road, Blairgowrie
Tel: (03) 5988 8088 Fax: (03) 5988 8499
Email: boat@pac.com.au (Mel Ref: 167 F1)

SORRENTO

Hotel Sorrento
'SEA' THE DIFFERENCE
Situated on the sparkling Port Phillip Bay, our crown jewel. Offering a range of accommodation, magnificent restaurant, friendly bars & a gaming room. Delivering satisfaction for a long, long time
5-15 Hotham Rd, Sorrento
Ph: (03) 5984 2206 • Fax: (03) 5984 3424
email: hotel@hotelsorrento.com.au
www.hotelsorrento.com.au

SORRENTO

Hotel Sorrento
The perfect accommodation venue on the Southern Peninsula. Choose from Sorrento on the Park apartments, refurbished historic hotel suites, or cottage-style B&B accommodation
5-15 Hotham Rd, Sorrento
Ph: (03) 5984 2206 • Fax: (03) 5984 3424
email: hotel@hotelsorrento.com.au
www.hotelsorrento.com.au

SORRENTO

Oceanic Sorrento – Whitehall Guesthouse
Historic Whitehall Guesthouse is ideally situated just minutes walk from Sorrento's historic village and spectacular ocean beach. A great holiday destination with Salt-water pool and tennis court.
231 Ocean Beach Rd, Sorrento 3943
Ph: (03) 5984 4166 • Fax: (03) 5984 3369
email: sorrento@oceanicgroup.com.au

SORRENTO

Antipodes Bookshop Gallery
A fine selection of **new release books** and **contemporary Australian art and craft**. Regularly changing exhibitions.
Open Daily
138 Ocean Beach Rd, Sorrento, 3943
Ph: (03) 5984 4217 • Fax: (03) 5984 0835
email: antipode@nex.net.au

SORRENTO

The First Settlement Gallery
One of the Peninsula's leading Galleries in the heart of Sorrento, with many of the region's prominent artists represented. Browse for hours amidst the vibrant display rooms filled to capacity with artistic treasures.
141 Ocean Beach Rd, Sorrento 3943
Ph: (03) 5984 2380 • Fax: (03) 5984 5716
email: fsg@bigpond.net.au

SORRENTO/QUEENSCLIFF

Queenscliff – Sorrento Car & Passenger Ferry
Ferry departs daily from Queenscliff Harbour and Sorrento Pier on the hour every hour, 7am-6pm. A 7pm trip operates from Boxing Day until the end of Daylight Saving.
Tel: (03) 5258 3244
www.searoad.com.au

SORRENTO

The Wooden Boat Shop
Manufacturers of the famous Coota Boat and Nepean Motor Launch.
Full service boatyard. Yanmar diesel agents. Full chandlery. 7 days a week.
129 Hotham Rd, Sorrento 3943
Ph: (03) 5984 4333 • Fax: (03) 5984 4570
email: wbs@woodenboatshop.com.au
www.woodenboatshop.com.au

BLAIRGOWRIE

Polperro Dolphin Swims
Hall of Fame Environmental Tourism Award
The marine adventure of a lifetime interacting with the wild bottlenose dolphins and seals of Port Phillip Bay. All gear supplied. Highly qualified crew. Bookings advised.
Trips depart Sorrento Pier,
PO Box 11, Blairgowrie
Tel: (03) 5988 8437 Fax: (03) 5988 8734
Email: crew@polperro.com.au

SORRENTO

Moonraker Seal & Dolphin Swims
We offer guests the chance to interact with these lovely creatures. Our cruises are specially focused on creating as little disturbance as possible to dolphins and to the pristine ecosystem.
2 St. Aubins Way, Sorrento (Mel Ref: 157 B7)
Tel: (03) 5984 4211 Fax: (03) 5984 4044
Email: info@moonrakercharters.com.au

PORTSEA

Point Nepean
Walk it, Bike it, Ride it…You'll be inspired! Tunnels and forts to explore. Nature walks, coastal walks and landscape. Views of the Rip, Bass Strait and Port Phillip Bay. Open everyday except Xmas day.
For further information Tel: (03) 5984 4276
Mornington Peninsula National Park,
end of Point Nepean Road, Portsea
Email: pointnepean@discoveryattraction.com

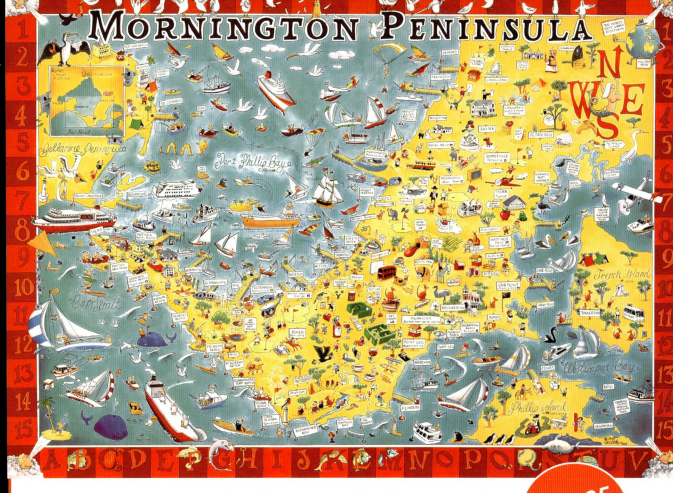

Mornington Peninsula "Images"
POSTER
ILLUSTRATED BY MATT GOLDING

Poster size: 60 cm x 84 cm

$9⁹⁵

The perfect present for those who love the Peninsula and a great way to discover its many delights, providing a humorous perspective on the diversity of this wonderful region.

Use it as a guide to find your next adventure or as an educational tool. The poster includes many Aboriginal place names, indigenous birds and animals and historic homesteads. Discover one of the seven walking trails through Greens Bush, to Bushrangers Bay or along the Ocean Coast. This lighthearted guide to the Peninsula will have you laughing time after time as you discover its offerings.

Get inspired – take an ocean kayak out to Chinaman's Hat, or swim with the seals, penguins and dolphins. Surf on the back beaches or sail on the bays. Have a hot springs bath and a massage to ease you into a blissful state of Peninsula life. Explore the wineries and restaurants or perhaps a horse ride along the beach or Hinterland.

Order by phone or mail, or purchase your copy at any of the leading Peninsula tourism attractions and retail outlets.

ORDER FORM
(FOR MULTIPLES OF 10)
FOR SINGLE POSTERS PLEASE PURCHASE FROM RETAIL OUTLETS

Mail to: Peninsula Hot Springs, 175 Devonport Drive, Fingal (Moonahgai), Mornington Peninsula, Vic. 3939.
Or call or fax your order: Tele: (03) 5988 6088   Fax: (03) 5988-6099

I enclose my cheque/money order for $95.00 (10 posters), or please charge my
Visacard ❑   Mastercard ❑   Bankcard ❑   Expiry date...............................

☐☐☐☐ ☐☐☐☐ ☐☐☐☐ ☐☐☐☐

Cardholders name..........................
Signature..........................
Send to Mr/Mrs/Ms..........................
Address..........................
.... Postcode ....
Daytime telephone..........................

*Please allow 14 days for delivery. Price includes GST and shipping and handling.
Wholesale enquiries contact Peninsula Hot Springs*

Acknowledgements

Alexandra and Barry Stevens for Publisher GippStar International Pty Ltd. would like to recognise the following individuals and organizations for their contribution.

Sponsors: Frankston City, Tourism and Events Coordinator Maxine Sando, Mornington Peninsula Shire, Jodie Clarke, and Public relations coordinator Kate Hopkins. Executive Tourism Officer, Alva Hemming, for her encouragement and assistance. Lindenderry of Red Hill, manager, Louise Page, and staff. Mark Rodman, President MPVA for introduction to wineries section. Ian Hickinbotham for his History of Peninsula Wineries. Cheryl Lee Executive Officer of the MPVA. John Mitchell, Montalto Vineyard and Marketing Committee, MPVA. Peter and Cathy Barker of Peter Barker Photography, Mornington for use of the magnificent Aerial photographs that contribute so much to the look of the publication. Media sponsors Peninsula Radio 3RPP, Visitor Publications and the Leader Group for their promotional support.

Special support from approximately 220 individual Listing Sponsors; who by their participation have made a valuable financial contribution in promoting their business and the Mornington Peninsula region.

In Frankston and on the Peninsula all those businesses and individuals who helped with accommodation and advice for material featured in the publication. Chris Yule for his assistance in securing much of the advertising support within the publication.

The Frankston, Mornington and Western Port Chambers of Commerce for their encouragement and assistance. All those who contributed text material and photographs for the publication a heartfelt thanks. Parks Victoria and the National Trust (Vic). HMAS Cerberus for access to their facilities for photographic and editorial purposes. Special thanks goes to all featured Wineries and Golf courses of the Southern Peninsula who continue to play an important role in the development of the region.

Photo credits

Unless otherwise indicated by page numbers all photographs have been taken by Barry Stevens.
Aerial views by Peter Barker Photography Pty Ltd, SKYPICS, Mornington.

P11.Frankston City. P14-15 Two Cans Antiques. P25 Jenny Pihan. P26 Frankston City files. P27 Geoff Atchison. P42 Sages Cottage. P50 Mornington Chamber of Commerce. P52 Sail Mornington Charters. P65 Mornington Peninsula Regional Gallery. P72 Rosemary Munro. P73 Perfumed Garden and Roseraie, Briars Park. P74 Original Oz Mt Martha. P75 Brian Thomas, Coolart Wetlands and Parks Victoria. P79 Mark Cairns, Moonlit Sanctuary Pearcedale. P82-83 Peter Barker SKYPICS Studio Mornington. P90 Victoriana's Restaurant. P93 Summerfield Country House. P100 Rain Hayne and Shine Farmyard. P110 Cipriani's Flinders Country Inn B&B and Restaurant, Ora Banda B&B, Papillon B&B. P120-121 David McCarthy, Nedlands Lavender Farm. P122-123 Sunny Ridge Strawberry Farm. P126-127 Arthurs Seat Maze. P129 Vines of Red Hill. P130 Langdons of Red Hill. P130-131 Summerhill Farm. P131 Roger Gould, Pennyroyal B&B. P133 Gordon Glass Studio. Peninsula Wineries Feature. **Several wineries supplied their own photographic material for the featured section.** P193 Moonah Links. P200-221 Heronswood Tarlei Kenyon. P220 Cape Schanck Shearwater Resort. P212 Neralie Thorp, Eagle Ridge Golf Course. P216 Nepean Country Club Resort. P218-219 Moonah Links. P224 Gunnamatta Equestrian Centre and Trail Rides. P235 & 237 Troy Muir, Polperro Dolphin Swims. P229 & 239 Liz and Wendy Watson.

Map Credits. Frankston and Mornington Peninsula Tourism
Maps used are meant as general reference only to the region. It is recommended that visitors requiring detailed street references consult a street DIRECTORY for more accurate detail. The Publishers do not except any responsibility for omissions or errors in the maps supplied and cannot be held libel.

PUBLISHER: GippStar International Pty Ltd.
AUTHOR: Alexandra Stevens
PHOTOGRAPHER: Barry Stevens
DESIGN, LAYOUT & REPRODUCTION: Captured Concepts, St Andrews
EDITOR: David Harrison.
PRINTED IN AUSTRALIA BY: BPA Books, Melbourne
PRE-PRESS: Mark Williams / Rob Brentnall.
PRINT MANAGER: Warwick Horgan

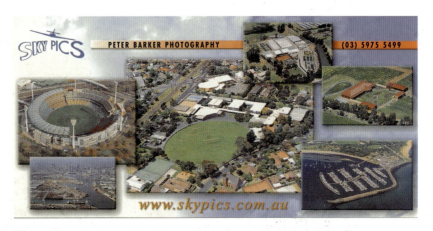